Table of Contents

Preface

The AP Chemistry Exam was changed in 2007. Don't use an old study guide to prepare for a new test!

College-level lectures, tests, quizzes, homework problems, and labs are to be evaluated in a 3-hour examination. It's just you and the AP exam. In preparing to do the very best job possible, you have four options:

1. Read your entire textbook again.
2. Do all of your homework problems again.
3. Buy a test preparation guide that has every conceivable type of problem in it and that in many cases is thicker than your textbook and that you will never be able to finish and that does not explain how to do well on the essay portion of the exam and does not review all of the laboratory experiments required and tested.
4. Use *CliffsAP Chemistry, 4th Edition* along with *CliffsAP 5 Chemistry Practice Exams.*

I'm glad you chose option 4. I've taught chemistry for over 33 years, and I've put together in this book what I believe are the most up-to-date types of questions that you will experience on the AP Chemistry Exam. Each question is thoroughly explained and the format of each practice exam is exactly what you will see when you take the actual exam. With other AP exams to study for and other time commitments, you need a quick set of practice exams that will cover everything you need to know. With *CliffsAP Chemistry, 4th Edition* to help you cover in more detail the topics covered in the practice exams, you will be absolutely prepared.

Study Guide Checklist

- ❑ Go through this checklist, placing a check in each box as you complete the task. When you've checked all the boxes on this page, you're ready for the AP Chemistry Exam.
- ❑ Become familiar with all of the resources available from the College Board for preparing for the AP Chemistry Exam: http://apcentral.collegeboard.com
- ❑ Read the Preface to this book.
- ❑ Read "Format of the NEW AP Chemistry Exam"
- ❑ Read "Topics Covered by the AP Chemistry Exam"
- ❑ Read "Questions Commonly Asked about the AP Chemistry Exam"
- ❑ Read "Strategies for Taking the AP Chemistry Exam"
- ❑ Read "Methods for Writing the Essays"
- ❑ Read and do all problems for Chapter 1, Atoms
- ❑ Read and do all problems for Chapter 2, Periodic Table
- ❑ Read and do all problems for Chapter 3, Bonding
- ❑ Read and do all problems for Chapter 4, Molecular Geometry-Hybridization
- ❑ Read and do all problems for Chapter 5, Stoichiometry
- ❑ Read and do all problems for Chapter 6, Gases
- ❑ Read and do all problems for Chapter 7, Liquids and Solids
- ❑ Read and do all problems for Chapter 8, Thermodynamics
- ❑ Read and do all problems for Chapter 9, Solutions
- ❑ Read and do all problems for Chapter 10, Equilibrium
- ❑ Read and do all problems for Chapter 11, Acids and Bases
- ❑ Read and do all problems for Chapter 12, Kinetics
- ❑ Read and do all problems for Chapter 13, Oxidation-Reduction (Redox)
- ❑ Read and do all problems for Chapter 14, Nuclear Chemistry
- ❑ Read and do all problems for Chapter 15, Organic Chemistry
- ❑ Read and do all problems for Chapter 16, Chemical Reactions
- ❑ Read and do all problems for Chapter 17, Laboratory Experiments
- ❑ Take Practice Exam 1 and go through your errors.
- ❑ Take Practice Exam 2 and go through your errors.
- ❑ If you need additional practice, use *CliffsAP 5 Chemistry Practice Exams.*

CliffsAP®

Chemistry

4TH EDITION

by

Bobrow Test Preparation Services

Wiley Publishing, Inc.

Author's Acknowledgments

I would like to thank my wife, Patti, and my two daughters, Kris and Erin, for their patience and understanding while I was writing this book. I would also like to acknowledge Dr. Jerry Bobrow of Bobrow Test Preparation Services and Christopher Bushée for their input, proofreading, and suggestions.

Publisher's Acknowledgments

Editorial

Project Editor: Donna Wright

Acquisitions Editor: Greg Tubach

Technical Editor: Christopher Bushée

Composition

Proofreader: Broccoli Information Management

Wiley Indianapolis Composition Services

CliffsAP Chemistry, 4th Edition

Published by:
Wiley Publishing, Inc.
111 River Street
Hoboken, NJ 07030-5774
www.wiley.com

Published by Wiley, Hoboken, NJ
Published simultaneously in Canada

Library of Congress Cataloging-in-Publication Data

CliffsAP chemistry / by Bobrow Test Preparation.—4th ed.
p. cm.
Rev. ed. of: CliffsAP chemistry / Gary S. Thorpe. 3rd ed. c2001.
ISBN-13: 978-0-470-13500-6
ISBN-10: 0-470-13500-X
1. Chemistry—Examinations—Study guides. 2. Universities and colleges—United States—Entrance examinations—Study guides. 3. Advanced placement programs (Education)—Examinations—Study guides. I. Thorpe, Gary S. Cliffs AP. II. Bobrow Test Preparation Services.
QD42.T49 2008
540.76—dc22

2007034615

Printed in the United States of America

10 9 8 7 6 5 4 3 2

Wiley Bicentennial Logo: Richard J. Pacifico

WILEY

Introduction

New Format of the AP Chemistry Exam

The AP Chemistry Exam has a new format that began in May 2007. This book reflects the NEW format. It is important to note that the content covered by the exam was not changed. Section I (the multiple-choice questions) and Section II (the essays) each contribute 50% toward the final grade.

Section I (90 minutes) consists of 75 multiple-choice questions with broad coverage of chemistry topics. Calculators are NOT permitted.

Section II (95 minutes) consists of a total of six free-response questions. Part A (55 minutes—calculators permitted) consists of three problems, the first of which is an equilibrium problem. Part B (40 minutes—calculators NOT permitted) consists of question 4 (reactions) and two essay questions. You will NOT be able to choose which questions you wish to answer in the NEW format.

Question 4 (reactions) assesses your knowledge about chemical reactions and will require you to write balanced chemical equations for three different sets of reactants and answer a short question about each of the three reactions.

The following chart summarizes the format of Section II of the NEW AP Chemistry Exam.

Section I Format: 50% of Total Score	***Section II Format: 50% of Total Score***	
75 Multiple-Choice Questions	**Part A, 55 minutes (with calculator)**	**% of Section Score**
	• Equilibrium problem	20%
	• Other problem*	20%
	• Other problem*	20%
90 Minutes	**Part B, 40 minutes (no calculator)**	**% of Section Score**
	• Reactions question (3 required)	10%
	• Essay question*	15%
Calculators NOT permitted	• Essay question*	15%
	One of the other problems or essays will be based on laboratory	

Topics Covered* by the AP Chemistry Exam

I. Structure of Matter (20%)

A. Atomic theory and atomic structure

1. Evidence for the atomic theory
2. Atomic masses; determination by chemical and physical means
3. Atomic number and mass number, isotopes
4. Electron energy levels: atomic spectra, quantum numbers, atomic orbitals
5. Periodic relationships including, for example, atomic radii, ionization energies, electron affinities, oxidation states

B. Chemical bonding

1. Binding forces
   - **a.** Types: ionic, covalent, metallic, hydrogen bonding, van der Waals (including London dispersion forces)
   - **b.** Relationships to states, structure, and properties of matter
   - **c.** Polarity of bonds, electronegativities
2. Molecular models
   - **a.** Lewis structures
   - **b.** Valence bond: hybridization of orbitals, resonance, sigma and pi bonds
   - **c.** VSEPR
3. Geometry of molecules and ions, structural isomerism of simple organic molecules and coordination complexes, dipole moments of molecules, relation of properties to structure

C. Nuclear chemistry: nuclear equations, half-lives, radioactivity, chemical applications

II. States of Matter (20%)

A. Gases

1. Laws of ideal gases
   - **a.** Equation of state for an ideal gas
   - **b.** Partial pressures
2. Kinetic-molecular theory
   - **a.** Interpretation of ideal gas laws on the basis of this theory
   - **b.** Avogadro's hypothesis and the mole concept
   - **c.** Dependence of kinetic energy of molecules on temperature
   - **d.** Deviations from ideal gas laws

B. Liquids and solids

1. Liquids and solids from the kinetic-molecular viewpoint
2. Phase diagrams of one-component systems
3. Changes of state, including critical points and triple points
4. Structure of solids, lattice energies

C. Solutions

1. Types of solutions and factors affecting solubility
2. Methods of expressing concentration (the use of formalities is not tested)
3. Raoult's law and colligative properties (nonvolatile solutes); osmosis
4. Non-ideal behavior (qualitative aspects)

** AP Course Description as published by the College Board*

III. Reactions (35–40%)

A. Reaction types

1. Acid-base reactions; concepts of Arrhenius, Brønsted-Lowry, and Lewis; coordination complexes, amphoterism
2. Precipitation reactions
3. Oxidation-reduction reactions
   - **a.** Oxidation number
   - **b.** The role of the electron in oxidation-reduction
   - **c.** Electrochemistry: electrolytic and galvanic cells, Faraday's laws, standard half-cell potentials, Nernst equation, prediction of the direction of redox reactions

B. Stoichiometry

1. Ionic and molecular species present in chemical systems: net ionic equations
2. Balancing of equations including those for redox reactions
3. Mass and volume relations with emphasis on the mole concept, including empirical formulas and limiting reactants

C. Equilibrium

1. Concept of dynamic equilibrium (physical and chemical), Le Chatelier's principle, equilibrium constants
2. Quantitative treatment
   - **a.** Equilibrium constants for gaseous reactions: K_p, K_c
   - **b.** Equilibrium constants for reactions in solution
     - **(1)** Constants for acids and bases: pK_a, pK_b, pH
     - **(2)** Solubility product constants and their application to precipitation and the dissolution of slightly soluble compounds
     - **(3)** Common ion effect, buffers, hydrolysis

D. Kinetics

1. Concept of rate of reaction
2. Use of experimental data and graphical analysis to determine reactant order, rate constants, and reaction rate laws
3. Effect of temperature change on rates
4. Energy of activation, the role of catalysts
5. The relationship between the rate-determining step and a mechanism

E. Thermodynamics

1. State functions
2. First law: change in enthalpy, heat of formation, heat of reaction, Hess's Law, heats of vaporization and fusion, calorimetry
3. Second law: entropy, free energy of formation, free energy of reaction, dependence of change in free energy on enthalpy and entropy changes
4. Relationship of change in free energy to equilibrium constants and electrode potentials

IV. Descriptive Chemistry (10–15%)

1. Chemical reactivity and products of chemical reactions
2. Relationships in the periodic table: horizontal, vertical, and diagonal with examples from alkali metals, alkaline earth metals, halogens, and the first series of transition elements
3. Introduction to organic chemistry: hydrocarbons and functional groups (structure, nomenclature, chemical properties)

V. Laboratory (5–10%)

The differences between college chemistry and the usual secondary school chemistry course are especially evident in the laboratory work. The AP Chemistry Exam includes some questions based on experiences and skills students acquire in the laboratory:

- making observations of chemical reactions and substances
- recording data
- calculating and interpreting results based on the quantitative data obtained
- communicating effectively the results of experimental work. The following list is a guideline for laboratory experiments that you should be familiar with:

1. Determination of the empirical formula of a compound
2. Determination of the percentage water in a hydrate
3. Determination of molar mass by vapor density
4. Determination of molecular mass by freezing point depression
5. Determination of the molar volume of a gas
6. Standardization of a solution using a primary standard
7. Determination of concentration by acid-base titration, including a weak acid or weak base
8. Determination of concentration by oxidation-reduction titration
9. Determination of mass and mole relationships in a chemical reaction
10. Determination of the equilibrium constant for a chemical reaction
11. Determination of appropriate indicators for various acid-base titrations, pH determination
12. Determination of the rate of a reaction and its order
13. Determination of enthalpy change associated with a reaction and Hess's Law
14. Separation and qualitative analysis of cations and anions
15. Synthesis of a coordination compound and its chemical analysis
16. Analytical gravimetric determination
17. Colorimetric or spectrophotometric analysis
18. Separation by chromatography
19. Preparation and properties of a buffer solution
20. Determination of electrochemical series
21. Measurement using electrochemical cells and electroplating
22. Synthesis, purification, and analysis of an organic compound

Questions Commonly Asked

Q. What is the AP Chemistry Exam?

A. The AP Chemistry Exam is given once a year to high school students and tests their knowledge of concepts in first-year college-level chemistry. The student who passes the AP exam may receive 1 year of college credit for taking AP chemistry in high school. Passing is generally considered to be achieving a score of 3, 4, or 5. The test is administered each May.

Q. What are the advantages of taking AP Chemistry?

A. There are several advantages of taking the AP Chemistry Exam:

- A student who passes the exam, at the discretion of the college in which the student enrolls, may be given full college credit for taking the class in high school.

- Taking the exam improves your chance of getting into the college of your choice. Studies show that students who successfully participate in AP programs in high school stand a much better chance of being accepted by selective colleges than students who do not.
- Taking the exam reduces the cost of a college education.
- Taking the exam may reduce the number of years needed to earn a college degree.
- If you take the course and the exam while still in high school, you will not be faced with the college course being closed or overcrowded.
- For those of you who are planning on a science career, passing the AP chemistry exam may fulfill the laboratory science requirement at the college, thus making more time available for you to take other courses.
- Taking AP chemistry greatly improves your chances of doing well in college chemistry. You will already have covered most of the topics during your high school AP chemistry program, and you will find yourself setting the curve in college.

Q. Do all colleges accept AP Exam scores for college credit?

A. Almost all of the colleges and universities in the United States and Canada, and many in Europe, take part in the AP program. The vast majority of the 3,000 U.S. colleges and universities that receive AP grades grant credit and/or advanced placement. Even colleges that receive only a few AP candidates and may not have specific AP policies are often willing to accommodate AP students who inquire about advanced placement work. To find out about a specific policy for the AP exam(s) you plan to take, contact the college's Director of Admissions.

Q. How is the AP exam graded and what do the scores mean?

A. The AP exam is graded on a five-point scale:

5: Extremely well qualified. About 17% of the students who take the exam earn this grade.

4: Well qualified. Roughly 15% earn this grade.

3: Qualified: Generally, 25% earn this grade.

2: Possibly qualified. Generally considered "not passing." About 22% of the students who take the exam earn this grade.

1: Not qualified. About 21% earn this grade.

Of the roughly 85,000 students from 6,500 high schools who take the AP chemistry exam each year, the average grade is 2.84.

Section I, the multiple-choice section, is machine graded. Each question has five answers to choose from, and there is a penalty for guessing: ¼ point is taken off for each wrong answer. A student generally needs to correctly answer 50% to 60% of the multiple-choice questions to obtain a 3 on the exam. Each answer in Section II, the free-response section, is read several times by different chemistry instructors who pay great attention to consistency in grading.

Q. Are there old exams available that I can look at?

A. Yes! Questions (and answers) from previous exams are available from The College Board. Request an order form by contacting apexams@ets.org.

Q. What materials should I take to the exam?

A. Be sure to take your admission ticket, some form of photo and signature identification, your social security number, several sharpened No. 2 pencils, a good eraser, a watch, and a scientific calculator with fresh batteries. You may bring a programmable calculator (it will not be erased or cleared), but it must not have a typewriter-style (QWERTY) keyboard. You may use the calculator only in Section II, Part A.

Q. When will I get my score?

A. The exam itself is generally given in the second or third week of May. The scores are usually available during the second or third week of July.

Q. Should I guess on the test?

A. Except in certain cases explained later in this book, you should not guess. There is a penalty for guessing on the multiple-choice section of the exam. As for the free-response section, it simply comes down to whether you know the material or not.

Q. Suppose I do not do well on the exam, may I cancel the test and/or scores?

A. You may cancel an AP grade permanently only if the request is received by June 15 of the year in which the exam was taken. There is no fee for this service, but a signature is required to process the cancellation. Once a grade is cancelled, it is permanently deleted from the records.

You may also request that one or more of your AP grades are not included in the report sent to colleges. There is a $5 fee for each score not included in the report.

Q. May I write on the exam?

A. Yes. Because scratch paper is not provided, you'll need to write in the test booklet. Make your notes in the booklet near the questions so that if you have time at the end, you can go back to your notes to try to answer the question.

Q. How do I register or get more information?

A. For further information contact:

AP Services
P.O. Box 6671
Princeton, NJ 08541-6671
Phone: (609) 771-7300 or (888) 225-5427 (*toll-free in the U.S. and Canada*)
E-mail: apexams@info.collegeboard.org

Strategies for Taking the AP Chemistry Exam

Section I: The Multiple-Choice Section

The "Plus-Minus" System

Many students who take the AP Chemistry Exam do not get their best possible score on Section I because they spend too much time on difficult questions and fail to leave themselves enough time to answer the easy ones. Don't let this happen to you. Because every question within each section is worth the same amount, consider the following guidelines:

1. Note in your test booklet the starting time of Section I. Remember that you have just over 1 minute per question.
2. Go through the entire test and answer all the easy questions first. Generally, the first 25 or so questions are considered by most to be the easiest questions, with the level of difficulty increasing as you move through Section I. Most students correctly answer approximately 60% of the first 25 multiple-choice questions, 50% of the next 25 questions, and only 30% of the last 25 questions (the fact that most students do not have time to finish the multiple-choice questions is factored into the percentages).
3. When you come to a question that seems impossible to answer, make a large minus sign (–) next to it in your test booklet. You are penalized for wrong answers, so do not guess at this point. Move on to the next question.
4. When you come to a question that seems solvable but appears too time-consuming, mark a large plus sign (+) next to that question in your test booklet. Do not guess; move on to the next question.
5. Your time allotment is just over 1 minute per question, so a "time-consuming" question is one that you estimate will take you several minutes to answer. Don't waste time deciding whether a question gets a plus or a minus. Act quickly. The intent of this strategy is to save you valuable time.

After you have worked all the easy questions, your booklet should look something like this:

1. C

+2.

3. B

–4.

5. A

etc.

6. After doing all the problems you can do immediately (the easy ones), go back and work on your "+" problems.
7. If you finish working your "+" problems and still have time left, you can do either of two things:

   Attempt the "–" problems, but remember not to guess under any circumstance.

   Forget the "–" problems, and go back over your completed work to be sure you didn't make any careless mistakes on the questions you thought were easy to answer.

You do not have to erase the pluses and minuses you made in your question booklet.

The Elimination Strategy

Take advantage of being able to mark in your test booklet. As you go through the "+" questions, eliminate choices from consideration by marking them out in your question booklet. Mark with question marks any choices you wish to consider as possible answers. See the following example:

~~A.~~

?B.

~~C.~~

~~D.~~

?E.

This technique will help you avoid reconsidering those choices that you have already eliminated and will thus save you time. It will also help you narrow down your possible answers.

If you are able to eliminate all but two possible answers, answers such as B and E in the previous example, you may want to guess. Under these conditions, you stand a better chance of raising your score by guessing than by leaving the answer sheet blank.

Section II: The Free-Response (Essay) Section

Many students waste valuable time by memorizing information that they feel they should know for the AP Chemistry Exam. Unlike the A.P. U.S. History Exam, for which you need to have memorized hundreds of dates, battles, names, and treaties, the AP Chemistry Exam requires you to have memorized comparatively little. Rather, it is generally testing whether you can *apply* given information to new situations. You will be frequently asked to explain, compare, and predict in the essay questions.

Section II of the AP Chemistry Exam comes with

- a periodic table
- an E°_{red} table
- a table of equations and constants

Method for Writing the Essays

The Restatement

In the second section of the AP Chemistry Exam, you should begin all questions by numbering your answer—the graders must be able to identify quickly which question you are answering. You may wish to underline key words or key concepts in your answer. However, do not underline too much, because doing so may obscure your reasons for underlining. In free-response questions that require specific calculations or the determination of products, you may also want to underline or draw a box around your final answer(s).

After you have written the problem number, restate the question in as few words as possible, but do not leave out any essential information. Often a diagram will help. By restating the question, you put the question in your own words and allow time for your mind to organize the way you intend to answer it. As a result, you eliminate a great deal of unnecessary language that clutters the basic idea.

If a question has several parts, such as (a), (b), (c), and (d), do not write all of the restatements together. Instead, write each restatement separately when you begin to answer that part. In these practice exams, you will see many samples of the uses of restatements.

Four Techniques for Answering Free-Response Questions

When you begin Section II, the essays, the last thing you want to do is start writing immediately. Take a minute and scan the questions. Find the questions that you know you will have the most success with, and put a star (*) next to them clearly in your response book.

After you have identified the questions that you will eventually answer, the next step is to decide what format each question lends itself to. There are four basic formats to answering free-response—essay questions. Let's do an actual essay question to demonstrate each format.

The Chart Format

In this format, you fill in a chart to answer the question. When you draw the chart, use the edge of your calculator case to make straight lines. Fill in the blanks with symbols, phrases, or incomplete sentences. The grid forces you to record all answers quickly and makes it unlikely that you will forget to give any part of the answer.

Essay 1

1. Given the molecules SF_6, XeF_4, PF_5, and ClF_3:

(a) Draw a Lewis structure for each molecule.
(b) Identify the geometry for each molecule.
(c) Describe the hybridization of the central atom for each molecule.
(d) Give the number of unshared pairs of electrons around the central atom.

Answer

1. Restatement: Given SF_6, XeF_4, PF_5, and ClF_3. For each, supply

(a) Lewis structure
(b) geometry
(c) hybridization
(d) unshared pairs

Characteristic	SF_6	XeF_4	PF_5	ClF_3
Lewis Structure	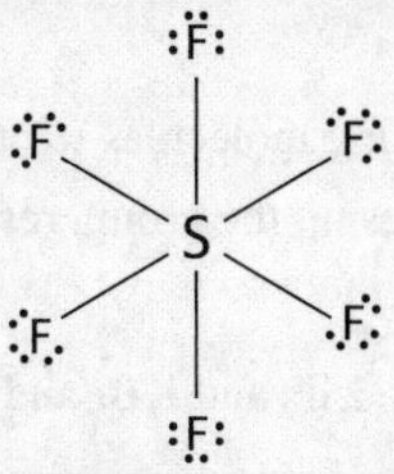	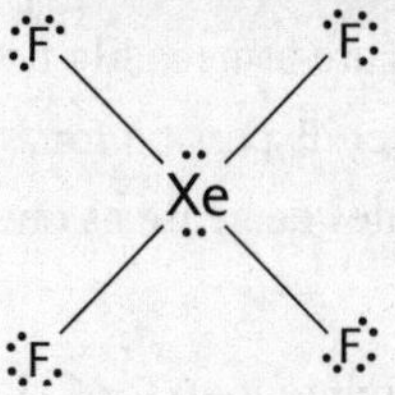	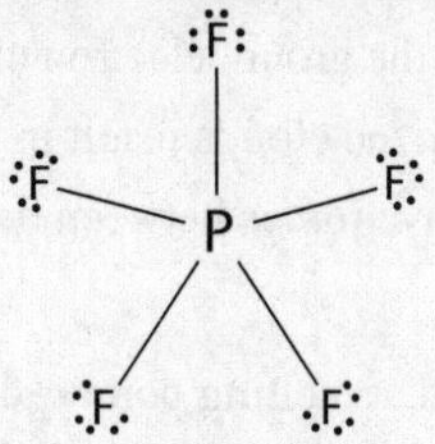	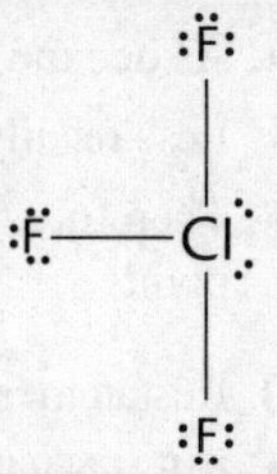
Geometry	Octahedral	Square planar	Triangular bipyramidal	T-shaped
Hybridization	sp^3d^2	sp^3d^2	sp^3d	sp^3d
Unshared pairs	0	2	0	2

The Bullet Format

The bullet format is also a very efficient technique because it, like the chart format, does not require complete sentences. In using this format, you essentially provide a list to answer the question. A "■" is a bullet, and each new concept receives one. Try to add your bullets in a logical sequence and leave room to add more bullets. You may want to come back later and fill them in. Don't get discouraged if you do not have as many bullets as the samples contain—it takes practice.

Essay 2

2. As one examines the periodic table, one discovers that the melting points of the alkali metals increase as one moves from cesium to lithium, whereas the melting points of the halogens increase from fluorine to iodine.

(a) Explain the phenomenon observed in the melting points of the alkali metals.
(b) Explain the phenomenon observed in the melting points of the halogens.
(c) Given the compounds CsI, NaCl, LiF, and KBr, predict the order of their melting points (from high to low) and explain your answer using chemical principles.

Answer

2. Given—melting points trends: alkali metals increase from Cs $\rightarrow$ Li; halogens increase from F $\rightarrow$ I

(a) Restatement: Explain alkali metal trend.

- ■ Observed melting point order: Li > Na > K > Rb > Cs
- ■ All elements are metals
- ■ All elements contain metallic bonds
- ■ Electrons are free to migrate in a "sea"
- ■ As one moves down the group, size (radius) of the atoms increases
- ■ As volume of atom increases, charge density decreases
- ■ Attractive force between atoms is directly proportional to melting point
- ■ Therefore, as attractive forces decrease moving down the group, melting point decreases

(b) Restatement: Explain halogen trend.

- ■ Observed melting point order: I > Br > Cl > F
- ■ All halogens are nonmetals
- ■ Intramolecular forces = covalent bonding
- ■ Intermolecular forces = dispersion (van der Waals) forces, which exist between molecules
- ■ Dispersion forces result from "temporary" dipoles caused by polarization of electron clouds

- As one moves up the group, the electron clouds become smaller
- Smaller electron clouds result in higher charge density
- As one moves up the group, electron clouds are less readily polarized
- Less readily polarized clouds result in weaker dispersion forces holding molecules to other molecules
- Therefore, attractive forces between molecules decrease as one moves up the group, resulting in lower melting points

(c) Restatement: Predict melting point order (high to low) for CsI, NaCl, LiF, and KBr and explain.

- LiF > NaCl > KBr > CsI
- All compounds contain a metal and a nonmetal ion
- Larger ionic radius results in lower charge density
- Lower charge density results in smaller attractive forces
- Smaller attractive forces result in lower melting point

The Outline Format

This technique is similar to the bullet format, but instead of bullets it uses the more traditional outline style that you may have used for years: Roman numerals, letters, and so on. The advantages of this format are that it does not require full sentences and that it progresses in a logical sequence. The disadvantage is that it requires you to spend more time thinking about organization. Leave plenty of room here because you may want to come back later and add more points.

Essay 3

3. The boiling points and electrical conductivities of six aqueous solutions are as follows:

Solution	Boiling Point	Relative Electrical Conductivity
0.05 *m* $BaSO_4$	100.025°C	0.03
0.05 *m* H_3BO_3	100.038° C	0.78
0.05 *m* NaCl	100.048° C	1.00
0.05 *m* $MgCl_2$	100.068° C	2.00
0.05 *m* $FeCl_3$	100.086° C	3.00
0.05 *m* $C_6H_{12}O_6$	100.025° C	0.01

Discuss the relationship among the composition, the boiling point, and the electrical conductivity of each solution.

Answer

3. Given: Boiling point data and electrical conductivities of six aqueous solutions, all at 0.05 *m*.

Restatement: Discuss any relationships between B.P. and electrical conductivities.

I. $BaSO_4$

A. $BaSO_4$ is an ionic compound.

B. According to known solubility rules, $BaSO_4$ is not very soluble.

1. If $BaSO_4$ were totally soluble, one would expect its B.P. to be very close to that of NaCl because $BaSO_4$ would be expected to ionize into two ions (Ba^{2+} and SO_4^{2-}) just as NaCl would (Na^+ and Cl^-). The substantial difference between the B.P. of the NaCl solution and that of the $BaSO_4$ solution suggests that the dissociation of the latter is negligible.
2. The electrical conductivity of $BaSO_4$ is closest to that of $C_6H_{12}O_6$, an organic molecule, which does not ionize; this observation further supports the previous evidence of the weak-electrolyte properties of $BaSO_4$.

II. H_3BO_3

A. H_3BO_3 is a weak acid.

B. In the equation $\Delta t = i \cdot m \cdot K_b$, where Δt is the boiling point elevation, m is the molality of the solution and K_b is the boiling point elevation constant for water. i (the van't Hoff factor) would be expected to be 4 if H_3BO_3 were completely ionized (3 H^+'s and 1 BO_3^-). According to data provided however, i is about 1.5. The BP of H_3BO_3 is about halfway in-between the aqueous solution of $C_6H_{12}O_6$ (a non-electrolyte, $n = 1$) and the aqueous solution of NaCl (an electrolyte, $n = 2$). Therefore, H_3BO_3 must have a relatively low K_a.

III. NaCl, $MgCl_2$, and $FeCl_3$

A. All three compounds are chlorides known to be completely soluble in water, so they are strong electrolytes and would increase electrical conductivities.

B. The van't Hoff factor (i) would be expected to be 2 for NaCl, 3 for $MgCl_2$, and 4 for $FeCl_3$.

C. Using the equation

$$\frac{\Delta t}{m \cdot K_b} = \frac{\text{B.P. of solution} - 100^\circ\text{C}}{(0.05 \text{ mole solute/kg})(0.512^\circ\text{C kg/mole solute})}$$

we find that the van't Hoff factors for these solutions are

Compound	Calculated i	Expected i
NaCl	1.9	2.0
$MgCl_2$	2.7	3.0
$FeCl_3$	3.4	4.0

which are in agreement.

D. The electrical conductivity data support the rationale just provided: the greater the number of particles, which in this case are ions, the higher the B.P.

IV. $C_6H_{12}O_6$

A. $C_6H_{12}O_6$, glucose, is an organic molecule. It would not be expected to dissociate into ions that conduct electricity. The reported electrical conductivity for glucose supports this.

B. Because $C_6H_{12}O_6$ does not dissociate, i is expected to be close to 1. The equation in III C gives i as exactly 1.

C. The boiling point elevation constant of 0.512°C · kg/mole would be expected to raise the B.P 0.026°C for a 0.05m solution when $i = 1$. The data show that the boiling point elevation is 0.026°C. This agrees with theory. Therefore, $C_6H_{12}O_6$ does not ionize. With few or no ions in solution, poor electrical conductivity is expected. This is supported by the evidence in the table.

The Free-Style Format

This method is the one most commonly used, although in my opinion, it is the method of last resort. Free-style often results in aimless, rambling, messy, incomplete answers. This method is simply writing paragraphs to explain the question. If you adopt this method for an answer (and many questions lend themselves only to this method) you MUST organize the paragraphs before writing. Adding thoughts at a later time is difficult with this approach because they will be out of logical sequence.

Essay 4

4. If one completely vaporizes a measured amount of a volatile liquid, the molecular weight of the liquid can be determined by measuring the volume, temperature, and pressure of the resulting gas. When one uses this procedure, one uses the ideal gas equation and assumes that the gas deviates from the ideal behavior. Explain the postulates of the ideal gas equation and explain why, when measurements are taken just above the boiling point, the calculated molecular weight of a liquid deviates from its true value.

Answer:

4. Restatement: Explain the ideal gas equation and explain why *MW* measurements taken just above the BP deviate.

The ideal gas equation, $PV = nRT$ stems from three relationships known to be true for gases under ordinary conditions:

1. The volume is directly proportional to the number of molecules, $V \sim n$
2. The volume is directly proportional to the absolute temperature, $V \sim T$
3. The volume is inversely proportional to the pressure, $V \sim 1/P$.

We obtain, n, the symbol used for the moles of gas, by dividing the mass of the gas by the molecular weight. In effect, $n = m / MW$. Substituting this relationship into the ideal gas law gives

$$PV = \frac{mRT}{MW}$$

Solving the equation for molecular weight gives

$$MW = \frac{mRT}{PV}$$

Real gas behavior deviates from the values obtained using the ideal gas equation because the ideal gas equation assumes that: (1) molecules do not occupy space; and (2) there is no attractive force between the individual molecules. However, at low temperatures (just above the boiling point of the liquid) these factors become significant and we must use an alternative equation known as the van der Waals equation.

At the lower temperatures, a greater attraction exists between the molecules, so the compressibility of the gas becomes a significant factor. This phenomenon causes the product of PV to be smaller than predicted. Since PV is found in the denominator, the calculated molecular weight would tend to be higher than the expected.

PART I

SUBJECT REVIEW

Atoms

You'll Need to Know

- ❑ what is the Aufbau Principle
- ❑ how to determine noble gas core abbreviation
- ❑ what is the Bohr model
- ❑ what are quantum numbers
- ❑ diamagnetism vs. paramagnetism
- ❑ important people, experiments, and theories
- ❑ energy and other relationships (amplitude, frequency, momentum, photoelectric effect, Planck's constant, Rydberg constant, velocity, wavelength, etc.)

The Aufbau Principle

Electrons are added to atoms in order of increasing energy: $1s^2 2s^2 2p^6 3s^2 3p^6 4s^2 3d^{10} 4p^6 5s^2 4d^{10} 5p^6 6s^2 4f^{14} 5d^{10} 6p^6 7s^2 5f^{14}$.

Noble Gas Core Abbreviation

Select the noble gas that most nearly precedes the element being considered. Place its symbol in square brackets, and continue from that point with the electron configuration. Example: Sr would be $[Kr]5s^2$.

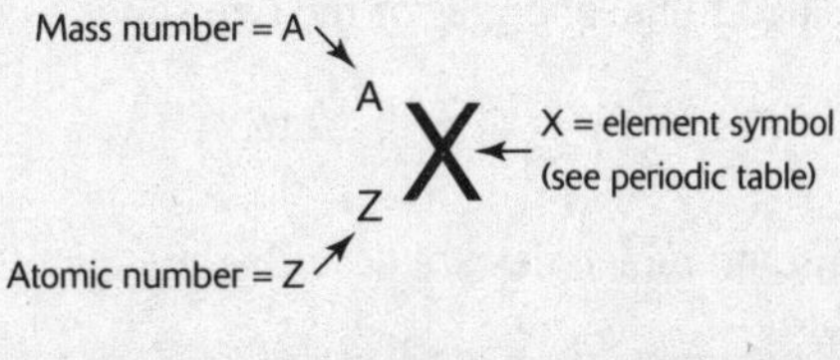

For neutral atoms, the number of electrons = the number of protons. The number of neutrons = A – Z.

Examples

Q. Write the electron configuration for Cl.

A. $1s^2 2s^2 2p^6 3s^2 3p^5$

Q. Write the electron configuration for Cl^-.

A. The "–" charge means to add an extra electron. $1s^2 2s^2 2p^6 3s^2 3p^6$. Cl^- is isoelectronic with Ar.

Q. Write the electron configuration for Ca^{2+}.

A. The 2+ charge means to subtract two electrons. It would be $1s^2 2s^2 2p^6 3s^2 3p^6$. Ca^{2+} is isoelectronic with Ar and Cl^-.

Q. Write the electron configuration for Cr.

A. [Ar] $4s^1 3d^5$ Extra stability is gained by having the *d* orbitals half-filled. You will find this same phenomenon with Cu: [Ar]$4s^1 3d^{10}$ in which the *d* orbitals are fully filled, providing a more stable configuration.

Q. Write the electron configuration for Mn^{3+}.

A. [Ar]$3d^4$ Transition metals characteristically have incompletely filled *d* orbitals and readily give rise to ions with incompletely filled *d* orbitals. This gives them distinct colors, ability to form paramagnetic compounds, catalytic activity, and the ability to form complex ions.

Q. How many unpaired electrons are there in the tungsten atom (W)?

A. Tungsten has 74 electrons. [Xe]$6s^2 4f^{14} 5d^4$. Each of the 5*d* electrons would be in a separate orbital, resulting in 4 unpaired electrons.

Bohr Model

A "solar system" model of the atom in which: (1) electrons moved in circular orbits around the nucleus; (2) only certain orbits with distinct radii were allowed (beginning of quantum theory); (3) energy of electron remained constant as long as it was within an orbit; (4) energy of the electron increased the farther its orbit was from the nucleus; (5) when energy was absorbed by the atom, the electron jumped to a higher energy orbit, farther from the nucleus; and (6) when energy was released by an atom, the electron jumped to a lower energy orbit, closer to the nucleus. Explained the source and observed wavelengths of lines in the hydrogen spectrum.

Quantum Numbers

Schrödinger described an atomic model with electrons in three dimensions and required three coordinates, or three quantum numbers, to describe where electrons could be found. The fourth quantum number(s) describes the spin of the electron. The three postulates of the quantum theory are: (1) atoms and molecules can exist only in discrete states, characterized by definite amounts of energy. When an atom or molecule changes state, it absorbs or emits just enough energy to bring it to another state; (2) when atoms or molecules absorb or emit light in moving from one energy state to another, the wavelength of the light is related to the energies of the two states as follows:

$$E_{\text{high}} - E_{\text{low}} = \frac{h \cdot c}{\lambda}$$

and (3) the allowed energy states of atoms and molecules are described by quantum numbers.

***n*: principal (shell) quantum number:** describes the energy level within the atom.

- 1 – 7 energy levels. As "*n*" increases, the shell is further away from the nucleus. Electrons have more energy the farther they are away from the nucleus.
- Maximum number of electrons in a shell (energy level) is $2n^2$.

***l*: momentum (subshell) quantum number:** describes the shape of the orbital. An orbital can hold a maximum of 2 electrons.

- Describes the sublevel in "*n*".
- Each energy level has "*n*" sublevels.
- Sublevels of different energy levels may have overlapping energies.
- Sublevels in the atoms of the known elements are:

  $l = 0$ (*s* orbital- spherical)
  $l = 1$ (*p* orbital- dumbbell shape)
  $l = 2$ (*d* orbital- cloverleaf shape)
  $l = 3$ (*f* orbital)

***m_l*: magnetic quantum number:** describes the direction or orientation in space for the orbital.

- *s* only has 1 orbital, coded as "0".
- *p* has 3 possible orbitals: p_x, p_y, and p_z; coded as –1, 0, 1 respectively.
- *d* has 5 possible orbitals: d_{z^2}, d_{xz}, d_{yz}, d_{xy}, $d_{x^2-y^2}$ coded as –2, –1, 0, 1, 2 respectively.
- *f* has 7 possible orbitals coded as –3, –2, –1, 0, 1, 2, 3.

***m_s*: spin quantum number:** describes the spin of the electron.

- Electrons in the same orbital must have opposite spins.
- Possible spins are clockwise (+½) or counterclockwise (–½).

Examples

Q. What are the possible values for an electron in a 4*d* orbital?

A. Principal energy level, $n = 4$. Since it is a *d* orbital, $l = 2$. m_l values can vary from $-l$ to l; therefore, m_l can be –2, –1, 0, 1, or 2.

Q. An atom has a principal quantum number of 3. How many orbitals are associated with $n = 3$?

A. For $n = 3$, there is one 3*s* orbital, three 3*p* orbitals; and five 3*d* orbitals for a total of 9.

Diamagnetism vs. Paramagnetism

Diamagnetic: all subshells are filled with electrons.

(Examples: He: $1s^2$; Be: $1s^22s^2$; Ne: $1s^22s^22p^6$). Elements are NOT affected by magnetic fields.

Paramagnetic: subshells are NOT completely filled with electrons.

(Examples: Li: $1s^22s^1$; N: $1s^22s^22p^3$; F: $1s^22s^22p^5$). Elements ARE affected by magnetic fields.

Example

Q. Is palladium (Pd) diamagnetic or paramagnetic?

A. Palladium has 46 electrons and an electron configuration $[Kr]4d^{10}$. Since the *d* orbitals are completely filled, palladium would be diamagnetic.

Important People, Experiments, and Theories

Neils **Bohr**	Electrons orbit the nucleus at specific fixed radii similar to planets orbiting the sun. Electrons can jump to higher energy levels after absorbing specific amounts of energy. Likewise, electrons dropping from higher to lower energy levels will release certain amounts of energy in the form of photons. Model was replaced with quantum mechanics.
Louis **de Broglie**	All matter has both particle and wave characteristics.
John **Dalton**	Elements are made up of unique atoms. Elements combine to make compounds. Compounds have constant ratios of atoms. Atoms are neither created nor destroyed in chemical reactions.
Albert **Einstein**	Photoelectric effect: When light with certain frequencies strikes a piece of metal, it emits electrons from the metal. Radiant energy behaves as a stream of tiny packets of energy (photons). Photons have properties of waves (wave-particle duality of nature).

Heisenberg Uncertainty Principle	It is not possible to know both the position and momentum of an electron at a particular moment. Electron orbitals are described in terms of probability.
Hund's Rule	Electrons will enter empty orbitals of equal energy when they are available.
James **Maxwell**	Maxwell provided a mathematical description of the general behavior of light. He described how energy in the form of radiation can travel through space as electric and magnetic fields.
Robert **Millikan**	Millikan calculated the charge of an electron.
Pauli Exclusion Principle	No two electrons in an atom have the same set of four quantum numbers.
Max **Planck**	Planck is the "father" of quantum mechanics. Energy can only be emitted or absorbed from atoms in fixed amounts (quanta).
Ernest **Rutherford**	Gold foil experiment: He shot a beam of alpha particles at a thin sheet of gold and found that the atoms in the foil must contain an extremely dense, positively charged core, sufficient to deflect the positively charged alpha particles. Atoms are mostly space. The nucleus is very dense positively charged center of atom. Electrons are small and travel around nucleus.
Erin **Schrödinger**	Through development of the Schrödinger equations, he was able to apply probability to describing the volume of space of where an electron would be located. Wave mechanics became the foundation for the development of the quantum model of the atom.
J.J. **Thomson**	"Plum Pudding Model": The atom consisted of a positively charged, spherical mass with negatively charged electrons scattered throughout.

Energy and Other Relationships

Amplitude (Ψ)	The vertical distance from the midline of a wave to the peak or trough.
Frequency (ν)	Number of waves that pass through a particular point in one second. Common units are hertz (Hz or sec^{-1}).
de Broglie equation	$\lambda = \frac{h}{m \cdot u}$
Electron charge (e^-)	$e^- = -1.602 \times 10^{-19}$ coulomb
Energy of an electron	$E_n = \frac{-2.178 \times 10^{-18}}{n^2}$ joules where E_n = energy of the electron and n = principal quantum number
Momentum	$p = m \cdot u$
Photoelectric effect	The emission of electrons from the surface of a metal when light shines on it. Electrons are emitted, however, only when the frequency of that light is greater than a certain threshold value characteristic of the particular metal.
Planck's constant (h)	$h = 6.63 \times 10^{-34}$ J · s
Rydberg constant	$R_H = 2.18 \times 10^{-18}$ J $\Delta E = h \cdot v = R_H\left(\frac{1}{n_i^2} - \frac{1}{n_f^2}\right)$
Speed of electromagnetic radiation (c)	$c = 3.00 \times 10^8$ m · s^{-1} ($c = \lambda \cdot \nu$)
Velocity (υ)	The speed of a wave. Common units are cm · sec^{-1}. $\upsilon = \lambda \cdot \nu$
Wavelength (λ)	Distance between identical points on successive waves. Common units are nanometers (10^{-9} m) or Angstrom (Å) (10^{-10} m).

Examples

Q. Calculate the speed of a wave whose wavelength is 17.5 cm and whose frequency is 89.0 Hz.

A. $\upsilon = \lambda \cdot \nu = 17.5\text{ cm} \cdot 89.0\text{ s}^{-1} = 1.56 \cdot 10^3\text{ cm} \cdot \text{s}^{-1}$

Q. Green light has a wavelength of 520 nm. What is the frequency of this light?

A. $$\nu = \frac{c}{\lambda} = \frac{3.00 \times 10^8\ \cancel{\text{m}}/\text{s}}{520\ \cancel{\text{nm}}} \times \frac{10^9\ \cancel{\text{nm}}}{1\ \cancel{\text{m}}} = 5.77 \times 10^{14} \cdot \text{s}^{-1}$$

Q. Calculate the energy (in joules) of a photon whose wavelength is 6.00 × 10⁴ nm.

A. $$E = \frac{h \cdot c}{\lambda} = \frac{(6.63 \times 10^{-34}\ \text{J} \cdot \text{s})(3.00 \times 10^8\ \cancel{\text{m}/\text{s}})}{6.00 \times 10^4\ \cancel{\text{nm}}} \times \frac{10^9\ \cancel{\text{nm}}}{1\ \cancel{\text{m}}} = 3.32 \times 10^{-21}\ \text{J}$$

Q. What is the wavelength (in nm) of a photon emitted during a transition from $n_i = 5$ state to the $n_f = 3$ state in the hydrogen atom?

$$\Delta E = h \cdot \nu = R_H\left(\frac{1}{n_i^2} - \frac{1}{n_f^2}\right) = 2.18 \times 10^{-18}\ \text{J}\left(\frac{1}{5^2} - \frac{1}{3^2}\right)$$

A. $$\Delta E = -1.53 \times 10^{-19}\ \text{J}\ \left(\textit{The} - \textit{sign indicates energy is being given off.}\right)$$

$$\lambda = \frac{c}{\nu} = \frac{c \cdot h}{\Delta E} = \frac{(3.00 \times 10^8\ \cancel{\text{m}}/\text{s})(6.63 \times 10^{-34}\ \cancel{\text{J}} \cdot \text{s})}{1.53 \times 10^{-19}\ \cancel{\text{J}}} \times \frac{10^9\ \text{nm}}{1\ \cancel{\text{m}}}$$

$$= 1.30 \times 10^3\ \text{nm}$$

Q. Calculate the wavelength of an electron in nanometers traveling at 61 m · s⁻¹. The mass of an electron is 9.1095 × 10⁻³¹ kg.

A. $$\lambda = \frac{h}{m \cdot \upsilon} = \frac{6.63 \times 10^{-34}\ \cancel{\text{J}} \cdot \cancel{\text{s}}}{(9.1095 \times 10^{-31}\ \cancel{\text{kg}})(61\ \cancel{\text{m}} \cdot \cancel{\text{s}^{-1}})} \times \frac{10^9\ \text{nm}}{1\ \cancel{\text{m}}} \times \frac{(\cancel{\text{kg}} \cdot \cancel{\text{m}^2}) \cdot \cancel{\text{s}^{-2}}}{1\ \cancel{\text{J}}}$$

$$= 1.2 \times 10^4\ \text{nm}$$

Multiple-Choice Questions

For Questions 1–5, choose from the following choices:

A. Max Planck
B. Niels Bohr
C. Werner Heisenberg
D. Louis de Broglie
E. Wolfgang Pauli

1. No two electrons in an atom can have the same set of four quantum numbers.

2. The theory that electrons travel in discrete orbits around the atom's nucleus, with the chemical properties of the element being largely determined by the number of electrons in the outer orbits. The idea that an electron could drop from a higher-energy orbit to a lower one, emitting a photon.

3. Wave-particle duality of nature.

4. Energy can only be absorbed or released in whole-number multiples of $h \cdot \nu$.

5. The simultaneous determination of both the position and momentum of a particle has an inherent uncertainty, the product of these being not less than a known constant.

6. How many electrons can be accommodated in all the atomic orbitals that correspond to the principal quantum number 4?

A. 2
B. 8
C. 18
D. 32
E. 40

7. The four quantum numbers that describe the valence electron in the cesium atom are

A. 6, 0, –1, ½
B. 6, 1, 1, ½
C. 6, 0, 0, ½
D. 6, 1, 0, ½
E. 6, 0, 1, –½

8. Which of the following does NOT represent a possible set of quantum numbers?

A. 2, 2, 0, ½
B. 2, 1, 0, –½
C. 4, 0, 0, –½
D. 3, 2, 0, ½
E. 4, 3, 1, ½

9. A photon was found to have a frequency of 3.00×10^{14} sec^{-1}. Calculate the wavelength of the photon given that the speed of light is 3.00×10^{8} $m \cdot s^{-1}$ and 1 meter = 10^{9} nm.

A. 1.00×10^{-6} nm
B. 3.00×10^{-3} nm
C. 1.00×10^{3} nm
D. 3.00×10^{3} nm
E. 3.00×10^{22} nm

10. Which of the following only has 1 electron in a *p* orbital?

A. carbon
B. fluorine
C. hydrogen
D. nitrogen
E. aluminum

11. Which of the following elements most readily shows the photoelectric effect?

A. noble gases
B. alkali metals
C. halogens
D. transition metals
E. chalcogens

12. An energy value of 3.313×10^{-19} joules is needed to break a chemical bond. What is the wavelength of energy needed to break the bond?

A. 5.00×10^{18} cm
B. 1.00×10^{15} cm
C. 2.00×10^{5} cm
D. 6.00×10^{-5} cm
E. 1.20×10^{-8} cm

13. Which of the following equations represents the energy of a single electron in a hydrogen atom when it is in the $n = 3$ state?

A. $\left(\frac{-2.178 \times 10^{-18}}{3}\right)$ joules

B. $\left(\frac{2.178 \times 10^{-18}}{3}\right)$ joules

C. $\left(\frac{3}{-2.178 \times 10^{-18}}\right)$ joules

D. $\left(\frac{-2.178 \times 10^{-18}}{9}\right)$ joules

E. $\left(\frac{-2.178 \times 10^{-18}}{2^3}\right)$ joules

14. What is the electron configuration of tin (Sn) in the ground state in order of filling orbitals from low energy to high energy?

A. $1s^22s^22p^63s^23p^64s^23d^{10}4p^65s^24d^{10}5p^2$
B. $1s^22s^22p^63s^23p^63d^{10}4s^24p^64d^{10}5s^25p^2$
C. $1s^22s^22p^63s^23p^63d^{10}4s^24p^64d^{10}5s^15p^3$
D. $1s^22s^22p^63s^23p^63d^{10}4s^24p^64d^{10}5s^25p^1$
E. $1s^22s^22p^63s^23p^63d^{10}4s^24p^64d^{10}4f^4$

15. Electrons will enter empty orbitals of equal energy when they are available. This is (the)

A. Heisenberg Uncertainty Principle
B. Hund's Rule
C. Pauli Exclusion Principle
D. de Broglie hypothesis
E. Schrödinger equation

16. The electron configuration for V^{3+} would be

A. $[Ar]3d^1$
B. $[Ar]3d^2$
C. $[Ar]3d^3$
D. $[Kr]3d^1$
E. $[Kr]3d^2$

17. The electron configuration for gold in its ground state would be

A. $[Au]6s^1 4f^{14} 5d^{10}$
B. $[Xe]6s^2 5d^9$
C. $[Xe]6s^1 4f^{14} 5d^{10}$
D. $[Xe]5s^1 4d^{10}$
E. $[Xe]5s^2 4d^9$

18. A Co^{3+} ion has _____ unpaired electron(s) and is _____.

A. 1, diamagnetic
B. 3, paramagnetic
C. 3, diamagnetic
D. 4, paramagnetic
E. 10, paramagnetic

For Questions 19–20:

I. carbon
II. selenium
III. calcium
IV. sulfur
V. germanium

19. Which two would have a valence electron configuration of ns^2np^4?

A. I and II
B. II and III
C. III and IV
D. II and IV
E. IV and V

20. Which two would have a valence electron configuration of ns^2np^2?

A. I and II
B. II and III
C. III and IV
D. II and IV
E. I and V

Free-Response Questions

1.

(a) Write the:

(i) complete ground-state electron configuration for an arsenic atom; and

(ii) use the noble gas core abbreviation method for electron configuration.

(b) Assuming arsenic to be in its ground state, write the four quantum numbers for:

(i) each of the two electrons in the 4*s* orbital; and

(ii) each of the three electrons in the 4*p* orbitals.

(c) Is the arsenic atom in its ground state diamagnetic or paramagnetic? Explain the difference.

(d) Write the formulas for and explain how the electron configuration of arsenic in its ground state is consistent with:

(i) sodium arsenide

(ii) arsenic(III) chloride

(iii) arsenic(V) fluoride

2. Answer the following questions about the element Cobalt, Co (atomic number = 27).

(a) Samples of natural cobalt show that there is 1 naturally occurring isotope, atomic mass = 59 while 33 other isotopes of cobalt have been discovered ranging from atomic mass of 48 to an atomic mass of 75. In terms of atomic structure, explain what these isotopes have in common and how they differ.

(b) Write the complete electron configuration for the cobalt atom (*e.g.*, $1s^2 2s^2$ . . . etc.) and the Co^{3+} ion.

(c) Indicate the number of unpaired electrons in the ground-state atom and the Co^{3+} ion and explain your reasoning.

(d) In terms of atomic structure, explain why the first ionization energy of cobalt (758 kJ/mol) is less than that of krypton (1351 kJ/mol) but greater than that of potassium (419 kJ/mol).

(e) Account for at least three properties of transition metals such as cobalt.

(f) Write the quantum numbers for at least three *d* electrons in the Co^{3+} ion.

Answers and Explanations

Multiple Choice

1. **E.**
2. **B.**
3. **D.**
4. **A.**
5. **C.**
6. **D.** A principal quantum number of 4 tells you that you are in the 4th energy level. The 4th energy level contains electrons in the *s*, *p*, *d* and *f* orbitals. Counting the maximum numbers of electrons available in each of the four types of sublevels; 2 in the *s*, 6 in the *p*, 10 in the *d*, and 14 in the *f* yields a total of 32. Alternatively, you can use the equation, $2n^2$ ($2 \cdot 4^2 = 32$).
7. **C.** The valence electron for the cesium atom is in the 6*s* orbital. In assigning quantum numbers, n = principal energy level = 6. The quantum number l represents the angular momentum (type of orbital). In this case, $l = 0$. The quantum number m_l is known as the magnetic quantum number and describes the orientation of the orbital in space. For *s* orbitals (as in this case), m_l always equals 0. The quantum number m_s is known as the electron spin quantum number and can take only two values, +½ and –½.
8. **A.** If $n = 2$, then l must be 0 or 1 (representing either an *s* or *p* orbital).
9. **C.** $\lambda = \frac{c}{\nu} = \frac{3.00 \times 10^8 \text{ m} \cdot \text{s}^{-1}}{3.00 \times 10^{14} \text{ s}^{-1}} \times \frac{10^9 \text{ nm}}{1 \text{ m}} = 1.00 \times 10^3 \text{ nm}$
10. **E.** $1s^22s^22p^63s^23p^1$
11. **B.** Alkali metals have only one electron in their valence shells and thus have the lowest threshold values that are susceptible to the photoelectric effect.
12. **D.** $\lambda = \frac{h \cdot c}{E} = \frac{6.626 \times 10^{-34} \text{ J} \cdot \text{sec} \cdot 3.00 \times 10^{10} \text{ cm} \cdot \times \text{sec}^{-1}}{3.313 \times 10^{-19} \text{ J}} = 6.00 \times 10^{-5} \text{ cm}$
13. **D.** The equation is $E_n = \frac{-2.178 \times 10^{-18}}{n^2}$ joules

    where E_n = energy of the electron and n = principal quantum number
14. **A.** The electron configuration follows the Aufbau process; there are no exceptions with tin.
15. **B.**
16. **B.**
17. **C.** Stability is achieved when the outer *d* orbitals are completely filled. The 5*d* orbitals are far enough away from the nucleus where small shifts in orbital location can occur that will favor stability.
18. **D.** The electron configuration for the Co^{3+} ion is $1s^22s^22p^63s^23p^63d^6$ and would have 24 electrons; 10 pairs of electrons and four unpaired electrons in the 3*d* orbits. Atoms in which one or more electrons are unpaired are paramagnetic.
19. **D.** Sulfur: $[Ne]3s^23p^4$; Selenium: $[Ar]4s^23d^{10}4p^4$
20. **E.** Carbon: $[He]2s^22p^2$; Germanium: $[Ar]4s^23d^{10}4p^2$

Free Response

Question 1

Maximum Points for Question 1
Part (a): 2 points
Part (b): 2 points
Part (c): 2 points
Part (d): 6 points
Total points: 12

1.	***2 points possible***
(a) Write the:	
(i) complete ground-state electron configuration for an arsenic atom: $1s^2\ 2s^22p^6\ 3s^23p^6\ 4s^23d^{10}4p^3$	*1 point for correctly writing the complete electron configuration.*
(ii) use the noble gas core abbreviation method for electron configuration: $[Ar]4s^23d^{10}4p^3$	*1 point for correctly writing the noble gas core abbreviation method for the electron configuration for arsenic.*
(b) Assuming arsenic to be in its ground state, write the four quantum numbers for:	***2 points possible***
(i) each of the two electrons in the 4s orbital: 4*s* 4, 0, 0, +½ and 4, 0, 0, −½	*1 point for correctly writing the electron configuration for an electron in the 4s.*
(ii) each of the three electrons in the 4p orbitals: 4*p* electrons 4, 1, −1, +½; 4, 1, 0, +½ and 4, 1, +1, +½	*1 point for correctly writing the electron configuration for an electron in a 4p orbital.*
(c) Is the arsenic atom in its ground state diamagnetic or paramagnetic? Explain the difference.	***2 points possible***
Paramagnetic. It has three unpaired electrons.	*1 point for correctly identifying that the arsenic atom is paramagnetic.* *1 point for explaining why it is paramagnetic.*

(d) Write the formulas for and explain how the electron configuration of arsenic in its ground state is consistent with: *(i) sodium arsenide* Na_3As: each Na gives up one electron to the As; the As has a complete octet; and the sodium atoms are ionically bonded to the arsenic. *(ii) arsenic(III) chloride* $AsCl_3$: the three chlorines each have one half-filled orbital and the arsenic has three. Three covalent bonds are created and the As has one non-bonding pair which forms a pyramidal structure. *(iii) arsenic(IV) fluoride* AsF_5: fluorine is highly electronegative. As such, it draws the two electrons of the non-bonding pair of $AsCl_3$ into bonding. A 4*d* orbital is involved in the sp^3d hybridization, and results in a trigonal bipyramidal geometry.	***6 points possible*** *1 point for each formula written correctly (3 points maximum).* *1 point each for a correct explanation of the bonding characteristics in each of the three examples (3 points maximum).*

Question 2

Maximum Points for Question 2
Part (a): 1 point
Part (b): 2 points
Part (c): 2 points
Part (d): 1 point
Part (e): 3 points
Part (f): 1 point
Total points: 10

2. Answer the following questions about the element Cobalt, Co (atomic number = 27). *(a) Samples of natural cobalt show that there is 1 naturally occurring isotope, atomic mass = 59 while 33 other isotopes of cobalt have been discovered ranging from atomic mass of 48 to an atomic mass of 75. In terms of atomic structure, explain what these isotopes have in common and how they differ.* The isotopes have the same number of protons (27) but different numbers of neutrons.	***1 point possible*** *No comment about the number of electrons is necessary.*

(b) Write the complete electron configuration for the cobalt atom (e.g., $1s^22s^2$ . . . etc.) and the Co^{3+} ion.	***2 points possible***
Co: $1s^22s^22p^63s^23p^64s^23d^7$	*1 point for Co.*
Co^{3+}: $1s^22s^22p^63s^23p^63d^6$	*1 point for Co^{3+}.*
(c) Indicate the number of unpaired electrons in the ground-state atom and the Co^{3+} ion and explain your reasoning.	***2 points possible***
Co: 3 unpaired	*1 point for Co.*
4*s* (↑↓) 3*d* (↑↓) (↑↓) (↑) (↑) (↑)	
Co^{3+}: 4 unpaired	
4*s* (↑↓) 3*d* (↑↓)(↑)(↑)(↑)(↑)	*1 point for Co^{3+}.*
(d) In terms of atomic structure, explain why the first ionization energy of cobalt (758 kJ/mol) is less than that of krypton (1351 kJ/mol) but greater than that of potassium (419 kJ/mol).	***1 point possible***
Ionization energy is the measure of how difficult it is to remove an electron from an atom. Since energy must be absorbed to bring about ionization, ionization energies are always positive quantities. The first ionization energy is the energy change required for the removal of the outermost electron from a gaseous atom to form a +1 ion. In general, the larger the ionization energy, the more difficult it is to remove an electron. Ionization energies increase from left to right across a period as more protons are being added (greater attraction of the electrons to the nucleus) and decrease down a group (the outermost electrons are moving farther away from the nucleus). While both potassium and krypton are in the same period as cobalt, potassium has 19 protons and krypton has 36 compared to cobalt with 27.	*1 point possible for properly explaining what ionization energy is and the reasons why ionization energy increases from left to right within a period.*
(e) Account for at least three properties of transition metals such as cobalt.	***3 points possible***
Moving from left to right across the periodic table, the five *d* orbitals for transition metals become more filled. The *d* electrons are loosely bound, which contributes to the high electrical conductivity and malleability of the transition elements. The transition elements have low ionization energies. They exhibit a wide range of oxidation states or positively charged forms. The positive oxidation states allow transition elements to form many different ionic and partially ionic compounds. The formation of complexes causes the *d* orbitals to split into two energy sublevels, which enables many of the complexes to absorb specific frequencies of light. Thus, the complexes form characteristic colored solutions and compounds. Complexation reactions sometimes enhance the relatively low solubility of some compounds.	*1 point for each property.*

(f) Write the quantum numbers for at least three d electrons in the Co^{3+} *ion.* 3,2,2,½; 3,2,2,–½; 3,2,1,½; 3,2,0,½; 3,2,–1,½; 3,2,–2,½	***1 point possible*** *Given any three, all three must be correct.* *Other combinations are possible.*

Periodic Table

You'll Need to Know

- ❑ how to determine the periodic trends (electron affinity, ionization energy, atomic radius, electronegativity, ionic radii, melting and boiling point relationships and shielding)
- ❑ what are chemical properties and periodicity
- ❑ metals vs. nonmetals
- ❑ important people, experiments, and theories

Periodic Trends

Electron affinity

Electron affinity is the amount of energy needed to remove an electron from a negatively charged ion. It's also the energy released when a single electron is combined with an isolated atom. The more negative the electron affinity, the greater the tendency of the atom to accept an electron. The tendency to accept electrons increases (electron affinity values become more negative) from left to right. Within a period, electron affinities of metals are more positive (less negative) than those of nonmetals. Halogens have the highest electron affinities.

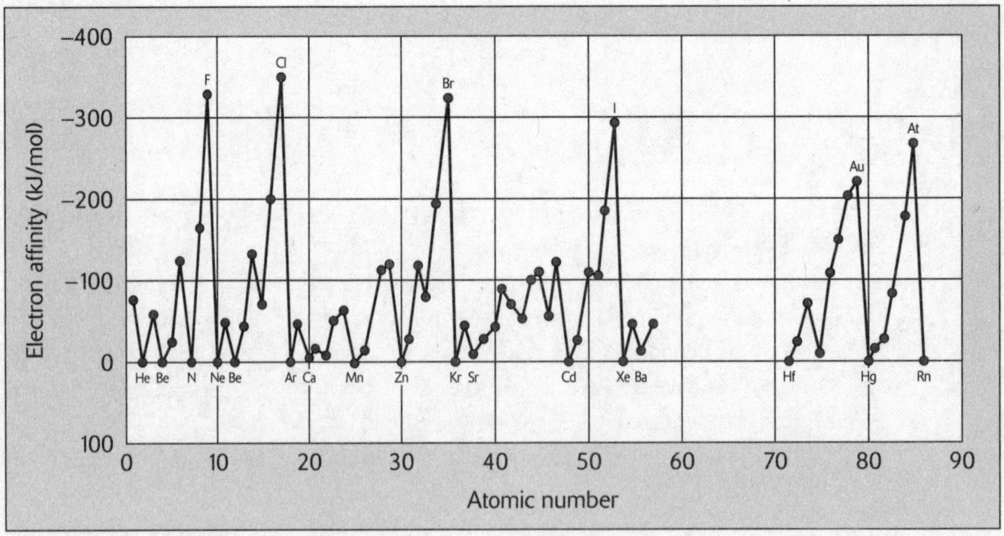

Ionization energy

Ionization energy is the amount of energy required to remove an electron from an atom to form a positive ion (cation). It measures how "tightly" an electron is held to an atom. Within a period, ionization increases from left to right with the metals having relatively low ionization energies, and the nonmetals have higher ionization energies. First, ionization energy (I_1) refers to the energy required to remove the highest energy electron from a neutral atom. Example: Neon has a higher first ionization energy (2,080 kJ/mol) than potassium (419 kJ/mol). The second ionization energy (I_2) is the energy needed to remove the next (i.e., the second) electron from the atom. The higher the value of the ionization energy, the more difficult it is to remove the electron. As electrons are removed, the positive charge from the nucleus remains unchanged; however, there is less repulsion between the remaining electrons:

- Z_{eff} increases with removal of electrons
- Greater energy is needed to remove remaining electrons (i.e., the ionization energy is higher for each subsequent electron)

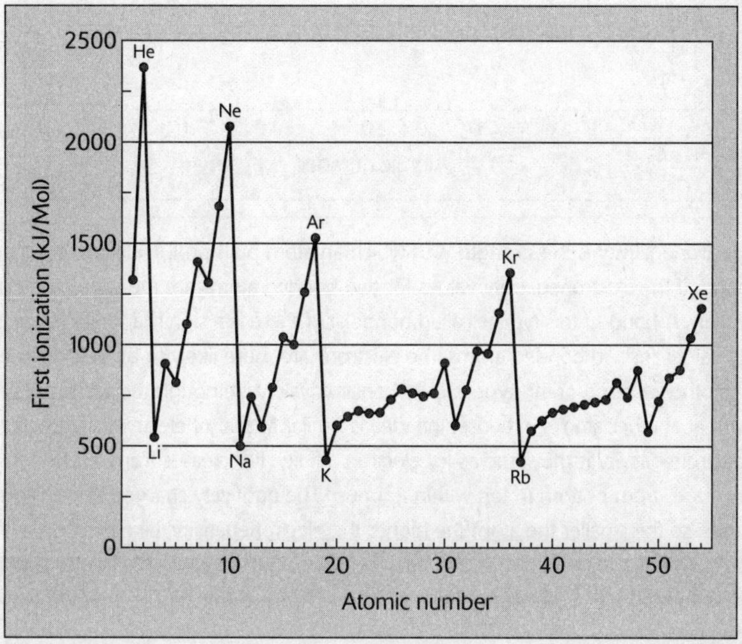

Atomic radius

Atomic radius is the distance from the atomic nucleus to the outermost stable electron orbital in an atom or, one-half the distance between nuclei of atoms of the same element when the atoms are bound by a single covalent bond or are in a metallic crystal. Two factors control atomic radius: (1) the value of the principal quantum number (*n*) and (2) the amount of positive charge in the nucleus. As one moves down a row on the periodic table, the elements have higher numbered shells occupied by electrons. Higher numbered shells have electrons farther from the nucleus; therefore, atomic radius increases as you go down a period as inner core electrons shield some of the positive charge from the outer electrons. As electron count increases, so does proton count. The nucleus gets progressively more positive as you go across a period. As you move across a period, each successive electron enters the same shell. Electrons in the same shell don't shield one another from the nucleus very well, yet the nucleus gets more positive. Therefore, the shells contract, and the atomic radius decreases across a period.

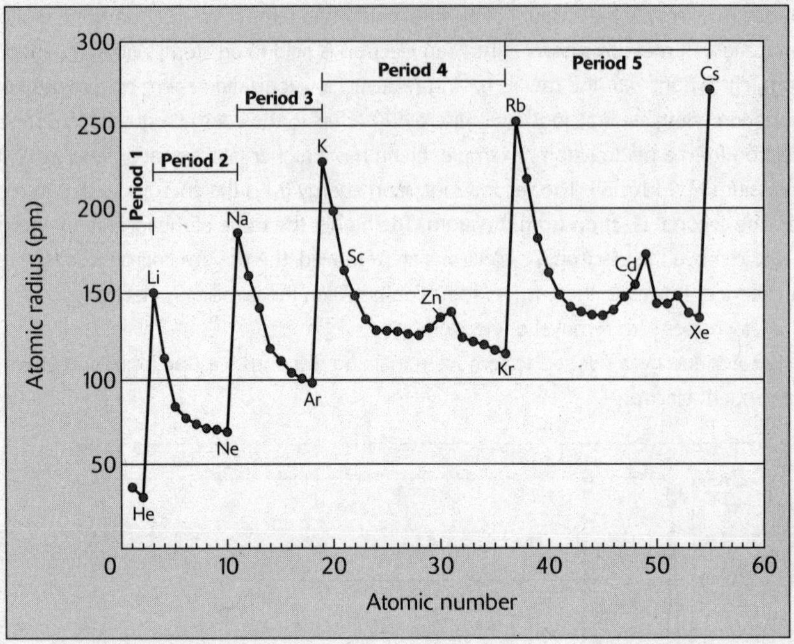

Electronegativity

Electronegativity is the strength with which an atom pulls on the electrons it shares in a covalent bond. If the electronegativity values for two bonded atoms are the same, the electrons are shared evenly. A bond of this type is called nonpolar. If there is a significant difference in the electronegativity values for two bonded atoms, the electrons are more likely to be found closer to one atom than the other. A bond of this type is called polar covalent. Although the atom does not gain an extra electron at another atom's expense, the idea is similar to that of electron affinity. The periodic trend for electronegativity is the same as for electron affinity: It increases from left to right across a period and increases from bottom to top within a group. The positively charged nucleus pulls on the outer electrons, so the smaller the atom the higher the electronegativity. Like electron affinity, the noble gases do not obey the trend due to the stability they gain from having full outer shells. There are several ways to report electronegativity values, one of which is the Pauling method (see diagram below).

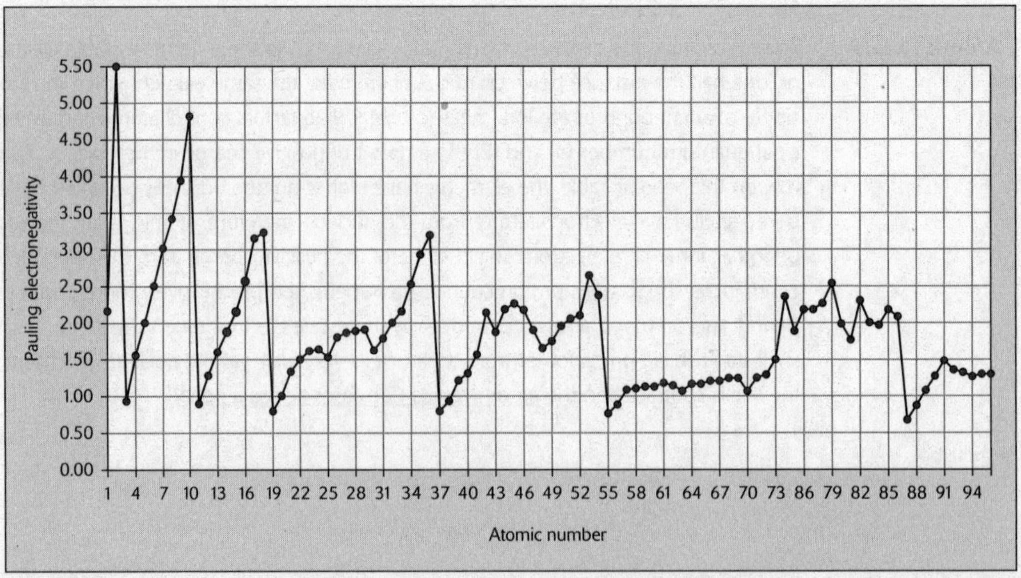

Ionic radii The radius of cations is always smaller than the radius of the atoms from which they are derived because whenever metals are converted to their cations, they always do so by losing the electrons in their highest energy level. Furthermore, since the ion has less electrons than the atom from which it was derived, there is less mutual repulsion among the electrons, and the electron orbitals "shrink" to some extent.

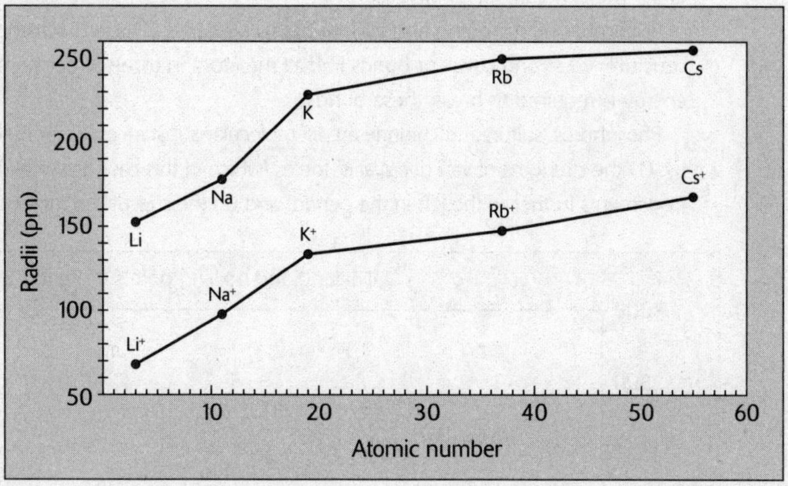

The radius of anions is always larger than the covalent radius of the atoms from which they are derived because the additional electrons increase the mutual repulsion among the electrons, which causes an expansion of the electron orbitals.

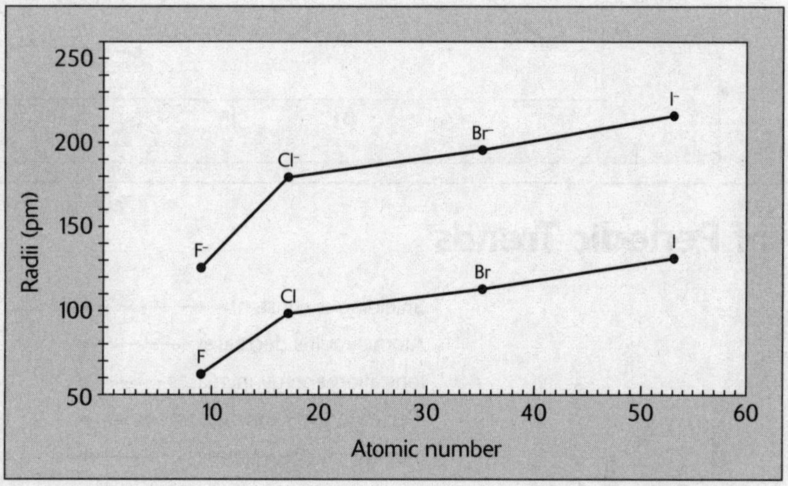

Melting points and boiling point

The melting points and boiling points, along with density, heat of vaporization, and heat of fusion depend on the bond strength and structure of the elements. On the AP Chemistry Exam if you understand what is happening in the third period, you'll understand the general trend. From Na to Al, the elements are metals. The melting points and boiling points increase because: (1) the atoms become smaller, (2) they have increasing effective nuclear charge (Z_{eff}), and (3) therefore, the strengths of the metal-metal bonds increase.

Silicon has high melting and boiling points because: (1) it is macromolecular with a diamond structure, (2) strong covalent bonds link all the atom in three dimensions, and (3) a great deal of energy is required to break these bonds.

Phosphorus, sulfur, and chlorine are all molecular substances. Their melting points are determined by: (1) the strengths of van der Waals' forces (which in this case are weak and easily broken compared to elements further to the left in the period) and (2) the size of the molecules.

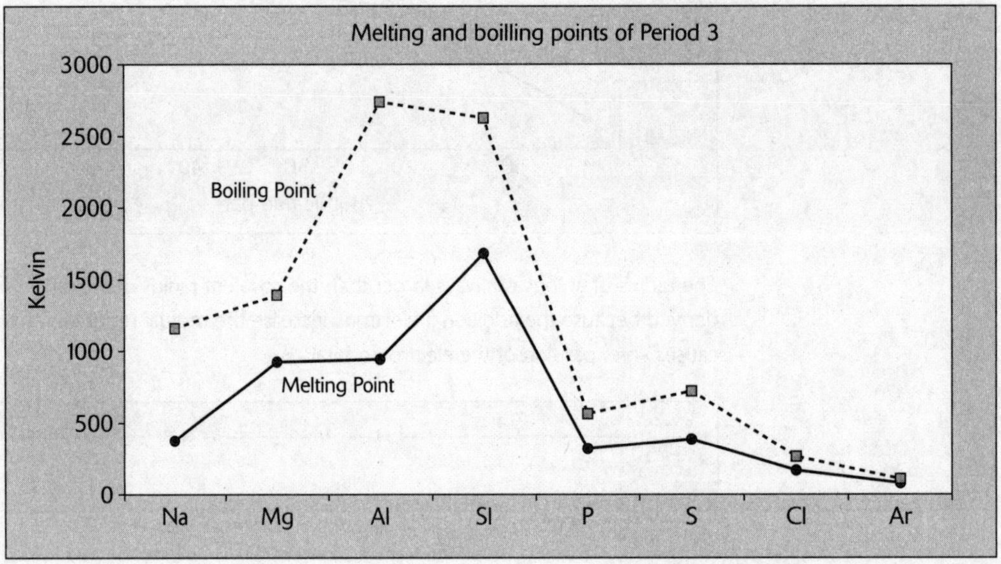

Summary of Periodic Trends

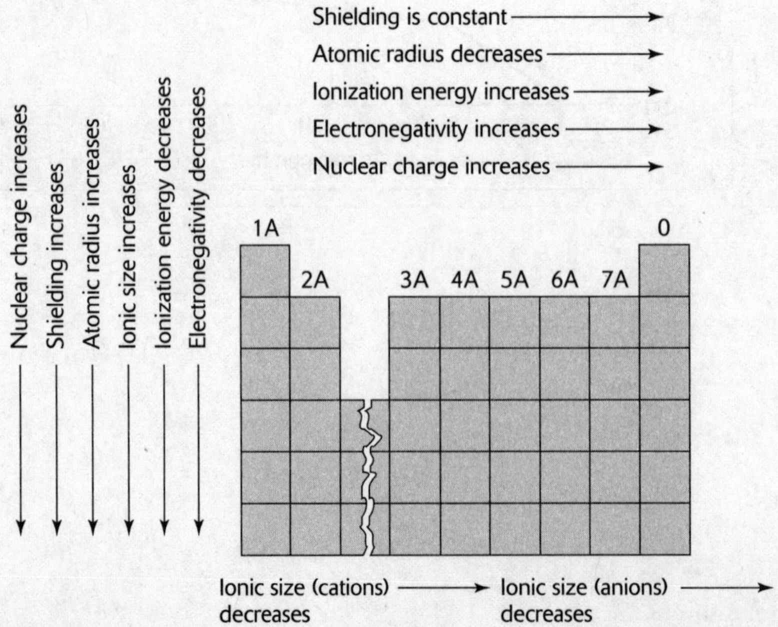

Examples

Account for each of the following in terms of principles of periodic trends

Q. Beryllium's first ionization energy is higher than the first ionization energy of boron.

A. The electron ionized in the case of Be is a 2*s* electron whereas in the case of B it is a 2*p* electron. 2*p* electrons are higher in energy than 2*s* electrons because 2*p* electrons penetrate the core to a lesser degree.

Q. Nitrogen's first ionization energy is higher than that of oxygen's.

A. The electron ionized in O is paired with another electron in the same orbital, whereas in N the electron comes from a singly occupied orbital. The ionization energy of the O electron is less because of the repulsion between two electrons in the same orbital.

Q. A potassium atom is larger than a zinc atom.

A. A zinc atom has more protons (11 more) than an atom of potassium. Electrons in the *d* orbitals of Zn have a lower principal quantum number; thus, they are not in orbitals that are farther from the nucleus.

Q. Nitrogen has a smaller radius and higher ionization energy than either oxygen or carbon.

A. Second row elements, specifically carbon, nitrogen, and oxygen have four subshells or orbitals in their valence shell: one *s* orbital and three *p* orbitals. The *s* orbital is slightly lower in energy and more tightly held than the *p* orbitals. In atomic carbon, there are four valence electrons (two in the lower-energy *s* orbital and one in each of two *p* orbitals). In atomic nitrogen, there are five valence electrons (two in the *s* orbital, and one in each of the three *p* orbitals). However, since the *p*-electrons are equally distant from the nucleus, they don't "shield" each other. Shielding occurs due to the decrease in the attraction between outer electrons and the nucleus, due to the presence of other electrons between them. Since nitrogen has one more proton than carbon, the atomic radius drops. In atomic oxygen, there are six valence electrons (two in the *s* orbital, one in each of two separate *p* orbitals and two in the third *p* orbital. The *p* electrons are attracted by a larger nuclear charge than found in nitrogen (+8 rather than +7), and therefore are more tightly held. However, the electron-electron repulsion is greater in oxygen than is found in nitrogen; the net effect being that the atomic radius of oxygen is slightly larger than that of nitrogen, just as oxygen's first ionization energy is slightly less.

Chemical Properties and Periodicity

Group 1A (alkali metals) (ns^1, $n \geq 2$)	Low ionization energies. Tendency to lose single valence electron. Highly reactive, never found in free form. React with water to produce hydrogen gas and metal hydroxide: $2M_{(s)} + 2H_2O_{(l)} \rightarrow 2MOH_{(aq)} + H_{2(g)}$. When combined with oxygen, they can form various oxides based on their stability: Li_2O, lithium oxide, peroxides (Na_2O_2, sodium peroxide) or superoxides (KO_2, potassium superoxide). Sodium oxide reacts with water to form a base, sodium hydroxide: $Na_2O_{(s)} + H_2O_{(l)} \rightarrow 2NaOH_{(aq)}$.
Group 2A (alkaline earth metals) (ns^2, $n \geq 2$)	Less reactive than Group 1A metals. Tendency to form M^{2+} ions increases as one moves down column. Be does not react with H_2O. Mg reacts slowly with steam. Calcium, strontium, and barium react with H_2O: $Ba_{(s)} + 2H_2O_{(l)} \rightarrow Ba(OH)_{2(aq)} + H_{2(g)}$. Reactivities of alkaline earth metals toward oxygen increase from Be to Ba. BeO and MgO are only formed at high temperatures. Mg, Ca, Sr, and Ba react with acid to produce hydrogen gas: $M_{(s)} + 2H^+_{(aq)} \rightarrow M^{2+}_{(aq)} + H_{2(g)}$. Magnesium oxide reacts with acids to form a salt and water (the usual products of an acid-base reaction): $MgO_{(s)} + 2HCl_{(aq)} \rightarrow MgCl_{2(aq)} + H_2O_{(l)}$.

Group 3A (ns^2np^1, $n \geq 2$)	B is a metalloid, does not form binary ionic compounds, and is unreactive towards oxygen and water. The rest are metals. Al reacts with oxygen gas: $4Al_{(s)} + 3O_{2(g)} \rightarrow 2Al_2O_{3(s)}$. Al reacts with acid: $2Al_{(s)} + 6H^+_{(aq)} \rightarrow 2Al^{3+}_{(aq)} + 3H_{2(g)}$. Aluminum oxide shows basic properties by reacting with acids to form a salt and water: $Al_2O_{3(s)} + 6HCl_{(aq)} \rightarrow 2AlCl_{3(aq)} + 3H_2O_{(l)}$. It also shows acidic properties by reacting with bases: $Al_2O_{3(s)} + 2NaOH_{(aq)} + 3H_2O_{(l)} \rightarrow 2NaAl(OH)_{4(aq)}$. Since it exhibits BOTH acidic and basic properties, Al_2O_3 is an amphoteric oxide. Other amphoteric oxides include ZnO, BeO and Bi_2O_3. Ga, In and Tl form +1 and +3 ions. +1 ions in this group are more stable than +3 ions due to the inert-pair effect (the two relatively stable and unreactive outer *s* electrons). Metallic elements in Group 3A also form molecular (covalent) compounds.
Group 4A (ns^2np^2, $n \geq 2$)	C is a nonmetal. Si and Ge are metalloids and do not form ionic compounds. Tin and lead do not react with water but do react with acid to produce hydrogen gas: $M_{(s)} + 2H^+_{(aq)} \rightarrow M^{2+}_{(aq)} + H_{2(g)}$. Form compounds in both +2 and +4 oxidation states (for carbon and silicon, +4 is most stable; i.e. CO_2 is more stable than CO). In lead compounds, +2 state is more stable due to inert-pair effect- lead loses the 6*p* electrons to form Pb^{2+}, not the 6*s* electrons.
Group 5A (ns^2np^3, $n \geq 2$)	Nitrogen and phosphorus are nonmetals. Arsenic and antimony are metalloids. Bi is a metal. Nitrogen reacts with oxygen to form $NO_{(g)}$ (nitric oxide), $N_2O_{(g)}$ (nitrous oxide), $NO_{2(g)}$ (nitrogen dioxide), $N_2O_{4(g)}$ (dinitrogen tetroxide) and $N_2O_{5(s)}$ (dinitrogen pentoxide). Nitrogen accepts 3 electrons to form the nitride ion, N^{3-} (isoelectronic with neon). Metallic nitrides are ionic (Li_3N, Mg_3N_2, etc.). Phosphorus exists as the allotrope P_4 (tetrahedron). P reacts with oxygen to form either P_4O_6 or P_4O_{10}. P_4O_{10} reacts with water to form phosphoric acid: $P_4O_{10(s)} + 6H_2O_{(l)} \rightarrow 4H_3PO_{4(aq)}$.
Group 6A (chalcogens) (ns^2np^4, $n \geq 2$)	O, S and Se are nonmetals. Te and Po are metalloids. Oxygen exists as either O_2 (oxygen gas) or O_3 (ozone). $3O_{2(g)} \rightarrow 2O_{3(g)}$ $\Delta H^\circ = +284.5$ kJ · mol^{-1}. Ozone is thermodynamically unstable and spontaneously reverts back into oxygen. Ozone is a strong oxidizing agent and is used in disinfection and blocks out UV radiation from the sun. Oxygen forms the oxide ion (O^{2-}) in most ionic compounds. Sulfur and selenium form the allotropes S_8 and Se_8, respectively. Sulfur trioxide reacts with water to form sulfuric acid: $SO_{3(g)} + H_2O_{(l)} \rightarrow H_2SO_{4(aq)}$. Elements in this group form a large variety of molecular compounds with nonmetals. Polonium is radioactive.
Group 7A (halogens) (ns^2np^5, $n \geq 2$)	All are nonmetals and are diatomic. Never found in the elemental form in nature due to their high reactivity. Astatine is radioactive. Fluorine reacts with water to produce oxygen gas: $2F_{2(g)} + 2H_2O_{(l)} \rightarrow 4HF_{(aq)} + O_{2(g)}$. Dichlorine heptoxide reacts with water to form perchloric acid: $Cl_2O_{7(g)} + H_2O_{(l)} \rightarrow 2HClO_{4(aq)}$. Halogens have high ionization energies and large negative electron affinities. The ions F^-, Cl^-, Br^- and I^- are known as halides. Can form ionic compounds (salts) such as NaCl or KBr or molecular (covalent) compounds such as ICl, BrF_3, PCl_5, NF_3, etc. Halogens react with hydrogen to produce hydrogen halides: $H_{2(g)} + X_{2(g)} \rightarrow 2HX_{(g)}$. Hydrogen halides dissolve in water to produce hydrohalic acids; most of which are strong acids, except HF (hydrofluoric), which is a weak acid.
Group 8A (inert or noble gases) (ns^2np^6, $n \geq 2$)	All are monoatomic. Very unreactive and highly stable. Some (krypton and xenon) have been made to react under special conditions. Helium (He) also belongs to this group and has a $1s^2$ electron configuration.
Oxides	As the metallic character decreases from left to right across a period, the metallic oxides change from basic to amphoteric to acidic. Normal metallic oxides are usually basic while most nonmetallic oxides are acidic. Transitional elements can form amphoteric oxides. Oxides of elements with larger atomic numbers (further down) tend to be more basic than those with smaller atomic numbers (due to the fact that metallic character increases as one moves down a column).

Metals vs. Nonmetals

Metals	*Nonmetals*
Good conductors of heat and electricity.	Generally poor conductors.
Show metallic luster.	Generally show no metallic luster.
Are malleable (can be pounded into sheets).	Are usually brittle and nonductile in the solid state.
Are ductile (can be bent or drawn into a wire).	Oxidize elemental metals and often oxidize other nonmetals that have less ability to attract electrons.
Reduce elemental nonmetals (except noble gases).	
Form oxides that may react with water to give hydroxides.	Form oxides that may react with water to give acids.
Form basic hydroxides.	Form acidic hydroxyl compounds (oxyacids).
React with O_2, F_2, H_2, and other nonmetals, usually giving ionic compounds.	React with O_2, F_2, H_2 and other nonmetals, giving covalent compounds.
Form binary metal hydrides that, if soluble, are strong bases.	Form binary hydrides that may be acidic.
	React with metals, often giving ionic compounds.
Have one to five electrons in outermost shell, usually not more than three.	Usually have four to eight electrons in outermost shell.
Readily form cations by loss of electrons.	Readily form anions by accepting electrons to fill outermost shell (except noble gases).
The properties characteristic of metallic behavior become less pronounced from left to right across a period.	The properties characteristic of nonmetallic character become more pronounced from left to right across a period.
Metallic character of elements increases going down a group.	Nonmetallic character decreases going down a group.
Metallic behavior of an element decreases as the positive oxidation number of the element in its compound increases.	Nonmetallic behavior increases as the positive oxidation number of the element in its compound increases.

Important People, Experiments, and Theories

Johann **Döbereiner**	Stated that many of the known elements could be arranged in groups of three similar elements, which he called triads, *e.g.* Li, Na, and K. When the three are written in ascending mass order, the middle element had properties close to the average of the outer two.
Dmitri **Mendeleev**	Arranged elements in order of increasing atomic mass. Current periodic table orders them by increasing atomic number.
Henry **Mosley**	An element's chemical properties are only roughly related to its atomic weight. What really matters is the element's atomic number, which he measured with X-rays. Discovered that, with few exceptions, increasing atomic numbers correlate with increasing atomic weights.
John **Newlands**	Suggested that when elements are arranged in order of atomic mass, any element had properties similar to one eight places in front and eight behind in the list. He called this his *"Law of Octaves"*.

Multiple-Choice Questions

1. Given the following atoms N, Si and P. If arranged in order of decreasing atomic radius the order would be

A. Si, P, N
B. N, P, Si
C. Si, N, P
D. P, N, Si
E. N, Si, P

2. The person responsible for concluding that an element's chemical properties are only roughly related to its atomic weight and that what really matters when arranging atoms is the element's atomic number, which he measured with X-rays, and who discovered that, with few exceptions, increasing atomic numbers correlate with increasing atomic weights was

A. Albert Einstein
B. Louis de Broglie
C. Niels Bohr
D. Dimitri Mendeleev
E. Henry Mosley

3. Given the following ions, (N^{3-}, Fe^{2+}, Ca^{2+}, and F^{-}) place them in order of increasing size

A. N^{3-}, Fe^{2+}, Ca^{2+}, F^{-}
B. F^{-}, Ca^{2+}, Fe^{2+}, N^{3-}
C. Fe^{2+}, Ca^{2+}, F^{-}, N^{3-}
D. N^{3-}, F^{-}, Ca^{2} , Fe^{2+}
E. Ca^{2+}, Fe^{2+}, F^{-}, N^{3-}

4. Given the following atoms (Ne, Xe, Na, and H) arrange them in order of increasing first ionization energies.

A. H, Ne, Na, Xe
B. Xe, Ne, Na, H
C. Na, Ne, H, Xe
D. Ne, Xe, H, Na
E. Na, H, Xe, Ne

5. Given the following elements (V, Cd, Pm, As, and Kr), which one is a metalloid?

A. vanadium
B. cadmium
C. promethium
D. arsenic
E. krypton

6. Which of the following pairs of elements would have similar chemical behavior?

A. Fe and Al
B. Be and Al
C. Ca and Ne
D. Cl and Na
E. H and O

7. Which is the smallest?

A. K
B. K^{+}
C. Ca
D. Ca^{2+}
E. Cs

8. Which series is ranked in order of increasing electronegativity?

A. O, S, Sc, Te
B. Cl, S, P, Si
C. In, Sn, N, O
D. C, Si, P, Se
E. Li, Rn, P, Mn

9. An amphoteric substance

A. has neither acid nor base properties.
B. turns litmus paper red and blue.
C. is insoluble in base, but dissolves in an acid.
D. reacts with both an acid and a base.
E. is insoluble in an acid, but dissolves in a base.

10. Which metal will react most vigorously with water?

A. Na
B. K
C. Mg
D. Ca
E. Zn

11. Which of the following isoelectronic ions should have the smallest ionic radius?

A. Sc^{3+}
B. Ca^{2+}
C. K^+
D. Cl^-
E. they all have the same ionic radius

12. Which element should have properties most like those of phosphorus?

A. Si
B. S
C. As
D. Sb
E. N

13. Which property decreases from left to right across the periodic table?

A. Electron affinity
B. Electrical conductivity
C. Ionization energy
D. Maximum oxidation state
E. Shielding

14. Which gaseous atom has the highest second ionization energy?

A. C
B. Li
C. F
D. Ne
E. H

15. The first ionization energy (potential) for S is lower than the first ionization energy for P because

A. Hund's rule is violated.
B. ionization potentials decrease across a representative period.
C. half-filled and filled sublevels are more stable than other electron configurations.
D. The statement above is false. Sulfur and phosphorus have identical first ionization potentials.
E. The statement above is false. The first ionization potential for S is higher than that for P.

16. The first ionization energy for a mole of calcium atoms is the energy required for the process

A. $Ca_{(s)} \rightarrow Ca_{(g)}$
B. $Ca_{(g)} \rightarrow Ca^+_{(g)} + 2e^-$
C. $Ca^+_{(g)} \rightarrow Ca^{2+}_{(g)} + e^-$
D. $Ca_{(g)} \rightarrow Ca^+_{(g)} + e^-$
E. $Ca_{(g)} \rightarrow Ca_{(s)} + e^-$

17. In their stable compounds, alkaline earth metals normally exist as

A. M^+ cations
B. M^{2+} cations
C. M atoms
D. M^- anions
E. M^{2+} anions

18. Which is the most electronegative atom?

A. P
B. H
C. Cl
D. Ne
E. F

19. For which pair of atoms is the electronegativity difference the greatest?

A. C, O
B. N, O
C. Na, Cl
D. H, I
E. C, Cl

20. Which element would be expected to have the highest melting point?

A. Li
B. Ca
C. Rh
D. At
E. C

Free-Response Questions

1. The table below shows data for successive ionization energies for elements in the third period.

Successive Ionization Energies (kJ per mole) for Period 3 Elements

Element	I_1	I_2	I_3
Na	495	4560	—
Mg	735	1445	7730
Al	580	1815	2740
Si	780	1575	3220
P	1060	1890	2905
S	1005	2260	3375
Cl	1255	2295	3850
Ar	1527	2665	3945

(a) Describe the concept of ionization energies and relate ionization energy to the trends found in the table above.

(b) Describe any four factors that can affect ionization energy.

(c) Sodium in the third period has a first ionization energy of 495 kJ/mol. Explain any ionization trends among sodium, magnesium, and aluminum.

2. Elements can be either classified as metals, nonmetals, or metalloids.

(a) Compare the physical and chemical properties of metals vs. nonmetals. Provide examples where necessary.

(b) Compare the general electron configurations of metals vs. nonmetals.

(c) Compare the number of metals vs. nonmetals in the periodic table and explain the reason for this phenomenon.

Answers and Explanations

Multiple Choice

1. **A.** N and P are in the same group; therefore, P > N (atomic radius increases as we go down a group). Both Si and P are in the third period, and Si is further to the left than P. Therefore, Si has a larger radius (atomic radius decreases as we move left to right across a period).

2. **E.**

3. **C.** F^- and N^{3-} are isoelectronic. N^{3-} by having three negative charges would be larger than F^-. Transitional metal ions (Fe^{2+}) in the center of the periodic table have the smallest ionic radii. Ca^{2+} has more protons than either F^- or N^{3-}, pulling the outer electrons in more tightly and making the ionic radius of F^- larger than that of Ca^{2+}.

4. **E.** Both Ne and Xe are inert gases and would be expected to have the highest first ionization energies. Ne, with fewer electron shells, would have the higher first ionization energy since there is less shielding. Group IA alkali metals have the lowest first ionization energies (they are farthest to the left on the periodic table). H is a nonmetal and would be expected to have a first ionization energy larger than the alkali metals.

5. **D.** Metalloids generally lie on a diagonal running from boron to astatine. They include boron, silicon, germanium, arsenic, antimony, tellurium, polonium and astatine.

6. **B.** Beryllium and aluminum exhibit a diagonal relationship. The principal kind of diagonal relationship occurs at the top (lowest-numbered periods) of the periodic table, and represents a kind of edge effect deviation from the main pattern of vertical relationships that led to the discovery of the periodic table. Beryllium and aluminum have a number of chemical similarities due to their similar charge densities: (1) Both form protective oxide coatings; (2) both elements are amphoteric; (3) both form carbides containing the C^{4-} anion; and (4) both give methane on reaction with water.

7. **D.** Atomic radius increases as one moves down a group or family. A potassium atom is larger than a calcium atom (fewer protons in K). A Ca^{2+} ion has lost its only two electrons in its outermost energy shell.

8. **C.** Electronegativity increases from left to right. Electronegativity increases as one moves up the periodic table. In is to the left of Sn. N is to the left of O. N and O are above In and Sn.

9. **D.** Examples of amphoteric substances include amino acids, proteins, and water. Amphoteric oxides include oxides of the metals zinc, tin, lead, aluminum, and beryllium. For example, zinc oxide (ZnO) reacts differently depending on the pH of the solution: in acid: $ZnO + 2H^+ \rightarrow Zn^{2+} + H_2O$; in base: $ZnO + H_2O + 2OH^- \rightarrow [Zn(OH)_4]^{2-}$. This effect can be used to separate different cations, such as zinc from manganese. For aluminum hydroxide dissolved in acid: $Al(OH)_3 + 3HCl \rightarrow AlCl_3 + 3H_2O$. In base: $Al(OH)_3 + NaOH \rightarrow NaAl(OH)_4$. Water can act as a base or acid simultaneously: $2H_2O \rightarrow H_3O^+ + OH^-$.

10. **B.** The Group IA (alkali metals) are the most active metals. Reactivity increases as one moves down the column.

11. **A.** Sc has the most protons of any species listed; therefore, it exerts the greatest "pull" on the outer electrons.

12. **C.** Phosphorus (P), arsenic (As), and antimony (Sb) are all members of Group 15 of the Periodic Table of the Elements. There is, however, little similarity between their properties and those of the corresponding derivatives of nitrogen, a member of the same group. Ordinary arsenic is a semi-metallic substance, steel-gray in color. There is also an unstable yellow crystalline form containing As_4 molecules, similar to the structure of P_4. Both arsenic and phosphorus are solids at room temperature; nitrogen is a gas at room temperature.

13. **B.**

14. **B.** The first ionization of lithium removes a valence electron, but the second ionization removes an inner electron in the first energy shell, characterized by extremely high ionization energies. Hydrogen only has 1 electron.

15. **C.**

16. **D.**

17. **B.** All Group IIA elements (alkaline earth metals) have two electrons in their valence shell. These elements lose 2 electrons to become positive +2 ions (cations).

18. **E.** According to the concept of electronegativity, each kind of atom has a certain attraction for the electrons involved in a chemical bond. This "electron-attracting" power of each atom can be listed numerically on an electronegativity scale. Fluorine, which has the greatest attraction for electrons in bond-forming situations, is assigned the highest value on this scale. Trends in electronegativity include:

Metals generally have low electronegativity values, while nonmetals have relatively high electronegativity values.

Electronegativity values generally increase from left to right within the Periodic Table of the Elements.

Electronegativity values generally decrease from top to bottom within each family of elements within the periodic table.

19. **C.** See answer #18 above.

20. **E.** Several factors affect a melting point, hence there is no clear pattern. Generally melting points increase across towards the metalloids, then decrease rapidly for nonmetals. Carbon has the highest melting/sublimation point of all elements. At atmospheric pressure it has no actual melting point as its triple point is at 10 MPa (100 bar) so it sublimes above 4,000 K. Thus it remains solid at higher temperatures than the highest melting point metals like tungsten or rhenium, regardless of its allotropic form.

Free Response

Question 1

Maximum Points for Question 1
Part (a): 3 points
Part (b): 4 points
Part (c): 3 points
Total points: 10

1. The table shows data for successive ionization energies for elements in the third period. *(a) Describe the concept of ionization energies and relate ionization energy to the trends found in the table.*	***3 points possible***
Ionization energy determines the ease with which an atom forms a positive ion. The first ionization energy of an atom is the energy required to remove the least tightly held electron from an isolated atom in the vapor state to form a positive ion. This endothermic process may be represented by a general equation as $X_{(g)} + \text{energy} \rightarrow X^{+}_{(g)} + e^{-}$ As the attraction between an electron and the nucleus increases, the energy required to remove the electron, the ionization energy, also increases. Ionization energies may be determined by spectroscopic analysis. The energy required to remove a second electron from the outer level of an atom (the second ionization energy) is always greater than that	*1 point for proper description of ionization energy.* *1 point each for each concept that relates ionization energy to the chart provided.*

required to remove the outermost electron. The removal of the outermost electron reduces the number of electrons and, consequently, the total electronic repulsion. This results in the electron cloud being drawn closer to the nucleus. The electron cloud is more compact and, due to the smaller radius, is subjected to a greater force of attraction by the nucleus. A greater force of attraction between an electron and its nucleus means that more energy is required to dislodge the electron to achieve ionization.	
(b) Describe any four factors that can affect ionization energy. **(1) The magnitude of the positive charge on the nucleus.** Other factors being constant, the greater the nuclear charge, the greater is the attraction for the outer level electron. As the force of attraction increases, more energy is needed to remove the electron from the atom. Thus, ionization energy increases with increased nuclear charge provided that other factors which normally influence the ionization energy are not considered. **(2) The radius of the atom.** The force of attraction between an electron and its nucleus is electrostatic. According to Coulomb's Law, the force varies inversely with the atomic radius. This means that the force of attraction decreases as the radius increases. Hence, other factors being constant, the energy required to remove an electron decreases as the distance from the nucleus increases. In general, the radii of atoms gradually decrease as we progress from left to right in a given horizontal row of the periodic table. This is because the atomic number (nuclear charge) increases. As the nuclear charge increases, all complete inner-electron clouds are drawn closer to the nucleus. The radii of the atoms generally increase from top to bottom in a given vertical column of the table. As you go down a family, the number of shells increases. Each additional shell of electrons shields the outer electrons from the attractive force of the nucleus. Consequently, as the attractive force decreases, the outer electrons are not attracted as strongly. Therefore, they are not pulled in as closely as in the case of atoms having fewer shells of electrons. **(3) Number of inner-level electrons underlying the outer energy level.** The inner-level electrons serve to shield the outer electron from the pull of the nuclear charge. This is known as the screening or shielding effect. Other factors being constant, as the number of inner energy levels increases, both the force of attraction and the ionization energy decrease. **(4) The number of occupied orbitals in the outer levels.** In general, *s* electrons penetrate the inner-electron levels better than *p* electrons which, in turn, penetrate the inner-electron levels better than *d* electrons. This penetrating ability plays an important role in determining atomic properties.	***4 points possible*** *1 point for each factor that affects ionization energy. Each factor must be explained correctly.*

(continued)

Since, in a given energy level, *s* electrons "feel" more of the nuclear charge than do the *p, d,* or *f* electrons, it follows that the ionization energies of the electrons in a principal-energy level decrease in the order *s, p, d, f.* It should be noted that two electrons occupying the same orbital have only a negligible influence in shielding each other from their respective nuclear charges. Increases in ionization energy are paralleled by increases in nonmetallic characteristics.	
(c) Sodium in the third period has a first ionization energy of 495 kJ/mol. Explain any ionization trends among sodium, magnesium, and aluminum.	***3 points possible***
The first ionization energy of magnesium is larger than sodium because magnesium has one more proton in its nucleus to hold on to the electrons in the 3*s* orbital. Mg: [Ne]$3s^2$	*1 point for correctly comparing the first ionization energy of sodium to ionization energies of elements in the third period.*
The second ionization energy of Mg is larger than the first because it always takes more energy to remove an electron from a positively charged ion than from a neutral atom. The third ionization energy of magnesium is large because the Mg^{2+} ion has a filled-shell electron configuration.	*1 point for correctly interpreting and comparing the ionization energies of magnesium to either sodium or aluminum.*
The same pattern can be seen in the ionization energies of aluminum. The first ionization energy of aluminum is smaller than magnesium. The second ionization energy of aluminum is larger than the first, and the third ionization energy is even larger. Although it takes a considerable amount of energy to remove three electrons from an aluminum atom to form an Al^{3+} ion, the energy needed to break into the filled-shell configuration of the Al^{3+} ion is extremely large in comparison. Therefore, the Al^{4+} ion is a very unlikely product of a chemical reaction.	*1 point for correctly interpreting and comparing the ionization energies of aluminum to either magnesium or sodium.*

Question 2

Maximum Points for Question 2
Part (a): 8 points
Part (b): 1 point
Part (c): 1 point
Total points: 10

2. Elements can be either classified as metals, nonmetals, or metalloids.

8 points possible

(a) Compare the physical and chemical properties of metals vs. nonmetals. Provide examples where necessary.

2 points awarded for at least 3 correct metallic physical properties with examples.

2 points awarded for at least 3 correct non-metallic physical properties with examples.

PHYSICAL PROPERTIES	**METALS**	**NONMETALS**
Structure	Cations surrounded by "sea of electrons"	Ions, atoms or molecules Examples: NaCl (ions), He (atom), H_2O (molecule)
Force between (inter) units	Metallic bond	Dipole-dipole (Example: ICl); ionic bond (NaCl); polar covalent bond (H_2O); and non-polar covalent bond (I_2)
Luster	High Example: Au	Low to none. Example: C
Electrical conductivity	Good Example: Cu	Poor to none Example: Ar
Melting point	Generally high but ranging from very low (Cs) to very high (Fe)	Generally low but ranging from very low (He) to very high (C)
Physical state	Generally solid (Fe) but can also be liquid (Hg)	Generally gas (Ne, O), but can also be solid (C or P) or liquid (Br_2)

CHEMICAL PROPERTIES	**METALS**	**NONMETALS**
Reactivity	React with nonmetals Example: $2Na + Cl_2 \rightarrow 2NaCl$	React with both metals (Example: $2Li + Br_2 \rightarrow 2LiBr$) and nonmetals (Example: $2H_2 + O_2 \rightarrow 2H_2O$)
Attraction to electrons	Electropositive Example: Al^{3+}	Electronegative Example: Cl^-
Acid-base characteristics	Oxides are either basic (Example: $Na_2O + 2H_2O \rightarrow 2\ Na^+ + 2OH^-$) or amphoteric (Example: reaction with acid: $Al_2O_3 + 6HCl \rightarrow 2AlCl_3 + 3H_2O$) or reaction with base: $Al_2O_3 + 2NaOH + 3H_2O \rightarrow 2NaAl(OH)_4$)	Oxides are acidic (Example: $SO_2 + H_2O \rightarrow H_2SO_3$)

(continued)

<table>
<tr><td>

CHEMICAL PROPERTIES	METALS	NONMETALS
Redox	Reducing agents (Example: $2Mg + O_2 \rightarrow 2MgO$. Magnesium has been oxidized because its oxidation number has increased and is the reducing agent because it donated electrons to O)	Oxidizing agents (Example: $4Fe + 3O_2 \rightarrow 2Fe_2O_3$. Oxygen has been reduced because its oxidation number has decreased and is the oxidizing agent because it took electrons from Fe)

</td><td>

2 points awarded for at least three correct metallic chemical properties with examples.

2 points awarded for at least three correct non-metallic chemical properties with examples.

</td></tr>
<tr><td>

(b) Compare the general electron configurations of metals vs. nonmetals.

Metals: Valence electrons in *s* or *d* sublevels of their atoms. (A few heavy elements have atoms with one or two valence electrons in *p* sublevels.)

Nonmetals: Valence electrons in *p* sublevels of their atoms (except for H and He, which have valence electrons in their 1*s* sublevels).

</td><td>

1 point possible

Metals: Valence electrons occur in either s or d sublevels.

Nonmetals: Valence electrons occur in p sublevel.

</td></tr>
<tr><td>

(c) Compare the number of metals vs. nonmetals in the periodic table and explain the reason for this phenomenon.

There are more metals than nonmetals because filling *d* orbitals within a given energy level involves the atoms of ten elements and filling the *f* orbitals within a given energy level involves the atoms of 14 elements. However, for nonmetals in the same energy levels, the maximum number of elements with atoms receiving *p* electrons is six.

</td><td>

1 point possible

1 point: metals fill d and f orbitals and nonmetals fill p orbitals.

</td></tr>
</table>

Bonding

You'll Need to Know

- ❑ Lewis dot diagrams including incomplete and expanded octets
- ❑ Ionic bonding
- ❑ Lattice energy
- ❑ Covalent bonding including bond length
- ❑ Intermolecular and intramolecular forces including network covalent, hydrogen bonding, metallic bonding, dipole-dipole, dipole-induced dipole, and London dispersion
- ❑ Atomic radii including covalent radii and van der Waals radii
- ❑ Radicals
- ❑ Bond strength
- ❑ Resonance

Lewis Dot Diagrams

Lewis dot diagrams consist of the symbol of the element and one dot for each valence electron. Except for helium, the number of dots is equal to the group number. Transition metals, lanthanides, and actinides all have incompletely filled inner shells, and generally you will not be responsible for drawing their Lewis dot diagram on the AP Chemistry Exam.

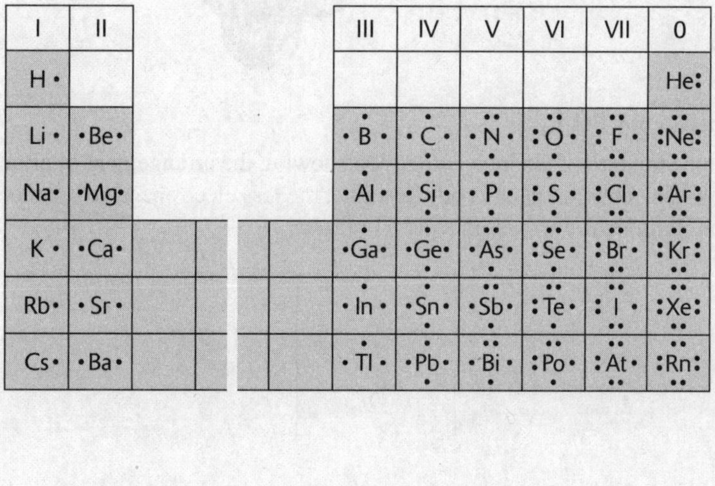
I
II
III
IV
V
VI
VII
0
H
He
Li
Be
B
C
N
O
F
Ne
Na
Mg
Al
Si
P
S
Cl
Ar
K
Ca
Ga
Ge
As
Se
Br
Kr
Rb
Sr
In
Sn
Sb
Te
I
Xe
Cs
Ba
Tl
Pb
Bi
Po
At
Rn

Incomplete Octets

Incomplete octets are atoms that are stable without having eight valence electrons. Examples: boron trifluoride (BF_3) and beryllium hydride (BeH_2).

$$\overset{\cdot\cdot}{\underset{\cdot\cdot}{:F:}}\,\,B:\overset{\cdot\cdot}{\underset{\cdot\cdot}{F}}: \qquad H:Be:H$$

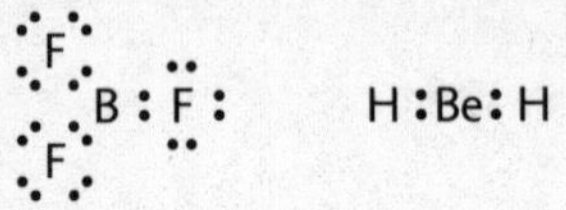

In these cases, boron is stable with six valence electrons, and beryllium is stable with four valence electrons.

Expanded Octets

Expanded octets occur when there are more than eight valence electrons around an atom and occur for elements in and beyond the third period; *d* orbitals may also be used in bonding.

••

Examples

Q. Draw the Lewis dot diagram for Bismuth.

A. $\cdot\overset{\cdot\cdot}{\underset{\cdot}{Bi}}\cdot$

Q. Draw the Lewis structure for phosphorus pentafluoride, PF_5.

A. Count up the total number of valence electrons ($5 + 5(7) = 40$). Place P in the middle, and draw five fluorine atoms around the P, each with a single bond. Subtract 10 electrons (2 for each single bond) ($40 - 10 = 30$). Distribute the 30 valence electrons around the fluorines. This is an example of an expanded octet.

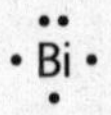

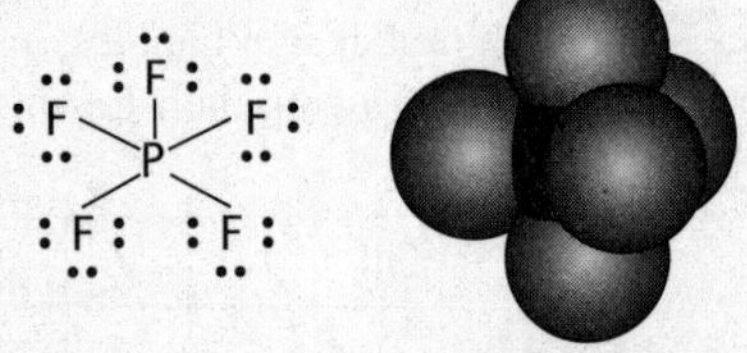

Q. Draw the Lewis structure for $PO_2F_2^-$.

A. **Step 1:** Draw a skeleton structure of the molecule or ion showing the arrangement of atoms and connect each atom to another with a single (one electron pair) bond. As a rule, the less electronegative element is often the central atom, except hydrogen. Ions are drawn within square brackets.

$$\left[\begin{array}{c} F \\ | \\ F-P-O \\ | \\ O \end{array}\right]^-$$

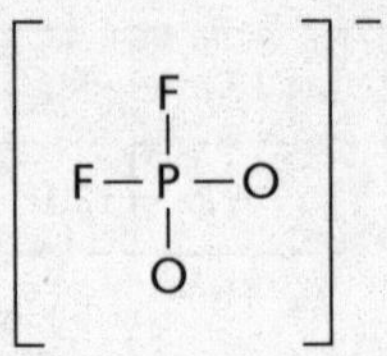

Step 2: Determine the total number of valence electrons in the molecule or ion. For a molecule, this is equal to the sum of the number of valence electrons on each atom. For a positive ion this is equal to the sum of the number of valence electrons minus the number of positive charges on the ion (one electron is lost for each single positive charge). For a negative ion, this is equal to the sum of the number of valence electrons plus the number of negative charges on the ion.

$$PO_2F_2^- = \text{Number of valence electrons} = 5(P\text{ atom}) + 6(O\text{ atom}) + 6(O\text{ atom}) +$$
$$7(F\text{ atom}) + 7(F\text{ atom}) + 1(\text{negative charge}) = 32.$$

Step 3: Deduct the two valence electrons that are used in each of the bonds written in Step 1. Distribute the remaining electrons as lone pairs so that each atom (except hydrogen) has eight electrons if possible. If there are too few electrons to give each atom eight electrons, convert single bonds to multiple bonds where possible. The ability to form multiple bonds is limited almost exclusively to bonds between carbon, nitrogen, and oxygen, although sulfur and selenium will sometimes form double bonds with carbon, nitrogen, and oxygen. In the case of $PO_2F_2^-$, the total of 32 valence electrons can be distributed as four electron pairs (eight electrons) in bonds and three lone pairs around each of the fluorine and oxygen atoms.

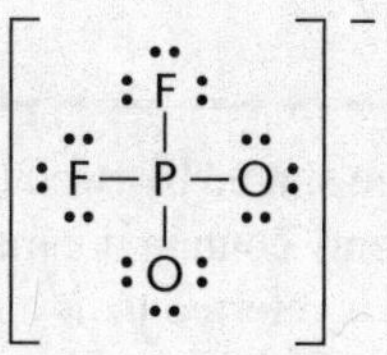

Step 4: In those molecules in which there are too many electrons to have only eight electrons around each atom, the central atom may have more than eight electrons in its valence shell (expanded octets).

Ionic Bonds

Atoms of elements with low ionization energies (Group 1A and 2A) tend to form cations ($Li \rightarrow Li^+ + e^-$), while elements with high negative electron affinities (Groups 6A and 7A) tend to form anions ($Cl + e^- \rightarrow Cl^-$). Since the ions formed are opposite in charge, there exists an attraction. The strength of the attraction can be measured using Coulomb's Law:

$$E = k\frac{(+q)(-q)}{d}$$

where E = electrostatic attractive energy, k = a proportionality constant, $+q$ = charge on the cation, $-q$ = charge on the anion, and d = the distance between the nuclei of the two ions. We can see that the potential energy between two ions in an ionic bond is directly proportional to the product of their charges and inversely proportional to the distance separating the ions. Ionic bonds can be determined by using the difference in electronegativity between the bonding atoms. In most cases, an electronegativity difference of 1.7 or more is considered an ionic bond while less than 1.7 it is classified as a covalent bond.

Examples

Q. The electronegativity of germanium is 1.8 while that of bromine is 2.8. Is the bond between germanium and bromine ionic?

A. 2.8 – 1.8 = 1.0. An electronegativity difference of 1.0 is below the threshold of 1.7 or higher required for a bond to be classified "ionic". Therefore, the bond is *not* ionic.

Q. Given MgO and NaI, which would you predict would have the higher melting point?

A. MgO since there is a +2 cation attracting a –2 anion as opposed to a +1 cation attracting a –1 anion as in NaI. This conclusion confirms that the potential energy between two ions in an ionic bond is directly proportional to the product of their charges according to Coulomb's Law.

Lattice Energy

Lattice energy is the energy required to completely separate one mole of a solid ionic compound into gaseous ions. It describes the stability of a solid ionic compound. Compounds with larger lattice energies are generally more stable and their ions are more tightly held which results in higher melting points. Compounds with more charges have higher lattice energies and generally higher melting points.

Covalent Bonds

A covalent bond is a bond in which two electrons are shared by two atoms. The term "molecule" is used to refer to compounds that are covalently bonded. Molecules only contain nonmetals. A single line (—) represents 1 pair of electrons being shared between atoms (*e.g.*, H—H) and is referred to as a single bond. A double line (=) represents two pairs of electrons being shared and is referred to as a double bond (*e.g.*, C = C). Three lines (≡) represent a triple bond in which 3 pairs of electrons are being shared (*e.g.*, C ≡ N). Sharing of electrons in covalent compounds involves only the valence (outer) electrons. Valence electrons that are not shared between atoms are called nonbonding electrons or lone pairs. Most molecules obey the octet rule; atoms other than hydrogen tend to form bonds until they are surrounded by eight valence electrons. There are exceptions known as incomplete octets, expanded octets, and radicals.

Examples

Q. Draw the Lewis structures for water, carbon dioxide, and nitrogen gas.

A.

```
 H
 ··      ··   ··
:O:H    :O=C=O:    :N≡N:
 ··
```

Q. Which of the following does NOT define a covalent bond?

- **A.** A shared pair of electrons
- **B.** An overlap of half-filled atomic or hybrid orbitals
- **C.** Increased electron density in the region between atoms of two nonmetals
- **D.** Electrostatic attraction between species in which one or more electrons has been transferred
- **E.** All of the above define a covalent bond.

A. D. Choice D defines an ionic bond.

Bond Length

Bond length is the distance between the nuclei of two bonded atoms in a molecule. For a given pair of atoms, triple bonds are shorter than double bonds, which are shorter than single bonds (*e.g.*, bond length of C ≡ C is 120 pm; whereas C = C is 133 pm and C—C is 154 pm).

Intermolecular and Intramolecular Forces

Many molecules contain bonds that fall between the extremes of ionic and covalent bonds. The difference between the electronegativities of the atoms in these molecules is large enough that the electrons aren't shared equally, and yet small enough that the electrons aren't drawn exclusively to one of the atoms to form positive and negative ions. The bonds in these molecules are said to be polar because they have positive and negative ends (or poles) and the molecules are often said to have a dipole moment. HCl molecules, for example, have a dipole moment because the hydrogen atom has a slight positive charge and the chlorine atom has a slight negative charge.

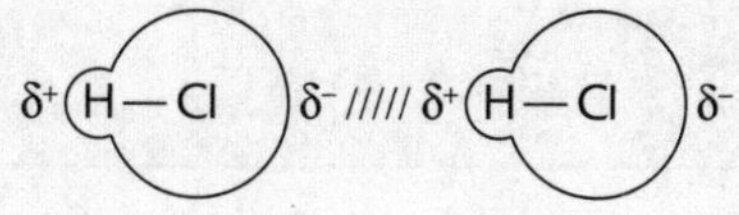

*Intra*molecular forces are forces that hold individual molecules together and are very strong. *Inter*molecular forces are attractive forces that occur between molecules and are much weaker. Intermolecular forces are responsible for the non-ideal behavior of gases and the existence of liquids and solids. Intramolecular forces stabilize individual molecules, whereas intermolecular forces are responsible for the general properties of matter (melting point, boiling point, etc.). Boiling point is a measure of the strength of intermolecular forces, *i.e.,* the higher the boiling point (or melting point), the stronger the intermolecular force. Dipole-dipole, dipole-induced dipole, and dispersion forces make up what are called "van der Waals forces". Dispersion forces are present between all molecules, whether they are polar or non-polar and are characterized by: (1) larger and heavier atoms and molecules exhibit stronger dispersion forces than smaller and lighter ones; (2) in a larger atom or molecule, the valence electrons are, on average, farther from the nuclei than in a smaller atom or molecule and are less tightly held and can therefore more easily form temporary dipoles; and (3) the ease with which the electron distribution around an atom or molecule can be polarized.

Network Covalent Bonds

Network covalent bonds have extensive three-dimensional structures and no discrete molecular units. They are very hard and have extremely high melting points. Examples include silicon dioxide (SiO_2), which is a major component in sand; silicon carbide (SiC), which is used in grinding and abrasives; and diamond (C).

Hydrogen Bonds

Hydrogen bonds are a type of intermolecular force that exists between two partial electric charges of opposite polarity. Although stronger than most other intermolecular forces, the typical hydrogen bond is much weaker than either an ionic or covalent bond. Hydrogen bonds involve the attractive force between a hydrogen atom of one molecule and an oxygen, nitrogen, or fluorine of another. In the compound containing hydrogen, the hydrogen atom itself must be attached to an oxygen, nitrogen, or fluorine.

Example

Q. Which of the following compounds would be capable of forming hydrogen bonds?

(a) C_2H_5OH (e) NH_3
(b) CH_3OCH_3 (f) CH_3F
(c) N_2H_4 (g) $(CH_3)_2CO$
(d) CH_3COOH (h) $[H—F—H]^+$

A. (a) yes; (b) no; (c) yes; (d) yes; (e) yes; (f) no; (g) no; (h) yes. Start by drawing the Lewis structures for each. An F, O, or N MUST be bonded to a hydrogen atom in a molecule for hydrogen bonding to occur.

Metallic Bonding

Metallic bonding occurs when an atom achieves a more stable configuration by sharing the electrons in its outer shell with many other atoms. Metallic bonds prevail in elements in which the valence electrons are not tightly bound with the nucleus, namely metals. In this type of bond, each atom in a metal crystal contributes all the electrons in its valence shell to all other atoms in the crystal. The valence electrons are not closely associated with individual atoms, but instead move around among the atoms within the crystal. Therefore, the individual atoms can "slip" over one another yet remain firmly held together by the electrostatic forces exerted by the electrons. This is why most metals can be hammered into thin sheets (malleable) or drawn into thin wires (ductile). When an electrical potential difference is applied, the electrons move freely between atoms and current flows.

Intermolecular Forces (forces between molecules)	*Properties*	*Examples*
Network covalent bonding	High melting point, hard, non-conducting. Covalent network solids.	C (diamond), SiO_2 (quartz)
Ionic	High melting point, brittle, hard. Ionic solids.	NaCl, MgO
Metallic bonding	Variable hardness and melting point (depending on the strength of metallic bonding), conducting. Metallic solids.	Fe, Li
Hydrogen bonding	Hydrogen bonds are a special type of dipole-dipole attraction. The bonds between the hydrogen atom of one molecule and the nitrogen, oxygen or fluorine of another molecule are exceptionally short and polar. The attractions between these specific bonds are particularly strong. Molecular solids.	H_2O, NH_3
Dipole-dipole	Dipole-dipole forces occur between two polar molecules and result from the attractive forces between the positive end of one polar molecule and the negative end of another polar molecule. They are much weaker than ionic or covalent bonds and have a significant effect only when the molecules involved are close together. Molecular solids.	HCl, CH_3F
Dipole-induced dipole	Forces that occur between an ion and a polar molecule. Strength of this force depends on charge and size of ion, magnitude of the dipole moment and size of molecule. Generally, cations interact more strongly with dipoles than anions due to charge concentrations. Hydration is an example of ion-dipole interaction. For example, in an aqueous solution of an ionic compound, such as sodium chloride, the sodium ion is attracted to the partial negative charge on neighboring water molecules and the chloride ion is attracted to the partial positive charge on neighboring water molecules. The solvent forms a shell around the ions, which gives them enough stability to counter the lattice energy.	NaCl dissolved in water.
London dispersion	London dispersion forces are the weakest intermolecular force. They are a temporary attractive force that results when the electrons in two adjacent atoms occupy positions that make the atoms form temporary dipoles. London (dispersion) forces are the attractive forces that cause non-polar substances to condense to liquids and to freeze into solids when the temperature is lowered sufficiently. Because of the constant motion of the electrons, an atom or molecule can develop a temporary (instantaneous) dipole when its electrons are distributed asymmetrically about the nucleus. Molecular solids.	H_2, Br_2

Examples

For Questions 1–5, choose from the following answers:

A. A network solid with covalent bonding
B. A molecular solid with zero dipole moment
C. A molecular solid with hydrogen bonding
D. An ionic solid
E. A metallic solid

Q. Solid ethyl alcohol (C_2H_5OH)

A. **C.** Ethyl alcohol contains H-bonding (between the O of one molecule and an H from another molecule).

Q. Silicon dioxide (SiO_2)

A. **A.** Silicon can only form a single covalent bond with an oxygen atom. Each silicon atom can bond to four oxygen atoms, which gives rise to a giant covalent network three dimensional structure in which each Si is bonded to four oxygens and each O to two silicon atoms which results in a 1:2 ratio between Si and O atoms; SiO_2 is really an empirical formula.

Q. Hafnium (Hf)

A. **E.** Hafnium, being located to the left in the periodic table, is a metal. All metal atoms bond to each other through metallic bonds.

Q. Strontium bromide ($SrBr_2$)

A. **D.** Strontium is a metal, bromine is a nonmetal.

Q. Dry ice (CO_2)

A. **B.** Molecular solids are characterized by relatively strong intramolecular bonds between the atoms that form the molecules and much weaker intermolecular forces between these molecules. Because the intermolecular forces are relatively weak, molecular solids are often soft substances with low melting points. The van der Waals forces holding the CO_2 molecules together are weak enough that dry ice sublimes; it passes directly from the solid to the gas phase at –78°C.

Q. Which of the following substances has the highest melting point?

- **A.** KCl
- **B.** ClO_2
- **C.** H_2
- **D.** $BiCl_3$
- **E.** SiO_2

A. **E.** Network solids contain no discrete molecular units. The atoms in the network solid are held together by conventional covalent bonds with neighboring atoms. The result is a single extended network or array. Two common examples of network solids are diamond (a form of pure carbon) and quartz (silicon dioxide).

Atomic Radii

Covalent Radii

The covalent radius of an atom is the radius of the sphere representing that atom when it is covalently bonded to another atom.

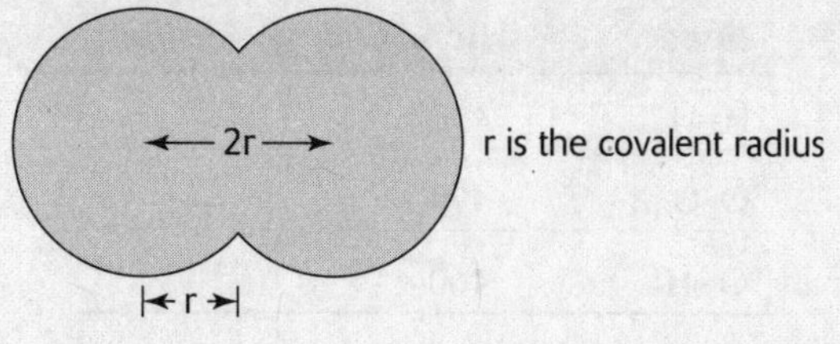

Van der Waals Radii

The van der Waals radius is the radius of the spherical space occupied by an atom when it is attracted to another atom by van der Waals forces. Van der Waals radii are significantly larger than covalent radii.

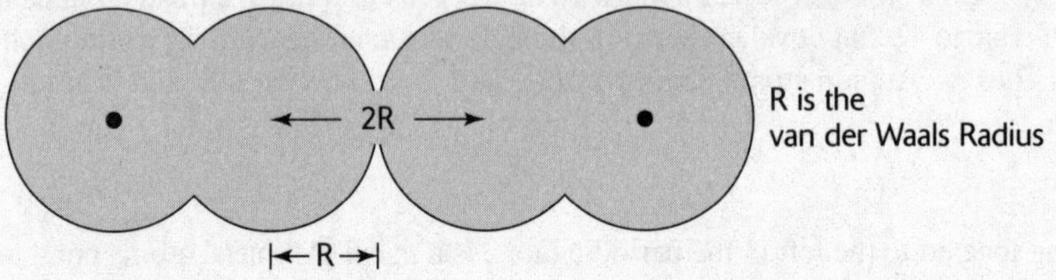

Radicals

Radicals are molecules in which the total number of valence electrons is an odd number. Some oxides of nitrogen fall into this category: nitric oxide (NO) and nitrogen dioxide (NO_2) which are major components of air pollution and sources of acid rain. In cases like these, the nitrogen, the less electronegative element, is left with an incomplete octet with an unpaired electron.

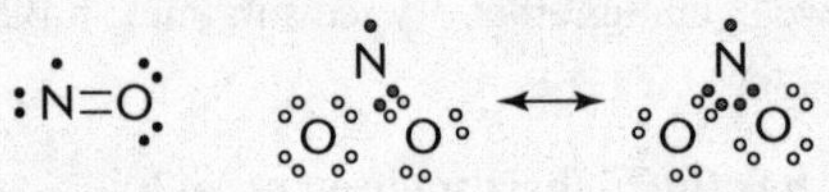

Bond Strength

The strength of a covalent bond is determined by the amount of energy required to break it (stronger bonds ~ higher bond energy). Bond energy (B.E.) is the amount of energy required to break a particular bond in one mole of gaseous molecules and is measured in kJ. Energy is always required (positive value for ΔH) to break chemical bonds, and chemical bond formation is always accompanied by a release of energy (negative value for ΔH). The enthalpy of a reaction is determined by the difference between the total energy required and the total energy released for the reaction to occur:

$$\Delta H^\circ = \Sigma \text{B.E.}_{(\text{reactants})} - \Sigma \text{B.E.}_{(\text{products})}$$

If ΔH° is positive, then the reaction is endothermic. If ΔH° is negative, then the reaction is exothermic.

Example

Q. Hydrogen gas reacts violently when sparked in the presence of oxygen gas. Using the following table of bond energies, estimate the enthalpy change for the combustion of hydrogen gas.

Bond	*Bond Energy (kJ/mol)*
H–H	436
O=O	499
O–H	460

A. $2H_{2(g)} + O_{2(g)} \rightarrow 2H_2O_{(g)}$

H—H + H—H + O=O → H—O—H + H—O—H

2 H—H bonds need to be broken: 2 (436 kJ) = 872 kJ

1 O = O bond need to be broken: 1(499 kJ) = 499 kJ

4 O—H bonds need to be formed: 4(460.) = 1840 kJ

$\Delta H° = \Sigma$B.E. bonds broken – ΣB.E. bonds formed = (872 kJ + 499 kJ) – 1840 kJ = –469 kJ

Resonance

There are a number of compounds and polyatomic ions that cannot be written using one single structure. Resonance happens when more than one valid Lewis dot diagram can be written for a molecule or ion. When this happens, the true structure is a "blend" of all the different possible structures. Example: NO_2:

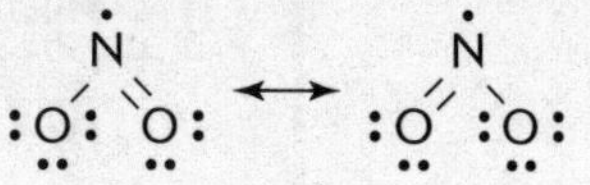

Example

Q. Draw the resonance structures for the nitrate ion (NO_3^-)

A.

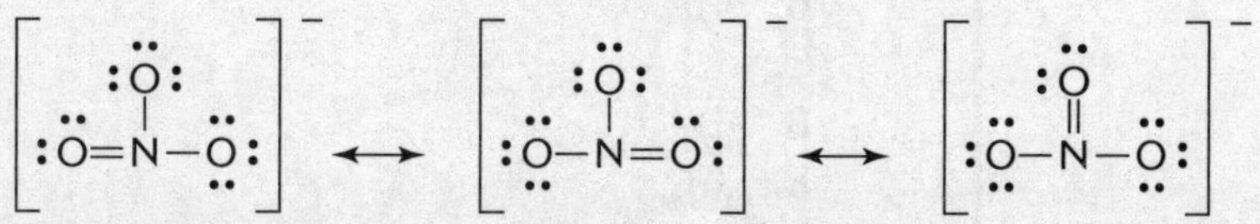

Multiple-Choice Questions

1. Determine the enthalpy of reaction for the combustion of ethane. Bond energies: C—H = 414 kJ/mol; C—C = 347 kJ/mol; O=O = 499 kJ/mol; C=C = 799 kJ/mol; and O—H = 460 kJ/mol.

A. –2760 kJ
B. –1380 kJ
C. 1380 kJ
D. 2760 kJ
E. 5520 kJ

2. Which of the following would represent a non-polar molecule containing polar bonds?

A. I_2
B. CO_2
C. PF_3
D. SO_2
E. H_2O

3. Which would be the most likely Lewis structure for HNO_2?

A. $H:\overset{..}{\underset{..}{O}}:\overset{..}{\underset{..}{N}}:\overset{..}{\underset{..}{O}}:$

B. $H:\overset{..}{\underset{..}{O}}:N::\overset{..}{\underset{..}{O}}:$

C. $H:\overset{..}{\underset{..}{O}}::N::\overset{..}{\underset{..}{O}}:$

D. $H:\overset{..}{\underset{..}{O}}:::N:\overset{..}{\underset{..}{O}}:$

E. $\overset{..}{\underset{..}{O}}=N-\overset{..}{\underset{..}{O}}-H$

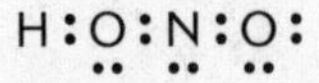

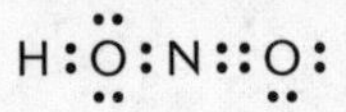

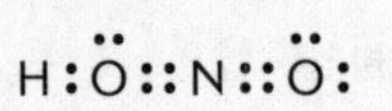

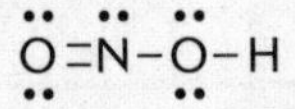

4. Which of the following would have the highest electrical conductivity at room temperature?

A. pure water
B. $0.10\ M\ NaCl_{(aq)}$
C. $1.0\ M\ NaCl_{(aq)}$
D. $2.0\ M\ C_6H_{12}O_6$
E. pure copper

5. A neutral molecule XF_3 has a zero dipole moment. Element X is most likely

A. Cl
B. N
C. C
D. B
E. Ar

6. What is the most likely formula for a compound composed of sulfur and indium?

A. InS
B. In_2S_3
C. In_3S_2
D. InS_3
E. S_3I_2

7. How many valence electrons are present in the SCN^- ion?

A. 14
B. 15
C. 16
D. 17
E. 18

8. Hydrogen fluoride has a boiling point of 19°C compared to hydrogen chloride's boiling point of −85°C. The difference in boiling points can best be explained in that

A. HCl molecules form strong intermolecular hydrogen bonds.
B. HF forms intramolecular hydrogen bonds.
C. HF forms intermolecular hydrogen bonds.
D. high dispersion forces exist between HF molecules.
E. there are strong van der Waals forces present between HF molecules.

9. In which of the following processes are covalent bonds broken?

A. $Br_{2(l)} \rightarrow Br_{2(g)}$
B. $NaCl_{(s)} \rightarrow Na^+_{(aq)} + Cl^-_{(aq)}$
C. $Al_{(s)} \rightarrow Al_{(l)}$
D. $Diamonds \rightarrow C_{(g)}$
E. $Na_3PO_{4(s)} \rightarrow Na_{(s)} + PO_{4(aq)}$

10. Which of the following molecules has the shortest covalent bond length?

A. CO
B. HI
C. KI
D. H_2
E. Cl_2

For Questions 11–15, refer to the following descriptions of bonding in different types of solids.

A. Composed of a crystal lattice consisting of positive and negative ions which are held together by electrostatic forces.
B. Macromolecules which are held together by strong covalent bonds.
C. A crystal lattice that is closely packed and contains delocalized electrons throughout the structure.
D. Strong multiple covalent bonds with weak intermolecular forces.
E. Strong single covalent bonds with weak intermolecular forces.

11. Silver, Ag

12. Table salt, NaCl

13. Dry ice, CO_2

14. Carbon tetrafluoride, CF_4

15. Quartz, SiO_2

16. Which of the following would NOT require one to consider an expanded octet?

A. PCl_5
B. I_3^-
C. SF_6
D. XeF_4
E. C_6H_6

17. Which end of the bonds in HCl, IBr, and CO would be more negative?

A. Cl, Br, O
B. H, I, C
C. H, Br, C
D. Br, I, O
E. Cl, I, C

18. How many resonance forms are possible for SO_3?

A. 1
B. 2
C. 3
D. 4
E. 5

19. $F_{2(g)}$ has a bond dissociation energy of of 157 kJ/mol. What is $\Delta H°_f$ for $F_{(g)}$?

A. 0 kJ/mol
B. 15.7 kJ/mol
C. 39.3 kJ/mol
D. 78.5 kJ/mol
E. 157 kJ/mol

20. The intermolecular force that is common for all molecules is

A. covalent bonding
B. dipole-dipole forces
C. van der Waals forces
D. dipole-induced dipole forces
E. London dispersion forces

Free-Response Questions

1. Explain each of the following in terms of atomic and molecular structures and/or intermolecular forces.

(a) Solid Mg has a higher melting point than solid sodium.

(b) $AsCl_3$ has a measurable dipole moment, whereas $AsCl_5$ does not.

(c) The boiling point of CCl_4 (350K) is greater than the boiling point of CH_4 (111K).

(d) $KI_{(s)}$ is very soluble in water whereas $I_{2(s)}$ is not.

(e) List by formula the following substances in order of increasing boiling point:

methoxymethane (dimethyl ether), $CH_3—O—CH_3$

1,2-ethanediol, $OH—CH_2—CH_2—OH$

ethanol, $CH_3—CH_2—OH$

ethane, $CH_3—CH_3$

2. Using principles of chemical bonding and/or intermolecular forces, explain each of the following:

(a) Fluorine and chlorine are gases, while bromine is a liquid and iodine is a solid.

(b) The hydride of oxygen (H_2O) is a liquid at room temperature (B.P 100°C at 1 atm) while the hydride of sulfur (H_2S) is a gas (B.P. –60.3°C at 1 atm).

(c) Hydrogen fluoride is a liquid at room temperature and a weak acid, but hydrogen chloride is a gas and a strong acid.

(d) The boiling point of ammonia (NH_3) at 240K is greater than the boiling point of phosphine (PH_3) at 185K.

(e) Acetic (ethanoic) acid is strongly associated in the liquid state.

Answers and Explanations

Multiple Choice

1. **A.** Begin by writing a balanced equation: $2C_2H_{6(g)} + 7O_{2(g)} \rightarrow 4CO_{2(g)} + 6H_2O_{(g)}$

Next, determine the number and types of bonds that need to be broken and formed:

Broken: 12 C—H @ 414 kJ/mol = 4968 kJ; 2 C—C @ 347 kJ/mol = 694 kJ; 7 O = O @ 499 kJ/mol = 3493 kJ.

Formed: 8 C = C @ 799 kJ/mol = 6392 kJ; 12 O—H @ 460 kJ/mol = 5520 kJ. Finally, use the formula $\Delta H = \Sigma BE_{(reactants)} - \Sigma BE_{(products)}$ = (4968 kJ + 694 kJ + 3493 kJ) – (6392 kJ + 5520 kJ) = 9155 kJ – 11915 kJ = –2760 kJ. The reaction is exothermic.

2. **B.** I_2 is a non-polar molecule but does not contain polar bonds. PF_3 is a polar molecule due to the presence of an unshared pair of electrons on the central atom. SO_2 is a polar molecule due to sulfur's unshared pair of electrons, which results in a bent molecule. Water is a polar molecule due to oxygen's two pairs of unshared electrons.

3. **E.** Choice E follows octet theory.

4. **E.** Metals have the highest electrical conductivity.

5. **D.** Boron has only three valence electrons.

6. **B.** Indium is a metal that loses its three electrons (In^{3+}). Sulfur is a nonmetal that gains two electrons (S^{2-}).

7. **C.** Sulfur has six valence electrons, carbon has four and nitrogen has five. Add one more due to the overall –1 charge.

8. **C.** The dashed lines in the diagram represent hydrogen bonding.

H– F---H– F---H– F

9. **D.** A diamond is composed of pure carbon and is an example of a network covalent compound. In the diamond structure the atoms are connected by covalent bonds, with each carbon atom bonded to four others in a tetrahedral geometry. In essence, a sample of diamond is one large molecule.

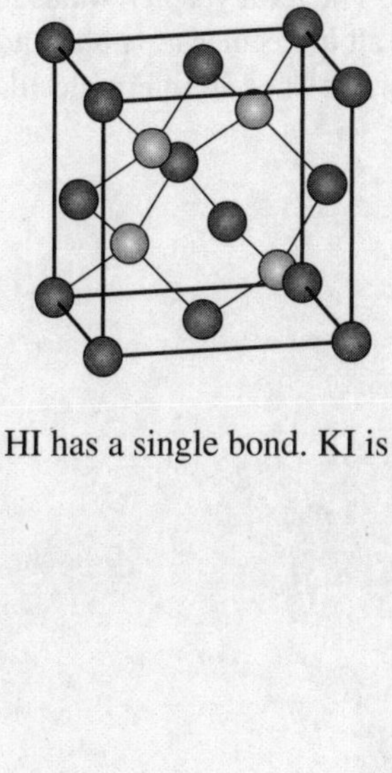

10. **A.** Carbon monoxide has a triple bond. HI has a single bond. KI is ionic. H_2 and Cl_2 both have single bonds.

11. C.

12. A.

13. D.

14. E.

15. B.

16. E. C_6H_6 is known as benzene and does not require the expanded octet model as each carbon is surrounded by the normal eight electrons.

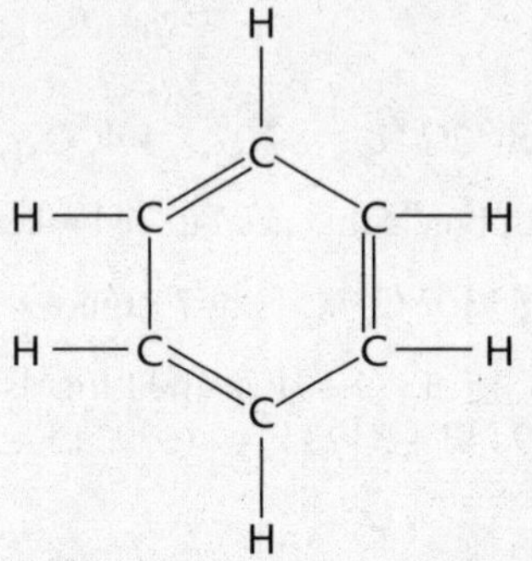

17. A. Electronegativity increases from left to right in the periodic table (Cl is more electronegative than H, O is more electronegative than C). Within the halogen family, electronegativity increases as one moves up the column, with fluorine being the most electronegative element (Br is more electronegative than I). All three molecules would be polar.

18. C.

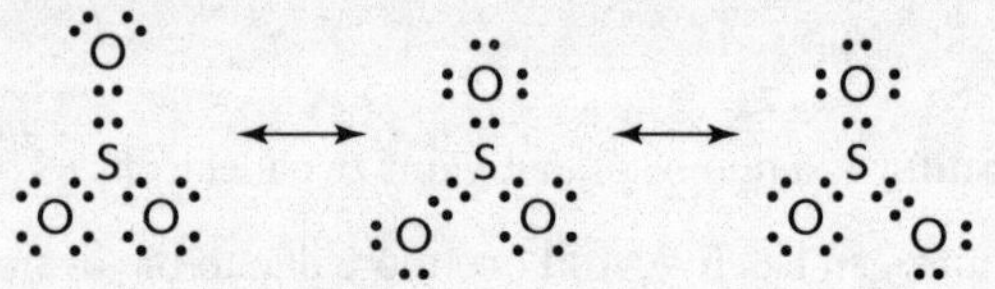

19. D. $F_{2(g)} \rightarrow 2F_{(g)} \quad \Delta H° = 157\text{ kJ}$

$\Delta H = 2\Delta H°_f(\text{F}) - \Delta H°_f(\text{F}_2)$

$157\text{ kJ} = (2\text{ mol})\ \Delta H°_f(\text{F}) - (1\text{ mol})\ (0)$ *(by definition, $\Delta H°_f$ of any element in its standard state= 0)*

$$\Delta H°_f(\text{F}) = \frac{157\text{ kJ}}{2\text{ mol}} = 78.5\text{ kJ/mol}$$

20. E. Covalent bonding is an intramolecular force. Dipole-dipole and London dispersion forces are grouped together and termed van der Waals forces. The term van der Waals forces refer to the fact that these forces produce non-ideal behavior in gases. Not all molecules are polar and have a dipole, so van der Waals forces is too inclusive. London dispersion forces, the weakest of all intermolecular forces is common to all molecules.

Free Response

Question 1

Maximum Points for Question 1
Part (a): 2 points
Part (b): 2 points
Part (c): 1 point
Part (d): 1 point
Part (e): 4 points
Total points: 10

1. Explain each of the following in terms of atomic and molecular structures and/or intermolecular forces. *(a) Solid Mg has a higher melting point than solid sodium.* Magnesium has the outer electronic structure $3s^2$. Both of these outer electrons become delocalized, so the "sea" has twice the electron density as it does in sodium with only one electron in its outer energy level. The remaining magnesium cation (Mg^{2+}) also has twice the charge and so there will be more attraction between the cations and the "sea". Each magnesium atom also has one more proton in the nucleus than a sodium atom has, and so not only will there be a greater number of delocalized electrons, but there will also be a greater attraction for them. Magnesium atoms have a slightly smaller radius than sodium atoms, and so the delocalized electrons are closer to the nuclei. Each magnesium atom also has 12 near-neighbors rather than sodium's 8, increasing the strength of the bond still further.	***2 points possible to include any of the following:*** *Explanation of metallic bonding for Mg* *Electron density of magnesium* *Greater cationic charge of Mg^{2+}-compared to Na^+ and its attractive forces on the sea of electrons* *Magnesium has 1 more proton than sodium* *Smaller atomic radius of Mg compared to Na* *12 near-neighbors for Mg compared to 8 for Na*
(b) $AsCl_3$ has a measurable dipole moment, whereas $AsCl_5$ does not. $AsCl_3$ does conform to the octet rule but $AsCl_5$ does not. $AsCl_3$ consists of four sp^3-hybridized orbitals, three of which are shared with electrons from three separate chlorine atoms and the fourth containing a nonbonding pair. Lone electron pairs interact and repel each other with the greatest electrostatic repulsion (more so than a lone pair-shared pair repulsion or a shared pair-shared pair repulsion). Lone pairs of electrons also take up more space than bonded pairs making the bond angle less than the pure tetrahedral angle of 109.5°. In doing so, they adopt a spatial arrangement such that they are as far apart as possible, and electrostatic repulsion is minimized. The result is that $AsCl_3$ has a trigonal pyramidal geometry and a measurable dipole moment. 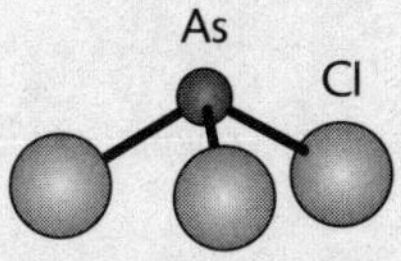 	***2 point possible to include any or all of the following:*** *A diagram showing a dipole in $AsCl_3$*

(continued)

$AsCl_5$ has trigonal bipyramidal geometry. $AsCl_5$ exhibits sp^3d hybridization and has five equivalent hybrid orbitals directed toward the corners of a trigonal bipyramid; three equatorial and two axial. The five dipoles, arranged symmetrically around the central As atom, cancel each other resulting in a nonpolar molecule. 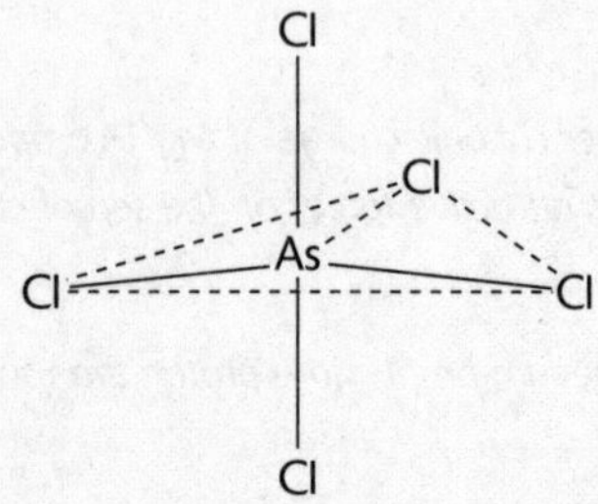	*Mentioning the geometry of the molecules* *Stating that the dipoles cancel each other out in $AsCl_5$* *Explaining $AsCl_3$ in terms of hybridization* *Explaining $AsCl_5$ in terms of hybridization*
(c) The boiling point of CCl_4 (350K) is greater than the boiling point of CH_4 (111K). CCl_4 would be expected to have a higher boiling point than CH_4 since it possesses more electrons than CH_4. Thus the magnitude of the dispersion forces present between CCl_4 molecules is higher than that between CH_4 molecules. The increased molecular mass of CCl_4 contributes only very slightly to the boiling point.	***1 point possible to include any or all of the following:*** *More electrons in CCl_4* *Increased molecular mass of CCl_4 is NOT the primary reason for higher boiling point*
(d) $KI_{(s)}$ is very soluble in water whereas $I_{2(s)}$ is not. KI has greater aqueous solubility than I_2 because KI is polar whereas I_2 is non-polar. H_2O, being polar, interacts with the ions of KI but not with I_2.	***1 point possible to include any or all of the following:*** *KI is ionic* *I_2 is non-polar* *"Like dissolves like" accepted if polarity of H_2O clearly indicated*
(e) List by formula the following substances in order of increasing boiling point: methoxymethane (dimethyl ether), $CH_3–O–CH_3$ 1,2-ethanediol, $OH–CH_2–CH_2–OH$ ethanol, $CH_3–CH_2–OH$ ethane, $CH_3–CH_3$. The C–O bonds of methoxymethane (dimethyl ether), $CH_3–O–CH_3$, are polar. The geometry of the molecule is angular, resulting in an overall molecular dipole. Hence the molecule will be subject to dipole-dipole and dipole-induced dipole interactions as well as the stronger dispersion forces.	***4 points possible to include any or all of the following:*** *Comparison of the polarity of the 4 molecules* *Resulting formation or cancellation of dipoles*

1,2-ethanediol ($OH-CH_2-CH_2-OH$), due to the presence of the O–H bonds, is capable of hydrogen bonding, which is usually the strongest intermolecular interaction. There are two sites for hydrogen bonding in this molecule, so this will enhance the possible hydrogen bonding interactions. This compound will of course also experience dispersion forces and dipole-dipole and dipole-induced dipole forces between molecules but the hydrogen bonding interaction would be most significant.	*Hydrogen bonding* *Number of sites for hydrogen bonding* *Dispersion forces* *Dipole-dipole forces* *Dipole-induced dipole forces*
Ethanol (CH_3CH_2OH) experiences the same types of intermolecular forces as 1,2-ethanediol but the hydrogen bonding can only occur at one site per molecule rather than two. This results in reduced interactions between molecules compared with 1,2-ethanediol but still more than in ethane and dimethyl ether, which lack hydrogen bonding between their molecules.	
Ethane (CH_3-CH_3) is non-polar, and subject only to dispersion forces.	
As hydrogen bonding is usually the strongest of the intermolecular forces, one would expect the boiling points of these compounds to correlate with hydrogen bonding interactions present. Hence ethanol would have a lower boiling point than 1,2-ethanediol but ethane and dimethyl ether would both have lower boiling points compared to ethanol. Of the latter two compounds, ethane is smaller than dimethyl ether so it has less dispersion forces and also it is non-polar so it lacks the dipole-dipole and dipole-induced dipole interactions which are present in the ether.	
Thus the order of increasing boiling point of all four compounds would be: $CH_3-CH_3 < CH_3-O-CH_3 < CH_3CH_2OH$ $< OH-CH_2-CH_2-OH$.	*Correct order*

Question 2

Maximum Points for Question 2
Part (a): 2 points
Part (b): 2 points
Part (c): 2 points
Part (d): 2 points
Part (e): 2 points
Total points: 10

2. Using principles of chemical bonding and/or intermolecular forces, explain each of the following: *(a) Fluorine and chlorine are gases, while bromine is a liquid and iodine is a solid.* All Group 17 elements (the halogens) have the same valence electron configuration and exhibit the same type of bonding. They all exist as covalent, diatomic molecules (F_2, Cl_2, Br_2, and I_2). Between individual molecules there exist dispersion forces, which arise from the randomness of electron distribution within the individual molecules. Dispersion forces are intermolecular forces, which are relatively weak when compared with covalent or ionic bonds, so the melting points of the halogens are low. The increase in melting point down the group is due to the increase in intermolecular dispersion forces experienced as a result of the increased number of electrons. The number of electrons in F_2 is 18, Cl_2 has 34, Br_2 has 70, and I_2 has 106.	***2 points possible to include any of the following:*** *Similarities of the Group 17 elements* *Diatomic molecules* *Dispersion forces* *Randomness of electron distribution* *Relative strength of dispersion forces correlated to melting and/or boiling point* *Increase in number of electrons results in increased in dispersion forces*
(b) The hydride of oxygen (H_2O), is a liquid at room temperature (B.P 100°C at 1 atm) while the hydride of sulfur (H_2S) is a gas (B.P. –60.3°C at 1 atm). The small size of the hydrogen atom and high electronegativity of oxygen result in highly polar O—H bonds in H_2O. These highly polar bonds lead to extensive hydrogen bonding between water molecules. Sulfur is larger and less electronegative than oxygen, so the S—H bonds in H_2S are much less polar and no hydrogen bonding between molecules occurs. These stronger intermolecular forces present between H_2O molecules require the supply of considerably more energy to break individual molecules from each other than is the case for H_2S molecules sufficient to give water a boiling point of 100°C. The weaker intermolecular forces present between H_2S molecules results in a boiling point of only –60.3°C (at 1 atm pressure).	***2 points possible to include any of the following:*** *Relative size of hydrogen vs. sulfur atom* *High electronegativity of oxygen* *Polar bonds* *Hydrogen bonding* *Energy required to break molecules*
(c) Hydrogen fluoride is a liquid at room temperature and a weak acid, but hydrogen chloride is a gas. Hydrogen fluoride exhibits hydrogen bonding between HF molecules. This results in a boiling point much higher than might be expected from consideration of molecular mass alone and thus hydrogen fluoride is a liquid at room temperature and pressure whereas the other hydrogen halides are all gases at those conditions. Conversely, HCl molecules do not hydrogen bond to each other or to water molecules, so it exists as a gas at room temperature and ionizes completely in water solution.	***2 points possible to include any of the following:*** *Hydrogen bonding between HF molecules which results in higher B.P.* *No hydrogen bonds in HCl*

(d) The boiling point of ammonia (NH_3) at 240K is greater than the boiling point of phosphine (PH_3) at 185K. NH_3 exhibits hydrogen bonding in addition to dispersion forces. This significantly increases the intermolecular force and raises the boiling point. PH_3 does not exhibit hydrogen bonding and the dominant intermolecular force holding these molecules together is dispersion forces.	***2 points possible to include any of the following:*** *NH_3 exhibits both hydrogen bonding and London dispersion forces* *Effect of hydrogen bonding on B.P.* *No hydrogen bonding in PH_3* *Only significant force between PH_3 molecules are dispersion forces*
(e) Acetic (ethanoic) acid is strongly associated in the liquid state. The hydrogen atom in the carboxyl group (–COOH) of acetic acid is donated as an H^+ ion (proton) giving acetic acid its acidic properties. Acetic acid is a weak, monoprotic acid such that less than 1% of the molecules are dissociated. Molecules of acetic acid pair up into dimers connected by hydrogen bonds. As water also contains hydrogen bonds, "like dissolves like". 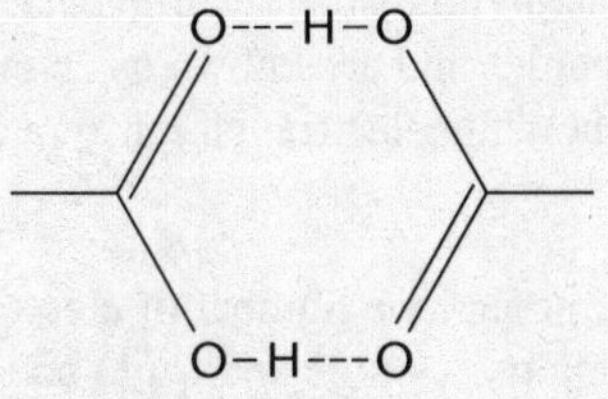 Cyclic Dimer 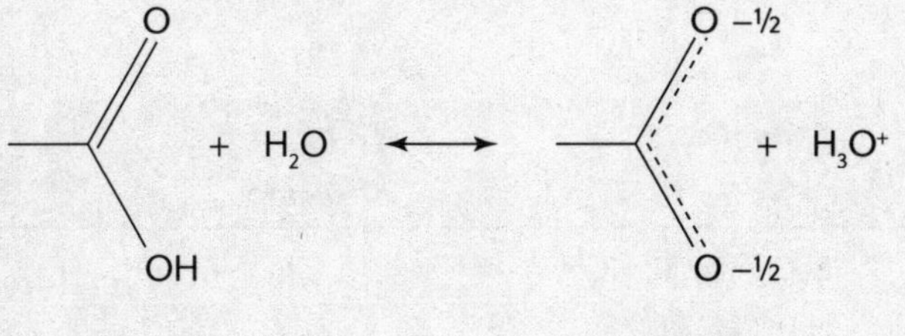 acetic acid acetate Acetic acid being a hydrophilic (polar) solvent can also dissolve polar compounds, such as inorganic salts and sugars but also non-polar compounds such as oils and elements such as sulfur and iodine. It can also mix (associate) with many other polar and non-polar solvents such as chloroform and hexane. This dissolving property and miscibility makes it widely used in industry.	***2 points possible to include any of the following:*** *Explanation of origin of H^+ when acetic acid is dissolved in water* *Acetic acid forms dimers in water* *Dimers are connected by hydrogen bonds* *Like dissolves like (acetic acid contains hydrogen bonds as does water)* *Diagram of cyclic dimers* *Diagram of acetic acid dissolving in water forming the acetate ion* *Other information relating to how acetic acid can dissolve other compounds and its industrial significance*

Molecular Geometry and Hybridization

You'll Need to Know

- ❑ Molecular geometry including linear, trigonal planar, tetrahedral, trigonal bipyramidal, octahedral, bent, trigonal pyramidal, distorted tetrahedron (seesaw), T-shaped, square pyramidal, and square planar
- ❑ Sigma and pi bonds
- ❑ Dipole moments
- ❑ Hybridization including *sp*, sp^2, sp^3, sp^3d, sp^3d^2

Molecular Geometry

The valence shell is the outermost electron-occupied shell of an atom and usually holds the electrons that are involved in bonding. Pairs of electrons, which are shared, hold atoms together in molecules and are known as "bonding pairs". The VSEPR model (valence-shell electron-pair repulsion) is used to predict how the electron clouds of atoms within compounds repel each other and results in an overall molecular geometry.

In attempting to predict molecular geometry: (1) draw the Lewis structure, (2) count the number of electron pairs (both bonding and lone pairs), and (3) use the following chart to "key out" the geometry. Double and triple bonds behave as if they were a single electron pair. When predicting bond angles, lone-pair vs. lone-pair repulsion is greater than lone-pair vs. bonding-pair repulsion is greather than bonding-pair vs. bonding-pair repulsion. In the following chart, A represents the central atom, B represents the other atoms that surround A, and E represents the number of lone pairs of electrons.

Type	***Number of Electron Pairs About A***	***Molecular Geometry***	***Examples***	***Generic Drawing***
AB_2	2	linear	$BeCl_2$, $HgCl_2$, HCN H : C ::: N :	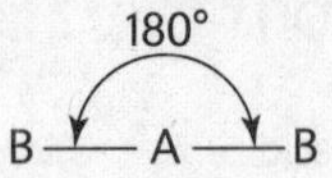
AB_3	3	trigonal planar	BF_3, SO_3, NO_3^- CO_3^{2-} 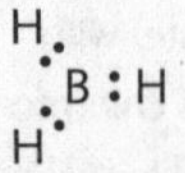	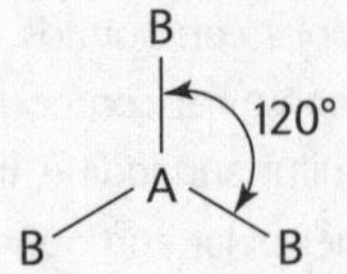
AB_4	4	tetrahedral	CH_4, NH_4^+, ClO_4^- SO_4^{2-}, PO_4^{3-}, SiF_4 	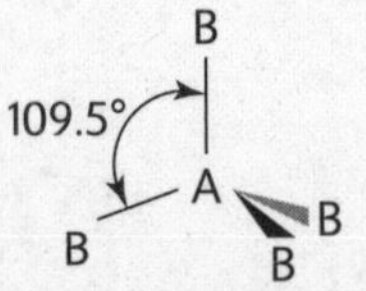

Type	*Number of Electron Pairs About A*	*Molecular Geometry*	*Examples*	*Generic Drawing*
AB_5	5	trigonal bipyramidal	PCl_5 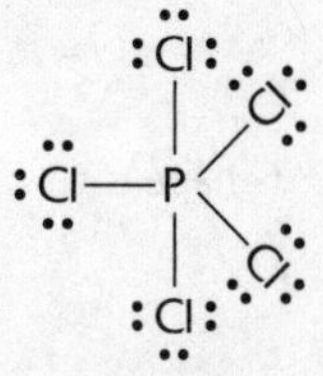	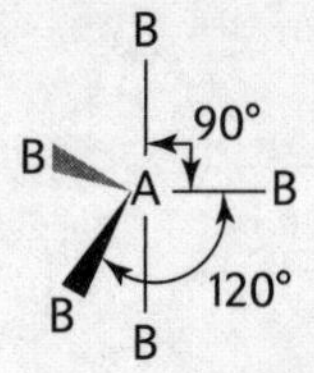
AB_6	6	octahedral	SF_6, SeF_6 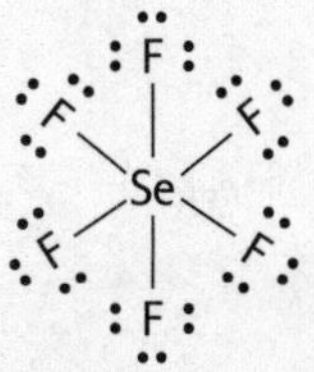	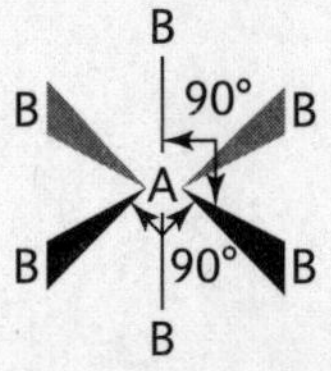
AB_2E	3	bent	SO_2, O_3 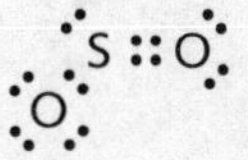	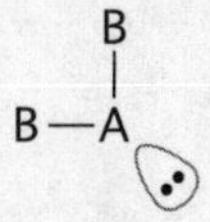 AB_2E
AB_3E	4	trigonal pyramidal	NH_3, PCl_3, AsH_3, SO_3^{2-} 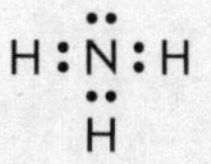	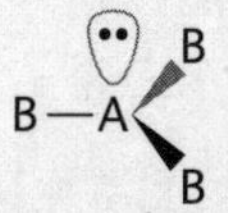 AB_3E
AB_2E_2	4	bent	H_2O, OF_2, NH_2^- 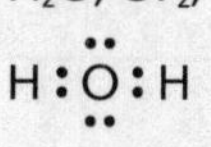	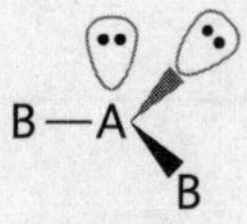 AB_2E_2
AB_4E	5	distorted tetrahedron (seesaw)	IF_4^+, SF_4, XeO_2F_2 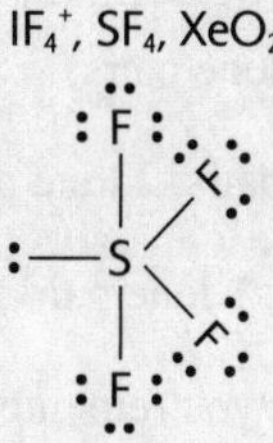	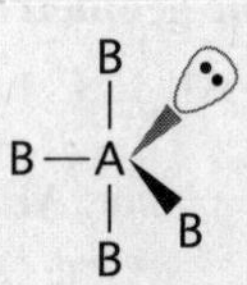 AB_4E

Type	*Number of Electron Pairs About A*	*Molecular Geometry*	*Examples*	*Generic Drawing*
AB_3E_2	5	T-shape	BrF_3, ICl_3 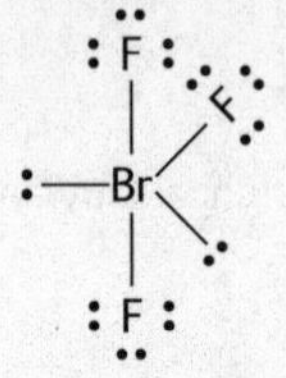	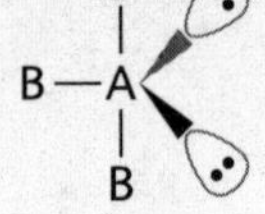 AB_3E_2
AB_2E_3	5	linear	XeF_2, I_3^- 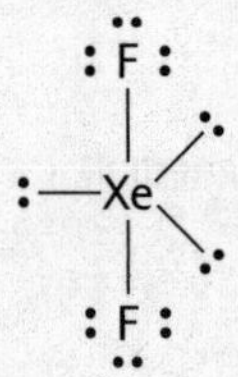	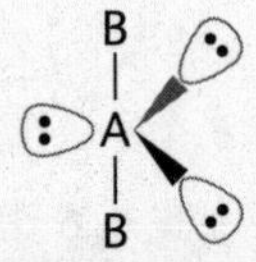 AB_2E_3
AB_5E	6	square pyramidal	BrF_5, $XeOF_4$, IF_5 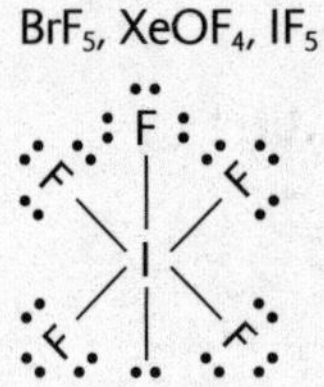	 AB_5E
AB_4E_2	6	square planar	XeF_4, ICl_4^- 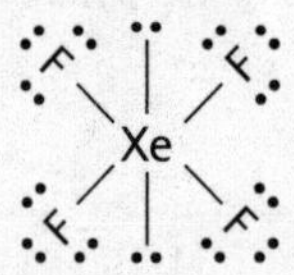	 AB_4E_2

Example

Q. Predict the geometries of (a) ICl_2^-, (b) XeF_4, (c) ClF_3, (d) CO_2.

A. (a) linear: AB_2E_3 (2 bonding pairs, 3 lone pairs)

(b) square planar: AB_4E_2 (4 bonding pairs, 2 lone pairs)

(c) T-shaped: AB_3E_2 (3 bonding pairs, 2 lone pairs)

(d) linear: AB_2 (2 bonding pairs). Did you remember to count each double bond as a single bonding pair?

Sigma and Pi Bonds

Orbitals that overlap end-to-end are known as sigma (σ) bonds. There are three types of sigma bonds: (1) σ_s which occurs when two electrons, both in *s* orbitals overlap; (2) σ_p, occurs when an electron in a *p* orbital overlaps end-to-end with another electron in a *p* orbital; and (3) σ_{sp}, when an electron in an *s* orbital overlaps with an electron in a *p* orbital. All single bonds are sigma. Pi (π) bonds occur when parallel *p* orbitals overlap. Double bonds contain one sigma and one pi bond; triple bonds contain one sigma and two pi bonds. Although π bonds are weaker than σ bonds, since the π bonds are found in multiple bonds together with π bonds, the combination is stronger than either bond by itself.

Example

Q. How many sigma and pi bonds are in the formaldehyde molecule, CH_2O?

A. Begin by drawing the Lewis structure.

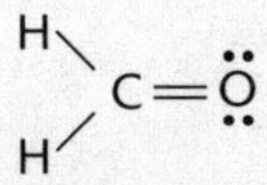

A σ bond is formed by the overlap of the sp^2 hybrid orbital of carbon with the sp^2 hybrid orbital of oxygen. A π bond is formed by the overlap of a 2*p* orbitals of the carbon and oxygen atom. The single bonds between the carbon and each hydrogen are both σ. The two lone pairs on oxygen are placed in the other two sp^2 orbitals of oxygen. Result: 3 σ and 1π.

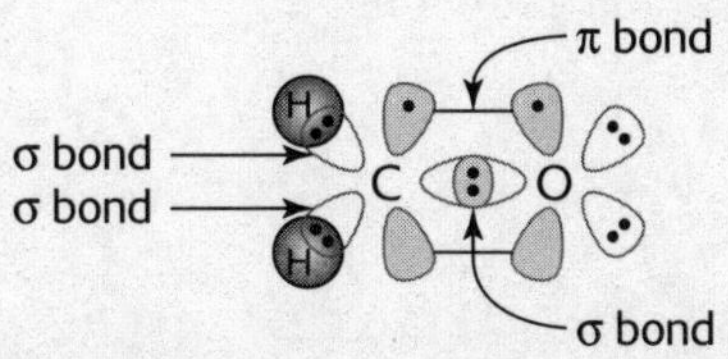

Dipole Moments

A dipole moment is a measure of the polarity of a bond and can be illustrated through vectors that can show both magnitude (how strong the polarity is) and direction (the overall result). All non-polar molecules have an overall zero dipole moment. In using vectors, the length of a line is directly proportional to the magnitude of the polarity, and the head of the arrow points to the more negative species. To illustrate dipole moments, we'll examine *cis*-dichloroethylene and *trans*-dichloroethylene.

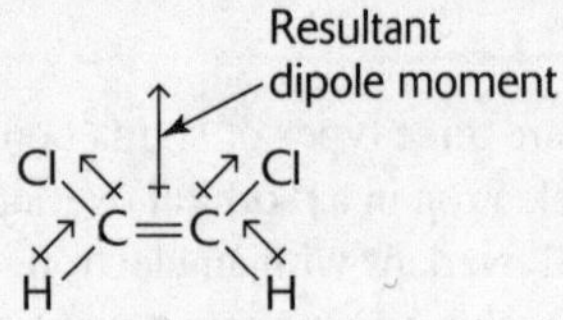 *cis*-dichlorocthylene	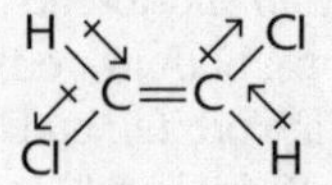 *trans*-dichlorocthylene
Chlorine is more electronegative than carbon (arrow points toward Cl). Carbon is slightly more electronegative than hydrogen (arrow points toward C). The lengths of the arrows are similar since the electronegativity differences between H–C and C–Cl are similar. The resultant vector shows that the molecule is polar with the chlorine side being much more negative.	In this arrangement, when all vectors are added, the resultant dipole vector is 0; therefore, *trans*-dichloroethylene is non-polar.

Example

Q. Predict whether the following molecules have an overall dipole moment: (a) ICl, (b) BF_3, (c) CH_3Br.

A.

(a) yes

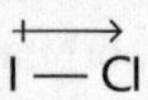

(b) no

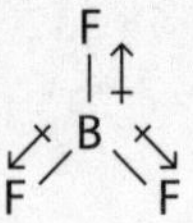

(c) yes

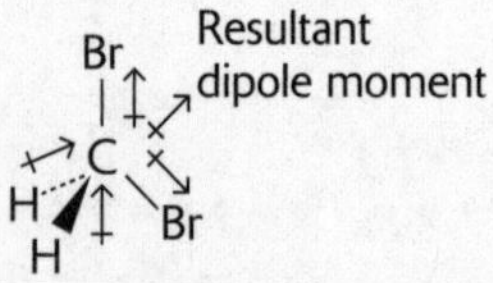

Hybridization

Hybridization is a concept that involves "blending" orbitals. The concept of hybridization explains why compounds can have a variety of three-dimensional molecular geometries. There are just five types of hybrid orbitals that you will be responsible for and which are summarized in the following table:

Hybridization	*Molecular Geometry*	*Total Electron Pairs Around Central Atom*	*Examples (central atom underlined)*
sp	linear	2	$\underline{Be}Cl_2$ The bonds in $BeCl_2$ arise from the overlap of two *sp* hybrid orbitals on the beryllium atom with the 3*p* orbitals on the two chlorine atoms. 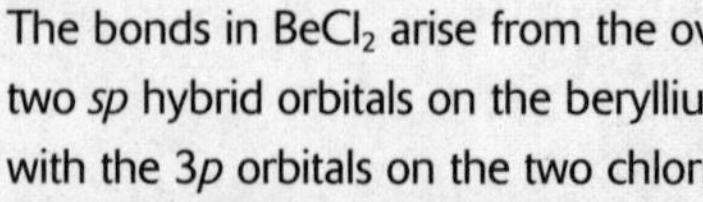

Hybridization	*Molecular Geometry*	*Total Electron Pairs Around Central Atom*	*Examples (central atom underlined)*
sp^2	trigonal planar	3	<u>B</u>F_3 The bonds in BF_3 arise from the overlap of three sp^2 hybrid orbitals on the boron atom with $2p$ orbitals on the three fluorine atoms. 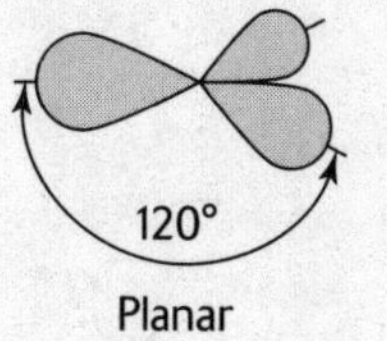
sp^3	tetrahedral	4	<u>C</u>H_4 Each of the four C–H bonds results from the overlap of a singly occupied (one electron in the orbit) carbon sp^3 hybrid orbital with a singly occupied hydrogen $1s$ orbital. 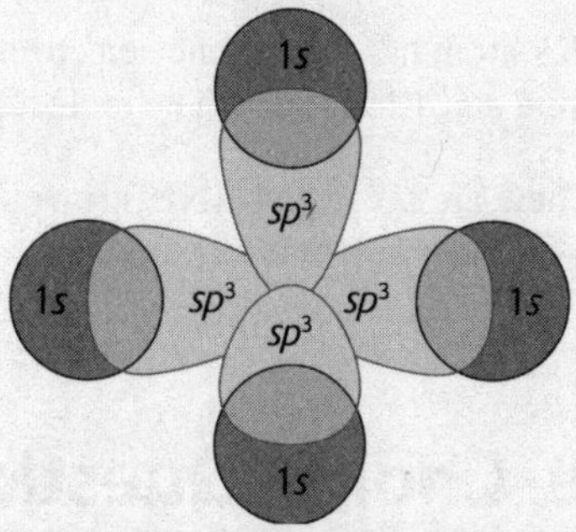
sp^3d	trigonal bipyramidal	5	<u>P</u>Cl_5 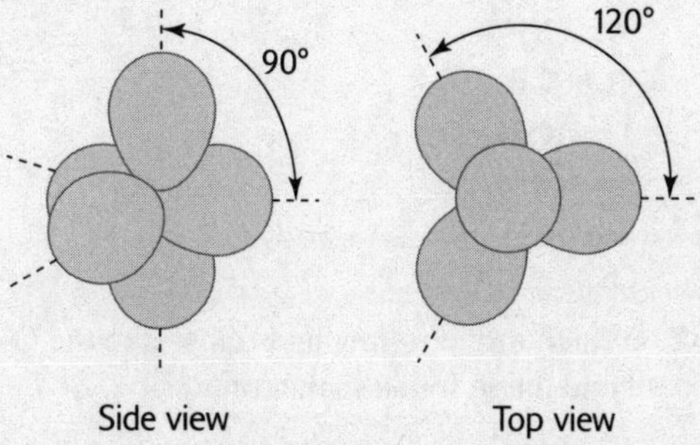
sp^3d^2	octahedral	6	<u>S</u>F_6  sp^3d^2 orbitals

Example

Q. Predict the hybridization of the central atom (underlined): (a) $\underline{C}H_2O$, (b) $\underline{Hg}Cl_2$, (c) $\underline{P}F_3$, (d) $[\underline{Co}(NH_3)_6]^{2+}$.

A. (a) sp^2. C has a double bond. Two of the sp^2 orbitals of the C atom form two sigma bonds with the H atoms, and the third sp^2 orbital forms a sigma bond with a sp^2 orbital of the O atom. A pi bond is formed from unhybridized *p* orbitals.

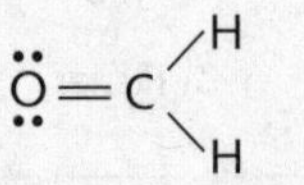

Lewis Structure

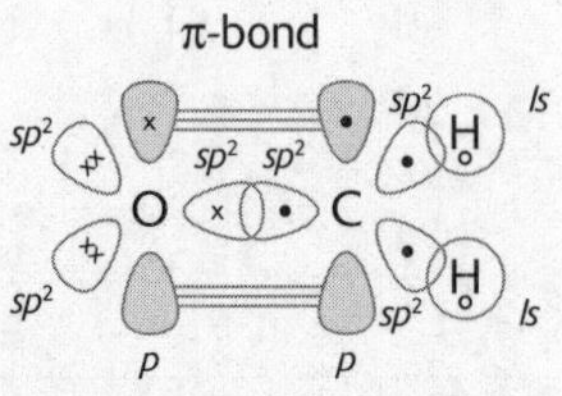

Valence Bond Description

(b) *sp*. There are a total of two bonding electron pairs around the Hg; there are no lone pairs. The two Hg–Cl bonds are formed by the overlap of the Hg *sp* hybrid orbitals with the 3*p* orbitals of the Cl atoms. The molecule is linear.

(c) sp^3. The P atom has five valence electrons, and there are a total of four electron pairs around the P atom (3 bonding and 1 lone pair). The molecule is tetrahedral.

(d) sp^3d^2. There are six ligands (NH_3) surrounding the central cobalt ion. The geometry would be octahedral which keys out sp^3d^2 hybridization.

Multiple-Choice Questions

1. Which species contains a central atom with sp^2 hybridization?

A. NF_3
B. ClF_3
C. O_3
D. Br_3^-
E. CH_4

2. Which of the following is closest to the O–Si–O bond angle found in quartz?

A. 90°
B. 110°
C. 120°
D. 145°
E. 180°

3. Which pair of substances will have the most similar geometry?

A. SO_3 and ICl_3
B. SO_3 and CO_3^{2-}
C. SO_3 and SO_4^{2-}
D. SO_4^{2-} and CO_3^{2-}
E. CH_4 and SF_4

4. Which of these molecules has/have nonbonding electron pair(s) on the central atom?

I. SF_4
II. IOF_3
III. ClF_3

A. I only
B. I and II only
C. I and III only
D. II and III
E. all of them

5. Which of the following diatomic molecules contains two pi bonds and one sigma bond?

A. O_2
B. Cl_2
C. Br_2
D. N_2
E. H_2

6. Of the following molecules, which one is polar?

A. BF_3
B. C_2H_4
C. $C_6H_{12}O_6$
D. CO_2
E. all are non-polar

7. Molecules which exhibit sp^3d^2 hybridization have their electron pairs directed toward the corners of a

A. triangle-based pyramid
B. square-based pyramid
C. triangle
D. distorted tetrahedron
E. an octahedron

8. Which molecule has the greatest bond energy?

A. CO
B. Cl_2
C. NO
D. F_2
E. H_2

9. Which of the following chlorine-oxygen species has a pyramidal structure?

A. ClO_2
B. ClO_2^-
C. ClO_3^-
D. ClO_4^-
E. Cl_2O

10. Which of the following organic compounds is polar?

A. CCl_4
B. CH_2Cl_2
C. C_2H_4
D. CH_4
E. C_6H_6

11. Arrange the following species in order of increasing N–H bond angle: NH_2^-, NH_3, NH_4^+.

A. $NH_2^- > NH_3 > NH_4^+$
B. $NH_3 > NH_4^+ > NH_2^-$
C. $NH_4^+ > NH_3 > NH_2^-$
D. $NH_2^- > NH_4^+ > NH_3$
E. $NH_3 > NH_2^- > NH_4^+$

12. Which compound listed below is geometrically bent and would require the use of resonance structures to explain its actual bond lengths?

A. O_2
B. O_3
C. OCN^-
D. NO_3^-
E. C_6H_6

13. The hybridization of each carbon in benzene (C_6H_6) would be classified as

A. sp
B. sp^2
C. sp^3
D. sp^3d
E. sp^3d^2

For Questions 14–18, refer to the following molecular geometries:

A. Square planar
B. Square pyramidal
C. T-shape
D. Distorted tetrahedron (seesaw)
E. Trigonal pyramidal

14. SF_4

15. IF_5

16. ICl_3

17. IF_4^-

18. SO_3^{2-}

19. Examine the following molecule

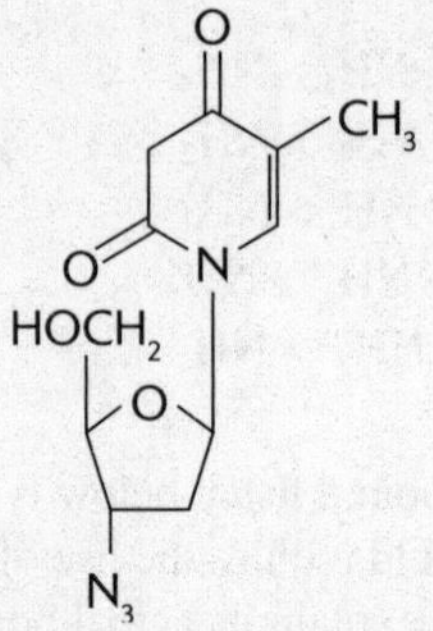

How many nitrogen atoms are sp^3 hybridized?

A. 0
B. 1
C. 2
D. 3
E. all nitrogen atoms are sp^3 hybridized

20. Given the following molecules: CCl_4, $BeCl_2$, $SbBr_3$, PF_5, and SCl_6, which of the following do NOT describe any of the molecules mentioned?

A. Trigonal bipyramidal
B. Octahedral
C. Linear
D. Tetrahedral
E. Square planar

Free-Response Questions

1. Given the molecules XeF_2 and XeF_4:

(a) Draw a Lewis dot diagram for each.

(b) Predict the geometry of each.

(c) Predict the ideal bond angle for each.

(d) Predict the hybridization of the central atom in each molecule.

(e) Give the number of sigma and pi bonds in each molecule.

2. C_3H_6 can exist in two different forms.

(a) Draw and name each isomer.

(b) Describe the geometry for each isomer.

(c) Identify the hybridization found on each carbon for both isomers.

(d) Which isomer would be more stable? Justify your answer.

Answers and Explanations

Multiple Choice

1. C.

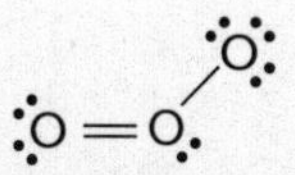

The hybridization for the oxygen to the left of the central oxygen in the diagram above and the central oxygen will be sp^2 with their electron-pair geometries being trigonal planar. The oxygen to the right of (and above) the central oxygen atom will be sp^3 with an electron-pair geometry of tetrahedral. The oxygen-oxygen-oxygen bond angle is 120°. The molecular geometry is bent.

2. B. The bonding for SiO_2 is

$$
\begin{array}{ccccccc}
 & O & & O & & O & \\
 & | & & | & & | & \\
-O-Si-O-Si-O-Si-O- \\
 & | & & | & & | & \\
 & O & & O & & O & \\
 & | & & | & & | & \\
-O-Si-O-Si-O-Si-O- \\
 & | & & | & & | &
\end{array}
$$

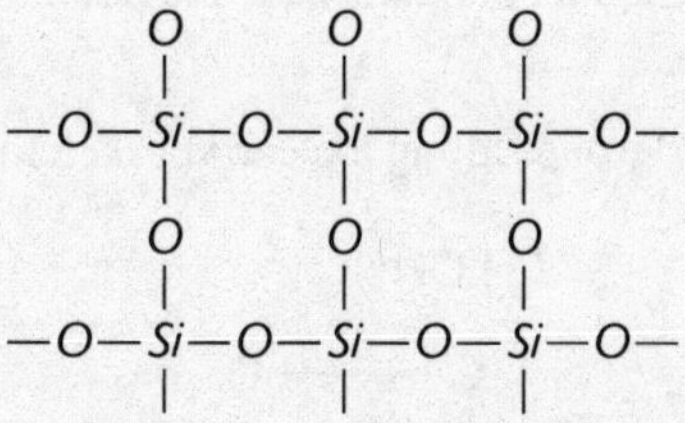

The three-dimensional structure of quartz is a crystal lattice

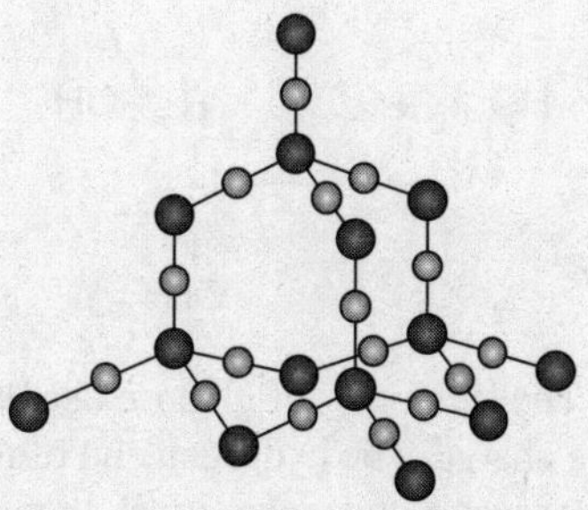

composed of a silicon atom tetrahedrally bonded to four oxygen atoms in repeating patterns. Electrons in a tetrahedral-shaped molecule are ideally 109.5° apart. Chains of tetrahedral quartz crystals bond in spirals which in turn link to form a precise, repeating latticework of molecules.

3. B.

A. SO_3 (trigonal planar) and ICl_3 (T-shape)
B. SO_3 and CO_3^{2-} (both trigonal planar)
C. SO_3 (trigonal planar) and SO_4^{2-} (tetrahedral)
D. SO_4^{2-} (tetrahedral) and CO_3^{2-} (trigonal planar)
E. CH_4 (tetrahedral) and SF_4 (distorted tetrahedron or seesaw)

4. E.

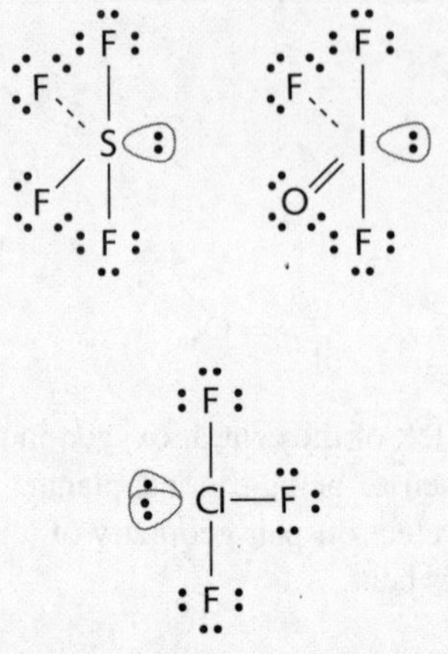

5. D. N_2 is the only diatomic molecule listed that contains a triple bond. A triple bond consists of two pi bonds and one sigma bond.

6. C. Glucose has five –O–H "hydroxyl" groups along the carbon skeleton.

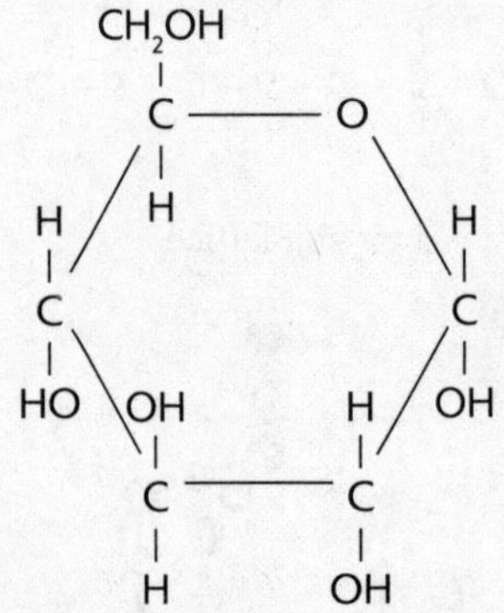

These –O–H groups are polar centers. The symmetry of glucose decreases the polarity of the molecule, but the "O" in each –O–H has a slight negative charge. The hydrogen end of the –O–H has a slight positive charge. Glucose dissolves in water because polar water molecules attach to the glucose molecules. The many –O–H groups in glucose are attracted to the water molecules by dipole-dipole forces. The strength of these forces can be greater than the glucose-glucose interactions. The hydrogen bonding between water molecules and glucose also makes the glucose more water soluble.

7. E.

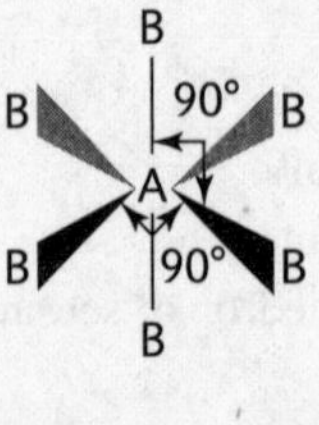

8. A. The strength of a chemical bond can be expressed in terms of the amount of energy needed to break the bond and liberate separate atoms, which is called the bond energy, and is measured in kJ/mol. By comparing bond energies of similar compounds, you can compare the strength of their bonds. Some compounds have relatively strong chemical bonds that are stable and are in a low state of potential energy so that large amounts of energy are required to break the compound into elements or simpler compounds. Carbon monoxide contains a triple bond with a large bond energy of 1074 kJ/mol.

9. C.

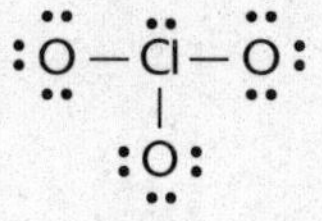

10. B.

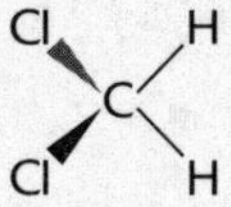

11. C. NH_4^+ is a perfect tetrahedron with N–H bond angles of 109.5°. In NH_3 the nitrogen has three bond pairs and one lone pair of electrons. The shape is trigonal pyramidal with a N–H bond angle of 107.3°. NH_2^- is bent with two lone pairs of unshared electrons that decrease the bond angle even more.

12. B. Ozone (O_3) is the only bent compound listed. The measured bond lengths between the central oxygen and the other two oxygens of ozone are identical:

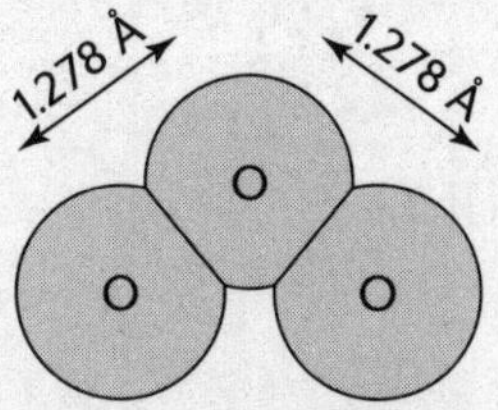

There is only one form of the ozone molecule; therefore, the bond lengths between the two oxygens are intermediate between characteristic single and double bond lengths leading to the concept of resonance:

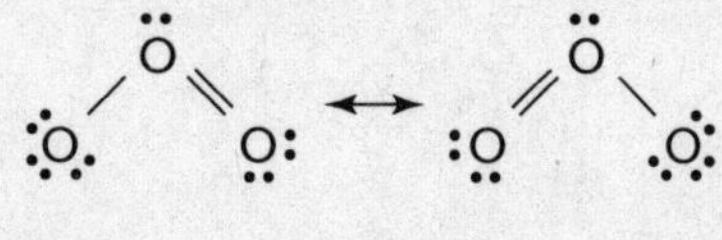

13. B. Benzene is built from hydrogen atoms ($1s^1$) and carbon atoms ($1s^2 2s^2 2p_x^1 2p_y^1$).

Each carbon atom has to join to three other atoms (one hydrogen and two carbons) and does not have enough unpaired electrons to form the required number of bonds, so one of the 2*s* electrons is promoted into the empty $2p_z$ orbital:

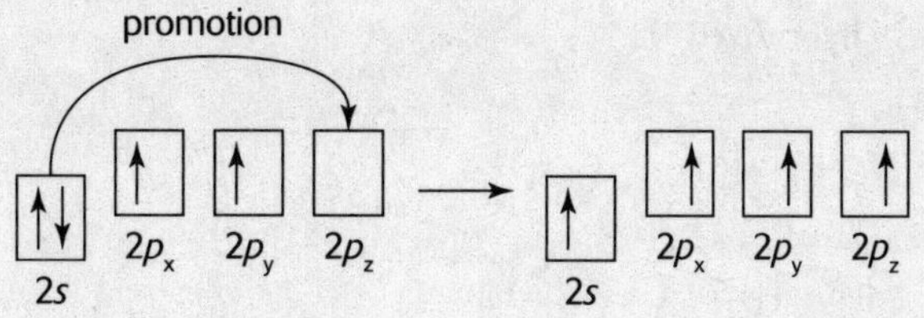

Because each carbon is only joining to three other atoms, when the carbon atoms hybridize their outer orbitals before forming bonds, they only need to hybridize three of the orbitals rather than all four. They use the 2*s* electron and two of the 2*p* electrons, but leave the other 2*p* electron unchanged. The new orbitals formed are called sp^2 hybrids, because they are formed by an *s* orbital and two *p* orbitals reorganizing themselves. The three sp^2 hybrid orbitals arrange themselves as far apart as possible—120° to each other in a plane.

14. D. four bond pairs; one lone pair

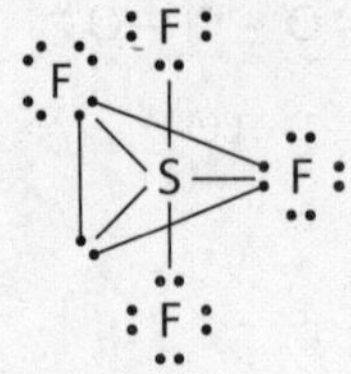

15. B. five bond pairs; one lone pair

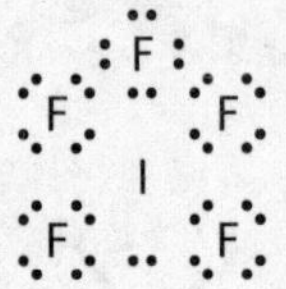

16. C. three bond pairs; two lone pairs

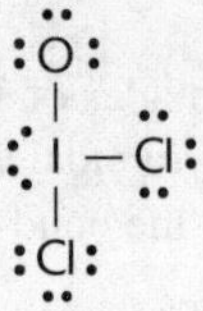

17. A. four bond pairs; two lone pairs

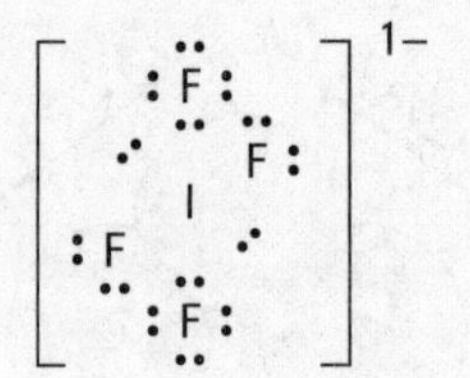

18. E. three bond pairs; one lone pair

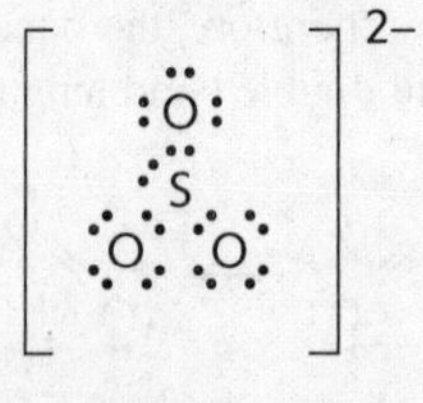

19. C. Hybridization of nitrogen can give four orbitals, one of which is filled with two electrons and does not participate in bonding (two 2*p* nonbonding electrons frequently called a lone electron pair). The remaining three hybrid orbitals form the normal σ bonds. Only the nitrogens that have single bonds emanating from them are sp^3 hybridized. The $-N_3$ part of the molecule has two double bonds; therefore, none of these three nitrogen atoms are sp^3 hybridized. The carbon atoms and nitrogen atoms marked with an asterisk (C and N*) are sp^2 hybridized; unmarked carbon atoms and nitrogen atoms marked with a diamond (C and N◆) are sp^3 hybridized; and the unmarked nitrogen atom is *sp* hybridized.

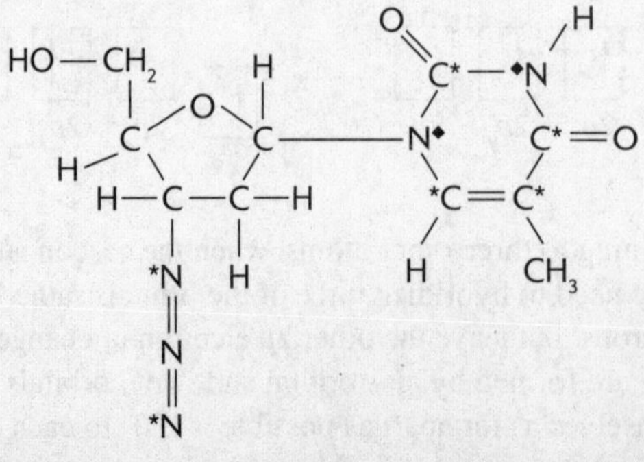

20. **E.** CCl_4 is tetrahedral, $BeCl_2$ is linear, $SbBr_3$ is trigonal pyramidal, PF_5 is trigonal bipyramidal, and SCl_6 is octahedral.

Free Response

Question 1

Maximum Points for Question 1
Part (a): 2 points
Part (b): 2 points
Part (c): 2 points
Part (d): 2 points
Part (e): 2 points
Total points: 10

1. *Given the molecules XeF_2 and XeF_4:*

   (a) Draw a Lewis dot diagram for each.

   (b) Predict the geometry of each.

   (c) Predict the ideal bond angle for each.

   (d) Predict the hybridization of the central atom in each molecule.

   (e) Give the number of sigma and pi bonds in each molecule.

	XeF_2	***XeF_4***
(a) Lewis Diagram (2 points each)		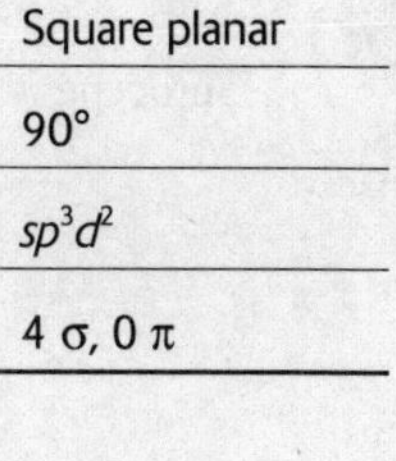
(b) Geometry *(2 points each)*	Linear	Square planar
(c) Bond angle *(2 points each)*	180°	90°
(d) Hybridization *(2 points each)*	sp^3d	sp^3d^2
(e) Type of bonds *(2 points each)*	$2\ \sigma, 0\ \pi$	$4\ \sigma, 0\ \pi$

Note to student: *Notice how the "grid" organizes the answer.*

Question 2

Maximum Points for Question 2
Part (a): 4 points
Part (b): 2 points
Part (c): 2 points
Part (d): 2 points
Total points: 10

2. C_3H_6 can exist in two different forms.

(a) Draw and name each isomer.

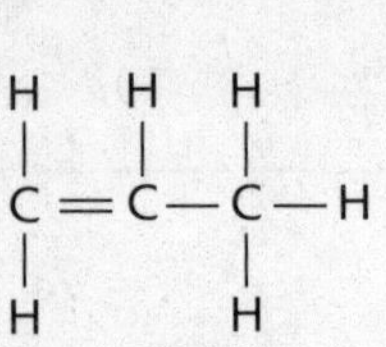

propene

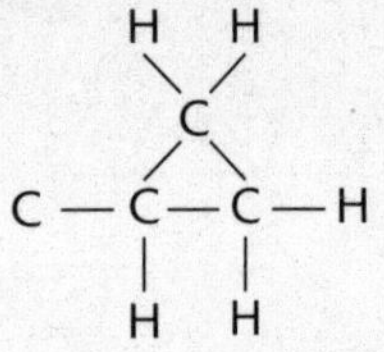

cyclopropane

4 points possible

1 point for each isomer drawn correctly.

1 point for each isomer named correctly.

(b) Describe the geometry for each isomer.

Propene: Geometry surrounding the #1 and #2 carbons below is trigonal planar. Geometry surrounding #3 carbon below is trigonal pyramidal.

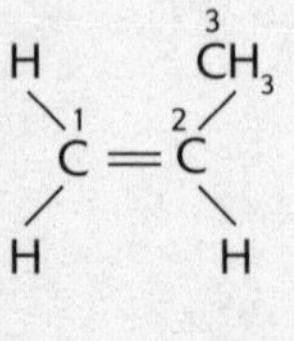

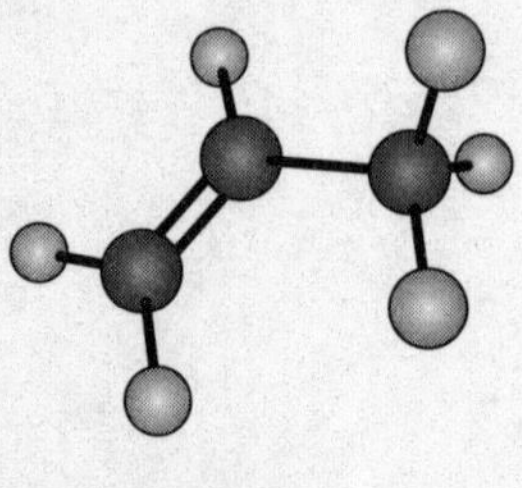

propene

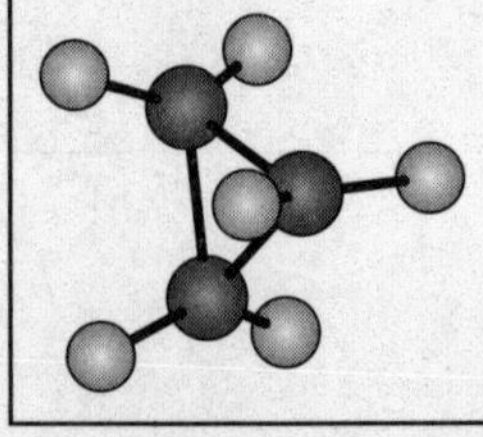

cyclopropane

2 points possible

1 point for propene being trigonal planar.

Cyclopropane: A planar molecule with the carbon atoms at the corners of an equilateral triangle. The 60° bond angles are much smaller than the optimum 109.5° angles of a normal tetrahedral carbon atom, and the resulting angle strain dramatically influences the chemical behavior.	*1 point for cyclopropane being planar.*
(c) Identify the hybridization found on each carbon for both isomers. All single bonded carbon atoms are sp^3 hybridized. Double-bonded carbon atoms are sp^2 hybridized.	***2 points possible*** *1 point for correctly identifying which carbons are sp^3 hybridized.* *1 point for correctly identifying which carbons are sp^2 hybridized.*
(d) Which isomer would be more stable? Justify your answer. Cyclopropane is quite unstable because the ring is very strained due to the enforced geometry; i.e., the C–C–C bond angle of 60°, rather than the usual "tetrahedral" bond system producing C–C–C angles of 109.5°. On heating or catalysis, isomerization occurs and cyclopropane is readily converted to the much more stable propene.	***2 points possible*** *1 point for identifying that propene is more stable.* *1 point for properly justifying the choice.*

Stoichiometry

Stoichiometry is a way of describing the quantitative relationships among elements in compounds and among substances as they undergo chemical changes.

You'll Need to Know

- ❑ how to express numbers to the correct number of significant figures
- ❑ how to use $\log_{10}$ and natural log (ln)
- ❑ how to solve problems using the factor-label method
- ❑ how to work with numbers in exponential form (add, subtract, multiply, and divide)
- ❑ how to work with moles
- ❑ how to balance chemical equations
- ❑ how to determine empirical and molecular formulas given data
- ❑ how to determine the percentage composition of a compound given data
- ❑ how to determine the limiting reactant
- ❑ how to determine theoretical and actual yields given data

Significant Figures

Note: The numbers that are underlined are significant.

(a) Nonzero digits and zeros between nonzero digits are significant.

$\underline{123}$ = 3 s.f.

$\underline{8.802}$ = 4 s.f.

$\underline{20304.007}$ = 8 s.f.

(b) Zeros at the end of a number and to the right of the decimal point are significant.

$\underline{56.000}$ = 5 s.f.

(c) Zeros to the left of the first nonzero digit are NOT significant.

$0.0\underline{1}$ = 1 s.f.

$0.000\underline{50800}$ = 5 s.f.

(d) Zeros at the end of a number greater than 1 are NOT significant, unless there is a decimal point.

$\underline{1,6}00$ = 2 s.f.

$\underline{1,600}.$ = 4 s.f.

(e) When multiplying or dividing, the answer should be rounded to contain the same number of significant figures as the least accurate number.

0.300 (3 s.f.) × 405.7009 (7 s.f.) = 3 s.f. in answer

5000. (4 s.f.) ÷ 10.32 × 10^{-10} (4 s.f.) = 4 s.f. in answer

(f) When adding or subtracting, the answer should have the same number of decimal places as the least accurate number used in the calculation.

84 + 87,600 + 9.005 = round answer to nearest whole number

10.00405 – 5,400.5 + 6.32 = round answer to nearest tenth

Log_{10} and Natural Log (ln)

If $10^x = y$, then $\log y = x$

If $e^x = y$, then $\ln y = x$

$e = 2.7183$

$\ln y = 2.303 \log y$

$\log (x \cdot y) = \log x + \log y$

$\log\left(\frac{x}{y}\right) = \log x - \log y$

Factor-Label Method

Throughout the rest of this book, we will use the factor-label method to solve problems involving mathematical setups. The following is a sample problem to illustrate the steps required using the factor-label method.

Example

Q. The Exxon Valdez spilled 240,000 barrels of oil into Prince William Sound, Alaska in 1989. It has been determined that a layer of oil can spread out on water to form a layer approximately 115 nanometers thick (1 nm = 10^{-9} m). Using factor-label methods, show how you would determine the number of square miles of ocean that could theoretically be covered by all of the oil spilled by the Exxon Valdez. (1 barrel = 31.5 U.S. gallons, 1 L = 1.057 qt., 4 qt = 1 gallon, 1 inch = 2.54 cm, and 5,280 ft = 1 mile). Calculations NOT required.

A. Volume = area × thickness; therefore, area = volume/thickness

$$\frac{2.4\times10^5\ \cancel{\text{barrels}}}{115\ \cancel{\text{nm}}}\times\frac{31.5\ \cancel{\text{gallons}}}{1\ \cancel{\text{barrel}}}\times\frac{4\ \cancel{\text{qt.}}}{1\ \cancel{\text{gallon}}}\times\frac{1\ \cancel{\text{L}}}{1.057\ \cancel{\text{qt.}}}\times\frac{10^3\ \cancel{\text{mL}}}{1\ \cancel{\text{L}}}\times\frac{1\ \cancel{\text{cm}^3}}{1\ \cancel{\text{mL}}}\times$$

$$\frac{(1\ \cancel{\text{m}})^3}{(100\ \cancel{\text{cm}})^3}\times\frac{(10^9\ \cancel{\text{nm}})^3}{(1\ \cancel{\text{m}})^3}\times\frac{(1\ \cancel{\text{m}})^2}{(10^9\ \cancel{\text{nm}})^2}\times\frac{(100\ \cancel{\text{cm}})^2}{(1\ \cancel{\text{m}})^2}\times$$

$$\frac{(1\ \cancel{\text{in}})^2}{(2.54\ \cancel{\text{cm}})^2}\times\frac{(1\ \cancel{\text{ft}})^2}{(12\ \cancel{\text{in}})^2}\times\frac{(1\ \text{mi})^2}{(5280\ \cancel{\text{ft}})^2} = X\ \text{mi}^2\ (\textit{The answer would be written to 2 s.f.}).$$

Moles

A mole (n, abbreviated as "mol") is the quantity of anything that has the same number of particles found in 12.000 grams of carbon-12. That number of particles is known as Avogadro's Number (N_A) and is equal to 6.02×10^{23}. 1 mole of pennies would be 6.02×10^{23} pennies.

$$1 \text{ mole} = 6.022 \times 10^{23} \text{ molecules}$$

The mole concept allows us to relate the atomic or molecular mass obtained from the periodic table to a more convenient, everyday unit of measurement called the gram.

$$\text{moles} = \text{grams/molar mass}$$

Therefore, 1 mole of phosphorus atoms (that would be 6.02×10^{23} atoms of phosphorus) would weigh 30.974 grams (the atomic mass of P). 6.02×10^{23} molecules of water (1 mole of water) would weigh 18.02 grams (MW H_2O = 18.02 g/mol).

Example

Q. A certain metallic oxide has the formula MO. A 40.00 gram sample of the compound is strongly heated in an atmosphere of hydrogen gas. At the end of the heating, 32.00 grams of the metal M is left. Calculate the atomic mass of metal M.

A. Heating the metallic oxide only in an atmosphere of hydrogen gas removes the oxygen. The oxygen combines with the hydrogen gas to form water. The mass of oxygen is 40.00 g MO – 32.00 g M = 8.00 g O. For every 1 mole of MO, there is 1 mole of M atoms and 1 mole of O atoms.

$$\frac{32.00\text{ g M}}{8.00\text{ }\cancel{\text{g O}}} \times \frac{16.00\text{ }\cancel{\text{g O}}}{1\text{ }\cancel{\text{mole O}}} \times \frac{1\text{ }\cancel{\text{mole O}}}{1\text{ mole M}} = 64.0\text{ g} \cdot \text{mol}^{-1}$$

Balancing Equations

Note: Balancing oxidation-reduction equations is covered in Chapter 13. Starting in 2007, there will be a new format for writing reactions (Question 4 of the Free-Response Section). Both practice exams in this book cover the new format.

Look for elements that appear only once on each side of the equation but in unequal numbers. Begin by trying suitable coefficients that will produce the same number of atoms of each element on both sides of the equation. Remember to only change coefficients, not subscripts. For example, if you were given the following equation to balance

$$?\ KClO_3 \rightarrow ?\ KCl + ?\ O_2$$

notice that you have 3 oxygen atoms on the left and 2 oxygen atoms on the right; the common denominator is 6. Therefore, you will need 6 oxygen atoms on both sides: $2KClO_3 \rightarrow ?\ KCl + 3O_2$. You now observe that you have 2K's and 2Cl's on the left and to complete the problem you will need the same number of K's and Cl's on the right. Simply place a 2 in front of the KCl and you're done: $2KClO_3 \rightarrow 2KCl + 3O_2$.

Example

Q. Balance the following equation: ? $NaHCO_3 \rightarrow$? Na_2CO_3 + ? H_2O + ? CO_2.

A. Do NOT start trying to balance the oxygens since they're all over the place on the right side. Starting with the carbons won't work either because they are in a 1:1 ratio. The one to start with is Na. Your coefficient in front of $NaHCO_3$ will be twice your coefficient in front of Na_2CO_3. Start with the smallest numbers possible: $\underline{2}NaHCO_3 \rightarrow 1Na_2CO_3$ + ? H_2O + ? CO_2. You will discover at this point that the 2 won't work since that gives you 6 O's on the left but you have 8 O's on the right without going further. Forget about trying a 3 since you can't get 3 Na's on the right (unless you use fractions, which is allowed but more complicated sometimes). So, try a 4: $4NaHCO_3 \rightarrow 2Na_2CO_3$ + ? H_2O + ? CO_2. Now you have 4 H's on the left, and it is possible to get 4 H's on the right: $4NaHCO_3 \rightarrow 2Na_2CO_3 + 2H_2O$ + ? CO_2. The last piece of the puzzle is to balance the O's. You have 12 O's on the left. It's possible to get 12 O's on the right by placing a 2 in front of CO_2: $4NaHCO_3 \rightarrow 2Na_2CO_3 + 2H_2O + 2CO_2$. The last step is to double check your work.

Determination of Empirical and Molecular Formulas

An empirical formula is the lowest, whole-number ratio for a compound. The actual formula for glucose is $C_6H_{12}O_6$; however, this can reduced to the empirical formula for glucose which would be CH_2O.

Example

Q. A 4.601 g sample of a compound only containing nitrogen and oxygen was found to contain 1.401 g N and 3.200 g O. The molecular mass of the compound is known to be 46.01 g · mol^{-1}. What is the most likely formula for this compound?

A. $n_N = 1.401\ \cancel{g\ N}\ (1\ mol\ N / 14.01\ \cancel{g\ N}) = 0.1000\ mol\ N$

$n_O = 3.200\ \cancel{g\ O}\ (1\ mol\ O / 16.00\ \cancel{g\ O}) = 0.2000\ mol\ O$

The empirical formula is $N_{0.1000}O_{0.2000} = NO_2$. Since the molecular mass of the empirical formula is the same as the known molecular mass given in the question, the formula for the compound is NO_2 (nitrogen dioxide).

Percentage Composition

Percentage composition is the percent by mass of each element that a compound contains. To determine the percentage composition, divide the mass of each element in 1 mole of the compound by the molar mass and then multiply by 100%.

$$\% = \frac{\textbf{mass of element}}{\textbf{molar mass of compound}} \times 100\%$$

Example

Q. What is the actual formula of a compound that contains 60.1% K, 18.4% C, and 21.5% N? The molecular mass of the compound is 65.118 g · mol^{-1}.

A. $\frac{60.1\,\cancel{g\,K}}{1} \times \frac{1\,\text{mol K}}{39.01\,\cancel{g\,K}} \approx 1.5\,\text{mol K}$

$\frac{18.4\,\cancel{g\,C}}{1} \times \frac{1\,\text{mol C}}{12.01\,\cancel{g\,C}} \approx 1.5\,\text{mol C}$

$\frac{21.5\,\cancel{g\,N}}{1} \times \frac{1\,\text{mol N}}{14.01\,\cancel{g\,N}} \approx 1.5\,\text{mol N}$

The empirical ratio would therefore be: $K_{1.5}C_{1.5}N_{1.5}$ = KCN. Since the molar mass of the empirical formula is the same value as the molar mass of the molecular compound, the molecular formula is KCN, known as potassium thiocyanate.

Average Atomic Mass

To calculate the average atomic weight, each exact atomic weight is multiplied by its percent abundance (expressed as a decimal). Then, the results are added together and rounded off to an appropriate number of significant figures.

Example

Silicon		
Mass Number	***Exact Weight***	***Percent Abundance***
28	27.976927	92.23
29	28.976495	4.67
30	29.973770	3.10

Q. Examine the data above. The average atomic mass of silicon is:

- **A.** 27.883
- **B.** 27.977
- **C.** 28.086
- **D.** 28.221
- **E.** 29.013

A. C. 0.9223 (27.976927) + 0.0467 (28.976495) + 0.0310 (29.973770) = 28.09

Limiting Reactant

The reactant that is used up first in a reaction is called the limiting reactant. After it is used up, the reaction stops. The rest of the reactants are "in excess".

Example

Q. The "hole in the ozone layer" is prominent over Antarctica. One of the causes of depletion of stratospheric ozone is the reaction of ozone with nitric oxide (NO) produced by high-flying aircraft. Ozone reacts with nitric oxide to produce nitrogen dioxide and oxygen gas.

(a) Write the balanced equation.

(b) If 0.960 g of ozone reacts with 0.900 g of nitric oxide, how many grams of nitrogen dioxide would be produced?

(c) How many molecules of excess reactant would be left?

A. (a) $O_{3(g)} + NO_{(g)} \rightarrow O_{2(g)} + NO_{2(g)}$

(b) $(0.960\ \cancel{g}\ O_3)\ (1\ \text{mol} \cdot 48\ \cancel{g}^{-1}) = 0.02\ \text{mol}\ O_3$

$(0.900\ \cancel{g}\ NO)\ (1\ \text{mol} \cdot 30.01\cancel{g}^{-1}) = 0.03\ \text{mol NO}$

Referring back to the balanced equation, 1 mole of O_3 combines with 1 mole of NO, and since we have more than 0.02 moles of NO, ozone is the limiting reactant. Now we can solve for grams of NO_2:

$$\frac{0.02\ \cancel{\text{mole}\ O_3}}{1} \times \frac{1\ \cancel{\text{mole}\ NO_2}}{1\ \cancel{\text{mole}\ O_3}} \times \frac{44.01\ \text{g}\ NO_2}{1\ \cancel{\text{mole}\ NO_2}} = 0.88\ \text{g}\ NO_2$$

(c) Since we can only use 0.02 moles of NO, there would be 0.01 moles of NO in excess.

$$\frac{0.01\ \cancel{\text{mol NO}}}{1} \times \frac{6.02 \times 10^{23}\ \text{moleculesNO}}{1\ \cancel{\text{mol NO}}} = 6.02 \times 10^{21}\ \text{molecules of NO in excess}$$

Theoretical and Actual Yield

The theoretical yield is the maximum amount of a product that could be produced when all of the limiting reactions has been used. The actual yield is what is actually produced. Reasons for not producing the maximum amount possible include errors in procedures, reversible reactions which do not proceed 100% to the right, difficulties in extracting materials from aqueous solutions, products may further react to produce other compounds, etc.

$$\textbf{\% yield} = \frac{\textbf{actual yield}}{\textbf{theoretical yield}} \times \textbf{100\%}$$

Example

Q. The explosion of nitroglycerin (NG) ($C_3H_5N_3O_9$) can be represented by the following balanced equation: $4C_3H_5N_3O_{9(l)} \rightarrow 6N_{2(g)} + 10H_2O_{(g)} + 12CO_{2(g)} + O_{2(g)}$.

(a) How many grams of oxygen gas can be produced from the explosion of 454.2 grams of nitroglycerin? *MW* of NG = 227.1 g/mol

(b) If only 8.00 g of oxygen gas was produced, what was the percent yield?

A. (a) $\frac{{}^{2}\cancel{454.2\ \text{g NG}}}{1} \times \frac{1\ \cancel{\text{mol NG}}}{{}_{1}\cancel{227.1\ \text{g NG}}} \times \frac{1\ \cancel{\text{mol}\ O_2}}{4\ \cancel{\text{mol NG}}} \times \frac{32.00\ \text{g}\ O_2}{1\ \cancel{\text{mol}\ O_2}} = 16.00\ \text{g}\ O_2$

(b) $\frac{8.00\ \cancel{\text{g}\ O_2}}{16.00\ \cancel{\text{g}\ O_2}} \times 100\% = 50.0\%$

Multiple-Choice Questions

1. How many moles of O_2 is needed to produce 56.8 grams of P_4O_{10} from P? (Molecular weight P_4O_{10} = 284)

A. 0.500 mole
B. 0.750 mole
C. 1.00 mole
D. 1.50 mole
E. 2.00 mole

2. If 2.806 gram of any alkene is burned in excess oxygen, what number of moles of H_2O is formed?

A. 0.1000 mole
B. 0.2000 mole
C. 0.3000 mole
D. 0.4000 mole
E. 0.5000 mole

3. When 100 grams of butane gas (C_4H_{10}, MW = 58.4) is burned in excess oxygen gas, the theoretical yield of H_2O (in grams) is:

A. $\frac{54.14 \times 18.02}{100 \times 5}$

B. $\frac{5 \times 58.4}{100 \times 18.02}$

C. $\frac{4 \times 18.02}{\frac{13}{2} \times 100} \times 100\%$

D. $\frac{5 \times 58.14 \times 18.02}{100}$

E. $\frac{100 \times 5 \times 18.02}{58.14}$

4. An unknown hydrocarbon was burned in excess oxygen to form 176.04 grams of carbon dioxide and 54.06 grams of water. What is a possible molecular formula of the hydrocarbon?

A. CH_4
B. C_2H_2
C. C_4H_3
D. C_4H_6
E. C_4H_{10}

5. How many grams of sulfuric acid, H_2SO_4, contain 32 grams of oxygen atoms?

A. 196 g
B. 98 g
C. 62 g
D. 49 g
E. 9.8 g

6. Hemoglobin is the oxygen-carrying protein of most mammals. Each molecule of hemoglobin contains 4 atoms of iron. The molecular weight of hemoglobin is about 64,000 g · mol^{-1}. How many iron atoms are in 0.128 g of hemoglobin?

A. 7.00×10^3
B. 7.99×10^{10}
C. 4.82×10^{18}
D. 8.03×10^{20}
E. 6.02×10^{23}

7. The mass of element X found in 1.00 mole of each of four different compounds is 40.0 grams, 60.0 grams, 80.0 grams, and 120. grams, respectively. A possible atomic weight of X is

A. 16.0
B. 20.0
C. 37.5
D. 56.25
E. 75.0

8. The simplest formula for an oxide of nitrogen that is 25.9% nitrogen by weight is

A. N_2O
B. NO
C. NO_2
D. N_2O_3
E. N_2O_5

9. Unknown element X combines with oxygen to form the compound XO_2. If 44.0 grams of element X combine with 8.00 grams of oxygen, what is the atomic mass of element X?

A. 16 amu
B. 44 amu
C. 88 amu
D. 176 amu
E. 352 amu

10. When a hydrate of $LiClO_4$ is heated until all the water is removed, it loses 33.7% of its mass. The formula of the hydrate is

A. $LiClO_4 \cdot 5H_2O$
B. $LiClO_4 \cdot 4H_2O$
C. $LiClO_4 \cdot 3H_2O$
D. $LiClO_4 \cdot 2H_2O$
E. $LiClO_4 \cdot H_2O$

11. When 0.600 mole of $BaCl_{2(aq)}$ is mixed with 0.250 mole of $K_3AsO_{4(aq)}$, what is the maximum number of moles of solid $Ba_3(AsO_4)_2$ that could be formed?

A. 0.125 mole
B. 0.200 mole
C. 0.250 mole
D. 0.375 mole
E. 0.500 mole

12. In which of the following compounds is the mass ratio of oxygen to nitrogen closest to 2.86 : 1.00?

A. NO
B. NO_2
C. N_2O
D. N_2O_3
E. N_2O_5

13. Which of the following would have an answer with three significant figures?

A. $103.1 + 0.0024 + 0.16$
B. $(3.0 \times 10^4)(5.022 \times 10^{-3}) / (6.112 \times 10^2)$
C. $(4.3 \times 10^5) / (4.225 + 56.0003 - 0.8700)$
D. $(1.43 \times 10^3 + 3.1 \times 10^1) / (4.11 \times 10^{-6})$
E. $(1.41 \times 10^2 + 1.012 \times 10^4) / (3.2 \times 10^{-1})$

14. When a 1.00-gram sample of limestone rock was dissolved in hydrochloric acid, 0.29 gram of CO_2 was generated. If the rock contained no carbonate other than $CaCO_3$, what was the percent of $CaCO_3$ by mass in the limestone?

A. 38%
B. 48%
C. 66%
D. 96%
E. 100%

15. A certain brand of rubbing alcohol is 90. wt. % solution of isopropyl alcohol (C_3H_8O) in water. How many grams of rubbing alcohol contain 9.0 grams of isopropyl alcohol?

A. 9.0 g
B. 10. g
C. 11. g
D. 90. g
E. 1.0×10^2 g

16. One atom of element *X* weighs 4.20×10^{-22} grams. The atomic mass of element *X* is closest to

A. $32\ g \cdot mol^{-1}$
B. $64\ g \cdot mol^{-1}$
C. $177\ g \cdot mol^{-1}$
D. $253\ g \cdot mol^{-1}$
E. $324\ g \cdot mol^{-1}$

17. A piece of copper is heated in a flame until it is coated with black copper oxide. The flame is extinguished. While still hot, the copper is bathed in hydrogen gas, and the original coppery color returns. What mass of Cu is produced when 0.0500 mol of CuO is reduced completely with excess H_2?

A. 3.18 g
B. 6.46 g
C. 12.9 g
D. 38.7 g
E. 48.9 g

18. A mining company supplies an ore that is 16% chalcocite (Cu_2S) by weight. How many metric tons of ore should be purchased in order to produce 600. metric tons of an alloy containing 13% Cu?

A. 5.0×10^{-1} metric tons
B. 1.0×10^1 metric tons
C. 2.0×10^2 metric tons
D. 3.0×10^2 metric tons
E. 6.0×10^2 metric tons

19. $C_4H_8O_3S_{(s)} + O_{2(g)} \rightarrow CO_{2(g)} + SO_{2(g)} + H_2O_{(g)}$

When the equation above is balanced and all coefficients are reduced to their lowest whole-number terms, the coefficient for $O_{2(g)}$ is?

A. 6
B. 7
C. 11
D. 22
E. 28

20. What is the average atomic mass of a hypothetical sample of element *X* if it is found that 20% of the sample contains an isotope with mass of 100, 50% of the sample contains an isotope of the element with mass of 102, and 30% of the sample contains an isotope of the element with a mass of 105?

A. 101.0
B. 101.5
C. 102.0
D. 102.5
E. 103.0

Free-Response Questions

1. A student suspended a clean piece of silver metal in an evacuated test tube. The empty test tube weighted 42.8973 grams. The silver weighed 1.7838 grams. Next, she introduced a stream of chlorine gas into the test tube and allowed it to react with the silver. After a few minutes, a white compound was found to have formed on the silver strip, coating it uniformly. She then opened the apparatus, weighed the coated strip, and found it to weigh 1.9342 grams. Finally, she washed the coated strip with distilled water, removing the entire white compound from the silver strip, and then dried the compound and the strip and reweighed. She discovered that the silver strip weighed 1.3258 grams.

(a) Show how she would determine

(i) the number of moles of chlorine gas that reacted.

(ii) the number of moles of silver that reacted.

(b) Show how she could determine the simplest formula for the silver chloride.

(c) Show how her results would have been affected if

(i) some of the white compound had been washed down the sink before it was dried and reweighed.

(ii) the silver strip was not thoroughly dried when it was reweighed.

2. Three compounds, D, E, and F, all contain element G. The percent (by weight) of element G in each of the compounds was determined by analysis. The experimental data are presented in the following chart.

Compound	Percentage by Weight of Element G	Molecular Weight
D	53.90	131.70
E	64.20	165.90
F	47.70	74.50

(a) Determine the mass of element G contained in 1.00 mole of each of compounds D, E, and F.

(b) What is the most likely value for the atomic weight of element G?

(c) Compound F contains carbon, hydrogen, and element G. When 2.19 grams of compound F is completely burned in oxygen gas, 3.88 grams of carbon dioxide and 0.80 grams of water are produced. What is the most likely formula for compound F?

Answers and Explanations

Multiple Choice

1. C. $4P + 5O_2 \rightarrow P_4O_{10}$

$$\frac{56.8\,\cancel{g\,P_4O_{10}}}{1} \times \frac{1\,\cancel{mol\,P_4O_{10}}}{284\,\cancel{g\,P_4O_{10}}} \times \frac{5\,mol\,O_2}{1\,\cancel{mol\,P_4O_{10}}} = 1.00\,mol\,O_2$$

2. B. Complete combustion of any hydrocarbon always produces carbon dioxide and water. Since any alkene will work, use C_2H_4. $C_2H_{4(g)} + 3O_{2(g)} \rightarrow 2CO_{2(g)} + 2H_2O_{(g)}$

$$\frac{2.806\,\cancel{g\,C_2H_4}}{1} \times \frac{1\,\cancel{mol\,C_2H_4}}{28.06\,\cancel{g\,C_2H_4}} \times \frac{2\,mol\,H_2O}{1\,\cancel{mol\,C_2H_4}} = 0.2000\,mol\,H_2O$$

3. E. Begin with a balanced equation: $C_4H_{10} + {}^{13}\!/\!_2\,O_2 \rightarrow 4CO_2 + 5H_2O$

Next, set-up the equation in factor-label method:

$$\frac{100\,\cancel{g\,C_4H_{10}}}{1} \times \frac{1\,\cancel{mole\,C_4H_{10}}}{58.14\,\cancel{g\,C_4H_{10}}} \times \frac{5\,\cancel{mole\,H_2O}}{1\,\cancel{mole\,C_4H_{10}}} \times \frac{18.02\,g\,H_2O}{1\,\cancel{mole\,H_2O}} = g\,H_2O$$

4. D. $$\frac{176.04\,\cancel{g\,CO_2}}{1} \times \frac{1\,mol\,CO_2}{44.01\,\cancel{g\,CO_2}} = 4\,moles\,CO_2$$

$$\frac{54.06\,\cancel{g\,H_2O}}{1} \times \frac{1\,mol\,H_2O}{18.02\,\cancel{g\,H_2O}} = 3\,mol\,H_2O$$

$C_4H_6 + {}^{11}\!/\!_2\,O_2 \rightarrow 4CO_2 + 3H_2O$

5. D. $$\frac{32\,\cancel{g\,O\,atoms}}{1} \times \frac{1\,\cancel{mol\,O\,atoms}}{16.00\,\cancel{g\,O\,atoms}} \times \frac{1\,\cancel{mol\,H_2SO_4}}{4\,\cancel{mol\,O\,atoms}} \times \frac{98.08\,g\,H_2SO_4}{1\,\cancel{mol\,H_2SO_4}} = 49\,g\,H_2SO_4$$

6. C. $$\frac{0.128\,\cancel{g\,hemoglobin}}{1} \times \frac{1\,\cancel{mol\,hemoglobin}}{64{,}000\,\cancel{g\,hemoglobin}} \times \frac{4\,\cancel{mol\,Fe}}{1\,\cancel{mol\,hemoglobin}} \times$$

$$\frac{6.02 \times 10^{23}\,Fe\,atoms}{1\,\cancel{mol\,Fe}} = 4.82 \times 10^{18}\,Fe\,atoms$$

7. B. The law of definite proportions, first defined by Joseph Louis Proust, states that in a pure compound, the elements combine in definite proportions to one another by mass. The lowest common multiple of all choices is 20.0.

8. E. $MW\,N_2O_5 = 108.02$

$$\frac{28.02\,g\,N_2}{108.02\,g\,N_2O_5} \times 100\% = 25.9\%$$

9. D. 8.00 g of oxygen atoms represent 0.500 moles.

$$\frac{8.00\,\cancel{g\,O}}{0.500\,\cancel{mole\,O}} \times \frac{2\,\cancel{moles\,O}}{1\,mole\,X} \times \frac{44.0\,g\,X}{8.00\,\cancel{g\,O}} = 176\,g\,X/mole\,X$$

10. C. $FW\,LiClO_4 = 106.39\,g \cdot mol^{-1}$ $FW\,LiClO_4 \cdot 3H_2O = 160.45\,g \cdot mol^{-1}$

$$\% = \frac{part}{whole} \times 100\% = \frac{106.39}{160.45} \times 100\% = 66.3\% \qquad 100.0\% - 66.3\% = 33.7\%\,H_2O$$

11. A. Begin by writing a balanced equation: $3BaCl_{2(aq)} + 2K_3AsO_{4(aq)} \rightarrow Ba_3(AsO_4)_{2(s)} + 6KCl_{(aq)}$

Next, realize that this problem is a limiting-reactant problem, that is, one of the two reactants will run out first, and when that happens, the reaction will stop. You need to determine which one of the reactants will run out first.

To do this, you need to be able to compare them on a 1:1 basis. But their coefficients are different, so you need to relate both reactants to a common product, say $Ba_3(AsO_4)_2$. Set the problem up like this:

$$\frac{0.600\ \text{mole BaCl}_2}{1} \times \frac{1\ \text{mole Ba}_3(\text{AsO}_4)_2}{3\ \text{moles BaCl}_2} = 0.200\ \text{mole Ba}_3(\text{AsO}_4)_2$$

$$\frac{0.250\ \text{mole K}_3\text{AsO}_4}{1} \times \frac{1\ \text{mole Ba}_3(\text{AsO}_4)_2}{2\ \text{moles K}_3\text{AsO}_4} = -0.125\ \text{mole Ba}_3(\text{AsO}_4)_2$$

Given the two amounts of starting materials, you discover that you can make a maximum of 0.125 moles of $Ba_3(AsO_4)_2$, because at that point you will have exhausted your supply of K_3AsO_4.

12. E. Oxygen: 5(16.00) = 80.00 Nitrogen: 2(14.01) = 28.02

$$\frac{80.00}{28.02} = 2.86$$

13. D. $(1.43 \times 10^3 + 3.1 \times 10^1) = 14.3 \times 10^2 + 0.31 \times 10^2 = 14.6 \times 10^2$

$$= \frac{14.6 \times 10^2}{4.11 \times 10^{-6}} = 3\,\text{s.f.}(3.55 \times 10^8)$$

14. C. *FW* $CaCO_3 = 100.09\ \text{g} \cdot \text{mol}^{-1}$

$$\frac{0.29\ \text{g CO}_2}{1.00\ \text{g sample}} \times \frac{12.01\ \text{g C}}{44.01\ \text{g CO}_2} \times \frac{100.09\ \text{g CaCO}_3}{12.01\ \text{g C}} \times 100\% = 66\%$$

15. B. $90.\ \text{mass\% alcohol} = \dfrac{9.0\ \text{g isopropyl alcohol}}{\text{total mass (g)}} \times 100$ total mass = 10. g

16. D. $\dfrac{4.20 \times 10^{-22}\ \text{g}}{1\ \text{atom}} \times \dfrac{6.02 \times 10^{23}\ \text{atoms}}{1\ \text{mol}} = 253\ \text{g} \cdot \text{mol}^{-1}$

17. A. Copper oxidizes slowly in air, corroding to produce a brown or green patina. At higher temperatures the process is much faster and produces mainly black copper(II) oxide (*copper(II) oxide is more stable than copper(I) oxide*): $2Cu_{(s)} + O_{2(g)} \rightarrow 2CuO_{(s)}$. The oxide can be reduced by hydrogen gas, which is a moderately strong reducing agent, producing a shiny, clean copper surface: $CuO_{(s)} + H_{2(g)} \rightarrow Cu_{(s)} + H_2O_{(g)}$

$$\frac{0.0500\ \text{mol CuO}}{1} \times \frac{1\ \text{mol Cu}}{1\ \text{mol CuO}} \times \frac{63.55\ \text{g Cu}}{1\ \text{mol Cu}} = 3.18\ \text{g Cu}$$

18. E. Do this problem by using the factor-label method (m.t. stands for metric tons, 1 m.t. = 10^3 kg).

$$\frac{600.\ \text{m.t.alloy}}{1} \times \frac{13\ \text{m.t.Cu}}{100.\ \text{m.t.alloy}} \times \frac{160\ \text{m.t.Cu}_2\text{S}}{130\ \text{m.t.Cu}} \times \frac{100.\ \text{m.t.ore}}{16\ \text{m.t.Cu}_2\text{S}} = 6.0 \times 10^2\ \text{m.t.ore}$$

19. C. Begin by balancing the carbons and lock in the coefficients: $\mathbf{1}C_4H_8O_3S + ?O_2 \rightarrow \mathbf{4}CO_2 + ?SO_2 + ?H_2O$. You can also lock in the coefficient for SO_2: $\mathbf{1}C_4H_8O_3S + ?O_2 \rightarrow \mathbf{4}CO_2 + \mathbf{1}SO_2 + ?H_2O$. Since you have 8 hydrogens on the left, balance the hydrogens on the right and lock in the coefficient: $1C_4H_8O_3S + ?O_2 \rightarrow 4CO_2 + 1SO_2 + \mathbf{4}H_2O$. The last step is to balance the oxygen on the left: $1C_4H_8O_3S + {}^{11}\!/_2\, O_2 \rightarrow 4CO_2 + 1SO_2 + 4H_2O$. But the question asked for whole numbers, so double all coefficients: $2C_4H_8O_3S + 11O_2 \rightarrow 8CO_2 + 2SO_2 + 8H_2O$.

20. D. Multiply the fraction of each isotope by its atomic mass and add the products: $(0.20 \times 100) + (0.50 \times 102) + (0.30 \times 105) = 20 + 51 + 31.5 = 102.5$

Free Response

Question 1

Maximum Points for Question 1
Part (a) (i): 2 points
Part (a) (ii): 2 points
Part (b): 2 points
Part (c) (i): 2 points
Part (c) (ii): 2 points
Total points: 10

1. A student suspended a clean piece of silver metal in an evacuated test tube. The empty test tube weighted 42.8973 grams. The silver weighed 1.7838 grams. Next, she introduced a stream of chlorine gas into the test tube and allowed it to react with the silver. After a few minutes, a white compound was found to have formed on the silver strip, coating it uniformly. She then opened the apparatus, weighed the coated strip, and found it to weigh 1.9342 grams. Finally, she washed the coated strip with distilled water, removing the entire white compound from the silver strip, and then dried the compound and the strip and reweighed. She discovered that the silver strip weighed 1.3258 grams. *(a) (i) Show how she would determine the number of moles of chlorine gas that reacted.* **Step 1:** Do a restatement of the general experiment. In this case, draw a sketch of the apparatus before and after the reaction, labeling everything. This will get rid of all the words and enable you to visualize the experiment. 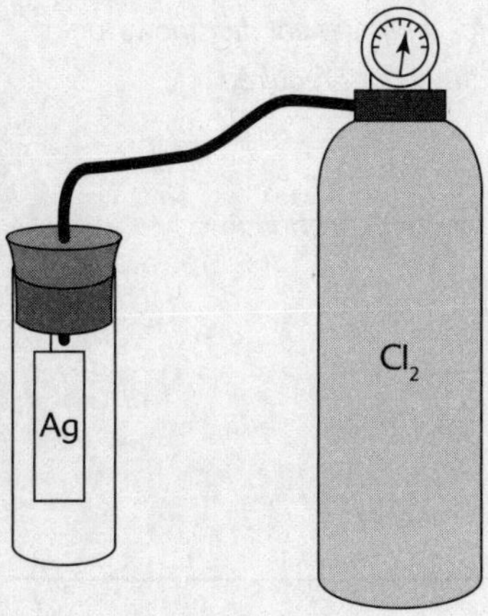 Initial: Empty test tube = 42.8973 g Ag strip = 1.7838 g Final: Coated strip = 1.9342 g Ag strip = 1.3258 g	***2 points possible***
Step 2: Write a balanced chemical equation that describes the reaction: Silver + chlorine gas yields silver chloride $2Ag_{(s)} + Cl_{2(g)} \rightarrow 2AgCl_{(s)}$	*1 point for balanced equation for the reaction of silver + chlorine gas.*

(continued)

Step 3: Begin to answer the questions asked. Remember to give a brief restatement for each question, label each specific question so that the AP grader knows which question you are answering, and underline the conclusion(s) where necessary. **Restatement:** Number of moles of chlorine gas that reacted. mass of chlorine that reacted = (mass of silver strip + compound) – mass of original silver strip 1.9342g – 1.7838 g = 0.1504 g of chlorine atoms moles of chlorine atoms that reacted = mass of chlorine atoms/atomic mass of Cl 0.1504 g Cl / 35.45 g · mol^{-1} = 0.004242 mol Cl atoms	 *1 point for the number of moles of chlorine gas that reacted.*
(a) (ii) Show how she would determine the number of moles of silver that reacted. **Restatement:** Moles of silver that reacted $\frac{(\text{mass of original strip} - \text{mass of dry strip after washing})}{\text{atomic mass of silver}}$ $= \frac{1.7838\text{g} - 1.3258\text{g}}{107.87\text{g} \cdot \text{mol}^{-1}} = 0.004246 \text{mol Ag atoms}$	***2 points possible*** *1 point for showing proper setup.* *1 point for correct answer of number of moles of Ag atoms.*
(b) Show how she could determine the simplest formula for the silver chloride. **Restatement:** Empirical formula for silver chloride Empirical formula = moles of silver atoms : moles of chlorine atoms $\frac{0.004246 \text{mol Ag}}{0.004242 \text{mol Cl}} = 1.001{:}1 \rightarrow \text{AgCl}$	***2 points possible*** *1 point for showing proper setup.* *1 point for correct answer for empirical formula.*
(c) (i) Show how her results would have been affected if some of the white compound had been washed down the sink before it was dried and reweighed. **Restatement:** Effect on the empirical formula if some of the white compound had been washed down the sink before the coated strip was dried and reweighed. The white product was silver chloride. Had she lost some before she weighed it, the mass of silver chloride would have been less than what it should have been. This would have made the number of grams of chlorine appear too low, which in turn would have made the number of moles of chlorine appear too low. Thus, in the ratio of moles of silver to moles of chlorine, the denominator would have been lower than expected and the ratio would have been larger. Because the mass of the compound does not enter into the calculations for the moles of silver that reacted, the moles of silver would not have been affected.	***2 points possible*** *1 point for an argument that shows logic; correct answer not required.* *1 point for correct conclusion.*

(c) (ii) Show how her results would have been affected if the silver strip was not thoroughly dried when it was reweighed.	***2 points possible***
Restatement: Effect on the empirical formula if the silver strip had not been dried thoroughly after being washed free of the silver chloride. Because the strip had been washed free of the compound (silver chloride), you would assume that any silver missing from the strip went into the making of the silver chloride. If the strip had been wet when you weighed it, you would have been led to think that the strip was heavier than expected, and therefore that less silver had gone into the making of the silver chloride. Thinking that less silver had been involved in the reaction, you would have calculated fewer moles of silver. The calculated ratio of moles of silver to moles of chlorine would have been less than expected.	*1 point for an argument that shows logic; correct answer not required.* *1 point for correct conclusion.*

Question 2

Maximum Points for Question 2
Part (a): 4 points
Part (b): 2 points
Part (c): 4 points
Total points: 10

2. Three compounds, D, E, and F, all contain element G. The percent (by weight) of element G in each of the compounds was determined by analysis. The experimental data are presented in the chart. *(a) Determine the mass of element G in 1.00 mole of compounds D, E, and F.* 0.539 × 131.70 g/mol = 71.0 g G/mole D 0.642 × 165.90 g/mol = 107 g G/mole E 0.477 × 74.5 g/mole = 35.5 g G/mol F	***4 points possible*** *1 point for proper setup showing how answers are obtained.* *1 point for each correct answer.*
(b) What is the most likely atomic weight of element G? According to the Law of Multiple Proportions, the ratios of the mass of element G to the masses of compounds D, E, and F must be small whole numbers. The largest common denominator of 71.0, 107, and 35.5 is 35.5; so our best estimate is that the atomic weight of G is 35.5 (chlorine).	***2 points possible*** *1 point for basing answer on the Law of Multiple Proportions.* *1 point for correct answer.*

(c) Compound F contains carbon, hydrogen, and element G. When 2.19 grams of compound F is completely burned in oxygen gas, 3.88 grams of carbon dioxide and 0.80 grams of water are produced. What is the most likely formula for compound F?	***4 points possible***
Compound F = $C_xH_yG_z$ or $C_xH_yCl_z$ $C_xH_yCl_{z(g)} + O_{2(g)} \rightarrow CO_{2(g)} + H_2O_{(l)} + Cl_{2(g)}$ $2.19\text{ g} + ?\text{ g} \rightarrow 3.88\text{ g} + 0.80\text{ g} + ?\text{ g } Cl_{2(g)}$	
Moles of carbon = moles of CO_2 $\frac{3.88\,g\,CO_2}{44.01\,g \cdot mol^{-1}} = 0.0882\,mol\,C$	*1 point for correctly determining the moles of carbon.*
Moles of hydrogen = 2 × moles H_2O $2 \times \frac{0.80\,g\,H_2O}{18.02\,g \cdot mol^{-1}} = 0.088\,mol\,H$	*1 point for correctly determining the moles of hydrogen.*
$\frac{2.19\,\text{grams of F}}{74.5\,g\,F/1\,mole\,F} = 0.0294\,mol\,F$	*1 point for correctly determining the moles of chlorine.*
This means that each mole of F contains 3 moles of C (0.0882/0.0294) and 3 moles of H (0.088), or 39 grams of CH. This leaves 74.5 – 39 = 36 grams, corresponding to 1 mole of element G (Cl); therefore, the empirical formula is C_3H_3Cl.	*1 point for correct answer.*

Gases

You'll Need to Know

- ❑ the properties of gases
- ❑ how to work with mole fractions
- ❑ how to calculate either pressure or temperatures given data and change from Celsius to Kelvin
- ❑ how to solve problems involving the following gas laws:
    - ❑ Avogadro's Law
    - ❑ Boyle's Law
    - ❑ Charles' Law
    - ❑ Combined Gas Law
    - ❑ Dalton's Law of Partial Pressure
    - ❑ gas density
    - ❑ Gay-Lussac's Law
    - ❑ Graham's Law of Diffusion-Effusion
    - ❑ Ideal Gas Law
    - ❑ van der Waals Equation
- ❑ the concepts of kinetic molecular theory
- ❑ how to answer questions that involve the Maxwell-Boltzmann Distribution

Properties of Gases

The following are some properties of gases:

- All elements in Group 8A are gases (noble gases).
- Elements that are gases at room temperature and pressure are nonmetals.
- Gases assume the volume and shape of their container.
- Gases have significantly lower densities and are more easily compressed than liquids or solids.
- Gases mix evenly and completely when confined to the same container.

Mole Fractions

A mole fraction is a dimensionless quantity that expresses the ratio of the number of moles of one component to the number of moles of all other components present. The symbol for the mole fraction of gas A is X_A, total pressure of all gases is P_T and the pressure of gas A is P_A.

$$X_A = \frac{P_A}{P_T} \text{ or } P_A = X_A \cdot P_T$$

Example

Q. A mixture of gases contains 1.00 mole of neon, 2.00 moles of argon, and 3.00 moles of xenon. The total pressure of the gas mixture is 2.00 atm. What is the partial pressure of the argon gas?

A. 0 atm
B. 0.333 atm
C. 0.667 atm
D. 1.50 atm
E. 3.33 atm

A. C. $X_{Ar} = \dfrac{n_{Ar}}{n_{Ne} + n_{Ar} + n_{Xe}} = \dfrac{2.00\ \cancel{mol}}{1.00\ \cancel{mol} + 2.00\ \cancel{mol} + 3.00\ \cancel{mol}} = 0.333$

$P_{Ar} = X_{Ar} \cdot P_T = 0.333 \times 2.00 \text{ atm} = 0.667 \text{ atm}$

Pressure and Temperature

- "Normal atmospheric conditions" are 25°C (298K) and 1 atm pressure.
- 760 mm Hg = 1 atm = 101.325 kPa, 1 torr = 1 mm Hg
- Gases that are collected after they have bubbled through water also contain water vapor molecules (i.e., the gas is "wet"). These water molecules must be gotten rid of as they increase the pressure of the system. Always subtract the water vapor pressure (given at various temperatures) from the total pressure of the gas to get just the pressure of the dry gas.
- When solving gas problems, always convert Celsius to Kelvin: °C + 273 = K

STP

Standard temperature is 0°C (273K) and standard pressure = 1 atm. Under these conditions, 1 mole of any gas (6.02×10^{23} particles) occupies 22.4 liters.

Gas Laws

Avogadro's Law $V_1n_2 = V_2n_1$	The volume of a gas is directly proportional to the number of moles of the gas present (pressure and temperature held constant). $V \propto n$ 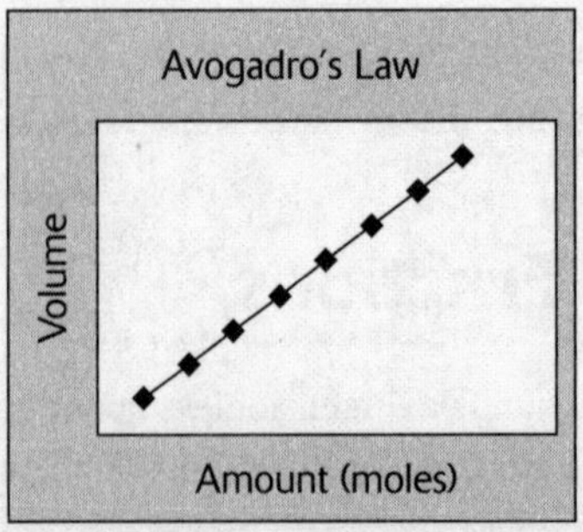

Boyle's Law $P_1V_1 = P_2V_2$	Volume is inversely proportional to pressure (temperature held constant). $V \propto \frac{1}{P}$ 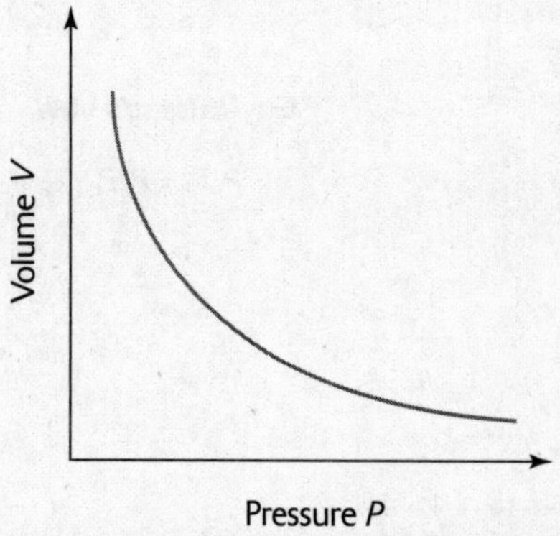
Charles' Law $V_1T_2 = V_2T_1$	Volume is proportional to the absolute temperature of a gas (pressure held constant). $V \propto T$ 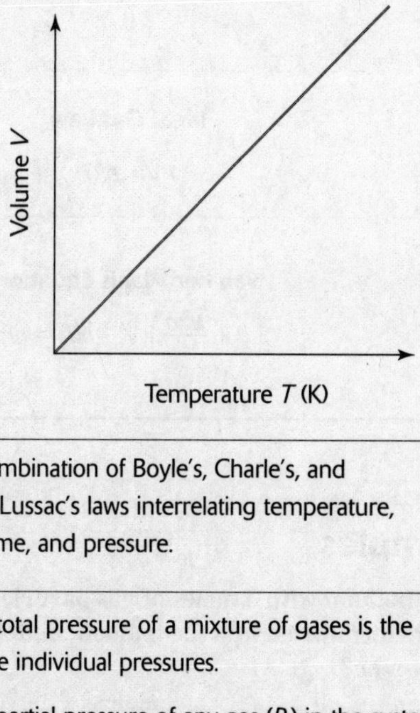
Combined Gas Law $\frac{P_1V_1}{T_1} = \frac{P_2V_2}{T_2}$	A combination of Boyle's, Charle's, and Gay-Lussac's laws interrelating temperature, volume, and pressure.
Dalton's Law of Partial Pressure $P_T = P_1 + P_2 + P_3 + \ldots$ $P_i = X_i \cdot P_T$	The total pressure of a mixture of gases is the sum of the individual pressures. The partial pressure of any gas (P_i) in the system is equal to the mole fraction of that gas (X_i) times the total pressure of the system (P_T).
Gas Density $d = \frac{m}{V} = \frac{P \cdot M}{R \cdot T}$	—

(continued)

Gay-Lussac's Law $P_1T_2 = P_2T_1$	At constant volume, the pressure exerted by a given mass of gas varies directly with the absolute temperature. $P \propto T$ 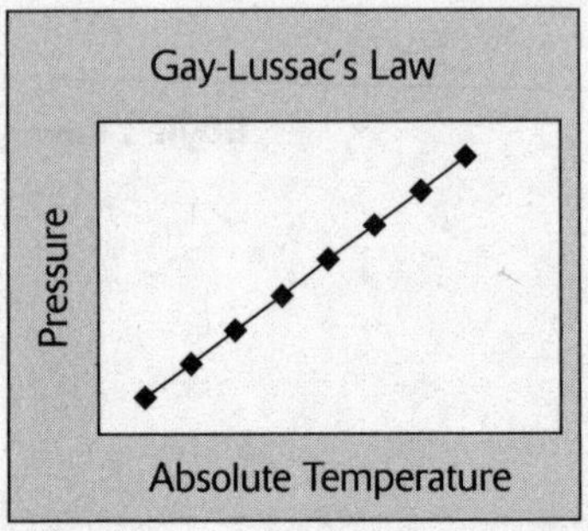
Graham's Law of Diffusion-Effusion $\frac{r_1}{r_2} = \frac{\sqrt{M_2}}{\sqrt{M_1}}$	The rates of diffusion (or effusion) for gases are inversely proportional to the square roots of their molecular masses. Diffusion is the gradual mixing of molecules of one gas with molecules of another. Effusion is the process by which a gas under pressure escapes from a small opening.
Ideal Gas Law $PV = nRT$	The equation of state of an ideal gas, which is a good approximation to real gases at sufficiently high temperatures and low pressures.
van der Waals Equation $\left(P + \frac{n^2 a}{V^2}\right)(V - nb) = nRT$	The behavior of real gases usually agrees with the predictions of the ideal gas equation to within ±5% at normal temperatures and pressures. At low temperatures or high pressures, real gases deviate significantly from ideal gas behavior.

Examples

Q. A balloon with 3 moles of gas particles has an initial volume of 7.0 L. If 6.0 additional moles of gas particles are introduced into the balloon, under conditions of constant *P* and *T*, what will the new volume of the balloon be?

A. $V_2 = V_1 \times \frac{n_2}{n_1} = 7.0\,\text{L} \times \frac{9\ \text{moles}}{3\ \text{moles}} = 21\,\text{L}$

Q. A balloon has a volume of 4.0 L at sea level on a day where the atmospheric pressure was measured at 1.0 atm. The balloon is let go and rises to a height of 4 miles where the pressure is about 0.40 atmospheres. What is the final volume of the balloon at this height (assume the temperature did not change)?

A. $V_2 = V_1 \times \frac{P_1}{P_2} = 4.0\,\text{L} \times \frac{1.0\ \text{atm}}{0.40\ \text{atm}} = 10.\,\text{L}$

Q. A 300. mL sample of oxygen gas is heated from 27°C to 77°C at constant pressure. What is the final volume?

A. Begin by changing temperatures to K: $T_1 = 27°\text{C} + 273 = 300\text{K}$ $T_2 = 77°\text{C} + 273 = 350\text{K}$

$$V_2 = V_1 \times \frac{T_2}{T_1} = 300.\,\text{mL} \times \frac{350\ \text{K}}{300\ \text{K}} = 350.\,\text{mL}$$

Q. A gas-filled balloon having a volume of 5.00 L at 3.00 atm and 27°C is set free and rises to an altitude where the temperature is –73°C and the pressure is 1.00 atm. Calculate the final volume of the balloon.

A. $P_1 = 3.00$ atm $V_1 = 5.00$ L $T_1 = 27°C + 273 = 300K$

$P_2 = 1.00$ atm $V_2 = ?$ $T_2 = -73°C + 273 = 200K$

$$V_2 = V_1 \frac{P_1}{P_2} \times \frac{T_2}{T_1} = 5.00\,\text{L} \times \frac{(3.00\,\cancel{\text{atm}})(200\,\cancel{\text{K}})}{(1.00\,\cancel{\text{atm}})(3500\,\cancel{\text{K}})} = 10.0\,\text{L}$$

Q. A mixture of gases contains 4.00 moles of neon, 1.00 mole of argon, and 3.00 moles of xenon. Calculate the partial pressures of the gases if the total pressure is 6.00 atm at a certain temperature.

A. $$\text{mole fraction of neon } X_{\text{Ne}} = \frac{n_{\text{Ne}}}{n_{\text{Ne}} + n_{\text{Ar}} + n_{\text{Xe}}} = \frac{4.00\,\cancel{\text{moles}}}{4.00\,\cancel{\text{mol}} + 1.00\,\cancel{\text{mol}} + 3.00\,\cancel{\text{mol}}} = 0.500$$

$P_{\text{Ne}} = X_{\text{Ne}} \cdot P_{\text{T}} = 0.500 \cdot 6.00 \text{ atm} = 3.00 \text{ atm}$

$$\text{mole fraction of argon } X_{\text{Ar}} = \frac{n_{\text{Ar}}}{n_{\text{Ne}} + n_{\text{Ar}} + n_{\text{Xe}}} = \frac{1.00\,\cancel{\text{moles}}}{4.00\,\cancel{\text{mol}} + 1.00\,\cancel{\text{mol}} + 3.00\,\cancel{\text{mol}}} = 0.125$$

$P_{\text{Ar}} = X_{\text{Ar}} \cdot P_{\text{T}} = 0.125 \times 6.00 \text{ atm} = 0.750 \text{ atm}$

$$\text{mole fraction of xenon } X_{\text{Xe}} = \frac{n_{\text{Xe}}}{n_{\text{Ne}} + n_{\text{Ar}} + n_{\text{Xe}}} = \frac{3.00\,\cancel{\text{moles}}}{4.00\,\cancel{\text{mol}} + 1.00\,\cancel{\text{mol}} + 3.00\,\cancel{\text{mole}}} = 0.375$$

$P_{\text{Xe}} = X_{\text{Xe}} \cdot P_{\text{T}} = 0.375 \cdot 6.00 \text{ atm} = 2.25 \text{ atm}$

Q. Calculate the density (in grams per liter) of a gas whose molar mass is 100. g · mol^{-1} at 380. mm Hg and 27°C.

A. $T = 27°C + 273 = 300$ K $MM = 100.\ \text{g} \cdot \text{mol}^{-1}$ $P = 380 \text{ mm Hg} / 760 \text{ mm Hg} = 0.50 \text{ atm}$

$$d = \frac{m}{V} = \frac{P \cdot MM}{R \cdot T} = \frac{(0.50\,\cancel{\text{atm}})(\overset{1}{\cancel{100.}}\,\text{g} \cdot \cancel{\text{mol}^{-1}})}{(0.0821\,\text{L} \cdot \cancel{\text{atm}} \cdot \cancel{\text{mol}^{-1}} \cdot \cancel{\text{K}^{-1}})(\underset{3}{\cancel{300\,\text{K}}})} \approx 2.0\,\text{g} \cdot \text{L}^{-1}$$

Q. The temperature of a gas sample is increased from 50.°C to 100.°C. By what factor must the pressure be changed if the volume is to be kept constant?

A. 0.5

B. 0.75

C. 1.15

D. 2.0

E. 4.0

A. C. Let $P_1 = 1.00$ atm $T_1 = 50.°C + 273 = 323$ K $T_2 = (100.°C + 273) = 373$ K

$$P_2 = \frac{P_1 T_2}{T_1} = \frac{(1.00\,\text{atm})(373\,\cancel{\text{K}})}{323\,\cancel{\text{K}}} = 1.15\,\text{atm}$$

Q. Gas A has a molar mass of 27.00 g · mol^{-1} while gas B has a molar mass of 3.00 g · mol^{-1}. How much faster or slower will gas B effuse from a small opening compared to gas A at the same temperature?

A. $$\frac{r_{\text{B}}}{r_{\text{A}}} = \frac{\sqrt{M_{\text{A}}}}{\sqrt{M_{\text{B}}}} = \frac{\sqrt{27.00\,\cancel{\text{g} \cdot \text{mol}^{-1}}}}{\sqrt{3.00\,\cancel{\text{g} \cdot \text{mol}^{-1}}}} = \sqrt{9.00} = 3.00$$

∴ Gas B will effuse 3 times faster than gas A.

Q. Calculate the volume (in liters) occupied by 88.02 grams of carbon dioxide gas at 27°C and 2.0 atm.

A. $n = \dfrac{88.02\ \cancel{g}\ CO_2}{44.01\ \cancel{g} \cdot mol^{-1}} = 2.000\ mol \quad P = 2.0\ atm \quad T = 27°C + 273 = 300\ K$

$$V = \frac{nRT}{P} = \frac{(2.000\ \cancel{mol})(0.0821\ L \cdot \cancel{atm})(300\ \cancel{K})}{(\cancel{mol} \cdot \cancel{K})(2.0\ \cancel{atm})} \approx 25\ L$$

Q. 2.50 moles of carbon dioxide gas at 500K has a volume of 5.00 L. The van der Waals correctional value for the attractiveness of gas molecules, (*a*) = 3.6 atm · L² · mol⁻² and the van der Waals correctional value for molecular size (*b*) = 0.05 L/mol. Without doing calculations, show how the problem would be set-up to solve for pressure.

A. $n = 2.50$ moles $\quad V = 5.00\ L \quad T = 500K \quad a = 3.6\ atm \cdot L^2 \cdot mol^{-2} \quad b = 0.05\ L/mol$

$$P = \frac{nRT}{(V - nb)} - \frac{an^2}{V^2}$$

$$\frac{(2.50\ \cancel{moles})(0.0821\ \cancel{L} \cdot atm \cdot \cancel{mol^{-1}} \cdot \cancel{K^{-1}})(500.\ \cancel{K})}{5.00\ \cancel{L} - (2.50\ \cancel{moles} \cdot 0.05\ \cancel{L/mol})} - \frac{(3.6\ atm \cdot \cancel{L^2} / \cancel{mol^2})(2.50\ \cancel{mol})^2}{(5.00\ \cancel{L})^2}$$

Kinetic Molecular Theory

The kinetic-molecular theory has five basic assumptions:

- Gases consist of large numbers of molecules (or atoms, in the case of the noble gases) that are in continuous, random motion.
- The volume of all the molecules of the gas is negligible compared to the total volume in which the gas is contained.
- Attractive and repulsive forces between gas molecules are negligible.
- The average kinetic energy of the molecules (K.E. = ½ mv^2) does not change with time (as long as the temperature of the gas remains constant). Energy can be transferred between molecules during collisions (but the collisions are perfectly elastic).
- The average kinetic energy of the molecules is proportional to absolute temperature. At any given temperature, the molecules of all gases have the same average kinetic energy. In other words, if you have two gas samples, both at the same temperature, then the average kinetic energy for the collection of gas molecules in one sample is equal to the average kinetic energy for the collection of gas molecules in the other sample.

The Maxwell-Boltzmann Distribution

In any mixture of gas particles, the molecular speeds will vary a great deal, from very slow particles (low energy) to very fast particles (high energy). Most of the particles however will be moving at a speed very close to the average. The Maxwell-Boltzmann distribution shows how the speeds (and hence the energies) of a mixture of moving particles varies at a particular temperature. Points to remember include:

- the area under the curve equals the total molecules in the sample and doesn't change
- there are no molecules with zero energy
- very few molecules have high energies
- there is no maximum energy for a molecule

- the most probable energy value is where the curve is at its highest
- if you increase the temperature of the sample, the distribution changes as shown in the diagram below. The curve becomes stretched out and has a lower peak, but *the area under the curve remains the same*

$$v_{rms} = \sqrt{\frac{3kT}{m}} = \sqrt{\frac{3RT}{M}}$$

where v_{rms} is known as the root mean square and is a measure of the velocity of particles in a gas and is defined as the square root of the average velocity-squared of the molecules in a gas.

m = mass, M = molar mass

KE per molecule = $\frac{1}{2}mv^2$

KE per mole = $(\frac{3}{2})RT$

$1\ J = 1\ kg \cdot m^2 \cdot s^{-2}$

$R = 8.314\ J \cdot K^{-1} \cdot mol^{-1}$

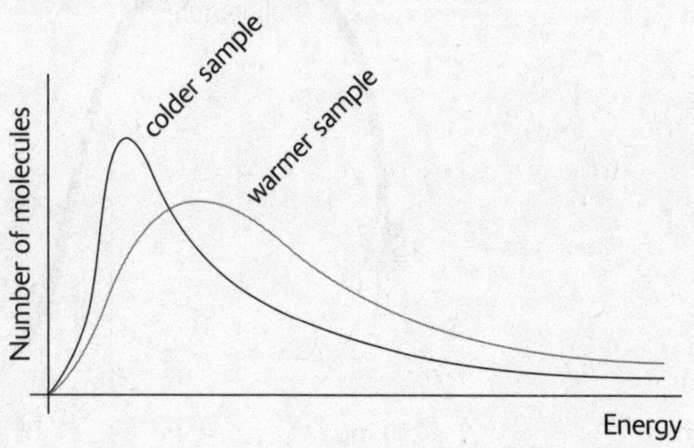

Multiple-Choice Questions

1. By what ratio will the average velocity of the molecules in a gas change when the temperature is raised from 50.0°C to 300.°C?

A. 1:1.33
B. 1.33:1
C. 1:6
D. 6:1
E. 1:1

2. A 41.08 gram sample of an unknown hydrocarbon was burned in excess oxygen to form 132.03 grams of carbon dioxide and 41.08 grams of water. What is a possible molecular formula of the hydrocarbon?

A. CH_4
B. C_3H_8
C. C_6H_6
D. C_6H_{10}
E. C_6H_{12}

3. A student collected a gas sample at a relatively low temperature and high pressure that seemed to be different than the volume she predicted it should be when she used the ideal gas law. The discrepancy could be explained by the fact that the ideal gas law does NOT include a correction factor for

A. density
B. mass
C. volume
D. kinetic energy
E. temperature

4. An ideal gas occupies a volume of 38.5 liters at a pressure of 722 torr (mm of Hg) and a temperature of 25.0°C. Which expression correctly calculates the volume of the gas at a pressure of 784 torr (mm of Hg) and a temperature of 50.0°C?

A. (38.5 L) (722/784) (323/298)
B. (38.5 L) (722/784) (298/323)
C. (38.5 L) (784/722) (298/323)
D. (38.5 L) (784/722) (323/298)
E. (38.5 L) (722/784) (50/25)

5. A student performed an experiment to determine the molecular mass of a gas and collected the gas using the following laboratory setup. Which of the following should the student use in his or her calculations but is NOT required to measure during the experiment?

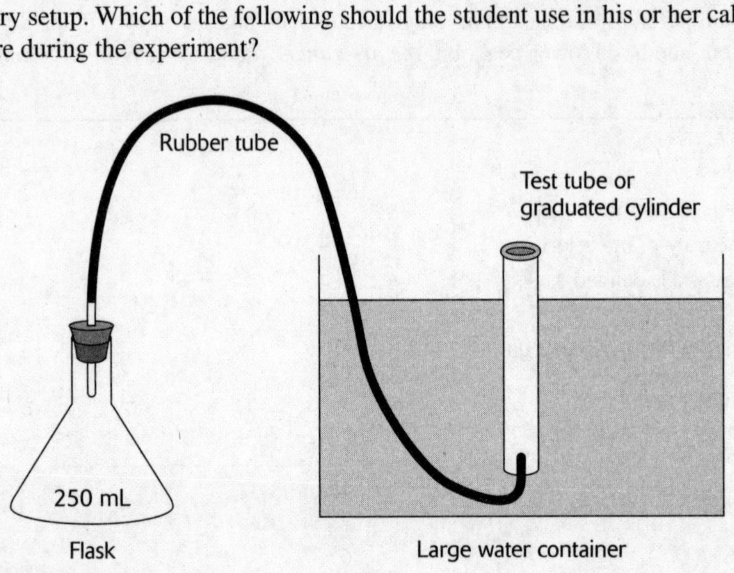

A. mass of the gas
B. vapor pressure of the water
C. pressure of the air in the lab
D. the volume of water that is displaced by the gas
E. temperature of the water in the container

6. If 22.4 grams of methanol is combined with 44.8 liters of oxygen, measured at STP, the number of moles of carbon dioxide which can be produced is

A. 0.0133
B. 0.699
C. 1.40
D. 1.33
E. 2.66

7. The density of an unknown gas at 173.0°C and a pressure of 720. torr (mm of Hg) is $3.14\ g \cdot L^{-1}$. What is the molar mass of the unknown gas?

A. $16.6\ g \cdot mol^{-1}$
B. $47.9\ g \cdot mol^{-1}$
C. $65.6\ g \cdot mol^{-1}$
D. $76.0\ g \cdot mol^{-1}$
E. $121\ g \cdot mol^{-1}$

8. Equal numbers of moles of helium and sulfur dioxide gas are placed in a container with a pinhole through which both can escape. What fraction of the sulfur dioxide gas escapes in the time required for one-half of the helium to escape?

A. ⅛
B. ¼
C. ½
D. ¾
E. none of the above

9. A mixture of Ar (0.30 mol), Kr (0.40 mol) and Xe (0.50 mol) exerts a pressure of 700 mm Hg. What would be the pressure of the Ar alone at the same temperature in the same container (in mm Hg)?

A. 50 mm Hg
B. 150 mm Hg
C. 175 mm Hg
D. 210 mm Hg
E. 280 mm Hg

10. How many molecules would be in 2.24 mL of water vapor maintained at STP conditions?

A. 3.01×10^{19}
B. 6.02×10^{19}
C. 6.02×10^{20}
D. 3.01×10^{21}
E. 6.02×10^{21}

For Questions 11–15, choose from the following:

A. Avogadro's Law
B. Boyle's Law
C. Charles' Law
D. Dalton's Law
E. Gay-Lussac's Law

11. The total pressure of a mixture of gases is the sum of the individual pressures.

12. Volume is inversely proportional to pressure (temperature held constant).

13. At constant volume, the pressure exerted by a given mass of gas varies directly with the absolute temperature.

14. The volume of a gas is directly proportional to the number of moles of the gas present (pressure and temperature held constant).

15. Volume is proportional to the absolute temperature of a gas (pressure held constant).

16. A hot-air balloon was inflated at sea level and rose to a height where the air pressure was ¾ that found at sea level and where the absolute temperature was ⅔ of the original temperature when the balloon was first inflated. By what factor does its volume change?

A. ¼
B. $\frac{8}{9}$
C. $\frac{9}{8}$
D. 2
E. 4

17. Gas A is mixed with gas B. The total pressure of the mixture is given by the equation

A. $P_A + P_B$
B. $P_A - P_B$
C. $P_A \times P_B$
D. $P_A \div P_B$
E. $X_A + X_B$

18. A sample of phosphine (PH_3) gas was placed in a flexible flask and occupied a volume of 800. cm^3. The initial temperature of 96.0°C and pressure of 760. mm Hg were maintained for several hours. At the conclusion of the experiment it was discovered that all of the phosphine had decomposed to $P_{4(g)}$ and $H_{2(g)}$. What was the total volume of the gaseous products?

A. 22.4 L
B. 457 cm^3
C. 800. cm^3
D. 1.40×10^3 cm^3
E. not enough information provided

For Questions 19–20, refer to the following experiment:

A 0.500 dm^3 flask contained a mixture of 1.50 grams of butane and another gas (X), the identity of which was unknown. The temperature of the mixture was 27.0°C and the total pressure was measured as 1.52×10^3 mm Hg.

19. The partial pressure of the butane was

A. 0.760 atm
B. 1.00 atm
C. 1.27 atm
D. 2.54 atm
E. 3.65 atm

20. The mole fraction of the unknown gas was

A. 0.111
B. 0.254
C. 0.365
D. 0.666
E. 0.750

Free-Response Questions

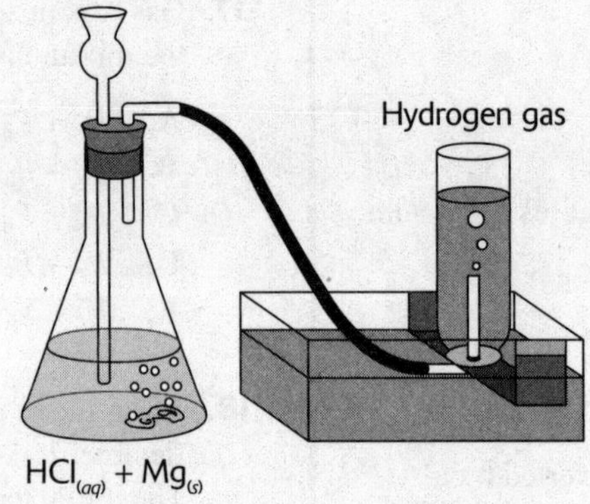

1. A student performed an experiment as diagrammed above and collected the following data:

Volume of Hydrogen Gas	*Temperature*	*Atmospheric Pressure*
45.0 mL	27°C	751 mm Hg

(a) Calculate the number of grams of hydrogen gas that the student collected. The vapor pressure of water at 27°C is 26.74 mm Hg.

(b) Calculate the mole fraction of:

(i) water vapor

(ii) hydrogen

(c) Calculate the ratio of the average speed of the water vapor molecules to the average speed of the hydrogen molecules in the sample.

(d) Describe both hydrogen gas and water vapor in terms of:

(i) molecular geometry

(ii) polarity

(iii) deviation from ideal gas behavior

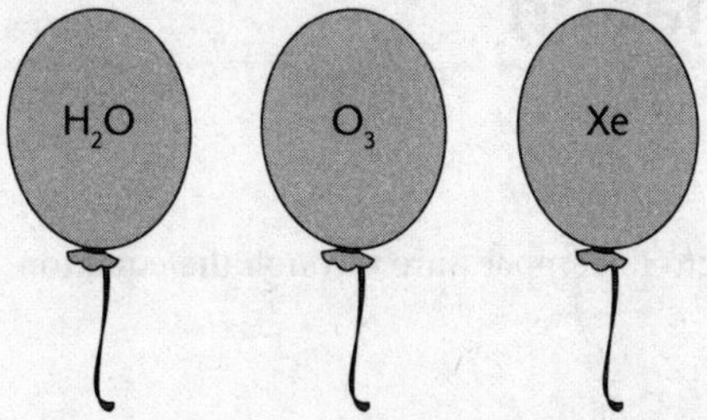

2. Three identical balloons are each filled with equal volumes of three separate gases as pictured above. All balloons are at 27°C and 1.5 atm pressure.

(a) Which balloon would have the least mass?

(b) Which balloon would have the

(i) greatest velocity?

(ii) greatest kinetic energy?

(c) Which gas would deviate the most from the behavior of an ideal gas? Explain.

(d) One day later, all balloons were appreciably smaller. If all factors were equal, which balloon would be the largest? Explain.

Answers and Explanation

Multiple Choice

1. **B.** The velocity of a gas is related to its temperature through the equation

$$v_{rms} = \sqrt{\frac{3RT}{MM}}$$

Since the molar mass of a gas is being held constant, the relationship becomes at

50.0°C: $\sqrt{3RT} = \sqrt{3(8.314\ \text{J/K}\cdot\text{mol})(50 + 273)\ \text{K}} = 89.76$

300.°C: $\sqrt{3RT} = \sqrt{3(8.314\ \text{J/K}\cdot\text{mol})(300 + 273)\ \text{K}} = 119.5$

119.5 / 89.76 = 1.33

2. **D.** Begin by writing as much information down as you can:

$C_xH_{y(g)} + O_{2(g)} \rightarrow CO_{2(g)} + H_2O_{(g)}$

41.08 g + excess → 132.03 g + 41.08 g

All of the carbon in the hydrocarbon ends up in the CO_2.

$$\frac{132.03\ \cancel{\text{g CO}_2}}{1} \times \frac{1\ \cancel{\text{mol CO}_2}}{44.01\ \cancel{\text{g CO}_2}} \times \frac{1\ \cancel{\text{mol C}}}{1\ \text{mol}\ \cancel{\text{CO}_2}} \times \frac{12.01\ \text{g C}}{1\ \cancel{\text{mol C}}} = 36.03\ \text{g C} = 3\ \text{moles C}$$

Since the entire hydrocarbon weighs 41.08 grams, 41.08 – 36.03 = 5.05 g of hydrogen in the hydrocarbon.

$$\frac{5.05\ \cancel{\text{g H}}}{1} \times \frac{1\ \text{mol H}}{1.01\ \cancel{\text{g H}}} = 5\ \text{mol H}$$

At this point we have C_3H_5, the empirical formula of C_6H_{10}.

3. **C.** The ideal gas equation ($PV = nRT$) is missing two characteristics real gases have: (1) the space the molecules themselves take up; i.e., ideal gases are treated as "point masses" that occupy no volume and (2) attractive forces between gas molecules. For gases near STP using the ideal gas equation causes no trouble and makes calculations easy. Measured temperatures, pressures, and volumes closely compare to those calculated. But at high pressure and/or low temperature, the ideal gas model does not predict gas behavior well.

4. **A.** $V_2 = V_1 \times \frac{P_1}{P_2} \times \frac{T_2}{T_1}$

5. **B.**

6. **B.** The equation for the complete combustion of methanol is

$$2CH_3OH_{(l)} + 3O_{2(g)} \rightarrow 2CO_{2(g)} + 4H_2O_{(g)}$$

$$\frac{44.8\ \cancel{\text{L O}_2}}{1} \times \frac{1\ \cancel{\text{mol O}_2}}{22.4\ \cancel{\text{L O}_2}} \times \frac{2\ \text{mol CO}_2}{3\ \cancel{\text{mol O}_2}} = 1.33\ \text{mol CO}_2$$

$$\frac{22.4\ \cancel{\text{g CH}_3\text{OH}}}{1} \times \frac{1\ \cancel{\text{mol CH}_3\text{OH}}}{32.05\ \cancel{\text{g CH}_3}\text{OH}} \times \frac{2\ \text{mol CO}_2}{2\ \cancel{\text{mol CH}_3\text{OH}}} = 0.699\ \text{mol CO}_2$$

7. **E.** $T = 173.0°\text{C} + 273 = 446\ \text{K}$

$$d = \frac{P\cdot MM}{R\cdot T} = \frac{(720.\ \cancel{\text{mm Hg}}/\ 760\ \cancel{\text{mm Hg}}\cdot\cancel{\text{atm}^{-1}})\cdot MM}{(0.0821\ \cancel{\text{L}}\cdot\cancel{\text{atm}}\cdot\text{mol}^{-1}\cdot\cancel{\text{K}^{-1}})\cdot 446\ \cancel{\text{K}}} = 3.14\ \text{g}\cdot\cancel{\text{L}^{-1}}$$

$MM = 121\ \text{g}\cdot\text{mol}^{-1}$

8. A. The question asks for the ratio of sulfur dioxide to one-half the amount of helium.

$$\frac{\text{rate sulfur dioxide}}{\text{rate helium}} = \frac{\frac{1}{2}\sqrt{MM_{\text{He}}}}{\sqrt{MM_{\text{SO}_2}}} = \frac{\frac{1}{2}\sqrt{4}}{\sqrt{64}} = \frac{\frac{1}{2}(2)}{8} = \frac{1}{8}$$

9. C. The pressure of an ideal gas in a mixture is equal to the pressure it would exert if it occupied the same volume alone at the same temperature. Ideal gas molecules are so far apart that they don't interfere with each other. A consequence of this is that the total pressure of a mixture of ideal gases is equal to the sum of the partial pressures of the individual gases in the mixture as stated by Dalton's Law of Partial Pressures.

Total moles = 0.30 + 0.40 + 0.50 = 1.20

$$X_{\text{Ar}} = \frac{0.30 \cancel{\text{ moles}} \text{ Ar}}{1.20 \cancel{\text{ total moles}}} = 0.25 \qquad 0.25(700 \text{ mm Hg}) = 175 \text{ mm Hg}$$

10. B. $\frac{2.24 \cancel{\text{mL } H_2O_{(g)}}}{1} \times \frac{1 \cancel{\text{L } H_2O_{(g)}}}{10^3 \cancel{\text{mL } H_2O_{(g)}}} \times \frac{1 \cancel{\text{mole } H_2O_{(g)}}}{22.4 \cancel{\text{L } H_2O_{(g)}}} \times \frac{6.02 \times 10^{23} \text{ molecules}}{1 \cancel{\text{mole } H_2O}} = 6.02 \times 10^{19} \text{ molecules}$

11. D.

12. B.

13. E.

14. A.

15. C.

16. B. $V_2 = V_1\left(\frac{P_1}{P_2}\right)\left(\frac{T_2}{T_1}\right) = V_1\left(\frac{4}{3}\right)\left(\frac{2}{3}\right) = V_1\left(\frac{8}{9}\right)$

17. A. Dalton's Law of Partial Pressures: The total pressure of a mixture of gases is the sum of the individual pressures.

18. D. $4PH_{3(g)} \rightarrow P_{4(g)} + 6H_{2(g)}$. Because the gases are at the same temperature and pressure, the molar ratio constructed from the coefficients in the balanced equation is equal to the volume ratio of the gases expressed in liters. Therefore, it is the only factor necessary to convert the volume of one gas into the stoichiometrically equivalent volume of the other. There are a total of 4 moles of gaseous reactants and 7 moles of gaseous products; therefore, the volume of the products must be 7/4 that of the reactant ($\frac{7}{4} \times 800. = 1.40 \times 10^3$).

19. C. Butane has the formula C_4H_{10}. The *MW* of butane = 58.12 g · mol^{-1}.

$$n = \frac{1.50 \text{ g } C_4H_{10}}{58.12 \text{ g } C_4H_{10} \cdot \text{mol}^{-1}} = 2.58 \times 10^{-2} \text{ mol} \qquad T = 27.0°\text{C} + 273 \text{ K} = 300. \text{ K}$$

$$P = \frac{nRT}{V} = \frac{2.58 \times 10^{-2} \cancel{\text{mol}}(0.0821 \cancel{\text{L}} \cdot \text{atm} \cdot \cancel{\text{mol}^{-1}} \cdot \cancel{\text{K}^{-1}})(300. \cancel{\text{K}})}{0.500 \cancel{\text{L}}} = 1.27 \text{ atm}$$

20. C. $\frac{1.27 \cancel{\text{atm}}}{1} \times \frac{760 \text{ mm Hg}}{1 \cancel{\text{atm}}} = 965 \text{ mm Hg}$

$$P_X = P_{\text{total}} - P_{C_4H_{10}} = 1520 \text{ mm Hg} - 965 \text{ mm Hg} = 555 \text{ mm Hg}$$

$$\frac{555 \cancel{\text{mm Hg}}}{1520 \cancel{\text{mm Hg}}} = 0.365$$

Free Response

Question 1

Maximum Points for Question 1
Part (a): 3 points
Part (b) (i): 1 point
Part (b) (ii): 1 point
Part (c): 2 points
Part (d) (i): 1 point
Part (d) (ii): 1 point
Part (d) (iii): 1 point
Total points: 10

1. A student performed an experiment and collected data: *(a) Calculate the number of grams of hydrogen gas that the student collected. The vapor pressure of water at 27°C is 26.74 mm Hg.*	***3 points possible***
PV = nRT	*1 point for using correct formula.*
$P_{H_2} = P_{total} - P_{H_2O}$ = 751 mm Hg – 26.74 mm Hg = 724 mm Hg	*1 point for correct setup.*
$\frac{724\,\text{mmHg}}{1} \times \frac{1\,\text{atm}}{760\,\text{mmHg}} = 0.953\,\text{atm}$ $\frac{45.0\,\text{mL}}{1} \times \frac{1\,\text{L}}{1000\,\text{mL}} = 0.0450\,\text{L}$	*1 point for correct answer.*
27°C + 273 = 300. K $n = \frac{PV}{RT} = \frac{0.953\,\text{atm} \times 0.0450\,\text{L}}{(0.0821\,\text{L}\cdot\text{atm}\cdot\text{mol}^{-1}\cdot\text{K}^{-1})\,300.\,\text{K}}$ $= \frac{1.74 \times 10^{-3}\,\text{moles}H_2}{1} \times \frac{2.02\,gH_2}{1\,\text{mol}H_2} = 3.51 \times 10^{-3}\,gH_2$	
(b) (i) Calculate the mole fraction water vapor	***1 point possible***
$\frac{26.74\,\text{mmHg}}{1} \times \frac{1\,\text{atm}}{760\,\text{mmHg}} = 0.03518\,\text{atm}$	*1 point for correct answer and showing setup.*
$n = \frac{PV}{RT} = \frac{(0.03518\,\text{atm}) \times 0.0450\,\text{L}}{(0.0821\,\text{L}\cdot\text{atm}\cdot\text{mol}^{-1}\cdot\text{K}^{-1})(300.\,\text{K})}$ $= 6.43 \times 10^{-5}$ mol $H_2O_{(g)}$ $X_{H_2O} = \frac{\text{mol}H_2O}{\text{total moles}} = \frac{6.43 \times 10^{-5}\,\text{mol}}{1.74 \times 10^{-3}\,\text{mol} + 6.43 \times 10^{-5}\,\text{mol}}$ $X_{H_2O} = 0.0356$	

(b) (ii) Calculate the mole fraction of hydrogen $\frac{1.74\times 10^{-3}\,\text{\sout{mol}}}{1.74\times 10^{-3}\,\text{\sout{mol}} + 6.43\times 10^{-5}\,\text{\sout{mol}}} = 0.964$	***1 point possible*** *1 point for correct answer and showing setup.*
(c) Calculate the ratio of the average speed of the water vapor molecules to the average speed of the hydrogen molecules in the sample. $\frac{r_{H_2O}}{r_{H_2}} = \frac{\sqrt{M_{H_2}}}{\sqrt{M_{H_2O}}} = \frac{\sqrt{2.02}}{\sqrt{18.02}} = 0.335{:}1$	***2 points possible*** *1 point for correct setup.* *1 point for correct answer.*
(d) (i) Describe both hydrogen gas and water vapor in terms of molecular geometry: H_2: linear H_2O: bent	***1 point possible*** *1 point for correct description of both hydrogen and water.*
(d) (ii) Describe both hydrogen gas and water vapor in terms of polarity: H_2 is non-polar since both hydrogen atoms making up the molecule have equal electronegativity so there is no net dipole. H_2O: The water molecule is electrically neutral, but the positive and negative charges are not distributed uniformly. The negative charge is concentrated at the oxygen end of the molecule, owing partly to the nonbonding electrons and to oxygen's high nuclear charge, which exerts stronger attractions on the electrons. This charge displacement constitutes an electric dipole.	***1 point possible*** *1 point for correct description of both hydrogen and water.*
(d) (iii) Describe both hydrogen gas and water vapor in terms of deviation from ideal gas behavior: H_2O deviates more from ideal behavior since the volume of the H_2O molecule is larger than that of the H_2 molecule, and the intermolecular forces among the H_2O molecules are stronger than those among H_2 molecules.	***1 point possible*** *1 point for correct description of both hydrogen and water.*

Question 2

Maximum Points for Question 2
Part (a): 2 points
Part (b) (i): 2 points
Part (b) (ii): 2 point
Part (c): 2 points
Part (d): 2 point
Total points: 10

2. Three identical balloons are each filled with equal volumes of three separate gases as pictured. All balloons are at 27°C and 1.5 atm pressure. *(a) Which balloon would have the least mass?* Given: H_2O, $MM = 18.02\ g \cdot mol^{-1}$ O_3, $MM = 48.00\ g \cdot mol^{-1}$ Xe, $MM = 131.30\ g \cdot mol^{-1}$ All three balloons have equal volumes. All three balloons are at 27°C and 1.5 atm. Since all three balloons have identical volumes, pressures, and temperatures, all three balloons would contain the same number of particles. The balloon filled with water vapor, which has the lowest molecular mass, would have the least mass.	***2 points possible*** *1 point for correct answer of water vapor.* *1 point for proper reasoning.*
(b) (i) Which would have the greatest velocity? H_2O since it is the lightest particle of the choices given; i.e., at the same temperature, lighter particles travel faster compared to heavier particles.	***2 points possible*** *1 point for correct answer of water vapor.* *1 point for proper reasoning.*
(b) (ii) Which balloon would have the greatest kinetic energy? All three balloons would have the same kinetic energy since they are all at the same temperature.	***2 points possible*** *1 point for correct answer of all three.* *1 point for proper reasoning.*
(c) Which gas would deviate the most from the behavior of an ideal gas? Explain. H_2O since H_2O molecules are polar. Hydrogen bonding does NOT occur when particles are in the gas phase. Even though Xe atoms have more electrons, individual atoms cannot be polar; only molecules can exhibit polarity.	***2 points possible*** *1 point for correct answer of water vapor.* *1 point for proper reasoning.*
(d) One day later, all balloons were appreciably smaller. If all factors were equal, which balloon would be the largest? The largest balloon (assuming all factors are equal) would be the one containing Xe gas since the Xe atoms are the heaviest gas particle. All factors being equal, heavier particles travel slower and have lower effusion rates (Graham's Law).	***2 points possible*** *1 point for correct answer of Xe.* *1 point for proper reasoning.*

Liquids and Solids

You'll Need to Know

- ❑ the properties of liquids
- ❑ what is surface tension and what affects it
- ❑ the difference between cohesion and adhesion
- ❑ the properties of water
- ❑ the properties of solids
- ❑ what is vaporization
- ❑ what is condensation
- ❑ what is dynamic equilibrium and what affects it
- ❑ how to determine the heat of vaporization
- ❑ how to determine the boiling point
- ❑ how to read the critical point from a phase diagram
- ❑ how to read critical pressure from a phase diagram
- ❑ how to read critical temperature from a phase diagram
- ❑ what are supercritical fluids
- ❑ how to determine melting-freezing point
- ❑ what is supercooling
- ❑ what is sublimation
- ❑ how to draw and interpret a phase diagram

Properties of Liquids

All liquids have a definite volume but assume the shape of their container. Liquids have higher densities than gases and are only slightly compressible. The molecules slide past each other freely.

- **Surface Tension:** The property of liquids arising from unbalanced molecular cohesive forces at or near the surface, as a result of which the surface tends to contract and has properties resembling those of a stretched elastic membrane.
- **Cohesion:** The intermolecular attraction between like molecules.
- **Adhesion:** The attraction between unlike molecules.
- **Viscosity:** A measure of a liquid's resistance to flow. Example: cold maple syrup has a high viscosity.

Properties of Water

The properties of water are (1) Excellent solvent for ionic compounds or other compounds capable of forming hydrogen bonds; (2) has a high specific heat due to hydrogen bonding, and therefore, water can absorb a substantial amount of heat while the temperature rises only slightly, which tends to stabilize global temperature; and (3) the liquid phase is more dense than the solid phase and results because water molecules are joined together in an extensive three-dimensional network in which each oxygen atom is tetrahedrally bonded to four hydrogen atoms—two by covalent bonds and two by hydrogen bonds.

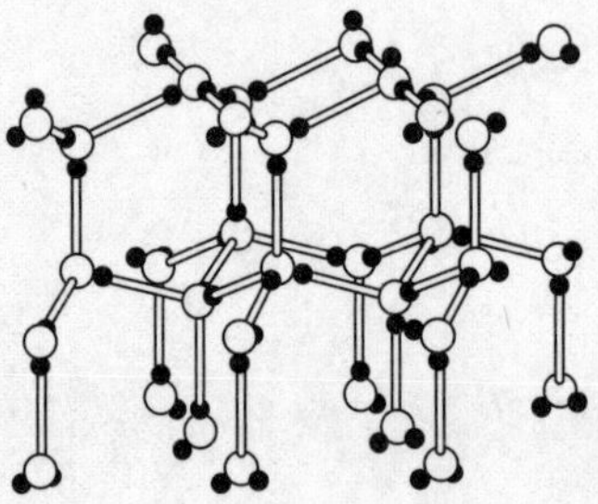

Example

Q. Using principles of chemical bonding, explain why water is most dense at 4°C, not 0°C, its freezing point.

A. Solid ice has a highly ordered three-dimensional structure, which keeps individual H_2O molecules apart from each other and results in "spaces" (these spaces increase the volume and decrease the density). When heat is applied to ice, some of the H_2O molecules have enough kinetic energy to break the hydrogen bonds and thereby separate from other H_2O molecules in the lattice. These H_2O molecules then become trapped in the spaces or cavities of the remaining three-dimensional ice structure. This results in more H_2O molecules per unit of volume than previously (higher density). At this point, 4°C, water is most dense. However, as the temperature increases (above 4°C), two processes occur: (1) the entire three-dimensional structure collapses and the spaces diminish, which tends to increase density and (2) thermal expansion predominates and causes water to expand and become less dense.

Properties of Solids

All solids: (1) have a definite volume and shape, (2) are usually more dense than the liquid phase of the same substance, (3) are virtually incompressible, and (4) vibrate about fixed positions. Solids are either classified as (1) amorphous (e.g., glass), lacking any defined arrangement of its molecules or (2) crystalline (e.g., iron, table salt), the atoms, ions or molecules are in specific positions. The net attractive intermolecular forces in solids are at their maximum and result from either ionic forces, covalent bonds, van der Waals forces, hydrogen bonds, or combinations of any of these.

Phase Changes

Liquid-Vapor Equilibrium

- **Vaporization:** A certain number of molecules at any temperature in a liquid possess enough kinetic energy to escape from the surface. In a closed system, these gaseous molecules exert a vapor pressure.
- **Condensation:** As the number of molecules increase in the vapor phase, some of them strike the surface of the liquid. Intermolecular forces between the molecules at the surface of the liquid and the gaseous molecule that strikes the surface cause the molecules to remain in the liquid phase.

- **Dynamic equilibrium:** Occurs when the rate of molecules leaving a liquid surface equals the rate of gaseous molecules returning to the liquid. The pressure at this point is called the equilibrium vapor pressure and is constant for any liquid at a given temperature $l \leftrightharpoons g$. Equilibrium vapor pressures increase with temperature.

Heat of Vaporization and Boiling Point

- **Molar heat of vaporization (ΔH_{vap}):** The energy (kJ/mol) required to vaporize one mole of a liquid. ΔH_{vap} is directly proportional to the strength of intermolecular forces of a liquid, which is reflected in its boiling point (stronger intermolecular forces ~ higher B.P.).
- **Critical point:** The temperature and pressure above which the liquid state can no longer exist.
- **Critical pressure (P_c):** The highest pressure at which a species can coexist as a liquid and a vapor.
- **Critical temperature (T_c):** The highest temperature at which a species can coexist as a liquid and a vapor.
- **Supercritical fluid:** A substance which is above its critical temperature and pressure.

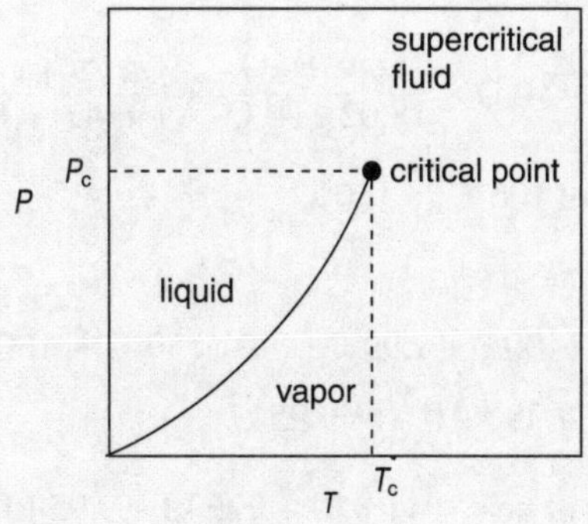

Liquid-Solid Equilibrium

- **Melting-freezing point:** The melting point of a solid (which is the same temperature as the freezing point of a liquid) is the temperature at which both solid and liquid phases exist in equilibrium, $l \leftrightharpoons s$. "Normal" refers to temperatures at 1 atm pressure. The energy required to melt one mole of a substance is called the molar heat of fusion (ΔH_{fus}). The heat of fusion is always smaller than the heat of vaporization for a substance since when a liquid vaporizes, its molecules become completely separated from each other, and more energy is required to overcome these attractive intermolecular forces. When a solid melts to become a liquid, intermolecular forces do not need to be broken, only rearranged.

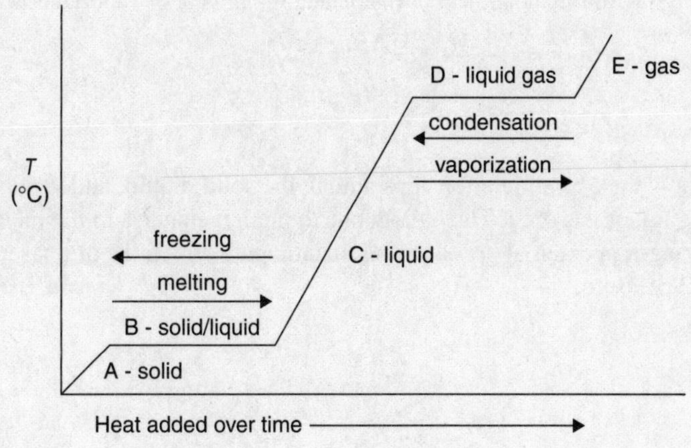

Example

Q. Calculate the amount of energy (in kJ) needed to heat 100. grams of liquid water from 0°C to 150°C. The specific heat of water is 4.184 J/(g · °C), the molar heat of vaporization of water = 40.79 kJ/mol, and the specific heat of steam is 1.99 J/(g · °C).

A. Break the problem into three parts:

(1) Energy to heat water from 0°C to 100°C

$$q_1 = m \cdot c \cdot \Delta t$$

$$= (100.\text{ g})\,(4.184\text{ J/(g}\cdot{}^\circ\text{C}))\,(100^\circ\text{C} - 0^\circ\text{C})$$

$$= 4.184 \times 10^4\text{ J} = 41.8\text{ kJ}$$

(2) Energy to vaporize 100. g of water at 100°C

$$q_2 = 100.\ \cancel{\text{g H}_2\text{O}} \times \frac{1\ \cancel{\text{mol H}_2\text{O}}}{18.02\ \cancel{\text{g H}_2\text{O}}} \times \frac{40.79\text{ kJ}}{1\ \cancel{\text{mol H}_2\text{O}}} = 226\text{ kJ}$$

(3) Energy to heat 100. g of steam from 100°C to 150°C

$$q_3 = m \cdot c \cdot \Delta t$$

$$= (100.\ \cancel{\text{g}})(1.99\text{ J}/\cancel{\text{g}}\cdot\cancel{{}^\circ\text{C}})(150\cancel{{}^\circ\text{C}} - 100\cancel{{}^\circ\text{C}})$$

$$= 9.95 \times 10^3\text{ J} = 9.95\text{ kJ}$$

Now, add $q_1 + q_2 + q_3$ for total amount of heat = 41.8 kJ + 226 kJ + 9.95 kJ = 278 kJ

- **Supercooling:** Occurs when a liquid is temporarily cooled below its freezing point. This temporary condition occurs because not enough time has passed for the molecules in the liquid phase to arrange into an ordered solid. Sometimes, a "seed" crystal or gentle stirring will speed up solidification.

Solid-Vapor Equilibrium

- **Sublimation:** The process by which molecules go directly from the solid into the gas phase (Example: dry ice, CO_2). The reverse process whereby molecules go directly from the gas phase into the solid phase is known as deposition (Example: formation of frost). The energy required to sublime one mole of a substance is called the molar heat of sublimation (ΔH_{sub}) and is the sum of the molar heat of fusion and molar heat of vaporization:

$$\Delta H_{sub} = \Delta H_{fus} + \Delta H_{vap}$$

Phase Diagrams

Phase diagrams graphically show the overall relationships among the solid, liquid, and vapor phases and summarize the conditions at which a solid, liquid, or gas exist. They allow one to predict changes in the melting point and boiling point of substances as a result of changes in external pressure and to anticipate directions of phase transitions brought about by changes in temperature and pressure.

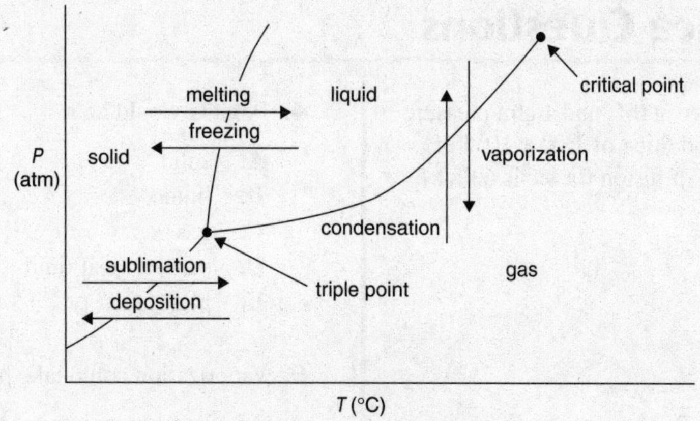

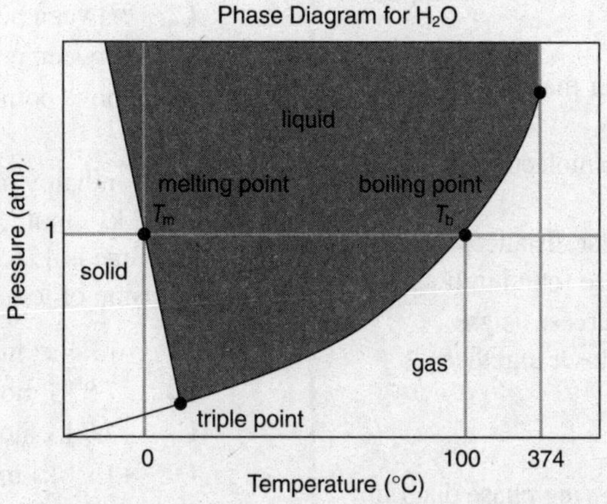

For water, the liquid phase is more dense than the solid phase due to hydrogen bonding.

Example

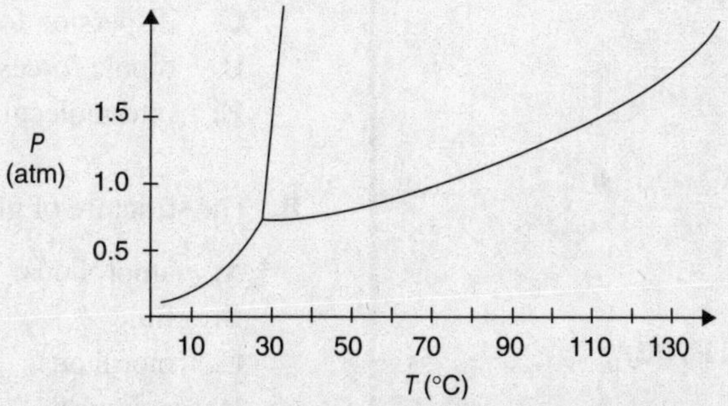

Q. The normal boiling point of the substance represented by the phase diagram above is

A. 15°C
B. 30°C
C. 70°C
D. greater than 70°C
E. cannot be determined from the diagram

A. C. Normal boiling point is the temperature at which a liquid's vapor pressure equals one atmosphere. Go up the Y axis to 1.0 atm, go straight across until you hit the liquid/gas equilibrium curve—go straight down.

Multiple-Choice Questions

1. How many grams of ice at 0°C and 1 atm pressure can be melted by the addition of 1.00×10^3 J of heat? (The molar heat of fusion for ice is 6.02 kJ · mol^{-1}).

A. 0.0180 g
B. 1.50 g
C. 2.99 g
D. 12.0 g
E. 15.0 g

2. Gases can be compressed more easily than liquids because

A. gas molecules are smaller than liquid molecules.
B. the kinetic energy of gas molecules is higher than that found in liquids.
C. the average intermolecular distances are greater in gases than those found in liquids.
D. intermolecular forces increase as gas molecules are brought closer together.
E. None of the above.

For Questions 3–7, refer to the following phase diagram:

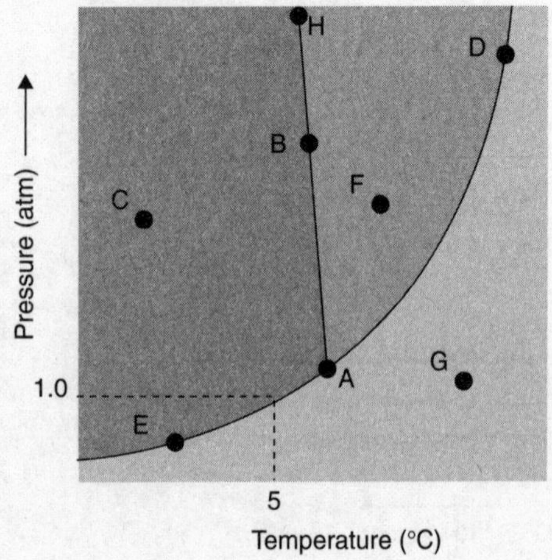

3. The point at which the solid, liquid, and gas phases exist simultaneously is point

A. A
B. B
C. C
D. D
E. E

4. Point G would be a

A. solid
B. liquid
C. gas
D. supercritical fluid
E. plasma

5. Vaporization could take place

A. between points A and B.
B. between points E and A.
C. between points A and D.
D. between points A and H.
E. above point D.

6. If the enthalpy of vaporization of iodine is +20.9 kJ · mol^{-1}, and the enthalpy of sublimation of iodine is +28.6 kJ · mol^{-1}, what is the enthalpy of fusion of iodine?

A. −13.4 kJ mol^{-1}
B. −7.8 kJ mol^{-1}
C. +7.7 kJ mol^{-1}
D. +13.1 kJ mol^{-1}
E. +49.5 kJ mol^{-1}

7. When solid carbon dioxide sublimes, what are the chemical forces that must be overcome?

A. intramolecular covalent bonds
B. hydrogen bonds
C. dispersion forces
D. dipole forces
E. intermolecular covalent bonds

8. The structure of glass is best described as

A. amorphous
B. fluid
C. morphous
D. polymer
E. lattice

For Questions 9–10, refer to the following phase diagram:

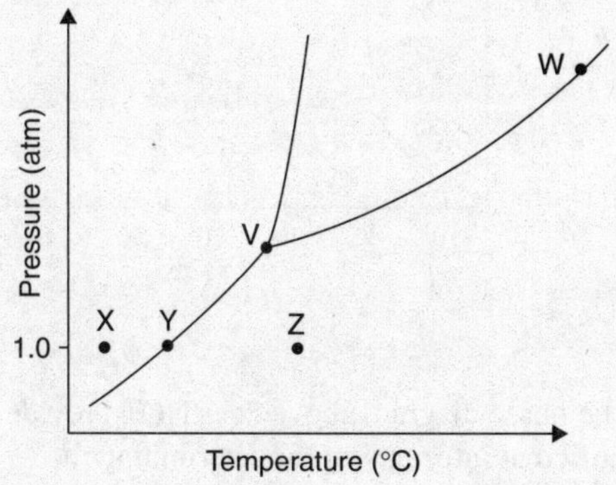

9. What will happen to the state of a substance represented by this phase diagram when its temperature is changed from Point X to Point Z (holding pressure constant)?

A. freezing
B. deposition
C. sublimation
D. melting
E. boiling

10. For this phase diagram, which of the following is true at the triple point (Point V)?

A. The vapor pressure of the solid phase is equal to the vapor pressure of the liquid phase.
B. The temperature is higher than the normal melting point.
C. The liquid and gas phases of the substance have the same density and are therefore indistinguishable.
D. The solid phase will melt if the pressure increases at constant temperature.
E. The liquid phase will vaporize if the pressure increases at constant temperature.

11. A 0.750 gram sample of an unknown volatile liquid in a sealed 2.00 L flask at 0.750 atm of pressure is completely vaporized at 102°C. The molecular weight of the substance is

A. 38.5 g/mol
B. 77.0 g/mol
C. 154 g/mol
D. 308 g/mol
E. none of the above

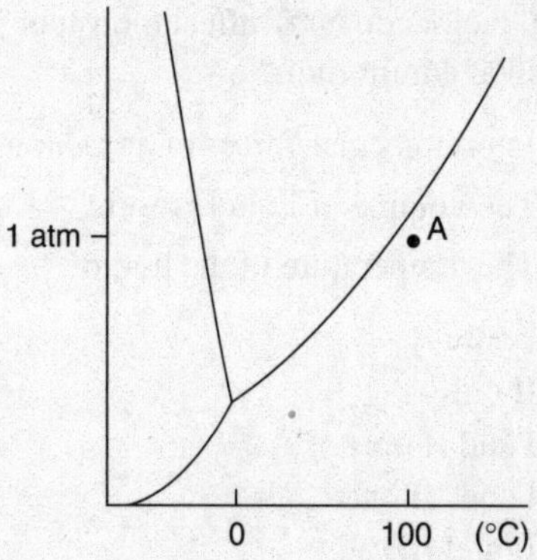

12. According to the phase diagram above, if the temperature is steadily decreased at constant pressure from point A, the physical change would be the same as

A. frost appearing on a lawn.
B. water vapor in clouds turning into rain.
C. dry ice undergoing sublimation.
D. an ice cube melting.
E. water freezing.

For Questions 13–14, you are given 2.50 grams of water at 27.0°C. The equilibrium vapor pressure of water at 27.0°C is 26.7 mm Hg.

13. The water is placed into a sealed 7.00 L flask kept at 27.0°C. How much liquid water will remain once equilibrium is established?

A. 0.00 g
B. 1.67 g
C. 2.32 g
D. 2.50 g
E. 3.00 g

14. Which of the following would be the minimum size flask that would be required if all of the water were to be completely vaporized?

A. 1.00 L
B. 2.00 L
C. 50.0 L
D. 100. L
E. 200. L

15. Which factors do NOT affect the vapor pressure of a liquid at equilibrium?

I. Intermolecular forces of attraction
II. The volume of liquid present
III. The temperature of the liquid

A. I only
B. II only
C. I and II only
D. I and III only
E. II and III only

16. Which of the following actions would be likely to change the boiling point of a sample of a pure liquid in an open container?

I. Placing the liquid in a larger container
II. Decreasing the amount of the liquid in the container
III. Moving the container and liquid to a lower altitude

A. I only
B. II only
C. III only
D. I and III only
E. I, II, and III

17. The normal boiling point of a liquid is defined as:

A. the boiling point of liquid under STP conditions.
B. the temperature at which a liquid changes to a gas.
C. the temperature at which the vapor pressure of a liquid equals 1 atm.
D. the temperature at which the vapor pressure of a liquid equals the barometric pressure.
E. the pressure at which a liquid changes to a gas.

18.

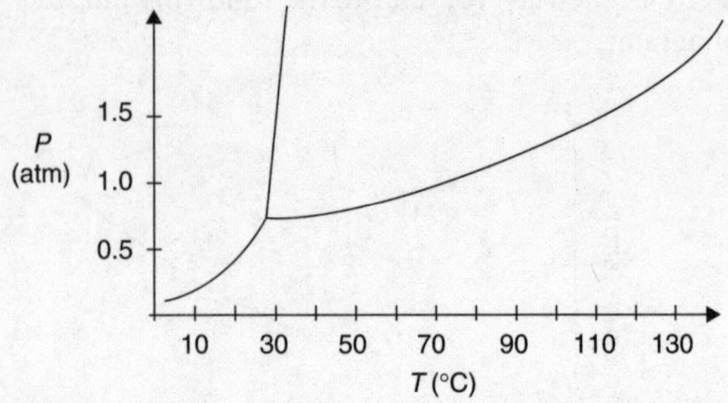

The phase diagram above does NOT provide sufficient information for determining the

A. conditions necessary for condensation.
B. conditions necessary for sublimation.
C. deviation from ideal gas behavior.
D. conditions necessary for vaporization.
E. conditions necessary for fusion.

19. In order to determine inter-atomic distances in a crystal, one would use (the)

A. Chadwick's equation
B. Graham's equation
C. Arrhenius equation
D. Clausius-Clapeyron equation
E. Bragg equation

20. Examine the following phase diagram for water:

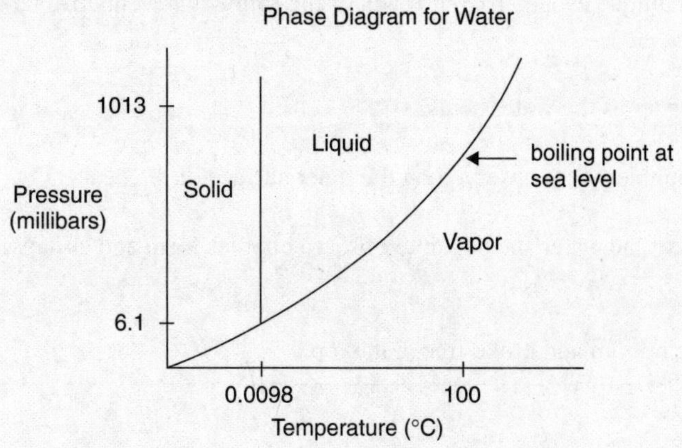

At pressures directly below the triple point (holding temperature constant at 0.0098°C), a substance can exist

- **A.** only as a gas.
- **B.** only as a solid.
- **C.** as a solid or a liquid.
- **D.** as a solid or a gas.
- **E.** as a liquid or a gas.

Free-Response Questions

1. Choose any five to discuss in terms of chemical principles:

(a) You are at the top of a high mountain at 8,000 feet. You're hungry, and you decide to boil an egg. You discover that the water gets to the boiling point faster than where you live on the coast. But you notice that after the amount of time it took to boil the egg at home, the egg boiled at the top of the mountain was not cooked.

(b) You and a friend are supposed to cook a meal for a party. But time is running out. Your friend says to use a pressure cooker.

(c) You are scheduled to compete in an ice-skating race. The salesman recommends a pair of ice skates with thinner blades, saying that they will make you skate faster.

(d) You are at a grocery store trying to decide on which coffee to buy. The store clerk says to buy freeze-dried coffee as it is much fresher than other types on the shelf.

(e) There has been a severe drought where you live. You turn to the local news, and they announce that the county has hired a firm to "seed" the clouds with granulated dry ice.

(f) You're reading an article on how the government plans to build a new magnetic rail system and supercomputers using superconductors.

2. A student places 500. mL of cold distilled water into a beaker. She then heats the distilled water with a Bunsen burner and notices several unique events. Explain each of the following events from a chemical and/or physical standpoint.

(a) Ripples occur in the water as the water heats.

(b) Around 80°C, small bubbles were observed on the inner surface of the beaker.

(c) As she continued to heat the water she began to observe bubbles form and collapse on the bottom of the beaker.

(d) Bubbles rose from the bottom and broke free at the top.

Answers and Explanations

Multiple Choice

1. **C.** $\frac{1.00\times 10^3\,\cancel{J}}{1}\times\frac{1\,\cancel{kJ}}{10^3\,\cancel{J}}\times\frac{1\,\cancel{mol\ ice}}{6.02\,\cancel{kJ}}\times\frac{18.02\text{ g ice}}{1\,\cancel{mol\ ice}}=2.99\text{ g ice}$

2. **C.** In a gas, the molecules are separated by a large distance and, as such, are able to be compressed by increasing the pressure. They move independently of one another because there is no appreciable intermolecular interaction among them.

3. **A.**

4. **C.**

5. **C.**

6. **C.** The quantity of heat required to convert a given amount of solid directly to a gas is the enthalpy (heat) of sublimation, which is equal to the sum of the enthalpy of fusion and the enthalpy of vaporization: $\Delta H_{\text{sublimation}} = \Delta H_{\text{fusion}} + \Delta H_{\text{vaporization}}$; therefore, $\Delta H_{\text{fusion}} = \Delta H_{\text{sublimation}} - \Delta H_{\text{vaporization}} = 28.6\text{ kJ}\cdot\text{mol}^{-1} - 20.9\text{ kJ}\cdot\text{mol}^{-1} = 7.7\text{ kJ mol}^{-1}$

7. **C.** Three types of forces can operate between covalent molecules: (1) dispersion forces also known as London Forces (also known as weak intermolecular forces or van der Waals Forces), (2) dipole-dipole interactions, and (3) hydrogen bonds. Intermolecular forces (dispersion forces, dipole-dipole interactions, and hydrogen bonds) are much weaker than intramolecular forces (covalent bonds, ionic bonds, or metallic bonds). Dispersion forces are the weakest intermolecular force (one hundredth to one thousandth the strength of a covalent bond) while hydrogen bonds are the strongest intermolecular force (about one-tenth the strength of a covalent bond): dispersion forces < dipole-dipole interactions < hydrogen bonds. Carbon dioxide (dry ice) is a non-polar molecule. Therefore, the only intermolecular forces present are dispersion forces that result from momentary dipoles occurring due to (1) uneven electron distributions in neighboring molecules as they approach one another and (2) the weak residual attraction of the nuclei in one molecule for the electrons in a neighboring molecule. The more electrons that are present in the molecule, the stronger the dispersion forces will be.

8. **A.** An amorphous solid is a solid in which there is no long-range order of the positions of the atoms. Solids in which there is long-range atomic order are called crystalline solids.

9. **C.** Point X is in the solid phase while point Z is in the gas phase. The transition does NOT pass through the liquid phase.

10. **A.**

11. **C.**

$$T = 102°\text{C} + 273 = 375\text{K}$$

$$PV = nRT = \frac{mRT}{MW} \rightarrow MW = \frac{m\cdot R\cdot T}{P\cdot V} = \frac{7.50\text{ g}\cdot(0.0821\,\cancel{L}\cdot\cancel{atm})\cdot 375\,\cancel{K}}{0.750\,\cancel{atm}\cdot(2.00\,\cancel{L})\cdot\text{mol}\cdot\cancel{K}} = 154\text{ g}\cdot\text{mol}^{-1}$$

12. **A.** The change that is occurring is known as deposition. Frost (also known as hoar frost) refers to the white ice crystals that are deposited on the ground or exposed objects and forms when the air is moist (high in water vapor) and the surface is cold. The water vapor does not pass through the liquid state. Frost is common on cold, clear autumn nights.

13. **C.**

$$T = 27.0°\text{C} + 273 = 300.\text{ K}$$

$$g = \frac{P\times V\times MM}{RT} = \frac{(26.7\,\cancel{mm\,Hg})(7.00\,\cancel{L})(18.0\text{ g}/\cancel{mol})}{(760.\,\cancel{mm\,Hg}\cdot\cancel{atm^{-1}})(0.0821\,\cancel{L}\cdot\cancel{atm}\cdot\cancel{mol^{-1}}\cdot\cancel{K^{-1}})(300.\,\cancel{K})} = 0.180\text{ g }H_2O_{(g)}$$

$$2.50\text{ g }H_2O_{(l)} - 0.180\text{ g }H_2O_{(g)} = 2.32\text{ g }H_2O_{(l)}$$

14. D. $V = \frac{g \cdot R \cdot T}{P \cdot MM} = \frac{(2.50\,\cancel{g})(0.0821\,L \cdot \cancel{atm} \cdot \cancel{mol^{-1}} \cdot \cancel{K^{-1}})(300.\,\cancel{K})}{(26.7\,\cancel{mm\,Hg})(1\,\cancel{atm} \cdot 760^{-1}\,\cancel{mm\,Hg^{-1}})(18.0\,\cancel{g} \cdot \cancel{mol^{-1}})} = 97.4\,L$

15. B. Substances with strong intermolecular forces (such as hydrogen bonds found in H_2O) will exhibit lower vapor pressures when compared to substances at the same temperature with similar molecular masses without such forces (e.g., H_2O [$MM = 18.02\ g \cdot mol^{-1}$] has a much lower vapor pressure than CH_4 [$MM = 16.05\ g \cdot mol^{-1}$]). Vapor pressures of substances increase with increasing temperature. As long as a substance is in equilibrium within a closed system, the amount of substance present does not affect the vapor pressure.

16. C. As altitude decreases, the air pressure increases. At sea level, the pressure on a square inch of surface is 14.7 pounds, while at 10,000 feet the pressure is only 10.2 pounds. This is a decrease of about 0.5 pounds per 1,000 feet. Therefore, with all other factors being held constant, a liquid will have a lower vapor pressure at lower altitudes. This is why water boils at 100°C at sea level, but boils at ~90°C at 10,000 feet. Therefore, it takes longer for a boiled egg to cook at 10,000 feet than it does at sea level (since the temperature of boiling water is lower at 10,000 feet).

17. C. The boiling point of a liquid is the temperature at which its vapor pressure is equal to the pressure of the gas above it. The "normal" boiling point of a liquid is the temperature at which its vapor pressure is equal to one atmosphere (760 torr).

18. C. Condensation is the phase change from vapor to liquid. Sublimation is the phase change from solid to vapor. Vaporization is the phase change from liquid to vapor. Fusion is the phase change from solid to liquid. The phase diagram provides information for all of these changes. The phase diagram provides no information on how a substance in the gas phase deviates from ideal behavior.

19. E. Bragg's equation is the result of experiments conducted at the start of the 20th century into the diffraction of X-rays from the surfaces of crystals. These diffractions only occur at certain angles. Although the equation ($d = n \cdot \gamma/(2\sin\theta)$) is simple, it confirmed the existence of particles on the atomic level. Bragg's equation indicates that diffraction is only observed when a set of planes makes a very specific angle with the incoming X-ray beam. This angle depends on the inter-plane spacing *d*, which itself depends on the size of the molecules which make up the structure.

20. A. The only phase that is directly below the triple point (holding the temperature constant) is the vapor phase.

Free Response

Question 1

Maximum Points for Question 1
Part (a): 2 points
Part (b): 2 points
Part (c): 2 points
Part (d): 2 points
Part (e): 2 points
Part (f): 2 points
Total points: 10

1 Choose any five to discuss in terms of chemical principles: *(a) You are at the top of a high mountain at 8,000 feet. You're hungry, and you decide to boil an egg. You discover that the water gets to the boiling point faster than where you live on the coast. But you notice that after the amount of time it took to boil the egg at home, the egg at the top of the mountain was not cooked.* Atmospheric pressure decreases with altitude. Since the boiling point of a liquid decreases with decreasing atmospheric pressure, water will boil at a lower temperature at higher altitudes. It is not the boiling action that cooks an egg but the amount of heat delivered to the egg. The amount of heat is proportional to the temperature.	***2 points possible*** *Atmospheric pressure decreases with altitude.* *Boiling point decreases with decreasing atmospheric pressure.* *Amount of heat that cooks an egg.*
(b) You and a friend are supposed to cook a meal for a party. But time is running out. Your friend says to use a pressure cooker. A pressure cooker is a sealed container that allows food to cook at higher pressures than normal. The pressure above the water in the pressure cooker is the sum of the atmospheric pressure and the pressure of the steam. At higher pressures, it takes more heat for water to boil. Consequently, the water in the pressure cooker will boil at temperatures above 100°C, and food will cook faster.	***2 points possible*** *How a pressure cooker works.* *Pressure above liquid in a pressure cooker is the sum of the atmospheric pressure and the pressure of the steam.* *More heat is required for water to boil at higher pressures.*
(c) You are scheduled to compete in an ice-skating race. The salesman recommends a pair of ice skates with thinner blades, saying that they will make you skate faster. The negative slope of the solid-liquid curve in a phase diagram for H_2O means that the melting point of ice decreases with increasing external pressure. Pressure is defined as force per unit area. With thinner blades, and keeping the weight of the skater constant, there is more pressure exerted on the ice. Consequently, at a temperature lower than 0°C, the ice under the skates melts and the film of water formed under the blades facilitates the movement of the skater over the ice.	***2 points possible*** *Melting point of ice decreases with increasing external pressure.* *Thinner blades result in higher pressures.*
(d) You are at a grocery store trying to decide on which coffee to buy. The store clerk says to buy freeze-dried coffee as it is much fresher than other types on the shelf. Freeze drying coffee first involves brewing the coffee. The coffee is then frozen within a container that continuously maintains a very low pressure. The lower pressure over the coffee causes the water to sublime (pass from the solid frozen state to the gaseous state). When most of the water that was used to brew the coffee has been removed, the solid coffee that remains is then packaged. The advantage of freeze-dried coffee is that the molecules responsible for flavor are not destroyed during prolonged heating.	***2 points possible*** *Frozen coffee is placed in a container with low pressure.* *The pressure above the frozen coffee is lowered.* *The solid, frozen coffee sublimes; the frozen H_2O turns directly into water vapor, which is removed.*

(e) There has been a severe drought where you live. You turn to the local news, and they announce that the county has hired a firm to "seed" the clouds with granulated dry ice. Clouds consist of fine water droplets. In order for rain to form, small particles are necessary for the water molecules to cluster to. As heat is removed from the water vapor due to the sublimation of CO_2, the temperature of the water vapor in the clouds decreases, eventually leading to ice-crystal formation.	***2 points possible*** *Small particles are required for rain to form.* *As heat is removed from the water vapor due to the sublimation of CO_2, the temperature of the water vapor in the clouds decreases.* *Ice-crystal formation results in particles around which water vapor can collect and form rain.*
(f) You're reading an article on how the government plans to build a new magnetic rail system and supercomputers using superconductors. At ordinary temperatures, metals have some resistance to the flow of electrons due to the vibration of the atoms, which scatter the electrons. As the temperature is lowered, the atoms vibrate less and the resistance eventually approaches zero. If an electrical current is started in a superconducting ring, it will continue essentially forever. Superconductors are also perfectly diamagnetic (i.e., they repel a magnetic field). A magnetic field induces a current in a conductor; conversely, a current induces a magnetic field. When a magnet approaches a superconductor, it induces a current in the superconductor. Because there is no resistance to the current, it continues to flow, thus inducing its own magnetic field which then repels the magnet's field. If the magnet is sufficiently small and strong, the repulsion will be enough to counterbalance the pull of gravity and the magnet will levitate above the surface of the superconductor.	***2 points possible*** *Metals at ordinary temperatures have some resistance to the flow of electrons.* *Lower temperatures result in less resistance to the flow of electrons.* *Resistance eventually reaches zero.* *Superconductors are diamagnetic and repel magnetic fields.* *Magnets induce electrical current in superconductors.* *Magnetic repulsion in superconductors will levitate the magnet.*

Question 2

Maximum Points for Question 2
Part (a): 3 points
Part (b): 2 points
Part (c): 2 points
Part (d): 3 points
Total points: 10

2. A student places 500. mL of cold distilled water into a beaker. She then heats the distilled water with a Bunsen burner and notices several unique events. Explain each of the following events from a chemical and/or physical standpoint. *(a) Ripples occur in the water as the water heats.* The ripples are called Schleeren patterns and arise from light being diffracted off of the regions of water with different temperatures and hence different densities. This is the same optical effect that gives rise to mirages. Since the water is being heated from below, the lighter, warm water will rise in the beaker causing cooler surface water to flow to the bottom.	***3 points possible*** *1 point: concept of diffraction.* *1 point: concept of density—warmer water will rise.* *1 point: connection between water at different temperatures will have different densities.*
(b) Around 80°C, small bubbles were observed on the inner surface of the beaker. These bubbles are the air that was dissolved in the water at room temperature coming out of solution. Air becomes less soluble in water as the temperature goes up.	***2 points possible*** *1 point: when water is heated, it cannot hold as much gas.* *1 point: bubbles at this point contain air.*
(c) As she continued to heat the water she began to observe bubbles form and collapse on the bottom of the beaker. These bubbles are the precursors to true boiling. The water on the bottom surface of the beaker is heated to the point where it converts to vapor, but this vapor cools rapidly as it expands and as it encounters slightly cooler water just above the bottom of the beaker.	***2 points possible*** *1 point: water near bottom of beaker converts to steam.* *1 point: gas cools as it expands.*
(d) Bubbles rose from the bottom and broke free at the top. As the bulk water in the beaker becomes hot, the bubbles begin to break free of the bottom and rise. The bubbles that form at the boiling point contain water vapor. In order for a bubble to exist, the pressure of the vapor in the bubble must be pushing against the water with exactly the same force that the water is pushing back. Vapor pressure is determined by both temperature and by intermolecular forces. Only when the water in the beaker is uniformly hot will the bubbles rise from the bottom and break free at the top. This is often called a rolling boil and is the point of true boiling.	***3 points possible*** *1 point: pressure inside bubble equals pressure outside of bubble.* *1 point: description of what causes vapor pressure.* *1 point: definition and explanation of true boiling.*

Thermodynamics

You'll Need to Know

- ❑ the definition of energy and it different forms
- ❑ what are the units in which energy can be expressed
- ❑ the difference between temperature and heat
- ❑ what constitutes a system vs. the surroundings
- ❑ what are state functions
- ❑ what constitutes "standard state"
- ❑ what are the Laws of Thermodynamics:
    - ❑ First Law
    - ❑ Second Law
    - ❑ Third Law
- ❑ what is enthalpy and how is it measured
- ❑ the difference between endothermic and exothermic
- ❑ how to calculate problems involving enthalpy
- ❑ what is Hess's Law and how to solve problems involving it
- ❑ what is heat of formation and how to solve problems involving it
- ❑ what is specific heat and how to solve problems involving it
- ❑ what is heat capacity and how to solve problems involving it
- ❑ what is calorimetry (both constant volume and constant pressure) and how to solve problems involving it
- ❑ what is entropy and how to solve problems involving it
- ❑ what is Gibbs Free Energy and how to solve problems involving it
- ❑ how to draw and interpret energy diagrams
- ❑ what catalysts are, how they function and how they affect energy diagrams

Energy

Energy is the capacity to do work. Two forms of energy important in chemistry are: (1) thermal energy, which is energy associated with the random motion of atoms and molecules and can be calculated from temperature measurements and (2) chemical energy, which is energy stored within the molecules and can be determined by the type and arrangement of atoms in a substance. Energy is usually expressed in kilojoules (kJ).

Temperature vs. Heat

Temperature is the measure of the average kinetic energy of the particles in a sample of matter—expressed in degrees. Heat is the transfer of thermal energy between two objects that are at different temperatures. Heat flows from hotter objects to colder objects. The study of heat that involves chemical reactions is called thermochemistry. A cup of boiling water at 100°C has a higher temperature than a swimming pool of water at 20°C; but, the water in the swimming pool would have more total thermal energy and, likewise, more heat content.

A System vs. Surroundings

A system involves just the substances involved in chemical and physical changes; everything else outside the system is known as the surroundings. There are three types of systems: (1) open, which can exchange mass and heat energy with the surroundings; (2) closed, only heat energy (not mass) is allowed to be transferred to the surroundings; and (3) isolated, neither mass nor energy is transferred to the surroundings.

State Functions

The values of state functions (e.g., ΔH, ΔG, ΔS) are fixed when temperature, pressure, composition, and physical form are specified. They depend ONLY on the change between the initial and final state of a system and do not depend on the process by which the change occurred; they are independent of the reaction pathway.

Standard State

If you see a "°" following a symbol (example: $\Delta H°$ or $\Delta G°$) it means conditions are "standard state". Standard state conditions are: all gases are at 1 atm pressure; all solids and liquids are pure; all solutions are 1-molar (1*M*) in concentration; and the temperature is 298K (25°C).

Laws of Thermodynamics

- The **First Law of Thermodynamics** is, the total quantity of energy in the universe is assumed to remain constant. Energy cannot be created nor destroyed, it can only be converted from one form to another.
- The **Second Law of Thermodynamics** says, reactions that are spontaneous must lead to an increase in the entropy of the universe ($\Delta S_{univ} > 0$). Reactions that are spontaneous in one direction cannot be spontaneous in the opposite direction (you can't have it both ways).
- The **Third Law of Thermodynamics** is the entropy of a perfect crystal at 0K is zero; this allows us to calculate the entropy of any substance.

Enthalpy

The change in enthalpy for a reaction (ΔH) is the overall measure of the energy that is absorbed to break bonds and the energy released when bonds form. A reaction is said to be "spontaneous" if it occurs without being driven by some outside force. There are two driving forces for all chemical reactions: enthalpy and entropy.

$$\Delta H = \Sigma H_{(products)} - \Sigma H_{(reactants)}$$

Exothermic ($-\Delta H$) gives off heat (favors spontaneous reactions)	Products have stronger bonds (lower enthalpy) than reactants.	Products are more stable than reactants.
Endothermic ($+\Delta H$) absorbs heat (favors non-spontaneous reactions)	Products have weaker bonds (higher enthalpy) than reactants.	Products are less stable than reactants.

Hess's Law

If you can break a chemical reaction up into a series of steps, just add up all the ΔH's for each step to get the overall ΔH for the reaction.

1. Write the overall equation for the reaction if not given.
2. Manipulate the given equations for the steps of the reaction so they add up to the overall equation. If you reverse an equation, reverse the sign of ΔH. If you multiply equations to obtain a correct coefficient, you must also multiply the ΔH by this coefficient.
3. Add up the equations canceling common substances in reactant and product.
4. Add up all the heats of the steps.

Example

Q. Calculate the heat of combustion of methane into gaseous H_2O given the information below:

$$2O_{(g)} \rightarrow O_{2\,(g)} \qquad \Delta H^\circ = -249\text{ kJ/mol}$$
$$2H_{(g)} + O_{(g)} \rightarrow H_2O_{(g)} \qquad \Delta H^\circ = -803\text{ kJ/mol}$$
$$C_{(graphite)} + 2O_{(g)} \rightarrow CO_{2\,(g)} \qquad \Delta H^\circ = -643\text{ kJ/mol}$$
$$C_{(graphite)} + 2H_{2\,(g)} \rightarrow CH_{4\,(g)} \qquad \Delta H^\circ = -75\text{ kJ/mol}$$
$$2H_{(g)} \rightarrow H_{2\,(g)} \qquad \Delta H^\circ = -436\text{ kJ/mol}$$

A. –100. kJ/mol
B. –201 kJ/mol
C. –402 kJ/mol
D. –804 kJ/mol
E. +804 kJ/mol

A. D.

$$CH_{4\,(g)} \rightarrow \cancel{C_{(graphite)}} + \cancel{2H_{2\,(g)}} \qquad \Delta H^\circ = +75\text{ kJ/mol*}$$
$$\cancel{C_{(graphite)}} + \cancel{2O_{(g)}} \rightarrow CO_{2\,(g)} \qquad \Delta H^\circ = -643\text{ kJ/mol*}$$
$$2O_{2\,(g)} \rightarrow \cancel{4O_{(g)}} \qquad \Delta H^\circ = 498\text{ kJ/mol*}$$
$$\cancel{4H_{(g)}} + \cancel{2O_{(g)}} \rightarrow 2H_2O_{(g)} \qquad \Delta H^\circ = -1606\text{ kJ/mol*}$$
$$\cancel{2H_{2\,(g)}} \rightarrow \cancel{4H_{(g)}} \qquad \Delta H^\circ = 872\text{ kJ/mol*}$$
$$CH_{4\,(g)} + 2O_{2\,(g)} \rightarrow CO_{2\,(g)} + 2H_2O_{(g)} \qquad \Delta H^\circ = -804\text{ kJ/mol}$$

** Remember to reverse the sign of ΔH° if the reaction is reversed. Also remember to multiply the value of ΔH° if necessary. For example, for $2O_{2(g)} \rightarrow 4O_{(g)}$, the reaction was reversed so the sign of ΔH° was changed from negative to positive AND the equation was doubled, therefore the value of ΔH° was likewise doubled.*

Heat of Formation (ΔH°_f)

The heat change that results when one mole of a compound is formed from its elements at a pressure of 1 atm. By convention, the standard enthalpy of formation for any element in its most stable form is 0.

Example

Q. The heat of formation of $CO_{2(g)}$ and $H_2O_{(l)}$ are –394 kJ/mole and –285.8 kJ/mole, respectively. Using the data for the following combustion reaction, calculate the heat of formation of $C_3H_{4(g)}$.

$$C_3H_{4(g)} + 4O_{2(g)} \rightarrow 3CO_{2(g)} + 2H_2O_{(l)} \qquad \Delta H = -1939.1 \text{ kJ}$$

A. To solve this problem, use Hess's Law and reverse the reaction above to make $C_3H_{4(g)}$ a product (remember to reverse the sign) and then add together the reactions for the heat of formation of $CO_{2(g)}$ and $H_2O_{(l)}$, remembering that the intermediates (H_2O, O_2, and CO_2) need to be eliminated so that all that ends up on the right side is $C_3H_{4(g)}$.

$$\cancel{3CO_{2(g)}} + \cancel{2H_2O_{(l)}} \rightarrow C_3H_{4(g)} + \cancel{4O_{2(g)}} \qquad \Delta H_1 = +1939.1 \text{ kJ}$$

$$3C_{(s)} + \cancel{3O_{2(g)}} \rightarrow \cancel{3CO_{2(g)}} \qquad \Delta H^\circ_f = 3(-394 \text{ kJ/mol})$$

$$2H_{2(g)} + \cancel{2\left(\frac{1}{2}\right)O_{2(g)}} \rightarrow \cancel{2H_2O_{(l)}} \qquad \Delta H^\circ_f = 2(-285.8 \text{ kJ/mol})$$

$$3C_{(s)} + 2H_{2(g)} \rightarrow C_3H_{4(g)} \qquad \Delta H^\circ_f = 185.5 \text{ kJ/mole}$$

Specific Heat and Heat Capacity

Specific heat (c) is the amount of heat required to raise the temperature of 1 gram of a substance by 1°C; the units are $J \cdot g^{-1} \cdot {}^\circ C^{-1}$. Heat capacity ($C_p$ for constant pressure, C_v for constant volume) is the amount of heat required to raise the temperature of a given quantity (m) of substance by 1°C and is measured in $J \cdot {}^\circ C^{-1}$. q represents the amount of heat released or absorbed and is measured in kJ (negative = exothermic, positive = endothermic).

$$C_p = m \cdot c$$

$$C_p = \frac{\Delta H}{\Delta T}$$

$$\text{where } \Delta T = T_{final} - T_{initial}$$

$$q = m \cdot c \cdot \Delta T$$

$$q = C_p \cdot \Delta T$$

Examples

Q. 100. grams of water is heated from 20°C to 30°C. The specific heat of water is 4.184 $J \cdot g^{-1} \cdot {}^\circ C^{-1}$. Calculate the amount of heat absorbed by the water.

A. $q = m \cdot c \cdot \Delta T = (100.\text{ g})(4.184 \text{ J} \cdot g^{-1} \cdot {}^\circ C^{-1})(30.0^\circ C - 20.0^\circ C) = 4.18 \times 10^3 \text{ J} = 4.18 \text{ kJ}$

Q. **100. grams of aluminum foil at 20.0°C is placed in contact with 10.0 grams of iron foil at 60.0°C. The specific heat of aluminum is 0.900 J · g^{-1} · °C^{-1} and the specific heat of iron is 0.444 J · g^{-1} · °C^{-1}. Assuming that no heat is lost to the surroundings, what is the final temperature of the combined metals?**

A. According to the Law of Conservation of Energy, the heat gained by the aluminum will be equal to the heat lost by the iron (heat flows from warmer objects to cooler objects): $q_{Al} = -q_{Fe}$.

$q_{Al} = m \cdot c \cdot \Delta T = (100.\ g)(0.900\ J \cdot g^{-1} \cdot {}^\circ C^{-1})(T_f - 20.0^\circ C)$

$q_{Fe} = m \cdot c \cdot \Delta T = (10.0\ g)(0.444\ J \cdot g^{-1} \cdot {}^\circ C^{-1})(T_f - 60.0^\circ C)$

$(100.\ g)(0.900\ J \cdot g^{-1} \cdot {}^\circ C^{-1})(T_f - 20.0^\circ C) = -(10.0\ g)(0.444\ J \cdot g^{-1} \cdot {}^\circ C^{-1})(T_f - 60.0^\circ C)$

$T_f = 17.9^\circ C$

Calorimetry

A coffee-cup calorimeter (see diagram below) can be used to determine heats of reactions for neutralization reactions and heats of dilution. The coffee cup is not sealed so the pressure is constant atmospheric air pressure. Furthermore, since the measurements are carried out at constant atmospheric pressure, $q_{rxn} = \Delta H$.

$$q_{rxn} = \Delta H$$
$$q_{rxn} = -(q_{soln} + q_{calorimeter})$$
$$q_{calorimeter} = C_{calorimeter} \cdot \Delta T$$

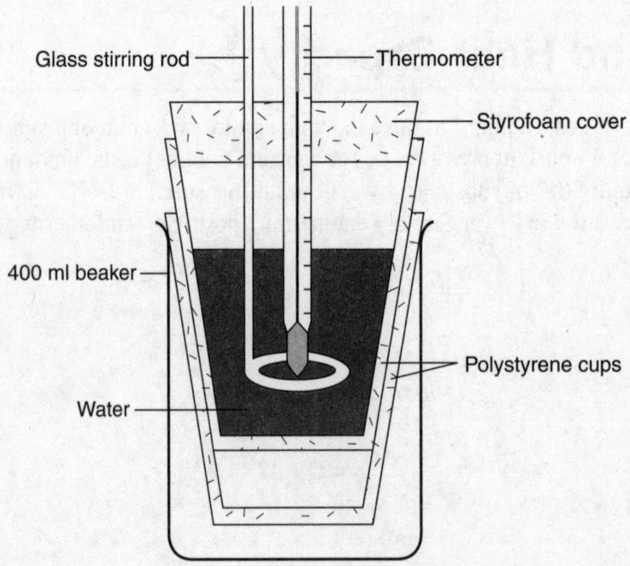

Example

Q. 100. mL of a 1.00 *M* HCl solution was mixed with 100. mL of 2.00 *M* NaOH in a coffee-cup calorime The coffee-cup calorimeter had a heat capacity of 500. J/°C. The temperatures of both the HCl and the NaOH solutions were initially both 30.0°C and at the end of the experiment, the final temperature reache was 40.0°C. Assume the densities and specific heats of both the HCl and the NaOH solutions were the same as the values for water (1.00 g/mL for density and 4.184 J · g^{-1} · °C^{-1} for specific heat). Calculate the heat of neutralization for the reaction.

A. $q_{rxn} = -(q_{soln} + q_{calorimeter})$

The limiting reactant is HCl (there are less moles of H^+ (0.100 L) (1.00 *M* HCl) = 0.100 mols than OH^- (0.100 L) (2.00 *M* NaOH) = 0.200 mols).

$100.\ \cancel{\text{mL}} \times 1.00\ \text{g}/\cancel{\text{mL}} = 100.\ \text{g}$

$q_{soln} = m \cdot c \cdot \Delta T = (100.\ \cancel{\text{g}} + 100.\ \cancel{\text{g}})\ (4.184\ \text{J} \cdot \cancel{\text{g}^{-1}} \cdot \cancel{°\text{C}^{-1}})\ (40.0\cancel{°\text{C}} - 30.0\cancel{°\text{C}})$

$= 8.37 \times 10^3\ \text{J}$

$q_{calorimeter} = C_{calorimeter} \cdot \Delta T = (500.\ \text{J}/\cancel{°\text{C}})\ (10.0\cancel{°\text{C}}) = 5.00 \times 10^3\ \text{J}$

$q_{rxn} = -(q_{soln} + q_{calorimeter}) = -(8.37 \times 10^3\ \text{J} + 5.00 \times 10^3\ \text{J}) = -1.34 \times 10^4\ \text{J} = -13.4\ \text{kJ}$

$$q_{neutralization} = \frac{-13.4\ \text{kJ}}{0.100\ \text{moles}\ H^+} = -134\ \text{kJ/mol HCl reacted}$$

Entropy (Δ*S*)

Entropy is a measure of the randomness or disorder of a system. The greater the disorder, the greater the entropy (e.g., dust in the air would have a higher entropy than atoms arranged in a crystal lattice). In terms of entropy: (1) gases have higher entropy than liquids and liquids have higher entropy than solids (g > *l* > s); (2) when a pure solid or liquid dissolves in a solvent, the entropy of the substance increases; (3) when a gas molecule escapes from a solvent, there is an increase in entropy; (4) entropy generally increases with increasing molecular complexity; and (5) reactions that increase the number of moles of particles often increase the entropy of the system.

$$\Delta S° = \Sigma S°_{products} - \Sigma S°_{reactants}$$

Examples

Q. Consider the following reactions and predict whether the entropy change (Δ*S*) is positive or negative.

(a) $Na^+_{(aq)} + Cl^-_{(aq)} \rightarrow NaCl_{(s)}$
(b) $NH_4Cl_{(s)} \rightarrow NH_{3(g)} + HCl_{(g)}$
(c) $2NH_{3(g)} + CO_{2(g)} \rightarrow NH_2CONH_{2(aq)} + H_2O_{(l)}$
(d) $C_2H_5OH_{(l)} + 3O_{2(g)} \rightarrow 2CO_{2(g)} + 3H_2O_{(g)}$

A. (a) Δ*S* is negative. The $Na^+_{(aq)}$ and $Cl^-_{(aq)}$ ions are free to move in solution. $NaCl_{(s)}$ is a solid and the particles are held in a crystal lattice. Furthermore, there are two particles on the reactant side and only one particle on the product side.

(b) Δ*S* is positive. The reaction proceeds from an orderly solid state to a disordered gaseous state.

(c) Δ*S* is negative. The initial reactants are gases (disorder) and the product are solution and liquid (more order).

(d) Δ*S* is positive. The number of total moles of gas for the final products is greater than the reactants.

... the standard entropy change (ΔS°_{rxn}) that occurs when methane combusts ... xide and water.

Substance	S° ($J \cdot K^{-1} \cdot mol^{-1}$)
$CH_{4(g)}$	186.19
$O_{2(g)}$	205.0
$CO_{2(g)}$	213.6
$H_2O_{(l)}$	69.9

A. $CH_{4(g)} + 2O_{2(g)} \rightarrow CO_{2(g)} + 2H_2O_{(l)}$

$$\Delta S^\circ_{rxn} = \Sigma S^\circ_{\text{products}} - \Sigma S^\circ_{\text{reactants}} = \left(S^\circ_{CO_2} + 2S^\circ_{H_2O}\right) - \left(S^\circ_{CH_4} + 2S^\circ_{O_2}\right)$$
$$= \left[213.6 + 2(69.9) - \left(186.19 + 2(205.0)\right)\right]$$
$$= -242.8\ \text{J} \cdot \text{K}^{-1}$$

Gibbs Free Energy (ΔG)

Gibbs free energy is the energy associated with a chemical reaction that can be used to do work. It can be used to determine if a reaction is spontaneous or not. Pure elements at standard conditions are assigned a $\Delta G_f^\circ = 0$. If $\Delta G < 0$, the reaction is spontaneous in the forward direction. If $\Delta G = 0$, the reaction is at equilibrium (this will be reviewed in Chapter 10, "Equilibrium"). If $\Delta G > 0$, then the reaction is nonspontaneous in the forward direction, but the reverse reaction will be spontaneous. The relationship $\Delta G = \Delta G^\circ + RT \ln K$ will be also be discussed in more detail in Chapter 10.

$$\Delta G^\circ = \Sigma \Delta G_f^\circ{}_{\text{(products)}} - \Sigma \Delta G_f^\circ{}_{\text{(reactants)}}$$
$$\Delta G^\circ = \Delta H^\circ - T\Delta S^\circ \text{ (standard state)}$$
$$\Delta G = \Delta H - T\Delta S \text{ (non-standard state)}$$
$$\Delta G = \Delta G^\circ + RT \ln K$$

ΔH	ΔS	$-T\Delta S$	ΔG
– exothermic	+ products more disordered	– favors spontaneity	– spontaneous at *all* T
– exothermic	– products less disordered	+ opposes spontaneity	(–) spontaneous at *low* T (+) non-spontaneous at *high* T *"Enthalpically-driven process"*
+ endothermic	+ products more disordered	– favors spontaneity	(+) non-spontaneous at *low* T (–) spontaneous at *high* T *"Entropically-driven process"*
+ endothermic	– products less disordered	+ opposes spontaneity	+ non-spontaneous at *all* T

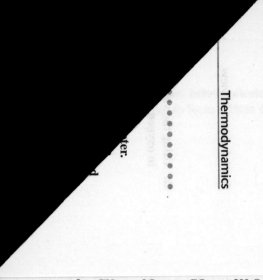

Examples

Q. Ammonium nitrate dissolves in water to form ammonium and nitrate ions. Given the following information at standard conditions, calculate $\Delta H°$, $\Delta S°$, and $\Delta G°$ and determine if the reaction is spontaneous or not.

A. $NH_4NO_{3(s)} \rightarrow NH_4{}^+{}_{(aq)} + NO_3{}^-{}_{(aq)}$

Compound	$\Delta H_f°$ ($kJ \cdot mol^{-1}$)	$S°$ ($J \cdot mol^{-1} \cdot K^{-1}$)
$NH_4NO_{3(s)}$	−366	151
$NH_4{}^+{}_{(aq)}$	−133	113
$NO_3{}^-{}_{(aq)}$	−205	146

$\Delta H° = \Sigma\Delta H_f°{}_{(products)} - \Sigma\Delta H_f°{}_{(reactants)}$

$\Delta H° = [(-133 \text{ kJ}) + (-205 \text{ kJ})] - (-366 \text{ kJ}) = 28 \text{ kJ}$

$\Delta S° = \Sigma S°{}_{(products)} - \Sigma S°{}_{(reactants)}$

$\Delta S° = (113 \text{ J} \cdot \text{K}^{-1} + 146 \text{ J} \cdot \text{K}^{-1}) - 151 \text{ J} \cdot \text{K}^{-1}$

$\Delta S° = 108 \text{ J} \cdot \text{K}^{-1} = 0.108 \text{ kJ} \cdot \text{K}^{-1}$

$T = 25°\text{C} + 273 = 298\text{K}$

$\Delta G° = \Delta H° - T\Delta S° = 28 \text{ kJ} - 298\cancel{\text{K}}(0.108 \text{ kJ} \cdot \cancel{\text{K}^{-1}}) = -4 \text{ kJ}$

$\therefore$ since $\Delta G° < 0$, the reaction is spontaneous.

Q. Calculate $\Delta G°$ at 298K for the Haber reaction starting with 1.0 atm $N_{2(g)}$, 3.0 atm $H_{2(g)}$, and 1.0 atm $NH_{3(g)}$. $\Delta G° = -33.3$ kJ

A. $N_{2(g)} + 3H_{2(g)} \rightleftharpoons 2NH_{3(g)}$

$\Delta G = \Delta G° + RT \ln K$

$K = 1.0^2 / (1.0 \times 3.0^3)$

$K = 3.7 \times 10^{-2}$

$\Delta G = -33.3 \text{ kJ} + [8.314 \text{ J}/\cancel{\text{K}} \times 298\cancel{\text{K}} \times \ln(3.7 \times 10^{-2})]$

$\Delta G = -33.3 \text{ kJ} - 8.17 \text{ kJ} = -41.5 \text{ kJ}$

The results follow Le Chatelier's principle: Adding more $H_{2(g)}$ would drive the reaction to the right.

** At standard conditions the pressure of all components is 1 atm. We use ΔG in this case because not all pressures are 1 atm.*

Energy Diagrams

Only a very small fraction of collisions that occur result in a reaction because: (1) The colliding molecules must be oriented in exactly the correct way for the product molecule bonds to be formed, and (2) the two molecules must collide with sufficient energy to overcome the activation energy of the reaction. The activation energy (E_a) is defined as the minimum energy needed to initiate a chemical reaction.

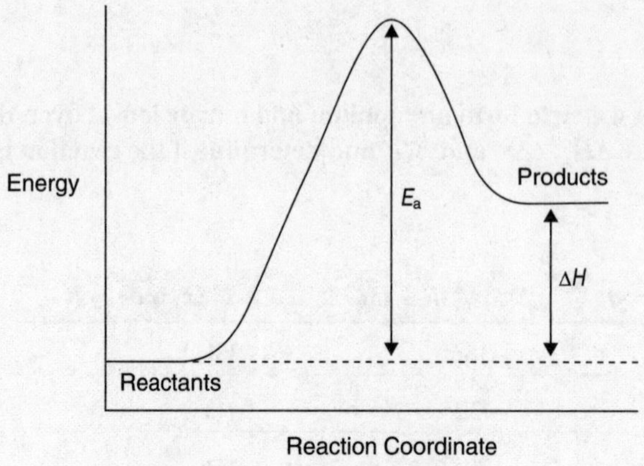

Endothermic

(The energy of the products is less than the energy of the reactants.)

Catalyst Added

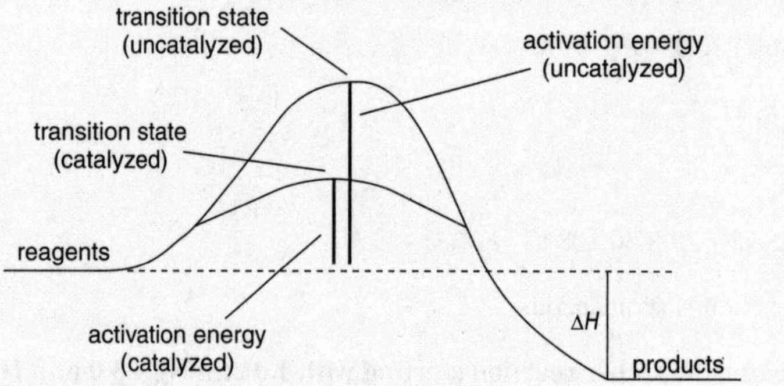

Because the catalyzed activation energy is lower than the uncatalyzed activation energy, this reaction will take place more quickly. Keep in mind, though, that the transition state is totally different for the catalyzed reaction.

Multiple-Choice Questions

1. 216 J of energy is required to raise the temperature of a piece of aluminum from 15.0°C to 35.0°C. Calculate the mass of the aluminum used. The specific heat capacity of aluminum is 0.90 J · °C^{-1} · g^{-1}.

A. 12.0 g
B. 15.0 g
C. 18.0 g
D. 21.0 g
E. 24.0 g

2. Two solutions, both at the same temperature, are mixed. After mixing, the temperature drops dramatically. Which of the following is/are true?

I. Products have stronger bonds (lower enthalpy) than reactants.

II. Products have weaker bonds (higher enthalpy) than reactants.

III. Products are more stable than reactants.

IV. Products are less stable than reactants.

A. I
B. III
C. I and III
D. II and IV
E. IV

3. In neutralizing 750 mL of 1.0 *M* HCl with 450 mL of 1.0 *M* NaOH, the temperature of the solution rises 5.0°C. Given that the density of the solution is 1.0 g/mL and the specific heat of the solution is 4.184 J/(g · °C), what is the approximate energy released from this experiment?

A. 5,000 J
B. 12,000 J
C. 25,000 J
D. 50,000 J
E. 100,000 J

4.

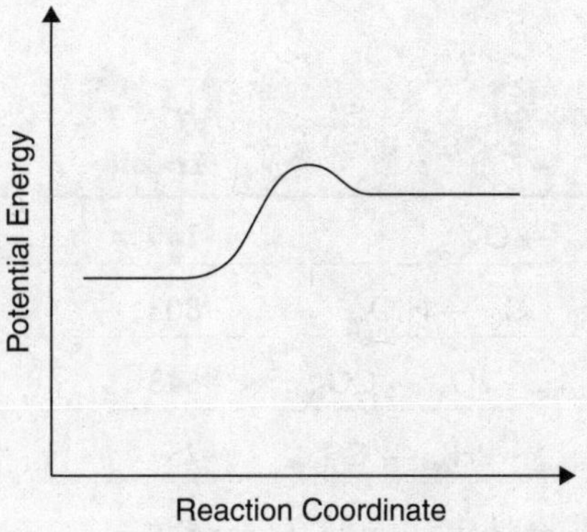

The graph above describes pathway of reaction that is

A. exothermic and with 0 activation energy requirements.
B. exothermic and with a low activation energy.
C. exothermic and with a high activation energy.
D. endothermic and with a low activation energy.
E. endothermic and with a high activation energy.

5. Use the bond energies below to estimate the enthalpy, ΔH, for the following reaction:

$$C_2H_{4(g)} + Cl_{2(g)} \rightarrow ClH_2C\text{–}CH_2Cl_{(g)}$$

Bond	Bond Energies (kJ · mol^{-1})
C–C	347
C=C	620
C–Cl	331
C–H	414
Cl–Cl	243

A. –279 kJ
B. –146 kJ
C. 0 kJ
D. 146 kJ
E. 279 kJ

6. A reaction has both positive $\Delta S°$ and $\Delta H°$ values. From this information alone, you can conclude that the reaction

A. can be spontaneous at any temperature.
B. cannot be spontaneous at any temperature.
C. cannot be spontaneous at high temperatures.
D. can be spontaneous only at low temperatures.
E. can be spontaneous only at high temperatures.

7. Using the reaction and information below, how much heat is released when 72.0 grams of ethanol is burned in excess oxygen?

$$C_2H_5OH_{(l)} + 3O_{2(g)} \rightarrow 2CO_{2(g)} + 3H_2O_{(l)}$$
$$\Delta H° = -1.40 \times 10^3 \text{ kJ}$$

A. 8.77×10^1 kJ
B. 1.53×10^2 kJ
C. 2.19×10^3 kJ
D. 2.80×10^3 kJ
E. 2.80×10^6 kJ

8. Which of the following is not expected to have a value of zero at 25°C and 1 atm?

A. ΔH°_f for $F_{2(g)}$
B. ΔG°_f for $Li_{(s)}$
C. S° for $Fe_{(s)}$
D. ΔH°_f for $Mg_{(s)}$
E. All choices have values equal to 0.

9. Consider the following hypothetical reaction (at 375K). The standard free energies in kJ/mol are given below each substance in parentheses. What is the value of the Gibb's free energy for the reaction at this temperature? Is the reaction spontaneous?

3A	→	B	+ 2C
(–30.0)		(150.0)	(–270.0)

A. –300.0 kJ; spontaneous
B. 0 kJ; at equilibrium
C. 300 kJ; non-spontaneous
D. 600.0 kJ; non-spontaneous
E. 900.0 kJ; spontaneous

10. What is ΔH for the reaction whose energy diagram is presented below?

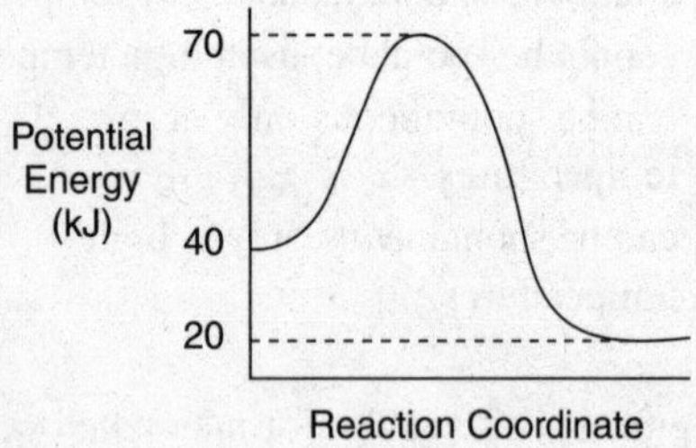

A. –70kJ
B. –30 kJ
C. –20 kJ
D. 20 kJ
E. 50 kJ

11. Which of the following are NOT exothermic processes or reactions?

I. The evaporation of a volatile liquid
II. The sublimation of dry ice
III. Water boiling to produce steam
IV. Water freezing to produce ice

A. I
B. II
C. III
D. II and IV
E. I, II and III

12.

Reaction	ΔH° (kJ · mol^{-1})
$2O_{(g)} \rightarrow O_{2(g)}$	–249
$2H_{(g)} + O_{(g)} \rightarrow H_2O_{(g)}$	–803
$C_{(graphite)} + 2O_{(g)} \rightarrow CO_{2(g)}$	–643
$C_{(graphite)} + 2H_{2(g)} \rightarrow CH_{4(g)}$	–75
$2H_{(g)} \rightarrow H_{2(g)}$	–436

Based on the information above, what is the standard enthalpy change for the combustion of methane?

A. –804 kJ · mol^{-1}
B. 0 kJ · mol^{-1}
C. 402 kJ · mol^{-1}
D. 804 kJ · mol^{-1}
E. 1608 kJ · mol^{-1}

13. Given the following reactions, which of them would involve a negative entropy change?

I. $2KClO_{3(s)} \rightarrow 2KCl_{(s)} + 3O_{2(g)}$
II. $C_{(s)} + O_{2(g)} \rightarrow CO_{2(g)}$
III. $2K_{(s)} + 2H_2O_{(l)} \rightarrow 2KOH_{(aq)} + H_{2(g)}$
IV. $O_{2(g)} \rightarrow 2O_{(g)}$
V. $2KOH_{(aq)} + CO_{2(g)} \rightarrow K_2CO_{3(aq)} + H_2O_{(l)}$

A. I and II
B. III and IV
C. IV and V
D. V
E. I, II, III, IV

14. An experiment was performed and it was determined that X + 2Y → 3Z. A catalyst was added to the reactants to speed up the reaction. From the data obtained, the following diagram was constructed.

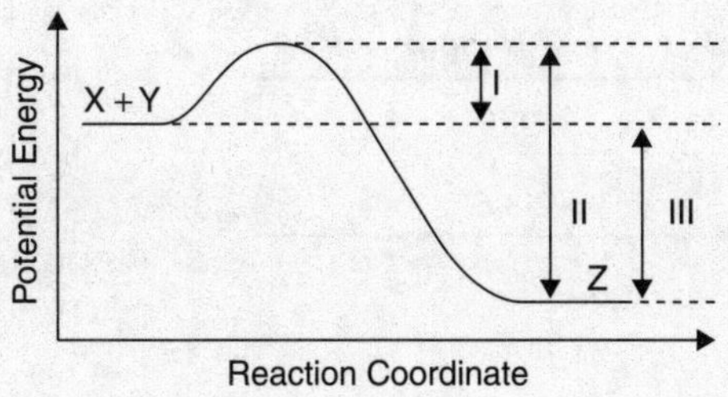

Which of the following will NOT be affected by the catalyst?

I. The rate of the reaction
II. The yield of Z
III. Arrow I
IV. Arrow II
V. Arrow III

A. I and II
B. II and III
C. II and V
D. I, II and III
E. I, III, and V

15. The standard molar heat of vaporization of methanol is 35.3 kJ · mol^{-1} and the boiling point at 1 atm is 64.6°C. What is $\Delta S°$ for the vaporization of 0.50 mol of methanol?

A. 17.4 J · mol · K^{-1}
B. 52.3 J · K^{-1}
C. 76.3 J · K · mol^{-1}
D. 88.4 J/K
E. 332 J · K^{-1}

16. A certain non-spontaneous reaction has a ΔH of 12.3 kJ and a ΔS of 42 J/K. At approximately what temperature would the reaction become spontaneous?

A. –20°C
B. 0°C
C. 20°C
D. 100°C
E. 200°C

17. A student volunteers to bring ice tea to a class picnic. She boils water to which she has added tea bags. Time is running short, so she places the hot tea into an insulated, steel thermos container, adds some ice cubes and then seals the thermos. Assume that there is no heat exchange with the surroundings. Which of the following would be true?

A. The total energy and entropy both remain constant.
B. The total energy decreases while the entropy increases.
C. The total energy and entropy decreases.
D. The total energy increases while the entropy decreases.
E. None of the above.

18. 0.30 kg of ice at 0.0°C is added to 1.0 kg of water at 45°C. What is the final temperature, assuming there is no heat exchange with the surroundings? Specific heat capacity of water is 4200 J · kg^{-1} · K^{-1} and the specific latent heat of fusion of ice is 3.4×10^5 J · kg^{-1}

A. 0°C
B. 8°C
C. 16°C
D. 22°C
E. 44°C

19. Which of the following is/are true when ice melts?

A. $\Delta H -$ $\Delta S -$ $\Delta V -$
B. $\Delta H +$ $\Delta S +$ $\Delta V +$
C. $\Delta H\ 0$ $\Delta S\ 0$ $\Delta V\ 0$
D. $\Delta H -$ $\Delta S -$ $\Delta V -$
E. $\Delta H +$ $\Delta S +$ $\Delta V -$

20. What are the signs and/or values of $\Delta H°$ and $\Delta S°$ for the condensation of benzene, C_6H_6?

A. $\Delta H° = +$, $\Delta S° = +$
B. $\Delta H° = +$, $\Delta S° = -$
C. $\Delta H° = -$, $\Delta S° = +$
D. $\Delta H° = -$, $\Delta S° = -$
E. $\Delta H° = 0$, $\Delta S° = 0$

Free-Response Questions

1. For the reaction, $2CO_{(g)} + O_{2(g)} \rightleftharpoons 2CO_{2(g)}$; $\Delta H° = -566.0$ kilojoules. The data in the table below were determined at 1 atm and 25°C.

	$\Delta H_f°$ ($kJ \cdot mol^{-1}$)	$\Delta G_f°$ ($kJ \cdot mol^{-1}$)	$S°$ ($J \cdot mol^{-1} \cdot K^{-1}$)
$CO_{(g)}$	−110.5	−137.3	+197.9
$CO_{2(g)}$	−393.5	−394.4	+213.6

(a) Calculate $\Delta G°$ for the reaction above at 25°C.

(b) Calculate K_{eq} for the reaction above at 25°C.

(c) Calculate $\Delta S°$ for the reaction above at 25°C.

(d) In the table above, there are no data for O_2. What are the values of $\Delta H_f°$, $\Delta G_f°$, and of the absolute entropy, $S°$, for O_2 at 25°C?

2. (a) State the physical significance of entropy and how it relates to the Second and Third Laws of Thermodynamics, providing examples where necessary.

(b) From each of the following pairs of substances, choose the one expected to have the greater absolute entropy. Explain your choice in each case. Assume 1 mole of each substance.

(i) $Br_{2(l)}$ or $C_{(diamond)}$ at the same temperature and pressure.

(ii) $Ne_{(g)}$ at 2 atmosphere or $Ne_{(g)}$ at 1 atmosphere, both at the same temperature.

(iii) $H_2O_{(l)}$ or $CH_3OCH_{3(l)}$ at the same temperature and pressure.

(iv) $Fe_{(s)}$ at 20°C or $Fe_{(s)}$ at 200°C, both at the same pressure.

Answers and Explanations

Multiple Choice

1. **A.** $q = m \times c \times (T_f - T_i) = 216\ \cancel{J} = m \times 0.90\ \cancel{J} \cdot \cancel{°C^{-1}} \cdot g^{-1} \times (35.0\cancel{°C} - 15.0\cancel{°C})$

   $m = 12.0$ g

2. **D.** Refer to the chart in the enthalpy section.

3. **C.**

   $$\text{mass of solution} = \frac{750\ \cancel{mL} + 450\ \cancel{mL}}{1} \times \frac{1.0\text{ g}}{1\ \cancel{mL}} = 1{,}200\text{ g}$$

   $$q_{soln} = m \cdot c \cdot \Delta T = (1{,}200\text{ g})(4{,}184\text{ J}/(\cancel{g} \cdot \cancel{°C}))(5.0\cancel{°C}) = 25{,}000\text{ J}$$

4. **D.** Refer to the graphs above in the section, "Energy Diagrams".

5. **B.**

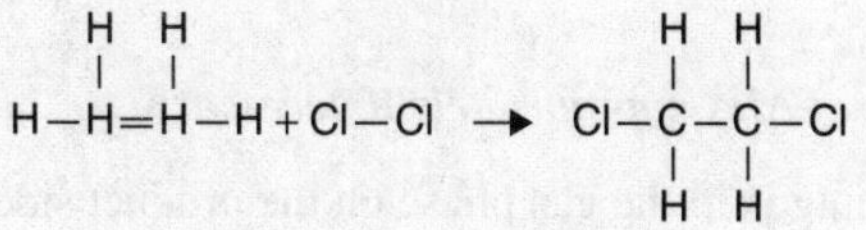

   Bonds broken: 4 C–H; 1 C=C; 1 Cl–Cl

   Bonds formed: 4 C–H; 1 C–C; 2 C–Cl

   $\Delta H° = \Sigma BE_{(reactants)} - \Sigma BE_{(products)}$ = total energy input – total energy released

   Note that the energy absorbed and released by the breaking and forming of the 4 C–H bonds cancels out.

   $\Delta H°$ = (620 kJ + 243 kJ) – [347 kJ + 2(331) kJ] = –146 kJ

6. **E.** With a positive value for ΔS, the $-T\Delta S$ term favors spontaneity. However, at low temperatures, its contribution will be small (magnitude of $-T\Delta S$ at low temperatures is small). In this case ΔH predominates and the reaction will be non-spontaneous (ΔG = positive). At higher temperatures, the magnitude of the $-T\Delta S$ term increases and can overwhelm the positive ΔH term. In this case, the $-T\Delta S$ predominates and the reaction is spontaneous (ΔG = negative at high temp).

7. **C.** $$\frac{1.40 \times 10^3\text{ kJ}}{1\ \cancel{mol\ C_2H_5OH}} \times \frac{1\ \cancel{mol\ C_2H_5OH}}{46.08\ \cancel{g\ C_2H_5OH}} \times \frac{72.0\ \cancel{g\ C_2H_5OH}}{1} = 2.19 \times 10^3\text{ kJ}$$

8. **C.** By definition, the standard enthalpy of formation of the most stable form of any element is zero because there is no formation reaction needed when the element is already in its standard state. The standard Gibbs free energy of formation of a compound is the change of energy that accompanies the formation of one mole of a substance from its component elements at their standard states (the most stable form of the element at 25°C and 1 atm). All elements in their standard states (O_2, $C_{(graphite)}$, etc.) have a $\Delta G°_f$ value of 0. The standard molar entropy is the entropy content of one mole of substance under conditions of standard temperature and pressure. The standard molar entropy is given the symbol $S°$, and the units are $J \cdot mol^{-1} \cdot K^{-1}$. According to the Third Law of Thermodynamics, unlike standard enthalpies of formation, the value of $S°$ is an absolute; that is, an element in its standard state has a nonzero value of $S°$ at room temperature, because only at 0 K is the entropy of an element $0\ J \cdot mol^{-1} \cdot K^{-1}$.

9. **A.** $\Delta G° = \Sigma \Delta G°_{(products)} - \Sigma \Delta G°_{(reactants)}$

   $\Delta G°$ = [150.0 kJ + 2(–270.0) kJ] – [3(–30.0) kJ] = –300.0 kJ

   $\Delta G°$ values that are negative are spontaneous.

10. **C.** The reaction is exothermic and ΔH must use a negative sign. Refer to the "Energy Diagrams" section above for review if you missed this question.

11. **E.** Evaporation (I), which occurs below the boiling point, and boiling (III) are transitions of a liquid to a vapor. Sublimation (II) is the transition of a solid to a vapor. Melting (fusion) is the transition of a solid to a liquid. All of these phase changes require the absorption of heat and so are endothermic. The reverse transitions give off heat and are exothermic.

12. **A.**

$$
\begin{array}{ll}
CH_{4\,(g)} \rightarrow \cancel{C_{(graphite)}} + \cancel{2H_{2\,(g)}} & \Delta H^\circ = 75\text{ kJ/mol*} \\
\cancel{C_{(graphite)}} + \cancel{2O_{(g)}} \rightarrow CO_{2\,(g)} & \Delta H^\circ = -643\text{ kJ/mol*} \\
2O_{2\,(g)} \rightarrow \cancel{4O_{(g)}} & \Delta H^\circ = 498\text{ kJ/mol*} \\
\cancel{4H_{(g)}} + \cancel{2O_{(g)}} \rightarrow 2H_2O_{(g)} & \Delta H^\circ = -1606\text{ kJ/mol*} \\
\cancel{2H_{2\,(g)}} \rightarrow \cancel{4H_{(g)}} & \Delta H^\circ = 872\text{ kJ/mol*} \\
\hline
CH_{4\,(g)} + 2O_{2\,(g)} \rightarrow CO_{2\,(g)} + 2H_2O_{(g)} & \Delta H^\circ = -804\text{ kJ/mol*}
\end{array}
$$

* *remember to reverse the sign of ΔH° and to multiply the value of ΔH° appropriately if necessary.*

13. **D.** I and III: One of the products is in the gas phase. II: Everything is in the gas phase on the product side, and CO_2 is a more complex molecule than O_2. IV: There are two gas-phase species on the product side and only one on the reactant side. V: The reactant side has a gas-phase molecule.

14. **C.** Catalysts do not affect the amount of product produced or the overall enthalpy of the reaction. Catalysts lower the activation required for a reaction to occur.

15. **B.** ***Hint:*** think of the units for ΔS° (J/K).

64.6°C + 273 = 337.6K

$$\Delta S^\circ_{vap} = \frac{\Delta H^\circ_{vap}}{T_{bp}} = \frac{0.50\ \cancel{\text{mol CH}_3\text{OH}}}{1} \times \frac{35.3\ \cancel{\text{kJ}}}{\cancel{\text{mol CH}_3\text{OH}} \cdot 337.6\text{ K}} \times \frac{10^3\text{ J}}{1\ \cancel{\text{kJ}}} = 52.3\text{ J/K}$$

16. **C.** $T = \frac{\Delta H}{\Delta S} = \frac{12{,}300\ \cancel{\text{J}}}{42\ \cancel{\text{J}}\text{/K}} = 293\text{ K} \qquad 293\text{ K} - 273 = 20^\circ\text{C}$

17. **E.** Isolated systems always maintain constant total energy while tending toward maximum entropy or disorder. The total energy in this isolated system remains constant, but the distribution of the energy changes with time. The Second Law of Thermodynamics says the entropy of a system will continue to increase until it attains some maximum value, which corresponds to the most probable state for the system (equilibrium). Heat will flow from the hot water to the ice cubes resulting in the ice cubes melting (entropy will increase as the solid changes to a liquid). At some point, the temperature will remain constant. In terms of energy, as long as the system is totally sealed from the surroundings, there will be no heat exchange and the energy within the system will remain constant. In practice, this does not occur with a thermos as some heat is always being lost to the surroundings.

18. **C.** Let x be the final temperature.

heat lost by water = heat gained in melting the ice + heat gained in warming the ice water

$$-(m_{H_2O})(c_{H_2O})(\Delta T_{H_2O}) = (m_{ice})(\Delta H_{fusion\,(ice)}) + (m_{ice})(c_{H_2O})(\Delta T_{melted\ ice})$$

$$-(1.0\text{ kg H}_2\text{O}) \times (4200\text{ J}\cdot\text{kg}^{-1}\cdot\text{K}^{-1}) \times (x - 45^\circ\text{C}) = (0.30\text{ kg}_{ice}) \times (3.4 \times 10^5\text{ J}\cdot\text{kg}^{-1}) + (0.30\text{ kg}_{ice}) \times (4200\text{ J}\cdot\text{kg}^{-1}\cdot\text{K}^{-1}) \times (x - 0.0^\circ\text{C})$$

$$-4200(x - 45) = (1.02 \times 10^5) + 1260x$$

$$(1.89 \times 10^5) - (1.02 \times 10^5) = 1260x + 4200x$$

$$x = 16^\circ\text{C}$$

19. **E.** Melting ice is an endothermic process (requires energy, $+\Delta H$). When H_2O goes from the solid state (ice) to the liquid state, the molecular arrangement is becoming more disordered (entropy increases, $\Delta S = +$). When ice melts to form liquid water, the uniform three-dimensional tetrahedral organization of the solid breaks down as thermal motions disrupt, distort, and occasionally break hydrogen bonds. It becomes denser and occupies less volume.

20. **D.** $C_6H_{6(g)} \rightarrow C_6H_{6(l)}$ (condensation) is an exothermic process, $\Delta H°$ is negative. A liquid, which results from the condensation of a gas, results in a more ordered system; therefore, $\Delta S°$ is negative.

Free Response

Question 1

Maximum Points for Question 1
Part (a): 2 points
Part (b): 2 points
Part (c): 2 points
Part (d): 3 points
Total points: 9

1. For the reaction, $2CO_{(g)} + O_{2(g)} \rightleftharpoons 2CO_{2(g)}$; $\Delta H° = -566.0$ kJ. The data in the table were determined at 1 atm and 25°C.	***2 points possible***
(a) Calculate $\Delta G°$ for the reaction above at 25°C.	
$\Delta G° = \Sigma\Delta G_f°{}_{\text{products}} - \Sigma\Delta G_f°{}_{\text{reactants}}$	*1 point for correct setup.*
$\Delta G° = 2(\Delta G_f°\ CO_{2(g)}) - [2(\Delta G_f°\ CO_{(g)}) + 0]$	
$\Delta G° = 2(-394.4\ \text{kJ/mol}) - [2(-137.3\ \text{kJ/mol}) + 0\ \text{kJ/mol}]$	
$\Delta G° = -514.2$ kJ/mol	*1 point for correct answer.*
(b) Calculate K_{eq} for the reaction above at 25°C.	***2 points possible***
$\Delta G° = -RT \ln K$ (or $-2.3\ RT \log K$)	*1 point for correct setup.*
25°C + 273 = 298 K	
$-514.2\ \cancel{\text{kJ}}/\cancel{\text{mol}} = -(8.31 \times 10^{-3}\ \cancel{\text{kJ}} \cdot \cancel{\text{mol}^{-1}} \cdot \cancel{\text{K}^{-1}})(298\cancel{\text{K}}) \ln K$	
$\ln K = 207.64$	
$K = \sim 2 \times 10^{90}$	*1 point for correct answer.*
(c) Calculate $\Delta S°$ for the reaction above at 25°C.	***2 points possible***
$\Delta G° = \Delta H° - T\Delta S°$	*1 point for correct setup.*
$-566.0\ \cancel{\text{kJ}} \times (10^3\ \text{J} / \cancel{\text{kJ}}) = -566{,}000$ J	
$-514{,}200\ \text{J} = -566{,}000\ \text{J} - 298\Delta S°$	
$\Delta S° = -51{,}800\ \text{J} / 298\ \text{K} = -174\ \text{J} \cdot \text{K}^{-1}$	*1 point for correct answer.*

(d) In the table there are no data for O_2. What are the values of ΔH_f°, ΔG_f°, and of the absolute entropy, S°, for O_2 at 25°C?	***3 points possible***
$\Delta H_f^\circ\ O_2 = 0$	
$\Delta G_f^\circ\ O_2 = 0$	*1 point for each correct answer.*
$\Delta S^\circ = \Sigma S^\circ_{products} - \Sigma S^\circ_{reactants}$	
$-174\ J \cdot K^{-1} = 2\ mol\ CO_2 \times 213.6\ J \cdot mol^{-1} \cdot K^{-1} - (2\ mol\ CO \times 197.9\ J \cdot mol^{-1} \cdot K^{-1} + S^\circ_{O_2})$	
$S^\circ = 206\ J \cdot mol^{-1} \cdot K^{-1}$	

Question 2

Maximum Points for Question 2
Part (a): 2 points
Part (b) (i): 2 points
Part (b) (ii): 2 points
Part (b) (iii): 2 points
Part (b) (iv): 2 points
Total points: 10

2 (a) State the physical significance of entropy and how it relates to the Second and Third Laws of Thermodynamics, providing examples where necessary.	***2 points possible***
Entropy is a measure of a system's energy that is: (a) unavailable for work or (b) the degree of a system's disorder.	*1 point for correct definition of entropy.*
When heat is added to a system held at constant temperature, the change in entropy is related to the change in energy, the pressure, the temperature, and the change in volume. The magnitude of entropy varies from zero to the total amount of energy in a system. Entropy is often presented as the Second Law of Thermodynamics, which states that entropy increases during irreversible processes such as spontaneous mixing of hot and cold gases, uncontrolled expansion of a gas into a vacuum, or combustion of a fuel and is regarded as a measure of the chaos or randomness of a system (e.g., dry ice or when a compound in the ordered solid state sublimes to a more disordered gaseous state). The Third Law of Thermodynamics states that the entropy of a pure substance approaches zero as the absolute temperature approaches zero.	*1 point for relating entropy to the Second and Third Laws of Thermodynamics.*

(b) From each of the following pairs of substances, choose the one expected to have the greater absolute entropy. Explain your choice in each case. Assume 1 mole of each substance. *(i) $Br_{2(l)}$ or $C_{(diamond)}$ at the same temperature and pressure.* Bromine. In the solid diamond lattice, neighboring carbon atoms are more localized by strong covalent bonds and are constrained to a certain position in the lattice. In the liquid state, a bromine molecule is free to move about the entire volume of the liquid. Molecules in a liquid have a higher degree of freedom than in a solid.	***2 points possible*** *1 point for correct answer.* *1 point for correct explanation.*
(ii) $Ne_{(g)}$ at 2 atmosphere or $Ne_{(g)}$ at 1 atmosphere, both at the same temperature $Ne_{(g)}$ at 1 atm. According to Boyle's Law, holding temperature constant, lower pressures result in larger volume. Therefore, 1 mole of neon gas at one atmosphere of pressure would occupy more space and result in higher entropy than one mole of neon gas held at 2 atm of pressure.	***2 points possible*** 1 point for correct answer. 1 point for correct explanation.
(iii) $H_2O_{(l)}$ or $CH_3OCH_{3(l)}$ at the same temperature and pressure. $CH_3OCH_{3(l)}$. $H_2O_{(l)}$ is capable of forming hydrogen bonds; dimethyl ether is not. Hydrogen bonds would tend to result in more order. Furthermore, dimethyl ether has more atoms than water and would result in more vibrations.	***2 points possible*** 1 point for correct answer. 1 point for correct explanation.
(iv) $Fe_{(s)}$ at 20°C or $Fe_{(s)}$ at 200°C, both at the same pressure. $Fe_{(s)}$ at 200°C. Higher temperatures result in higher kinetic energy. Higher kinetic energy results in faster vibrations of the iron atoms in the crystal lattice.	***2 points possible*** 1 point for correct answer. 1 point for correct explanation.

Solutions

You'll Need to Know

- ❑ how to determine molarity
- ❑ how to determine molality
- ❑ how to determine the density of a solution
- ❑ how to determine the concentration of a solution in percent
- ❑ how to determine either initial molarities or volumes involving dilution
- ❑ how to determine mole fraction and fractional distillation
- ❑ what are colligative properties
- ❑ how to work with problems involving boiling point elevation
- ❑ how to work with problems involving freezing point depression
- ❑ how to solve problems involving vapor pressure lowering (Raoult's Law)
- ❑ how to determine the osmotic pressure of a solution

Solutions are homogenous mixtures of two or more substances. Most (although not all) solution problems on the AP Chemistry Exam will involve a water solvent. The solute is the item being dissolved and is usually the smaller amount. Solutions that contain the maximum amount of solute in a given amount of solvent are called saturated solutions. Solutions that contain less solute than they have the capacity to dissolve are known as unsaturated solutions. Supersaturated solutions are solutions that contain more solute than is present in the saturated condition. The lower the temperature and/or the higher the pressure, the more soluble a gas will be in a solution.

Molarity

Molarity is the molar concentration of a solution, which is usually expressed as the number of moles of solute per liter of solution. The symbol for molarity is *M*.

$$M = \frac{\textbf{moles of solute}}{\textbf{liter of solution}}$$

Example

Q. 70. mL of a 2.0-molar Na_2CO_3 solution is added to 30. mL of 1.0-molar $NaHCO_3$ solution. What is the resulting concentration of Na^+?

A. $Na_2CO_3 \rightarrow 2Na^+ + CO_3^{2-}$

$(2 \text{ moles } Na^+ / \cancel{\text{mole } Na_2CO_3}) \times (2.0 \cancel{\text{ mol } Na_2CO_3} / \text{L sol'n}) = 4 \text{ moles } Na^+ / \text{L sol'n}$

$$\frac{70.\ \cancel{\text{mL}}}{1} \times \frac{1\ \cancel{\text{L}}}{10^3\ \cancel{\text{mL}}} \times \frac{4 \text{ moles Na}^+}{\cancel{\text{L soln}}} = 0.28 \text{ moles Na}^+ \text{ in } 70.0 \text{ mL}$$

$NaHCO_3 \rightarrow Na^+ + HCO_3^-$

$$\frac{30.\ \cancel{\text{mL}}}{1}\ \frac{1\ \cancel{\text{L}}}{10^3\ \cancel{\text{mL}}} \times \frac{1 \text{ mole Na}^+}{\cancel{\text{L sol'n}}} = 0.030 \text{ moles Na}^+ \text{ in } 30.0 \text{ mL}$$

$$\frac{0.28 \text{ moles Na}^+ + 0.030 \text{ moles Na}^+}{70.0\ \cancel{\text{mL}} + 30.\ \cancel{\text{mL}}} \times \frac{10^3\ \cancel{\text{mL}}}{1 \text{L}} = 3.1\,M$$

Molality

Molality is the molal concentration of a solute, which is usually expressed as the number of moles of solute per 1,000 grams of solvent. The symbol for molality is *m*.

$$m = \frac{\textbf{moles of solute}}{\textbf{kg of solvent}}$$

Example

Q. What is the molality of an aqueous sucrose ($C_{12}H_{22}O_{11}$, $MM = 342 \text{ g} \cdot \text{mol}^{-1}$) solution that is 10.0% sucrose by mass?

A. 10.0% sucrose sol'n = 90.0 g H_2O + 10.0 g $C_{12}H_{22}O_{11}$

$$\frac{10.0\ \cancel{\text{g } C_{12}H_{22}O_{11}}}{90.0\ \cancel{\text{g } H_2O}} \times \frac{1 \text{ mole } C_{12}H_{22}O_{11}}{342\ \cancel{\text{g } C_{12}H_{22}O_{11}}} \times \frac{10^3\ \cancel{\text{g } H_2O}}{1 \text{ kg } H_2O} = 0.325\,m$$

Density and Percent

$$d = \frac{\textbf{mass of solution}}{\textbf{volume of solution}}$$

Solutions can be expressed as either $\%_{(w/w)}$, which is a percentage based on mass, or $\%_{(v/v)}$, which is a percentage based on volume. $\%_{(v/v)}$ is typically used for mixtures of liquids. If 30 mL of ethanol is mixed with 70 mL of water, the percent ethanol by volume will be 30%, but the total volume of the solution will NOT be 100 mL (although it will be close because ethanol and water molecules interact differently with each other than they do with themselves).

$$\%_{(w/w)} = \frac{\textbf{mass of solute}}{\textbf{mass of solution}} \times 100\%$$

$$\%_{(v/v)} = \frac{\textbf{volume solute}}{\textbf{volume solute(s) + volume solvent}} \times 100\%$$

Note: Dilution is the procedure for preparing a less concentrated solution from a more concentrated one.

$$M_i V_i = M_f V_f$$

Examples

Q. What is the density (g · mL^{-1}) of a 29.0%$_{(w/w)}$ H_2SO_4 solution that is 2.90 *M*? (*MM* H_2SO_4 = 98.08 g · mol^{-1}).

A. $$\frac{100.\text{ g sol'n}}{29.0\ \cancel{\text{g } H_2SO_4}} \times \frac{98.08\ \cancel{\text{g } H_2SO_4}}{1\ \cancel{\text{mol } H_2SO_4}} \times \frac{2.90\ \cancel{\text{moles } H_2SO_4}}{\cancel{\text{L sol'n}}} \times \frac{1\ \cancel{\text{L sol'n}}}{10^3\text{ mL}} = 0.981\text{ g/mL}$$

Q. What is the molarity of a solution that is made by diluting 15.0 mL of a 2.00 *M* H_2SO_4 (*MM* = 98.08 g · mol^{-1}) solution to a volume of 60.0 mL?

A. $M_i V_i = M_f V_f$ (2.00 *M*) (0.015 L) = (M_f) (0.06 L) M_f = 0.500 *M*

Mole Fraction and Fractional Distillation

$$\text{mol fraction of component A} = X_A = \frac{\text{moles of A}}{\text{sum of moles of all components}}$$

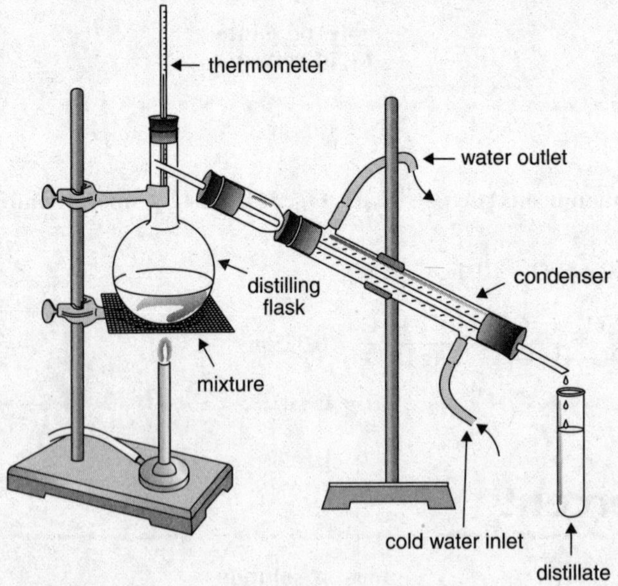

Example

Q. A mixture of 320.4 grams of methanol that boils at 64.6°C at 1 atm of pressure is mixed with 18.02 grams of water ($P°$ = 184 mm Hg at 64.6°C). If the mixture is distilled at 64.6°C, what is the mole fraction of methanol in the distillate?

A. $$\frac{320.4\ \cancel{g\ CH_3OH}}{1} \times \frac{1\ mol\ CH_3OH}{32.04\ \cancel{g\ CH_3OH}} = 10.00\ mol\ CH_3OH$$

$$\frac{18.02\ \cancel{g\ H_2O}}{1} \times \frac{1\ mol\ H_2O}{18.02\ \cancel{g\ H_2O}} = 1.000\ mol\ H_2O$$

$$\text{mol fraction methanol} = X_M = \frac{10.00\ mol\ CH_3OH}{1.000\ mol\ H_2O + 10.00\ mol\ CH_3OH} = 0.9091$$

$$\text{mol fraction water} = X_W = \frac{1.000\ mol\ H_2O}{1.000\ mol\ H_2O + 10.00\ mol\ CH_3OH} = 0.09091$$

Since distillation occurs at the boiling point, the vapor pressure of pure methanol is the atmospheric pressure.

partial pressure of methanol = $P_m = X_m P° = (0.9091)\ (760.\ mm\ Hg) = 691\ mm\ Hg$

partial pressure of water vapor = $P_w = X_w P° = (0.09091)\ (184\ mm\ Hg) = 16.7\ mm\ Hg$

total vapor pressure = 691 mm Hg + 16.7 mm Hg = 708 mm Hg

The moles of methanol and moles of water in the vapor are proportional to the partial pressures. Therefore, the ratio of partial pressures will also be equal to the ratio of moles.

$$X_m(\text{in vapor}) = \frac{691\ mm\ Hg}{708\ mm\ Hg} = 0.976$$

Colligative Properties

Colligative properties depend only on the number of dissolved particles in solution and not on their identity. The van't Hoff factor (i) is the number of moles of solute actually in solution per mole of solid solute added; i.e, a $1M$ solution of NaCl is actually $2M$ in total ions ($1M\ NaCl_{(aq)} \rightarrow 1M\ Na^+_{(aq)} + 1M\ Cl^-_{(aq)}$).

Boiling Point Elevation

The boiling point of a solution made of a liquid solvent with a nonvolatile solute is greater than the boiling point of the pure solvent. The boiling point of a liquid is defined as the temperature at which the vapor pressure of that liquid equals the atmospheric pressure.

$$\Delta T_b = iK_b m$$

Example

Q. What is the boiling point of a solution made by mixing 46.07 grams of ethanol and 500.00 grams of water?

A. solute = 46.07 g ethanol solvent = 500.00 g H_2O

$\Delta T = iK_b\, m$ $K_b = 0.52°C / m$ $i = 1$ (ethanol is molecular)

$$\frac{46.07\ \cancel{g\ C_2H_5OH}}{1} \times \frac{1\ mol\ C_2H_5OH}{46.07\ g\ \cancel{C_2H_5OH}} = 1.000\ mol\ C_2H_5OH$$

$$kg\ H_2O = \frac{500.00\ \cancel{g\ H_2O}}{1} \times \frac{1\ kg\ H_2O}{1000\ \cancel{g\ H_2O}} = 0.50000\ kg\ H_2O$$

$$m = \frac{1.000\ mol\ C_2H_5OH}{0.50000\ kg\ H_2O} = 2.000\ m$$

$$\Delta T = K_b \cdot m = \frac{0.52°C}{\cancel{m}} \times \frac{2.000\ \cancel{m}}{1} = 1.04°C$$

BP = 100.00°C + 1.04°C = 101.04°C

Recall that 100°C is defined as the BP of water. It is therefore an exact number with infinite significant figures.

Freezing Point Depression

Freezing point depression occurs when a solute is added to a solvent and the freezing point lowers.

$$\Delta T_f = iK_f\, m$$

Example

Q. What is the freezing point of a 0.500 *m* aqueous solution of NaCl?

A. $i = 2$ since NaCl ionizes into Na^+ and Cl^-

$$\Delta T = i \cdot K_f \cdot m = (2)\frac{1.86°C}{\cancel{m}} \times \frac{0.500\ \cancel{m}}{1} = 1.86°C$$

F.P. = 0.00°C – 1.86°C = –1.86°C

Vapor Pressure Lowering (Raoult's Law)

When a nonvolatile solute is added to a liquid to form a solution, the vapor pressure above that solution decreases.

$$VP_{solution} = VP_{solvent} \cdot X_{solvent} \text{ where } X_{solvent} = \frac{\text{moles solvent}}{\text{total moles}}$$

$$X_{solvent} = (1 - X_{solute})$$

$$VP_{solvent} - VP_{solution} = \Delta P = X_{solute} \cdot VP_{solvent}$$

Example

Q. What is the vapor pressure of a mixture 9.01 grams of water and 0.200 mol sugar at 29°C? The vapor pressure of water at 29°C is 30.0 torr.

A. $\frac{9.01\,\cancel{g\,H_2O}}{1} \times \frac{1\,mol\,H_2O}{18.02\,\cancel{g\,H_2O}} = 0.500\,mol\,H_2O$

$$\text{mol fraction } H_2O = \frac{0.500\,mol\,H_2O}{0.500\,mol\,H_2O + 0.200\,mol\,sugar} = 0.714$$

$$VP_{solution} = VP_{solvent} \cdot X_A = (30.0\text{ torr})\,(0.714) = 21.4\text{ torr}$$

Osmotic Pressure

Osmosis refers to the flow of solvent molecules through a semi-permeable membrane. When a solution and the pure solvent used in making that solution are placed on either side of a semi-permeable membrane, it is found that more solvent molecules flow out of the pure solvent side of the membrane than solvent flows into the pure solvent from the solution side of the membrane. That flow of solvent from the pure solvent side makes the volume of the solution rise. When the height difference between the two sides becomes large enough, the net flow through the membrane ceases due to the extra pressure exerted by the excess height of the solution chamber. Converting that height of solvent into units of pressure (atmospheres) gives a measure of the osmotic pressure exerted on the solution by the pure solvent.

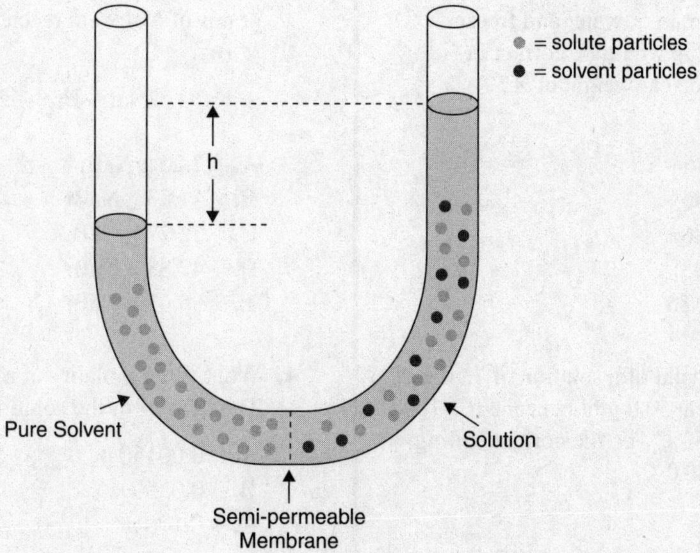

$$\pi = iMRT$$

Example

Q. What is the osmotic pressure of 13.73 mg of PCl_3 in 500.0 mL of an ethanol solution at 27°C? (*MM* PCl_3 = 137.30 g · mol^{-1})

A. $\pi = iMRT$

$$\frac{13.73 \cancel{\text{mg PCl}_3}}{1} \times \frac{1 \cancel{\text{g}}}{10^3 \cancel{\text{mg}}} \times \frac{1 \text{ mol PCl}_3}{137.30 \cancel{\text{g PCl}_3}} = 1.000 \times 10^{-4} \text{ mol PCl}_3$$

$$\frac{500.0 \cancel{\text{mL}}}{1} \times \frac{1 \text{ L}}{10^3 \cancel{\text{mL}}} = 0.5000 \text{ L} \qquad M = \frac{1.000 \times 10^{-4} \text{ mol PCl}_3}{0.5000 \text{ L}} = 2.000 \times 10^{-4} \, M \text{ PCl}_3$$

$R = 0.0821 \text{ L} \cdot \text{atm} \cdot \text{mol}^{-1} \cdot \text{K}^{-1}$ $\qquad T = 27°\text{C} + 273 = 300. \text{ K}$

PCl_3 does not ionize, $\therefore i = 1$

$\pi = iMRT = (1)(2.000 \times 10^{-4} \cancel{\text{mol}} \cdot \cancel{\text{L}^{-1}})(0.0821 \cancel{\text{L}} \cdot \text{atm} \cdot \cancel{\text{mol}^{-1}} \cdot \cancel{\text{K}^{-1}})(300. \cancel{\text{K}})$

$\pi = 4.93 \times 10^{-3}$ atm

Multiple-Choice Questions

1. A solution of a non-electrolyte, X, contains 93 grams of X per kilogram of water and freezes at –1.46°C. What setup would be correct in determining the molecular weight of X? (K_f = 1.86°C / *m*)

A. 93 × 1.86 × 1.46
B. 93 × (1.86 / 1.46)
C. 93 × (1.46 / 1.86)
D. 1.46 × (1.86 / 93)
E. (1.46 × 93) + 1.86

2. What is the boiling point of a solution of 7.50 g of naphthalene ($C_{10}H_8$) in 50.0 g of benzene (C_6H_6)? (K_b of benzene is 2.53°C / *m*; the normal boiling point of benzene = 80.0°C).

A. 80.3°C
B. 81.5°C
C. 83.0°C
D. 85.0°C
E. 273°C

3. How many grams of NaBr could be formed if 17.2 grams of NaI were reacted with 50.0 mL of 0.700 *M* Br_2?

$$2NaI + Br_2 \rightarrow 2NaBr + I_2$$

A. 7.20 g NaBr
B. 11.83 g NaBr
C. 32.77 g NaBr
D. 42.88 g NaBr
E. 55.63 g NaBr

4. What is the molality of a 0.250 *M* $HCl_{(aq)}$ solution? The density of the solution is 1.030 g/mL.

A. 0.00150 *m*
B. 0.0550 *m*
C. 0.100 *m*
D. 0.245 *m*
E. 0.550 *m*

5. Which aqueous solution should have the highest boiling temperature (assume equimolar solutions)?

A. CH_4
B. C_2H_4
C. SiC
D. NaCl
E. K_2SO_4

6. A 20.0-milliliter sample of 0.200-molar potassium dichromate solution is added to 30.0 milliliters of 0.400-molar silver nitrate solution. Silver chromate precipitates. The concentration of silver ion, Ag^+, in solution after reaction is

A. 0.080 *M*
B. 0.160 *M*
C. 0.200 *M*
D. 0.240 *M*
E. 0.267 *M*

7. How many grams of H_2SO_4 ($MW = 98.08\ g \cdot mol^{-1}$) are in 75.0 milliliters of a 4.00-*M* solution?

A. 14.2 g
B. 29.4 g
C. 36.7 g
D. 44.7 g
E. 55.2 g

8. A chemist wants to make 500. mL of 0.050 *M* HCl by diluting a 6.0 *M* HCl solution. How much of the 6.0 *M* solution should be used?

A. 4.2 mL
B. 5.0 mL
C. 6.0 mL
D. 8.0 mL
E. 9.0 mL

9. The freezing point of a 0.0100 *m* solution of $XY_{(aq)}$ is –0.0186°C. What is the percentage of the XY molecules that remain undissociated?

A. 0%
B. 0.186%
C. 1.86%
D. 18.6%
E. 100%

10. Seawater ($i = 1.8$, density = $1.03\ g \cdot mL^{-1}$) averages 0.60 *M* NaCl (some oceans are saltier than others). Assuming no other compounds are present in the sea water, which of the following is true?

A. Sea water is 3.40% NaCl and has an osmotic pressure of 27 atm at 27°C.
B. Sea water has a density of 3.40% and an osmotic pressure of 0.27 atm at 27°C.
C. Sea water has a density of 1.03% and an osmotic pressure of 27 atm at 27°C.
D. Sea water has a density of 3.40% and an osmotic pressure of 1 atm.
E. Sea water has a density of 3.40% and an osmotic pressure of 1.8 atm at 27°C.

11. The freezing point of a solution that contains 1.00 g of an unknown non-ionizing compound, X, dissolved in 10.0 g of benzene is found to be 3.00°C. The freezing point of pure benzene is 5.48°C. The molal-freezing point depression constant of benzene is 5.12°C / *m*. What is the molecular weight of the unknown compound?

A. $17.4\ g \cdot mol^{-1}$
B. $48.4\ g \cdot mol^{-1}$
C. $207\ g \cdot mol^{-1}$
D. $484\ g \cdot mol^{-1}$
E. $512\ g \cdot mol^{-1}$

12. What is the vapor pressure of a solution at 25.0°C when 20.0 grams of urea ($MW = 60.0\ g \cdot mol^{-1}$), a non-ionizing solute, are dissolved in 54.0 grams of H_2O? The vapor pressure of pure water at 25.0°C is 23.8 torr.

A. 7.74 torr
B. 11.3 torr
C. 19.4 torr
D. 21.4 torr
E. 23.8 torr

13. The molarity of a 1.00 *m* HCl solution can be obtained by using which of the following?

A. freezing point
B. density of the solution
C. volume of solvent
D. solubility of HCl
E. temperature of the solution

14. A 1.00 *m* solution of acetic acid (CH_3COOH) in benzene has a freezing point depression of 2.5°C. K_f for benzene = 5.0°C · m^{-1}. Which of the following statements is true?

A. i = 0.50; the acetic acid dimerized in the benzene and formed $(CH_3COOH)_2$
B. i = 0.50; the acetic acid did not dimerize- it stayed as acetic acid
C. i = 0.50; the benzene dimerized into $(C_6H_6)_2$
D. i = 2.0; the acetic acid dimerized in the benzene and formed $(CH_3COOH)_2$
E. i = 2.0; the benzene dimerized into $(C_6H_6)_2$

15. A student wishes to prepare 3.00 liters of a 0.200 *M* KCl solution (*MW* KCl = 74.55 g · mol^{-1}). The proper procedure is to weigh out

A. 89.5 grams of KCl and add H_2O until the final homogeneous solution has a volume of 3.00 liters.
B. 74.55 grams of KCl and add H_2O until the final homogeneous solution has a volume of 3.00 liters.
C. 14.9 g of KCl and 3.00 kg of H_2O.
D. 44.73 g of KCl and add it to 3.00 liters of water.
E. 44.73 grams of KCl and add H_2O until the final homogeneous solution has a volume of 3.00 liters.

16. Which of the following solutions would have the lowest freezing point (assuming 100% ionization)?

A. 0.600 *M* sucrose
B. 0.200 *M* K_2SO_4
C. 0.300 *M* NaCl
D. 0.150 *M* $AlCl_3$
E. All solutions would have the same freezing point.

17. When table salt is dissolved in water, the resulting solution

A. has a higher freezing point than pure water.
B. has a higher boiling point than pure water.
C. has a higher vapor pressure than pure water.
D. has a lower osmotic pressure than pure water.
E. All of the above are true.

18. A solution of xylene (*MW* = 106.16 g · mol^{-1}) in toluene (*MW* = 92.14 g · mol^{-1}) is prepared. The mole fraction of xylene in the solution is 0.300. What is the molality of the solution?

A. 0.0100 *m*
B. 2.23 *m*
C. 4.67 *m*
D. 8.92 *m*
E. 17.33 *m*

19. How many grams of water must be used to dissolve 100. grams of sucrose ($C_{12}H_{22}O_{11}$, *MW* = 342.30 g/mol) to prepare a 0.200 mole fraction of sucrose in the solution?

A. 1.4 g
B. 7.5 g
C. 21.1 g
D. 200. g
E. 500. g

20. The freezing point depression of a 0.10 *m* solution of $HF_{(aq)}$ solution is –0.201°C. Calculate the percent dissociation of $HF_{(aq)}$.

A. 0%
B. 8.00%
C. 56.0%
D. 92.0%
E. 100.%

Free-Response Questions

1. (a) A solution containing 6.30 grams of an unknown compound dissolved in 100.0 grams of water freezes at –0.651°C. The solution does not conduct electricity. Calculate the molecular weight of the compound. (The molal freezing point depression constant for H_2O is 1.86°C/*m*.)

(b) Elemental analysis of this unknown compound yields the following percentages by weight: C = 40.0%; H = 6.70%; O = 53.3%. Determine the molecular formula of the compound.

(c) Complete combustion of a 2.50-gram sample of the compound with the stoichiometric amount of oxygen gas produces a mixture of $H_2O_{(g)}$ and $CO_{2(g)}$. What is the total pressure of the product gases when they are contained in a 2.00-liter flask at 150.°C?

2. A solution of camphor ($C_{10}H_{16}O$, *MM* = 152.23 g · mol^{-1}; density = 0.990 g · mL^{-1}) is prepared by mixing 50.0 g of camphor with 1.50 L of chloroform ($CHCl_3$, *MM* = 119.40 g · mol^{-1}; density = 1.48 g · cm^3). Assume volumes are additive.

(a) Determine the mass percent of camphor in the solution.

(b) Determine the concentration of camphor in parts per million.

(c) Determine the molarity of the solution.

(d) Determine the molality of the solution.

(e) The vapor pressure of pure chloroform at 20.°C is 159 mm Hg. Determine the vapor pressure of the chloroform in the solution at 20.°C.

(f) Determine the osmotic pressure of the camphor-chloroform solution at 20.°C.

(g) Determine the boiling point of the solution. The normal boiling point of chloroform is 62.0°C. K_b = 3.63°C / *m*

(h) A 0.350 g sample of an unknown molecular compound was dissolved in 15.0 g of chloroform, and the freezing point depression was determined to be 0.240°C. Calculate the molar mass of the molecular compound (K_f for chloroform is 4.70°C · kg · mol^{-1}).

Answers and Explanations

Multiple Choice

1. B. $$\frac{93\text{ grams X}}{1\,\cancel{\text{kg H}_2\text{O}}}\times\frac{1.86^\circ\cancel{\text{C}}}{\text{mole X}\cdot\cancel{\text{kg H}_2\text{O}^{-1}}\cdot\left(0^\circ\cancel{\text{C}}-\left(-1.46^\circ\cancel{\text{C}}\right)\right)}$$

2. C. $C_{10}H_8 = 10(12.01) + 8(1.01) = 128.19\text{ g}\cdot\text{mol}^{-1}$

$$\frac{7.50\,\cancel{\text{g}}\,C_{10}H_8}{128.19\,\cancel{\text{g}}\cdot\text{mol}^{-1}} = 0.0585\text{ moles }C_{10}H_8$$

$$\frac{50.0\,\cancel{\text{g}}\text{ benzene}}{1}\times\frac{1\text{ kg}}{10^3\,\cancel{\text{g}}} = 0.0500\text{ kg benzene}$$

$$m = \frac{0.0585\text{ moles }C_{10}H_8}{0.500\text{ kg benzene}} = 1.17\,m$$

$$\Delta T = K_b\cdot m = \frac{2.53^\circ\text{C}}{\cancel{m}}\times\frac{1.17\,\cancel{m}}{1} = 2.96^\circ\text{C}$$

$$\text{BP} = 80.0^\circ\text{C} + 2.96^\circ\text{C} = 83.0^\circ\text{C}$$

3. A. This is a limiting-reactant problem.

$$\frac{17.2\,\cancel{\text{g NaI}}}{1}\times\frac{1\,\cancel{\text{mol NaI}}}{149.89\,\cancel{\text{g NaI}}}\times\frac{2\text{ mol NaBr}}{2\,\cancel{\text{mol NaI}}} = 0.115\text{ mol NaBr}$$

$$\frac{50.0\,\cancel{\text{mL sol'n Br}_2}}{1}\times\frac{1\,\cancel{\text{L sol'n Br}_2}}{1000\,\cancel{\text{mL sol'n Br}_2}}\times\frac{0.700\,\cancel{\text{moles Br}_2}}{1\,\cancel{\text{L Br}_2\text{ sol'n}}}\times\frac{2\text{ mol NaBr}}{1\,\cancel{\text{mol Br}_2}} = 0.0700\text{ mol NaBr}$$

$\therefore$ $Br_{2(aq)}$ is the limiting reactant

$$\frac{0.0700\,\cancel{\text{mol NaBr}}}{1}\times\frac{102.9\text{ g NaBr}}{1\,\cancel{\text{mol NaBr}}} = 7.20\text{ g NaBr}$$

4. D. Total mass of 1 L of 0.250 *M* HCl solution:

$$\frac{1\,\cancel{\text{L sol'n}}}{1}\times\frac{10^3\,\cancel{\text{mL sol'n}}}{1\,\cancel{\text{L sol'n}}}\times\frac{1.030\text{ g sol'n}}{1\,\cancel{\text{mL sol'n}}} = 1030.\text{ g}$$

Amount of water in solution:

$$1030.\text{ g sol'n}-\left(\frac{0.250\,\cancel{\text{mol HCl}}}{1}\times\frac{36.46\text{ g HCl}}{1\,\cancel{\text{mol HCl}}}\right) = 1021\text{ g H}_2\text{O}$$

$$m = \frac{0.250\text{ mol HCl}}{1021\,\cancel{\text{g H}_2\text{O}}}\times\frac{10^3\,\cancel{\text{g H}_2\text{O}}}{1\text{ kg H}_2\text{O}} = 0.245\,m$$

5. E. Choices A and B are hydrocarbons and generally not very soluble in water. The van't Hoff factor describes how many parts a solute breaks into when it dissolves. Non-ionic compounds (choices A, B and C) have a van't Hoff factor of 1. K_2SO_4 breaks up into three particles (two K^+ ions and one SO_4^{2-} ion) while NaCl breaks up into two particles (Na^+ and Cl^-).

6. A. Begin by writing the balanced equation:

Overall ionic equation:

$$2K^+_{(aq)} + CrO_4^{2-}{}_{(aq)} + 2Ag^+_{(aq)} + 2NO_3^-{}_{(aq)} \rightarrow 2K^+_{(aq)} + 2NO_3^-{}_{(aq)} + Ag_2CrO_{4(s)}$$

Net ionic equation: $2Ag^+_{(aq)} + CrO_4^{2-}{}_{(aq)} \rightarrow Ag_2CrO_{4(s)}$

Moles of each reactant: $\frac{0.200 \text{ moles } K_2CrO_4}{1 \cancel{L}} \times \frac{1 \cancel{L}}{10^3 \cancel{mL}} \times \frac{20.0 \cancel{mL}}{1} = 0.004 \text{ mol } K_2CrO_4$

$$\frac{0.400 \text{ mol } AgNO_3}{1 \cancel{mL}} \times \frac{1 \cancel{L}}{10^3 \cancel{mL}} \times \frac{30.0 \cancel{mL}}{1} = 0.012 \text{ mol } AgNO_3$$

Determine limiting factor:

$$\frac{0.004 \cancel{\text{mol } K_2CrO_4}}{1} \times \frac{1 \text{ mol } Ag_2CrO_4}{1 \cancel{\text{mol } K_2CrO_4}} = 0.004 \text{ mol } Ag_2CrO_4$$

$$\frac{0.012 \cancel{\text{mol } AgNO_3}}{1} \times \frac{1 \text{ mol } Ag_2CrO_4}{2 \cancel{\text{mol } AgNO_3}} = 0.006 \text{ mol } Ag_2CrO_4$$

K_2CrO_4 is the limiting reagent. Therefore, a maximum of 0.004 mol Ag_2CrO_4 can be made. In 0.004 mol Ag_2CrO_4 there are:

$$\frac{0.004 \cancel{\text{mol } Ag_2CrO_4}}{1} \times \frac{2 \text{ mol } Ag^+}{1 \cancel{\text{mol } Ag_2CrO_4}} = 0.008 \text{ mol } Ag^+$$

You started with 0.012 mol Ag^+ and you used up 0.008 in the precipitate; therefore, 0.004 moles of Ag^+ is left (0.012 – 0.008).

$$\frac{0.004 \text{ mol } Ag^+}{20.0 \text{ mL} + 30.0 \text{ mL}} = \frac{0.008 \text{ mol } Ag^+}{50.0 \cancel{mL}} \times \frac{10^3 \cancel{mL}}{1 \text{ L}} = 0.080\ M$$

7. B. $\frac{4.00 \cancel{\text{moles } H_2SO_4}}{\cancel{\text{L sol'n}}} \times \frac{1 \cancel{\text{L sol'n}}}{10^3 \cancel{mL}} \times \frac{75.0 \cancel{mL}}{1} \times \frac{98.08 \text{ g } H_2SO_4}{1 \cancel{\text{mol } H_2SO_4}} = 29.4 \text{ g } H_2SO_4$

8. A. $M_iV_i = M_fV_f$ $\quad$ $(6.0\ M)\ (V_i) = (0.050\ M)\ (0.500 \text{ L})$

$$V_i = \frac{(0.050 \cancel{M})(0.500 \text{ L})}{(6.0 \cancel{M})} = 0.0042 \text{ L} = 4.2 \text{ mL}$$

9. A. Since i works out to be exactly 1.00, there is no dissociation.

$$i = \frac{\Delta T_f}{k_f \cdot m} = \frac{0.0186°\text{C} \cdot \cancel{m}}{1.86°\text{C} \cdot 0.0100 \cancel{m}} = 1.00$$

10. A. $\frac{0.60 \cancel{\text{moles NaCl}}}{1 \cancel{\text{L solution}}} \times \frac{58.44 \text{ g NaCl}}{1 \cancel{\text{mol NaCl}}} \times \frac{1 \cancel{\text{L solution}}}{10^3 \cancel{\text{mL solution}}} \times \frac{1 \cancel{\text{mL sol'n}}}{1.03 \text{ g sol'n}} = \frac{0.0340 \text{ g NaCl}}{\text{g sol'n}}$

$= 3.40\%_{(w)}$ NaCl $\qquad$ *(density is NOT measured in percent)*

$T = 27°\text{C} + 273 = 300.\text{K}$

$\pi = iMRT = (1.8)\ (0.60 \cancel{\text{mol/L}})\ (0.0821 \cancel{L} \cdot \text{atm} \cdot \cancel{\text{mol}^{-1}} \cdot \cancel{K^{-1}})\ (300.\cancel{K}) = 27 \text{ atm}$

When 1 mole of NaCl ionizes in solution it produces one mole of Na^+ ions and one mole of Cl^- ions; therefore, the van't Hoff factor would theoretically be equal to 2. The actual value of 1.8 is due to ion pairing; i.e., in solution, a certain number of Na^+ ions and Cl^- ions will randomly come together and form NaCl ion pairs. This reduces the total number of particles in solution, thereby reducing the van't Hoff factor.

11. C. $\Delta T_f = 5.48°\text{C} - 3.00°\text{C} = 2.48°\text{C}$

$\Delta T_f = (K_f)\ (m)$

$m = (2.48°\cancel{C})\ /\ (5.12°\cancel{C}/\ m)$

$m = 0.484$ mol X / kg benzene

moles X = (0.484 mol X / ~~kg benzene~~) (0.0100 ~~kg benzene~~) = 4.84×10^{-3} mol X

molecular weight of X = (1.00 g X) / (4.84×10^{-3} mol X)

X = 207 g/mol

12. D. $\frac{20.0\ \cancel{\text{g urea}}}{1} \times \frac{1\ \text{mol urea}}{18.02\ \cancel{\text{g urea}}} = 0.333\ \text{mol urea}$

$$\frac{\cancel{54.0\ \text{g}\ H_2O}}{1} \times \frac{1\ \text{mol}\ H_2O}{18.02\ \cancel{\text{g}\ H_2O}} = 3.00\ \text{mol}\ H_2O$$

$$X_{\text{urea}} = \frac{\text{moles urea}}{\text{total moles}} = \frac{0.333}{0.333 + 3.00} = 0.0999$$

$$\Delta P = VP_{\text{solvent}} - VP_{\text{solution}} = X_{\text{solute}} \cdot VP_{\text{solvent}}$$

$$P_1 = P_1^\circ - (X_{\text{urea}})(P_1^\circ) = 23.8\ \text{torr} - 0.0999(23.8\ \text{torr}) = 23.8\ \text{torr} - 2.38\ \text{torr} = 21.4\ \text{torr}$$

13. B. Since we have a value for molality, let's assume we are working with exactly 1.00 kg water. Let's also assume that we were given the density of the solution as 1.030 g/mL.

$m \times \text{kg} = \text{mol HCl} = (1.00\ m)\ (1\ \text{kg}) = 1.00\ \text{mol HCl}$

$$\frac{1.00\ \cancel{\text{mol HCl}}}{1} \times \frac{36.45\ \text{g HCl}}{1\ \cancel{\text{mol HCl}}} = 36.45\ \text{g HCl}$$

g solution = 1000.00 g H_2O + 36.45 g HCl = 1036.45 g

$$\frac{1036.45\ \cancel{\text{g solution}}}{1} \times \frac{1\ \cancel{\text{mL sol'n}}}{1.030\ \cancel{\text{g sol'n}}} \times \frac{1\ \text{L sol'n}}{1000\ \cancel{\text{mL sol'n}}} = 1.006\ \text{L sol'n}$$

$$M = \frac{\text{mol HCl}}{\text{L sol'n}} = \frac{1.00\ \text{mol HCl}}{1.006\ \text{L sol'n}} = 0.994\ M$$

Notice that although the values for molality and molarity are similar, the value for molarity will be slightly less. The difference normally becomes larger at higher concentrations.

14. A. $\Delta T = i \cdot K_f \cdot m$

$2.5°C = (x)\ (5.0°C \cdot \cancel{m^{-1}})\ (1.00\ \cancel{m})$ $\qquad x = 0.50.$

For every two molecules of acetic acid (CH_3COOH) that originally went into the solution, only one molecule [$(CH_3COOH)_2$, the dimer] was present in solution.

15. E. $\frac{3.00\ \cancel{\text{L sol'n}}}{1} \times \frac{0.200\ \cancel{\text{moles KCl}}}{\cancel{\text{L sol'n}}} \times \frac{74.55\ \text{g KCl}}{1\ \cancel{\text{mol KCl}}} = 44.7\ \text{g KCl}$

16. E. Colligative properties depend only on the number of dissolved particles and not their identity and include vapor pressure lowering, freezing point depression, boiling point elevation, and osmotic pressure. Choices A–D each contain 0.600 moles of particles in 1 liter of solution.

17. B. If you missed this question, review colligative properties and their effect on water.

18. C. Since the mole fraction of xylene is less than the mole fraction of toluene; the toluene is considered the solvent. Assume 1.00 kg of toluene.

$$\frac{1.00\ \cancel{\text{kg toluene}}}{1} \times \frac{10^3\ \cancel{\text{g}}}{1\ \cancel{\text{kg}}} \times \frac{1\ \text{mol toluene}}{92.14\ \cancel{\text{g toluene}}} = 10.9\ \text{mol toluene}$$

$X_{\text{toluene}} + X_{\text{xylene}} = 1.00 \qquad X_{\text{toluene}} = 1.00 - 0.300 = 0.700$

$$X_{\text{toluene}} = 0.700 = \frac{\text{mol toluene}}{\text{mol toluene} + \text{mol xylene}} = \frac{10.9}{10.9 + x}$$

x = 4.67 moles xylene

$$m = \frac{\text{moles solute}}{\text{kg solvent}} = \frac{4.67\ \text{moles xylene}}{1.00\ \text{kg toluene}} = 4.67\ m$$

19. C. $\frac{100.\ \text{g C}_{12}\text{H}_{22}\text{O}_{11}}{1} \times \frac{1\ \text{mole C}_{12}\text{H}_{22}\text{O}_{11}}{342.30\ \text{g C}_{12}\text{H}_{22}\text{O}_{11}} = 0.292\ \text{moles C}_{12}\text{H}_{22}\text{O}_{11}$

Let x = moles H_2O

$$X_{sucrose} = 0.200 = \frac{\text{moles C}_{12}\text{H}_{22}\text{O}_{11}}{\text{moles C}_{12}\text{H}_{22}\text{O}_{11} + \text{moles H}_2\text{O}} = \frac{0.292}{0.292 + x}$$

$0.200 = 0.292 / (0.292 + x)$

$0.200\ (0.292 + x) = 0.0584 + 0.200x = 0.292$

$x = (0.292 - 0.0584) / 0.200 = 1.17$ moles H_2O

$$\frac{1.17\ \text{mols H}_2\text{O}}{1} \times \frac{18.02\ \text{g H}_2\text{O}}{1\ \text{mol H}_2\text{O}} = 21.1\ \text{g H}_2\text{O}$$

20. B. $\Delta T = i \cdot K_f \cdot m$

$0.201°\text{C} = (x)\ (1.86°\text{C} \cdot m^{-1})\ (0.10m)$ $x = 1.08$

$$\% = \frac{(\text{observed value} - \text{expected value})}{\text{expected value}} \times 100\% = \frac{1.08 - 1.00}{1.00} \times 100\% = 8.00\%$$

Free Response

Question 1

Maximum Points for Question 1
Part (a): 4 points
Part (b): 3 points
Part (c): 3 points
Total Points: 10

1. *(a) A solution containing 6.30 grams of an unknown compound dissolved in 100.0 grams of water freezes at –0.651°C. The solution does not conduct electricity. Calculate the molecular weight of the compound. (The molal freezing point depression constant for H_2O is 1.86°C / m.)*	***4 points possible***
$\Delta T_f = K_f \cdot m$ $0.651°\text{C} = (1.86°\text{C} \cdot m^{-1}) \cdot m$	*1 point for correct setup for determining molality.*
$m = 0.350$ moles solute · kg solvent^{-1}	*1 point for correct molality.*
$\frac{6.30\ \text{g solute}}{100.0\ \text{g solvent}} \times \frac{10^3\ \text{g}}{1\ \text{kg}} = 63.0\ \text{g solute/kg solvent}$	*1 point for correct setup for determining molecular mass.*
$\frac{63.0\ \text{g solute/kg solvent}}{0.350\ \text{mole solute/kg solvent}} = 180.\ \text{g} \cdot \text{mol}^{-1}$	*1 point for correct molecular mass.*

(b) Elemental analysis of this unknown compound yields the following percentages by weight: C = 40.0%; H = 6.70%; O = 53.3%. Determine the molecular formula of the compound. Per 100 g of compound: $\frac{40.0\,\cancel{gC}}{1} \times \frac{1\,mol\,C}{12.01\,\cancel{gC}} = 3.33\,mol\,C$ $\frac{6.70\,\cancel{gH}}{1} \times \frac{1\,mol\,H}{1.01\,\cancel{gH}} = 6.63\,mol\,H$ $\frac{53.3\,\cancel{gO}}{1} \times \frac{1\,mol\,O}{16.00\,\cancel{gO}} = 3.33\,mol\,O$ Empirical formula is CH_2O ($MW = 30.0$) $180.\ g \cdot mol^{-1} / 30.0\ g \cdot mol^{-1} = 6$ Molecular formula is $(CH_2O)_6$ or $C_6H_{12}O_6$	***3 points possible*** *1 point for correctly determining moles of each element.* *1 point for correctly determining the empirical formula.* *1 point for correctly determining the actual molecular formula.*
(c) Complete combustion of a 2.50-gram sample of the compound with the stoichiometric amount of oxygen gas produces a mixture of $H_2O_{(g)}$ and $CO_{2(g)}$. What is the total pressure of the product gases when they are contained in a 2.00-liter flask at 150.°C? $C_6H_{12}O_{6(s)} + 6O_{2(g)} \rightarrow 6H_2O_{(g)} + 6CO_{2(g)}$ Combustion produces 12 moles gaseous products per 1 mole $C_6H_{12}O_6$ moles $C_6H_{12}O_6$ = 2.50 g / 180. g/mol = 0.0139 mole moles gases = 12 (0.0139) = 0.167 $PV = nRT$ $T = 150.°C + 273 = 423\ K$ $P = \frac{(0.167\,\cancel{moles})(0.0821\,\cancel{L} \cdot atm \cdot \cancel{mol^{-1}} \cdot \cancel{K^{-1}})(423\,\cancel{K})}{2.00\,\cancel{L}}$ $P = 2.90\ atm$	***3 points possible*** *1 point for correctly balanced equation.* *1 point for proper setup.* *1 point for correct pressure.*

Question 2

Maximum Points for Question 2
Part (a): 1 point
Part (b): 1 point
Part (c): 1 point
Part (d): 1 point
Part (e): 2 points
Part (f): 1 point
Part (g): 1 point
Part (h): 2 points
Total points: 10

2. A solution of camphor ($C_{10}H_{16}O$, MM = 152.23 g · mol^{-1}; density = 0.990 g · mL^{-1}) is prepared by mixing 50.0 g of camphor with 1.50 L of chloroform ($CHCl_3$, MM = 119.40 g · mol^{-1}; density = 1.48 g · mL^{-1}). Assume volumes are additives. *(a) Determine the mass percent of camphor in the solution.* chloroform: $\frac{1.50\not{L}}{1} \times \frac{10^3\,\not{mL}}{1\not{L}} \times \frac{1.48g}{\not{mL}} = 2220g$ camphor: 50.0 g $\%_{mass} = \frac{50.0g}{50.0g + 2220g} \times 100\% = 2.20\%$	***1 point possible*** *1 point for correct answer.*
(b) Determine the concentration of camphor in parts per million. $2.20\% = \frac{2.20g}{100.\,g\,solution} = \frac{x}{1{,}000{,}000}$ $x = 2.20 \times 10^4$ ppm	***1 point possible*** *1 point for correct answer.*
(c) Determine the molarity of the solution. $M = \frac{moles\ camphor}{L\ sol'n}$ $moles\ camphor = \frac{50.0g\,C_{10}H_{16}O}{152.23g \cdot mol^{-1}} = 0.328\ moles$ L sol'n = L camphor + L chloroform $L\ camphor = \frac{50.0\not{g\,C_{10}H_{16}O}}{1} \times \frac{1\not{mL}}{0.990\not{g}} \times \frac{1L}{10^3\not{mL}} = 0.0505L$ Total liters of solution = 1.50 L + 0.0505 L = 1.55 L = 0.328 moles / 1.55 L = 0.212 *M*	***1 point possible*** *1 point for correct answer.*
(d) Determine the molality of the solution. $m = \frac{moles\ camphor}{kg\ chloroform}$ *m* = 0.328 moles camphor / 2.220 kg chloroform = 0.148 *m*	***1 point possible*** *1 point for correct answer.*
(e) The vapor pressure of pure chloroform at 20.°C is 159 mm Hg. Determine the vapor pressure of the chloroform in the solution at 20.°C. $\frac{2220\,\not{g\,CHCl_3}}{1} \times \frac{1mol\,CHCl_3}{119.40\not{g\,CHCl_3}} = 18.6mol\,CHCl_3$ $X_{solute} = \frac{0.328moles\,C_{10}H_{16}O}{0.328mol\,C_{10}H_{16}O + 18.6mol\,CHCl_3} = 0.0173$ $VP_{solution} = VP_{solvent} \cdot X_{solvent}$ = 159 mm Hg (1 − 0.0173) = 156 mm Hg	***2 points possible*** *1 point for correct setup.* *1 point for correct answer.*

(f) Determine the osmotic pressure of the camphor-chloroform solution at 20.°C. 20.°C + 273 = 293K $\pi = iMRT$ $= (1)\ (0.212\ \cancel{moles} \cdot \cancel{L^{-1}})\ (0.0821\ \cancel{L} \cdot atm \cdot \cancel{mol^{-1}} \cdot \cancel{K^{-1}})\ (293\ \cancel{K})$ = 5.10 atm	***1 point possible*** *1 point for correct answer.*
(g) Determine the boiling point of the solution. The normal boiling point of chloroform is 62.0°C. $K_b = 3.63°C / m$ $\Delta T = iK_b\,m$ (1) (3.63°C / $\cancel{m}$) (0.148 $\cancel{m}$) = 0.537°C 62.0°C + 0.537°C = 62.5°C	***1 point possible*** *1 point for correct answer.*
(h) A 0.350 g sample of an unknown molecular compound was dissolved in 15.0 g of chloroform, and the freezing point depression was determined to be 0.240°C. Calculate the molar mass of the molecular compound (K_f for chloroform is 4.70°C · kg · mol^{-1}). $\Delta T_f = K_f \cdot m$ $m = \Delta T_f \cdot K_f^{-1}$ $m = \frac{0.240\cancel{°C}}{4.70\cancel{°C} \cdot kg/mol} = 0.051m$ moles of solute = molality × kg solvent moles of solute = (0.051 m) (0.015 kg) = 7.65×10^{-4} moles 0.350 g / 7.65×10^{-4} moles = 457.5 g/mol	***2 points possible*** *1 point for correct setup.* *1 point for correct answer.*

Equilibrium*

You'll Need to Know

- ❑ the definition of equilibrium
- ❑ how to setup an equilibrium expression
- ❑ how to calculate and interpret the value for K_c
- ❑ how to calculate and interpret the value for K_p
- ❑ how to calculate and interpret the value for K_{sp}
- ❑ how to solve problems involving Le Chatelier's Principle
- ❑ how to calculate and interpret the value for the reaction quotient, Q_c or Q_p
- ❑ how to determine free energy (ΔG) given the reaction quotient, Q
- ❑ how to solve problems that involve the common ion effect

* K_a *and* K_b *are covered in Chapter 11.*

Equilibrium results when the rate of the forward reaction is equal to the rate of the reverse reaction. This means that reactants are being formed at the same rate as products are being formed, indicated by double arrows, $\rightleftharpoons$.

When a chemical reaction has reached equilibrium, collisions are still occurring (i.e., the reaction is occurring in each direction at the same rate). At equilibrium, the reaction can lie far to the right (there are more products) or far to the left (there are more reactants). The concentration of the reactants and products in a reaction at equilibrium can be expressed by an equilibrium constant (K_{eq} or K_c, K_p, K_a, K_b, K_{sp}, etc.), where square brackets represent the concentrations in molarity. Homogeneous equilibrium refers to reactions in which all reacting species are in the same phase. Heterogeneous equilibrium applies to reactions in which the reacting species are in different phases.

For the general reaction $a\text{A} + b\text{B} \rightleftharpoons c\text{C} + d\text{D}$

$$K = \frac{[\text{C}]^c[\text{D}]^d}{[\text{A}]^a[\text{B}]^b}$$

Here are some general rules to follow when solving equilibrium problems:

1. Pure solids and pure liquids (including water) do not appear in the equilibrium expression.
2. When a reactant or product is preceded by a coefficient, its concentration is raised to the power of that coefficient in the equilibrium expression.
3. The equilibrium constant of a reaction occurring in the reverse direction (K^{-1}) is the inverse of the K of the reaction occurring in the forward direction.
4. The equilibrium constant of a net reaction that has two or more steps is found by the product of the equilibrium constants for each of the steps: $K = K_1 \times K_2 \times K_3 \ldots$

Interpretation of *K*

- $K > 1$ indicates more product(s) than reactant(s) at equilibrium.
- $K \approx 1$ indicates about equal amounts of reactant(s) and product(s).
- $K < 1$ indicates less product(s) than reactant(s) at equilibrium.
- The exact value of K is dependent on temperature. Since heat can shift equilibrium concentrations, the K is listed at a certain temperature.
- The value of K is independent of concentration.
- The units for K will vary from reaction to reaction, and are often not listed with units.

$$aA + bB \rightleftharpoons cC + dD$$

$$K_{eq} = \frac{[C]^c[D]^d}{[A]^a[B]^b}$$

$$K_p = K_c(RT)^{\Delta n\ gas}$$

Example

Q. A 100.0 gram sample of PCl_5 (B.P. 160.°C) is placed in an empty 20.0 liter container at 200.°C.

(a) What is the molarity of the PCl_5 in the container prior to decomposition?

(b) What is the pressure in atmospheres of the PCl_5 in the container before any decomposition occurs?

(c) After a period of time, the $PCl_{5(g)}$ had partially decomposed into $PCl_{3(g)}$ and $Cl_{2(g)}$. It was determined experimentally that the PCl_5 had decomposed 45.0% when equilibrium had been established at 200.°C. Calculate both K_c and K_p.

A. (a) $MW\ PCl_5 = 30.9738 + 5(35.453) = 208.239\ g \cdot mol^{-1}$

$$\frac{100.0\ \cancel{g\ PCl_5}}{208.239\ \cancel{g} \cdot mol^{-1}} \times \frac{1}{20.0\ L} = 0.0240\ M$$

(b) $T = 200.°C + 273 = 473K$

$P = nRT \cdot V^{-1}$

$= [(100.0\ \cancel{g\ PCl_5} / 208.239\ \cancel{g} \cdot \cancel{mol^{-1}})(0.0821\ \cancel{L} \cdot atm \cdot \cancel{mol^{-1}} \cdot \cancel{K^{-1}})(473\cancel{K})] / 20.0\ \cancel{L} = 0.932\ atm$

(c) $[PCl_3] = [Cl_2] = (0.02402\ mol / L) \times 0.450 = 1.08 \times 10^{-2}\ M$

$[PCl_5] = (0.02402\ mol / L) \times 0.550 = 1.32 \times 10^{-2}\ M$

$K_c = ([PCl_3][Cl_2]) \div [PCl_5] = (1.08 \times 10^{-2})^2 \div (1.32 \times 10^{-2}) = 8.84 \times 10^{-3}$

$P_{PCl_3} = P_{Cl_2} = 0.932\ atm \times 0.450 = 0.419\ atm$

$P_{PCl_5} = 0.932\ atm \times 0.550 = 0.513\ atm$

$K_p = \left(P_{PCl_3} \times P_{Cl_2}\right) \div P_{PCl_5} = (0.419)^2 \div 0.513 = 3.42 \times 10^{-1}$

K_{sp}

Solubility product constants are used to describe saturated solutions of ionic compounds of relatively low solubility. A saturated solution is in a state of dynamic equilibrium between the dissolved, dissociated ionic compound and the undissolved solid. The solubility of a substance is dependent on the forces holding the crystal together (the lattice energy) and the solvent (usually water) acting on these forces. As a solid dissolves, the ions in solution are surrounded by water molecules by a process called hydration. During hydration, energy is released. The extent to which the energy of hydration is greater than the lattice energy determines the solubility. The solubility product constant is the product of the molar concentrations of the constituent ions, each raised to the power of its stoichiometric coefficient in the equilibrium equation. The smaller the K_{sp}, the less soluble the compound.

For the reaction $A_xB_{y(s)} \rightleftharpoons xA^{y+}{}_{(aq)} + yB^{x-}{}_{(aq)}$

$$K_{sp} = [A^{y+}]^x\,[B^{x-}]^y$$

Example

Q. At 25°C, calcium carbonate has a K_{sp} of 8.7×10^{-9} while that of calcium fluoride has a K_{sp} of 4.0×10^{-11}.

(a) Calculate the molar solubility of calcium carbonate in pure water at 25°C.

(b) Calculate the molar solubility of calcium fluoride in pure water at 25°C.

(c) An aqueous solution of calcium nitrate was added slowly to 1.0 liters of 0.030 moles F^- and 0.070 mole CO_3^{2-} at 25°C (the calcium nitrate does not appreciably affect the total volume). Determine which salt precipitates first.

(d) Calculate the concentration of the calcium ion when the first precipitate forms.

(e) As the student adds more calcium nitrate to the mixture in (c), she notices another precipitate forming. At that point, what percent of the anion of the first precipitate is still in solution?

A. (a) $CaCO_{3(s)} \rightleftharpoons Ca^{2+}{}_{(aq)} + CO_3^{2-}{}_{(aq)}$ at equilibrium: $[CO_3^{2-}] = [Ca^{2+}] = x$

$K_{sp} = (x)\,(x) = 8.7 \times 10^{-9}$ $x = 9.3 \times 10^{-5}\,M$

(b) $CaF_{2(s)} \rightleftharpoons Ca^{2+}{}_{(aq)} + 2F^-{}_{(aq)}$ at equilibrium: $[Ca^{2+}] = x$, $[F^-] = 2x$

$K_{sp} = [Ca^{2+}]\,[F^-]^2 = (x)\,(2x)^2 = 4.0 \times 10^{-11}$

$4x^3 = 4.0 \times 10^{-11}$ $x^3 = 1.0 \times 10^{-11}$ $x = 2.2 \times 10^{-4}\,M$

(c) $CaF_{2(s)} \rightleftharpoons Ca^{2+}{}_{(aq)} + 2F^-{}_{(aq)}$ at equilibrium: $[Ca^{2+}] = x$, $[F^-] = 2x$

$K_{sp} = [Ca^{2+}]\,[F^-]^2 = 4.0 \times 10^{-11}$

$(x)\,(0.030\text{ mole} / 1.0\text{ L})^2 = 4.0 \times 10^{-11}$ $x = 4.4 \times 10^{-8}\,M$

$CaCO_{3(s)} \rightleftharpoons Ca^{2+}{}_{(aq)} + CO_3^{2-}{}_{(aq)}$ at equilibrium: $[CO_3^{2-}] = [Ca^{2+}] = x$

$K_{sp} = (y)\,(0.070 / 1.0\text{ L}) = 8.7 \times 10^{-9}$ $y = 1.2 \times 10^{-7}\,M$

$\therefore$ Since $4.4 \times 10^{-8} < 1.2 \times 10^{-7}$, CaF_2 will precipitate first.

(d) $[Ca^{2+}] = 4.4 \times 10^{-8}\,M$

(e) $CaCO_3$ would be the second precipitate to form. This occurs when $[Ca^{2+}] = 1.2 \times 10^{-7}$.

$K_{sp} = [Ca^{2+}]\,[F^-]^2 = 4.0 \times 10^{-11} = (1.2 \times 10^{-7})\,(z)^2 = 4.0 \times 10^{-11} \qquad z = 1.8 \times 10^{-2}$

$\%\ F^-$ still in solution $= (1.8 \times 10^{-2} / 3.0 \times 10^{-2}) \times 100\% = 60.\%$

Le Chatelier's Principle

If stress is applied to a system at equilibrium, the position of the equilibrium will shift in the direction that reduces the stress to reinstate equilibrium.

Rule	*Example*
If more reactants are added to the system, the reaction will shift in the forward direction.	$A + 2B \rightleftharpoons C + D$ $\longrightarrow$ The position of equilibrium moves to the right if you increase the concentration of A.
A temperature increase favors an endothermic reaction and a temperature decrease favors an exothermic reaction. If heat is added to the system and the reaction is exothermic (heat is a product), the reaction will shift to the left.	$A + 2B \rightleftharpoons C + D \quad \Delta H = -250\ \text{kJ mol}^{-1}$ $\longrightarrow$ The position of equilibrium moves to the left if you increase the temperature.
Addition of pressure will cause the reaction to shift in the direction that results in the fewer number of moles of a gas.	$A(g) + 2B(g) \rightleftharpoons C(g) - D(g)$ $\longrightarrow$ The position of equilibrium moves to the right if you increase the pressure or the reaction.

Example

$$2CO_{(g)} + O_{2(g)} \rightleftharpoons 2CO_{2(g)} \qquad \Delta H < 0$$

Q. Which of the following changes alone would cause a decrease in the value of K_{eq} for the reaction represented above?

A. Decreasing the temperature
B. Increasing the temperature
C. Decreasing the volume of the reaction vessel
D. Increasing the pressure within the reaction vessel
E. Adding a catalyst

A. **B.** To decrease K_{eq} means less product is produced (i.e., CO_2). $\Delta H < 0$ means that the reaction is exothermic (gives off heat). Therefore, the reaction could be written $2CO_{(g)} + O_{2(g)} \rightleftharpoons 2CO_{2(g)}$ + heat. Adding more heat on the right side of the equation would shift the equilibrium to the left, resulting in less CO_2. Decreasing the volume of a reaction vessel has the same effect as increasing the pressure. Increasing the pressure for this particular reaction would shift in the direction that results in the fewer number of moles of a gas, which would result in a higher concentration of $CO_{2(g)}$. Pressure changes and catalysts have no effect on the value of K_{eq}.

Reaction Quotient, Q_c or Q_p

The reaction quotient, Q_c or Q_p, is determined in the same manner as K_c or K_p and concentrations can represent either initial partial pressures or initial molar concentrations. Q is used to determine which direction a reaction will shift to reach equilibrium but uses initial conditions, not conditions at equilibrium.

$$aA + bB \rightleftharpoons cC + dD$$

$$Q = \frac{[C]^c[D]^d}{[A]^a[B]^b}$$

If $Q < K$, then products are favored (reaction goes from left to right)

If $Q > K$, then reactants are favored (the reaction goes from right to left)

If $Q = K$, the reaction is at equilibrium.

Example

Q. 0.035 moles of SO_2, 0.500 moles of SO_2Cl_2, and 0.080 moles of Cl_2 were initially combined in an evacuated 5.00 L flask and heated to 100.°C. K_c for the decomposition of SO_2Cl_2 is 0.078 at 100.°C. Which direction will the reaction proceed in order to establish equilibrium?

A. $SO_2Cl_{2(g)} \rightleftharpoons SO_{2(g)} + Cl_{2(g)} \quad K_c = 0.078$ at 100.°C

$$Q_c = \frac{[SO_2][Cl_2]}{[SO_2Cl_2]} = \frac{(0.035\text{ mole}/5.00\text{L})(0.080\text{ mole}/5.00\text{L})}{(0.500\text{ mole}/5.00\text{L})} = \frac{(0.0070)(0.016)}{(0.100)}$$

$$Q_c = 0.0011$$

Since $Q_c < K_c$, the reaction will proceed in the forward direction in order to increase the concentrations of both SO_2 and Cl_2 and decrease that of SO_2Cl_2 until $Q_c = K_c$.

Free Energy and Equilibrium Constants

The following equation relates the standard-state free energy of reaction with the free energy of reaction at any moment in time during a reaction (not necessarily at standard-state conditions):

$$\Delta G° = -RT \ln K$$

$$\Delta G = \Delta G° + R \cdot T \cdot \ln Q$$

where ΔG = free energy at any moment, $\Delta G°$ = standard-state free energy; R = ideal gas constant (8.314 J · mol^{-1} · K^{-1}); T is temperature in Kelvin; ln Q = natural log of the reaction quotient, and ln K is the natural log of the equilibrium constant.

K	$\Delta G°$	*Comments*
> 1	–	Products are favored over reactants at equilibrium.
= 1	0	Products and reactants are equally favored at equilibrium.
< 1	+	Reactants are favored over products at equilibrium.

Example

Q. Given the following reaction and data below occurring at 27°C, calculate ΔG and predict whether the reaction is spontaneous or not.

$N_{2(g)} + 3H_{2(g)} \rightleftharpoons 2NH_{3(g)}$ $\quad \Delta G° = -33.2$ kJ

$P_{NH_3} = 0.75$ atm $\quad P_{N_2} = 1.50$ atm $\quad P_{H_2} = 0.500$ atm

A. $Q = \dfrac{(P_{NH_3})^2}{(P_{N_2})(P_{H_2})^3} = \dfrac{(0.75)^2}{(1.50)(0.500)^3} = \dfrac{0.56}{0.188} = 3.0$

$T = 27°C + 273 = 300K$

$R = 8.3148\ J \cdot K^{-1} \cdot mol^{-1}$

$\Delta G° = -33.2$ kJ/mol $= -3.32 \times 10^4$ J/mol

$\Delta G = \Delta G° + RT \ln Q$

$\Delta G = (-3.32 \times 10^4\ J) + (8.3148\ J \cdot K^{-1} \cdot mol^{-1})\ (300.K) \ln (3.0)$

$\Delta G = (-3.32 \times 10^4\ J) + (2.74 \times 10^3\ J) = -3.05 \times 10^4\ J$

Since ΔG is negative, the reaction will occur spontaneously.

Common Ion Effect

The common ion effect occurs when there are two sources of the same ion involved in an equilibrium reaction.

Example

Q. Calculate the solubility of silver bromide (in g/L) in a 5.8×10^{-3} *M* silver nitrate solution. K_{sp} AgBr = 7.7×10^{-13}.

A. All nitrates are soluble.

$$AgNO_{3\,(s)} \xrightarrow{H_2O} Ag^+_{(aq)} + NO_3^-{}_{(aq)}$$

let s = molar solubility of AgBr in $AgNO_3$ solution.

$AgBr_{(s)} \rightleftharpoons Ag^+_{(aq)} + Br^-_{(aq)}$

	$Ag^+_{(aq)}$	$Br^-_{(aq)}$
Initial (*M*)	5.8×10^{-3} *M*	0.0
Change (*M*)	$+s$	$+s$
Equilibrium (*M*)	$(5.8 \times 10^{-3} + s)$	s

$K_{sp} = [Ag^+]\,[Br^-]$

$7.7 \times 10^{-13} = (5.8 \times 10^{-3} + s)\,(s)$

Since AgBr is rather insoluble, and Ag^+ from $AgNO_3$ lowers the solubility of AgBr even more, $s < 5.8 \times 10^{-3}$. Therefore, $5.8 \times 10^{-3} + s \approx 5.8 \times 10^{-3}$

$7.7 \times 10^{-13} = 5.8 \times 10^{-3}\,(s)$

$s = 1.3 \times 10^{-10}\,M$

At equilibrium: $[Ag^+] = (5.8 \times 10^{-3} + 1.3 \times 10^{-10})M = 5.8 \times 10^{-3}\,M$

$[Br^-] = 1.3 \times 10^{-10}\,M$

$$\text{solubility in AgNO}_3\text{ solution} = \frac{1.3 \times 10^{-10}\ \cancel{\text{mol AgBr}}}{1\text{ L sol'n}} \times \frac{187.8\text{ g AgBr}}{1\ \cancel{\text{mol AgBr}}} = 2.4 \times 10^{-8}\text{ g/L}$$

Multiple-Choice Questions

1. Using molar concentrations, what are the units of K_c?

$$2Cl_{2(g)} + 2H_2O_{(g)} \rightleftharpoons 4HCl_{(g)} + O_{2(g)}$$

A. M^{-2}
B. M^{-1}
C. M^0
D. M^1
E. M^2

2. Which of the following is true?

A. $K_c = K_c^{-1}$
B. $K_c + K_c^{-1} = 1$
C. $K_c \cdot K_c^{-1} = 1$
D. $K_c - K_c^{-1} = 0$
E. $K_c \div K_c^{-1} = 1$

3. $2CO_{(g)} + O_{2(g)} \rightleftharpoons 2CO_{2(g)}$

At 1000°C, the K_c for the reaction above was determined to be 6.02×10^{23}. What is the K_p at the same temperature?

A. 4.88×10^{-3}
B. 5.39×10^{7}
C. 7.42×10^{19}
D. 8.34×10^{20}
E. 5.76×10^{21}

4. $H_{2(g)} + CO_{2(g)} \rightleftharpoons H_2O_{(g)} + CO_{(g)}$

For the reaction above, K_c was determined to be 0.534 at 700.°C. In an equilibrium mixture of these four gases at 700.°C, which of the following are true?

A. [CO] will always be greater than $[CO_2]$
B. [CO] will always be less than $[CO_2]$
C. [CO] will always be equal to $[CO_2]$
D. [CO] will never be equal to $[CO_2]$
E. none of the above are true

5. 3.00 moles of $NO_{2(g)}$ was initially placed in a 2.00-L reaction vessel maintained at 500.°C. After equilibrium was established, it was found that 25.0% of the $NO_{2(g)}$ had dissociated into $NO_{(g)}$ and $O_{2(g)}$. The equilibrium constant, K_c for the reaction is

A. 2.07×10^{-2}
B. 4.63×10^{-1}
C. 3.11
D. 8.38×10^{1}
E. 4.91×10^{2}

6. For the reaction

$$A_{(g)} + B_{(g)} \rightleftharpoons C_{(g)} + D_{(g)}$$

in order to increase the amount of D, you could

A. add more C for D to react with.
B. remove some C.
C. decrease the volume of the container.
D. increase the volume of the container.
E. add a catalyst to speed up the reaction to make more D.

7. The equilibrium constant K_c for the reaction

$$COCl_{2(g)} \rightleftharpoons CO_{(g)} + Cl_{2(g)}$$

is 1.67×10^2 at 850.°C. The initial pressures of each gas are as follows: $COCl_{2(g)} = 0.500$ atm; $CO_{(g)} = 0.250$ atm; and $Cl_{2(g)} = 0.750$ atm. Which of the following are true?

A. The system will change such that the pressures of $CO_{(g)}$ and $Cl_{2(g)}$ will decrease while that of $COCl_{2(g)}$ will increase.
B. The system will change such that the pressures of $CO_{(g)}$ and $Cl_{2(g)}$ will increase while that of $COCl_{2(g)}$ will decrease.
C. The system will not change. All pressures will remain constant and in equilibrium.
D. The system will change such that only the pressure of $COCl_{(g)}$ will increase while all other gases will maintain the same pressure.
E. None of the above are true.

8. Referring to Question 7 above, what are the final pressures of each gas when equilibrium is achieved?

A. $[COCl_2] = 0.033$ atm; $[CO] = 0.153$ atm; $[Cl_2] = 5.442$ atm
B. $[COCl_2] = 0.336$ atm; $[CO] = 3.66$ atm; $[Cl_2] = 3.22$ atm
C. $[COCl_2] = 0.006$ atm; $[CO] = 0.744$ atm; $[Cl_2] = 3.556$ atm
D. $[COCl_2] = 0.006$ atm; $[CO] = 0.744$ atm; $[Cl_2] = 1.244$ atm
E. $[COCl_2] = 17.3$ atm; $[CO] = 0.554$ atm; $[Cl_2] = 2.558$ atm

9. Given the following reaction:

$$2A_{(g)} \rightleftharpoons B_{2(g)} + 3C_{(g)} \qquad \Delta H° = +78.4 \text{ kJ}$$

To achieve the maximum amount of products, the reaction should be carried out at

A. low *T*, low *P*.
B. low *T*, high *P*.
C. high *T*, high *P*.
D. high *T*, low *P*.
E. None of the above.

10. What is the concentration of $Ag^+_{(aq)}$ for a 0.13 *M* solution of $Ag(CN)_2^-$ ($K_f = 3.0 \times 10^{20}$)?

A. 6.3×10^{-21} *M*
B. 8.8×10^{-17} *M*
C. 1.5×10^{-11} *M*
D. 3.7×10^{-9} *M*
E. 4.7×10^{-7} *M*

11. Given $2NOCl_{(g)} \rightleftharpoons 2NO_{(g)} + Cl_{2(g)}$, $K_c = 4.4 \times 10^{-6}$ at 250.°C, what is the equilibrium constant for $6NO_{(g)} + 3Cl_{2(g)} \rightleftharpoons 6NOCl_{(g)}$ at the same temperature?

A. 2.2×10^3
B. 4.4×10^6
C. 1.2×10^{16}
D. 8.8×10^{18}
E. 1.32×10^{19}

12. The solubility of silver carbonate (Ag_2CO_3) in water at 25°C is given as 0.036 g · L^{-1}. The K_{sp} of Ag_2CO_3 at this temperature is

A. 8.8×10^{-12}
B. 4.4×10^{-6}
C. 2.2×10^{-3}
D. 1.1×10^3
E. 2.2×10^6

13. If the K_{sp} of barium fluoride (BaF_2) is 1.7×10^{-6} at 25°C, a solution where $[Ba^{2+}]$ is 1.0 *M* may have a concentration (*M*) of $F^-_{(aq)}$

A. not greater than $(K_{sp})^{1/2}$.
B. not less than $(K_{sp})^{1/2}$.
C. not greater than $(K_{sp})^2$.
D. not less than 2.0 *M*.
E. not greater than 2.0 *M*.

14. If 300. mL of 0.0500 *M* barium fluoride is added to 400. mL of 0.0750 *M* sodium sulfate, which of the following is true? (K_{sp} $BaSO_4 = 1.1 \times 10^{-10}$)

A. Barium sulfate will precipitate out, $Q > K_{sp}$.
B. Barium sulfate will not precipitate out, $Q > K_{sp}$.
C. Barium sulfate will precipitate out, $Q < K_{sp}$.
D. Barium sulfate will not precipitate out, $Q < K_{sp}$.
E. Barium sulfate will not precipitate out since it is soluble.

For Questions 15–17: Solid sodium bromide (NaBr) is slowly added to a solution that was made by adding 250. mL of 0.100 *M* $CuNO_3$ and 250. mL of 0.100 *M* $AgNO_3$. K_{sp} CuBr = 4.2×10^{-8}; K_{sp} AgBr = 7.7×10^{-13}.

15. Which one of the following will precipitate first?

A. CuBr
B. AgBr
C. NaBr
D. $NaNO_3$
E. $Ag_{(s)}$

16. The concentration of Ag^+ when CuBr just begins to precipitate is

A. 7.7×10^{-13} *M*
B. 5.3×10^{-12} *M*
C. 8.2×10^{-9} *M*
D. 4.2×10^{-8} *M*
E. 9.2×10^{-7} *M*

17. What percent of the $Ag^+_{(aq)}$ remains in solution when CuBr just begins to precipitate out?

A. 0%
B. 1.8×10^{-3} %
C. 39%
D. 52%
E. 100%

18. How many grams of magnesium carbonate (MW = 84.32 g · mol^{-1}) will dissolve in 3.00 L of 0.075 *M* $Mg(NO_3)_2$? K_{sp} $MgCO_3$ = 4.0×10^{-5}

A. 0 g
B. 0.025 g
C. 0.13 g
D. 1.6 g
E. 32 g

19. Given the following statements, which one is true?

I. The equilibrium constant for an exothermic reaction is always negative.
II. Increasing the pressure on a system at equilibrium always causes the system to adjust so as to relieve the stress.
III. A homogeneous equilibrium is one involving only one substance.
IV. The rate at which substances reach equilibrium may be increased by adding a catalyst.

A. I and II
B. I and IV
C. II and III
D. III and IV
E. IV

20. Given the following thermodynamic data, calculate K_p at 25°C for the following reaction:

$$N_{2(g)} + 3H_{2(g)} \rightleftharpoons 2NH_{3(g)}$$

$\Delta H°_{rxn} = -92.6$ kJ $\quad \Delta S°_{rxn} = -199$ J · K^{-1}

A. 4.96×10^2
B. 9.40×10^3
C. 4.33×10^4
D. 6.60×10^5
E. 4.50×10^6

Free-Response Questions

1. Ammonium chloride (NH_4Cl), sometimes known as sal ammoniac, is in its pure form, a clear white, water-soluble crystalline salt with a biting, slightly sour taste. When heated, it decomposes into ammonia gas and hydrogen chloride gas as follows:

$$NH_4Cl_{(s)} \rightarrow NH_{3(g)} + HCl_{(g)}$$

(a) A sample of solid ammonium chloride is placed in an 1.00-L evacuated flask and heated until it decomposes into ammonia gas and hydrogen chloride gas. After equilibrium was attained (with some solid NH_4Cl remaining at the bottom of the flask), the total pressure inside the flask was determined to be 0.750 atmospheres at a temperature of 286°C. Calculate K_p at this temperature.

(b) Later, extra ammonia gas is injected into the flask and the mixture is allowed to come back into equilibrium (temperature remained constant). It was then discovered that the partial pressure of ammonia gas was three times the partial pressure of the hydrogen chloride gas. Calculate the partial pressure of the ammonia gas and the partial pressure of the hydrogen chloride gas.

(c) In a separate experiment, $NH_{3(g)}$ and $HCl_{(g)}$ are injected into the same empty 1.00-L vessel at 286°C. The initial pressure of each gas was 1.50 atm. Calculate the number of grams of solid NH_4Cl that was present when equilibrium was established. (MM $NH_4Cl = 53.49\ g \cdot mol^{-1}$).

2. The K_{sp} of calcium hydroxide, $Ca(OH)_2$, is 8.0×10^{-6} at 25°C.

(a) Write a balanced equation for the solubility equilibrium.

(b) Determine the solubility of calcium hydroxide in grams per liter.

(c) Calculate the pH of a saturated solution of calcium hydroxide at 25°C.

(d) A 75.0-mL sample of 2.50×10^{-2} M $CaSO_4$ solution is added to 75.0-mL of a 3.00×10^{-2} molar NaOH solution. Does a precipitate of $Ca(OH)_2$ form? Explain and show calculations to support your answer.

Answers and Explanations

Multiple Choice

1. D. $K_c = \frac{[HCl]^4[O_2]^1}{[Cl_2]^2[H_2O]^2} = \frac{M^5}{M^4} = M$

2. C. This relationship is universally true. Any number multiplied by its reciprocal is equal to 1. Chemical equilibrium results when the forward chemical reactions proceed at the same rate as their reverse reactions. The rates of the forward and reverse reactions are generally not zero but, being equal, there are no net changes in any of the reactant or product concentrations.

3. E. $K_p = K_c(0.0821\ T)^{\Delta n}$

$T = 1000°C + 273 = 1273K$

$\Delta n = 2 - 3 = -1$

$K_p = 6.02 \times 10^{23}(0.0821 \times 1273)^{-1} = 5.76 \times 10^{21}$

4. E. The relationship $[H_2O]\ [CO]\ /\ [CO_2]\ [H_2]$ at 700.°C must always have the value of K_c, regardless of the relationship of $[CO]\ /\ [CO_2]$.

5. A. $2NO_{2(g)} \rightleftharpoons 2NO_{(g)} + O_{2(g)}$

$[NO_2]_0 = \frac{3.00\ \text{mol}}{2.00\ \text{L}} = 1.50\ M$

After 25.0% dissociation at equilibrium:

$[NO_2] = (1 - 0.250)\ (1.50\ M) = 1.13\ M$

$[NO] = (0.250)\ (1.50\ M) = 0.375\ M$

$[O_2] = 1/2\ (0.250)\ (1.50\ M) = 0.188\ M$

$K_c = \frac{[NO]^2[O_2]}{[NO_2]^2} = \frac{(0.375)^2(0.188)}{(1.13)^2} = 2.07 \times 10^{-2}$

6. B. Removing C shifts the equilibrium to the right, producing more D. Changing the volume of the container would change the concentrations of all species, but no shift would occur because there are equal numbers of moles of gas on both sides of the equation.

7. B. $Q_p = \frac{(P_{CO})(P_{Cl_2})}{P_{COCl_2}} = \frac{(0.250)(0.750)}{0.500} = 0.375$

The calculated Q_P is less than K_P for this system; therefore, the system will change in a way to increase Q_P until it is equal to K_P. To achieve this, the pressures of $CO_{(g)}$ and $Cl_{2(g)}$ must increase and the pressure of $COCl_{2(g)}$ must decrease.

8. D.

	$COCl_2$	CO	Cl_2
Initial	0.500 atm	0.250 atm	0.750 atm
Change	$-x$	$+x$	$+x$
Equilibrium	$0.500 - x$	$0.250 + x$	$0.750 + x$

$$K_p = \frac{(P_{CO})(P_{Cl_2})}{P_{COCl_2}} = \frac{(0.250 + x)(0.750 + x)}{0.500 - x} = 1.67 \times 10^2$$

$(0.250 + x)\ (0.750 + x) = (0.500 - x)\ (1.67 \times 10^2)$ ***(Hint:** Quadratic equation is required).*

$x = 0.494$ Therefore, $[COCl_2] = 0.500 - 0.494 = 0.006$ atm

$[CO] = 0.250 + 0.494 = 0.744$ atm $[Cl_2] = 0.750 + 0.494 = 1.244$

9. D. heat + $2A_{(g)} \rightleftharpoons B_{2(g)}\ 3C_{(g)}$ More heat shifts the equilibrium to the right (products). Low pressure favors the formation of the larger number of moles of gas.

10. C. $Ag^+_{(aq)} + 2CN^-_{(aq)} \rightleftharpoons Ag(CN)_2^-{}_{(aq)}$

$$K_f = \frac{[Ag(CN)_2^-]}{[Ag^+][CN^-]^2}$$

	Ag^+	CN^-	$Ag(CN)_2^-$
Initial Conc. (*M*)	0	0	0.13
Change	$+x$	$+2x$	$-x$
Equilibrium (*M*)	x	$2x$	$0.13 - x$

$$3.0 \times 10^{20} = \frac{(0.13 - x)}{x(2x)^2}$$

Assuming x is small, since K greatly favors the complex ion:

$$3.0 \times 10^{20} = \frac{(0.13)}{x(2x)^2} \qquad x = 4.8 \times 10^{-8}\ M = [Ag^+]$$

Note: This problem comes from the perspective of K_f, the reverse of K_{sp}. It's a good idea to be able to understand how to solve these types of problems from either direction.

11. C. The reaction is both reversed and multiplied by 3 when compared to the original. Therefore,

$$K_c = \frac{1}{K_c^3} = \frac{1}{(4.4 \times 10^{-6})^3} = 1.2 \times 10^{16}$$

12. A. $Ag_2CO_{3(s)} \rightleftharpoons 2Ag^+_{(aq)} + CO_3^{2-}{}_{(aq)}$

$$\frac{0.036\ \text{g } Ag_2CO_3}{1\text{ L sol'n}} \times \frac{1\text{ mol g } Ag_2CO_3}{275.8\text{ g } Ag_2CO_3} = 1.3 \times 10^{-4}\ M$$

$[CO_3^{2-}] = 1.3 \times 10^{-4}\ M$

$[Ag^+] = 2 \times [CO_3^{2-}] = 2.6 \times 10^{-4}\ M$

$K_{sp} = [Ag^+]^2[CO_3^{2-}] = (2.6 \times 10^{-4})^2\ (1.3 \times 10^{-4}) = 8.8 \times 10^{-12}$

Hint: Knowing from the solubility rules that silver carbonate is not very soluble, you could easily rule out choices D and E.

13. **A.** $BaF_{2(s)} \rightleftharpoons Ba^{2+}_{(aq)} + 2F^{-}_{(aq)}$ $\quad K_{sp} = [F^{-}]^2 [Ba^{2+}]$

BaF_2 will begin to precipitate if $[F^{-}] = (K_{sp} / [Ba^{2+}])^{1/2}$

14. **A.** $Ba^{2+}_{(aq)} + SO_4^{2-}{}_{(aq)} \rightarrow BaSO_{4(s)}$

Number of moles of $Ba^{2+}_{(aq)}$ initially present:

$$\frac{300.\ \cancel{mL}}{1} \times \frac{1\ \cancel{L}}{10^3\ \cancel{mL}} \times \frac{0.0500\ mol\ Ba^{2+}}{1\ \cancel{L\ sol'n}} = 1.50 \times 10^{-2}\ mol\ Ba^{2+}$$

Total volume: 300. mL + 400. mL = 700. mL = 0.700 L

$$[Ba^{2+}] = \frac{1.50 \times 10^{-2}\ mol\ Ba^{2+}}{0.700\ L} = 2.14 \times 10^{-2}\ M$$

Number of moles of $SO_4^{2-}{}_{(aq)}$ initially present:

$$\frac{400.\ \cancel{mL}}{1} \times \frac{1\ \cancel{L}}{10^3\ \cancel{mL}} \times \frac{0.0750\ mol\ SO_4^{2-}}{1\ \cancel{L\ sol'n}} = 3.00 \times 10^{-2}\ moles$$

$[SO_4^{2-}] = 3.00 \times 10^{-2}$ moles / 0.700 L = $4.29 \times 10^{-2}\ M$

$Q = [Ba^{2+}]\ [SO_4^{2-}] = (2.14 \times 10^{-2})\ (4.29 \times 10^{-2}) = 9.18 \times 10^{-4}$

Therefore, since Q $(9.18 \times 10^{-4}) > K_{sp}$ (1.1×10^{-10}), a precipitate will be formed.

15. **B.** AgBr has the smallest K_{sp} value.

16. **E.** When $CuBr_{(s)}$ first begins to precipitate out, the solubility product expression will equal K_{sp}.

250. mL of 0.100 M $CuNO_3$
+250. mL of 0.100 M $AgNO_3$
500. mL of solution

$$mol\ Cu^{+} = \frac{0.100\ mol\ Cu^{+1}}{\cancel{L\ sol'n}} \times \frac{0.250\ \cancel{L\ sol'n}}{1} = 0.025\ mol\ Cu^{+}$$

$[Cu^{+}] = 0.025$ mol Cu^{+} / 0.500 total L sol'n = $0.0500\ M\ Cu^{+}$

$K_{sp} = [Cu^{+}]\ [Br^{-}] = (0.0500)\ [Br^{-}] = 4.2 \times 10^{-8}$ $\qquad [Br^{-}] = 8.4 \times 10^{-7}\ M$

$$[Ag^{+}] = \frac{K_{sp}}{[Br^{-}]} = \frac{7.7 \times 10^{-13}}{8.4 \times 10^{-7}} = 9.2 \times 10^{-7}\ M$$

17. **B.**

$$\%\ Ag^{+}_{(aq)} = \frac{9.2 \times 10^{-7}\ M}{0.0500\ M} \times 100\% = 1.8 \times 10^{-3}\ \%$$

18. **C.** Let x = the molar solubility of $MgCO_3$ in the solution.

$$MgCO_{3(s)} \rightleftharpoons Mg^{2+}_{(aq)} + CO_3^{2-}{}_{(aq)}$$

	Mg^{2+}	CO_3^{2-}
Initial Conc (M)	0.075	0
Change	$+x$	$+x$
Final Conc (M)	$0.075 + x$	$+x$

$K_{sp}\ MgCO_3 = [Mg^{2+}]\ [CO_3^{2-}] = (0.075 + x)\ (x) = 4.0 \times 10^{-5}$

Assume that $0.075 + x = 0.075$; therefore,

$$x = \frac{4.0 \times 10^{-5}}{0.075} = 5.3 \times 10^{-4}\,M$$

$$\frac{3\,\cancel{\text{L sol'n}}}{1} \times \frac{5.3 \times 10^{-4}\,\cancel{\text{mol MgCO}_3}}{1\,\cancel{\text{L}}} \times \frac{84.32\,\text{g MgCO}_3}{1\,\cancel{\text{mol MgCO}_3}} = 0.13\,\text{g MgCO}_3$$

19. **E.** A catalyst provides an easier path for the reaction, the path for the reverse reaction is made equally easier. A catalyst will not shift an equilibrium position because both rates are equally increased. The equilibrium is achieved quicker in time and under easier conditions, however.

20. **D.** $\Delta G° = \Delta H° - T\Delta S°$ $\quad T = 25°C + 273 = 298K$

$= -92{,}600\text{ J} - (298\cancel{K})(-199\text{ J}\cdot \cancel{K^{-1}}) = -3.33 \times 10^4\text{ J}$

$\Delta G° = -RT \ln K_p$

$-3.33 \times 10^4\text{ J} = -(8.314\text{ J/K}\cdot\text{mol})(298K) \ln K_p$

$\ln K_p = 13.4 \quad K_p = 6.60 \times 10^5$

Free Response

Question 1

Maximum Points for Question 1
Part (a): 3 points
Part (b): 3 points
Part (c): 4 points
Total points: 10

1. Ammonium chloride (NH_4Cl), sometimes known as sal ammoniac, is in its pure form, a clear white, water-soluble crystalline salt with a biting, slightly sour taste. When heated, it decomposes into ammonia gas and hydrogen chloride gas as follows: $NH_4Cl_{(s)} \rightarrow NH_{3(g)} + HCl_{(g)}$ *(a) A sample of solid ammonium chloride is placed in an evacuated 1.00-L flask and heated until it decomposes into ammonia gas and hydrogen chloride gas. After equilibrium was attained (with some solid NH_4Cl remaining at the bottom of the flask), the total pressure inside the flask was determined to be 0.750 atmospheres at a temperature of 286°C. Calculate K_p at this temperature.*	***3 points possible***
$K_p = (P_{NH_3})(P_{HCl})$	*1 point for showing that $K_p = (P_{NH_3})(P_{HCl})$.*
$P_{NH_3} = P_{HCl} = (0.750\text{atm}/2) = 0.375\text{atm}$	*1 point for showing that $P_{NH_3} = P_{HCL} = (750\,\text{atm}/2)$.*
$K_p = (0.375\text{ atm})(0.375\text{ atm}) = 0.141\text{ atm}^2$	*1 point for correct answer for K_p.*

(b) Later, extra ammonia gas is injected into the flask and the mixture is allowed to come back into equilibrium (temperature remained constant). It was then discovered that the partial pressure of ammonia gas was three times the partial pressure of the hydrogen chloride gas. Calculate the partial pressure of the ammonia gas and the partial pressure of the hydrogen chloride gas. $P_{NH_3} = 3P_{HCl}$ Let $x = P_{HCl}$ $(3x)(x) = 0.141\ \text{atm}^2$ $x = 0.217\ \text{atm} = P_{HCl}$ $3x = 0.651\,\text{atm} = P_{NH_3}$	***3 points possible*** *1 point for showing that* $P_{NH_3} = 3P_{HCl}$. *1 point for correct partial pressure of* NH_3. *1 point for correct partial pressure of HCl.*
(c) In a separate experiment, $NH_{3(g)}$ *and* $HCl_{(g)}$ *are injected into the same empty 1.00-L vessel at 286°C. The initial pressure of each gas was 1.50 atm. Calculate the number of grams of solid* NH_4Cl *that was present when equilibrium was established. (MM* $NH_4Cl = 53.49\ g \cdot mol^{-1}$*)* The temperature of 286°C (559K) was the same as that used to determine K_p in section (a) above. $K_p = 0.141$. The size of the flask also was the same. $P_{NH_{3(g)}} = P_{HCl_{(g)}} = (1.50 - x)^2 = K_p = 0.141$ $x = 1.12\ \text{atm}$ $n = \frac{PV}{RT} = \frac{(1.12\,\text{atm})(1.00\,\text{L})}{(0.0821\,\text{L}\cdot\text{atm}\cdot\text{mol}^{-1}\cdot\text{K}^{-1})(559\,\text{K})}$ $= 2.44 \times 10^{-2}\ \text{mol}$ $\frac{2.44 \times 10^{-2}\ \text{mol}\ NH_4Cl}{1} \times \frac{53.49\text{g}}{1\ \text{mol}} = 1.31\text{g}$	***4 points possible*** *1 point for showing that* P_{NH_3} *that has reacted* $= P_{HCl}$. *1 point for correct* P_{NH_3} *that reacted.* *1 point for correct use of* $PV = nRT$. *1 point for correct number of grams of* NH_4Cl.

Question 2

Maximum Points for Question 2
Part (a): 1 point
Part (b): 3 points
Part (c): 2 points
Part (d): 4 points
Total points: 10

2. The K_{sp} of calcium hydroxide, $Ca(OH)_2$, is 8.0×10^{-6} at 25°C.	***1 point possible***
(a) Write a balanced equation for the solubility equilibrium.	
$Ca(OH)_{2(s)} \rightarrow Ca^{2+}{}_{(aq)} + 2OH^{-}{}_{(aq)}$	*1 point for correctly balanced equation.*
(b) Determine the solubility of calcium hydroxide in grams per liter.	***3 points possible***
$K_{sp} = [Ca^{2+}]\,[OH^{-}]^2$	
Let $x = [Ca^{2+}]$; $2x = [OH^{-}]$	*1 point for correct K_{sp} expression.*
$K_{sp} = (x)\,(2x)^2 = 4x^3 = 8.0 \times 10^{-6}$	
$x = 0.0126\ M$	*1 point for correct setup.*
$\dfrac{0.0126\ \text{moles}\ Ca(OH)_2}{L} \times \dfrac{74.093\,g\ Ca(OH)_2}{1\ \text{mol}\ Ca(OH)_2}$	*1 point for correct answer.*
$= 0.933\ g \cdot L^{-1}$	
(c) Calculate the pH of a saturated solution of calcium hydroxide at 25°C.	***2 points possible***
From *(b)* above: $x = [Ca^{2+}]$; $2x = [OH^{-}]$	*1 point for correct setup.*
$x = 0.0126\ M$; $[OH^{-}] = 2x = 2(0.0126) = 0.0252\ M$	
$[H^{+}] = 1.0 \times 10^{-14} / [OH^{-}]$	*1 point for correct answer.*
$= 1.0 \times 10^{-14} / 0.0252$	
$= 3.97 \times 10^{-13}$	
$pH = -\log [H^{+}] = 12.4$	
(d) A 75.0-mL sample of 2.50×10^{-2} M $CaSO_4$ solution is added to 75.0-mL of a 3.00×10^{-2} molar NaOH solution. Does a precipitate of $Ca(OH)_2$ form? Explain and show calculations to support your answer.	***4 points possible***
Total volume = 75.0 mL + 75.0 mL = 150.0 mL	*1 point for correct Ca^{2+} concentration.*
$V_1M_1 = V_2M_2$	
$[Ca^{2+}]$: $(0.075\ L)\,(2.50 \times 10^{-2}\ M) = (x\ M)\,(0.150\ L) = 1.25 \times 10^{-2}\ M$	*1 point for correct OH^{-} concentration.*
$[OH^{-}] = (0.075\ L)\,(3.00 \times 10^{-2}\ M) = (x\ M)\,(0.150\ L) = 1.50 \times 10^{-2}\ M$	
$Q = [Ca^{2+}]\,[OH^{-}]^2$	*1 point for correct value of Q.*
$= (1.25 \times 10^{-2})\,(1.50 \times 10^{-2})^2 = 2.81 \times 10^{-6}$	
Precipitate will NOT form since $Q\ (2.81\ 10^{-6}) < K_{sp}\ (8.0 \times 10^{-6})$	*1 point for correct conclusion that a precipitate will not form.*

Acids and Bases

You'll Need to Know

- ❑ what is the Brønsted-Lowry acid-base theory
- ❑ what is the Arrhenius acid-base theory
- ❑ what is the Lewis acid-base theory
- ❑ how to identify conjugate acids and bases
- ❑ how to solve pH and pOH problems
- ❑ how to solve problems involving K_a and pK_a
- ❑ how to solve problems involving K_b and pK_b
- ❑ how to solve problems involving polyprotic acids
- ❑ how to determine the relative strengths of oxyacids
- ❑ the acid-base properties of common ions in aqueous solution
- ❑ molecular structure and correlation with acid strength
- ❑ how to solve problems involving titration
- ❑ how to draw and interpret titration curves
- ❑ how to determine the % ionization of a weak acid or basic solution
- ❑ what are buffers and how to solve problems that involve buffers (Henderson-Hasselbalch equation)
- ❑ how indicators work and solve problems involving indicators
- ❑ what are anhydrides and how to write equations involving anhydrides
- ❑ what are amphoteric substances and how to solve problems involving them

Brønsted-Lowry Theory

Any compound that can transfer (donate) a proton (H^+) to any other compound is a Brønsted acid, and the compound that accepts the proton is a Brønsted base.

Example

Q. Which one of the following CANNOT act as both a Brønsted acid and a Brønsted base?

A. HS^-
B. $H_2PO_4^-$
C. H_2O
D. NH_4^+
E. HCO_3^-

A. **D.** NH_4^+ can only donate a proton: $NH_4^+ \rightarrow NH_3 + H^+$ and act as a Brønsted acid. All other choices can either accept a proton or donate a proton.

Brønsted Acid	*Brønsted Base*
$HS^- \rightarrow H^+ + S^{2-}$	$HS^- + H^+ \rightarrow H_2S$
$H_2PO_4^- \rightarrow H^+ + HPO_4^{2-}$	$H_2PO_4^- + H^+ \rightarrow H_3PO_4$
$H_2O \rightarrow H^+ + OH^-$	$H_2O + H^+ \rightarrow H_3O^+$
$HCO_3^- \rightarrow H^+ + CO_3^{2-}$	$HCO_3^- + H^+ \rightarrow H_2CO_3$

Arrhenius Theory

Acid: any substance which delivers hydrogen ion (H^+) to the solution ($HA \rightarrow H^+ + A^-$).

Base: any substance which delivers hydroxide ion (OH^-) to the solution ($XOH \rightarrow X^+ + OH^-$).

Example

Q. **Which equation below represents an Arrhenius acid/base reaction?**

A. $Cu^{+2} + 6H_2O \rightleftharpoons Cu(H_2O)_6^{+2}$
B. $HCl + NH_3 \rightleftharpoons NH_4Cl$
C. $H_2SO_4 + H_2O \rightleftharpoons H_3O^+ + HSO_4^-$
D. $HNO_3 + NaOH \rightarrow NaNO_3 + H_2O$
E. $Cu^{2+} + 4NH_3 \rightleftharpoons Cu(NH_3)_4^{2+}$

A. **D.** NaOH delivers OH^- to the solution. HNO_3 delivers H^+ to the solution.

Lewis Acid-Base Theory

A Lewis acid is an electron pair acceptor. A Lewis base is an electron pair donor.

Example

Q. **Which one of the following is a Lewis acid?**

A. H_2O
B. F^-
C. NH_3
D. OH^-
E. BCl_3

A. **E.** The reaction of BCl_3 with ammonia demonstrates how BCl_3 can accept a pair of electrons. The B in BCl_3 is sp^2-hybridized. The vacant, unhybridized $2p$ orbital accepts the pair of electrons from NH_3.

```
   Cl  H              Cl  H
   |   |              |   |
Cl – B + : N – H  →  Cl – B – N – H
   |   |              |   |
   Cl  H              Cl  H

  acid    base
```

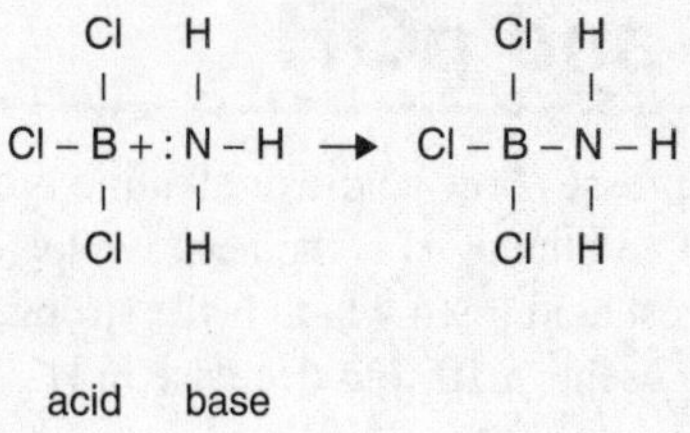

Conjugate Acids and Bases

Removal of a proton from an acid forms its conjugate base. Addition of a proton to a base forms its conjugate acid. Conjugate pair formulas differ by a proton.

Examples

Q. Compare HCl, HOAc, NaCl, and NaOAc. Identify the acid, base, conjugate acid, and conjugate base.

A. HCl is a stronger acid than HOAc. NaCl is a weaker base than NaOAc. Stronger acids have weaker conjugate bases.

HCl	+	NaOAc	→	HOAc	+	NaCl
stronger acid		stronger base		weaker conjugate acid		weaker conjugate base

Q. Compare HCl, NaOH, and NaCl. Identify the acid, base, conjugate acid, and conjugate base.

A. HCl is a stronger acid than water. NaCl is a weaker base than NaOH. Strong acids react with strong bases to form weaker acids and bases.

HCl	+	NaOH	→	H_2O	+	NaCl
stronger acid		stronger base		weaker conjugate acid		weaker conjugate base

Q. Compare NaOH, NH_3, H_2O, and NH_4Cl. Identify the acid, base, conjugate acid, and conjugate base.

A. NaOH is a stronger base than NH_3. Water is a weaker acid than NH_4Cl. Weaker bases have stronger conjugate acids. NH_3 is a weak base, but its conjugate acid, NH_4Cl, is a stronger acid.

NH_4Cl	+	NaOH	→	H_2O	+	NH_3
stronger acid		stronger base		weaker conjugate acid		weaker conjugate base

pH and pOH

pH expresses how acidic or alkaline is a solution. The pH of a solution is the negative log of the hydrogen ion concentration and the pOH is the negative log of the hydroxide ion concentration. The pH scale runs from 0, which is the strongest acid to 14 which is the strongest base. A pH of 7 is neutral, $[H^+] = [OH^-] = 1 \times 10^{-7}$ *M*. A shift in 1 pH value up represents a 10-fold decrease in H^+.

$$pH = -\log [H^+]$$
$$pOH = -\log [OH^-]$$
$$pH + pOH = 14$$
$$K_w = [H^+][OH^-] = 1.0 \times 10^{-14}$$

Examples

Q. What is the pH of a solution that has a $[H^+] = 0.002$ *M*?

A. With a graphing calculator: Press (–), LOG, enter concentration (2.0×10^{-3}), press (=) **answer = 2.7**

Q. The pH of a solution is 3.5. What is the $[H^+]$?

A. With a graphing calculator: Enter 2nd function, then LOG button, press (–) key, put in pH value, press Enter **answer = 3.16×10^{-4}**

K_a and pK_a

The acid ionization constant (K_a) is a measurement of the degree to which an acid ionizes. The –log of the K_a is known as the pK_a.

For the reaction $HA_{(aq)} \rightleftharpoons H_3O^+_{(aq)} + A^-_{(aq)}$

$$K_a = \frac{[H_3O^+][A^-]}{[HA]}$$
$$pK_a = -\log K_a$$

Strong acids have large K_a values (i.e., the equilibrium lies far to the right; the acid is almost completely dissociated to H_3O^+ and A^-). Weak acids have small K_a values (at equilibrium, significant amounts of HA and A^- exist together in solution; moderate levels of $H_3O^+_{(aq)}$ are present, and the acid is only partially dissociated). Most organic acids are weak acids.

Example

Q. Hydrocyanic acid (HCN) is a weak acid with an equilibrium constant (K_a) of 4.9×10^{-10} at 25°C. A 0.500-liter solution of 0.500 *M* HCN was prepared.

(a) Write the equilibrium expression for hydrocyanic acid.

(b) Calculate the pH of this solution at 25°C.

(c) To 0.250 liters of this solution, 1.00 gram of potassium cyanide (KCN) was added (assume that it dissolved completely). Calculate the pH of this solution at 25°C.

(d) To the remaining 0.250 liters of the original solution, 0.100 liters of 1.25 *M* NaOH solution was added. Calculate the pH of this solution at 25°C.

A.

(a) $K_a = \dfrac{[H^+][CN^-]}{[HCN]}$

(b) $4.9 \times 10^{-10} = \dfrac{x^2}{0.500}$ $\quad x = [H^+] = 1.6 \times 10^{-5}$

(c) $[CN^-] = ((1.00 \text{ gram} / (1 \text{ mole} / 65.12 \text{ g})) / 0.250 \text{ L} = 0.061\ M$

$4.9 \times 10^{-10} = ([H^+]\ (0.061)) / 0.500$

$[H^+] = 4.0 \times 10^{-9}\ M$ $\quad$ pH = 8.40

(d) (0.100 L) (1.25 *M*) = 0.125 mol NaOH

(0.250 L) (0.500 *M*) = 0.125 mol HCN

$OH^-_{(aq)} + HCN_{(aq)} \rightarrow H_2O_{(l)} + CN^-_{(aq)}$

Neutralization is complete and yields 0.125 mol CN^-

$$\text{Final}\,[CN^-] = \frac{0.125 \text{ mol } CN^-}{0.250 \text{ L} + 0100 \text{ L}} = 0.357\ M$$

$CN^-_{(aq)} + H_2O_{(l)} \rightarrow HCN_{(aq)} + OH^-_{(aq)}$

$$K_b = K_w / K_a = \frac{1.0 \times 10^{-14}}{4.9 \times 10^{-10}} = \frac{[HCN][OH^-]}{[CN^-]} = \frac{x^2}{0.357\ M}$$

$x = [OH^-] = 2.7 \times 10^{-3}\ M$ $\quad$ pOH = –log $(2.7 \times 10^{-3}] = 2.56$

pH = 14 – pOH = 14 – 2.56 = 11.44

K_b and pK_b

The base ionization constant (K_b) is a measurement of the degree to which a base ionizes. The –log of the K_b is known as the pK_b.

For the reaction $B_{(aq)} + H_2O_{(l)} \rightleftharpoons HB^+_{(aq)} + OH^-_{(aq)}$

$$K_b = \frac{[HB^+][OH^-]}{[B]}$$

$$pK_b = -\log K_b$$

$$K_b = \frac{K_w}{K_a}$$

Example

Q. Methyl amine (CH_3NH_2) is a weak base that dissociates in water at 25°C ($K_b = 4.4 \times 10^{-4}$) according to the following reaction:

$$CH_3NH_{2(aq)} + H_2O_{(l)} \rightleftharpoons CH_3NH_3^+{}_{(aq)} + OH^-_{(aq)}$$

(a) Calculate the $[OH^-]$ of a 0.200 *M* solution of methyl amine at 25°C.
(b) Calculate the pH of the solution made in (a).
(c) Calculate the % dissociation of the solution in (a) at 25°C.

A.

(a) $[CH_3NH_3^+] = [OH^-] = x$ $[CH_3NH_2] = 0.200 - x$

$$K_b = \frac{[CH_3NH_3^+][OH^-]}{[CH_3NH_2]} = 4.4 \times 10^{-4} = \frac{x^2}{(0.200 - x)} \approx \frac{x^2}{0.200}$$

$x = [OH^-] = 9.4 \times 10^{-3}\ M$

(b) pH + pOH = 14

$[OH^-] = 9.4 \times 10^{-3}$ pOH = 2.03 pH = 14 – pOH = 14 – 2.03 = 11.97

(c) $\%\ \text{dissociation} = \frac{[OH^-]}{0.200\ M} \times 100\% = \frac{9.4 \times 10^{-3}}{0.200} \times 100\% = 4.7\%$

Polyprotic Acids

Polyprotic acids, which are acids that contain more than one ionizable hydrogen (H^+) per molecule, ionize in a step wise manner. There is an ionization constant for each step. The pH of the solution is determined primarily by the first dissociation (primary source of H^+) with $K_{a1} > K_{a2} > K_{a3}$. Example: Phosphoric acid (H_3PO_4) is a triprotic acid and goes through three separate ionization steps:

Step 1:	$H_3PO_{4(aq)} \rightleftharpoons H^+_{(aq)} + H_2PO_4^-{}_{(aq)}$	$K_{a_1} = \frac{[H^+][H_2PO_4^-]}{[H_3PO_4]} = 7.5 \times 10^{-3}$
Step 2:	$H_2PO_4^-{}_{(aq)} \rightleftharpoons H^+_{(aq)} + HPO_4^{2-}{}_{(aq)}$	$K_{a_2} = \frac{[H^+][HPO_4^{2-}]}{[H_2PO_4^-]} = 6.2 \times 10^{-8}$
Step 3:	$HPO_4^{2-}{}_{(aq)} \rightleftharpoons H^+_{(aq)} + PO_4^{3-}{}_{(aq)}$	$K_{a_3} = \frac{[H^+][PO_4^{3-}]}{[HPO_4^{2-}]} = 4.8 \times 10^{-13}$

Example

Q. Calculate the pH of a 0.10 *M* H_2SO_4 solution. $K_{a2} = 1.3 \times 10^{-2}$.

A. H_2SO_4 is a diprotic acid and undergoes two successive ionizations.

First ionization: $H_2SO_{4(aq)} \rightarrow H^+_{(aq)} + HSO_4^-{}_{(aq)}$.

Note: Sulfuric acid is a strong acid, so the first dissociation is almost 100%, therefore, use a "$\rightarrow$" in the reaction (not a "$\rightleftharpoons$").

	$H_2SO_{4(aq)}$	$H^+_{(aq)}$	$HSO_4^-{}_{(aq)}$
Initial (*M*)	0.10	0.00	0.00
Change (*M*)	–0.10	+0.10	+0.10
Final (*M*)	0.00	0.10	0.10

Second ionization: $HSO_4^-{}_{(aq)} \rightleftharpoons H^+{}_{(aq)} + SO_4^{2-}{}_{(aq)}$. In this case, $HSO_4^-{}_{(aq)}$ is a weak acid and is in equilibrium with H^+ and its conjugate base.

	$HSO_4^-{}_{(aq)}$	$H^+{}_{(aq)}$	$SO_4^{2-}{}_{(aq)}$
Initial (*M*)	0.10	0.10 (from the first ionization)	0.00
Change (*M*)	$-x$	$+x$	$+x$
Equilibrium (*M*)	$(0.10 - x)$	$(0.10 + x)$	x

$$K_{a_2} = \frac{[H^+][SO_4^{2-}]}{[HSO_4^-]} = 1.3 \times 10^{-2} = \frac{(0.10 + x)(x)}{(0.10 - x)}$$

Since K_{a_2} is fairly large, we have to use the quadratic formula:

$x^2 + 0.11x - 0.0013 = 0; \quad x = 1.1 \times 10^{-2}\ M$

The total $[H^+]$ at equilibrium is the sum of both ionizations $(0.10 + 0.011) = 0.11\ M$.

$pH = -\log[H^+] = 0.96$

Oxoacids

Oxoacids (acids that contain oxygen) donate protons from a hydroxyl group (–OH), in which the acid proton is on a hydroxyl group with an oxo group attached to the same atom. Oxoacids are found where the central atom has a high oxidation number. Oxoacids are named the same as the oxoanion except that the endings "ite" and "ate" are replaced by "ous" and "ic". Examples: SO_3^{2-} = sulfite, H_2SO_3 = sulfurous acid; SO_4^{2-} = sulfate, H_2SO_4 = sulfuric acid. Neutralization of oxoacids replaces the hydrogen with a metal ion; the oxoanions then change from being in molecular compounds (the acid) to an ionic compound. (Example: $HNO_{3(aq)} + NaOH_{(aq)} \rightarrow H_2O_{(l)} + Na^+{}_{(aq)} + NO_3^-{}_{(aq)}$). When the central atom has the same number of oxygen atoms, acid strength increases from bottom to top within a group (e.g., $H_2SO_4 > H_2SeO_4$; $HNO_3 > H_3PO_3$). When the central atoms have the same number of oxygen atoms, acid strength increases from left to right (*e.g.* $HClO_4 > H_2SO_4 > H_3PO_4$). When the same central atoms have a different number of oxygen atoms, acid strength increases with the number of oxygens (e.g., $HClO_4 > HClO_3$; $H_2SO_4 > H_2SO_3$).

Example

Q. The strongest acid is

A. $HClO_4$
B. $HClO_3$
C. $HClO_2$
D. $HClO$
E. They are all equally strong.

A. A. When the same central atoms have a different number of oxygen atoms, acid strength increases with the number of oxygens.

Acid-Base Properties of Common Ions in Aqueous Solution

The following table summarizes the acid-base properties of both cations and anions.

	Anions (–)	*Cations (+)*
acidic	HSO_4^-, $H_2PO_4^-$	NH_4^+, Mg^{2+}, Al^{3+}, transition metal ions
basic	$C_2H_3O_2^-$, CN^-, CO_3^{2-}, F^-, HCO_3^-*, HPO_4^{2-}, HS^-, NO_2^-, PO_4^{3-}, S^{2-}	none
neutral	Cl^-, Br^-, I^-, ClO_4^-, NO_3^-, SO_4^{2-}	Li^+, Na^+, K^+, Ca^{2+}, Ba^{2+}, Sr^{2+}

** close to neutral*

Salts

A salt (an ionic compound formed by the reaction between an acid and a base) is the combination of the anion of an acid combined with the cation of a base; i.e., $HCl + NaOH \rightarrow NaCl + H_2O$ (NaCl is the salt). Salts are strong electrolytes that dissociate in water and in many cases react with water (often affecting the pH of the solution) in a process known as salt hydrolysis. Salts containing an alkali metal ion or alkaline earth metal ion (except Be^{2+}) and the conjugate base of a strong acid (e.g., Cl^-, Br^-, NO_3^-) do not undergo hydrolysis and therefore, do not affect pH. Solutions of a salt derived from a strong base and a weak acid (e.g., $NaC_2H_3O_2$, in which the $C_2H_3O_2^-$ is the conjugate base of acetic acid and has an affinity for H^+) are basic. The pH of a salt will depend on the type of anion and cation, the solubility of the salt, the temperature of the solution, and the concentration of the salt if less than saturated.

- Salts made of the anion of a strong acid and the cation of a strong base will be neutral salts, $pH \approx 7$. (Example: sodium chloride).
- Salts made of the anion of a strong acid and the cation of a weak base will be acidic salts. (Example: ammonium chloride)
- Salts made of the anion of a weak acid and a cation of a strong base will be basic salts. (Example: sodium bicarbonate)

Example

Q. Classify each of the salts listed below as acidic, basic, or neutral.

1. $Fe(NO_3)_3$
2. $MgSO_4$
3. $Ni(ClO_4)_2$

A. (1) $Fe(NO_3)_3$—This salt was formed from the reaction of a weak base (iron(III) hydroxide) with a strong acid (nitric acid). This means that the salt will be acidic.

(2) $MgSO_4$—This salt was formed from the reaction of a strong base (magnesium hydroxide) with strong acid (sulfuric acid). This reaction results in a neutral salt.

(3) $Ni(ClO_4)_2$—This salt was formed from the reaction of a weak base (nickel(II) hydroxide) with a strong acid (perchloric acid). This is an acidic salt.

Molecular Structure and Acid Strength

Acid (HX) strengths are determined by:

Extent to which the acid ionizes

The weaker the H–X bond, the stronger the acid.

Strong acids (listed in decreasing strength) are: $HClO_4$ (perchloric); HI (hydroiodic); HBr (hydrobromic); HCl (hydrochloric); H_2SO_4 (sulfuric); and nitric (HNO_3)

Polarity of the H–X bond

When all other factors are kept constant, acids become stronger as the H–X bond becomes more polar.

	K_a	pH (0.1 *M*)	Electronegativity Difference
HF	7.2×10^{-4}	2.1	1.9
H_2O	1.0×10^{-14}	7	1.4
NH_3	1×10^{-33}	11.1	0.9
CH_4	1×10^{-49}	–	0.4

Size of the X atom

Acids become stronger as the H–X bond becomes weaker, and bonds generally become weaker as the atoms get larger.

	K_a	Bond Dissociation Energy (kJ/mol)
HF	7.2×10^{-4}	569
HCl	1×10^{6}	431
HBr	1×10^{9}	370
HI	3×10^{9}	300

Charge on the acid or base

Compounds become less acidic and more basic as the negative charge increases.

	pH (0.1 *M*)
H_3PO_4	1.5
$H_2PO_4^-$	4.4
HPO_4^{2-}	9.3
PO_4^{3-}	12.0

Oxidation state of the central atom

Acidity increases significantly as the oxidation state of the central atom becomes larger.

Oxyacid	K_a	Oxidation Number of the Chlorine
HOCl	2.9×10^{-8}	+1
HOClO	1.1×10^{-2}	+3
$HOClO_2$	5.0×10^{2}	+5
$HOClO_3$	1×10^{3}	+7

Example

Q. Given that HSO_4^- is a stronger acid than HCOOH, predict the direction of the following reaction in aqueous solution:

$$HSO_4^-{}_{(aq)} + HCOO^-{}_{(aq)} \rightleftharpoons HCOOH_{(aq)} + SO_4^{2-}{}_{(aq)}$$

A. $HCOO^-$ would be a stronger base than SO_4^{2-}. The reaction as written will proceed from left to right since HSO_4^- is a better proton-donor than HCOOH (and therefore, $HCOO^-$ is a better proton acceptor than SO_4^{2-}).

Titration

Titration is a technique where a solution of known concentration is used to determine the concentration of an unknown solution. Typically, the titrant (the known solution) is added from a buret to a known quantity of the analyte (the unknown solution) until the reaction is complete (an exact number of moles of acid neutralize the same exact number of moles of base). Knowing the volume of titrant added allows the determination of the concentration of the unknown. Often, an indicator is used to signal the end of the reaction, the endpoint (equivalence point).

$$\text{moles of acid} = \text{moles of base}$$

$$M_aV_a = M_bV_b$$

Example

Q. Calculate the molarity of an acetic acid solution if 34.57 mL of this solution are needed to neutralize 25.19 mL of 0.1025 *M* sodium hydroxide.

A. $CH_3COOH_{(aq)} + NaOH_{(aq)} \rightarrow Na^+{}_{(aq)} + CH_3COOH^-{}_{(aq)} + H_2O_{(l)}$

$$M_aV_a = M_bV_b$$

$$(M_a)\,(0.03457\ \cancel{L}) = (0.1025\ \text{moles}/\cancel{L})\,(0.02519\ \cancel{L})$$

$$M_a = 7.469 \times 10^{-2}\ M$$

Titration Curves

A titration curve is a graph of the pH as a function of the amount of titrant (acid or base) added.

Acid + Base → Water + Salt

Strong Acid-Strong Base

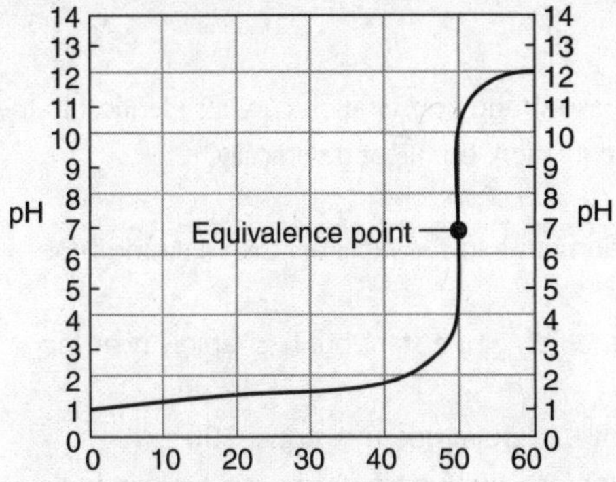

mL 0.100*M* NaOH added to 50.00mL 0.100*M* HCl

Example: 0.100 *M* NaOH is being added to 50.0 mL of 0.100 *M* HCl:

For strong acid-strong base titrations, the pH = 7.00 at the equivalence point. However, in other types of titrations, this is not the case. Notice that the pH increases slowly at first, then rapidly as it nears the equivalence point, since the pH scale is logarithmic, which means that a pH of 1 will have 10 times the hydronium ion concentration than a pH of 2. Thus, as the hydronium ion is initially removed, it takes a lot of base to change its concentration by a factor of 10, but as more and more hydronium ion is removed, less base is required to change its concentration by a factor of 10. Near the equivalence point (which is detected through the use of a chemical indicator that changes color (e.g., phenolphthalein), a change of a factor of 10 occurs very quickly, which is why the graph is extremely steep at this point. As the hydronium ion concentration becomes very low, it will again take a lot of base to increase the hydroxide ion concentration by 10 fold to change the pH significantly.

Weak acid being titrated by a strong base

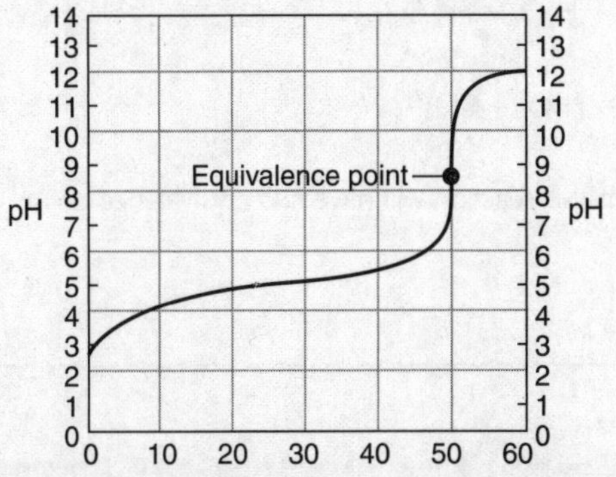

mL 0.100*M* NaOH added to 50.00mL 0.100*M* $HC_2H_3O_2$

Example: 0.100 *M* NaOH is being added to 50.0 mL of 0.100 *M* acetic acid to produce a basic salt solution.

(1) The weak-acid solution has a higher initial pH than a strong-acid solution.
(2) The pH rises more rapidly at the start, but less rapidly near the equivalence point.
(3) The pH at the equivalence point does not equal 7.00.
(4) The equivalence point for a weak acid-strong base titration has a pH > 7.00 while the equivalence point for a strong acid-weak base titration would have a pH < 7.00.

For a strong acid-weak base or weak acid-strong base titration, the pH will change rapidly at the very beginning and then have a gradual slope until near the equivalence point. The gradual slope results from a buffer solution being produced by the addition of the strong acid or base, which resists rapid change in pH until the added acid or base exceeds the buffer's capacity and the rapid pH change occurs near the equivalence point. At the half-equivalence point, enough base has been added to convert exactly half of the acid into the conjugate base (in this case 25 mL). Therefore, at this point the concentration of the acid equals the concentration of the conjugate base (pH = pK_a)

(continued)

Acid + Base → Water + Salt *(continued)*

Weak base being titrated by a strong acid

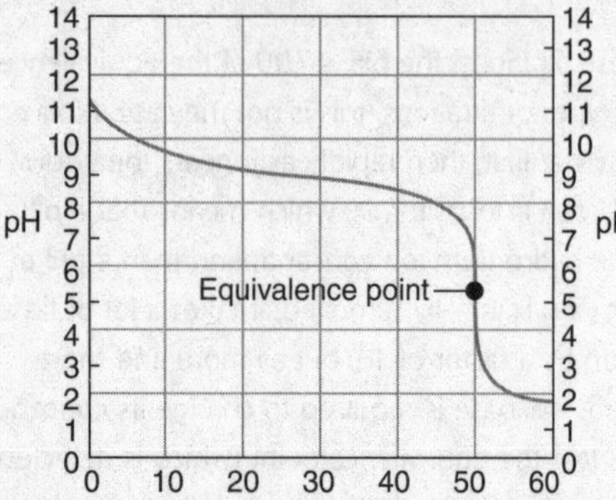

mL 0.100*M* HCl added to 50.00mL 0.100*M* NH_3

Example: 0.100 *M* HCl is being added to 50.0 mL of 0.100 *M* ammonia solution.

(Note that the strong base-strong acid titration curve is identical to the strong acid-strong base titration, but flipped vertically.)

1. The weak-base solution has a lower initial pH than a strong-base solution.
2. The pH drops more rapidly at the start, but less rapidly near the equivalence point.
3. The pH at the equivalence point does not equal 7.00.
4. The equivalence point for a weak base-strong acid titration has a pH < 7.00.

Titrations of Polyprotic Acids

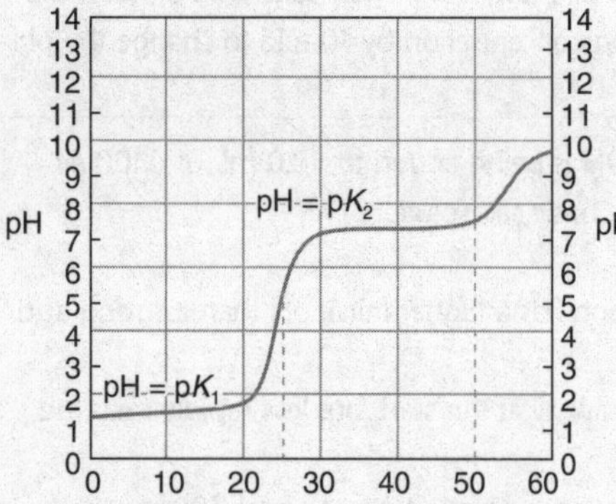

mL 0.100*M* NaOH added to 25.00mL 0.100*M* H_2CO_3

Example: 0.100 *M* NaOH is being added to 25 mL of 0.100 *M* H_2CO_3

H_2CO_3 is an example of a polyprotic acid which neutralizes in two steps:

$H_2CO_{3(aq)} + OH^-_{(aq)} \rightarrow H_2O_{(l)} + HCO_3^-{}_{(aq)}$

$HCO_3^-{}_{(aq)} + OH^-_{(aq)} \rightarrow H_2O_{(l)} + CO_3^{2-}{}_{(aq)}$

The titration curve for this reaction will have two equivalence points.

Examples

Use the titration curve below to answer Questions 1–3.

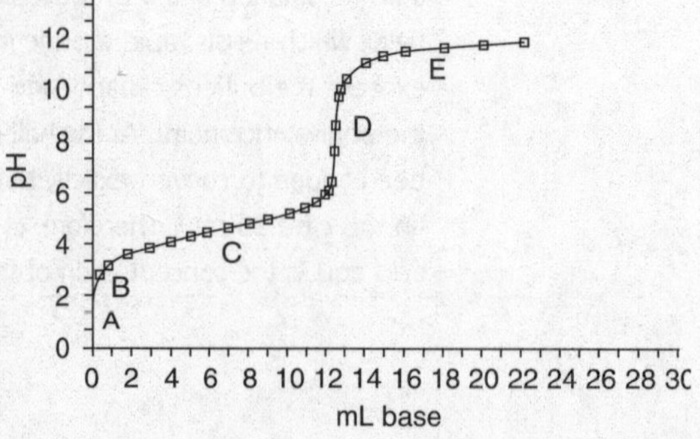

Q. Which point indicates the region where the solution behaves as a buffer?

A. A
B. B
C. C
D. D
E. E

A. C.

Q. Which point indicates the equivalence point of the titration?

A. A
B. B
C. C
D. D
E. E

A. D.

Q. The titration curve describes a titration between

A. a strong acid and a strong base
B. a strong acid and weak base
C. a weak acid and a strong base
D. a weak acid and a weak base
E. none of the above

A. C.

% Ionization

Given a monoprotic acid HA, % ionization tells you what percent of the original acid (HA_o) has dissociated into $H^+_{(aq)}$. It is another measurement of acid strength.

$$\% \text{ ionization} = \frac{[H^+]}{[HA]_0} \times 100\%$$

Example

Q. Calculate the percent ionization of a 0.50 *M* HF solution. K_a HF = 7.1×10^{-4}

A. Let $x = [H^+]$ and $[F^-]$ at equilibrium.

$$HF_{(aq)} \rightleftharpoons H^+_{(aq)} + F^-_{(aq)}$$

	$HF_{(aq)}$	$H^+_{(aq)}$	$F^-_{(aq)}$
Initial (*M*)	0.50	0.00	0.00
Change (*M*)	$-x$	$+x$	$+x$
Equilibrium (*M*)	$(0.50 - x)$	x	x

$$K_a = \frac{[H^+][F^-]}{[HF]} = 7.1 \times 10^{-4} = \frac{x^2}{0.5 - x}$$ Since HF is a weak acid, $0.50 - x \approx 0.50$.

$$\frac{x^2}{0.50} = 7.1 \times 10^{-4} \qquad x^2 = 3.6 \times 10^{-4} \qquad x = 1.9 \times 10^{-2}\, M$$

$$\% \text{ ionization} = \frac{1.9 \times 10^{-2}\, \cancel{M}}{0.50\, \cancel{M}} \times 100\% = 3.8\%$$

Buffers

Mixtures of a weak acid and its conjugate base are called buffers (e.g., acetic acid and the acetate ion). Buffers lessen or absorb the drastic change in pH that occurs when small amounts of acids or bases are added to water.

Henderson-Hasselbalch Equation

The Henderson-Hasselbalch equation expresses the pH of a buffer solution as a function of the concentration of the weak acid or base and the salt components of the buffer.

$$\mathbf{pH = p}K_a \mathbf{+ \log \frac{[conjugate\ base]}{[weak\ acid]}}$$

$$\mathbf{pOH = p}K_b \mathbf{+ \log \frac{[conjugate\ acid]}{[weak\ base]}}$$

Example

Q. Acetic acid, CH_3COOH, has a K_a of 1.80×10^{-5}.

(a) Calculate the $[H^+]$ of a 0.30-molar solution of acetic acid (HOAc).

(b) What is the % ionization of acetic acid molecules in a 0.30-molar solution?

(c) What is the ratio of $[CH_3COO^-]$ to $[CH_3COOH]$ in a buffer solution that has a pH of 5.50?

A.

(a) $K_a = \frac{[H^+][Ac^-]}{[HOAc]} = 1.8 \times 10^{-5} = \frac{x^2}{0.30\, M} \qquad x = [H^+] = 2.3 \times 10^{-3}\, M$

(b) % dissociation = $[H^+] / [HOAc] = 2.3 \times 10^{-3}\, M / 0.30\, M = 0.77\%$

(c) pH = pK_a + log ([base] / [acid])

$K_a = 1.8 \times 10^{-5}$; therefore p$K_a = -\log K_a = -\log 1.8 \times 10^{-5} = 4.74$

$5.50 = 4.74 + \log([Ac^-] / [HOAc])$

$\log([Ac^-] / [HOAc]) = 0.76$

$[Ac^-] / [HOAc] = 5.8$

Indicators

Indicators are weak acids or weak bases (often derived from plant pigments) that have distinctly different colors in their ionized and non-ionized forms and which are related to the pH of the solution being tested. Different indicators change colors at different pH's. Take for example the weak acid indicator, HIn. In solution it achieves equilibrium $HIn_{(aq)} \rightleftharpoons H^+_{(aq)} + In^-_{(aq)}$. If the indicator is placed in an acidic solution, the equilibrium shifts left and the solution is the color of HIn. If the solution is more basic, the equilibrium shifts right and the solution takes on the color of $In^-_{(aq)}$. If $[HIn] \approx [In^-]$, then the color is a combination of colors between those of HIn and In^-. An indicator is chosen for a titration so that its color change coincides with the equivalence point of the titration—the point at which the amount of added base (or acid) is stoichiometrically equivalent to the amount of acid (or base) originally present in the solution. The equivalence point in the titration of an acid with a base occurs at pH 7 or higher; when a base is titrated with an acid, the equivalence point has pH 7 or lower. Generally, an indicator changes color over a pH range of 2 units, centered about the value of pK_{In} ($-\log K_{In}$).

Example

Q. You are given the following titration curve and a list of indicators and their pH range. Which indicator should have been used in the titration?

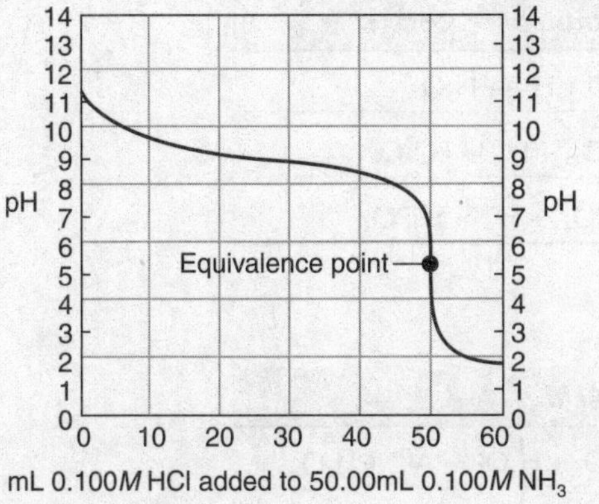

Indicator	*pH Range*
thymol blue	1.2 – 2.8
chlorophenol blue	4.8 – 6.4
cresol red	7.2 – 8.8
phenolphthalein	8.3 – 10.0

A. thymol blue
B. chlorophenol blue
C. cresol red
D. phenolphthalein
E. An equimolar mixture of cresol red and thymol blue

A. B. The steep portion of the pH curve covers the pH range between 3 and 7; therefore, the most suitable indicator would be chlorophenol blue.

Anhydrides

Anhydride means "without water." When an acidic anhydride reacts with water it forms an acid. In most cases, acidic anhydrides are nonmetallic oxides (Examples: $CO_{2(g)} + H_2O_{(l)} \rightarrow H_2CO_{3(aq)}$; $SO_{3(g)} + H_2O_{(l)} \rightarrow H_2SO_{4(aq)} \rightarrow H^+_{(aq)} + HSO_4^-{}_{(aq)}$). When a basic anhydride reacts with water, it forms a base. In most cases, basic anhydrides are metallic oxides. (Examples: $MgO_{(s)} + H_2O_{(l)} \rightarrow Mg(OH)_{2(aq)}$; $K_2O_{(s)} + H_2O_{(l)} \rightarrow 2K^+_{(aq)} + 2OH^-_{(aq)}$.)

Example

Q. Which compound is the anhydride of phosphoric acid?

A. PO
B. PO_2
C. P_2O_3
D. P_2O_5
E. none of the above

A. D. $3H_2O + P_2O_5 \rightarrow 2H_3PO_4$

Amphoteric Substances

Amphoteric substances can act as either acids or bases. Examples of amphoteric hydroxides include $Al(OH)_3$, $Be(OH)_2$, $Cr(OH)_3$ and $Zn(OH)_2$.

Substance	*Acting as an Acid (proton donor)*	*Acting as a Base (proton acceptor)*
H_2O	$H_2O \rightarrow H^+ + OH^-$	$H_2O + H^+ \rightarrow H_3O^+$
HSO_4^-	$HSO_4^- \rightarrow H^+ + SO_4^{2-}$	$HSO_4^- + H^+ \rightarrow H_2SO_4$
$H_2PO_4^-$	$H_2PO_4^- \rightarrow H^+ + HPO_4^{2-}$	$H_2PO_4^- + H^+ \rightarrow H_3PO_4$

	In Base	*In Acid*
Al_2O_3	$Al_2O_3 + OH^- \rightleftharpoons Al(OH)_4^-$	$Al_2O_3 + H_3O^+ \rightleftharpoons Al^{3+} + H_2O$
$Al(OH)_3$	$Al(OH)_3 + OH^- \rightleftharpoons Al(OH)_4^-$	$Al(OH)_3 + H_3O^+ \rightarrow Al^{3+} + H_2O$
$Be(OH)_2$	$Be(OH)_2 + OH^- \rightleftharpoons Be(OH)_4^{2-}$	$Be(OH)_2 + H_3O^+ \rightarrow Be^{2+} + H_2O$
$Cr(OH)_3$	$Cr(OH)_3 + OH^- \rightleftharpoons Cr(OH)_4^-$	$Cr(OH)_3 + H_3O^+ \rightarrow Cr^{3+} + H_2O$
$Sn(OH)_2$	$Sn(OH)_2 + OH^- \rightleftharpoons Sn(OH)_3^-$	$Sn(OH)_2 + H_3O^+ \rightarrow Sn^{2+} + H_2O$
$Zn(OH)_2$	$Zn(OH)_2 + OH^- \rightleftharpoons Zn(OH)_4^{2-}$	$Zn(OH)_2 + H_3O^+ \rightarrow Zn^{2+} + H_2O$

Multiple-Choice Questions

For Questions 1–3, choose from the following:

A. Arrhenius base
B. Brønsted acid
C. Brønsted base
D. Lewis acid
E. Lewis base

1. In the reaction $BF_3 + NH_3$, the BF_3 acts as a(n) ____?

2. In the reaction $HCO_3^-{}_{(aq)} + OH^-{}_{(aq)} \rightleftharpoons CO_3^{2-}{}_{(aq)} + H_2O_{(l)}$, the $HCO_3^-{}_{(aq)}$ and the $H_2O_{(l)}$ are acting as a(n) ______?

3. A student titrates a solution of hydrochloric acid to which some phenolphthalein had been added with a 3.0 *M* sodium hydroxide solution. The sodium hydroxide solution is acting as a(n) ______?

4. Lemon juice, with a pH of about 2.3 has a $[OH^-]$ of

A. 0 *M*
B. 2.3×10^{-1} *M*
C. 5.0×10^{-3} *M*
D. 2.0×10^{-12} *M*
E. 4.0×10^{-12} *M*

5. Which of the following ions would give an acidic solution upon addition to water?

A. K^+
B. Ba^{2+}
C. ClO_4^-
D. HPO_4^{2-}
E. NH_4^+

For Questions 6–7: A student prepares a buffer by mixing 0.20 mol of $HC_2H_3O_{2(aq)}$ ($K_a = 1.8 \times 10^{-5}$) with 0.20 mol of $KC_2H_3O_{2(aq)}$.

6. What is the pH of the buffer?

A. 2.56
B. 3.39
C. 4.74
D. 5.87
E. 7.00

7. What is the pH of the buffer after the students adds 25 mL of 2.0 *M* NaOH?

A. 4.63
B. 4.97
C. 5.00
D. 5.28
E. 7.00

8. Given the following information

	K_a
$HC_2H_3O_2$	1.8×10^{-5}
H_2CO_3	4.2×10^{-7}

What is *K* for the following reaction?

$$H_2CO_{3(aq)} + C_2H_3O_2^-{}_{(aq)} \rightarrow HCO_3^-{}_{(aq)} + HC_2H_3O_{2(aq)}$$

A. 2.4×10^{-2}
B. 3.8×10^{-1}
C. 8.2×10^{0}
D. 3.9×10^{1}
E. 7.3×10^{1}

9. Solid sodium hydroxide is added to a 0.10 *M* solution of calcium nitrate until the pH of the solution reaches 12.00. Assuming no volume change, what is *Q* for the reaction and will a precipitate form? K_{sp} $Ca(OH)_2 = 1.3 \times 10^{-6}$

A. $Q = 1.3 \times 10^{-6}$; a precipitate will form
B. $Q = 1.3 \times 10^{-6}$; a precipitate will not form
C. $Q = 1.00$; the reaction is at equilibrium so a precipitate will not form
D. $Q = 1.0 \times 10^{-5}$; a precipitate will form
E. $Q = 1.0 \times 10^{-5}$; a precipitate will not form

10. A student makes a buffer in the lab by adding 600. mL of 0.15 *M* acetic acid to 400. mL of 0.10 *M* sodium acetate. What is the maximum amount of HCl that can be added to this buffer system without exceeding the capacity of the buffer?

A. 0.020 mol
B. 0.030 mol
C. 0.040 mol
D. 0.050 mol
E. 1.00 mol

11. The K_a values for HPO_4^{2-} and HSO_3^- are 4.8 × 10^{-13} and 6.3 × 10^{-8} respectively. Therefore HPO_4^{2-} is a ______ acid than HSO_3^- and PO_4^{3-} is a ______ base than SO_3^{2-}.

A. stronger, weaker
B. weaker, stronger
C. stronger, stronger
D. weaker, weaker
E. none of the above

12. What is the pH of a 0.300-molar ammonia solution? $K_b = 1.8 \times 10^{-5}$

A. 9.88
B. 10.52
C. 11.36
D. 12.55
E. 13.91

13. Given the following oxides

Na_2O, Al_2O_3, CaO

if arranged in order of increasing pH (least basic → most basic) the order would be

A. $Na_2O < Al_2O_3 <$ CaO
B. $Al_2O_3 < Na_2O <$ CaO
C. CaO $< Na_2O < Al_2O_3$
D. CaO $< Al_2O_3 < Na_2O$
E. $Al_2O_3 <$ CaO $< Na_2O$

14. What is the pH of a 0.20 *M* solution of $AlCl_{3(aq)}$? K_a for $Al(H_2O)_6{}^{3+}{}_{(aq)}$ is 1.4 × 10^{-5}.

A. 2.77
B. 3.32
C. 4.38
D. 7.00
E. 7.86

15. What is the conjugate base of $C_5H_5NH^+$?

A. $C_5H_5N^-$
B. C_5H_5NH
C. $C_5H_5NH_2^+$
D. $C_5H_5N^+$
E. C_5H_5N

16. Boron trichloride gas is bubbled through an aqueous solution of ammonia. The Lewis acid is ______________ and the Lewis base is ______________.

A. BCl_3, $Cl_3B{:}NH_3$
B. NH_3, BCl_3
C. $Cl_3B{:}NH_3$, BCl_3
D. NH_3, $Cl_3B{:}NH_3$
E. BCl_3, NH_3

17.

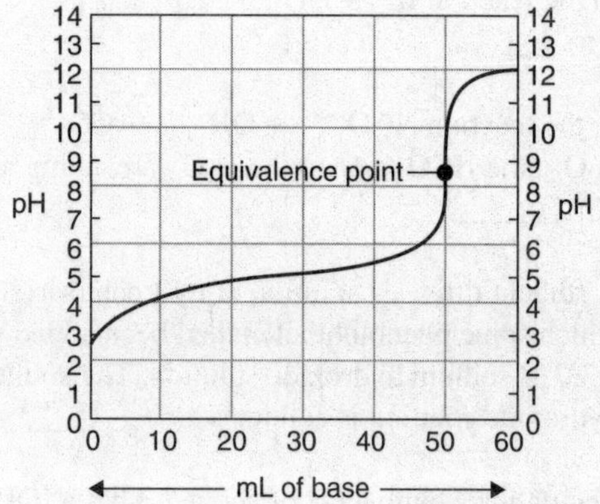

The titration curve above would best represent the titration of

A. ethanoic acid with sodium hydroxide.
B. sulfuric acid with ammonia.
C. hydrofluoric acid with ammonia.
D. sulfuric acid with sodium hydroxide.
E. hydrochloric acid with sodium hydroxide.

18. What is the percent ionization of a 0.50 *M* nitrous acid (HNO_2) solution? K_a $HNO_2 = 4.5 \times 10^{-4}$?

A. 0%
B. 1.5%
C. 3.0%
D. 6.0%
E. 9.0%

19. Which of the following would NOT make an effective buffer system?

A. NaH_2PO_4 and H_3PO_4
B. $KClO_4$ and $HClO_4$
C. KCH_3COO and CH_3COOH
D. $NaHCO_3$ and Na_2CO_3
E. Na_2HPO_4 and NaH_2PO_4

20. A student was working in the lab and splashed a strong acid in his eye. The student should immediately

- **A.** run to the nurse's office.
- **B.** splash a strong base into the eye to neutralize the acid.
- **C.** continuously flush the eye with water.
- **D.** find some distilled water to flush out the eye.
- **E.** call 911 and wait for trained medical personnel.

Free-Response Questions

1. A student was asked to determine the molecular weight of a weak monoprotic dry acid (HX). She was provided the following laboratory equipment: a balance (accurate to 0.001 g), distilled water, a 100.00 mL volumetric flask, a supply of sodium hydroxide solution of unknown concentration, a bottle of phenolphthalein, a 100.00 mL graduated cylinder (accurate to 0.01 mL), and a supply of oxalic acid dihydrate ($H_2C_2O_4 \cdot 2H_2O$).

(a) Describe the theory of titration and how it is used.

(b) Suppose the student had used 20.00 grams of the acid and dissolved the acid in distilled water to bring the volume to exactly 100.00 mL. She then added several drops of phenolphthalein to the acidic solution. She then titrated a 50.00 mL sample of this acidic solution with the sodium hydroxide solution and found that it took 42.33 mL of NaOH to reach the end point. She repeated her procedure and found that it took 42.89 mL of NaOH to reach the end point. In order to determine the molarity of the sodium hydroxide solution, she discovered that it took exactly 50.00 mL of sodium hydroxide solution to neutralize 1.500 grams of oxalic acid dihydrate.

(i) Determine the molarity of the NaOH solution.

(ii) Calculate the molecular weight of the unknown acid.

(c) Sketch a titration curve of what the titration of the dry acid vs. sodium hydroxide might look like and explain the diagram.

2. Sodium ascorbate is a highly reactive antioxidant used as a food preservative with the formula $C_6H_7NaO_6$ and is a salt of the weak acid, ascorbic acid ($C_6H_8O_6$), also known as vitamin C.

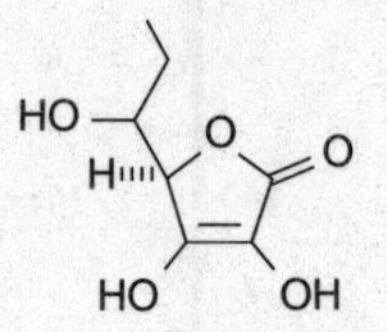

A 0.10-molar solution of sodium ascorbate was found to have a pH of 8.55 at room temperature.

(a) Calculate the [OH$^-$] in the sodium ascorbate solution described above.

(b) Calculate the value for the equilibrium constant for the reaction

$$C_6H_7O_6^-{}_{(aq)} + H_2O_{(l)} \rightleftharpoons C_6H_8O_{6(aq)} + OH^-{}_{(aq)}$$

(c) Calculate the value of K_a, the acid dissociation constant for ascorbic acid.

(d) A saturated solution of ascorbic acid is prepared by adding excess solid ascorbic acid to pure water at room temperature. Since this saturated solution has a pH of 3.50, calculate the molar solubility of ascorbic acid at room temperature.

Answers and Explanations

Multiple Choice

1. **D.** $BF_3 + NH_3 \rightarrow F_3B{:}NH_3$. A Lewis acid is an electron pair acceptor.

2. **B.** Both species are proton donors.

3. **A.** An Arrhenius base is any substance which delivers hydroxide ion (OH^-) to the solution.

4. **D.** $pH = -\log [H^+] = 2.3 \qquad [H^+] = 10^{-2.3} = 5.0 \times 10^{-3}$

$$[OH^-] = \frac{K_w}{[H^+]} = \frac{1.0 \times 10^{-14}}{5.0 \times 10^{-3}} = 2.0 \times 10^{-12}\,M$$

5. **E.** $NH_4^+{}_{(aq)} + H_2O_{(l)} \rightleftharpoons NH_{3(aq)} + H_3O^+{}_{(aq)}$

6. **C.** $[H^+] = 1.8 \times 10^{-5} \times \frac{[HC_2H_3O_2]}{[C_2H_3O_2]} = 1.8 \times 10^{-5} \times \frac{(0.20)}{(0.20)} = 1.8 \times 10^{-5}$

$pH = -\log (1.8 \times 10^{-5}) = 4.74$

7. **B.**

$$\frac{25\,\cancel{mL}}{1} \times \frac{1\,\cancel{L}}{10^3\,\cancel{mL}} \times \frac{2\,mol\,OH^-}{\cancel{L}} = 0.05\,mol\,OH^-$$

$$[H^+] = 1.8 \times 10^{-5} \times \frac{(0.20 - 0.05)}{(0.20 + 0.05)} = 1.08 \times 10^{-5}$$

$pH = -\log [H^+] = -\log (1.08 \times 10^{-5}) = 4.97$

8. **A.**

$$C_2H_3O_2^-{}_{(aq)} + \cancel{H^+_{(aq)}} \rightarrow HC_2H_3O_{2\,(aq)} \qquad K_1 = 1/K_a = 1/1.8 \times 1^{-5} = 5.6 \times 10^4$$

$$H_2CO_{3\,(aq)} \rightarrow \cancel{H^+_{(aq)}} + HCO_3^-{}_{(aq)} \qquad K_2 = K_a = 4.2 \times 10^{-7}$$

$$H_2CO_{3\,(aq)} + C_2H_3O^-{}_{(aq)} \rightarrow HCO^-{}_{(aq)} + HC_2H_3O_{2\,(aq)}$$

$K = K_1 \times K_2 = (5.6 \times 10^4)\,(4.2 \times 10^{-7}) = 2.4 \times 10^{-2}$

9. **D.** $Ca(OH)_{2(aq)} \rightleftharpoons Ca^{2+}{}_{(aq)} + 2OH^-{}_{(aq)}$

$$[OH^-] = \frac{K_w}{[H^+]} = \frac{1.0 \times 10^{-14}}{1.0 \times 10^{-12}} = 1.0 \times 10^{-2}\,M$$

$Q = [Ca^{2+}]\,[OH^-]^2 = (0.10)\,(1.0 \times 10^{-2})^2 = 1.0 \times 10^{-5}$

Since $Q > K_{sp}$, a precipitate will form.

10. **C.** Buffers are mixtures of a weak acid (acetic acid) and its conjugate base (acetate ion): $NaC_2H_3O_{2(aq)} \rightarrow Na^+{}_{(aq)} + C_2H_3O_2^-{}_{(aq)}$. The acetate ion ($C_2H_3O_2^-$) functions to absorb excess H^+ ($H^+ + C_2H_3O_2^- \rightarrow HC_2H_3O_2$). When the acetate ion in solution is exhausted, the buffer will no longer function. Therefore, the capacity of the buffer is limited by the concentration of the acetate ion: $0.400\,L \times 0.10\,M = 0.040$ mol. 0.040 mol of acetate will neutralize just 0.040 mol of H^+ from the HCl added to the system.

11. **B.** The larger the K_a value, the stronger the acid (more H^+). A strong acid will have a weak conjugate base, and a strong base will have a weak conjugate acid.

12. **C.** $NH_{3(aq)} + H_2O_{(l)} \rightleftharpoons NH_4^+{}_{(aq)} + OH^-{}_{(aq)}$

	NH_3	NH_4^+	OH^-
Initial (*M*)	0.300	0.000	0.000
Change (*M*)	–*x*	+*x*	+*x*
Equilibrium (*M*)	0.300 – *x*	*x*	*x*

$$K_b = \frac{[NH_4^+][OH^-]}{[NH_3]} = 1.8 \times 10^{-5} \qquad \frac{x^2}{0.300 - x} = 1.8 \times 10^{-5}$$

$$0.300 - x \approx 0.300$$

$$\frac{x^2}{0.300} = 1.8 \times 10^{-5} \qquad x = 2.3 \times 10^{-3}\,M$$

$$pOH = -\log(2.3 \times 10^{-3}) = 2.64 \qquad pH = 14.00 - 2.64 = 11.36$$

13. **E.** The most basic oxides occur with metal ions having the lowest positive charge (or lowest oxidation numbers): Al^{3+}, Ca^{2+}, Na^+.

14. **A.** $Al(H_2O)_6^{3+}{}_{(aq)} + H_2O_{(l)} \rightleftharpoons H_3O^+{}_{(aq)} + Al(H_2O)_5(OH)^{2+}{}_{(aq)}$

$$K_a = 1.4 \times 10^{-5} = \frac{[H_3O^+][Al(H_2O)_5(OH)^{2+}]}{[Al(H_2O)_6^{3+}]} \approx \frac{x^2}{0.20}$$

$$x = [H_3O^+] = 1.7 \times 10^{-3}\,M$$

$$pH = -\log(1.7 \times 10^{-3}) = 2.77$$

15. **E.** Removal of a proton from an acid forms its conjugate base ($C_5H_5NH^+ \rightarrow C_5H_5N + H^+$). Addition of a proton to a base forms its conjugate acid.

16. **E.** A Lewis acid is an electron pair acceptor. A Lewis base is an electron pair donor. Boron trichloride is surrounded by only six valence electrons in a trigonal planar arrangement. The boron atom uses three sp^2 hybrid orbitals to bond to three Cl atoms and has a vacant 2*p* valence orbital that can accept a share in a pair of electrons from the Lewis base (NH_3).

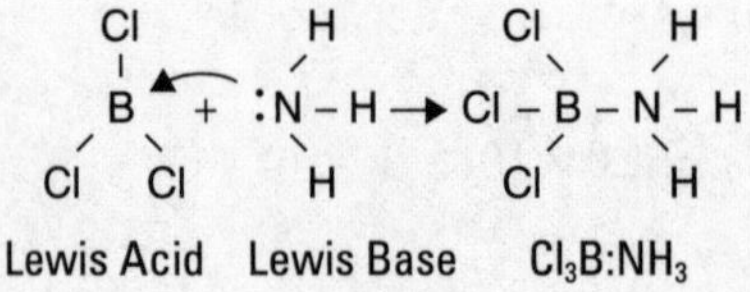

17. **A.** For the titration of a weak acid with a strong base, the equivalence point is greater than pH 7.00. Before the equivalence point, added $NaOH_{(aq)}$ titrant is neutralized by the weak acid in the analyte solution to produce a salt and water:

$$OH^-{}_{(aq)} + CH_3CO_2H_{(aq)} \rightarrow CH_3CO_2^-{}_{(aq)} + H_2O_{(l)}$$

Overall, the added base is neutralized, acid is consumed, and a solution of the salt (sodium ethanoate) is produced. However, the conjugate base of a weak acid is generally a strong base and so the conjugate base of the ethanoic acid (the ethanoate anion) can react further. The ethanoate anion combines with hydronium ions in solution, $H_3O^+{}_{(aq)}$, reducing their concentration and raising the pH. The overall result is that the pH rises faster before the equivalence point than in a strong acid/strong base titration. At the equivalence point the acid has just been neutralized by the base to give a solution of sodium ethanoate in water. However, the ethanoate anion is a base which combines with hydronium ions in solution, reducing their concentration and raising the pH. The result is that the pH value of the solution at the equivalence point is greater than pH 7.0. After the equivalence point, the dominant factor is the continued addition of hydroxide ions, $OH^-_{(aq)}$, from the burette and so the curve follows a similar pattern to a strong acid/strong base titration.

18. **C.** $HNO_{2(aq)} \rightleftharpoons H^+_{(aq)} + NO_2^-{}_{(aq)}$

	HNO_2	H^+	NO_2^-
Initial (*M*)	0.50	0.00	0.00
Change (*M*)	$-x$	$+x$	$+x$
Equilibrium (*M*)	$(0.50 - x)$	x	x

$$K_a = 4.5 \times 10^{-4} = \frac{[H^+][NO_2^-]}{[HNO_2]} = \frac{x^2}{0.50 - x} \approx \frac{x^2}{0.50}$$

$$x = 0.015\,M \qquad \%\text{ ionization} = \frac{0.015}{0.50} \times 100\% = 3.0\%$$

19. **B.** Buffers consist of mixtures of a weak acid and its conjugate base. In (B), $HClO_4$ is a strong acid and its conjugate base (ClO_4^-) is a very weak base; therefore, ClO_4^- cannot combine with H^+ to produce $HClO_4$.

20. **C.** The eye should be immediately flushed with water non-stop for at least 20 minutes. During this time, trained emergency providers should be called.

Free Response

Question 1

Maximum Points for Question 1
Part (a): 2 points
Part (b) (i): 4 points
Part (b) (ii): 4 points
Part (c): 2 points
Total points: 12

1. A student was asked to determine the molecular weight of a weak monoprotic dry acid (HX). She was provided the following laboratory equipment: a balance (accurate to 0.001 g), distilled water, a 100.00 mL volumetric flask, a supply of sodium hydroxide solution of unknown concentration, a bottle of phenolphthalein, a 100.00 mL graduated cylinder (accurate to 0.01 mL), and a supply of oxalic acid dihydrate ($H_2C_2O_4 \cdot 2H_2O$). *(a) Describe the theory of titration and how it is used.*	***2 points possible***

(continued)

Titration (also known as volumetric analysis) is a common laboratory technique that can be used to determine the concentration of a known reactant. A reagent (titrant) of known concentration (standard solution), and volume is used to react with a measured quantity of reactant (analyte). Using a calibrated burette to add the titrant, it is possible to determine the exact amount that has reacted when the endpoint is reached (usually the point at which the number of moles of titrant is equal to the number of moles (or multiples) of analyte through the use of a visual indicator which changes color at the endpoint. Due to the logarithmic nature of the pH curve, the transitions in color of the indicator are generally pronounced.	*1 point discussion of moles of titrant = moles of analyte.* *1 point use of indicators.*
(b) Suppose the student had used 20.00 grams of the acid and dissolved the acid in distilled water to bring the volume to exactly 100.00 mL. She then added several drops of phenolphthalein to the acidic solution. She then titrated a 50.00 mL sample of this acidic solution with the sodium hydroxide solution and found that it took 42.33 mL of NaOH to reach the end point. She repeated her procedure and found that it took 42.89 mL of NaOH to reach the end point. In order to determine the molarity of the sodium hydroxide solution, she discovered that it took exactly 50.00 mL of sodium hydroxide solution to neutralize 1.500 grams of oxalic acid dihydrate. *(i) Determine the molarity of the NaOH solution.* $MM\ H_2C_2O_4 \cdot 2H_2O = 126.07\ g \cdot mol^{-1}$ $1.500\ g\ H_2C_2O_4 \cdot 2H_2O / 126.07\ g \cdot mol^{-1}$ $= 0.01190\ mol\ H_2C_2O_4 \cdot 2H_2O$ $H_2C_2O_4 + 2NaOH \rightarrow Na_2C_2O_4 + 2H_2O$ $\frac{0.01190 \cancel{mol\ H_2C_2O_4 \cdot 2H_2O}}{1} \times \frac{2\ mol\ NaOH}{1 \cancel{mol\ H_2C_2O_4 \cdot 2H_2O}}$ $= 0.0238\ mol\ NaOH$ $M_{NaOH} = \frac{0.0238 mol\ NaOH}{0.05000 L\ NaOH} = 0.476\ M$	**4 points possible** *1 point for mol $H_2C_2O_4 \cdot 2H_2O$.* *1 point for $H_2C_2O_4 + 2NaOH \rightarrow Na_2C_2O_4 + 2H_2O$.* *1 point for mol NaOH.* *1 point for mol NaOH.*
(ii) Calculate the molecular weight of the unknown acid. mol HX = mol NaOH (42.33 mL NaOH + 42.89 mL NaOH) / 2 = 42.61 mL NaOH = 0.04261 L average 0.476 *M* NaOH × 0.04261 L NaOH = 0.0203 mol NaOH = mol HX $\frac{20.00 g\ HX}{0.10000 \cancel{L}} \times \frac{0.0500 \cancel{L}}{0.0203 mol HX} = 493 g \cdot mol^{-1}$	**4 points possible** *1 point for mol HX = mol NaOH.* *1 point for use of and correct average of mL NaOH.* *1 point for correct mols of HX.* *1 point for correct MM of HX.*

(c) Sketch a titration curve of what the titration of the dry acid vs. sodium hydroxide might look like and explain the diagram. 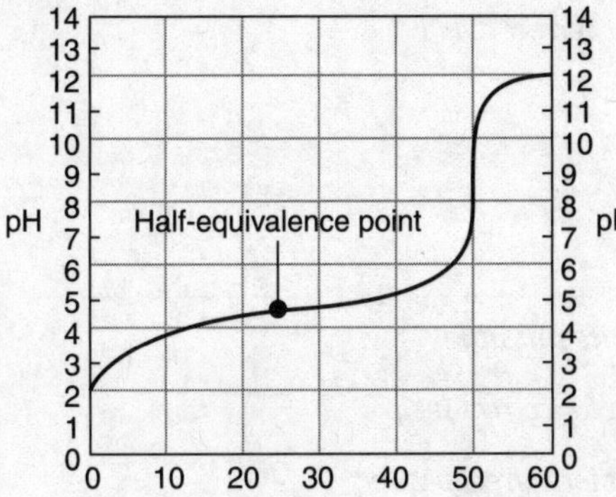 For a strong acid-weak base or weak acid-strong base titration, the pH will change rapidly at the very beginning and then have a gradual slope until near the equivalence point. The gradual slope results from a buffer solution being produced by the addition of the strong acid or base, which resists rapid change in pH until the added acid or base exceeds the buffer's capacity and the rapid pH change occurs near the equivalence point. At the half-equivalence point, enough base has been added to convert exactly half of the acid into the conjugate base (in this case 25 mL). Therefore, at this point the concentration of the acid equals the concentration of the conjugate base (pH = pK_a).	***2 points possible*** *1 point for correct sketch.* *1 point for correct interpretation.*

Question 2

Maximum Points for Question 2
Part (a): 2 points
Part (b): 2 points
Part (c): 2 points
Part (d): 3 points
Total points: 9

2. Sodium ascorbate is a highly reactive antioxidant used as a food preservative with the formula $C_6H_7NaO_6$ and is a salt of the weak acid, ascorbic acid ($C_6H_8O_6$), also known as vitamin C. 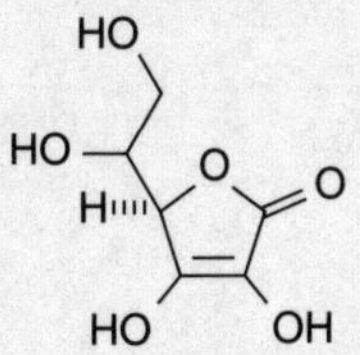	***2 points possible***

(continued)

A 0.10-molar solution of sodium ascorbate was found to have a pH of 8.55 at room temperature. *(a) Calculate the [OH⁻] in the sodium ascorbate solution described above.* pH = 8.55 $[H^+] = 1.00 \times 10^{-8.55}\ M = 2.81 \times 10^{-9}\ M$ $[OH^-] = (1 \times 10^{-14}) / (2.81 \times 10^{-9}) = 3.56 \times 10^{-6}\ M$	*1 point correct [H⁺].* *1 point correct [OH⁻].*
(b) Calculate the value for the equilibrium constant for the reaction $C_6H_7O_6^-{}_{(aq)} + H_2O_{(l)} \rightleftharpoons C_6H_8O_{6(aq)} + OH^-{}_{(aq)}$ $K = ([C_6H_8O_6]\ [OH^-]) / [C_6H_7O_6^-]$ $= \{(3.56 \times 10^{-6})\ (3.56 \times 10^{-6})\} / (0.10 - 3.56 \times 10^{-6}) = 1.27 \times 10^{-10}$	***2 points possible*** *1 point for correct setup.* *1 point for correct answer.*
(c) Calculate the value of K_a, the acid dissociation constant for ascorbic acid. $C_6H_8O_6 \rightleftharpoons C_6H_7O_6^- + H^+$ $K_a = ([H^+]\ [C_6H_7O_6^-]) / [C_6H_8O_6]$ $= \{(2.81 \times 10^{-9})\ (0.10)\} / (3.56 \times 10^{-6}) = 7.89 \times 10^{-5}$	***2 points possible*** *1 point for correct setup.* *1 point for correct answer.*
(d) A saturated solution of ascorbic acid is prepared by adding excess solid ascorbic acid to pure water at room temperature. Since this saturated solution has a pH of 3.50, calculate the molar solubility of ascorbic acid at room temperature. $C_6H_8O_6 \rightleftharpoons C_6H_7O_6^- + H^+$ pH = 3.50 $[H^+] = 1 \times 10^{-3.50}\ M = 3.16 \times 10^{-4}\ M$ $K_a = ([H^+]\ [C_6H_7O_6^-]) / [C_6H_8O_6]$ $7.89 \times 10^{-5} = \{(3.16 \times 10^{-4})\ (3.16 \times 10^{-4})\} / x$ $x = 1.27 \times 10^{-3}\ M$ Total $C_6H_8O_6$ in solution = $(1.27 \times 10^{-3} + 3.16 \times 10^{-4})\ M$ $= 1.59 \times 10^{-3}\ M$	***3 points possible*** *1 point for correct [H⁺].* *1 point for correct $[C_6H_8O_6]$.* *1 point for correct total $C_6H_8O_6$ in solution.*

Kinetics

You'll Need to Know

- ❑ the concept of "reaction rate"
- ❑ the concept of a rate constant and how to write rate law expressions
- ❑ what a zero-order reaction means and how to solve problems involving zero-order reactions
- ❑ what a first-order reaction means and how to solve problems involving first-order reactions
- ❑ what a second-order reaction means and how to solve problems involving second-order reactions
- ❑ collision theory (Maxwell-Boltzmann distribution)
- ❑ how to solve for activation energy (E_a)
- ❑ how to interpret graphs involving E_a and identify factors that affect E_a
- ❑ the relationship between kinetics and equilibrium and how to solve problems involving equilibrium
- ❑ what are catalysts (heterogeneous and homogeneous) and how they affect the reaction rate

Reaction Rates

The rate of a reaction changes as a reaction proceeds because the concentrations of reactants and products change over time. Rate laws are differential equations because the rate of a reaction is the rate of change of the extent of the reaction with time (*dt*).

Given the reaction

$$A + B \rightarrow C + D, \text{ the rate} = k[A]^m[B]^n$$

where *k* is known as the "rate constant". The value of *m* describes the order of the reaction; whereby if $m = 0$, the reaction is zero order with respect to A and the rate is independent of the concentration of A (i.e., doubling the concentration of A has no effect on the rate). If $m = 1$, then the reaction is first order with respect to A; whereby the rate is directly proportional to the concentration of A. Doubling the concentration of A increases the rate by a factor of 2. And finally, if $m = 2$, then the reaction is second order with respect to A and the rate is equal to the square of the concentration of A. Doubling the concentration of A increases the rate by a factor of 4. The overall order of the reaction is the sum of the orders with respect to each reactant. If for example, $m = 0$ and $n = 1$, then the overall order for the reaction would be $0 + 1 = 1$.

Zero Order

The rate of the reaction is independent of the concentration of any reactant. A zero-order reaction will give a straight-line plot if measured values of reactant concentration, [*X*], are plotted against time. The absolute value of the slope of the plot will be the apparent zero-order rate constant. The units for a zero order rate constant are commonly moles · L^{-1} · sec^{-1}.

$$\textbf{rate} = k$$

$$[\textbf{A}]_0 - [\textbf{A}] = kt$$

$$t_{1/2} = [\textbf{A}]_0 / 2k$$

linear plot: [A] vs. *t*

Examples

Q. A 125 mg / mL drug suspension decays by zero-order kinetics with a rate constant of 0.50 mg · mL^{-1} · hr^{-1}. What is the concentration of the drug remaining after 3 days?

A. $[A] = -kt + [A]_0 = -(0.50\ \text{mg} / (\text{mL} \cdot \text{hr}))\ (72\ \text{hr}) + 125\ \text{mg} / \text{mL} = 89\ \text{mg} / \text{mL}$

Q. What is $t_{1/2}$ for the drug suspension?

A. $t_{1/2} = [A]_0 / 2k = (125\ \text{mg} / \text{mL}) \div [2(0.50\ \text{mg} / (\text{mL} \cdot \text{hr}))] = 125\ \text{hr}$ *(130 hrs, 2 s.f.)*

Q. How long will it take to reach 90.% of the original concentration?

A. $0.90(125\ \text{mg} / \text{mL}) = 112.5\ \text{mg} / \text{mL}$

$[A] = -kt + [A]_0,\ t = ([A] - [A]_0) / -k = (112.5 - 125) / -0.50 = 25\ \text{hr}$

First Order

The first order is the rate that is proportional to the concentration of one of the reactants.

$$\textbf{rate} = k[\text{A}]$$

$$\ln [\text{A}] = -kt + \ln [\text{A}]_0$$

$$t_{1/2} = 0.693 / k$$

linear plot: ln[A] vs. *t*

Examples

Q. Dinitrogen pentoxide decomposes to nitrogen dioxide and oxygen gas via a first-order reaction with a rate constant of 5.1 × 10^{-4} s^{-1} at 45°C. If the initial concentration of N_2O_5 is 0.30 *M*, what is the concentration after 180. sec?

A. $2N_2O_{5(g)} \rightarrow 4NO_{2(g)} + O_{2(g)}$

$$\ln\frac{[A]_0}{[A]} kt = \ln\frac{0.30\,M}{[A]} = (5.1\times10^{-4}\,\text{s}^{-1})(180.\ \text{sec})$$

$$\ln\frac{0.30\,M}{[A]} = 0.092$$

$$\frac{0.30\,M}{[A]} = e^{0.092} = 1.1 \qquad [A] = 0.27\,M$$

Q. How long will it take (in sec) for the concentration of N_2O_5 to decrease in half (from 0.30 *M* to 0.15 *M*)?

A. $\ln\frac{[A]_0}{[A]} = kt = \ln\frac{0.30\,M}{0.15\,M} = (5.1\times10^{-4}\,\text{s}^{-1})\,t$

$\ln 2 = (5.1\times10^{-4}\ \text{s}^{-1})\ t$

$0.69 = (5.1\times10^{-4}\ \text{s}^{-1})\ t \qquad t = 1.4\times10^{3}\ \text{s}$

Q. How long will it take to convert 75% of the starting material?

A. Amount left after time t = 100% – 75% = 25%

$$\frac{[A]}{[A]_0} = \frac{0.25}{1.0} = 0.25$$

$$t = \frac{1}{k}\ln\frac{[A]_0}{[A]} = \frac{1}{5.1\times10^{-4}\,s^{-1}}\ln\frac{1.0}{0.25} = 2.7\times10^{3}\,s$$

Second Order

Second order is the rate proportional to the square of the concentration of one of the reactants, or it might be proportional to the product of two different concentrations.

$$\textbf{rate} = k[A]^2$$

$$\frac{1}{[A]} - \frac{1}{[A]_0} = kt$$

$$t_{\frac{1}{2}} = \frac{1}{k[A]_0}$$

linear plot: 1 / [A] vs. *t*

Examples

The following data were measured for the reaction

$$BF_{3(g)} + NH_{3(g)} \rightarrow F_3BNH_{3(g)}$$

Experiment	*[BF$_3$]*	*[NH$_3$]*	*Initial Rate (M / s)*
1	0.250	0.250	0.2130
2	0.250	0.125	0.1065
3	0.200	0.100	0.0682
4	0.350	0.100	0.1193
5	0.175	0.100	0.0596

Q. What is the rate law for the reaction?

A. Comparing 1 and 2: When the concentration of ammonia is halved (0.250 *M* to 0.125 *M*), the rate slows down to half its value (0.213 *M* / *s* to 0.1065 *M* / *s*), therefore, this reaction is first order in ammonia.

Comparing 4 and 5: When the concentration of boron trifluoride is halved (0.350 *M* to 0.175 *M*), the rate also reduces to half its value (0.1193 *M* / *s* to 0.0596 *M* / *s*), therefore, this reaction is first order in boron trifluoride.

The rate law is therefore: rate = $k\,[BF_3]\,[NH_3]$

Q. What is the overall order of the reaction?

A. 1 + 1 = 2

Q. What is the value of the rate constant for this reaction?

A. For each of the experiment, divide the rate by $[BF_3]$ and $[NH_3]$, then take the average of all experiments:

(1) 0.2130 $(M / s) / (0.250\ M)(0.250\ M) = 3.41\ M^{-1} \cdot s^{-1}$

(2) 0.1065 $(M / s) / (0.250\ M)(0.125\ M) = 3.41\ M^{-1} \cdot s^{-1}$

(3) 0.0682 $(M / s) / (0.200\ M)(0.100\ M) = 3.41\ M^{-1} \cdot s^{-1}$

(4) 0.1193 $(M / s) / (0.350\ M)(0.100\ M) = 3.41\ M^{-1} \cdot s^{-1}$

(5) 0.0596 $(M / s) / (0.175\ M)(0.100\ M) = 3.41\ M^{-1} \cdot s^{-1}$

Final answer: $3.41\ M^{-1} \cdot s^{-1}$

Summary

Reaction Order	*Differential Rate Law*	*Integrated Rate Law*	*Linear Plot*	*Slope of Linear Plot*	*Units of Rate Constant*
0	$-d[A] / dt = k$	$[A] = [A]_0 - kt$	$[A]$ vs t	$-k$	$mol \cdot L^{-1} \cdot s^{-1}$
1st	$-d[A] / dt = k[A]$	$\ln[A] = \ln[A]_0 - kt$	$\ln[A]$ vs t	$-k$	s^{-1}
2nd	$-d[A] / dt = k[A]^2$	$1 / [A] = (1 / [A]_0) + kt$	$1 / [A]$ vs t	k	$L \cdot mol^{-1} \cdot s^{-1}$

Collision Theory

The collision theory explains how chemical reactions occur and why reaction rates differ. For a reaction to occur, the reactant particles must collide. However, only a certain fraction of the total collisions are "successful" to cause a chemical change. The successful or effective collisions have: (1) sufficient activation energy at the moment of impact to break the existing bonds and form new bonds, which results in the formation of the products and (2) the correct spatial orientation (steric factor) with respect to each other. The reaction rate is a function of the number of effective collisions per unit of time. Three factors affect collision frequency: (1) concentration—higher concentrations result in greater collision frequencies; (2) temperature—higher temperatures result in higher kinetic energies of the reactant particles and a larger proportion of particles having sufficient activation energies (Maxwell-Boltzmann distribution); and (3) surface area—smaller reactant particles (e.g., powder) result in larger surface areas and higher probabilities of effective collisions.

Activation Energy (E_a)

In order for collisions to be effective, there must be considerable force in the collisions. Slower moving molecules do not have enough kinetic energy to react when they collide . . . they bounce off one another and retain their identity. Only those molecules moving at high speed by either having lower molecular masses or being at higher temperatures have enough energy for collisions to result in a reaction (Maxwell-Boltzmann distribution).

Molecular Speed Distribution for Noble Gases (T constant)

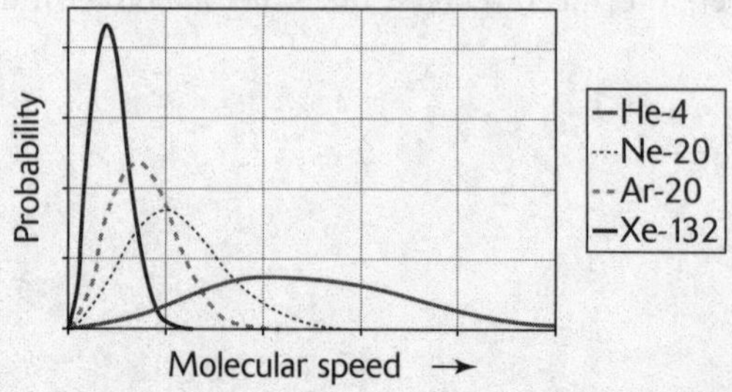

Molecular Speed Distribution at Various Temperatures (MW constant)

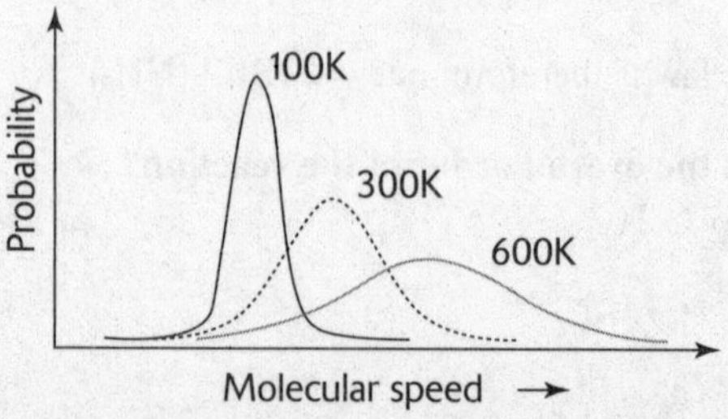

Activation energy, E_a, is expressed in kJ/mol and it is a positive quantity, $E_a > 0$. E_a depends on the nature of the reaction—"fast" reactions usually have a small E_a while those with a large E_a usually proceed slowly. E_a **is also** independent of temperature and concentrations.

$$\ln k = (-E_a / RT) + \ln[A]$$
$$R = 8.314\ J / (K \cdot mol)$$

Example

Q. A reaction necessary for cellular metabolism was found to have an activation energy of 45.0 kJ / mole at a normal body temperature (37°C). Without a catalyst, the rate constant for the reaction was determined to be $5.0 \times 10^{-4}\ s^{-1}$. To be effective in the human body, where the reaction is catalyzed by a specific enzyme, the rate constant must be at least $2.0 \times 10^{-2}\ s^{-1}$. How much must the enzyme lower the activation energy of the reaction to achieve the desired rate?

A. $k = Ae^{-E_a/RT}$

$$\ln k = (-E_a/RT) + \ln[A]$$
$$\ln k_1 = (-E_{a_1}/RT) + \ln[A]$$
$$\ln k_2 = (-E_{a_2}/RT) + \ln[A]$$

Hint: Subtract the second equation from the first to get rid of ln A

$$\ln(k_1/k_2) = (1/RT)(-E_{a_1} + E_{a_2}) \qquad E_{a_2} - E_{a_1} = RT(\ln(k_1/k_2))$$

$T = 37°C + 273 = 310K$

$= (8.314\ J / K \cdot mol)\ (310K)\ \ln(5.0 \times 10^{-4}\ s^{-1} / 2.0 \times 10^{-2}\ s^{-1})$

$= -9.5 \times 10^3\ J / mol = -9.5\ kJ / mole$

Reaction Mechanisms

Only elementary reactions (those which occur in one step) can give the rate law. The rate law of an elementary process follows from the coefficients of its balanced equation. However, most chemical reactions occur by mechanisms that involve more than one step. As a result, the rate law cannot be directly deduced from the stoichiometry of a single balanced chemical equation. Among the steps in a multi-step reaction, there is always one that is the slowest and acts like a "bottleneck." This slowest step limits the overall reaction rate and is called the rate-determining step.

Examples

Given the following reaction: $2A_{(g)} + B_{(g)} \rightarrow 3C_{(g)} + D_{(g)}$

A series of experiments were performed by mixing different concentrations of A and B. The following data was collected:

Experiment	*[A]*	*[B]*	*Rate of Formation of A* ($M \cdot hr^{-1}$)
1	0.240 *M*	0.120 *M*	2.00
2	0.120 *M*	0.120 *M*	0.500
3	0.240 *M*	0.0600 *M*	1.00
4	0.0140 *M*	1.35 *M*	?

Q. Write the rate law expression.

A. When [A] is doubled, the rate quadruples when comparing experiments 1 and 2; A is second order. When [B] is doubled, the rate doubles when comparing experiments 1 and 3; B is first order. Therefore; rate = $k[A]^2[B]$

Q. Calculate *k* and provide the proper units.

A. Using Experiment 1: $2.00\ M / \text{hr} = k(0.240\ M)^2\ (0.120\ M)$

$k = 289\ M^{-2} \cdot \text{hr}^{-1}$

Q. Calculate the rate for Experiment 4

A. rate = $(289\ M^{-2} \cdot \text{hr}^{-1})\ (0.0140\ M)^2\ (1.35\ M) = 0.0765\ M \cdot \text{hr}^{-1}$

Q. What is the final [C] for Experiment 1?

A. $\frac{0.240\ M\ \text{A}}{1} \times \frac{3\ \text{mol C}}{2\ \text{mol A}} = 0.360\ M\ \text{C}$

$\frac{0.120\ M\ \text{B}}{1} \times \frac{3\ \text{mol C}}{1\ \text{mol B}} = 0.360\ M\ \text{C}$

[C] = 0.360 *M* *(had the initial concentrations of A and B been different, the smaller answer, based on the limiting reactant, would have been the correct answer)*

Q. Propose a reaction mechanism.

A.

$$\begin{array}{l} \text{A} + \text{B} \rightleftharpoons \text{Y (fast)} \\ \text{Y} + \text{A} \rightarrow 3\text{C} + \text{D (slow)} \\ \hline 2\text{A} + \text{B} \rightarrow 3\text{C} + \text{D} \end{array}$$

K = [Y] / ([A] [B]). The overall rate constant (*k*) has the equilibrium constant for the fast reaction incorporated into it.

The rate-determining step is the slowest mechanism. Since rate laws generally must be in terms of stable reactants and products (not intermediates), Y needs to be expressed in terms of A and B ([Y] = [A] [B]). Therefore, rate = $k[Y]\ [A] = k[A][B][A] = k[A]^2[B]$ which agrees with the observed rate. There could be other answers that would also be correct.

Kinetics and Equilibrium

The reactants are initially the only molecules present, and they react to form products. The amount of reactant(s) decreases over time and the forward reaction slows down. At the same time, the amount of product(s) is increasing and begins to form reactant(s). The rate for this reverse reaction increases as the amount of product(s) increases. Eventually there comes a time when the forward reaction rate and the reverse reaction rates are equal and the mixture is at equilibrium. At equilibrium, the numbers of reactant and product molecules stay constant.

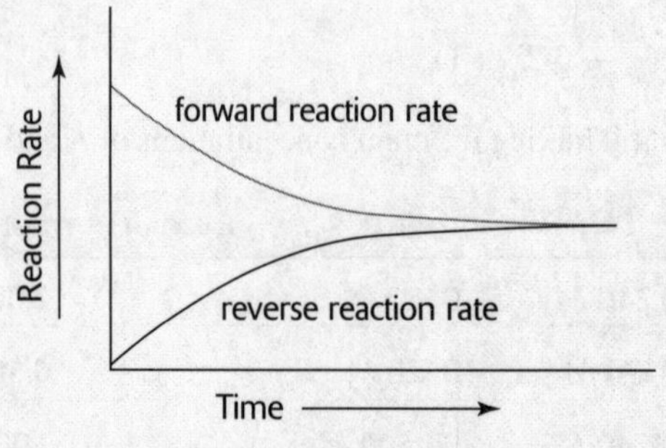

$$K_{eq} = \frac{k_f}{k_r}$$

Example

Q. An experiment is performed to study the following reaction: $A_{(g)} \rightleftharpoons B_{(g)}$

3.00 moles of A are placed in a 3.00-liter vessel. The initial rate of formation of B is found to be 0.020 $M \cdot s^{-1}$. When the system finally reaches equilibrium, 1.00 mole of B is obtained. What is the rate constant (k_r) of the reverse process, $B_{(g)} \rightleftharpoons A_{(g)}$?

A. $K_{eq} = [B] / [A] = k_f / k_r$

$k_f [A] = k_r [B]$

At equilibrium, 1.00 mole of B is present. For every one mole of B formed, one mole of A is used. Thus, at equilibrium, 2.00 moles of A should be present. Thus,

$K_{eq} = [B] / [A] = 1.00 / 2.00 = 0.500$

Volume is constant and cancels out.

rate = $0.020\ M / s = k_f [A] = k_f$ (3.00 moles / 3.00 L)

$k_f = 0.020\ s^{-1}$

$k_r = k_f / K_{eq} = 0.020\ s^{-1} / 0.500 = 0.040\ s^{-1}$

Catalysis

A catalyst is a substance that increases the rate of a chemical reaction without itself being consumed. Catalysts work by providing a set of elementary steps with more favorable kinetics than those that exist in its absence and by lowering the activation energy for the reaction. By lowering the activation energy required, catalysts also enhance the rate of the reverse reaction to the same extent as they do in the forward direction.

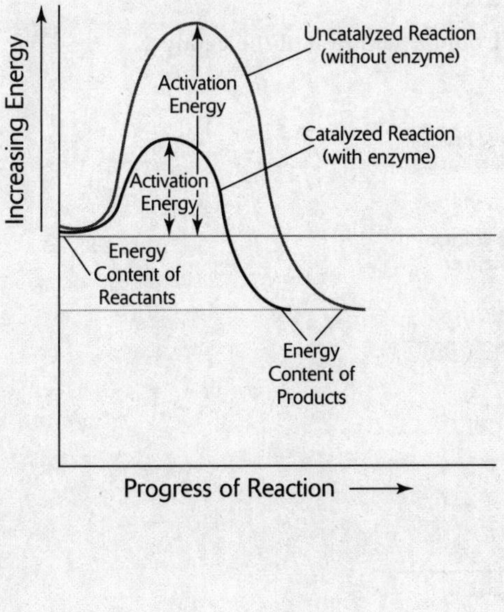

Type of Catalyst	Description	Examples
Heterogeneous	Reactants and catalyst are in different phases	Examples: (1) Haber process: $N_{2(g)} + 3H_{2(g)} \rightarrow 2NH_{3(g)}$. N_2 and H_2 gases dissociate on a solid metal surface; (2) Ostwald process: manufacture of nitric acid that utilizes a solid platinum-rhodium catalyst in the presence of gaseous ammonia and oxygen; and (3) Catalytic converters: solid catalysts of Pd, Pt, CuO or Cr_2O_3 are used to dissociate NO gas into N_2 and O_2 and also oxidize CO gas and unburned hydrocarbons to CO_2 and H_2O.
Homogeneous	Reactants, catalysts, and products are all in same phase	Example: Acidic catalyst in the reaction of ethyl acetate with water to form acetic acid and ethanol, in which all species are in the aqueous state.
Enzyme	Catalyst found in living organisms. Homogenous in nature.	Increase rate of biological reactions 10^6 to 10^{12} times. Highly specific—a unique enzyme catalyzes only one biological reaction by reacting with a specific substrate (molecule). A single cell may include up to 3,000 different enzymes.

Examples

Q. The synthesis of compound C is an elementary process that proceeds as follows:

$$A_{(g)} + B_{(g)} \rightleftharpoons C_{(g)} + D_{(g)} \qquad \Delta H° = -25 \text{ kcal}$$

The forward reaction is slow at room temperature but becomes rapid when a catalyst is added.

(a) Draw a diagram of potential energy versus reaction coordinate for the uncatalyzed reaction. On this diagram label

(1) the axes

(2) the energies of the reactants and the products

(3) the energy of the activated complex

(4) all significant energy differences

(5) the change(s) that result from the addition of the catalyst

A.

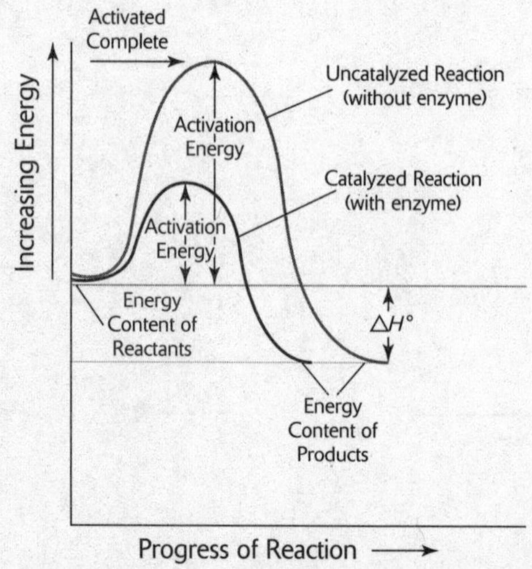

Q. If the temperature is decreased, what will happen to the ratio k_f / k_r?

A. If the temperature is decreased for this exothermic reaction, mechanisms consistent with Le Chatelier's Principle will cause the equilibrium to shift right causing the ratio k_f / k_r to increase. Second, at lower temperatures, fewer molecules will have attained sufficient velocities resulting in lower kinetic energies which is consistent with Maxwell-Boltzmann distributions. Third, a lower temperature will lower the value $T\Delta S$ and influence the magnitude of ΔG.

Multiple-Choice Questions

1. Hydrogen iodide decomposes to give a mixture of hydrogen and iodine:

$$2HI_{(g)} \rightarrow H_{2(g)} + I_{2(g)}$$

	Initial [HI]	*Initial Rate of Reaction*
Trial 1	$1.0 \times 10^{-2}\ M$	$4.0 \times 10^{-6}\ M/s$
Trial 2	$2.0 \times 10^{-2}\ M$	$1.6 \times 10^{-5}\ M/s$
Trial 3	$3.0 \times 10^{-2}\ M$	$3.6 \times 10^{-5}\ M/s$

The order of the decomposition of HI in the gas phase is

A. 0
B. 1
C. 2
D. 3
E. 4

2. The equation C → A + B which was found to be second order, had a rate of $0.40\ M \cdot s^{-1}$ and with an initial concentration of C of 0.25 *M*. If the concentration of C was increased to 0.75 *M*, then the rate would change to

A. $0.028\ M \cdot s^{-1}$
B. $0.125\ M \cdot s^{-1}$
C. $0.50\ M \cdot s^{-1}$
D. $0.75\ M \cdot s^{-1}$
E. $3.6\ M \cdot s^{-1}$

3. The following reaction is first order: $2N_2O_{5(g)} \rightarrow 4NO_{2(g)} + O_{2(g)}$. If it takes 30 minutes for half of the N_2O_5 to decompose, the rate constant *k* is approximately

A. $0.011\ min^{-1}$
B. $0.023\ min^{-1}$
C. $15\ min^{-1}$
D. $30\ min^{-1}$
E. 60 minutes

4. Which of the following is a graph that describes the pathway of reaction that is exothermic and has relatively high activation energy?

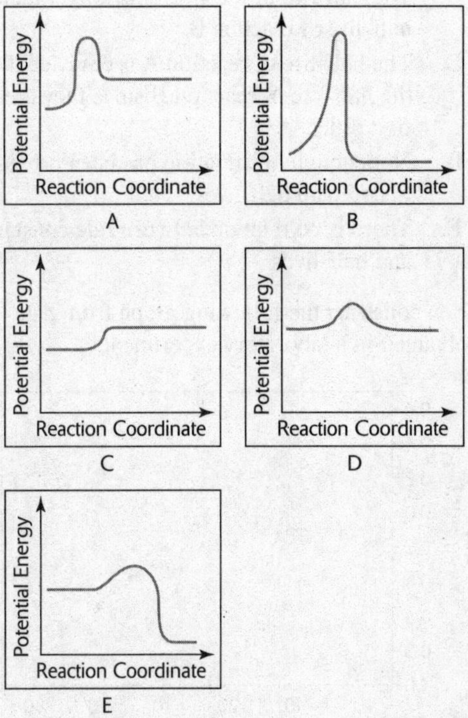

5. Which of the following, if increased, does NOT increase reaction rate?

A. reactant concentration
B. surface area
C. pressure
D. activation energy
E. temperature

6. The first order rate constant of reaction A is 0.050 h^{-1} and the first-order rate constant of reaction B is 0.10 h^{-1}. Which of the following is true?

A. The half-life of reaction B is longer than the half-life of reaction A.
B. The half-life of reaction A is longer than the half-life of reaction B.
C. The half-life of reaction A is equivalent to the half-life of reaction B since they are both first order.
D. Not enough information has been provided to compare half-lives.
E. There is no relation between rate constants and half-lives.

7. You construct the following graph from data obtained in a laboratory experiment:

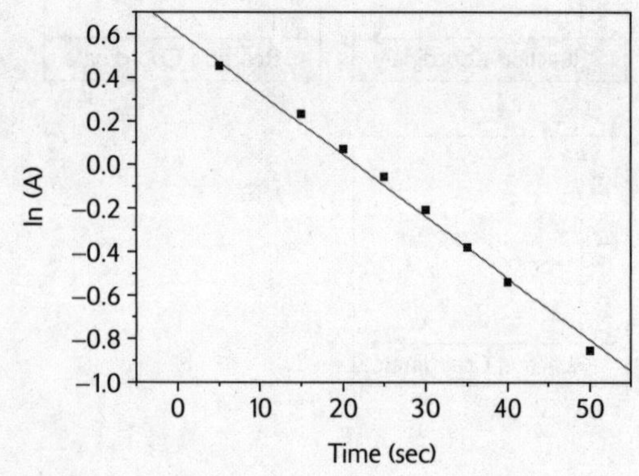

From the graph, you know that the reaction is

A. zero order
B. first order
C. second order
D. third order
E. You cannot determine the order of the reaction from this graph.

8. $A \rightarrow 2B + C$

What is the order of the reaction above given the following information?

time (min)	*[A] (M)*
0.00	1.000
10.00	0.8000
20.00	0.6667
40.00	0.5000

A. zero order
B. first order
C. second order
D. third order
E. You cannot determine the order of the reaction from the information provided.

For Questions 9–14: Consider the following reaction

$A + B + C \rightarrow$ Products

A student performed a series of experiments and obtained the following data.

Trial	*$[A]_0$ (M)*	*$[B]_0$ (M)*	*$[C]_0$ (M)*	*Initial Rate (M / s)*
1	0.151	0.213	0.398	0.480
2	0.251	0.105	0.325	0.356
3	0.151	0.213	0.525	1.102
4	0.151	0.250	0.480	0.988

9. What is the order of C?

A. 0
B. 1
C. 2
D. 3
E. Cannot be determined

10. What is the order of B?

- **A.** 0
- **B.** 1
- **C.** 2
- **D.** 3
- **E.** Cannot be determined

11. What is the order of A?

- **A.** 0
- **B.** 1
- **C.** 2
- **D.** 3
- **E.** Cannot be determined

12. What is the overall order of the reaction?

- **A.** 1
- **B.** 2
- **C.** 3
- **D.** 6
- **E.** 8

13. The rate constant *k* is equal to

- **A.** $1.57 \times 10^{-1}\ L^4 \cdot mol^{-5} \cdot s^{-1}$
- **B.** $1.57 \times 10^{-5}\ L^5 \cdot mol^{-5} \cdot s^{-3}$
- **C.** $1.57 \times 10^{3}\ L^5 \cdot mol^{-1} \cdot s^{-5}$
- **D.** $1.57 \times 10^{3}\ L^{-5} \cdot mol^{5} \cdot s^{-1}$
- **E.** $1.57 \times 10^{3}\ L^5 \cdot mol^{-5} \cdot s^{-1}$

14. What is the initial rate of the reaction when all the reactants are at 0.100 *M* concentrations?

- **A.** $2.93 \times 10^{-5}\ M \cdot s^{-1}$
- **B.** $4.25 \times 10^{-4}\ M \cdot s^{-1}$
- **C.** $1.57 \times 10^{-3}\ M \cdot s^{-1}$
- **D.** $1.06 \times 10^{-2}\ M \cdot s^{-1}$
- **E.** $8.33 \times 10^{-1}\ M \cdot s^{-1}$

15. Relatively fast rates of chemical reaction are associated with which of the following?

- **A.** The absence of a catalyst
- **B.** Low temperature
- **C.** Low concentration of reactants
- **D.** Relatively weak bonds in reactant molecules
- **E.** High activation energy

16. You sprinkle lighter fluid onto some charcoal in order to start a barbeque. You wait 30 seconds and then you throw a lighted match onto the charcoal. The lighted match

- **A.** decreases the energy of activation for the slow step.
- **B.** acts as a catalyst.
- **C.** supplies some of the energy of activation for the combustion reaction.
- **D.** provides a more favorable activated complex for the combustion reaction.
- **E.** provides the heat of vaporization for the volatile hydrocarbon.

17. Dinitrogen pentoxide decomposes into dinitrogen tetroxide and oxygen gas as a first-order reaction:

$$2N_2O_{5(g)} \rightarrow 2N_2O_{4(g)} + O_{2(g)}$$

The half-life of the reaction at 45.0°C is 1.12×10^3 min. How much time would be required for 80.0% of the N_2O_5 to decompose at this temperature?

- **A.** 1.30×10^3 min
- **B.** 2.60×10^3 min
- **C.** 2.60×10^4 min
- **D.** 2.60×10^5 min
- **E.** 2.60×10^6 min

18. The thermal decomposition of PH_3 obeys first-order kinetics. At 680.°C, a plot of $\ln[PH_3]$ versus *t* gives a slope of $-0.0198\ s^{-1}$. What is the half-life of the reaction?

- **A.** 35.0 min
- **B.** 70.0 min
- **C.** 140.0 min
- **D.** 175.0 min
- **E.** 210.0 min

19. The reaction

$$2NO_{2(g)} + F_{2(g)} \rightarrow 2NO_2F_{(g)}$$

follows the mechanism

(i.) $NO_2 + F_2 \rightarrow NO_2F + F$ (slow)

(ii.) $NO_2 + F \rightarrow NO_2F$ (fast)

The rate law would be consistent with

A. $k\,[NO_2]^3\,[F_2]^2$
B. $k\,[NO_2]^2\,[F_2]$
C. $k\,[NO_2]\,[F_2]$
D. $k\,[NO_2]^2\,[F_2]^2$
E. $k\,[NO_2]\,[F_2]^2$

20. Calcium carbonate ($CaCO_3$) can exist in a variety of different structural forms, the most common of which are aragonite and calcite.

aragonite $\rightleftharpoons$ calcite $\Delta G = -0.85\ \text{kJ} \cdot \text{mol}^{-1}$

Even though calcite is thermodynamically more stable than aragonite, aragonite fossils that are hundreds of millions of years old are common. The time taken for 10.0% of a mass of aragonite to be converted to calcite in the absence of water was measured at a range of temperatures and presented below. Also presented is a plot of ln(t) vs. $1/T$. Determine the activation energy (E_a).

Temperature (K)	*Time (hours)*
651	316
680	10
693	2.51
714	0.126
739	0.040

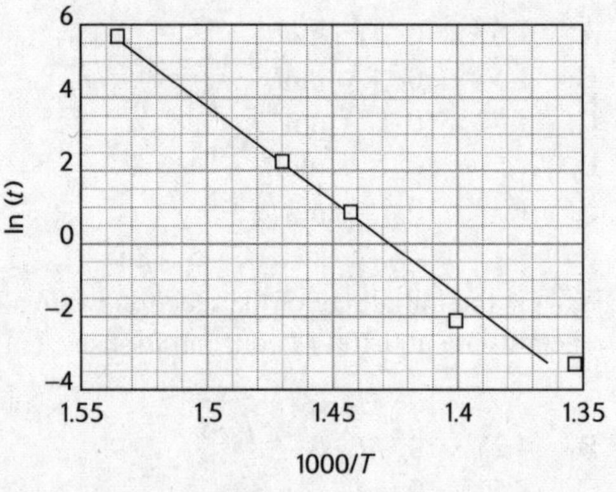

A. $-440\ \text{kJ} \cdot \text{mol}^{-1}$
B. $440\ \text{kJ} \cdot \text{mol}^{-1}$
C. $880\ \text{kJ} \cdot \text{mol}^{-1}$
D. $1{,}784\ \text{kJ} \cdot \text{mol}^{-1}$
E. $4{,}397\ \text{kJ} \cdot \text{mol}^{-1}$

Free-Response Questions

1. The reaction between Q and S is believed to occur in the following three-step process.

$$Q + Q \rightleftharpoons R \quad \text{(fast)}$$
$$R + S \rightarrow T + U \quad \text{(slow)}$$
$$T + S \rightarrow V + U \quad \text{(fast)}$$

(a) Write a balanced equation for the overall reaction.

(b) Identify the intermediates in the reaction. Explain your reasoning.

(c) The following data was obtained from an experiment between S and Q at 700.°C:

Trial	*S (M)*	*Q (M)*	*Initial Rate (M / s)*
1	0.010	0.025	2.4×10^{-6}
2	0.0050	0.025	1.2×10^{-6}
3	0.010	0.0125	6.0×10^{-7}

Determine the rate law of the reaction from the above data.

(d) Determine the overall order of the reaction.

(e) Calculate the rate constant, *k*.

(f) Which of the following mechanisms can be ruled out on the basis of the rate law determined in part (c)? Explain your reasoning.

Mechanism I: $S + Q \rightarrow U + W$ (slow)
$W + Q \rightarrow V + X$ (fast)
$X + S \rightarrow U$ (fast)

Mechanism II: $S + 2Q \rightarrow T + U$ (slow)
$T + S \rightarrow V + U$ (fast)

Meachnism III: $2Q \rightleftharpoons R$ (fast equilibrium)
$R + S \rightarrow T + U$ (slow)
$T + S \rightarrow V + U$

(g) Explain why an increase in temperature increases the rate constant, *k*, given the rate law determined in part (c).

2. 2.00 moles of hydrogen gas and 3.00 moles of nitrogen monoxide gas, both at 25.0°C are introduced into a 5.00 L container. The total pressure of the gases in the container is 2.50 atm.

(a) Write a balanced equation.

(b) Calculate the partial pressure of each gas.

(c) Using the following thermodynamic data, calculate $\Delta H°$.

Substance	*ΔH° (kJ / mol)*
$NO_{(g)}$	90.4
$H_2O_{(g)}$	−241.8

(d) The rate law was determined to be $k = [H_2]\,[NO]^2$. Predict the effect of each of the following changes on the initial rate of the reaction and explain your prediction.

(i) Doubling the concentration of hydrogen gas at constant temperature and volume.

(ii) Doubling the concentration of nitrogen monoxide at constant temperature and volume.

(iii) Addition of a catalyst. In your explanation, include a diagram of potential energy versus reaction coordinate.

(iv) Decrease in temperature. In your explanation, include a diagram showing the number of molecules as a function of energy.

(v) Decreasing the volume of the container from 5.00 L to 2.00 L.

Answers and Explanations

Multiple Choice

1. **C.** $\frac{\text{rate trial 2}}{\text{rate trial 1}} = \frac{1.6 \times 10^{-5}\ M/s}{4.0 \times 10^{-6}\ M/s} = 4$ when [HI] is doubled

$\frac{\text{rate trial 3}}{\text{rate trial 1}} = \frac{3.6 \times 10^{-5}\ M/s}{4.0 \times 10^{-6}\ M/s} = 9$ when [HI] is tripled

The rate of this reaction is proportional to the square of the HI concentration. The reaction is therefore second order in HI; rate = $k(\text{HI})^2$

2. **E.** The concentration of C increases from 0.25 *M* to 0.75 *M* (a three-fold increase). Being second order, the rate would increase $3^2 = 9$ times: $9\ (0.40\ M \cdot s^{-1}) = 3.6\ M \cdot s^{-1}$

3. **B.** $k = 0.693 / t_{1/2} = 0.693 / 30.\ \text{min} = 0.023\ \text{min}^{-1}$

4. **B.** In this diagram, the reactants possess more potential energy than the products; therefore, energy was released to the environment (exothermic). This diagram also contains the highest barrier (activation energy) for the reactants to overcome.

5. **D.** Reactant concentration, if increased, usually makes the reaction occur faster. In reactions on surfaces, which take place for example during heterogeneous catalysis, the rate of reaction increases as surface area increases (i.e., coal dust will burn faster than solid coal) due to the fact that more particles of the solid are exposed and can be hit by reactant molecules. By increasing pressure, molecules are forced closer together increasing the frequency of collisions. Higher activation energies imply that a reaction will be more difficult to start, and hence slower. Raising temperatures increases the frequency of molecular collisions. Catalysts lower the activation energy.

6. **B.** The half-life is inversely related to the rate constant. Since reaction A has a smaller rate constant than reaction B, its half-life will be longer.

7. **B.** If the reaction is first order, a plot of the natural log of the concentration versus time will be a straight line. Thus, the change in the natural log of the concentration divided by the elapsed time will be constant.

8. **C.** If the reaction is second order, a plot of the inverse concentration versus time will be linear. Thus, the change in inverse concentration (1 / [A]) divided by the elapsed time (Δt) will be constant:

$(1 / 0.800 - 1/1.000) / 10 = 0.0250$

$(1 / 0.6667 - 1/0.8000) / 10 = 0.0250$

$(1 / 0.5000 - 1/1.000) / 40 = 0.0250$

The rate constant is $0.0250\ M^{-1} \cdot \text{min}^{-1}$

9. **D.** rate = $k[\text{A}]^a [\text{B}]^b [\text{C}]^c$. Isolate the effect of the concentration of one of the reactants. In runs number 1 and 3, the only change of initial concentrations is that of reactant C, a change from 0.398 *M* to 0.525 *M* with a change in rate from 0.480 *M/s* to 1.102 *M/s*.

The ratio of the initial rates of runs 1 and 3 is then:

$$\frac{\text{trial 1}}{\text{trial 3}} = \frac{0.480\ \cancel{M/s}}{1.102\ \cancel{M/s}} = \frac{k\,\cancel{(0.151\,M)^a}\,\cancel{(0.213\,M)^b}\,(0.398\,M)^c}{k\,\cancel{(0.151\,M)^a}\,\cancel{(0.213\,M)^b}\,(0.525\,M)^c}$$

$$0.4356 = \frac{(0.398\,M)^c}{(0.525\,M)^c} = 0.7851^c$$

$$\ln(0.4356) = \ln(0.7581)^c = c \cdot \ln(0.7581)$$

$$c = \frac{\ln(0.4356)}{\ln(0.7581)} = 3.00 \text{ order}$$

10. B. Pick another pair of runs that have a change in the initial concentration of C and just one other reactant.

$$\frac{\text{trial 1}}{\text{trial 4}} = \frac{0.480\ \cancel{M/s}}{0.988\ \cancel{M/s}} = \frac{\cancel{k(0.151\,M)^{a}}(0.213\,M)^{b}(0.398\,\cancel{M})^{3}}{\cancel{k(0.151\,M)^{a}}(0.250\,M)^{b}(0.480\,\cancel{M})^{3}}$$

$0.4858 = (0.8520)^b\ (0.5701)$

$\ln (0.8521) = b \cdot \ln (0.8520)$

b = 1.00 = first order

11. C. Use a pair of runs where the initial concentration of A changes.

$$\frac{\text{trial 1}}{\text{trial 2}} = \frac{0.480\ \cancel{M/s}}{0.356\ \cancel{M/s}} = \frac{k(0.151\,\cancel{M})^{a}(0.213\,\cancel{M})^{1}(0.398\,\cancel{M})^{3}}{k(0.251\,\cancel{M})^{a}(0.105\cancel{M})^{1}(0.325\,\cancel{M})^{3}}$$

$1.3483 = (0.6016)^a\ (2.0286)^1\ (1.2246)^3$

$\ln (0.3619) = a \cdot \ln (0.6016)$

a = 2.00 order

12. D. a = 2; b = 1; c = 3; 2 + 1 + 3 = 6

13. E. The rate constant for the reaction may now be evaluated from any of the experimental runs:

$0.480\ M/s = k\ (0.151\ M)^2\ (0.213\ M)^1\ (0.398\ M)^3$

$k = 1.57 \times 10^3\ M^{-5} \cdot s^{-1}$

14. C. rate $= k[A]^a\ [B]^b\ [C]^c = (1.57 \times 10^3\ M^{-5} \cdot s^{-1})\ (0.100\ M)^2\ (0.100\ M)^1\ (0.100\ M)^3$

$= 1.57 \times 10^{-3}\ M \cdot s^{-1}$

15. D. It takes energy to break bonds. If reactant bonds are weak, it will take less energy to break them resulting in a faster reaction. All other choices will slow down reactions.

16. C. Ignition temperature is the minimum temperature to which the fuel (in this case the lighter fluid) mixture (or a portion of it) must be heated in order for the combustion reaction to occur. A high ignition temperature means the fuel is difficult to ignite and a low ignition temperature means the fuel ignites easily making the fuel potentially hazardous (high vapor pressure). The greater the activation energy of a reaction, the higher the ignition temperature will be. A match and its striking surface contain a fuel and its oxidizer with a low activation energy and therefore low ignition temperature, so low that the friction of striking the match generates enough heat to raise the temperature sufficiently for ignition to occur. A spark is needed to raise the temperature of the mixture sufficiently near the spark for the mixture to ignite. The heat of reaction generated heats up more of the mixture so the reaction becomes self-sustaining.

17. B. $k = \dfrac{0.693}{t_{\frac{1}{2}}} = \dfrac{0.693}{1.12 \times 10^3\ \text{min}} = 6.19 \times 10^{-4}\ \text{min}^{-1}$

The value of [A] after 80.0% of the reactant has decomposed is $0.200\ [A]_0$

$$t = \frac{1}{k}\ln\frac{[A]_0}{[A]} = \frac{1}{6.19 \times 10^{-4}\ \text{min}^{-1}}\ln\frac{[A]_0}{0.200[A]_0} = \frac{\ln 5}{6.19 \times 10^{-4}\ \text{min}^{-1}}$$

2.60×10^3 min

18. **A.** $4PH_{3(g)} \rightarrow P_{4(g)} + 6H_{2(g)}$

For first order reactions, the slope of the line is equal to $-k$. Therefore, $k = 0.0198\ s^{-1}$.

$$t_{\frac{1}{2}} = \frac{0.693}{k} = \frac{0.693}{0.0198\,s^{-1}} = 35.0\,\text{min}$$

19. **C.** Since step i is the rate-determining step, the rate law is

$$\text{rate} = k\,[NO_2]\,[F_2]$$

Addition of i and ii gives the overall reaction:

$$NO_2 + F_2 \rightarrow NO_2F + \cancel{F}$$
$$NO_2 + \cancel{F} \rightarrow NO_2F$$
$$\overline{2NO_2 + F_2 \rightarrow 2NO_2F}$$

This problem illustrates that the overall reaction equation has nothing to do with the order of the reaction. The elementary process in the rate-determining step determines the order.

Other possible elementary steps in this reaction are:

$$F + F \rightarrow F_2$$
$$F + F_2 \rightarrow F_2 + F$$
$$NO_2F + F \rightarrow F + NO_2F$$

20. **B.** The slope of the line is equal to $-E_a / R$ and ~ –53,000. Multiply this by R (8.314 J / (K · mol)) and reverse the sign to get a value of 440,642 J · mol^{-1} = ~ 440. kJ · mol^{-1} for E_a.

Free Response

Question 1

Maximum Points for Question 1
Part (a): 1 point
Part (b): 2 points
Part (c): 2 points
Part (d): 1 point
Part (e): 1 point
Part (f): 2 points
Part (g): 1 point
Total points: 10

1. The reaction between Q and S is believed to occur in the following three-step process. *Q + Q ⇌ R (fast)* *R + S → T + U (slow)* *T + S → V + U (fast)*	***1 point possible***
(a) Write a balanced equation for the overall reaction. Q + Q ⇌ ~~R~~ (fast) ~~R~~ + S → ~~T~~ + U (slow) ~~T~~ + S → V + U (fast) 2Q + 2S → V + 2U	*1 point for correctly balanced overall reaction.*
(b) Identify the intermediates in the reaction. Explain your reasoning. R and T are intermediates because they appear in the mechanism but not in the overall products (or reactants).	***2 points possible*** *1 point for correct intermediates.* *1 point for correct explanation.*
(c) Data was obtained from an experiment between S and Q at 700°C: *Determine the rate law of the reaction from the data.* The overall rate law is of the general form rate = $k\,[S]^x\,[Q]^y$. Comparing Experiment 1 and Experiment 2: The concentration of Q is constant and the concentration of S has decreased by one-half. The initial rate has also decreased by one-half. Therefore, the initial rate is directly proportional to the concentration of S; x = 1. Comparing Experiment 1 and Experiment 3: The concentration of S is constant and the concentration of Q has decreased by one-half. The initial rate has decreased by one-fourth. Therefore, the initial rate is proportional to the squared concentration of Q; y = 2. Overall rate law: rate = $k\,[S]\,[Q]^2$	***2 points possible*** *1 point for correct rate law.* *1 point for correct reasoning.*
(d) Determine the overall order of the reaction. The overall order of the reaction is the sum of the exponents: 1 + 2 = 3.	***1 point possible*** *1 point for correct overall order of the reaction.*

(e) Calculate the rate constant, k. rate = k [S][Q]^2 $k = \frac{\text{rate}}{[S][Q]^2}$ $k = \frac{2.4 \times 10^{-6}\ M/s}{(0.010\,M)(0.025\,M)^2} = 0.38/\left(M^2 \cdot s\right)$	***1 point possible*** *1 point for correct rate constant.*
(f) Which of the following mechanisms can be ruled out on the basis of the rate law determined in part (c)? Explain your reasoning. Mechanism I: $S + Q \rightarrow U + W$ (slow) $W + Q \rightarrow V + X$ (fast) $X + S \rightarrow U$ (fast) Mechanism II: $S + 2Q \rightarrow T + U$ (slow) $T + S \rightarrow V + U$ (fast) Mechanism III: $2Q \rightleftharpoons R$ (fast equilibrium) $R + S \rightarrow T + U$ (slow) $T + S \rightarrow V + U$ (fast) The rate law determined in part (c) is: rate = k [S][Q]^2 In Mechanism I, the slow step is bimolecular and the rate law would be rate = k [S][Q] and is not consistent with the rate law determined in part (c). In Mechanism II, the rate-determining step involves the simultaneous collision of two Q molecules with one S molecule. The rate law would be rate = k[S] [Q]^2 and is consistent with the rate law determined in part (c). In Mechanism III, the forward and reverse reaction in the first step are in dynamic equilibrium; therefore, their rates are equal: $k_f[Q]^2 = k_r[R]$. The slow step is bimolecular and involves the collision of an S molecule with a molecule of R. The rate would therefore be rate = k_2[S] [R]. Solving the dynamic equilibrium equation of the first step for [R] and substituting into the above equation, we get the following rate law $\text{rate} = \frac{k_2 \cdot k_f}{k_r}[S][Q]^2 = k[S][Q]^2$ which is consistent with the rate law determined in part (c).	***2 points possible*** *1 point for correctly identifying Mechanisms II and III as being possible and ruling out Mechanism I.* *1 point for correct reasoning.*

(g) Explain why an increase in temperature increases the rate constant, k, given the rate law determined in part (c).	***1 point possible***
In the rate equation the temperature dependent quantity is the rate constant, *k*; the rate of reaction changes with a change in temperature because *k* changes. The quantitative effect is given by the Arrhenius equation:	
$k = Ae^{-E_a/RT}$. Since the activation energy E_a is always a positive quantity, the result is that an increase in temperature always results in an increase in *k*. This should mean that for every reaction an increase in temperature increases the rate. Excluded from this are enzyme-mediated reactions; the rate of these will fall with increasing temperature beyond the optimum for the enzyme since the enzyme becomes denatured (inactive) at high temperatures. Another reason is that at higher temperatures, molecules are traveling faster with a higher percentage of them having enough energy for effective collisions that result in a reaction, consistent with the Maxwell-Boltzmann distribution.	*1 point for a correct reason which can include Arrhenius (outside scope of AP Chemistry); Maxwell-Boltzmann, etc.*

Question 2

Maximum Points for Question 2
Part (a): 1 point
Part (b): 2 points
Part (c): 1 point
Part (d) (i): 1 point
Part (d) (ii): 1 point
Part (d) (iii): 2 points
Part (d) (iv): 2 points
Part (d) (v): 1 point
Total points: 11

2. 2.00 moles of hydrogen gas and 3.00 moles of nitrogen monoxide gas, both at 25.0°C, are introduced into a 5.00 L container. The total pressure of the gases in the container is 2.50 atm. *(a) Write a balanced equation.*	***1 point possible***
$2H_{2(g)} + 2NO_{(g)} \rightarrow N_{2(g)} + 2H_2O_{(g)}$	*1 point for correctly balanced equation.*
(b) Calculate the partial pressure of each gas. $X_{H_2} = \frac{n_{H_2}}{n_{H_2} + n_{NO}} = \frac{2.00\text{moles}}{2.00\text{moles} + 3.00\text{moles}} = 0.400$ $X_{NO} = \frac{n_{NO}}{n_{H_2} + n_{NO}} = \frac{3.00\text{moles}}{2.00\text{moles} + 3.00\text{moles}} = 0.600$	***2 points possible*** *1 point for correct partial pressure of H_2.*

$P_{H_2} = X_{H_2} \cdot P_T = 0.400(2.50\text{atm}) = 1.00\text{atm}$ $P_{NO} = X_{NO} \cdot P_T = 0.600\ (2.50\ \text{atm}) = 1.50\ \text{atm}$	*1 point for correct partial pressure of NO.*
(c) Using the thermodynamic data, calculate ΔH°. $\Delta H^\circ_{rxn} = \Sigma\Delta H^\circ_{f\,(products)} - \Sigma\Delta H^\circ_{f\,(reactants)}$ $= 2\Delta H^\circ_f H_2O_{(g)} - 2\Delta H^\circ_f NO_{(g)}$ $= 2(-241.8\ \text{kJ} \cdot \text{mol}^{-1}) - 2(90.4\ \text{kJ} \cdot \text{mol}^{-1})$ $= -438.6\ \text{kJ} - 180.8\ \text{kJ}$ $= -619.4\ \text{kJ}$	***1 point possible*** *1 point for correct ΔH° and correctly showing work.*
(d) The rate law was determined to be $k = [H_2]\,[NO]^2$. Predict the effect of each of the following changes on the initial rate of the reaction and explain your prediction. *(i) Doubling the concentration of hydrogen gas at constant temperature and volume.* Since the reaction is first order in H_2, doubling the concentration would double the rate. The inclusion of H_2 in the rate law indicates it participates in the rate-determining step.	***1 point possible*** *1 point for correct conclusion and supporting argument.*
(ii) Doubling the concentration of nitrogen monoxide at constant temperature and volume. Since the reaction is second order in NO, the rate is proportional to the square of the concentration of NO; i.e., doubling the concentration of NO would increase the rate four times.	***1 point possible*** *1 point for correct conclusion and supporting argument.*
(iii) Addition of a catalyst. In your explanation, include a diagram of potential energy versus reaction coordinate. Addition of a catalyst will increase the rate of both forward and reverse reactions by lowering the activation energy. 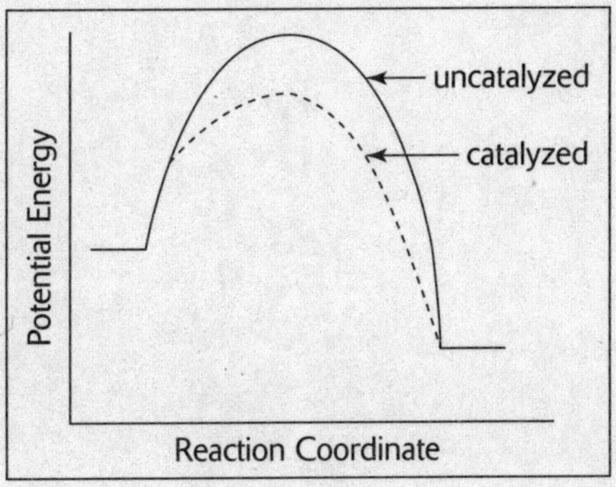 	***2 points possible*** *1 point for correct conclusion.* *1 point for correct diagram.*

<table>
<tr>
<td>

(iv) Decrease in temperature. In your explanation, include a diagram showing the number of molecules as a function of energy.

The initial rate of reaction will decrease since molecules will be moving slower and possess less kinetic energy. Less kinetic energy results in less effective collisions between molecules and fewer activated complexes.

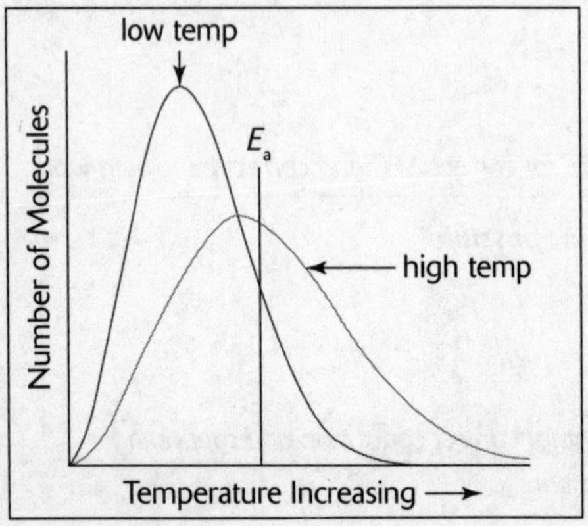

</td>
<td>

2 points possible

1 point for correct conclusion.

1 point for correct diagram and supporting argument.

</td>
</tr>
<tr>
<td>

(v) Decreasing the volume of the container from 5.00 L to 2.00 L.

The initial rate would increase. Decreasing the volume would increase the concentration of both reactants. At the higher concentration, there would be a larger number of overall collisions (due to less distance between individual molecules) leading to a larger number of effective collisions.

</td>
<td>

1 point possible

1 point for correct conclusion and supporting argument.

</td>
</tr>
</table>

Oxidation-Reduction (Redox)

You'll Need to Know

- ❑ what oxidation state means
- ❑ how to determine the oxidation number of an element within a compound
- ❑ what the difference is between oxidation and reduction
- ❑ how to determine what is being oxidized and what is being reduced
- ❑ how to determine the oxidizing agent
- ❑ how to determine the reducing agent
- ❑ how to balance redox reactions
- ❑ how to solve problems involving galvanic (voltaic) cells
- ❑ how to draw and label a simple voltaic cell given sufficient information
- ❑ how to draw and label an electrolytic cell given sufficient information
- ❑ how to solve problems that involve the Nernst equation.

Oxidation States

The following are some oxidation rules:

1. The oxidation state (charge) of any element such as Fe, H_2, or S_8 is zero (0).
2. The oxidation state of oxygen in its compounds is –2, except for peroxides like H_2O_2 or Na_2O_2, in which the oxidation state for O is –1.
3. The oxidation state of hydrogen is +1 in its compounds, except for metal hydrides, such as NaH, LiH, etc., in which the oxidation state for H is –1.
4. The oxidation states of other elements are then assigned to make the algebraic sum of the oxidation states equal to the net charge on the molecule or ion.
5. The following elements usually have the same oxidation states in their compounds:
   - +1 for alkali metals: Li, Na, K, Rb, Cs
   - +2 for alkaline earth metals: Be, Mg, Ca, Sr, Ba
   - –1 for halogens except when they form compounds with oxygen or one another

Examples

Q. What is the oxidation number of S in $S_2O_3^{2-}$?

A. O usually has the oxidation number of –2 (Rule 2 above), so S must be +2 for the anion to have a net charge of –2.

Q. What is the oxidation number of Au in $KAuCl_4$?

A. K has a charge of +1. Cl has a charge of –1. $1(+1) + 1(x) + 4(-1) = 0$. $x = +3$

Q. What is the oxidation number of I in H_5IO_6?

A. H will have a +1 oxidation number since it is combined with nonmetals. Iodine will have a + charge because it is less electronegative than oxygen.

$5\,H + I + 6\,O = 0 \qquad 5(+1) + (I?) + 6(-2) = 0 \qquad (+5) + (I?) + (-12) = 0$

$(I?) + (-7) = 0 \qquad I? = +7$

Oxidation

The loss of electrons from an atom, compound, or molecule.

OIL = **O**xidation **I**s **L**oss of electrons

Reduction

The gain of electrons by an atom, compound, or molecule.

RIG = **R**eduction **I**s **G**ain of electrons

Example

Q. In the reaction $SO_{2(g)} + 2H_2S_{(g)} \rightarrow 3S_{(s)} + 2H_2O_{(g)}$

- **A.** sulfur is oxidized and hydrogen is reduced
- **B.** sulfur is reduced and there is no oxidation
- **C.** sulfur is reduced and hydrogen is oxidized
- **D.** sulfur is both reduced and oxidized
- **E.** oxygen is both reduced and oxidized

A. D.

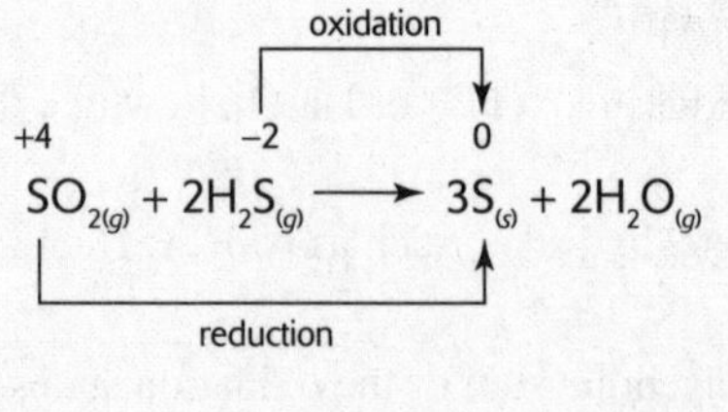

Oxidizing and Reducing Agents

An oxidizing agent is the substance in an oxidation-reduction reaction that gains electrons, and whose oxidation number is reduced. Oxidation is the loss of electrons (OIL: oxidation is loss).

A reducing agent is the substance in an oxidation-reduction reaction that gives up electrons, and whose oxidation number is increased. Reduction is the gain of electrons (RIG: reduction is gain).

Example

Q. Given the following equation, identify the oxidizing and reducing agents.

$$Cu(NO_3)_{2(aq)} + Mg_{(s)} \rightarrow Cu_{(s)} + Mg(NO_3)_{2(aq)}$$

A. Begin by writing a net ionic reaction: $Cu^{2+}{}_{(aq)} + Mg_{(s)} \rightarrow Cu_{(s)} + Mg^{2+}{}_{(aq)}$

Through examination, it can be seen that the copper(II) ion is gaining two electrons to become $Cu_{(s)}$; therefore, the $Cu^{2+}{}_{(aq)}$ ion is undergoing reduction and is acting as the oxidizing agent. The magnesium atom is changing to a magnesium(II) ion and is therefore losing electrons and is undergoing oxidation. Therefore, by definition, magnesium is the reducing agent.

Activity Series

The activity or electromotive series of metals is a listing of the metals in decreasing order of their reactivity with hydrogen-ion sources such as water or acids. In the reaction with a hydrogen-ion source, the metal is oxidized to a metal ion, and the hydrogen ion is reduced to H_2. The ordering of the activity series can be related to the standard reduction potential of a metal cation and can be correlated with its electronegativity. The more positive the standard reduction potential of the cation, the more difficult it is to oxidize the metal to a hydrated metal cation and the later that metal falls in the series.

Characteristics include:

1. **Very electropositive metals:** The most active metals have low electronegativities (EN < 1.4), and their cations generally have reduction potentials of –1.6 V or below. Examples: Li, Na, and K.
   (a) react with water to release hydrogen
   (b) good reducing agents (not very good oxidizing agents)
   (c) ions can't be reduced to the metal in aqueous solution
2. **Electropositive metals:** Metals in this group have electronegativities that fall between 1.4 and 1.9. Cations of these metals generally have standard reduction potentials between 0.0 and –1.6 V. Examples: Fe, Co, Ni, Zn, and Sn.
   (a) do not react very readily with water to release hydrogen
   (b) react with H^+
3. **Electronegative metals:** Metals in this group have electronegativities between 1.9 and 2.54. Cations of these metals generally have positive standard reduction potentials. Examples: Pt, Au, Hg, and Pb.
   (a) metals are not oxidized by H^+
   (b) good oxidizing agents
   (c) oxidize H_2 producing H^+ and deposits the metal from an aqueous solution
   (d) cations of these less active metals will oxidize more active metals to a cation. The less active metal is deposited as the metal.

Balancing Oxidation-Reduction (Redox) Reactions

The following steps are used to balance redox reactions:

1. Write the unbalanced equation in net-ionic form.
2. Separate the net-ionic equation into two half-reactions (an oxidation half-reaction and a reduction half-reaction).
3. Balance the atoms other than O and H in each half reaction separately.

4. Add H_2O to balance the O atoms and H^+ to balance the H atoms.
5. Add electrons to one side of each half-reaction to balance the charges. If required, equalize the number of electrons in the two half-reactions by multiplying one or both half-reactions by appropriate coefficients.
6. Add the two half-reactions together and balance the final equation by inspection. The electrons on both sides must cancel.
7. Double check your work by making sure that there are equal numbers of atoms on both sides of the equation and that the overall charge is the same on both sides.
8. If the reaction is in basic solution, add an equal number of OH^- ions as there are H^+ ions to both sides of the equation. Combine H^+ and OH^- ions to form H_2O.

Example

Q. Balance the following redox reaction in basic aqueous solution:

$$SO_3^{2-} + CrO_4^{2-} \rightarrow SO_4^{2-} + Cr(OH)_3$$

A. Step 1: Write the unbalanced equation in net-ionic form:

$$SO_3^{2-} + CrO_4^{2-} \rightarrow SO_4^{2-} + Cr(OH)_3$$

Step 2: Separate the net-ionic equation into two half-reactions (an oxidation half-reaction and a reduction half-reaction):

$$\text{OX: } SO_3^{2-} \rightarrow SO_4^{2-}$$
$$\text{RED: } CrO_4^{2-} \rightarrow Cr(OH)_3$$

Step 3: Balance the atoms other than O and H in each half-reaction separately.

$$\text{OX: } SO_3^{2-} \rightarrow SO_4^{2-}$$
$$\text{RED: } CrO_4^{2-} \rightarrow Cr(OH)_3$$

Step 4: Add H_2O to balance the O atoms and H^+ to balance the H atoms.

$$\text{OX: } SO_3^{2-} + H_2O \rightarrow SO_4^{2-} + 2H^+$$
$$\text{RED: } CrO_4^{2-} + 5H^+ \rightarrow Cr(OH)_3 + H_2O$$

Step 5: Add electrons to one side of each half-reaction to balance the charges. If required, equalize the number of electrons in the two half-reactions by multiplying one or both half-reactions by appropriate coefficients.

$$\text{OX: } SO_3^{2-} + H_2O \rightarrow SO_4^{2-} + 2H^+ + 2e^-$$
$$\text{RED: } CrO_4^{2-} + 5H^+ + 3e^- \rightarrow Cr(OH)_3 + H_2O$$
$$\text{OX: } 3(SO_3^{2-} + H_2O \rightarrow SO_4^{2-} + 2H^+ + 2e^-) \rightarrow 3SO_3^{2-} + 3H_2O \rightarrow 3SO_4^{2-} + 6H^+ + \cancel{6e^-}$$
$$\text{RED: } 2(CrO_4^{2-} + 5H^+ + 3e^- \rightarrow Cr(OH)_3 + H_2O) \rightarrow 2CrO_4^{2-} + 10H^+ + \cancel{6e^-} \rightarrow 2Cr(OH)_3 + 2H_2O$$

Step 6: Add the two half-reactions together and balance the final equation by inspection. The electrons on both sides must cancel.

$$\text{OX: } 3SO_3^{2-} + 3H_2O \rightarrow 3SO_4^{2-} + 6H^+$$
$$\text{RED: } 2CrO_4^{2-} + 10H^+ \rightarrow 2Cr(OH)_3 + 2H_2O$$
$$\overline{3SO_3^{2-} + 2CrO_4^{2-} + 4H^+ + H_2O \rightarrow 3SO_4^{2-} + 2Cr(OH)_3}$$

Step 7: Double-check your work, by making sure that there are equal numbers of atoms on both sides of the equation and that the overall charge is the same on both sides.

Step 8: If the reaction is in basic solution, add an equal number of OH^- ions as there are H^+ ions to both sides of the equation. Combine H^+ and OH^- ions to form H_2O.

$$3SO_3^{2-} + 2CrO_4^{2-} + 4H^+ + H_2O + 4OH^- \rightarrow 3SO_4^{2-} + 2Cr(OH)_3 + 4OH^-$$

$$3SO_3^{2-} + 2CrO_4^{2-} + 5H_2O \rightarrow 3SO_4^{2-} + 2Cr(OH)_3 + 4OH^-$$

Galvanic (Voltaic) Cells

Voltaic cells use spontaneous chemical reactions to produce electrical energy (flow of electrons). Let's look at an example to illustrate. If zinc metal is placed in a copper(II) sulfate solution, the following reaction takes place: $Zn_{(s)}$ + $CuSO_{4(aq)} \rightarrow ZnSO_{4(aq)} + Cu_{(s)}$ or in net-ionic form: $Zn_{(s)} + Cu^{2+}_{(aq)} \rightarrow Zn^{2+}_{(aq)} + Cu_{(s)}$. *(If we examine the activity series of metals, we find zinc higher than copper.)* If we break the reaction down into two half-reactions we obtain: OX: $Zn_{(s)} \rightarrow Zn^{2+}_{(aq)} + 2e^-$ ($E°_{ox} = +0.76$ V) and RED: $Cu^{2+}_{(aq)} + 2e^- \rightarrow Cu_{(s)}$ ($E°_{red} = +0.34$ V); total voltage produced by cell = $E°_{ox}$ + $E°_{red} = 0.76 + 0.34 = 1.10$ V. A salt bridge (in this case filled with Na_2SO_4) is required to complete the circuit. We can use a short-hand method to represent this cell: $Zn|Zn^{2+}||Cu^{2+}|Cu$.

Anode	*Cathode*
Oxidation occurs	Reduction occurs
Electrons are produced	Electrons are consumed
Anions migrate towards anode	Cations migrate toward cathode
Has negative sign	Has positive sign

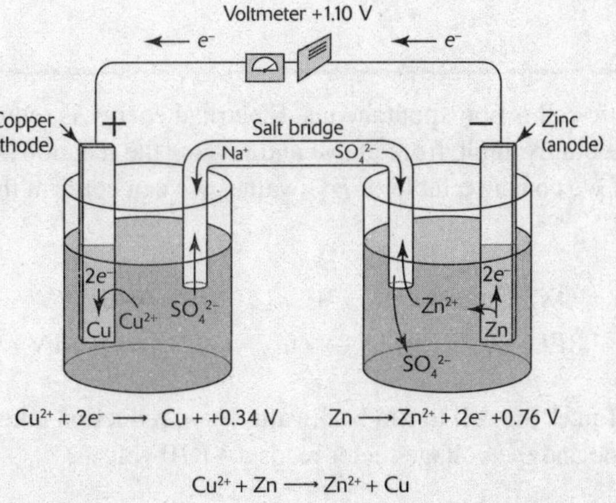

Example

Half-Reaction	E° (V)
$Co^{2+}_{(aq)} + 2e^- \rightarrow Co_{(s)}$	–0.28
$Fe^{2+}_{(aq)} + 2e^- \rightarrow Fe_{(s)}$	–0.44

Q. Using the information in the table above, what is the voltage produced from the following reaction at 298K if $[Co^{2+}] = 1.00\ M$ and $[Fe^{2+}] = 3.00\ M$?

$$Co_{(s)} + Fe^{2+}_{(aq)} \rightarrow Co^{2+}_{(aq)} + Fe_{(s)}$$

A. –0.15 V, cell is not spontaneous
B. +0.15 V, cell is spontaneous
C. +0.25 V, cell is spontaneous
D. +0.30 V, cell is spontaneous
E. +0.72 V, cell is spontaneous

A. A.

$$\text{OX: } Co_{(s)} \rightarrow Co^{2+}_{(aq)} + 2e^- \qquad E^\circ_{ox} = +0.28\text{ V}$$

$$\text{RED: } Fe^{2+}_{(aq)} + 2e^- \rightarrow Fe_{(s)} \qquad +E^\circ_{red} = -0.44\text{ V}$$

$$E^\circ = -0.16\text{ V}$$

$$E = E^\circ - \frac{0.0591\text{ V}}{n}\log\frac{[Co^{2+}]}{[Fe^{2+}]} = -0.16\text{ V} - \frac{0.0591\text{ V}}{2}\log\frac{1.00}{3.00}$$

$$E = -0.16\text{ V} + 0.0141 = -0.15\text{ V}$$

Electrolytic Cells

The redox reaction in an electrolytic cell is non-spontaneous. Electrical energy is required (usually a battery) to induce the electrolysis reaction. Let's take our example from above and reverse the reaction so that it is NOT spontaneous: $Cu_{(s)} + Zn^{2+}_{(aq)} \rightarrow Cu^{2+}_{(aq)} + Zn_{(s)}$. If we consult a table of E°_{red} values we can confirm that the reaction is non-spontaneous ($E^\circ = -1.10$ V).

$$\text{OX: } Cu_{(s)} \rightarrow Cu^{2+}_{(aq)} + 2e^- \qquad E^\circ_{ox} = -0.34\text{ V}$$

$$\text{RED: } Zn^{2+}_{(aq)} + 2e^- \rightarrow Zn_{(s)} \qquad E^\circ_{red} = -0.76\text{ V}$$

The battery in an electrolytic cell forces the cell to run backward. Now, reduction takes place at the Zn electrode and oxidation occurs at the Cu electrode and the voltage meter reads a +1.10 volts.

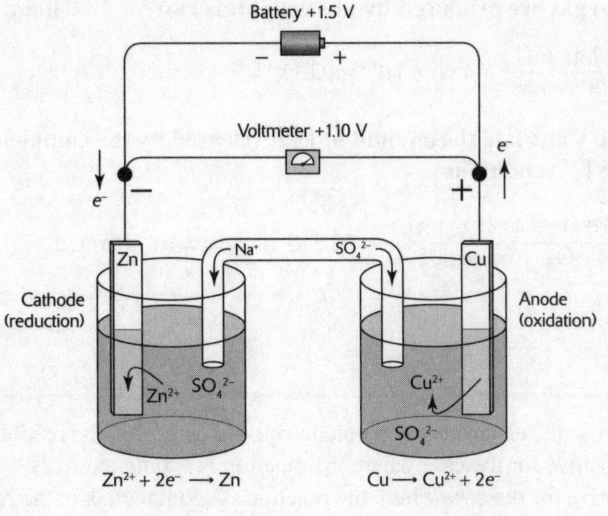

Examples

A battery charger was used in the electrolysis of water—a small amount of hydrochloric acid was added to the water.

Q. Sketch the apparatus that was used in this experiment and label all necessary components.

A.

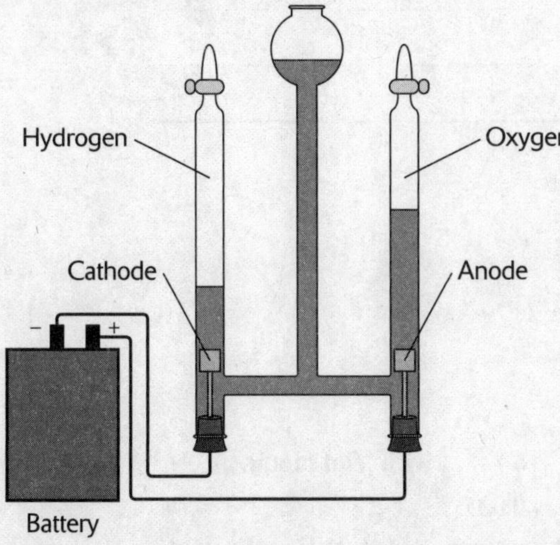

Q. Write the balanced half-reaction that occurs at the anode.

A. $2H_2O \rightarrow O_2 + 4H^+ + 4e^-$ or $2O^{2-} \rightarrow O_2 + 4e^-$

Q. Write the balanced half-reaction that occurs at the cathode.

A. $2H_2O + 2e^- \rightarrow H_2 + 2OH^-$ or $2H^+ + 2e^- \rightarrow H_2$

Q. Write the overall reaction.

A. $2H_2O \rightarrow 2H_2 + O_2$ or $4H^+ + 2O^{2-} \rightarrow 2H_2 + O_2$

Q. A current of 5.00 amperes was passed through the cell. Compute the coulombs of charge that passed through the cell in 1 hour.

A. 1 coulomb = 1 ampere × 1 second

$$\text{coulombs} = \frac{5.00 \text{ amperes}}{1} \times \frac{1 \cancel{\text{hour}}}{1} \times \frac{60 \cancel{\text{min}}}{1 \cancel{\text{hour}}} \times \frac{60 \text{ sec}}{1 \cancel{\text{min}}} = 1.80 \times 10^4 \text{ C}$$

Q. How many moles of oxygen gas are produced by this cell if it is run for 1.00 hour at 5.00 amperes?

A. $$\frac{1.80\times10^{4}\ \cancel{C}}{1}\times\frac{1\ \cancel{\text{mole } e^-}}{96{,}500\ \cancel{C}}\times\frac{1\ \text{mole } O_2}{4\ \cancel{\text{mole } e^-}}=4.66\times10^{-2}\ \text{mole } O_2$$

Q. $\Delta H_f\ H_2O_{(g)} = -241.8$ kJ/mol. Calculate the amount of heat released by the complete combustion of the hydrogen that was produced at STP conditions.

A. $$\frac{4.66\times10^{-2}\ \cancel{\text{mol } O_2}}{1}\times\frac{2\ \cancel{\text{moles } H_2O}}{1\ \cancel{\text{mole } O_2}}\times\frac{-241.8\ \text{kJ}}{1\ \cancel{\text{mol } H_2O}}=22.5\ \text{kJ of heat was liberated}$$

Spontaneity

A positive voltage that forms across the electrodes of a voltaic cell indicates that the oxidation-reduction reaction is spontaneous. Thus, $E°$ will be positive for the case where the reaction is spontaneous; $E° = 0$ for a redox reaction at equilibrium, and $E°$ will be negative for the case where the reaction is spontaneous in the reverse direction. Free energy change, ΔG, and $E°_{cell}$ are measures of the spontaneity of a chemical reaction or process and are related through the equation $\Delta G° = -nFE°$, where n is the number of moles of electrons and the constant F (stands for Faraday) is the charge on one mole of electrons and has the value of 96,486 coulombs.

$\Delta G°$	K	$E°_{cell}$	*Reaction Under Standard State Conditions*
–	> 1	+	Spontaneous
0	= 1	0	At equilibrium
+	< 1	–	Non-spontaneous

$$\Delta G° = -nFE°_{cell}$$

$$E°_{cell} = \frac{RT}{nF}\ln K$$

$$K_c = 10^{nE°_{cell}/0.0591}$$

Examples

Q. Vanadium can be reduced in an acidic solution from $VO^{2+}{}_{(aq)}$ to $V^{3+}{}_{(aq)}$ with lead metal. $E°_{red}$ $Pb^{2+}{}_{(aq)} \rightarrow Pb_{(s)} = -0.13$ V and $E°_{red}$ for $VO^{2+}{}_{(aq)} \rightarrow V^{3+}{}_{(aq)}$ is 0.337 V. Write a balanced equation for the reaction of $VO^{2+}{}_{(aq)}$ with lead in acidic solution and calculate $E°_{cell}$.

A.

OX: $Pb_{(s)} \rightarrow Pb^{2+}{}_{(aq)} + \cancel{2e^-}$ $\qquad E°_{ox} = 0.13$ V

RED: $2VO^{2+}{}_{(aq)} + \cancel{2e^-} + 4H^+{}_{(aq)} \rightarrow 2V^{3+}{}_{(aq)} + 2H_2O_{(l)}$ $\qquad E°_{red} = 0.337$ V

$Pb_{(s)} + 2VO^{2+}{}_{(aq)} + 4H^+{}_{(aq)} \rightarrow Pb^{2+}{}_{(aq)} + 2V^{3+}{}_{(aq)} + 2H_2O_{(l)}$ $\qquad E°_{cell} = 0.47$ V

Q. How many grams of lead metal is necessary for the reduction of a 75.0-mL sample of a 0.200 *M* solution of $VO^{2+}{}_{(aq)}$?

A. $$\frac{75.0\ \cancel{mL}}{1}\times\frac{1\ \cancel{L}}{10^3\ \cancel{mL}}\times\frac{0.200\ \cancel{\text{mol } VO^{2+}}}{\cancel{L}}\times\frac{1\ \cancel{\text{mol Pb}}}{2\ \cancel{\text{mol } VO^{2+}}}\times\frac{207.2\ \text{g Pb}}{1\ \cancel{\text{mol Pb}}}=1.55\ \text{g Pb}$$

Q. How many seconds is required to reduce another 75.0-mL sample of the 0.200 *M* $VO^{2+}{}_{(aq)}$ solution with a current of 0.80 amperes?

A. $$\frac{75.0\ \cancel{mL}}{1}\times\frac{1\ \cancel{L}}{10^3\ \cancel{mL}}\times\frac{0.200\ \cancel{\text{mol } VO^{2+}}}{\cancel{L}}\times\frac{1\ \cancel{\text{mol } e^-}}{1\ \cancel{\text{mol } VO^{2+}}}\times\frac{96{,}487\ \cancel{C}}{1\ \cancel{\text{mol } e^-}}\times\frac{1\ \cancel{\text{amp}}\ \text{sec}}{1\ \cancel{C}}\times\frac{1}{0.80\ \cancel{\text{amp}}}=1.81\times10^3\ \text{seconds}$$

Q. Calculate the standard free energy change for the reaction described in the first question.

A. $\Delta G^\circ = -nFE^\circ = -\frac{2\ \text{mol}\ e^-}{1} \times \frac{96{,}487\ \text{coulombs}}{1\ \text{mol}\ e^-} \times \frac{0.47\ \text{V}}{1} \times \frac{1\ \text{J}}{1\ \text{V} \cdot \text{C}}$

$= -9.1 \times 10^4$ J (Since ΔG° is negative, the reaction is spontaneous and is in agreement with the positive sign of E°_{cell} found in the first question which also indicates spontaneity.)

Voltage and Equilibrium

The Nernst equation allows you to: (1) calculate the voltage of an electrochemical cell under any conditions, or (2) find the concentration of one of the components.

$$E = E^\circ - \frac{2.303\,RT}{nF}\log Q$$

$$\text{or at 298K, } E = E^\circ - \frac{0.0591\,V}{n}\log Q$$

$$E = E^\circ - \frac{RT}{nF}\ln Q$$

Examples

Q. A zinc electrode is immersed in an acidic solution of 1.50 *M* $Zn^{2+}_{(aq)}$ solution. A salt bridge connects this beaker to another beaker filled with a 1.50 *M* $Ag^+_{(aq)}$ solution in which a silver electrode is immersed. Write the half-cell reaction that is occurring at the anode.

A. The first step is to determine in which beaker oxidation is occurring and in which beaker reduction is occurring. In order for the cell to be spontaneous, the E° must be positive. Referring to the standard reduction potential table, E°_{red}: $Zn^{2+}_{(aq)} + 2e^- \rightarrow Zn_{(s)} = -0.76$ V and E°_{red}: $Ag^+_{(aq)} + e^- \rightarrow Ag_{(s)} = +0.80$ V. The only possible way to obtain a positive E° is for Zn to be oxidized (+0.76 V) and silver to be reduced (+0.80 V). An OX (oxidation occurs at the anode): $Zn_{(s)} \rightarrow Zn^{2+}_{(aq)} + 2e^-$.

Q. Write the half-cell reaction that is occurring at the cathode.

A. Reduction occurs at the cathode (RED CAT): $Ag^+_{(aq)} + e^- \rightarrow Ag_{(s)}$

Q. Write the balanced chemical equation for the overall spontaneous cell reaction that occurs and calculate E°.

A.

$$\begin{array}{ll} Zn_{(s)} \rightarrow Zn^{2+}_{(aq)} + \cancel{2e^-} & E^\circ_{ox} = +0.76\text{ V} \\ 2Ag^+_{(aq)} + \cancel{2e^-} \rightarrow 2Ag_{(s)} & E^\circ_{red} = +0.80\text{ V} \\ \hline Zn_{(s)} + 2Ag^+_{(aq)} \rightarrow Zn^{2+}_{(aq)} + 2Ag_{(s)} & E^\circ = 1.56\text{ V} \end{array}$$

Q. Calculate the equilibrium constant for this reaction at 298K.

A. at 298K, $\log K = \frac{nE^\circ}{0.0591\text{V}}$ $\quad n = 2$

$\log K = \frac{(2)(1.56\text{ V})}{0.0591\text{ V}} = 52.8 \qquad K = 6 \times 10^{52}$

Q. A new cell is constructed such that the initial concentration of $Zn^{2+}_{(aq)}$ is changed to 0.80 *M* and the initial concentration of $Ag^+_{(aq)}$ is changed to 1.30 *M*. Calculate the initial voltage, *E*, of this cell at 298K.

A. at 298 K, $E = E^\circ - \frac{0.0591\text{ V}}{n}\log Q$

$Q = [Zn^{2+}] / [Ag^+]^2 = (0.80) / (1.69) = 0.47$

$E = 1.56\text{ V} - (0.0591 / 2)\log(0.47) = 1.57\text{ V}$

Multiple-Choice Questions

1. The proper cell notation for the reaction written below is

$$Ni_{(s)} + Sn^{4+}_{(aq)} \rightarrow Ni^{2+}_{(aq)} + Sn^{2+}_{(aq)}$$

A. $Ni^{2+}|Ni \,||\, (Pt)\ Sn^{2+}|Sn^{4+}$
B. $(Pt)\ Sn^{4+}|Sn^{2+} \,||\, Ni^{2+}|Ni$
C. $Ni|Ni^{2+} \,||\, (Pt)\ Sn^{4+}|Sn^{2+}$
D. $(Pt)\ Sn^{4+}|Sn^{2+} \,||\, Ni|Ni^{2+}$
E. $Sn^{2+}|Ni^{2+} \,||\, (Pt)\ Sn^{4+}|Ni$

2. Given the following cell

$$Zn|Zn^{2+}||Sn^{2+}|Sn$$

in order to increase the voltage, one could

A. increase the concentration of Zn^{2+}.
B. increase the concentration of Sn^{2+}.
C. use more Zn.
D. use more Sn.
E. use more Zn and Sn.

3. The oxidation number of V in $VOCl_3$ is

A. –6
B. 0
C. +5
D. +6
E. +8

For Questions 4–6, use the following reaction:

$$MnO_4^-{}_{(aq)} + SO_3^{2-}{}_{(aq)} \rightarrow MnO_4^{2-}{}_{(aq)} + SO_4^{2-}{}_{(aq)}$$

4. In the equation above, which species contains the element that is being reduced?

A. $MnO_4^-{}_{(aq)}$
B. $SO_3^{2-}{}_{(aq)}$
C. $MnO_4^{2-}{}_{(aq)}$
D. $SO_4^{2-}{}_{(aq)}$
E. Oxidation numbers remain constant. This is NOT a redox reaction.

5. Which species is the oxidizing agent?

A. $MnO_4^-{}_{(aq)}$
B. $SO_3^{2-}{}_{(aq)}$
C. $MnO_4^{2-}{}_{(aq)}$
D. $SO_4^{2-}{}_{(aq)}$
E. Oxidation numbers remain constant. This is NOT a redox reaction.

6. What is the smallest whole number coefficient of $OH^-_{(aq)}$ in the balanced equation if the reaction occurs in basic solution?

A. 0
B. 1
C. 2
D. 3
E. 4

7. Consulting a table of standard reduction potentials, which one of the following reactions will NOT occur spontaneously?

A. $Mg_{(s)} + 2Ag^+_{(aq)} \rightarrow Mg^{2+}_{(aq)} + 2Ag_{(s)}$
B. $Hg^{2+}_{(aq)} + Zn_{(s)} \rightarrow Hg_{(l)} + Zn^{2+}_{(aq)}$
C. $Cu^{2+}_{(aq)} + Zn_{(s)} \rightarrow Cu_{(s)} + Zn^{2+}_{(aq)}$
D. $2Ag_{(s)} + Ni^{2+}_{(aq)} \rightarrow 2Ag^+_{(aq)} + Ni_{(s)}$
E. All reactions will occur spontaneously.

For Questions 8–9:

$$W + X^+ \rightarrow W^+ + X$$
$$X + Z^+ \rightarrow X^+ + Z$$
$$Y^+ + Z \rightarrow \text{no reaction}$$
$$X + Y^+ \rightarrow X^+ + Y$$

8. Using the reactions listed above, when arranged in order of their redox activity, they are

A. $W > X > Y > Z$
B. $X > Y > Z > W$
C. $Y > Z > W > X$
D. $Z > W > X > Y$
E. $Y > W > Z > X$

9. Which of the following reactions would occur?

A. $W^+ + Y \rightarrow W + Y^+$
B. $W^+ + Y \rightarrow W + Z$
C. $X^+ + Y \rightarrow X + Y^+$
D. $Z + Y^+ \rightarrow Z^+ + Y$
E. $W + Z^+ \rightarrow W^+ + Z$

For Questions 10–11: Choose from the following answer choices. A question may have more than one answer.

A. Oxidizing agent
B. Reducing agent
C. Substance undergoing oxidation
D. Substance undergoing reduction
E. Substance undergoing neither oxidation nor reduction.

10. Oxidation number increases.

11. Oxidation number decreases.

For Questions 12–13: A student is involved in an iodine-clock redox titration that utilizes the following two half-reactions:

$$\text{OX: } 2S_2O_3^{2-}{}_{(aq)} \rightarrow S_4O_6^{2-}{}_{(aq)} + 2e^-$$
$$\text{RED: } I_{2(s)} + 2e^- \rightarrow 2I^-{}_{(aq)}$$

12. How many grams of I_2 are present in a solution if 45.0 mL of 0.250 *M* $Na_2S_2O_3$ solution is needed to titrate the iodine solution?

A. 0.793 g
B. 1.43 g
C. 1.84 g
D. 2.07 g
E. 2.22 g

13. How many mL of the 0.250 *M* $Na_2S_2O_3$ solution would be needed to titrate 2.50 g of $I_{2(s)}$?

A. 49.8 mL
B. 62.3 mL
C. 71.4 mL
D. 78.8 mL
E. 85.8 mL

14. Consulting a table of standard reduction potentials, what is the standard free-energy change at 25°C that occurs when solid iron is oxidized to $Fe^{2+}{}_{(aq)}$ by the oxidizing agent, $Cu(NO_3)_2$?

A. –294 kJ
B. –114 kJ
C. 55.0 kJ
D. 98.4 kJ
E. 114 kJ

15. A student constructs a galvanic cell using the reaction

$$Mg_{(s)} + 2H^+{}_{(aq)} \rightarrow Mg^{2+}{}_{(aq)} + H_{2(g)}$$

What is the cell potential when $[H^+] = 2.0\ M$, $[Mg^{2+}] = 0.0050\ M$, and $P_{H_2} = 0.40$ atm

A. 0.00 V
B. 0.57 V
C. 0.73 V
D. 1.62 V
E. 2.47 V

16. A student sets up the following galvanic cell

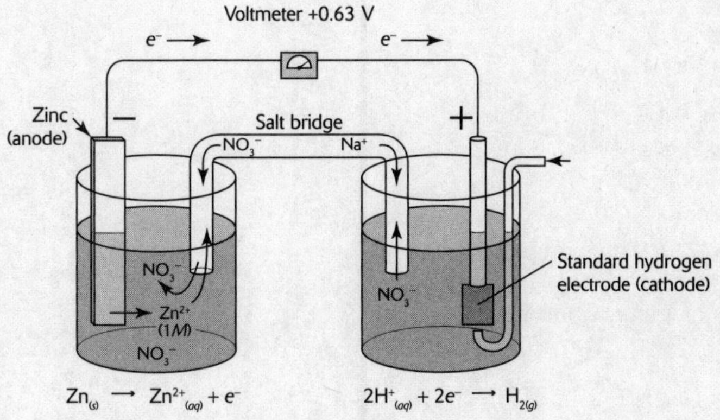

What is the pH of the solution in the beaker on the right if the solution is at 25°C?

A. 2.2
B. 3.2
C. 4.7
D. 5.4
E. 6.3

17. Using a table of standard reduction potentials, what is *K* for the overall reaction produced from the following half-reactions?

OX: $SO_{2(g)} + 2H_2O_{(l)} \rightarrow SO_4^{2-}{}_{(aq)} + 4H^+{}_{(aq)} + 2e^-$
$E°_{ox} = -0.20$ V

RED: $Cr_2O_7^{2-}{}_{(aq)} + 14H^+{}_{(aq)} + 6e^- \rightarrow 2Cr^{3+}{}_{(aq)} + 7H_2O_{(l)}$
$E°_{red} = +1.33$V

A. 115
B. 115^{10}
C. 10^{115}
D. 10^{1115}
E. none of the above

For Questions 18–20: A current of 25.0 A is continuously passed through an aqueous solution of KCl for 90.0 minutes.

18. The reaction that occurs at the anode is:

A. $2H_2O_{(l)} + 2e^- \rightarrow H_{2(g)} + 2OH^-{}_{(aq)}$
B. $KCl_{(s)} \rightarrow K^+{}_{(aq)} + Cl^-{}_{(aq)}$
C. $K^+{}_{(aq)} + Cl^-{}_{(aq)} \rightarrow KCl_{(s)}$
D. $2Cl^-{}_{(aq)} \rightarrow Cl_{2(g)} + 2e^-$
E. $K^+{}_{(aq)} + 2Cl^-{}_{(aq)} \rightarrow K_{(s)} + Cl_{2(g)}$

19. How many grams of KOH are produced?

A. 3.22 grams
B. 22.4 grams
C. 56.11 grams
D. 69.3 grams
E. 78.6 grams

20. How many liters of chlorine gas at STP are produced?

A. 3.2 L
B. 10.3 L
C. 14.7 L
D. 15.7 L
E. 22.4 L

Free-Response Questions

1. An aqueous solution of NaCl is electrolyzed using a battery.

(a) Write the cathode half-reaction that is consistent with the observation above and describe what is happening.

(b) Write the anode half-reaction that is consistent with the observation above and describe what is happening.

(c) Sketch an apparatus that can be used for such an experiment and label its necessary components.

(d) List the experimental measurement that would be needed in order to determine from such an experiment the value of the Faraday.

2. An electrochemical cell consists of a silver electrode in an acidic solution of 1.00-molar Ag^+ connected by a salt bridge to a second compartment with a copper electrode in an acidic solution of 1.00-molar Cu^{2+}.

(a) Using a table of standard reduction potentials, write the balanced chemical equation for the overall spontaneous cell reaction that occurs when the circuit is complete. Calculate the standard voltage, $E°$, for this cell reaction.

(b) Write the equation for the half-cell reaction occurring at each electrode. Indicate which half-reaction occurs at the anode.

(c) Sketch a diagram of the cell, labeling all parts.

(d) Calculate the equilibrium constant for this cell reaction at 298K.

(e) A cell similar to the one described above is constructed with solutions that have initial concentrations of 1.00-molar Cu^{2+} and 0.0200-molar Ag^+. Calculate the initial voltage, E, of this cell.

Answers and Explanations

Multiple Choice

1. **C.** Nickel is oxidized to $Ni^{2+}{}_{(aq)}$ at a nickel anode and $Sn^{4+}{}_{(aq)}$ is reduced to $Sn^{2+}{}_{(aq)}$ at an inert electrode (in this case platinum).

2. **B.** Begin by converting cell notation into a chemical equation:

$$\begin{array}{ll} \text{OX: } Zn_{(s)} \rightarrow Zn^{2+}{}_{(aq)} + \cancel{2e^-} & E^\circ{}_{ox} = +0.76\text{ V} \\ \text{RED: } Sn^{2+}{}_{(aq)} + \cancel{2e^-} \rightarrow Sn_{(s)} & E^\circ{}_{red} = -0.14\text{ V} \\ \hline Zn_{(s)} + Sn^{2+}{}_{(aq)} \rightarrow Zn^{2+}{}_{(aq)} + Sn_{(s)} & E^\circ = +0.62\text{ V} \end{array}$$

By properly using the setup for the Nernst equation (required since we will be changing from standard conditions of 1 *M*), we can see that as Sn^{2+} becomes larger, *E* becomes greater.

$$E = E^\circ - \frac{0.0591\text{ V}}{2}\log\frac{[Zn^{2+}]}{[Sn^{2+}]}$$

To demonstrate this, let's set $[Zn^{2+}]$ at 0.50 *M* and solve for *E* with $[Sn^{2+}]$ at 0.20 *M* and again at 3.00 *M*. At $[Sn^{2+}] = 0.20$ *M*, *E* works out to 0.61 V. However, if we solve for *E* by increasing the concentration of $[Sn^{2+}]$ to 3.00 *M*, *E* works out to become 0.64 V.

3. **C.** $10(-2) + 3\text{ Cl}^-(-1) + 1\text{ V}(?) = 0 \qquad V = +5$

4. **A.** Mn in MnO_4^- has an oxidation number of +7. Mn in MnO_4^{2-} has an oxidation number of +6.

5. **A.** The species that causes an oxidation by accepting electrons is known as the oxidizing agent.

6. **C.** $2MnO_4^-{}_{(aq)} + SO_3^{2-}{}_{(aq)} + 2OH^-{}_{(aq)} \rightarrow 2MnO_4^{2-}{}_{(aq)} + SO_4^{2-}{}_{(aq)} + H_2O_{(l)}$

   Note: If you got this problem wrong, go back and review how to balance redox reactions.

7. **D.** There are two ways to do this problem. The first way would be add up $E^\circ{}_{red}$ and $E^\circ{}_{ox}$ values for each answer choice and determine if any are negative or non-spontaneous. Another way would be to quickly look at the relative positions on the species in the table and draw the proper conclusion.

8. **A.** Any element higher in the activity series will react with the ion of any element lower in the activity series.

   $W + X^+ \rightarrow W^+ + X$; therefore, W is higher than X.

   $Y^+ + Z \rightarrow$ no reaction; therefore, Y is higher than Z.

   $X + Z^+ \rightarrow X^+ + Z$; therefore, X is higher than Z.

   $X + Y^+ \rightarrow X^+ + Y$; therefore, X is higher than Y.

9. **E.** Any element higher in the activity series will react with the ion of any element lower in the activity series.

10. **B** and **C.** Let's use the reaction $Zn_{(s)} + Sn^{2+}{}_{(aq)} \rightarrow Zn^{2+}{}_{(aq)} + Sn_{(s)}$. In this example $Zn^\circ{}_{(s)}$ is going from pure zinc with an oxidation number of 0 to $Zn^{2+}{}_{(aq)}$. Zinc is being oxidized. The oxidation number is increasing. The reducing agent is Zn.

11. **A** and **D.** Using this same example, $Sn^{2+}{}_{(aq)}$ is being reduced to $Sn^\circ{}_{(s)}$. The oxidation number is decreasing. The oxidizing agent is $Sn^{2+}{}_{(aq)}$.

12. **B.** $I_{2(aq)} + 2S_2O_3^{2-}{}_{(aq)} \rightarrow S_4O_6^{2-}{}_{(aq)} + 2I^-{}_{(aq)}$

$$\frac{0.045\,\cancel{L}}{1} \times \frac{0.250\,\cancel{mol\,S_2O_3^{2-}}}{\cancel{L}} \times \frac{1\,\cancel{mol\,I_2}}{2\,\cancel{mol\,S_2O_3^{2-}}} \times \frac{253.8\text{ g }I_2}{1\,\cancel{mol\,I_2}} = 1.43\text{ g }I_2$$

13. **D.** $\dfrac{2.50\,\cancel{g\,I_2}}{1} \times \dfrac{1\,\cancel{mol\,I_2}}{253.8\,\cancel{g\,I_2}} \times \dfrac{2\,\cancel{mol\,S_2O_3^{2-}}}{1\,\cancel{mol\,I_2}} \times \dfrac{10^3\text{ mL}}{0.250\,\cancel{mol\,S_2O_3^{2-}}} = 78.8\text{ mL}$

14. B. Begin with the information provided and a table of standard reduction potentials to write an overall reaction and determine $E°$.

$$\begin{array}{ll} \text{OX: } Fe_{(s)} \rightarrow Fe^{2+}_{(aq)} + \cancel{2e^-} & E°_{ox} = +0.440\text{ V} \\ \text{RED: } Cu^{2+}_{(aq)} + \cancel{2e^-} \rightarrow Cu_{(s)} & E°_{red} = +0.150\text{ V} \\ \hline Fe_{(s)} + Cu^{2+}_{(aq)} \rightarrow Fe^{2+}_{(aq)} + Cu_{(s)} & E° = +0.590\text{ V} \end{array}$$

$$\Delta G° = -nFE° = -(2\ \cancel{\text{mol } e^-})(96{,}500\ \cancel{\text{C}}/\cancel{\text{mol } e^-})(0.590\ \cancel{\text{V}})(\text{J}\cdot\cancel{\text{C}}^{-1}\cdot\cancel{\text{V}}^{-1}) = -113{,}870\text{ J} = -114\text{ kJ}$$

15. E.

$$\begin{array}{ll} \text{OX: } Mg_{(s)} \rightarrow Mg^{2+}_{(aq)} + \cancel{2e^-} & E°_{ox} = 2.37\text{ V} \\ \text{RED: } 2H^+_{(aq)} + \cancel{2e^-} \rightarrow H_{2\,(g)} & E°_{red} = +0.00\text{ V} \\ \hline Mg_{(s)} + 2H^+_{(aq)} \rightarrow Mg^{2+}_{(aq)} + H_{2\,(g)} & E° = 2.37\text{ V} \end{array}$$

$$E = E° - \frac{0.0592}{n}\log Q = E° - \frac{0.0592}{2}\log\frac{[Mg^{2+}](P_{H_2})}{[H^+]^2} = 2.37\text{ V} - \left(\frac{0.0592\text{ V}}{2}\right)\log\frac{(0.0050)(0.40)}{(2.0)^2} = 2.47\text{ V}$$

16. A. The beaker on the right is where reduction is taking place: $2H^+_{(aq)} + 2e^- \rightarrow H_{2(g)}$. pH is a function of the concentration of $H^+_{(aq)}$; pH = –log [H^+]. Utilizing a table of standard reduction potentials, we can setup the following half-reactions in order to determine $E°$:

$$\begin{array}{ll} \text{OX: } Zn_{(s)} \rightarrow Zn^{2+}_{(aq)} + \cancel{2e^-} & E°_{ox} = +0.76\text{ V} \\ \text{RED: } 2H^+_{(aq)} + \cancel{2e^-} \rightarrow H_{2\,(g)} & E°_{red} = 0.00\text{ V} \\ \hline Zn_{(s)} + 2H^+_{(aq)} \rightarrow Zn^{2+}_{(aq)} + H_{2\,(g)} & E° = +0.76\text{ V} \end{array}$$

$$E = E° - \left(\frac{0.0592}{n}\right)\log\frac{(P_{H_2})[Zn^{2+}]}{[H^+]^2} = 0.76\text{ V} - \left(\frac{0.0592\text{ V}}{2}\right)\log\frac{(1)(1)}{[H^+]^2}$$

$$0.63\text{ V} = 0.76\text{ V} - \left(\frac{0.0592\text{ V}}{2}\right)\log\frac{(1)(1)}{[H^+]^2} = 0.76\text{ V} - (0.0296\text{ V})\log[H^+]^{-2}$$

$-0.13\text{ V} = 0.0592\log[H^+]$ $\quad$ pH = –log [H^+] = 0.13 / 0.0592 = 2.2

17. C.

$$\begin{array}{ll} \text{OX: } 3\left(SO_{2\,(g)} + 2H_2O_{(l)} \rightarrow SO_4^{2-}{}_{(aq)} + 4H^+_{(aq)} + 2e^-\right) & E°_{ox} = -0.20\text{ V} \\ \text{OX: } 3\ SO_{2\,(g)} + 6H_2O_{(l)} \rightarrow 3SO_4^{2-}{}_{(aq)} + 12H^+_{(aq)} + \cancel{6e^-} & E°_{ox} = -0.20\text{ V} \\ \text{RED: } Cr_2O_7^{2-}{}_{(aq)} + 14H^+_{(aq)} + \cancel{6e^-} \rightarrow 2Cr^{3+}_{(aq)} + 7H_2O_{(l)} & E°_{red} = +1.33\text{ V} \\ \hline 3SO_{2\,(g)} + Cr_2O_7^{2-}{}_{(aq)} + 2H^+_{(aq)} \rightarrow 3SO_4^{2-}{}_{(aq)} + 2Cr^{3+}_{(aq)} + H_2O_{(l)} & E° = +1.13\text{ V} \end{array}$$

$$\log K = \frac{nE°}{0.0592} = \frac{6(1.13\text{ V})}{0.0592\text{ V}} = 115 \qquad K = 10^{115}\text{ at }25°\text{C}$$

18. D. Reduction occurs at the cathode (RED CAT): $2H_2O_{(l)} + 2e^- \rightarrow H_{2(g)} + 2OH^-_{(aq)}$

Oxidation occurs at the anode (AN OX): $2Cl^-_{(aq)} \rightarrow Cl_{2(g)} + 2e^-$

Overall: $2H_2O_{(l)} + 2Cl^-_{(aq)} \rightarrow H_{2(g)} + 2OH^-_{(aq)} + Cl_{2(g)}$

19. E. $$\text{Charge} = \frac{25.0\ \cancel{\text{A}}}{1}\times\frac{\text{C}}{1\ \cancel{\text{A}}\cdot\cancel{\text{s}}}\times\frac{60\ \cancel{\text{s}}}{1\ \cancel{\text{min}}}\times\frac{90.0\ \cancel{\text{min}}}{1} = 1.35\times10^5\text{ C}$$

$$\text{moles of } e^-: \frac{1.35\times10^5\ \cancel{\text{C}}}{1}\times\frac{1\text{ mol } e^-}{96{,}500\ \cancel{\text{C}}} = 1.40\text{ mol } e^-$$

$$\frac{1.40\ \cancel{\text{mol } e^-}}{1}\times\frac{2\ \cancel{\text{mol KOH}}}{2\ \cancel{\text{mol } e^-}}\times\frac{56.11\text{ g KOH}}{1\ \cancel{\text{mol KOH}}} = 78.6\text{ g KOH}$$

20. D. $$\frac{1.40\ \cancel{\text{mol } e^-}}{1}\times\frac{1\ \cancel{\text{mol } Cl_{2(g)}}}{2\ \cancel{\text{mol } e^-}}\times\frac{22.4\text{ L } Cl_{2(g)}}{1\ \cancel{\text{mol } Cl_{2(g)}}} = 15.7\text{ L } Cl_2$$

Free Response

Question 1

Maximum Points for Question 1
Part (a): 2 points
Part (b): 2 points
Part (c): 4 points
Part (d): 2 points
Total points: 10

1. An aqueous solution of NaCl is electrolyzed using a battery. *(a) Write the cathode half-reaction that is consistent with the observation above and describe what is happening.* The cathode is the negative (–) terminal. Two reactions are potentially occurring at the cathode: $Na^+_{(aq)} + e^- \rightarrow Na_{(s)}$ $E^\circ_{red} = -2.71$ V $2H_2O_{(l)} + 2e^- \rightarrow H_{2(g)} + 2OH^-_{(aq)}$ $E^\circ_{red} = -0.83$ V Because it is much easier to reduce water than Na^+ ions, the only product formed at the cathode is hydrogen gas.	***2 points possible*** *1 point for correctly identifying the reaction that would occur at the cathode.* *1 point for describing what is occurring at the cathode.*
(b) Write the anode half-reaction that is consistent with the observations above and describe what is happening. The anode is the positive (+) terminal. There are also two substances that can be oxidized at the anode: Cl^- ions and water molecules. $2Cl^-_{(aq)} \rightarrow Cl_{2(g)} + 2e^-$ $E^\circ_{ox} = -1.36$ V $2H_2O_{(l)} \rightarrow O_{2(g)} + 4H^+_{(aq)} + 4e^-$ $E^\circ_{ox} = -1.23$ V The standard-state potentials for these half-reactions are so close to each other that we might expect to see a mixture of Cl_2 and O_2 gas collect at the anode. In practice, however, the only product of this reaction is $Cl_{2(g)}$. At first glance, it would seem easier to oxidize water ($E^\circ_{ox} = -1.23$ volts) than Cl^- ions ($E^\circ_{ox} = -1.36$ volts). However, the cell is never allowed to reach standard-state conditions. The solution is typically 25% NaCl by mass, which significantly increases the oxidation potential of the Cl^- ion. The pH of the cell is also kept very high, which decreases the oxidation potential for water. The deciding factor is a phenomenon known as overvoltage, which is the extra voltage that must be applied to a reaction to get it to occur at the rate at which it would occur in an ideal system.	***2 points possible*** *1 point for correctly identifying the reaction that would occur at the anode.* *1 point for describing what is occurring at the anode.*

(c) Sketch an apparatus that can be used for such an experiment and label its necessary components. 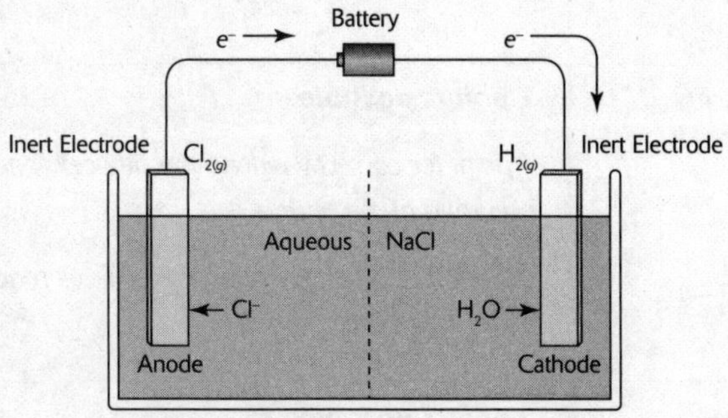	***4 points possible*** *1 point for correctly showing what is occurring at the anode.* *1 point for correctly showing what is happening at the cathode.* *1 point for correctly showing the flow of electrons.* *1 point for correctly showing how the battery would be connected.*
(d) List the experimental measurement that would be needed in order to determine from such an experiment the value of the Faraday. The Faraday (*F*) is the electrical charge on 1 mole of electrons and is equivalent to 96,485 Coulombs. The value of the Faraday could be obtained through the equation $\Delta G = -nFE$. To determine the value of *F*, one would need to: (1) Measure mass of electrode(s) before and after the experiment. (2) Measure current. (3) Measure time. (4) If gases are collected, measure their volume, temperature, and pressure.	***2 points possible*** *1 point for correctly defining the Faraday and showing the proper equation from which the value could be obtained.* *1 point for correctly identifying the factors that would be needed in order to determine its value.*

Question 2

Maximum Points for Question 2
Part (a): 2 points
Part (b): 2 points
Part (c): 2 points
Part (d): 2 points
Part (e): 2 points
Total points: 10

2. An electrochemical cell consists of a silver electrode in an acidic solution of 1.00-molar Ag^+ connected by a salt bridge to a second compartment with a copper electrode in an acidic solution of 1.00-molar Cu^{2+}. *(a) Using a table of standard reduction potentials, write the balanced chemical equation for the overall spontaneous cell reaction that occurs when the circuit is complete. Calculate the standard voltage, E°, for this cell reaction.*	***2 points possible*** *1 point for correctly writing the balanced reaction.*

(continued)

OX: $Cu_{(s)} \rightarrow Cu^{2+}_{(aq)} + 2e^-$ $E^\circ_{ox} = -0.340\,V$ RED: $Ag_{(aq)} + e^- \rightarrow Ag_{(s)}$ $E^\circ_{red} = +0.800\,V$ $2Ag^+_{(aq)} + Cu_{(s)} \rightarrow 2Ag_{(s)} + Cu^{2+}_{(aq)}$ $E^\circ = 0.460\,V$	*1 point for correctly determining the value of E°.*
(b) Write the equation for the half-cell reaction occurring at each electrode. Indicate which half-reaction occurs at the anode. OXIDATION (– terminal) (anode): $Cu_{(s)} \rightarrow Cu^{2+}_{(aq)} + 2e^-$ REDUCTION (+ terminal) (cathode): $Ag^+_{(aq)} + e^- \rightarrow Ag_{(s)}$	***2 points possible*** *1 point for correctly writing the half-cell reaction occurring at the anode.* *1 point for correctly writing the half-cell reaction occurring at the cathode.*
(c) Sketch a diagram of the cell, labeling all parts. 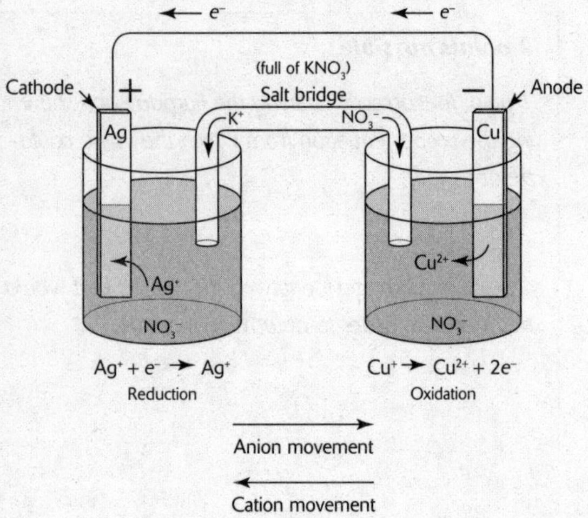	***2 points possible*** *1 point for correctly drawing the anode compartment.* *1 point for correctly drawing the cathode compartment.*
(d) Calculate the equilibrium constant for this cell reaction at 298K. $E^\circ = \frac{0.0592}{n} \log K$ $\log K = \frac{nE^\circ}{0.0592} = \frac{2(0.460\,V)}{0.0592} = 15.5$ $K = 10^{15.5}$	***2 points possible*** *1 point for correct setup.* *1 point for the correct value of K.*
(e) A cell similar to the one described above is constructed with solutions that have initial concentrations of 1.00-molar Cu^{2+} and 0.0200-molar Ag^+. Calculate the initial voltage, E, of this cell. $E = E^\circ - \frac{0.0592}{n} \log Q$ $= 0.460 - \frac{0.0592}{2} \log \frac{[Cu^{2+}]}{[Ag^+]^2}$ $= 0.460 - \frac{0.0592}{2} \log \frac{[1.00]}{[0.0200]^2}$ $= 0.460 - \frac{0.0592}{2} \log 2500.$ $= 0.359\,V$	***2 points possible*** *1 point for correct setup.* *1 point for the correct value of E.*

Nuclear Chemistry

You'll Need to Know

- ❑ how nuclear reactions differ from chemical reactions
- ❑ what is alpha emission and how to write an equation that involves alpha emission
- ❑ what is beta emission and how to write an equation that involves beta emission
- ❑ what is positron emission and how to write an equation that involves positron emission
- ❑ what is electron capture and how to write an equation that involves electron capture
- ❑ what are gamma rays and how to write an equation that involves gamma rays
- ❑ how to balance nuclear reactions
- ❑ the concept of nuclear stability and how to make predictions of decay modes
- ❑ what is nuclear half-life and how to solve problems involving the concept
- ❑ what are binding energy and mass defect and how to write a short paragraph about the concepts
- ❑ the difference between nuclear fission and nuclear fusion and how to identify the processes when given a reaction

Nuclear Reactions

Nuclear reactions differ from ordinary chemical reactions:

1. Chemical reactions involve rearrangement of valence shell electrons (breaking and/or formation of chemical bonds) while leaving the identity of the participating atoms unchanged. In nuclear reactions, the atom's nucleus is transformed, often changing the identity of the atom.
2. Changing pressure or temperature or adding a catalyst has no effect on nuclear reactions.
3. The chemical environment (isolated atom vs. atom in a compound) doesn't influence the outcome of a nuclear reaction.
4. Energy changes in nuclear reactions are much larger ($> 10^5$ times larger).
5. Isotopes of an element (same atomic number but different mass number) exhibit the same chemical reactivity but different nuclear reactions.

Types of Nuclear Decay

All radioactive decays obey first-order kinetics.

Alpha (α) Emission

Subtract 4 from the mass number.

Subtract 2 from the atomic number.

Add a helium nucleus $^{4}_{2}He$.

Alpha particles are helium nuclei released from an unstable nucleus. It is classified as ionizing radiation. The alpha particle is positively charged containing two protons, two neutrons, and no electrons. The alpha particle will be able to pick up two electrons from nearby atoms. The symbol for the alpha particle is ${}^{4}_{2}He$. Alpha particles are emitted from the nucleus of an atom at ~ 10% the speed of light. The penetrating power of the alpha particle is very low since it will not be able to penetrate a thin sheet of paper. Because of this low penetrating power, the alpha particle will do severe damage to the cells if taken into the body. One method of entering the body is by inhalation.

Example

Q. Uranium-238 decays by alpha emission. Write a balanced equation for this nuclear decay.

A. ${}^{238}_{92}U \rightarrow {}^{234}_{90}Th + {}^{4}_{2}He$. In this reaction U-238 is changed into Th-234 by emission of an alpha particle. Notice that both the mass number of the element and the atomic number decrease. During alpha decay, the mass number of the element undergoing the change decreases by four and the atomic number by two.

Beta (β) Emission

Mass number stays the same.

Add 1 to the atomic number.

Add an electron ${}^{0}_{-1}e$.

Beta particles are identical to electrons. Since electrons do not exist in the nucleus of an atom they come from a neutron by the following reaction: $n \rightarrow p + \beta$. A beta particle is written by use of the following symbol, ${}^{0}_{-1}e$. The –1 represents the atomic number of the electron. Since the electron has a very small mass compared to the proton, the mass number of the electron is zero. Beta particles are emitted from the nucleus at 0.9 times the velocity of light. Beta particles' penetrating power is greater than that of the alpha particle. Aluminum foil approximately 1 centimeter in thickness will stop the beta particle. Beta particles are also harmful if ingested into the body. Beta particles have an ionizing effect on gases.

Example

Q. Bromine-82 decays by beta emission. Write a balanced equation for this nuclear reaction.

A. ${}^{82}_{35}Br \rightarrow {}^{0}_{-1}e + ?$

The atomic number for the new element is 36:

$$35 = -1 + x \qquad x = 36$$

The mass number for the new element is 82 since the proton and neutron have equal mass. The mass number does not change. When referring to the periodic table, krypton (Kr) has the atomic number of 36. Therefore the nuclear equation is:

$${}^{82}_{35}Br \rightarrow {}^{0}_{-1}e + {}^{82}_{36}Kr$$

Positron (${}^{0}_{+1}e$) Emission

Mass number stays the same.

Subtract 1 from the atomic number.

Add a positron ${}^{0}_{+1}e$.

Some nuclei emit positrons. Positrons have the same mass as an electron but are positively charged. The positrons last a very short time. The symbol for a positron is

$$^{0}_{+1}e$$

No positrons exist in the nucleus of an atom; however, the emission of the positron can result from the conversion of a proton to a neutron:

$$^{1}_{1}\text{H} \rightarrow {}^{1}_{0}n + {}^{0}_{+1}e$$

Within about 10^{-9} seconds, the positron combines with an electron and is converted to gamma rays (γ). Positrons are similar to beta particles in velocity and ionizing effect, however they have very low penetrating power.

Example

Q. Oxygen-15 decays by positron emission. Write a balanced equation for this nuclear reaction.

A. $^{15}_{8}\text{O} \rightarrow {}^{0}_{+1}e + ?$

The atomic number for the new element is 7, and the mass number is 15.

$$8 = 1 + x \qquad x = 7$$

From the periodic table, the new element is nitrogen (N), and the equation for this nuclear reaction is:

$^{15}_{8}\text{O} \rightarrow {}^{0}_{+1}e + {}^{15}_{7}\text{N}$

Electron Capture ($^{0}_{-1}e$)

Mass number stays the same.

Subtract 1 from the atomic number.

Add an electron $^{0}_{-1}e$.

Example: $^{40}_{19}\text{K} + {}^{0}_{-1}e \rightarrow {}^{40}_{18}\text{Ar} + hv$

1. An electron from the closest energy level falls into the nucleus, which causes a proton to become a neutron and leads to a decrease of one in the charge on the nucleus.
2. The energy given off in this reaction is carried by an X-ray photon, which is represented by the symbol hv, where h is Planck's constant and v is the frequency of the X-ray.
3. Another electron falls into the empty energy level and so on causing a cascade of electrons falling. One free electron, moving about in space, falls into the outermost empty level.
4. The atomic number goes down by one, and mass number remains unchanged.
5. The electron captured by the nucleus in this reaction is usually a 1*s* electron because electrons in this orbital are the closest to the nucleus.

Example

Q. Write out the full electron capture equation for $^{239}_{96}\text{Cm}$.

A. $^{239}_{96}\text{Cm} + {}^{0}_{-1}e \rightarrow {}^{239}_{95}\text{Am} + hv$

Gamma (γ) Rays

Gamma rays represent electromagnetic radiation of very short wavelength—in general, the shorter the wavelength, the greater the energy of electromagnetic radiation. Gamma rays are very similar to X-rays having no charge and no mass. When gamma rays are emitted from the nucleus, a loss of energy occurs in the nucleus of the atom. Because gamma rays are electromagnetic radiation, they travel at the velocity of light. Gamma rays have high energy and great penetration power. These rays can easily penetrate the body and may have an effect on DNA sequences. Gamma rays have a very slight ionizing effect, less than beta particles.

Balancing Nuclear Equations

The number of nucleons and the total electric charge are conserved in simple nuclear reactions. If the mass numbers and atomic numbers of the particles emitted from a nucleus are known, the product nucleus can be identified by balancing mass numbers and atomic numbers in the nuclear equation.

Step 1: Identify the type of particle emitted by the decay and write the nuclear equation, with the mass number (A) and the atomic number (Z) of the daughter nucleus ${}^{A}_{Z}X$.

Step 2: Find the values of A and Z for the daughter nucleus from the requirement that the sums of the mass numbers and the nuclear charges remain unchanged in the decay.

Step 3: Use A and Z to identify the daughter nucleus in the periodic table.

Examples

Q. Write the nuclear equation for the α decay of thorium-232.

A. Write the equation with ${}^{A}_{Z}X$ representing the daughter nucleus:

$${}^{232}_{90}\text{Th} \rightarrow {}^{A}_{Z}\text{X} + {}^{4}_{2}\text{He}$$

To balance mass, we find from 232 = A + 4 that A = 228. To balance charge, Z must equal 90 – 2 = 88, so the daughter nucleus is ${}^{228}_{88}\text{Ra}$. The balanced nuclear equation is

$${}^{232}_{90}\text{Th} \rightarrow {}^{228}_{88}\text{Ra} + {}^{4}_{2}\text{He}$$

Q. Write the nuclear equation for the β decay of lithium-9.

A. Write the equation with ${}^{A}_{Z}X$ representing the daughter nucleus:

$${}^{9}_{3}\text{Li} \rightarrow {}^{A}_{Z}\text{X} + {}^{0}_{-1}e$$

To balance mass, we find from 9 = A + 0 that A = 9. To balance charge, Z must equal 3 – (–1) = 4, so the daughter nucleus is ${}^{9}_{4}\text{Be}$. The balanced nuclear equation is

$${}^{9}_{3}\text{Li} \rightarrow {}^{9}_{4}\text{Be} + {}^{0}_{-1}e$$

Nuclear Stability

Nuclei undergo changes (nuclear decay) to become more stable. The principal factor for determining whether a nucleus is stable or not is the neutron-to-proton ratio.

- For stable atoms of elements of low atomic number, the neutron-to-proton ratio is close to 1. As the atomic number increases, the neutron-to-proton ratios of the stable nuclei become greater than 1.
- Nuclei that contain 2, 8, 20, 50, 82, or 126 protons or neutrons are generally more stable than nuclei that do not possess these numbers.
- Nuclei with even numbers of both protons and neutrons are generally more stable than those with odd numbers of these particles.
- All isotopes of the elements starting with polonium (Z = 84) are radioactive.

In general, for isotopes whose:

mass number > stable atomic weight (i.e., $^{14}_{6}C$), predict beta (β) decay.

Example: $^{14}_{6}C \rightarrow\, ^{14}_{7}N + \,^{0}_{-1}\beta$

mass number < stable atomic weight (i.e., $^{11}_{6}C$), predict positron emission or electron capture.

Example (positron emission): $^{11}_{6}C \rightarrow\, ^{11}_{5}B + \,^{0}_{+1}e$

Example (electron capture): $^{11}_{6}C + \,^{0}_{-1}e \rightarrow\, ^{11}_{5}B + hv$

atomic number > 60, predict alpha (α) emission.

Example (alpha emission): $^{189}_{83}Bi \rightarrow\, ^{4}_{2}He + \,^{185}_{81}Tl$

atomic number > 90, predict spontaneous fission. Nuclides with atomic numbers of 90 or more undergo a form of radioactive decay known as spontaneous fission in which the parent nucleus splits into a pair of smaller nuclei. The reaction is usually accompanied by the ejection of one or more neutrons:

$$^{252}_{98}Cf \rightarrow\, ^{140}_{54}Xe + \,^{108}_{44}Ru + 4\,^{1}_{0}n$$

For all but the very heaviest isotopes, spontaneous fission is a very slow reaction. Spontaneous fission of U-238, for example, is almost two million times slower than the rate at which this nuclide undergoes α-decay.

Examples

For Questions 1–5, choose from the following:

- **A.** electron emission
- **B.** positron emission
- **C.** electron capture
- **D.** alpha emission
- **E.** gamma-ray emission

Q. $^{60}_{27}Co \rightarrow\, ^{60}_{27}Co + \gamma$

A. E.

Q. $^{40}_{19}K + \,^{0}_{-1}e \rightarrow\, ^{40}_{18}Ar + hv$

A. C.

Q. $^{40}_{19}K \rightarrow\, ^{40}_{20}Ca + \,^{0}_{-1}e$

A. A.

Q. $^{238}_{92}U \rightarrow ^{234}_{90}Th + ^{4}_{2}He$

A. D.

Q. $^{40}_{19}K \rightarrow ^{40}_{18}Ar + ^{0}_{+1}e$

A. B.

Half-life

The time required for half of the atoms in any given quantity of a radioactive isotope to decay is the half-life of that isotope. Each particular isotope has its own half-life. For example, the half-life of U-238 is 4.5 billion years; i.e., in 4.5 billion years, half of the U-238 on Earth will have decayed into other elements, in another 4.5 billion years, half of the remaining U-238 will have decayed, and so on. In this case, one-fourth of the original material will remain on Earth after 9 billion years. The half-life of C-14 is 5,730 years and is often used for dating archaeological material. Nuclear half-lives range from tiny fractions of a second to many times the age of the universe.

$$t_{\frac{1}{2}} = \frac{0.693}{k}$$

$$\ln\left(\frac{N}{N_o}\right) = -0.693\left(\frac{t}{t_{\frac{1}{2}}}\right)$$

where N = amount of material left

N_o = original amount of material

t = time

$t_{1/2}$ = half-life

k = rate constant

Example

Q. Phosphorus-32 is a radioactive isotope that has a half-life of 14.28 days and is used in treating leukemia patients. Starting with 45.0 grams of P-32, how many grams would be left after 35.0 days?

A. $\ln\left(\frac{N}{N_o}\right) = -0.693\left(\frac{t}{t_{\frac{1}{2}}}\right) = -0.693\left(\frac{35.0}{14.28}\right) = -1.70$

$\frac{N}{45.0} = 0.183 \qquad N = 8.24\ g$

Binding Energy and Mass Defect

You do NOT need to calculate binding energy on the AP Chemistry Exam.

Nuclear binding energy is derived from the strong nuclear force and is the energy required to disassemble a nucleus into free unbound neutrons and protons. A mass defect is produced because a bound system is at a lower energy level than its unbound constituents; i.e., its mass must be less than the total mass of its unbound constituents.

Hydrogen through sodium	Increasing binding energy per nucleon as atomic number increases. Generated by increasing forces per nucleon as each additional nucleon is attracted by all of the other nucleons and thus is more tightly bound to the whole.
Magnesium through xenon	Region of relative stability (saturation). The nucleus has become large enough that nuclear forces no longer completely extend efficiently across its width. Attractive nuclear forces in this region, as atomic mass increases, are nearly balanced by repellant electromagnetic forces between protons, as atomic number increases.
Elements heavier than xenon	Decreasing binding energy per nucleon as atomic number increases. In this region, electromagnetic repulsive forces are beginning to gain against strong nuclear forces.

Fission vs. Fusion

Nuclear fission occurs when the nucleus of an atom splits into two or more smaller nuclei as fission products and usually some by-product particles. Hence, fission is a form of elemental transmutation. The by-products include free neutrons, photons (usually in the form gamma rays) and other nuclear fragments such as alpha and beta particles. Fission of heavy elements is an exothermic reaction and can release substantial amounts of useful energy both as gamma rays and as kinetic energy of the fragments.

$$\text{Example: } {}^{235}_{92}\text{U} + {}^{1}_{0}\text{n} \rightarrow {}^{90}_{38}\text{Sr} + {}^{143}_{54}\text{Xe} + 3\,{}^{1}_{0}\text{n}$$

Nuclear fusion can occur when extremely high temperatures (~1.5×10^7 °C) are used to force nuclei of isotopes of lightweight atoms to fuse together, which causes large amounts of energy to be released. An example of nuclear fusion reactions are the following reactions which occur in the sun:

$${}^{1}_{1}\text{H} + {}^{2}_{1}\text{H} \rightarrow {}^{3}_{2}\text{He} \qquad {}^{3}_{2}\text{He} + {}^{3}_{2}\text{He} \rightarrow {}^{4}_{2}\text{He} + 2\,{}^{1}_{1}\text{H} \qquad {}^{1}_{1}\text{H} + {}^{1}_{1}\text{H} \rightarrow {}^{2}_{1}\text{H} + {}^{0}_{+1}\beta$$

Example

Q. Is the following process an example of fission or fusion?

$${}^{235}_{92}\text{U} + {}^{1}_{0}\text{n} \rightarrow {}^{146}_{57}\text{La} + {}^{87}_{35}\text{Ba} + 3\,{}^{1}_{0}\text{n}$$

A. Fission. Fission occurs when a large nucleus is bombarded by a small particle, such as a neutron. The result is two smaller nuclei and additional neutrons, and a chain reaction process begins.

Multiple-Choice Questions

For Questions 1–4, use the following key:

1. Keep mass number the same.
2. Subtract 2 from the atomic number.
3. Subtract 4 from the mass number.
4. Add 1 to the atomic number.
5. Subtract 1 from the atomic number.
6. Add a helium nucleus.
7. Add an electron.
8. Add a positron.

1. Which of the following are necessary steps when writing a balanced equation for alpha-particle emission?

A. 1, 2, 8
B. 1, 5, 7
C. 2, 3, 8
D. 2, 3, 6
E. 1, 4, 7

2. Which of the following are necessary steps when writing a balanced equation for beta-particle emission?

A. 2, 6, 8
B. 1, 4, 7
C. 2, 3, 6
D. 1, 5, 7
E. 2, 3, 8

3. Which of the following are necessary steps when writing a balanced equation for positron emission?

A. 6, 7, 8
B. 5, 6, 7
C. 1, 4, 7
D. 2, 3, 8
E. 1, 5, 8

4. Which of the following are necessary steps when writing a balanced equation for electron capture?

A. 1, 5, 7
B. 1, 4, 6
C. 4, 6, 7
D. 7, 8
E. 5, 7, 8

5. Which of the following is NOT a characteristic of a nuclear reaction?

A. Elements (or isotopes of the same element) are converted from one to another.
B. Protons, neutrons, electrons and other elementary particles may be involved.
C. Only electrons in atomic orbitals are involved in the breaking and forming of bonds.
D. Reactions are accompanied by absorption or release of great amounts of energy.
E. Rates of reaction are normally not affected by temperature, pressure and/or catalysts.

6. A certain radioactive series starts with $^{238}_{92}U$ and ends up as $^{206}_{82}Pb$. In this process, ______ α-particles and ______ β-particles are emitted.

A. 6, 8
B. 8, 6
C. 10, 32
D. 32, 10
E. 28, 10

For Questions 7–9, predict the mode of decay using the following key:

1. Alpha emission
2. Beta emission
3. Electron capture
4. Positron emission
5. Spontaneous fission

7. Pu-240

A. 1
B. 1 and 5
C. 2
D. 3
E. 3 and 4

8. Na-20

A. 1
B. 2
C. 3
D. 4
E. 3 and 4

9. Po-212

A. 1
B. 2
C. 3
D. 4
E. 5

For Questions 10–12: Strontium-90 undergoes β-emission and has a half-life of 28.1 years.

10. The balanced equation for the decay of Sr-90 is

A. $^{90}_{38}Sr + ^{4}_{2}He \rightarrow ^{94}_{40}Sr$
B. $^{90}_{38}Sr \rightarrow ^{86}_{36}Kr + ^{4}_{2}He$
C. $^{90}_{38}Sr + ^{0}_{+1}e \rightarrow ^{90}_{39}Y$
D. $^{90}_{38}Sr \rightarrow ^{90}_{39}Y + ^{0}_{-1}e$
E. $^{90}_{38}Sr \rightarrow ^{90}_{38}Sr + h\nu$

11. The rate constant is

A. 4.33×10^{-4} yr
B. 6.33×10^{-3} yr^{-1}
C. 2.47×10^{-2} yr^{-1}
D. 4.36×10^{-1} yr^{-1}
E. 5.33×10^{2} yr^{-1}

12. How long will it take for 90.0% of a sample of Sr-90 to decay?

- **A.** 56.2 years
- **B.** 93.1 years
- **C.** 148 years
- **D.** 176 years
- **E.** 253 years

13. A group of anthropologists discover a piece of charcoal at the site of an excavation. They send the charcoal to a lab and it was determined that there were 6.00×10^{-14} grams of C-14 for every one gram of C-12. A piece of charcoal produced this year from the site was found to contain 8.00×10^{-14} grams of C-14 for every one gram of C-12. The half-life of C-12 is 5,720 years. How old was the site?

- **A.** 390 years
- **B.** 633 years
- **C.** 2,370 years
- **D.** 4,740 years
- **E.** 9,877 years

14. Given the following types of radiation

1. Alpha particles
2. Beta particles
3. Gamma rays

if arranged in decreasing ability to penetrate a piece of lead the order would be

- **A.** $1 > 2 > 3$
- **B.** $2 > 3 > 1$
- **C.** $3 > 2 > 1$
- **D.** $1 > 3 > 2$
- **E.** $2 > 1 > 3$

15. Assume the diameter of an average spherical U-238 nucleus is 1.6×10^{-2} pm (1 pm = 10^{-12} m). The density of the nucleus is

- **A.** 8.3×10^{11} g / cm^3
- **B.** 1.9×10^{14} g / cm^3
- **C.** 3.9×10^{16} g / cm^3
- **D.** 2.7×10^{17} g / cm^3
- **E.** 8.7×10^{18} g / cm^3

For Questions 16–8: Predict the most likely mode of decay of the following nuclides using the following choices:

- **A.** Alpha decay
- **B.** Beta decay
- **C.** Positron emission
- **D.** Electron capture
- **E.** Electron emission

16. F-17

17. Ag-105

18. Ta-185

19. A becquerel (Bq) is one disintegration per second. A curie (Ci) is 3.70×10^{10} disintegrations per second (dps). The most abundant isotope of uranium is U-238; 99.276% of the atoms in a sample of uranium are U-238. What is the activity (in μCi) of the U-238 in 1 L of a 1.00 *M* solution of the uranyl ion, UO_2^{2+}? Assume that the rate constant for the decay of this isotope is 4.87×10^{-18} Bq.

- **A.** 79.2 μCi
- **B.** 92.6 μCi
- **C.** 134 μCi
- **D.** 357 μCi
- **E.** 736 μCi

20. A carbon-based artifact was recently discovered at a native American burial site. The half-life of C-14 is 5,720 years and decays first-order. How old was the artifact if it retains 65.0% of its original C-14 activity?

- **A.** 2,789 years
- **B.** 3,560 years
- **C.** 4,781 years
- **D.** 6,883 years
- **E.** 7,833 years

Free-Response Questions

1. (a) Balance the following nuclear equation: ${}^{243}_{95}Am \rightarrow {}^{239}_{93}Np + ?$

(b) From the balanced equation above, predict the type of nuclear decay.

(c) In the decay of Americium-241 which is used in smoke detectors, Am-241 loses a total of 8 alpha particles and 3 beta particles. Predict the final isotope that is produced.

(d) Americium-241 has a half-life of 432.2 years. What is the rate constant?

(e) What percentage of Am-241 remains after 75.0 years?

2. Explain each of the following in terms of nuclear models.

(a) The mass of an atom of C-12 is less than the sum of the masses of 6 protons, 6 neutrons, and 6 electrons.

(b) Gamma radiation will penetrate much further through material than either alpha or beta particles. Which form(s) of radiation are generally useful in medicine?

(c) Draw a sketch of how α, β, and γ rays might behave if they passed through an electric field.

(d) Discuss the role of binding energy in the processes of nuclear fission and fusion.

(e) Discuss why binding energy is highest in medium-sized nuclei.

Answers and Explanations

Multiple Choice

1. **D.** Example: ${}^{239}_{94}\text{Pu} \rightarrow {}^{235}_{92}\text{U} + {}^{4}_{2}\text{He}$
2. **B.** Example: ${}^{14}_{6}\text{C} \rightarrow {}^{14}_{7}\text{N} + {}^{0}_{-1}e$
3. **E.** Example: ${}^{118}_{54}\text{Xe} \rightarrow {}^{0}_{1}e + {}^{118}_{53}\text{I}$
4. **A.** Example: ${}^{204}_{84}\text{Po} + {}^{0}_{-1}e \rightarrow {}^{204}_{83}\text{Bi} + hv$
5. **C.** If you missed this question, review the first part of this chapter.
6. **B.** An alpha particle is a helium nucleus, ${}^{4}_{2}\text{He}$. A beta particle is an electron, ${}^{0}_{-1}e$.

   ${}^{238}_{92}\text{U} \rightarrow {}^{206}_{82}\text{Pb} + 8\,{}^{4}_{2}\text{He} + 6\,{}^{0}_{-1}\beta$
7. **B.** Since the atomic number is both > 60 and > 90, we can predict both alpha-decay and spontaneous fission.

   Alpha emission: ${}^{240}_{94}\text{Pu} \rightarrow {}^{236}_{92}\text{U} + {}^{4}_{2}\text{He}$

   Spontaneous fission: ${}^{240}_{94}\text{Pu} \rightarrow {}^{93}_{40}\text{Zr} + {}^{144}_{54}\text{Xe} + 3\,{}^{1}_{0}\text{n}$
8. **E.** Since the mass number (20) < stable atomic weight (22.99), we can predict positron emission or electron capture.

   Positron emission: ${}^{20}_{11}\text{Na} \rightarrow {}^{20}_{10}\text{Ne} + {}^{0}_{+1}\beta$

   Electron capture: ${}^{20}_{11}\text{Na} + {}^{0}_{-1}e \rightarrow {}^{20}_{10}\text{Ne} + hv$
9. **A.** Since the atomic number (84) > 60 (but less than 90), predict alpha (α) emission.

   Alpha emission: ${}^{212}_{84}\text{Po} \rightarrow {}^{208}_{82}\text{Pb} + {}^{4}_{2}\text{He}$
10. **D.** A beta particle is an electron.
11. **C.** $k = 0.693 / 28.1\text{ yr} = 2.47 \times 10^{-2}\text{ yr}^{-1}$
12. **B.** $\log_{10}(100/10) = 1.0 = (2.47 \times 10^{-2}\text{ yr}^{-1})(t) / 2.30$

    $t = 93.1$ years

    Note: This problem was worked out using $\log_{10}$ for those students whose classroom experience or preference is working in this mode.
13. **C.** $k = 0.693 / (t_{1/2}) = 0.693 / (5720) = 1.21 \times 10^{-4}$

    $$\ln\left(\frac{N}{N_o}\right) = -0.693\left(\frac{t}{t_{\frac{1}{2}}}\right) = \ln\left(\frac{6.00 \times 10^{-14}}{8.00 \times 10^{-14}}\right) = -0.693\left(\frac{t}{5{,}720}\right)$$

    $t = 2{,}370$ years
14. **C.** Alpha and beta particles are physical particles of matter. An alpha particle consists of two protons and two neutrons, and consequently is relatively very heavy and slow. A beta particle is simply an electron. The beta particle may be moving from very slow to very fast, and the speed is an indication of its energy level. Gamma radiation is true electromagnetic energy, and moves at or near the speed of light. Alpha particles can be blocked by a piece of paper. Beta particles can only penetrate a thin piece of aluminum. Gamma radiation can penetrate inches of lead.

15. B. This problem is a good review of the factor-label method.

$$r = d/2 = 1.6 \times 10^{-2}\,\text{pm}/2 = \frac{8.0 \times 10^{-3}\,\cancel{\text{pm}}}{1} \times \frac{10^{-12}\,\cancel{\text{m}}}{1\,\cancel{\text{pm}}} \times \frac{10^{2}\,\text{cm}}{1\,\cancel{\text{m}}} = 8.0 \times 10^{-13}\,\text{cm}$$

$$V = 4/3\,\pi\,r^3 = 1.33\,(3.14)\,(8.0 \times 10^{-13}\,\text{cm})^3 = 2.1 \times 10^{-36}\,\text{cm}^3$$

$$\frac{238\,\cancel{\text{amu}}}{1} \times \frac{1\,\text{g}}{6.022 \times 10^{23}\,\cancel{\text{amu}}} = 3.95 \times 10^{-22}\,\text{g}$$

$$d = \frac{m}{v} = \frac{3.95 \times 10^{-22}\,\text{g}}{2.1 \times 10^{-36}\,\text{cm}^3} = 1.9 \times 10^{14}\,\text{g/cm}^3$$

16. C. The atomic weight of fluorine is 18.998 amu. Because the mass of a F-17 nuclide is smaller than the average fluorine atom, the F-17 nuclide must contain fewer neutrons. It is therefore likely to be a neutron poor. Because it is a relatively light nuclide, F-17 it should decay by positron emission:

$${}^{17}_{9}\text{F} \rightarrow {}^{17}_{8}\text{O} + {}^{0}_{+1}e$$

17. D. The atomic weight of silver is 107.868 amu. Because the mass of the Ag-105 nuclide is smaller than the average silver atom, this nuclide contains fewer neutrons than the stable isotopes of silver. Since Ag-105 is a relatively heavy neutron-poor nuclide, it should decay by electron capture:

$${}^{105}_{47}\text{Ag} + {}^{0}_{-1}e \rightarrow {}^{105}_{46}\text{Pd} + h\nu$$

18. E. The atomic weight of tantalum is 180.948 amu. The Ta-185 isotope is therefore likely to be a neutron-rich isotope, which decays by electron emission:

$${}^{185}_{73}\text{Ta} \rightarrow {}^{185}_{74}\text{W} + {}^{0}_{-1}e$$

19. A. The rate at which the U-238 isotope decays depends on the rate constant for this reaction (k) and the number of uranium atoms in the sample (N). One liter of 1.00 M UO_2^{2+} solution contains 1 mole of uranium atoms.

$$\text{rate} = kN = (4.87 \times 10^{-18}\,\text{s}^{-1})\,(6.02 \times 10^{23}\,\text{atoms}) = 2.93 \times 10^{6}\,\text{atom} \cdot \text{s}^{-1}$$

To calculate the activity of this sample, convert from disintegrations per second to curies:

$$\frac{2.93 \times 10^{6}\,\cancel{\text{atoms}}}{\cancel{\text{s}}} \times \frac{1\,\cancel{\text{Ci}}}{3.70 \times 10^{10}\,\cancel{\text{atoms} \cdot \text{s}^{-1}}} \times \frac{10^{6}\,\mu\text{Ci}}{1\,\cancel{\text{Ci}}} = 79.2\mu\text{Ci}$$

20. B. Because C-14 decays by first-order kinetics, the log of the ratio of the C-14 in the sample today (N) to the amount that would be present if it was still alive (N_0) is proportional to the rate constant for this decay and the time since death:

$$\ln\left[\frac{(N)}{(N_0)}\right] = -kt$$

The rate constant for this reaction can be calculated from the half-life of C-14, which is 5,720 years:

$$k = \frac{\ln 2}{t_{\frac{1}{2}}} = \frac{0.693}{5{,}720\,\text{yr}} = 1.21 \times 10^{-4}\,\text{yr}$$

If the sample retains 65.0% of its activity, the ratio of the activity today (N) to the original activity (N_0) is 0.650.

$\ln(0.650) = -(1.21 \times 10^{-4}\,\text{yr}^{-1})(t)$ $\quad t = 3{,}560$ years

Free Response

Question 1

Maximum Points for Question 1
Part (a): 2 points
Part (b): 2 points
Part (c): 2 points
Part (d): 2 points
Part (e): 2 points
Total points: 10

1. (a) Balance the following nuclear equation: ${}^{243}_{95}Am \rightarrow {}^{239}_{93}Np + ?$ ${}^{243}_{95}Am \rightarrow {}^{239}_{93}Np + {}^{4}_{2}He$	***2 points possible*** *2 points for correctly balanced equation.*
(b) From the balanced equation above, predict the type of nuclear decay. Alpha decay. Spontaneous fission is also possible.	***2 points possible*** *2 points for correct answer.*
(c) In the decay of Americium-241 which is used in smoke detectors, Am-241 loses a total of 8 alpha particles and 3 beta particles. Predict the final isotope that is produced. 241 = 32 + 0 + 209 95 = 16 + (−3) + 82 ${}^{241}_{95}Am \rightarrow 8\,{}^{4}_{2}He + 3\,{}^{0}_{-1}e + {}^{209}_{82}Pb$	***2 points possible*** *1 point for correctly showing work.* *1 point for correct answer.*
(d) Americium-241 has a half-life of 432.2 years. What is the rate constant? $k = \frac{0.693}{t_{\frac{1}{2}}} = \frac{0.693}{432.2\,yr} = 1.60 \times 10^{-3}\,yr^{-1}$	***2 points possible*** *1 point for correctly showing work.* *1 point for correct answer.*
(e) What percentage of Am-241 remains after 75.0 years? $\ln\left(\frac{N}{N_0}\right) = -0.693\left(\frac{t}{t_{\frac{1}{2}}}\right)$ $= -0.693\left(\frac{75.0\,\cancel{yrs}}{432.2\,\cancel{yrs}}\right) = -0.120$ $\frac{N}{N_0} = e^{-0.120} = 0.887$ $\frac{N}{100\%} = 0.887 \qquad N = 88.7\%$	***2 points possible*** *1 point for correctly showing work.* *1 point for correct answer.*

Question 2

Maximum Points for Question 2
Part (a): 2 points
Part (b): 2 points
Part (c): 2 points
Part (d): 2 points
Part (e): 2 points
Total points: 10

2. Explain each of the following in terms of nuclear models. *(a) The mass of an atom of C-12 is less than the sum of the masses of 6 protons, 6 neutrons, and 6 electrons.* When nucleons are combined in nuclei, some of their mass is converted to energy (binding energy) which is released and stabilizes the nucleus. The equation that relates the loss in mass to the energy released is $E = mc^2$.	***2 points possible*** *The concept of binding energy.* *The use of $E = mc^2$ to account for the amount of matter lost.* *Concept of stability as reason for loss in mass.*
(b) Gamma radiation will penetrate much further through material than either alpha or beta particles. Which form(s) of radiation are generally useful in medicine? Alpha particles have a greater mass than beta particles. Thus their speed (penetrating potential) is less. Though the most massive and most energetic of radioactive emissions, the alpha particle is the shortest in range because of its strong interaction with matter. Because of its very large mass (more than 7000 times the mass of the beta particle) and its charge, it has a very short range. It is generally not suitable for radiation therapy because its range is less than a tenth of a millimeter inside the body. Its main radiation hazard comes when it is ingested into the body. The electron of beta radioactivity strongly interacts with matter and also has a limited range. Gamma radiation is not composed of particles. The electromagnetic gamma ray is extremely penetrating, even penetrating considerable thicknesses of concrete and lead.	***2 points possible*** *Discussion of relative mass between alpha and beta particles.* *Effect of differences in mass resulting in differences in speed.* *Correct discussion of the uses of various forms of radiation and which are most useful in medicine.*

(c) Draw a sketch of how α, β, and γ rays might behave if they passed through an electric field. 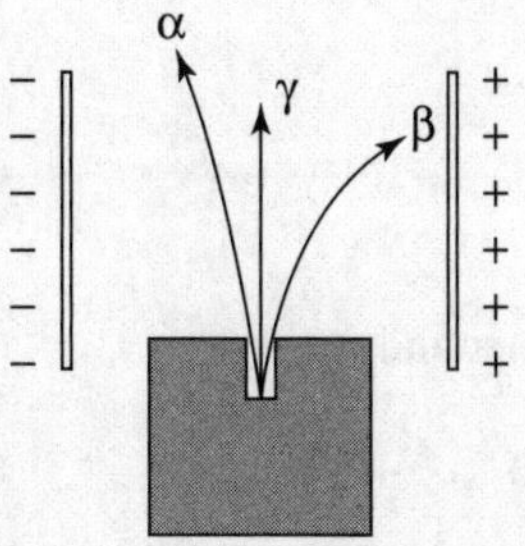 In an electric field the path of the beta particles (–) is greatly deflected toward the positive electric pole, that of the alpha particles (+) to a lesser extent toward the negative pole, and gamma rays are not deflected at all.	***2 points possible*** *Deflection of alpha particle towards negative pole.* *Deflection of beta particle towards positive pole.* *Gamma ray does not deflect.*
(d) Discuss the role of binding energy in the processes of nuclear fission and fusion. Large amounts of energy are needed to initiate fusion reactions in order to overcome the repulsive forces between the positively charged nuclei. Large amounts of energy are not required to cause large nuclei to split. Nuclear fusion produces energy by combining the very lightest elements into more tightly bound elements (such as hydrogen into helium), and nuclear fission produces energy by splitting the heaviest elements (such as uranium or plutonium) into more tightly bound elements such as barium and krypton. Both processes produce energy because mid-sized nuclei are the most tightly bound of all.	***2 points possible*** *Relative amounts of energy required to initiate a fusion vs. a fission reaction.* *Discussion of fission.* *Discussion of fusion.* *Relating binding energy to fission and fusion.* *Discussion of mid-sized nuclei.*
(e) Discuss why binding energy is highest in medium-sized nuclei. The existence of a maximum in binding energy in medium-sized nuclei is a consequence of the trade-offs in the effects of two opposing forces which have different range characteristics. The attractive nuclear force (strong nuclear force) which binds protons and neutrons equally to each other has a limited range due to a rapid exponential decrease in this force with distance. However, the repelling electromagnetic force, which acts between protons to force nuclei apart, falls off with distance much more slowly (as the inverse square of distance). At the peak of binding energy is nickel and iron which have tightly bound nuclei and is the reason why iron and nickel are very common metals in planetary cores as they are produced in large quantities as end products during supernova explosions. For nuclei larger than about four nucleons in diameter, the increase in the repelling force of additional protons more than offsets the increase in strong force interactions of additional nucleons. Such nuclei become less and less tightly bound as their size increases, though most of them are still stable. Finally, nuclei containing more than 209 nucleons are all too large to be stable and are subject to spontaneous decay to smaller nuclei.	***2 points possible*** *Concept of decreasing force with distance.* *Difference between nuclear force and electromagnetic force.* *Influence of repelling electromagnetic force.* *Comparison of forces with other sized nuclei.*

Organic Chemistry

You'll Need to Know

- ❑ the properties of organic compounds and how they are different from non-organic compounds
- ❑ how to draw condensed formulas
- ❑ how to draw and name various hydrocarbon compounds including:
    - ❑ alkanes
    - ❑ alkenes
    - ❑ alkynes
    - ❑ cyclic hydrocarbons
- ❑ how to draw and name various ring (aromatic) compounds
- ❑ how to draw and name compounds containing various functional groups including:
    - ❑ alcohols
    - ❑ carboxylic acids
    - ❑ amides
    - ❑ amines
    - ❑ aldehydes
    - ❑ ketones
    - ❑ esters
    - ❑ ethers
- ❑ how to draw and name various isomers including:
    - ❑ structural
        - ❑ chain
        - ❑ positional
        - ❑ functional
    - ❑ stereisomerism
        - ❑ geometric
        - ❑ optical

Properties of Organic Compounds

Organic compounds are any of a large class of chemical compounds whose molecules contain carbon, with the exception of carbides (i.e., SiC), carbonates (i.e., $CaCO_3$), and carbon oxides (i.e., CO_2). Organic compounds are generally covalently bonded and allow for unique structures such as long carbon chains and rings. The reason carbon is excellent at forming unique structures and that there are so many carbon compounds is that carbon atoms form very stable covalent bonds with one another (catenation).

Some general properties of organic compounds include:

1. They usually have low melting points. In contrast to most inorganic materials, organic compounds typically melt, boil, sublime or decompose below 300°C.
2. They usually are non-polar (unless they contain functional groups). Neutral organic compounds tend to be less soluble in water compared to many inorganic salts, with the exception of certain compounds such as low molecular weight alcohols and carboxylic acids where hydrogen bonding occurs.
3. They are usually nonconductors of electricity.
4. They can exist in solid, liquid, and gaseous form. Compounds with:
   - 1–4 carbons tend to be gases at room temperature; butane and propane are among the lightest hydrocarbons and are used for fuel.
   - 5–10 carbons tend to be in the liquid state at room temperature; compounds that fall in this size range are used to make gasoline and solvents.
   - 12–18 carbons make up jet fuels and kerosene.
   - More than 18 carbons tend to be solids at room temperature.

Organic compounds can exist as polymers, in which many repeating units called monomers, make up a larger molecule. Amino acids are monomers of proteins when amino acids are bonded in a chain and make a polypeptide or protein. Starches are polymers of the monomer glucose. Plastics are polymers of organic molecules extracted from crude oil.

Some common examples include:

- Polyethylene—many ethenes (ethylenes) strung together with covalent bonds. Example: shopping bags and plastic bottles.
- Polypropylene—many propenes strung together. Example: glues and carpets.
- Polystyrene—a clear, hard, brittle polymer used in CD cases; if you blow carbon dioxide into it during manufacture you get the soft, opaque, foamy polymer used in coffee cups.

Condensed Formulas

Structures are condensed by leaving off the lone pairs and grouping the hydrogens with the carbon they are bonded to. Oxygens are also grouped with the carbon they are bonded to. For example, COH implies an alcohol group, whereas CHO implies an aldehyde.

A very condensed structure might consist only of lines representing carbon–carbon bonds. A carbon is assumed at every point where the line segments join. If that does not make four bonds around the carbon, it is also assumed that carbon–hydrogen bonds make up the missing bonds. The hydrogens are not written.

Examples

Q. How many hydrogen and carbon atoms are in each of the following structures?

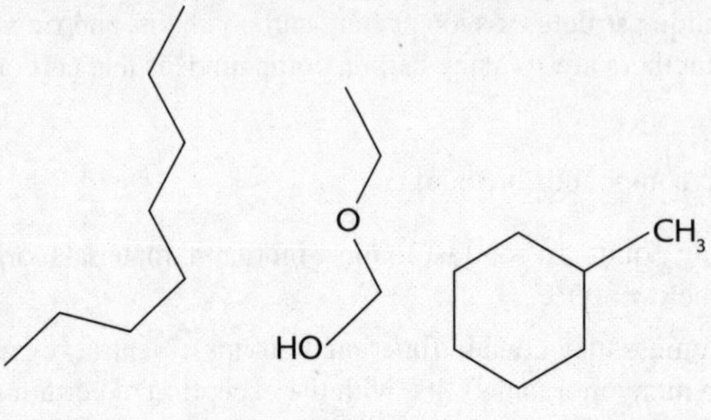

A. B. C.

A. (a) 8 carbons, 18 hydrogens.

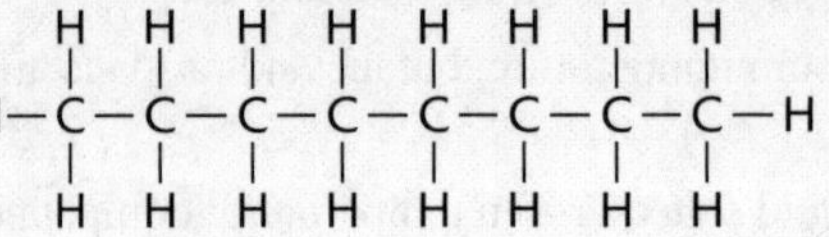

(b) 3 carbons, 8 hydrogens.

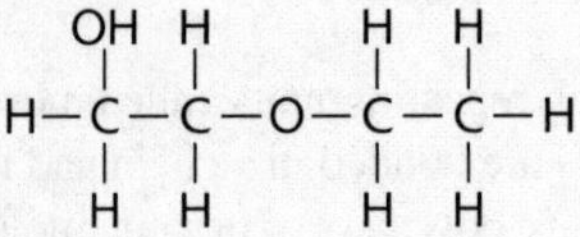

(c) 7 carbons, 14 hydrogens.

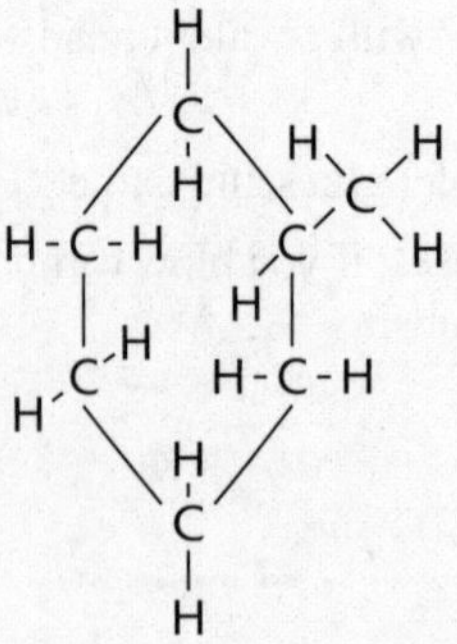

Hydrocarbons

A hydrocarbon is any chemical compound that consists only of the elements carbon and hydrogen. Aliphatic hydrocarbons do not contain a benzene ring whereas aromatic hydrocarbons do. All hydrocarbons contain a carbon backbone, called a carbon skeleton, and have hydrogen atoms attached to that backbone. Most hydrocarbons are combustible. There are essentially three types of hydrocarbons: (1) aromatic hydrocarbons, which have at least one benzene ring; (2) saturated hydrocarbons, also known as alkanes, which do not have double, triple, or aromatic bonds; and (3) unsaturated hydrocarbons, which have one or more double or triple bonds between carbon atoms and can be further divided into alkenes and alkynes.

Alkanes

Alkanes are also known as saturated hydrocarbons (ending in "*ane*"). The saturated open-chain hydrocarbons form a homologous series called the alkane, or paraffin, series. The composition of each of the members of the series corresponds to the formula C_nH_{2n+2}, where n is the number of carbon atoms in the molecule. Among the members of the series are methane, CH_4; ethane, C_2H_6; propane, C_3H_8; and butane, C_4H_{10}. All the members of the series are unreactive; that is, they do not react readily at ordinary temperatures with such reagents as acids, alkalis, or oxidizers; however, they are combustible at high enough temperatures. The first four members of the series are gases at ordinary temperature and pressure; intermediate members are liquids; and the heavier members are semi-solids or solids. Petroleum contains a great variety of saturated hydrocarbons, and such petroleum products as gasoline, heavy fuel oil, lubricating oils, and paraffin consist principally of mixtures of paraffin hydrocarbons, which range from the lighter liquid members to the solid members.

$$C_nH_{2n+2}$$

Root Word and Number of Carbons				
meth- (1)	eth- (2)	prop- (3)	but- (4)	pent- (5)
hex- (6)	hept- (7)	oct- (8)	non- (9)	dec- (10)

Examples

methane

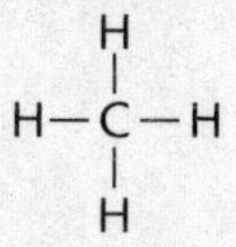

CH_4

ethane

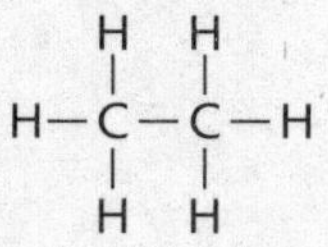

C_2H_6

propane

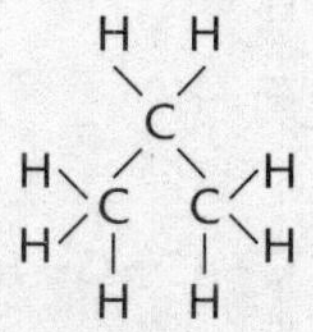

C_3H_8

butane

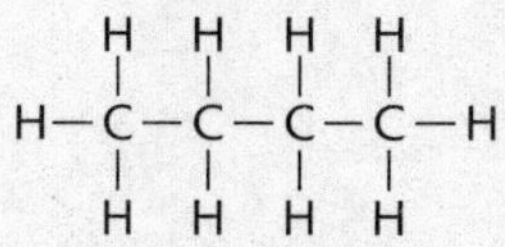

C_4H_{10}

isobutane

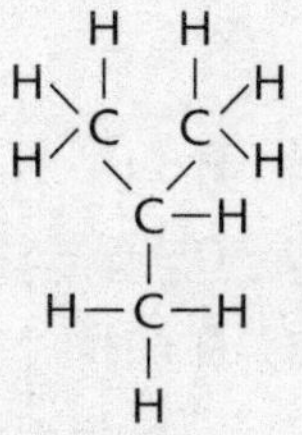

C_4H_{10}

Common Alkyl Groups	
methyl	$-CH_3$
ethyl	$-CH_2-CH_3$
n-propyl	$-CH_2-CH_2-CH_3$
n-butyl	$-CH_2-CH_2-CH_2-CH_3$
isopropyl	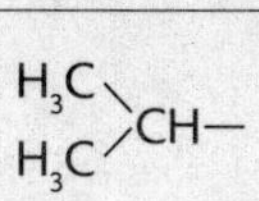
t-butyl	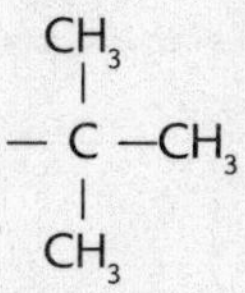

Common Functional Groups	
amino	$-NH_2$
fluoro	–F
chloro	–Cl
bromo	–Br
iodo	–I
nitro	$-NO_2$
vinyl	$-CH{=}CH_2$

Example

Q. Draw all of the structural isomers of C_6H_{14} and name each.

A.

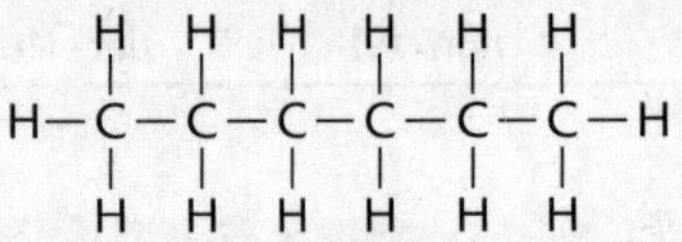

n-hexane

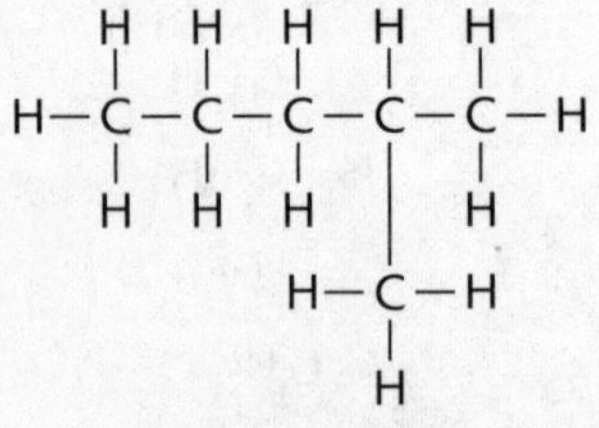

2-methylpentane

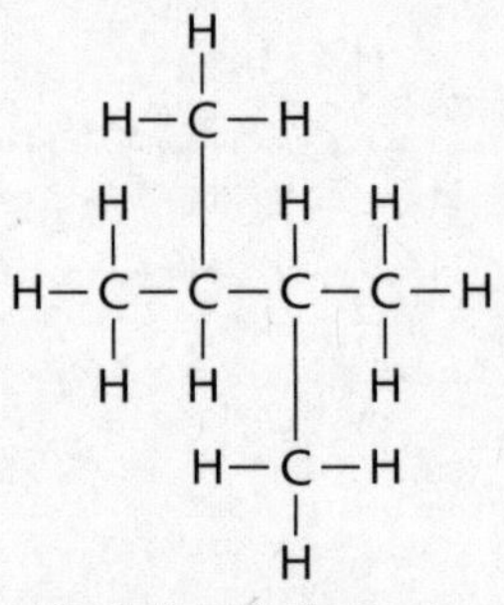

2, 3-dimethylbutane

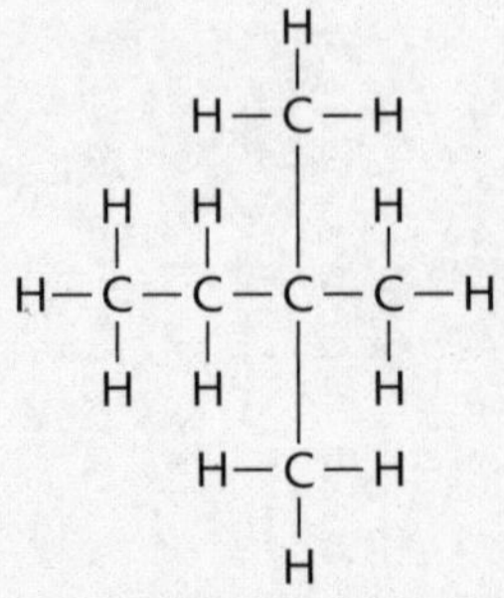

2, 2-dimethylbutane

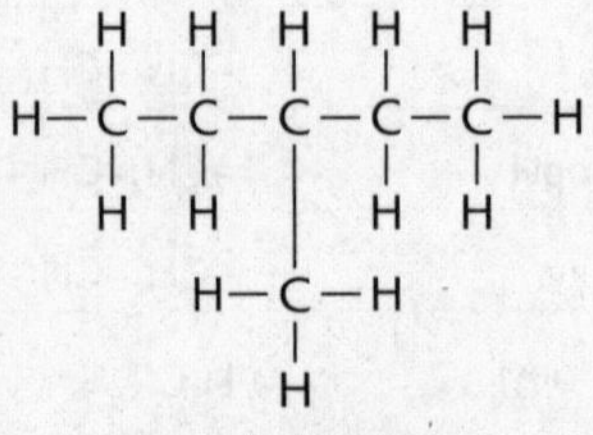

3-methylpentane

Alkenes

Ending in "*ene*," the alkene, or olefin series of chain hydrocarbons are those in which a double bond exists between two carbon atoms. The general formula for the series is C_nH_{2n}, where *n* is the number of carbon atoms. As in the alkane series, the lower members are gases, intermediate compounds are liquids, and the higher members of the series are solids. The alkene series compounds are more active chemically than the saturated compounds. They easily react with substances such as halogens, adding atoms at the double bonds. They are found to some extent in natural products, and are produced in the destructive distillation of complex natural substances, such as coal, and are formed in large amounts in petroleum-refining.

$$C_nH_{2n}$$

Examples

ethylene or ethene

$$H{\Large\diagdown}C=C{\Large\diagup}H$$
$$H{\Large\diagup}\qquad{\Large\diagdown}H$$

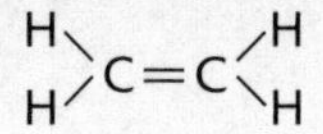

C_2H_4

propene

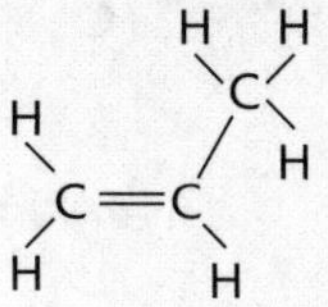

C_3H_6

- -

Example

Q. Draw all isomers of pentene, C_5H_{10}, and label them.

A. $CH_2=CHCH_2CH_2CH_3$ $CH_3CH=CHCH_2CH_3$

 1-pentene 2-pentene

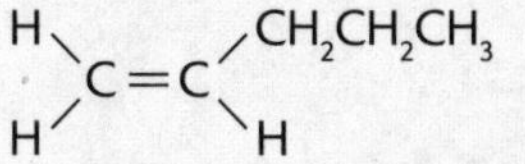

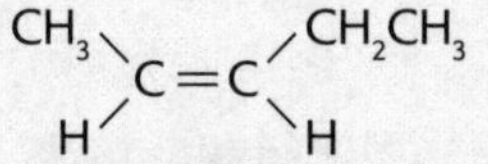

cis-2-pentene trans-2-pentene

- -

Alkynes

The members of the alkyne series contain a triple bond between two carbon atoms in the molecule. They are very active chemically and are not found free in nature. They form a series analogous to the alkene series. The first and most important member of the series is ethyne, C_2H_2.

$$C_nH_{2n-2}$$

Examples	Name	Structural Formula	
C_2H_2	ethyne	$H-C\equiv C-H$	
C_3H_4	propyne	$H-\overset{\displaystyle H}{\underset{\displaystyle H}{C}}-C\equiv C-H$	
C_4H_6	butyne	$H-\overset{H}{\underset{H}{C}}-\overset{H}{\underset{H}{C}}-C\equiv C-H$	$H-\overset{H}{\underset{H}{C}}-C\equiv C-\overset{H}{\underset{H}{C}}-H$
		1-butyne	2-butyne

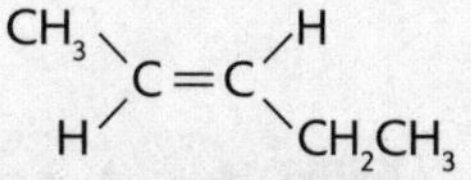

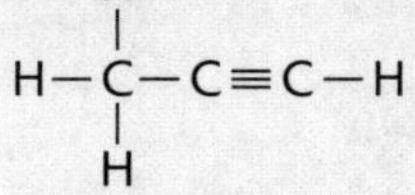

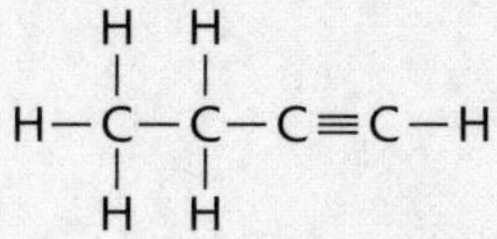

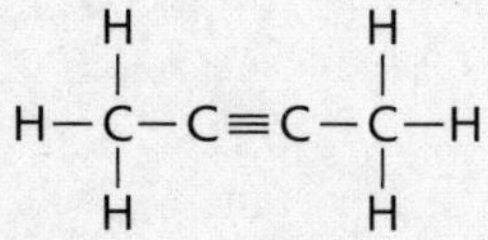

Example

Q. Draw all of the structural isomers of pentyne and name each.

A.

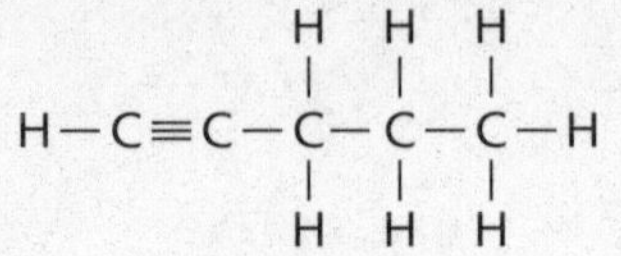

1-pentyne

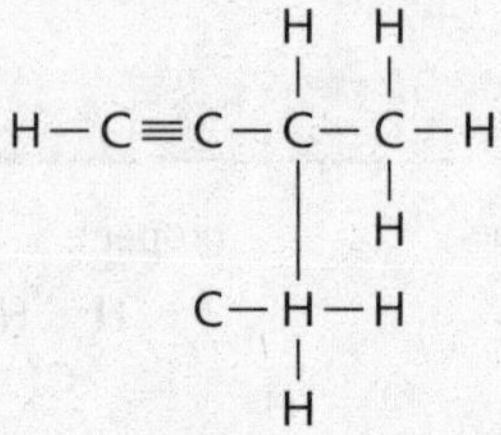

3-methyl-1-butyne

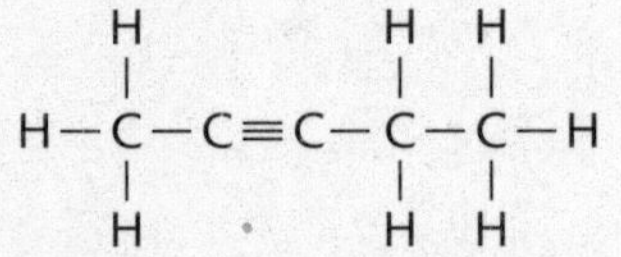

2-pentyne

Cyclic Hydrocarbons

A cyclic compound is one in which a series of carbon atoms are connected together to form a loop or ring. The simplest of the saturated cyclic hydrocarbons, or cycloalkanes, is cyclopropane, C_3H_6; the molecules of which are made up of three carbon atoms to each of which two hydrogen atoms, are attached. Cyclopropane is somewhat more reactive than the corresponding open-chain alkane, propane, C_3H_8.

$$C_nH_{2n}$$

Examples	*Name*	*Structural Formula*
C_3H_6	cyclopropane	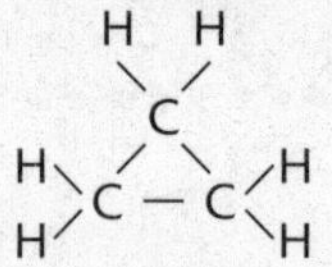
C_4H_8	cyclobutane	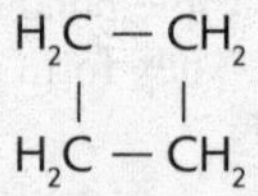
C_5H_{10}	cyclopentane	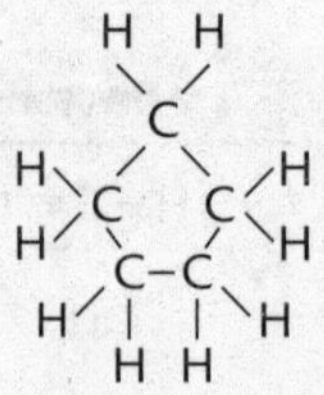

Ring (Aromatic) Compounds

All aromatic compounds are based on benzene, C_6H_6, which has a ring of six carbon atoms and has the symbol:

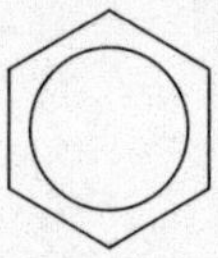

Each corner of the hexagon has a carbon atom with a hydrogen attached. A phenyl group, C_6H_5, is formed by removing a hydrogen from a benzene ring. There are three ways in which a pair of substituents can be placed on an aromatic ring. In the *ortho* (*o*) isomer, the substituents are in adjacent positions on the ring. In the *meta* (*m*) isomer, they are separated by one carbon atom. In the *para* (*p*) isomer, they are on opposite ends of the ring. The three isomers of dimethylbenzene, or xylene, are shown below.

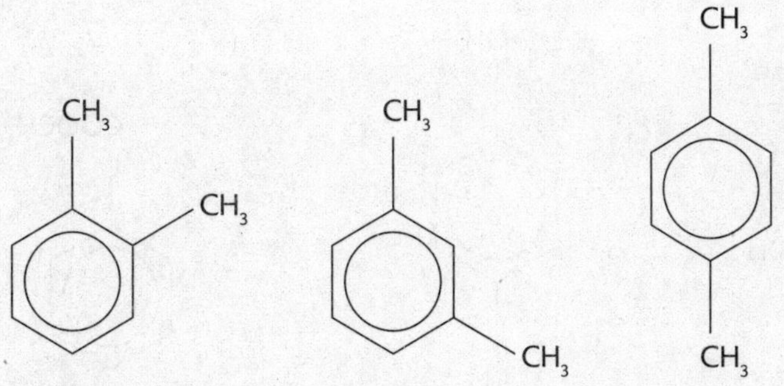

ortho *meta* *para*

Examples

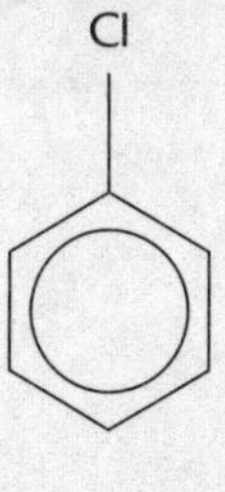

chlorobenzene

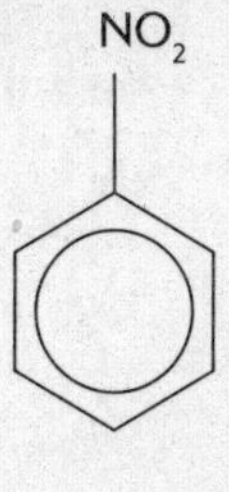

nitrobenzene

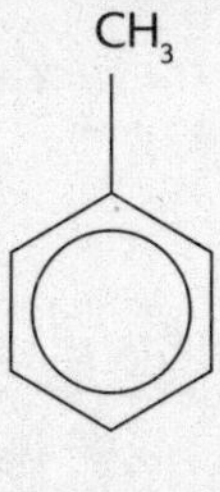

methylbenzene

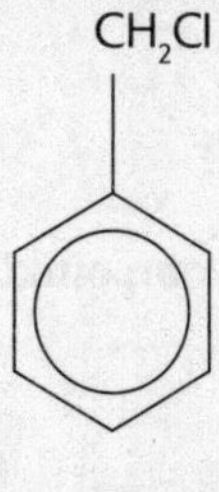

chloromethylbenzene

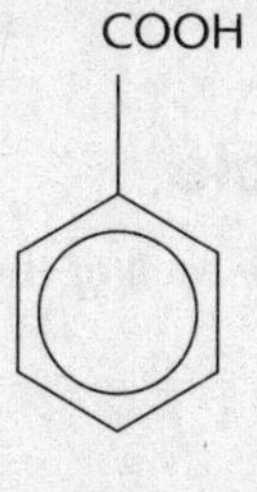

benzoic acid

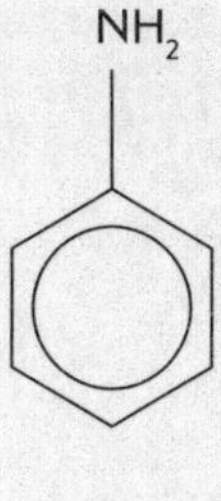

phenylamine

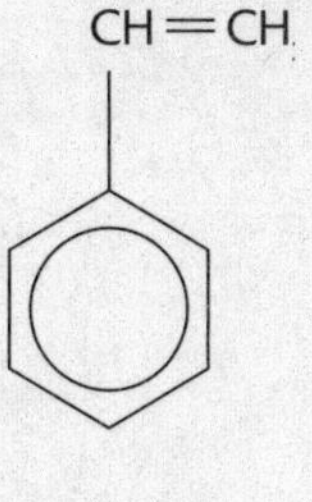

phenylethene

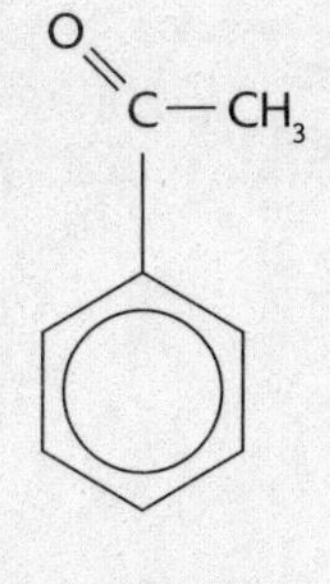

phenylethanone

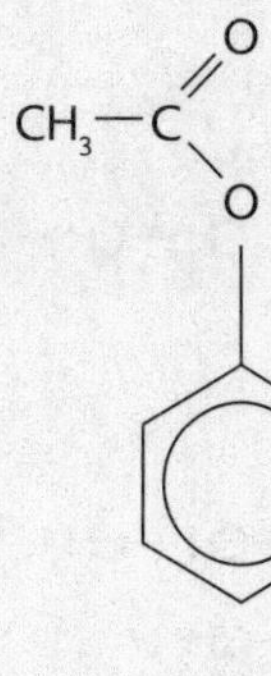

phenylethanoate

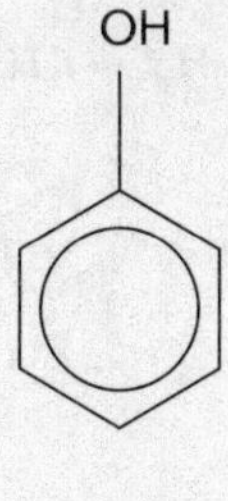

phenol

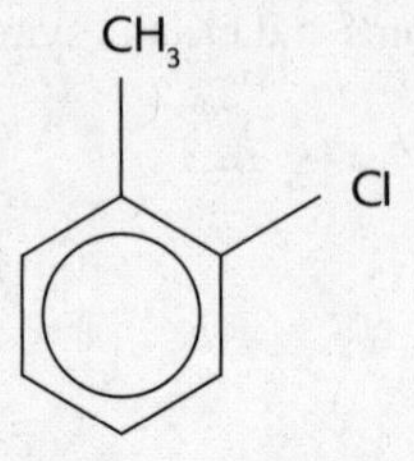

2-chloromethylbenzene 3-chloromethylbenzene 4-chloromethylbenzene

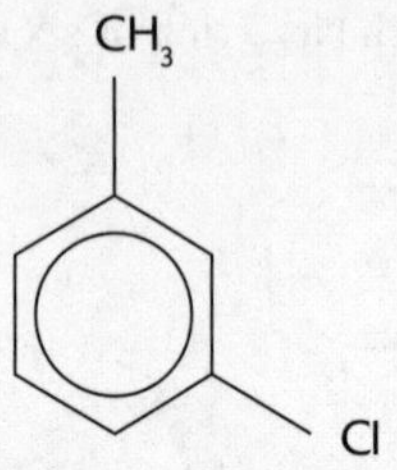

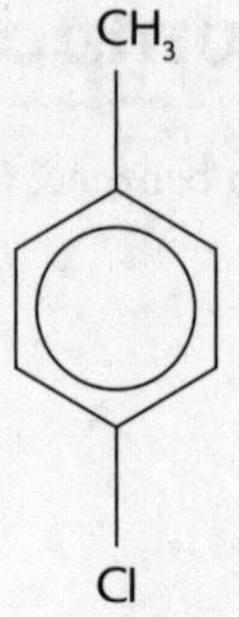

derivatives of methylbenzene

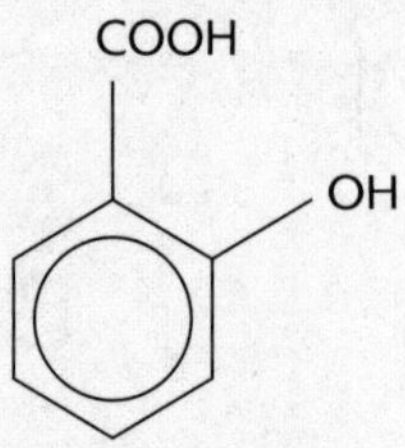

2-hydroxybenzoic acid 2, 4, 6-trichlorophenol methyl-3-nitrobenzoate

• •

Example

Q. Name each of the following compounds.

(a)

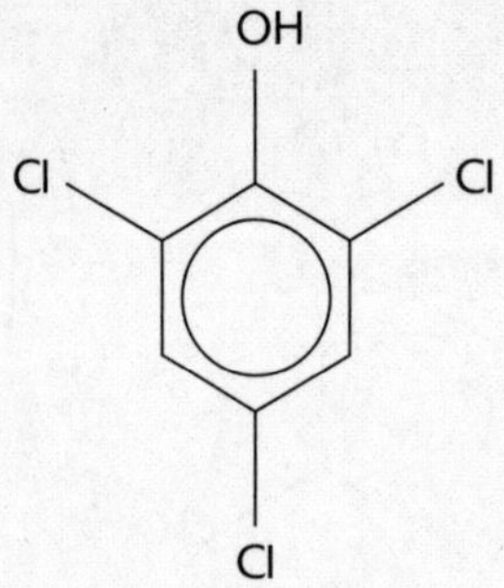

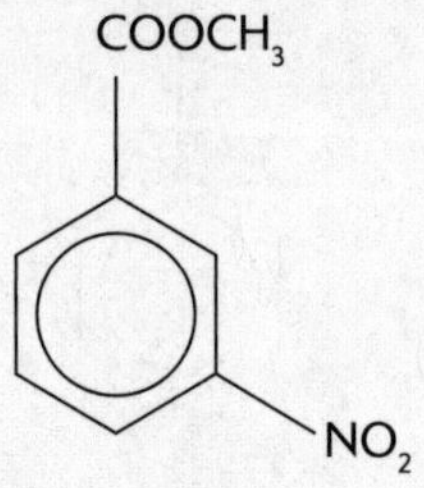

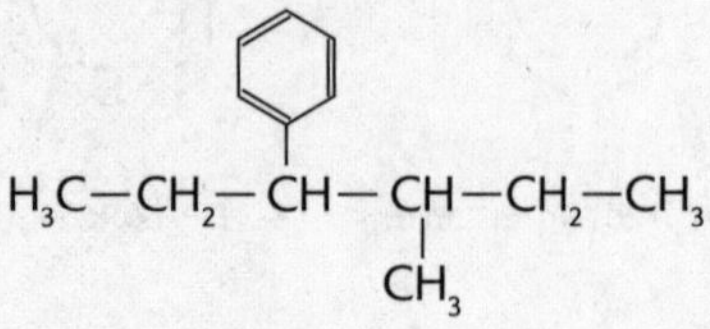

$$H_3C-CH_2-CH-CH-CH_2-CH_3$$
$$\qquad\qquad\;\; CH_3$$

(b)

$$H_3C-CH-CH=CH-CH_2-CH_2-CH_2-CH_3$$

(c)

$$H_2C-CH-CH_2-CH-CH_2-CH_2-CH_3$$
$$\qquad\qquad\qquad\; CH_3-CH_3$$

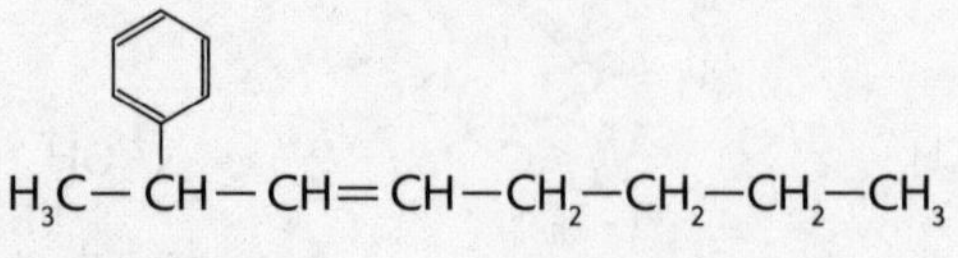

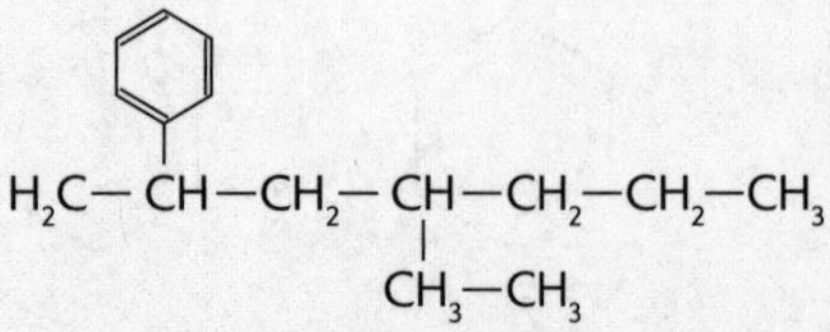

A. (a) 3-methyl-4-phenylhexane; (b) 2-phenyl-3-octene; (c) 4-ethyl-2-phenylheptane

• •

Functional Groups

Alcohols

The hydroxyl group (–OH) found in alcohols makes alcohols more soluble in polar solvents than the hydrocarbon from which they were derived and also increases the boiling point due to hydrogen bonding formed between the alcohol molecules. When naming alcohols, remove the ending of the hydrocarbon and replace with "*ol*"; e.g., ethane becomes ethanol.

—OH

Examples

methanol

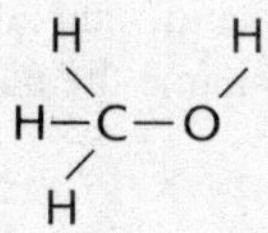

CH_3OH

ethanol

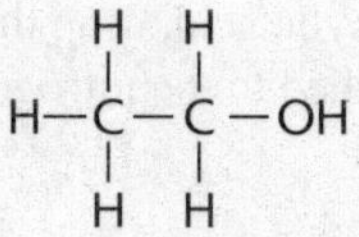

C_2H_5OH

propanol

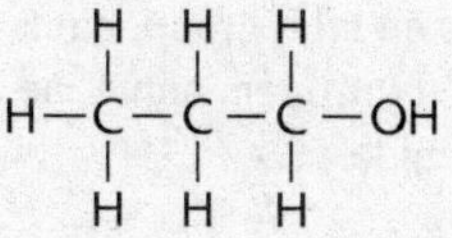

1-propanol

2-propanol (isopropyl alcohol or isopropanol)

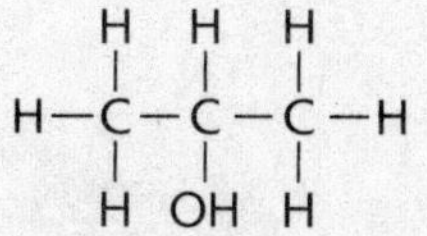

C_3H_7OH

Example

Q. Name the following alcohols.

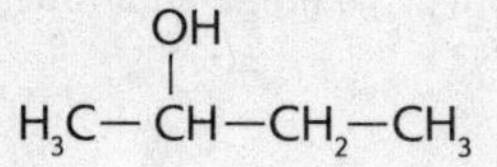

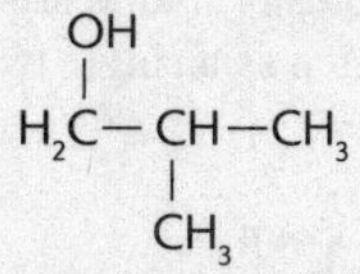

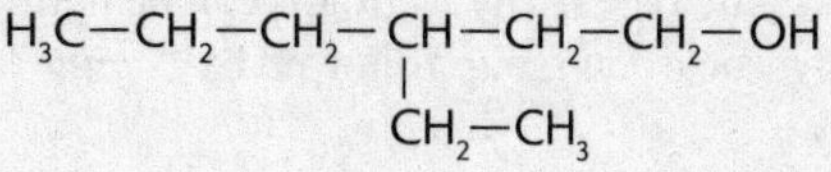

A. (a) 2-butanol; (b) 2-methyl-1-propanol; (c) 3-ethyl-1-hexanol

Organic (Carboxylic) Acids

The functional group of an organic acid is known as a carboxyl group (—COOH). Carboxylic acids are weak acids. To name organic acids, replace the ending with "*oic acid*".

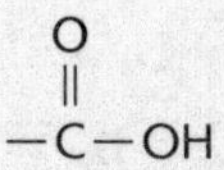

Examples

methanoic (formic) acid	ethanoic (acetic) acid	propanoic acid
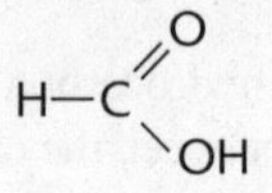	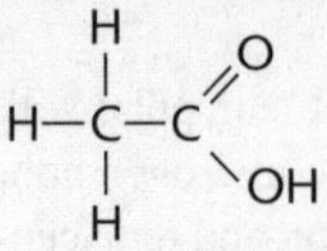	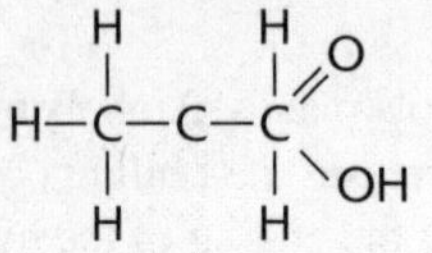
HCOOH	CH_3COOH	CH_3CH_2COOH

Amides

Amides are commonly formed from the reaction of a carboxylic acid with an amine which forms peptide bonds between amino acids. Amides can participate in hydrogen bonding as hydrogen bond acceptors and donors, but do not ionize in aqueous solution. Amide formation plays a role in the synthesis of some condensation polymers, such as nylon and Kevlar. For amides with an NH_2 group, name the parent carboxylic acid, drop the "–oic acid" and add "*–amide*". For amides with a substituted nitrogen, name the alkyl groups attached to the nitrogen, then name the parent acid, drop the "–oic acid" and add "–amide".

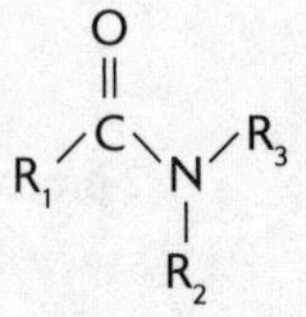

Name	***Structural Formula***
acetamide or ethanamide	
CH_3CONH_2	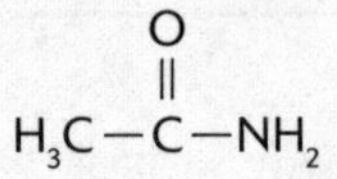

Amines

Amines are organic bases. The R groups can be hydrogen atoms or hydrocarbon groups. To name an amine, use the name of the hydrocarbon group followed by "*amine*" all written as a single word.

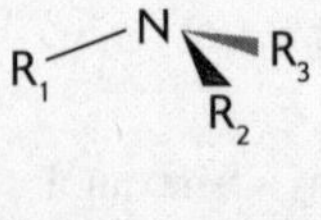

Examples

methylamine	methylethylamine	diethylamine
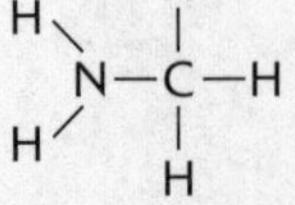 CH_3NH_2	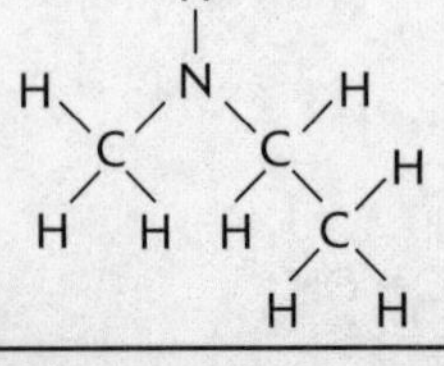	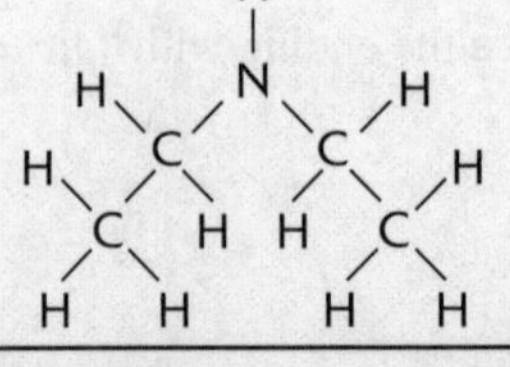

Example

Q. Name the following amines.

a)
$$CH_3$$
$$|$$
$$CH_2$$
$$|$$
$$H_3C-CH_2-N-CH_2-CH_3$$

b) $H_3C-CH_2-CH_2-NH-CH_2-CH_2-CH_2-CH_3$

c)
$$CH_3$$
$$|$$
$$H_2N-CH-CH_3$$

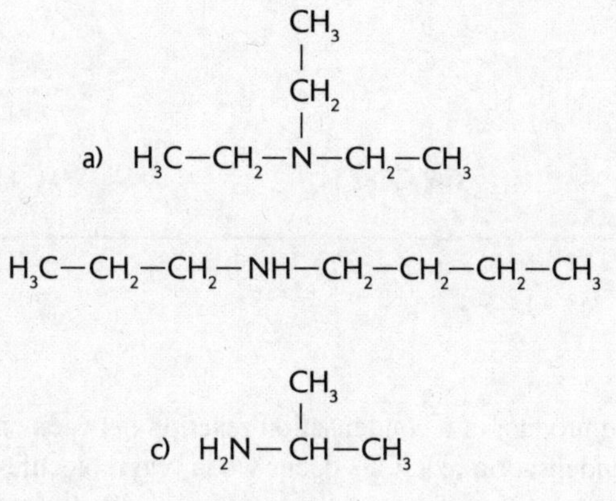

A. (a) triethylamine (b) *n*-butyl-*n*-propylamine (c) isopropylamine

Aldehydes

Aldehydes contain a carbonyl group (C = O) to which at least one hydrogen is attached and the carbonyl group must be attached to the last carbon of the chain. To name an aldehyde, add the suffix *-al*.

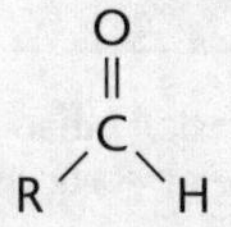

Examples

methanal (formaldehyde)

CH_2O

ethanal (acetaldehyde)

CH_3CHO

propanal (propionaldehyde)

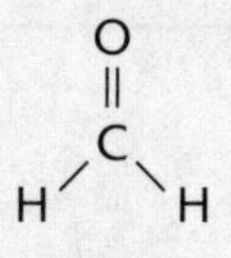

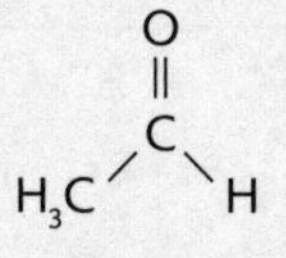

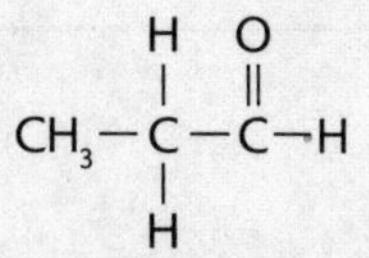

CH_3CH_2CHO

Ketones

Ketones have a carbonyl group (C=O) attached to an interior carbon atom. Ketones are commonly used as organic solvents due to their polarity. To name ketones, replace the ending of the molecule with the suffix *-one* and use a number to indicate the position of the carbonyl group in the molecule.

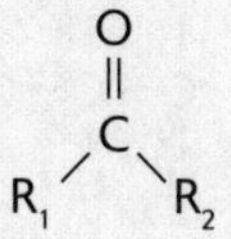

Examples

propanone (acetone)

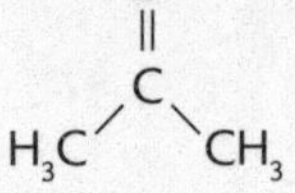

CH_3COCH_3

2-butanone (methyl ethyl ketone)

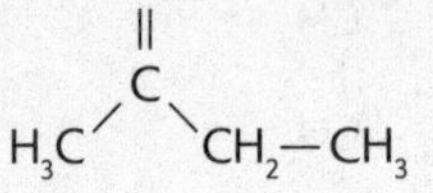

$CH_3COC_2H_5$

acetophenone

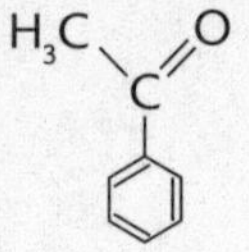

C_8H_8O

cyclohexanone

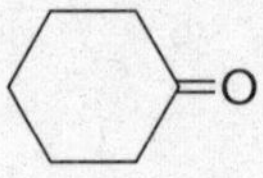

$C_6H_{10}O$

Esters

Esters are commonly formed as the product of a condensation reaction between an acid (usually an organic acid) and an alcohol (or phenol compound). Condensation reactions occur when two molecules are joined together and eliminate a small molecule, e.g., H_2O. A condensation reaction to form an ester is called esterification. To name esters, use the name of the group derived from the alcohol followed by the name of the group derived from the acid, end with "*-oate*".

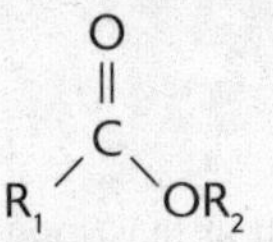

Examples

methyl methanoate (methyl formate)

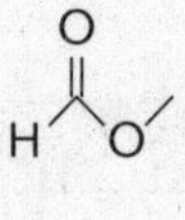

$HCOOCH_3$

methyl ethanoate (methyl acetate or acetic acid methyl ester)

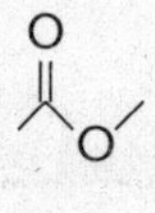

$C_3H_6O_2$

ethyl ethanoate (ethyl acetate)

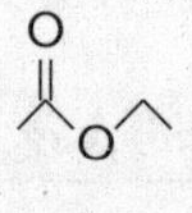

$C_4H_8O_2$

Ethers

Ethers are formed by the condensation reaction between two alcohols. To name ethers, place the names (in alphabetical order) of the two R groups before the word "ether".

$$R_1—O—R_2$$

Examples

dimethyl ether

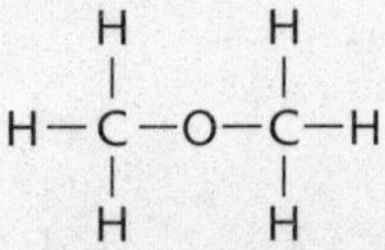

CH_3OCH_3

ethyl methyl ether

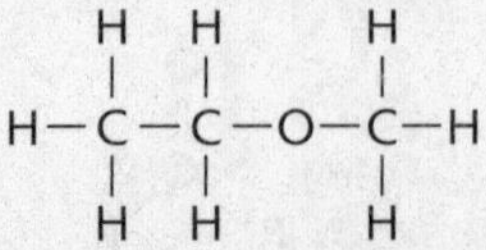

$C_2H_5OCH_3$

diethyl ether

$C_2H_5OC_2H_5$

Isomers

Isomers are compounds with the same formula but different properties that result from different structures. There are two broad classes of isomers: structural isomers and stereoisomers.

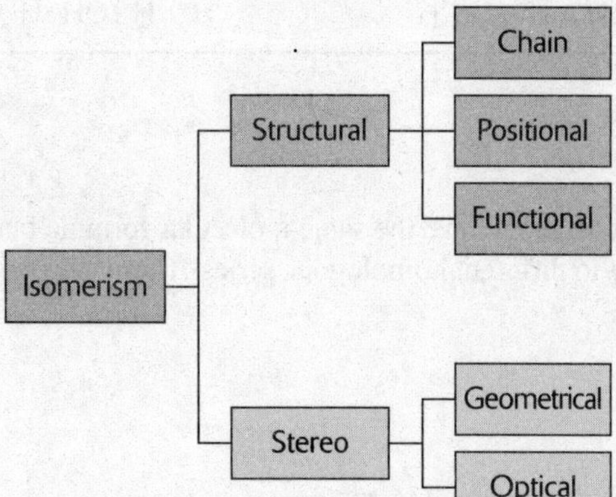

Structural Isomerism

Structural isomerism occurs when two or more organic compounds have the same molecular formula, but different structures. These differences tend to give the molecules different chemical and physical properties. Structural isomers have the same molecular formula but different molecular structures (different connectivities or different numbers and kinds of chemical bonds). Organic examples of structural isomers: CH_3OCH_3 (dimethyl ether) and CH_3CH_2OH (ethyl alcohol). There are three types of structural isomerism: chain isomerism, positional isomerism, and functional isomerism.

Chain Isomerism

Chain isomerism, also called nuclear isomerism, occurs when the way carbon atoms are linked together is different from compound to compound. There are three chain isomers of C_5H_{12} shown below. Note that these isomers have the same molecular formula as pentane, but different conformations.

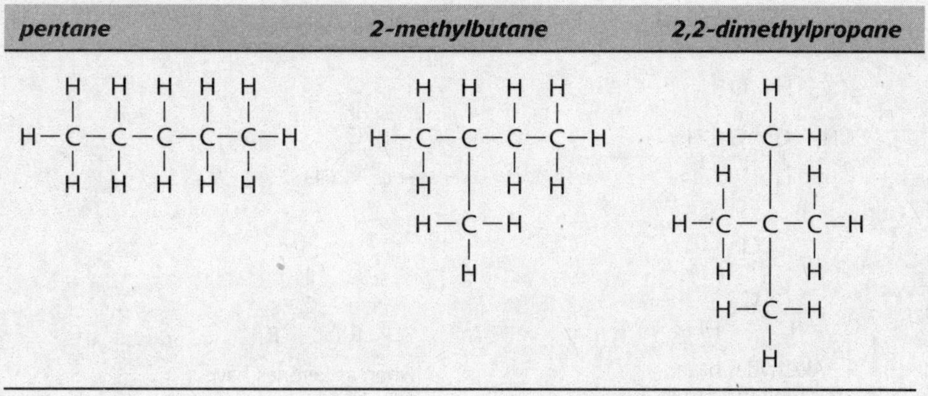

Positional Isomerism

Positional isomerism occurs when functional groups are in different positions on the same carbon chain. Positional isomers of alcohols, alkenes, and aromatics are common. Below are models of the positional isomers of butanol:

1-butanol	*2-butanol*
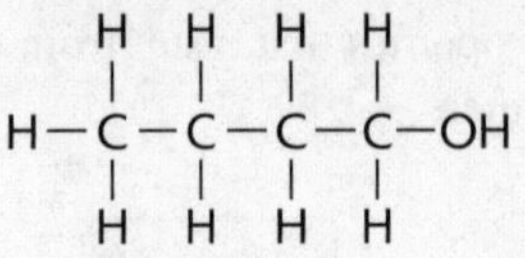	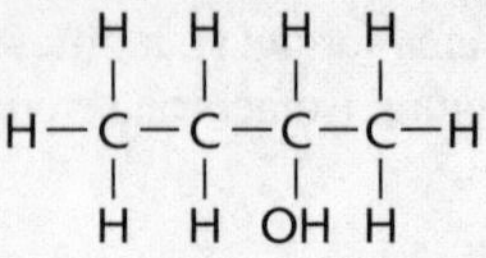

Functional Isomerism

Functional isomerism occurs when substances have the same molecular formula but different functional groups. This means that functional isomers belong to different homologous series. There are two functional group isomers of which you need to be aware of:

- alcohols and ethers
- aldehydes and ketones

Below are models of the functional isomers ethanol and methoxymethane.

ethanol (alcohol)	*methoxymethane (ether)*
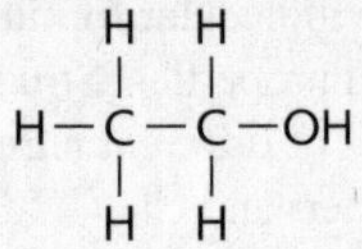	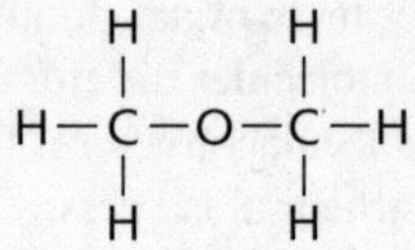
Alcohols have the hydroxyl group –OH.	Ethers have the functional group R–O–R′.

Below are the models of the functional isomers propanal and propanone both of which have 3 carbons, 6 hydrogens, and 1 oxygen.

propanal (aldehyde)	*propanone (ketone)*
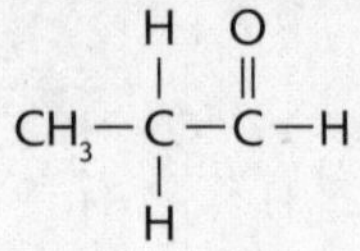	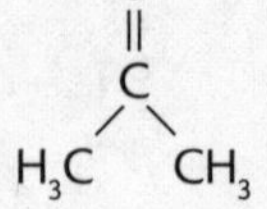
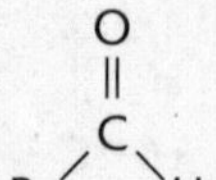	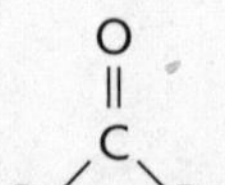
Aldehydes have this funtional group	whereas ketones have this functional group

Stereisomerism

When the atoms in a molecule can have different arrangements in space, stereisomerism occurs. There are two types of stereoisomerism: geometrical isomerism and optical isomerism.

Geometric Isomerism

Geometric isomerism occurs when substances have the same molecular formula, but a different arrangement of their atoms in space. When like groups are on the same side of the double bond, we call it a *cis* isomer; when they are on opposite sides it is called a *trans* isomer.

cis-2-butene

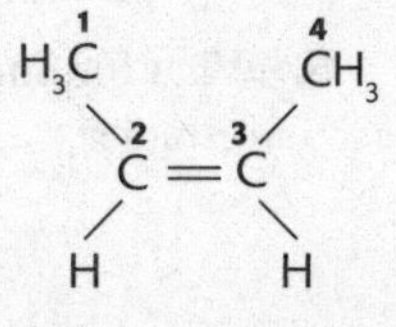

trans-2-butene

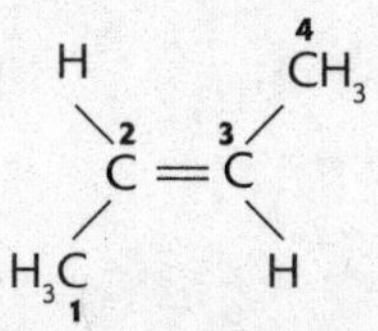

Optical Isomerism

Optical isomerism occurs when substances have the same molecular and structural formula, but one cannot be superimposed on the other; i.e., mirror images of each other. No matter how hard you try, the molecule on the left will not turn into the molecule on the right. Molecules like this are said to be chiral (pronounced ky-ral), and the different forms are called enantiomers.

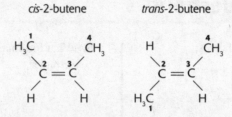

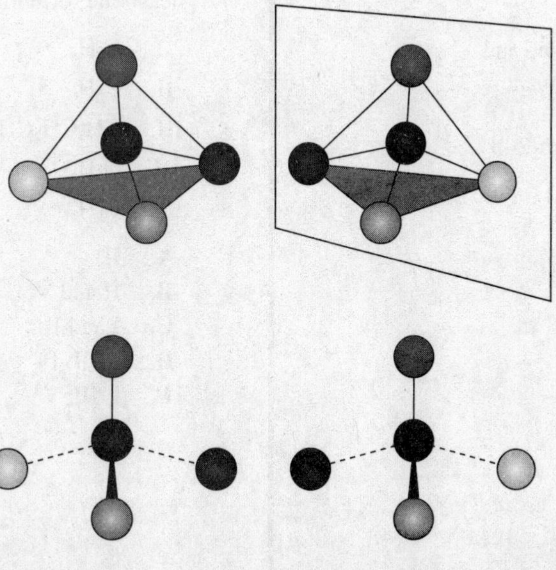

Optical isomers can occur when there is an asymmetric carbon atom. An asymmetric carbon atom is one which is bonded to four different groups; there must be four groups, and they must be different. Optical isomers can rotate the plane of polarization of plane-polarized light: one enantiomer rotates the polarized light clockwise (to the right) and is the (+) enantiomer and the other rotates the polarized light counterclockwise (to the left) and is called the (–) enantiomer. A mixture containing equal concentrations of the (+) and (–) enantiomers is not optically active—i.e., will not rotate polarized light and is called a racemic mixture. Below are models of the optical isomers of 2-hydroxypropanoic acid (lactic acid). Lactic acid is a fairly common and simple example of optical isomerism. The (+) enantiomer of lactic acid is found in muscles. Sour milk contains a racemic mixture of the two enantiomers.

(+) lactic acid	(–) lactic acid
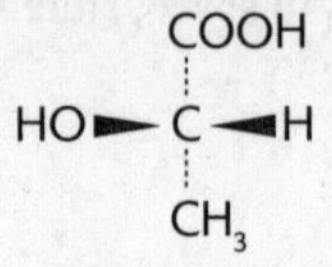	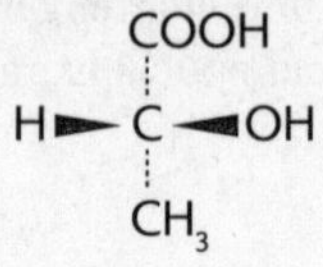

See Chapter 16 for organic reactions.

Multiple-Choice Questions

For Questions 1–5, use the following choices:

A. positional isomerism
B. geometric isomerism
C. functional isomerism
D. chain isomerism
E. optical isomerism

1. Butane and 2-propane

2. 1-butene and 2-butene

3. propanal and propanone (acetone)

4. *cis*-1,2-dichlorocyclopropane and *trans*-1,2-dichlorocyclopropane

5. (+) butan-2-ol and (–) butan-2-ol

6. What formula describes the following condensed formula?

A. $CH_3CH_2CH_2CH_3$
B. $CH_3CH_2CH_2CH_2$
C. CH_3CHCH_2CH
D. $CH_3CH_2CH_2CH_2CH_3$
E. $CH_3CH_2CHCH_2$

7. Which of the following compounds contain at least one form that is saturated?

I. C_2H_6
II. C_6H_6
III. $CH_3CH_2CH_2CH_3$
IV. C_5H_8
V. C_6H_{12}

A. II
B. II and V
C. I and III
D. I, III, IV
E. I, III, V

8. The following structures all have the same molecular formula: C_6H_{14}. Which of these structures represent the same molecule?

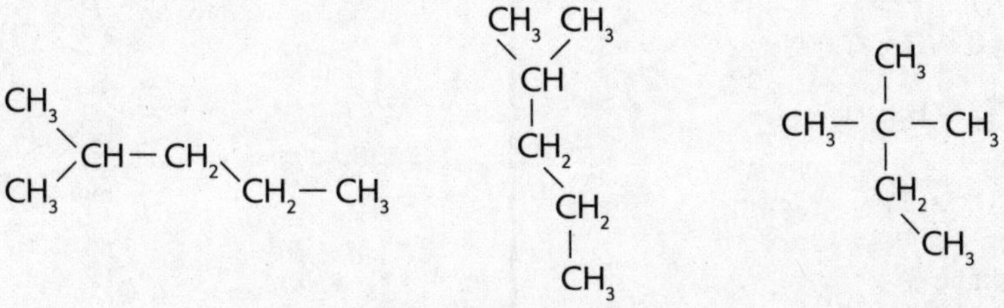

I II III

- **A.** I and II
- **B.** II and III
- **C.** I and III
- **D.** I, II, and III
- **E.** they are all different molecules

9. How many isomers of hexane are there?

- **A.** 0
- **B.** 1
- **C.** 2
- **D.** 3
- **E.** 5

10. The name of the following compound is

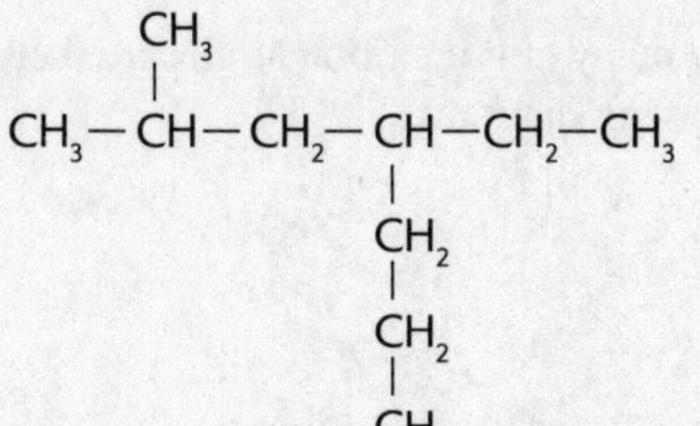

- **A.** decane
- **B.** 4-ethyl-6-methylhexane
- **C.** 2-methyl-4-ethylheptane
- **D.** 4-ethyl-2-methylheptane
- **E.** 6-methyl-4-ethylhexane

11. The name of the following compound

$$CH_2{=}CHCH{=}CH_2$$

is

- **A.** 1, 3-butene
- **B.** 1, 4-butene
- **C.** 1, 3-butadiene
- **D.** *n*-dibutene
- **E.** dibutene

12. The name of the following compound

$$CH_3CH{=}CHCH_2C{\equiv}CH$$

is

- **A.** *n*-hexyne
- **B.** 2-ene-5-hexyne
- **C.** 1-yne-4-hexene
- **D.** 2-ene-5-yne hexyne
- **E.** 4-hexen-1-yne

13. The name of the following compound

$$H-\underset{\underset{H}{|}}{\overset{\overset{H}{|}}{C}}-\underset{\underset{H}{|}}{\overset{\overset{H}{|}}{C}}=\underset{}{\overset{\overset{H}{|}}{C}}-\underset{\underset{H}{|}}{\overset{\overset{H}{|}}{C}}-\underset{\underset{H}{|}}{\overset{\overset{H}{|}}{C}}-N\overset{H}{\underset{H}{}}$$

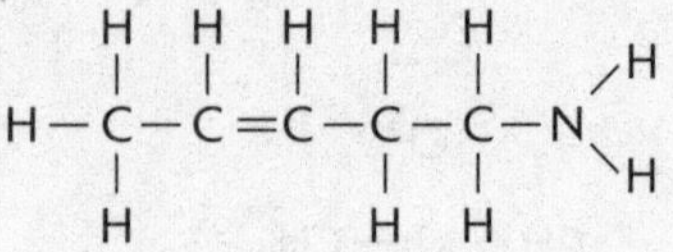

is

A. 5-amino-2-hexane
B. 2-amide-4-hexene
C. 2-amino-4-hexene
D. 5-amino-2-hexene
E. 2-amino-5-hexene

14. The name of the following compound

$$\overset{O}{\overset{||}{CH_3COCH_2CH_3}}$$

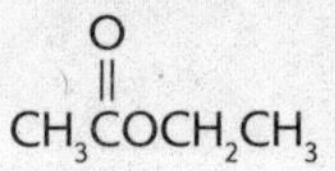

is

A. methyl-ethanoic acid
B. ethyl ethanoate
C. methy-ethyl ether
D. butanol
E. trans-2-ethanoate

15. The name of the following compound

$$CH_3CH_2CO_2H$$

is

A. propyl carbonate
B. ethyl ester
C. propyl ether
D. propionic acid
E. ethanone

16. The name of the following compound

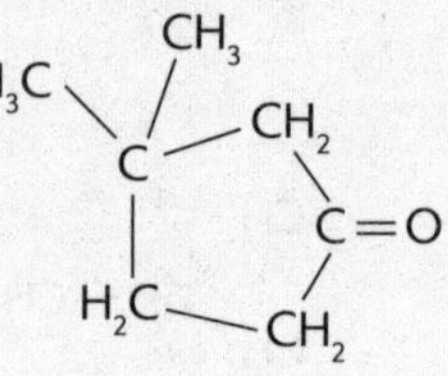

is

A. 3,3-dimethylcyclopentyl ether
B. 3,3-dimethylcyclopentanone
C. 1,1-dimethyl-3-one
D. 1,1-dimethylcyclopentanoic acid
E. 1,1-dimethylcyclopentaldehyde

17. The name of the following compound

$$CH_3CH_2CH_2\overset{\overset{H}{|}}{C}=O$$

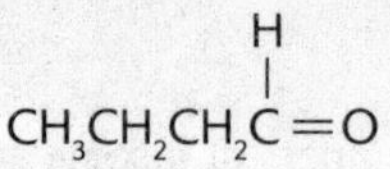

is

A. *n*-butyraldehyde
B. pentanoic acid
C. pentyl ether
D. pentone
E. 1-pentyne-5-one

18. How many chiral carbon atoms are there in the following diagram?

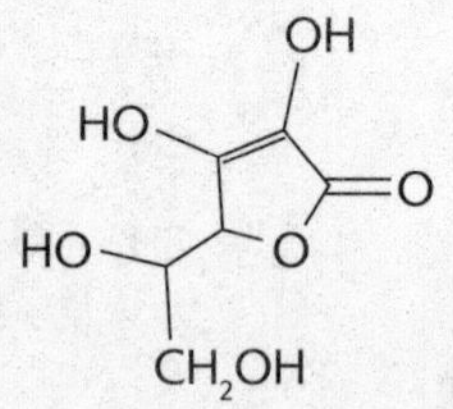

A. 0
B. 1
C. 2
D. 3
E. 4

19. An ester is formed by the reaction between

 A. two acids.

 B. two alcohols.

 C. two aldehydes.

 D. an acid and an alcohol.

 E. an acid and a ketone.

20. When these compounds are arranged in order of increasing boiling point, what is the correct order?

 1. $CH_3CH_2CH_2CH_2CH_3$

 2. $CH_3CH_2CH(CH_3)CH_3$

 3. $CH_3C(CH_3)_2CH_3$

 A. $1 < 2 < 3$

 B. $2 < 1 < 3$

 C. $2 < 3 < 1$

 D. $3 < 2 < 1$

 E. $1 < 3 < 2$

Free-Response Questions

1. Given the following alkyl halide

$$\begin{array}{ccccc} & H & & CH_3 & \\ & | & & | & \\ CH_3 - & C & - & C & - CH_3 \\ & | & & | & \\ & Br & & H & \end{array}$$

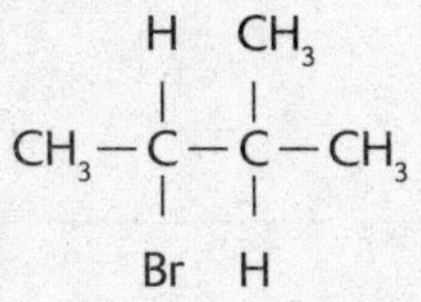

(a) What is the name of the alkyl halide?

(b) What is the name of the alkane from which it is derived?

(c) Draw the structure of the alkene formed when HBr is eliminated from the alkyl halide.

(d) Name the alkene in (c).

(e) Given C_5H_{12}, draw all of the possible structural diagrams and name each.

(f) Draw the structural diagrams and name all of the alkenes isomeric with that given in (d) above.

(g) Draw the structural diagram and name the alcohol that is formed when this alkyl halide undergoes substitution with an OH^- ion.

(h) Draw the structural diagram and name the species that is formed when the species in (g) reacts with formic acid.

(i) How many chiral carbon atoms are there in this alkyl halide? Indicate which carbon(s) are chiral.

2. Pentane, a 5-carbon alkane, also known as amyl hydride, is a liquid mainly used as a fuel or solvent.

(a) Draw the structural diagram and name all isomers of pentane.

(b) Predict the order of increasing boiling point for the isomers and explain your reasoning.

(c) Draw the structural diagram and name each of the following (you may use structural, condensed or Lewis diagrams):

(i) a 5-carbon carboxylic acid

(ii) a 5-carbon ether

(iii) a 5-carbon ester

(iv) a 5-carbon ketone

(v) a 5-carbon aldehyde

(vi) a 5-carbon alcohol

(vii) a 5-carbon ring (cyclic) alkane

Answers and Explanations

Multiple Choice

1. D.

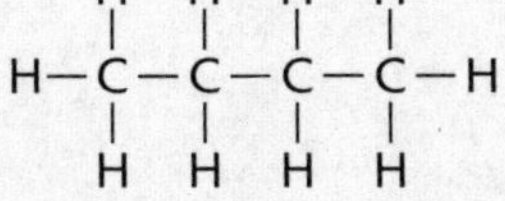

butane

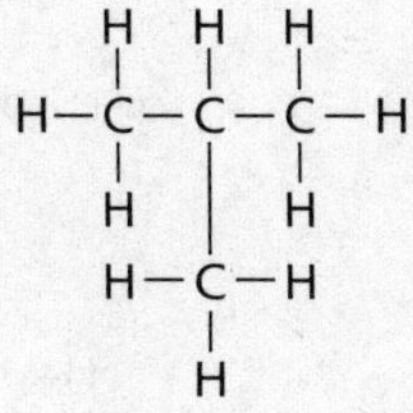

2-methyl propane

2. A.

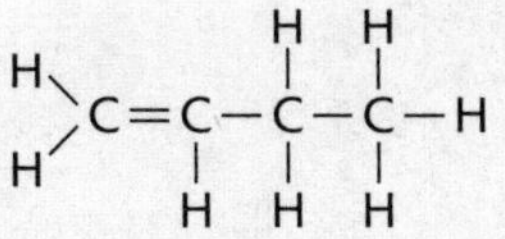

1-butene

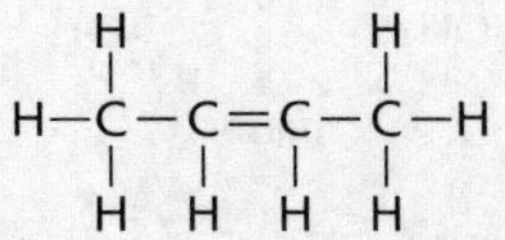

2-butene

3. C.

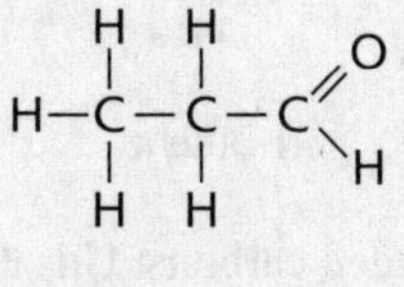

propanal

propanone (acetone)

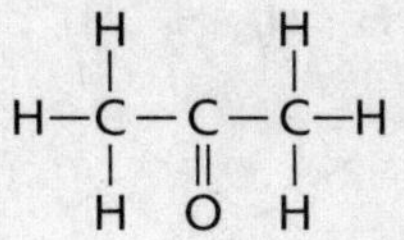

C_3H_6O

Aldehydes and ketones both have the carbonyl group C=O. In ketones this is attached to two carbon atoms; in aldehydes it is attached to 1 or 2 hydrogen atoms.

4. B.

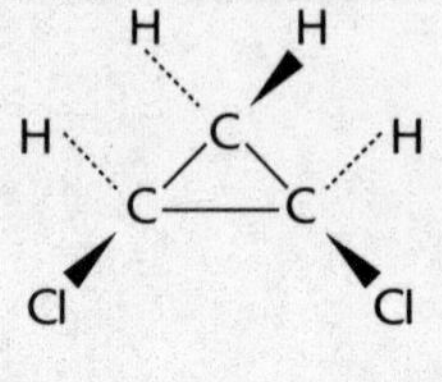

cis-1, 2-dichlorocyclopropane

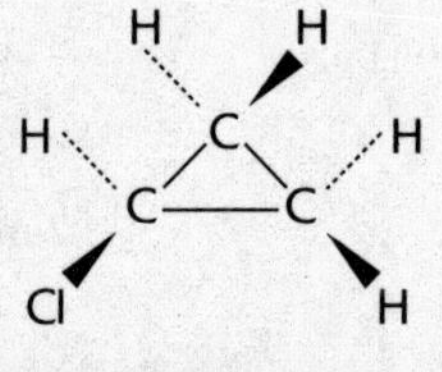

trans-1, 2-dichlorocyclopropane

5. E.

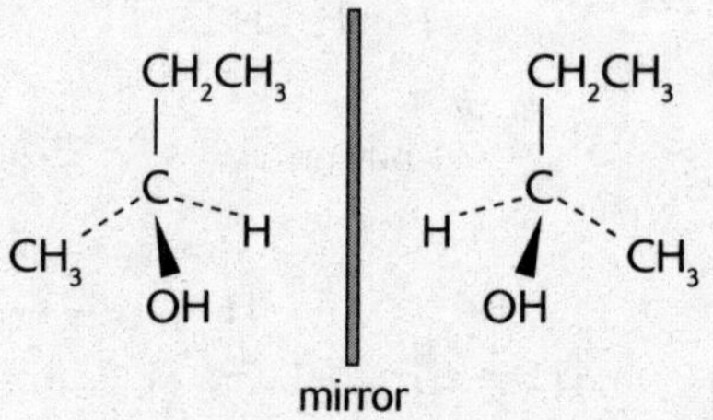

6. E.

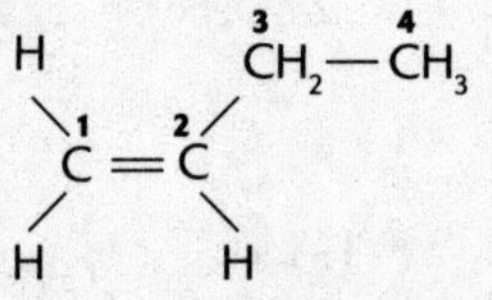

1-butene

7. C. Saturated compounds all have single-bonded carbons. Unsaturated compounds have either double or triple bonds.

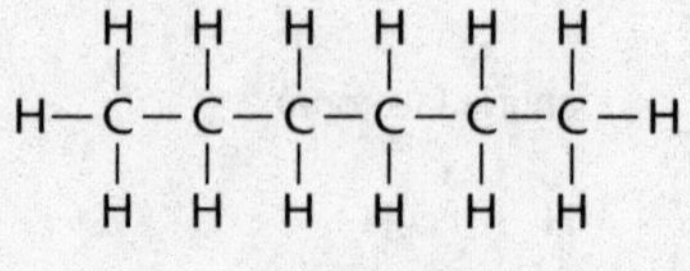

hexane

n-butane

i-butane

8. A. There is no difference between compounds *I* and *II*; they both contain a five-carbon chain with a branch on the second carbon. Compound *III*, on the other hand, contains a four-carbon chain with two branches on the second carbon atom.

9. E. There are five isomers of hexane. There is the straight-chain form.

$$CH_3 — CH_2 — CH_2 — CH_2 — CH_2 — CH_3$$

There are two isomers with a single carbon branch.

$$
\begin{array}{c}
CH_3 \\
| \\
CH_3 — CH — CH_2 — CH_2 — CH_3
\end{array}
$$

$$
\begin{array}{c}
CH_3 \\
| \\
CH_3 — CH_2 — CH — CH_2 — CH_3
\end{array}
$$

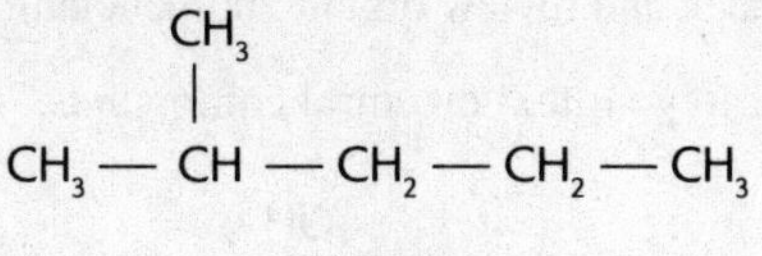

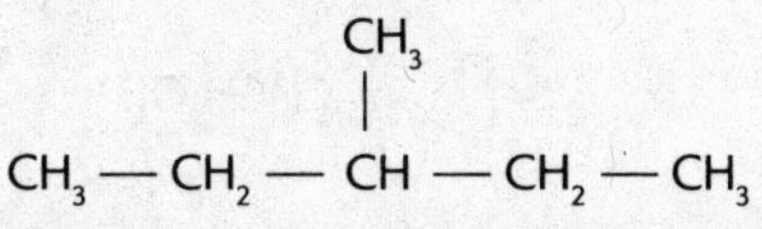

And there are two isomers with two branches.

$$
\begin{array}{cc}
CH_3 & CH_3 \\
| & | \\
CH_3 — CH & — CH — CH_3
\end{array}
$$

$$
\begin{array}{c}
CH_3 \\
| \\
CH_3 — C — CH_2 — CH_3 \\
| \\
CH_3
\end{array}
$$

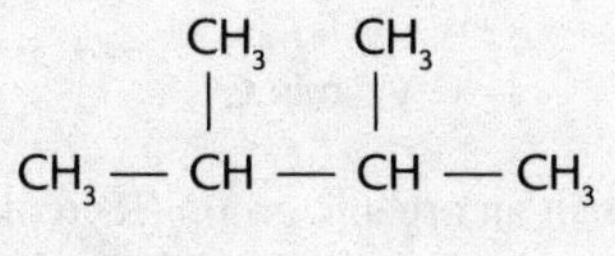

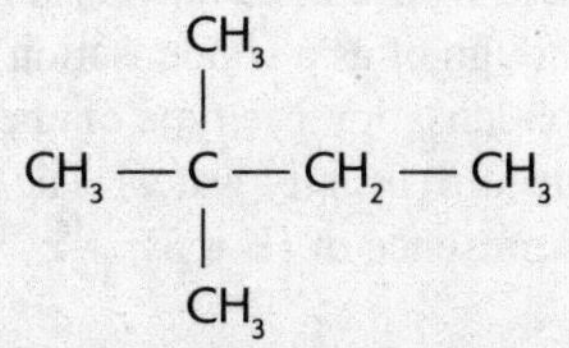

10. D. The longest continuous chain in the skeleton structure of this compound contains seven carbon atoms. It is therefore named as a derivative of heptane.

$$
\begin{array}{c}
^1CH_3 \\
| \\
CH_3 — CH — CH_2 — {}^4CH — CH_2 — CH_3 \\
\ \ \ \ \ _2 \ \ \ \ \ \ _3 \ \ \ \ \ \ \ | \\
_5 CH_2 \\
| \\
_6 CH_2 \\
| \\
_7 CH_3
\end{array}
$$

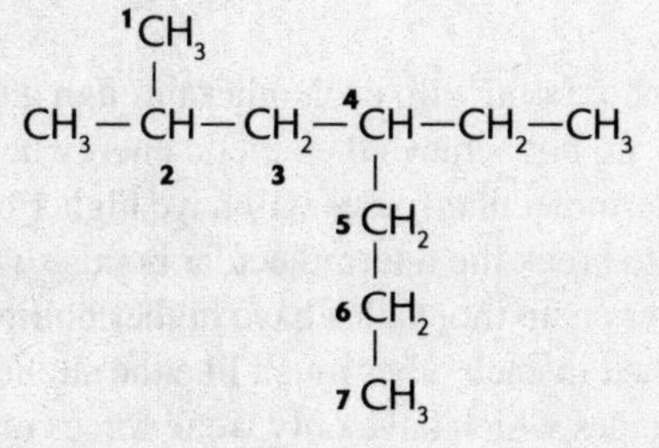

The heptane chain contains two substituents, a methyl group on the second carbon atom and an ethyl group on the fourth carbon atom.

$$
\begin{array}{c}
CH_3 \\
| \\
\boxed{CH_3} — CH — CH_2 — CH — \boxed{CH_2 — CH_3} \\
Methyl \ \ \ \ \ \ \ \ \ \ \ \ \ | \ \ \ \ \ \ \ \ Ethyl \\
CH_2 \\
| \\
CH_2 \\
| \\
CH_3
\end{array}
$$

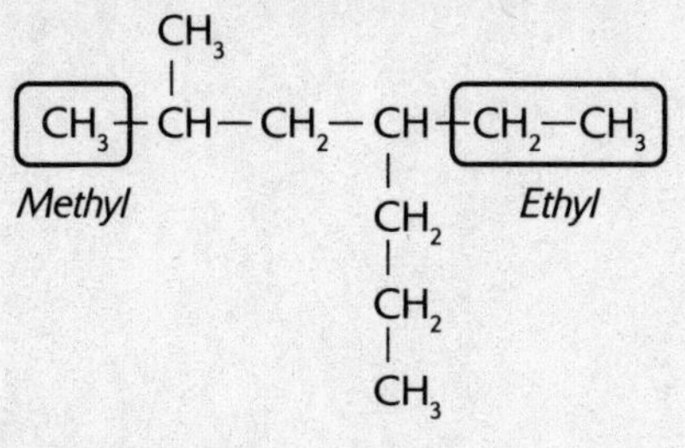

Because the substituents are listed in alphabetical order, the systematic name for this compound is 4-ethyl-2-methylheptane.

11. **C.** If you missed this question, go back and review organic nomenclature of alkenes.

12. **E.** If you missed this question, go back and review organic nomenclature of alkynes.

13. **D.** If you missed this question, go back and review organic nomenclature of amines.

14. **B.** If you missed this question, go back and review organic nomenclature of esters.

15. **D.** If you missed this question, go back and review organic nomenclature of carboxylic acids.

16. **B.** If you missed this question, go back and review organic nomenclature of ketones.

17. **A.** If you missed this question, go back and review organic nomenclature of aldehydes.

18. **B.** If you missed this question, refer to your text on chiral compounds.

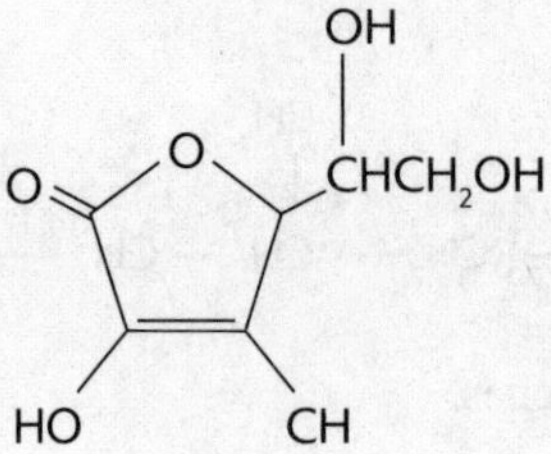

Vitamin C

19. **D.** Esters are organic compounds in which an organic group (R) replaces a hydrogen atom (or more than one) in a hydroxyl group. An oxygen acid is an acid whose molecule has an —OH group from which the hydrogen can dissociate as an H^+ ion. An ester can be though of as a condensation reaction of an acid (usually an organic acid) and an alcohol (or phenol compound). Condensation is a type of chemical reaction in which two molecules are joined together and eliminate a small molecule (usually water). The reaction to produce an ester is called esterification and can be catalyzed by the presence of H^+ ions.

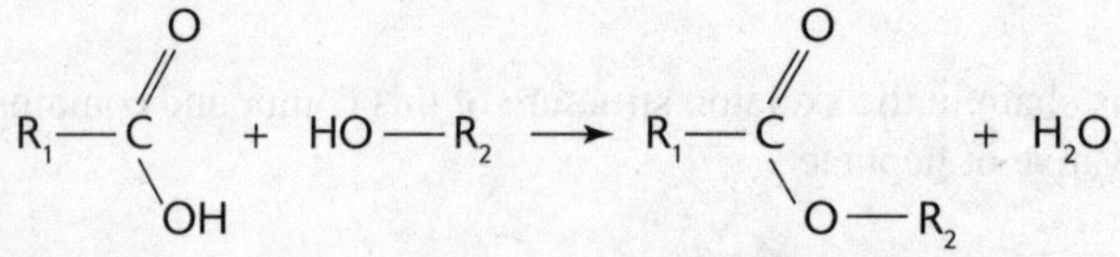

20. **D.** Molecules which strongly interact or bond with each other through a variety of intermolecular forces cannot move easily or rapidly and therefore, do not achieve the kinetic energy necessary to escape the liquid state. Therefore, molecules with strong intermolecular forces will have higher boiling points. This is a consequence of the increased kinetic energy needed to break the intermolecular bonds so that individual molecules may escape the liquid as gases. The reason that longer chain molecules have higher boiling points is that longer chain molecules become wrapped around and enmeshed in each other much like the strands of spaghetti. More energy is needed to separate them than short chain molecules which have only weak forces of attraction for each other.

Free Response

Question 1

Maximum Points for Question 1
Part (a): 1 point
Part (b): 1 point
Part (c): 1 point
Part (d): 1 point
Part (e): 3 points
Part (f): 6 points
Part (g): 2 points
Part (h): 2 points
Part (i): 2 points
Total points: 19

1. Given the following alkyl halide 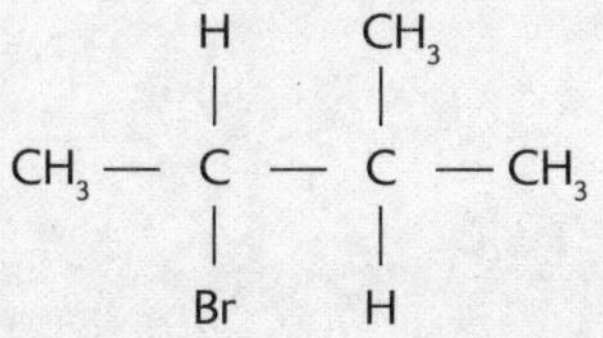 *(a) What is the name of the alkyl halide?* 3-bromo-2-methylbutane	***1 point possible*** *1 point for properly naming the alkyl halide.*
(b) What is the name of the alkane from which it is derived? 2-methylbutane	***1 point possible*** *1 point for properly naming the alkane from which it is derived.*
(c) Draw the structure of the alkene formed when HBr is eliminated from the alkyl halide. 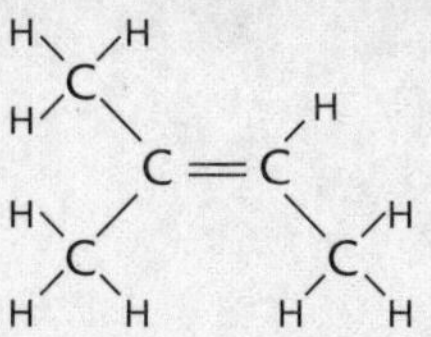	***1 point possible*** *1 point for properly drawing the structure of the alkene formed when HBr is eliminated from the alkyl halide.*
(d) Name the alkene in (c). 2-methyl-2-butene	***1 point possible*** *1 point for naming the alkene in (c).*

(e) Given C_5H_{12}, draw all of the possible structural diagrams and name each. $CH_3 — CH_2 — CH_2 — CH_2 — CH_3$ pentane (*n*-pentane) CH₃ | $CH_3 — CH — CH_2 — CH_3$ methylbutane (isopentane) CH₃ | $CH_3 — C — CH_3$ | CH₃ dimethylpropane (neopentane)	***3 points possible*** *1 point for each proper drawing and labeling each of the alkanes isomeric with that given in (b).*
(f) Draw the structural diagrams and name all of the alkenes isomeric with that given in (d) above. 1-pentene cis-2-pentene trans-2-pentene 2-methyl-1-butene 2-methyl-2-butene	***6 points possible*** *1 point for each drawn structural isomer properly labeled.*

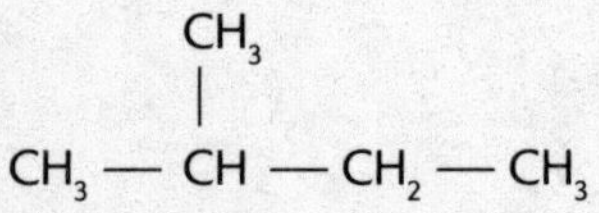

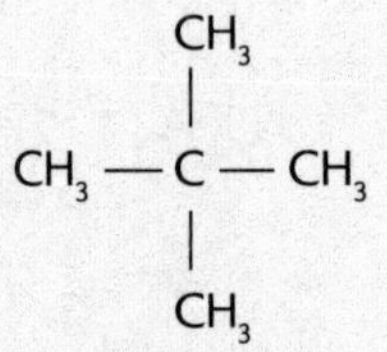

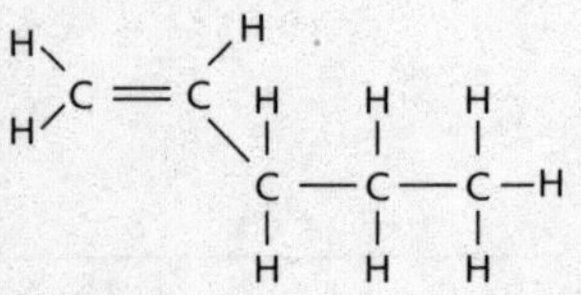

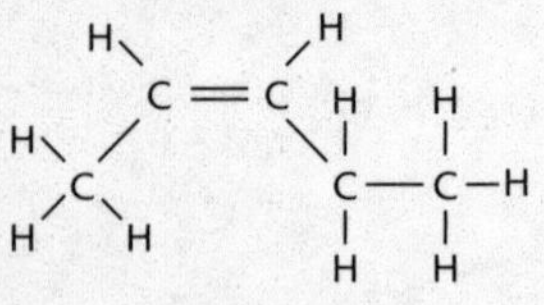

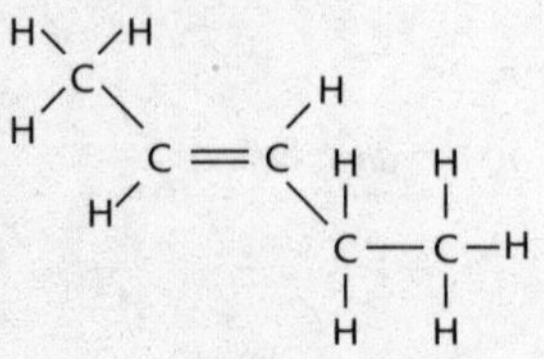

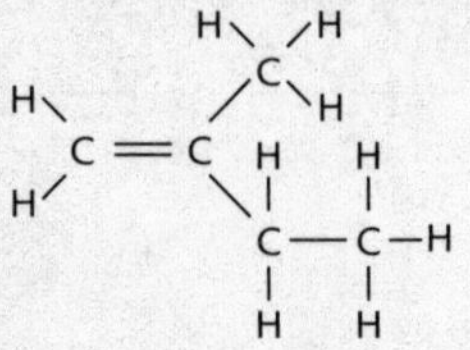

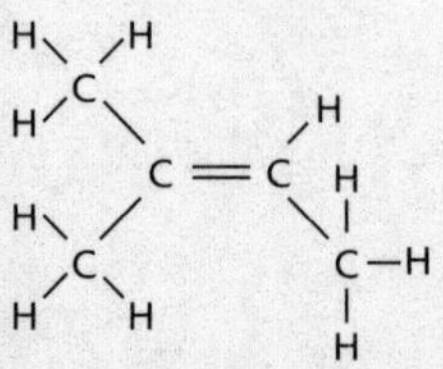

3-methyl-1-butene 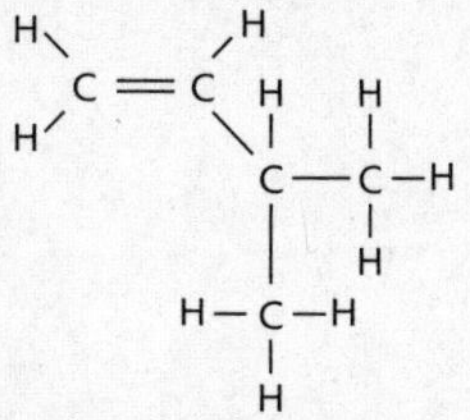	
(g) Draw the structural diagram and label the alcohol that is formed when this alkyl halide undergoes substitution with an OH^- ion. 3-methyl-2-butanonol 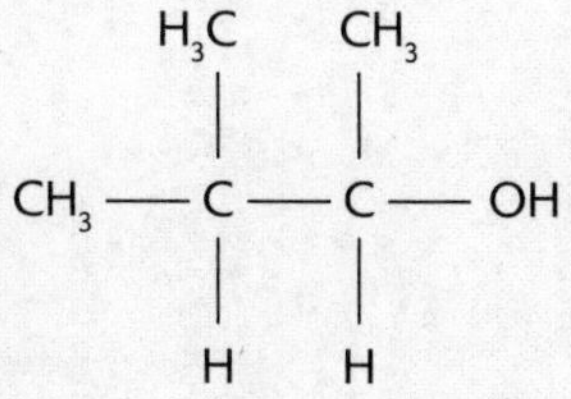	***2 points possible*** *2 points for properly drawing and labeling the alcohol that is formed when this alkyl halide undergoes substitution with an OH^- ion.*
(h) Draw the structural diagram and name the species that is formed when the species in (g) reacts with formic acid. 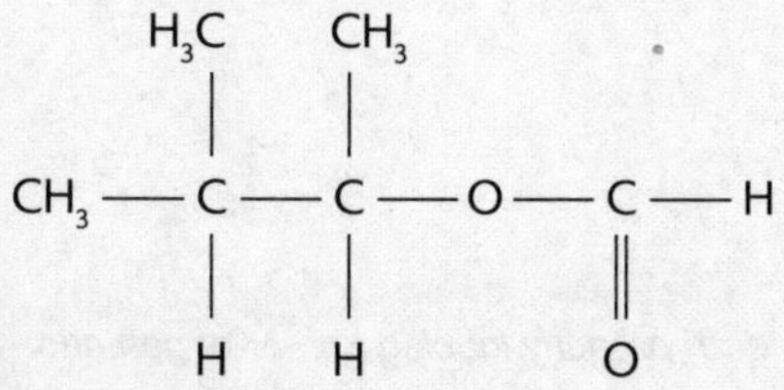 1,2-dimethyl propyl formate	***2 points possible*** *2 points for properly drawing and labeling the species that is formed when the species in (g) reacts with formic acid.*
(i) How many chiral carbon atoms are there in this alkyl halide? Indicate which carbon(s) are chiral. 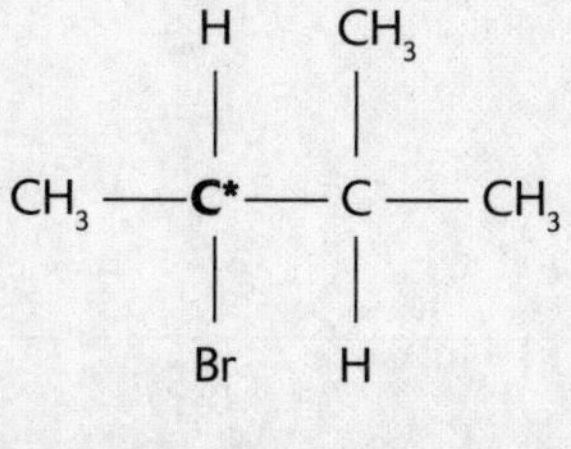 1 chiral carbon*	***2 points possible*** *1 point for correctly determining the number of chiral carbons.* *1 point for correctly identifying the carbon that is chiral.*

Question 2

Maximum Points for Question 2
Part (a): 3 points
Part (b): 2 points
Part (c) (i): 1 point
Part (c) (ii): 1 point
Part (c) (iii): 1 point
Part (c) (iv): 1 point
Part (c) (v): 1 point
Part (c) (vi): 1 point
Part (c) (vii): 1 point
Total points: 12

2. Pentane, a 5-carbon alkane, also known as amyl hydride, is a liquid mainly used as a fuel or solvent. *(a) Draw the structural diagram and name all isomers of pentane.* $CH_3 — CH_2 — CH_2 — CH_2 — CH_3$ pentane (*n*-pentane) 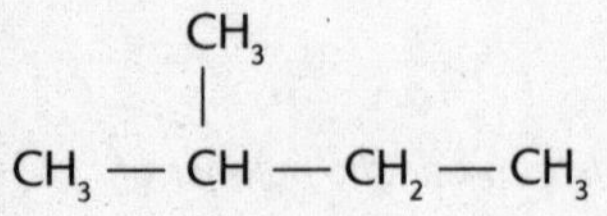 methylbutane (isopentane) 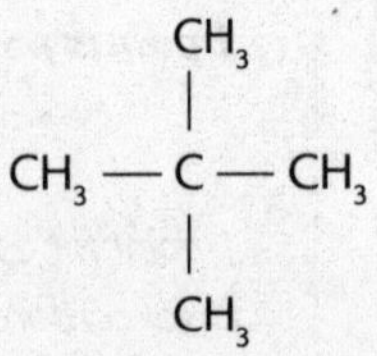 dimethylpropane (neopentane)	***3 points possible*** *1 point for each properly labeled isomer of pentane.*
(b) Predict the order of increasing boiling point for the isomers and explain your reasoning. dimethylpropane < isopentane < *n*-pentane Stronger intermolecular forces develop in long chains. Straight chain isomers have higher boiling points than their more compact branched isomers because there are fewer contacts (lower dispersion forces) in the branched molecule.	***2 points possible*** *1 point for correct order.* *1 point for correct explanation.*

(c) Draw the structural diagram and name each of the following (you may use structural, condensed, or Lewis diagrams): *(i) a 5-carbon carboxylic acid* 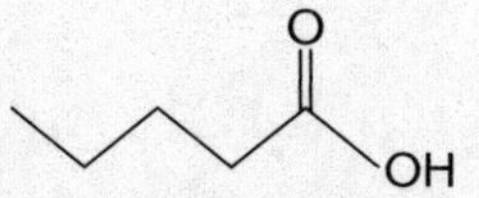 pentanoic acid	***1 point possible*** *1 point for a properly drawn and labeled diagram.*
(ii) a 5-carbon ether $C_3H_7-O-C_2H_5$ ethyl propyl ether	***1 point possible*** *1 point for a properly drawn and labeled diagram.*
(iii) a 5-carbon ester $CH_3-CH_2-C(=O)-O-CH_2-CH_3$ ethyl propanoate	***1 point possible*** *1 point for a properly drawn and labeled diagram.*
(iv) a 5-carbon ketone 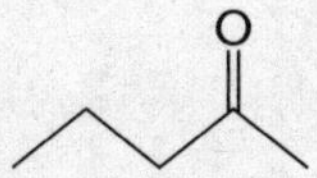 methyl propyl ketone or 2-pentanone or pentan-2-one	***1 point possible*** *1 point for a properly drawn and labeled diagram.*
(v) a 5-carbon aldehyde 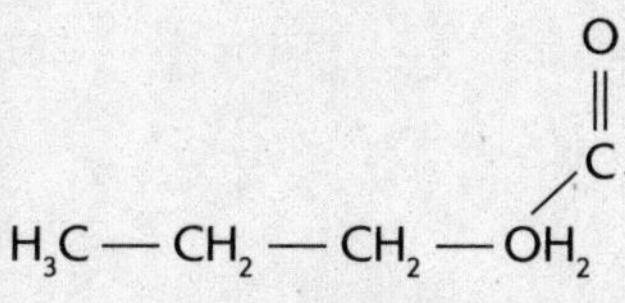 pentanal	***1 point possible*** *1 point for a properly drawn and labeled diagram*
(vi) a 5-carbon alcohol 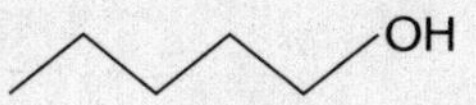 1-pentanol	***1 point possible*** *1 point for a properly drawn and labeled diagram.*

(vii) a 5-carbon ring (cyclic) alkane 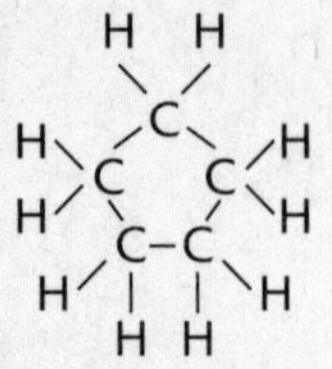 cyclopentane	***1 point possible*** *1 point for a properly drawn and labeled diagram.*

Chemical Reactions

Changes in the 2007 AP Exam will require you to balance the equation and answer some questions regarding the reaction. Please refer to the Practice Exams at the end of this book to see what this new format will look like. We will only focus on writing and predicting reactions in this chapter.

You'll Need to Know

- ❑ solubility rules
- ❑ how to write net ionic reactions
- ❑ how to identify and predict synthesis reactions
- ❑ how to identify and predict decomposition reactions
- ❑ how to identify and predict single displacement reactions
- ❑ how to identify and predict double displacement (metathesis) reactions
- ❑ how to identify and predict combustion reactions
- ❑ how to identify and predict reactions involving
  - ❑ a metallic oxide + water
  - ❑ a nonmetallic oxide + water
  - ❑ a metallic oxide + an acid
  - ❑ a nonmetallic oxide + a base
  - ❑ a metallic oxide + a nonmetallic oxide
  - ❑ an acid + a metal
  - ❑ a base + an amphoteric metal
  - ❑ a strong acid + a salt of a weak acid
  - ❑ a weak acid + a weak base
  - ❑ a weak acid + a strong base
  - ❑ a strong acid + a weak base
  - ❑ an acid + a carbonate
  - ❑ a metallic oxide + a nonmetallic oxide
- ❑ how to identify and predict redox (oxidation-reduction) reactions
- ❑ how to identify and predict the products of a precipitation reaction
- ❑ how to identify and predict reactions involving complex ions
- ❑ how to identify and predict reactions involving a strong acid + a strong base

- ❑ how to identify and predict organic reactions involving:
  - ❑ addition of Br_2 or Cl_2 to an alkene
  - ❑ addition of Br_2 or Cl_2 to an alkyne
  - ❑ addition of H_2 to an alkene
  - ❑ addition of H_2O to an alkene
  - ❑ addition of HX to an alkene or an alkyne
  - ❑ dehydration of an alcohol
  - ❑ halogenation of an aromatic ring
  - ❑ nitration of an aromatic ring
  - ❑ oxidation of a primary alcohol
  - ❑ oxidation of a secondary alcohol
  - ❑ oxidation of an aldehyde
  - ❑ reduction of an aldehyde
  - ❑ esterification
  - ❑ formation of an ether
  - ❑ reduction of a ketone

Solubility Rules

Generally Soluble (MUST be memorized)

Group	*Exceptions*
Alkali metals (Li^+, Na^+, K^+, Rb^+, Cs^+)	none
Ammonium (NH_4^+)	none
Acetates ($C_2H_3O_2^-$)	$AgC_2H_3O_2$
Chlorates (ClO_3^-)	none
Chlorides, bromides, or iodides (Cl^-, Br^-, I^-)	Those containing Ag^+, Hg_2^{2+} or Pb^{2+}. CuCl is not soluble whereas $CuCl_2$ is soluble.
Nitrates (NO_3^-)	none
Perchlorates (ClO_4^-)	none
Sulfates (SO_4^{2-})	Those containing Ag^+, Ca^{2+}, Sr^{2+}, Ba^{2+}, Hg_2^{2+}, or Pb^{2+}

Generally NOT Soluble (MUST be memorized)	
Group	***Exceptions***
Carbonates (CO_3^{2-})	Those containing alkali metals (or ammonium) are soluble.
Chromates (CrO_4^{2-})	Those containing alkali metals (or ammonium) are soluble.
Hydroxides (OH^-)	Those containing alkali metals are soluble and those containing Ca^{2+}, Sr^{2+}, or Ba^{2+} are slightly soluble.
Phosphates (PO_4^{3-})	Those containing alkali metals (or ammonium) are soluble.
Sulfides (S^{2-})	Those containing alkali metals, alkaline earth metals, and ammonium are soluble.
Sulfites (SO_3^{2-})	Those containing alkali metals (or ammonium) are soluble.

Writing Net Ionic Reactions

Net ionic equations are useful in that they show only those chemical species participating in a chemical reaction. The key to being able to write net ionic equations is the ability to recognize monatomic and polyatomic ions, and the solubility rules. If you are weak in these areas, a review of these concepts would be helpful before attempting to write net ionic equations. First start with a complete chemical equation and see how the net ionic equation is derived. Take for example the reaction of lead(II) nitrate with hydrochloric acid to form lead(II) chloride and nitric acid, shown below:

$$Pb(NO_3)_{2(aq)} + 2HCl_{(aq)} \rightarrow PbCl_{2(s)} + 2HNO_{3(aq)}$$

This complete equation may be rewritten in ionic form by using the solubility rules, and by recognizing strong acids. All nitrates are soluble, therefore the lead(II) nitrate will be dissociated. Both hydrochloric acid and nitric acid are strong acids and will therefore also be dissociated. The lead(II) chloride, however is insoluble—all halides are soluble except silver, lead(II), copper(I), and mercury(I). The above equation written in dissociated form is:

$$Pb^{2+}{}_{(aq)} + 2NO_3^-{}_{(aq)} + 2H^+{}_{(aq)} + 2Cl^-{}_{(aq)} \rightarrow PbCl_{2(s)} + 2H^+{}_{(aq)} + 2NO_3^-{}_{(aq)}$$

At this point, you may cancel out those ions which have not participated in the reaction. *Notice how the nitrate ions and hydrogen ions remain unchanged on both sides of the reaction.*

$$Pb^{2+}{}_{(aq)} + \cancel{2NO_3^-}{}_{(aq)} + \cancel{2H^+}{}_{(aq)} + 2Cl^-{}_{(aq)} \rightarrow PbCl_{2(s)} + \cancel{2H^+}{}_{(aq)} + \cancel{2NO_3^-}{}_{(aq)}$$

What remains is the net ionic equation, showing only those chemical species participating in a chemical process. For the AP Exam, DO NOT include (*aq*), (*s*), (*g*), etc.

$$Pb^{2+} + 2Cl^- \rightarrow PbCl_2$$

Spectator ions are usually Group I and II cations (unless they form a precipitate) and anions of strong acids such as Br^-, Cl^-, ClO_4^-, I^-, and NO_3^-.

A "salt" (*as used in this book*) is any of a class of compounds formed by the replacement of one or more hydrogen atoms of an acid with elements or groups, which are composed of anions and cations, and which usually ionize in solution and is a product formed by the neutralization of an acid by a base.

Refer to the Appendix for the list of common polyatomic ions and the list of common strong and weak acids and bases.

I. Synthesis (A + B → AB): two or more substances react together to form a single compound

Examples

metal + nonmetal → binary ionic compound

Solid potassium is added to a flask of oxygen gas.

$K + O_2 \rightarrow KO_2$

---

metallic oxide + carbon dioxide → metallic carbonate

Finely powdered magnesium oxide is added to a container filled with carbon dioxide gas.

$MgO + CO_2 \rightarrow MgCO_3$

---

concentrated ammonia + metal ion → amine complex ion

A concentrated solution of ammonia is added to a solution of zinc iodide.

$Zn^{2+} + NH_3 \rightarrow [Zn(NH_3)_4]^{2+}$ or $Zn^{2+} + NH_3 + H_2O \rightarrow Zn(OH)_2 + NH_4^+$

---

electron pair donor + electron pair acceptor → complex ion

Sodium iodide is mixed with cadmium(II) nitrate.

I^- *(Lewis base-electron pair donor)* + Cd^{2+} *(Lewis acid-electron pair acceptor)* → CdI_4^{2-}

---

alkene + hydrogen → alkane

Under high pressure and in the presence of a catalyst, hydrogen gas is added to ethene gas.

$H_2 + CH_2{=}CH_2 \rightarrow CH_3\text{-}CH_3$

---

metal ion + hydroxide ion → hydroxo complex ion

A 6*M* solution of potassium hydroxide is added to a 6*M* solution of aluminum nitrate.

$Al^{3+} + OH^- \rightarrow [Al(OH)_4]^-$

metal oxide + sulfur dioxide → metallic sulfites

Solid calcium oxide is heated in an atmosphere of sulfur dioxide gas.

$CaO + SO_2 \rightarrow CaSO_3$

nonmetallic oxide + water → acid

Carbon dioxide gas is bubbled through water.

$CO_2 + H_2O \rightarrow H_2CO_3$

soluble metallic oxide + water → base

Barium oxide is dissolved in hot distilled water.

$BaO + H_2O \rightarrow Ba^{2+} + OH^-$

Quick Quiz #1

Directions: Please write the chemical equations for each statement below.

1. Hot steam is mixed with propene gas.

2. A sample of pure 2-butene gas is heated in the presence of hydrogen chloride gas.

3. Excess bromine gas is added to pure acetylene.

4. Ethene (ethylene) gas is bubbled through a solution of chlorine.

5. Fine pieces of aluminum are heated in bromine gas.

See end of chapter for answers.

II. Decomposition (AB → A + B): a compound breaks apart into two or more substances

Examples

metallic chlorates → metallic chloride + oxygen

Manganese dioxide (acting as a catalyst) is added to a solid sample of potassium chlorate and the mixture is then heated.

$KClO_3 \xrightarrow{MnO_2} KCl + O_2$

metallic carbonates → metallic oxides + carbon dioxide

A sample of calcium carbonate is heated.

$CaCO_3 \rightarrow CaO + CO_2$

binary ionic compounds $\xrightarrow{electrolysis}$ metal + nonmetal

A solution of copper(II) nitrate is electrolyzed using inert electrodes.

$Cu^{2+} + H_2O \rightarrow Cu + O_2 + H^+$

ammonium carbonate → ammonia + water + carbon dioxide

Solid ammonium carbonate is heated.

$(NH_4)_2CO_3 \rightarrow NH_3 + CO_2 + H_2O$

---

oxyacid → nonmetallic oxide + water

A dilute solution of carbonic acid is heated.

$H_2CO_3 \rightarrow CO_2 + H_2O$

---

hydrogen peroxide → water + oxygen

Hydrogen peroxide is gently warmed.

$H_2O_2 \rightarrow H_2O + O_2$

---

metallic hydroxides → metallic oxide + water vapor

The Group 1 metal hydroxides do not readily decompose on heating, except for lithium hydroxide which forms lithium oxide and water vapor: $LiOH_{(s)} \rightarrow Li_2O_{(s)} + H_2O_{(g)}$. Alkali metal hydroxides are white solids that dissolve in water to give an alkaline solution. Upon heating Group II metal hydroxides including lead, aluminum—and transition metal hydroxides—these decompose to form the metal oxide and water vapor.

Aluminum hydroxide is strongly heated.

$Al(OH)_3 \rightarrow Al_2O_3 + H_2O$

---

nitrate salt (Group I metals) → nitrite salt + oxygen gas

The Group 1 metal nitrates decompose to form the nitrite salt and oxygen gas. They are white soluble solids giving neutral solutions: $MNO_3 \rightarrow MNO_2 + O_2$ where M = Na or K.

Potassium nitrate is strongly heated.

$KNO_3 \rightarrow KNO_2 + O_2$

---

nitrate salt (Group II metals) → metallic oxide + NO_2 + O_2

The Group II, lead, aluminum, and transition metal nitrates decompose to form the metal oxide, nitrogen dioxide gas, and oxygen gas when strongly heated. These are all water soluble neutral salts:

$M(NO_3)_2 \rightarrow MO_{(s)} + NO_{2(g)} + O_{2(g)}$, where M = Mg, Ca, or Zn.

Calcium nitrate is strongly heated.

$Ca(NO_3)_2 \rightarrow CaO + NO_2 + O_2$

---

hydrate → anhydride + water

Copper(II) sulfate pentahydrate is heated.

$CuSO_4 \cdot 5H_2O \rightarrow CuSO_4 + 5H_2O$

---

metallic oxide → metal + oxygen

Solid mercury(II) oxide is strongly heated.

$HgO \rightarrow Hg + O_2$

Quick Quiz #2

Directions: Please write the chemical equations for each statement below.

1. Iron(III) hydroxide is strongly heated.

____

2. Nitrous acid decomposes.

____

3. A solution of sodium iodide is electrolyzed using inert electrodes.

____

III. Single Displacement ($A + BX \rightarrow AX + B$)

Examples

active free halogens replace less active halide ions → halogen + halide ion

Activity series for the halogens: $F_2 > Cl_2 > Br_2 > I_2$

Chlorine gas is bubbled through a strong solution of potassium bromide.

$Cl_2 + Br^- \rightarrow Cl^- + Br_2$

(This is a Redox reaction. The original reaction would have looked like $Cl_2 + KBr \rightarrow KCl + Br_2$*. However, you MUST write the reaction as a net-ionic—and not include spectator ions.)*

---

active free metals replace hydrogen in acids → metallic ion + hydrogen gas

Calcium metal is dropped into a dilute solution of hydrochloric acid.

$Ca + H^+ \rightarrow Ca^{2+} + H_2$

---

active free metals replace hydrogen in water → metallic hydroxide + hydrogen gas

A small pellet of calcium metal is added to warm water.

$Ca + H_2O \rightarrow Ca^{2+} + OH^- + H_2$

---

active free metals replace less active metals → metal + metal ion

Activity series for free metals arranged in order of the metal's ability to displace hydrogen from an acid or water; i.e., in order of most active to least active: Li > K > Ba > Sr > Ca > Na > Mg > Al > Mn > Zn > Fe > Cd > Co > Ni > Sn > Pb > H > Cu > Ag > Hg > Au

Aluminum shot is added to a 6*M* silver nitrate solution.

$Al + Ag^+ \rightarrow Al^{3+} + Ag$

Quick Quiz #3

Directions: Please write the chemical equations for each statement below.

1. Powdered lead is added to a warm solution of copper(II) sulfate.

2. Strontium turnings are added to a 4*M* sulfuric acid solution.

IV. Double Displacement (metathesis) (AX + BY → AY + BX)

Examples

two soluble ions → precipitate

Equimolar solutions of sodium iodide and lead nitrate are mixed.

$I^- + Pb^{2+} \rightarrow PbI_2$

metal sulfide + acid → salt + hydrogen sulfide

Aqueous potassium sulfide is allowed to react with nitric acid.

$S^{2-} + H^+ \rightarrow H_2S$ *(Remember: K^+ and NO_3^- are spectator ions.)*

metallic carbonate + acid → salt + carbon dioxide + water

Small chunks of calcium carbonate are dropped into sulfuric acid.

$CaCO_3 + H^+ + HSO_4^- \rightarrow CaSO_4 + CO_2 + H_2O$

metallic sulfite + acid → salt + sulfur dioxide + water

A solution of sodium sulfite is mixed with hydrobromic acid.

$SO_3^{2-} + H^+ \rightarrow SO_2 + H_2O$ *(Remember: Na^+ and Br^- are spectator ions.)*

---

ammonium salt heated in presence of soluble strong hydroxide → salt + ammonia + water

Ammonium sulfate is added to a 6*M* sodium hydroxide solution and then heated.

$(NH_4)_2SO_4 + OH^- \rightarrow SO_4^{2-} + NH_3 + H_2O$

---

acid + base → salt + water

50 mL of 6*M* sulfuric acid is added to 50 mL of 6*M* sodium hydroxide.

$H^+ + OH^- \rightarrow H_2O$

---

salt (produced from strong acid + weak base) + water → strong acid + weak base

An aqueous solution of manganese(II) sulfate is undergoing hydrolysis.

$Mn^{2+} + SO_4^{2-} + H_2O \rightarrow Mn(OH)_2 + H^+ + HSO_4^-$

---

salt (produced from weak acid + strong base) + water → weak acid + strong base

Solid sodium cyanide is added to distilled water.

$NaCN + H_2O \rightarrow HCN + Na^+ + OH^-$

Quick Quiz #4

Directions: Please write the chemical equations for each statement below.

1. A dilute solution of acetic acid is added to pieces of solid magnesium carbonate.

2. Equimolar solutions of ammonium sulfate and sodium hydroxide are mixed.

3. A 0.4*M* barium nitrate solution is added to an alkaline 0.4*M* potassium chromate solution.

4. A 9*M* solution of hydrochloric acid is added to small pieces of manganese(II) sulfide.

5. Magnesium nitride is added to water.

V. Combustion: Substance + Oxygen → Oxides of Elements

Combustion is the reaction of a substance with oxygen. The usual products are the oxides of the elements present in the original substances in their higher valence state. When N, Cl, Br, or I are present in the original compound, they are usually released as free elements, not the oxides (compounds containing carbon, hydrogen, and oxygen burn in oxygen to produce carbon dioxide and water). If sulfur is present, SO_2 is formed. If nitrogen is present, NO_2 is formed.

Examples

Solid copper(II) sulfide is heated strongly in oxygen gas.

$CuS + O_2 \rightarrow CuO + SO_2$ or $Cu_2O + SO_2$

Carbon disulfide gas is burned in excess oxygen gas.

$CS_2 + O_2 \rightarrow CO_2 + SO_2$

Methanol is burned completely in air.

$CH_3OH + O_2 \rightarrow CO_2 + H_2O$

All alcohols (as well as hydrocarbons and carbohydrates) burn in oxygen gas to produce CO_2 and H_2O. "Air" usually means oxygen gas.

Silane is combusted in a stream of oxygen gas.

$SiH_4 + O_2 \rightarrow SiO_2 + H_2O$

Hot iron filings are exposed to pure oxygen gas.

$Fe + O_2 \rightarrow Fe_2O_3$ *(Note that iron is in its higher valence state, +3.)*

Quick Quiz #5

Directions: Please write the chemical equations for each statement below.

1. Magnesium nitride is burned in oxygen gas.

____

2. Ammonia and oxygen gases are heated in the presence of a platinum catalyst.

____

3. A piece of sodium is ignited in air.

____

4. Diborane gas (B_2H_6) is burned in excess oxygen.

____

VI. Metallic Oxide + $H_2O \rightarrow$ Base (metallic hydroxide)

A metallic oxide is often referred to as a basic oxide because when it dissolves in water it will react to form a base. Metallic oxides are also known as basic anhydrides.

Examples

Lithium oxide is added to water.

$Li_2O + H_2O \rightarrow Li^+ + OH^-$

Calcium oxide is added to water.

$CaO + H_2O \rightarrow Ca(OH)_2$ *(Calcium hydroxide is only slightly soluble.)*

Quick Quiz #6

Directions: Please write the chemical equations for each statement below.

1. A solid piece of potassium oxide is dropped into cold water.

2. Sodium oxide is added to water.

VII. Nonmetallic Oxide + $H_2O \rightarrow$ Acid

A nonmetallic oxide is often called an acidic oxide because when it dissolves in water it will react to form an acid. Nonmetallic oxides are sometimes called acid anhydrides.

Examples

Dinitrogen pentoxide is added to water.

$N_2O_5 + H_2O \rightarrow H^+ + NO_3^-$

Carbon dioxide gas is bubbled through water.

$CO_2 + H_2O \rightarrow H_2CO_3$ *(Carbonic acid is a weak acid so do NOT write it as $H^+ + HCO_3^-$.)*

Sulfur trioxide gas is bubbled through water.

$SO_3 + H_2O \rightarrow H^+ + HSO_4^-$ (or $H^+ + SO_4^{2-}$)

Phosphorus(V) oxytrichloride is added to water.

$POCl_3 + H_2O \rightarrow H^+ + H_3PO_4 + Cl^-$

Quick Quiz #7

Directions: Please write the chemical equations for each statement below.

1. Solid phosphorus(V) oxide is mixed with distilled water.

2. Sulfur dioxide gas is bubbled through water.

VIII. Metallic Oxide + Acid → Metal Ion + H_2O

Examples

Ferric oxide is added to hydrochloric acid.

$Fe_2O_3 + H^+ \rightarrow Fe^{3+} + H_2O$

Copper(II) oxide is added to nitric acid.

$CuO + H^+ \rightarrow Cu^{2+} + H_2O$

Quick Quiz #8

Directions: Please write the chemical equations for each statement below.

1. Solid copper(II) oxide is dropped into sulfuric acid.

____

2. Chunks of magnesium oxide are dropped into hydrochloric acid.

____

IX. Nonmetallic Oxide (acidic anhydride) + Base → Salt + Water

Examples

Carbon dioxide gas is bubbled through a solution of sodium hydroxide.

$CO_2 + OH^- \rightarrow CO_3^{2-} + H_2O$

(Na_2CO_3 would be the salt; however, Na^+ is a spectator ion.)

Sulfur dioxide gas is bubbled through a solution of lithium hydroxide.

$SO_2 + OH^- \rightarrow SO_3^{2-}$ (or HSO_3^-) $+ H_2O$

(Li_2SO_3 would be the salt; however, Li^+ is a spectator ion.)

Quick Quiz #9

Directions: Please write the chemical equations for each statement below.

1. Carbon dioxide gas is bubbled through a solution of lye.

2. Dinitrogen pentoxide gas is bubbled through a solution of concentrated ammonia.

X. Metallic Oxide + Nonmetallic Oxide → Complex (non-binary) Salt

Examples

Magnesium oxide is heated in carbon dioxide gas.

$MgO + CO_2 \rightarrow MgCO_3$

Calcium oxide is heated in an environment of sulfur trioxide gas.

$CaO + SO_3 \rightarrow CaSO_4$

Quick Quiz #10

Directions: Please write the chemical equations for each statement below.

1. Carbon dioxide gas is passed over hot, solid sodium oxide.

2. Potassium oxide is heated in an atmosphere of sulfur trioxide.

XI. Acid + Metal → Salt + Hydrogen Gas

Examples

Sulfuric acid is added to a solid strip of zinc.

$H^+ + Zn \rightarrow H_2 + Zn^{2+}$ *(SO_4^{2-} is a spectator ion.)*

A piece of magnesium is dropped into a beaker of 6*M* hydrochloric acid.

$Mg + H^+ \rightarrow Mg^{2+} + H_2$ *(Cl^- is a spectator ion.)*

Solid copper shavings are added to a concentrated nitric acid solution.

$Cu + H^+ + NO_3^- \rightarrow Cu^{2+} + H_2O + NO_2$

(Nitric acid is an oxidizing agent. It oxidized Cu° to Cu^{2+}. The N atom was reduced from +5 to +4.)

Quick Quiz #11

Directions: Please write the chemical equations for each statement below.

1. Calcium metal is added to a solution of 4*M* HCl.

2. Lead shot is dropped into hot, concentrated sulfuric acid.

XII. Base + Amphoteric Metal → Complex Ion (containing oxygen) + Hydrogen Gas

Amphoteric metals (such as Al, Zn, Pb, and Hg) have properties that may be intermediate between those of metals and those of nonmetals. They will react with a base to form a complex ion with oxygen. *This is a rare problem.*

Examples

A piece of solid aluminum is added to a 6*M* solution of sodium hydroxide.

$Al + OH^- \rightarrow AlO_3^{3-}$ *[or Al(OH)$_4$]$^-$* $+ H_2$ *(Na$^+$ is a spectator ion.)*

A solid piece of zinc is added to a 6*M* solution of potassium hydroxide.

$Zn + OH^- \rightarrow ZnO_2^{2-} + H_2$ *(K$^+$ is a spectator ion.)*

Quick Quiz #12

Directions: Please write the chemical equations for each statement below.

1. Silicon is allowed to react with sodium hydroxide.

2. Pieces of tin are dropped into a hot potassium hydroxide solution.

XIII. Strong Acid + Salt of a Weak Acid → Salt of Strong Acid + Weak Acid

Examples

Hydrochloric acid is added to potassium acetate.

$H^+ + C_2H_3O_2^- \rightarrow HC_2H_3O_2$

(K$^+$ and Cl$^-$ are spectator ions. You may see the acetate ion sometimes written as Ac$^-$.)

A 9*M* nitric acid solution is added to a solution of potassium carbonate.

$H^+ + CO_3^{2-} \rightarrow H_2CO_3$ *(K^+ and NO_3^- are spectator ions.)*

Quick Quiz #13

Directions: Please write the chemical equations for each statement below.

1. Sulfuric acid is added to a solution of sodium nitrite.

2. Perchloric acid is added to a solution of ammonium oxalate.

XIV. Weak Acid + Weak Base → Conjugate Base + Conjugate Acid

Examples

A solution of ammonia is mixed with an equimolar solution of hydrofluoric acid.

$NH_3 + HF \rightarrow NH_4^+ + F^-$

Acetic acid is added to a solution of ammonia.

$HC_2H_3O_2 + NH_3 \rightarrow CH_3COO^- + NH_4^+$

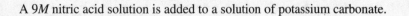

Quick Quiz #14

Directions: Please write the chemical equations for each statement below.

1. Sulfurous acid is added to a solution of the weak base hydrazine (N_2H_4).

XV. Weak Acid + Strong Base → Water + Conjugate Base

Examples

Hydrofluoric acid is added to a solution of sodium hydroxide.

$HF + OH^- \rightarrow H_2O + F^-$

A solution of vinegar (acetic acid) is titrated with lye (sodium hydroxide).

$HC_2H_3O_2 + OH^- \rightarrow H_2O + C_2H_3O_2^-$

Nitrous acid is added to sodium hydroxide.

$HNO_2 + OH^- \rightarrow H_2O + NO_2^-$

Hydrogen sulfide gas is bubbled through a solution of potassium hydroxide.

$H_2S + OH^- \rightarrow S^{2-}$ (or HS^-) $+ H_2O$

Quick Quiz #15

Directions: Please write the chemical equations for each statement below.

1. Excess potassium hydroxide solution is added to a solution of potassium dihydrogen phosphate.

2. 3*M* sodium hydroxide is added to a solution of oxalic acid.

3. Equal volumes of equimolar solutions of phosphoric acid and potassium hydroxide are mixed.

XVI. Strong Acid + Weak Base → Conjugate Acid

Examples

Hydrochloric acid is added to a solution of ammonia.

$H^+ + NH_3 \rightarrow NH_4^+$

Sulfuric acid is added to a solution of sodium fluoride.

$H^+ + F^- \rightarrow HF$

Hydrochloric acid is added to sodium carbonate.

$H^+ + CO_3^{2-} \rightarrow HCO_3^-$ or H_2CO_3 or $CO_2 + H_2O$

Sodium acetate is added to a weak solution of nitric acid.

$H^+ + C_2H_3O_2^- \rightarrow HC_2H_3O_2$

Quick Quiz #16

Directions: Please write the chemical equations for each statement below.

1. Equal volumes of equimolar solutions of disodium hydrogen phosphate and hydrochloric acid are mixed.

2. Hydrobromic acid is mixed with ammonia.

XVII. Acid + Carbonate → Salt + CO_2 + Water

Examples

Hydrochloric acid is added to a sodium carbonate solution.

$H^+ + CO_3^{2-} \rightarrow CO_2 + H_2O$ (or H_2CO_3 or HCO_3^-)

Hydroiodic acid is mixed with solid calcium carbonate.

$H^+ + CaCO_3 \rightarrow Ca^{2+} + CO_2 + H_2O$

Quick Quiz #17

Directions: Please write the chemical equations for each statement below.

1. Dilute hydrochloric acid is added to a solution of potassium carbonate.

2. A strong acetic acid solution is added to a beaker containing solid magnesium carbonate.

XVIII. Metallic Oxide + Nonmetallic Oxide (acidic anhydride + basic anhydride) → Salt

Examples

Sulfur trioxide gas is heated in the presence of sodium oxide.

$SO_3 + Na_2O \rightarrow Na_2SO_4$

Carbon dioxide gas is heated in the presence of powdered magnesium oxide.

$CO_2 + MgO \rightarrow MgCO_3$

Sulfur dioxide gas is passed over solid calcium oxide.

$SO_2 + CaO \rightarrow CaSO_3$

Quick Quiz #18

Directions: Please write the chemical equations for each statement below.

1. Solid calcium oxide is heated in the presence of sulfur trioxide gas.

2. Barium oxide is heated in the presence of carbon dioxide gas.

XIX. Redox

Oxidation–reduction (redox) reactions are characterized by changes in oxidation numbers. However, it is often possible to notice that oxidation numbers are changing without actually calculating them. Some clues that redox is occurring are the following:

(a) An element is uncombined (with any different element) on one side of the reaction and combined on the other.

(b) The number of oxygens or hydrogens associated with element changes.

(c) The charge on the element changes.

Common Oxidizing Agents	***Formula***	***Reduced to***
dichromate/chromate	$Cr_2O_7^{2-}$, CrO_4^{2-}	Cr^{3+} (with acid); $Cr(OH)_3$ (with base)
hydrogen peroxide	H_2O_2	H_2O
iodate	IO_3^-	I^-
iron(III)	Fe^{3+}	Fe^{2+}
chlorine/fluorine	Cl_2/F_2	Cl^-/F^-
nitrate	NO_3^-	NO_2 (with concentrated acid); NO with dilute acid)
oxygen	O_2	H_2O or OH^-
permanganate	MnO_4^-	Mn^{2+} (with acid); MnO_2 (with base)
sulfate	SO_4^{2-}	SO_2 (with acid); H_2S (with hot, concentrated acid)
tin(IV)	Sn^{4+}	Sn^{2+}

Common Reducing Agents	***Formula***	***Oxidized to***
hydrogen gas	H_2	H^+
hydrogen peroxide	H_2O_2	O_2
iodide	I^-	I_2
metal	M^0	M^+
oxalic acid	$H_2C_2O_4$	CO_2
sulfite (in acid solution, sulfites produce sulfur dioxide and water; i.e., $SO_3^{2-} + H^+ \rightarrow SO_2 + H_2O$; no change in oxidation number for sulfur).	SO_3^{2-}	SO_4^{2-}
thiosulfate	$S_2O_3^{2-}$	SO_4^{2-}; $S_2O_6^{2-}$ with I_2; S and SO_2 with H^+

Examples

A strip of zinc metal is added to a solution of copper(II) nitrate.

$Zn + Cu^{2+} \rightarrow Zn^{2+} + Cu$

A piece of aluminum is dropped into a hot solution of lead chloride*.

$Al + Pb^{2+} \rightarrow Pb + Al^{3+}$

**Lead chloride is a slightly soluble salt, with a solubility of 10 g/L at 20°C and is one of only three commonly insoluble chlorides, the other two being silver chloride and mercury(I) chloride. The solubility of $PbCl_2$ increases very rapidly as the temperature rises. At 100°C it has a solubility of 33.5 g/L. However, $PbCl_2$ precipitates very slowly, particularly when other ions that form insoluble chlorides are not present. $PbCl_2$ dissolves in excess chloride ion as a result of the formation of a complex ion, tetrachloroplumbate(II) ion: $PbCl_{2(s)} + 2Cl^-_{(aq)} \rightleftharpoons [PbCl_4]^{2-}_{(aq)}$.*

Chlorine gas is bubbled through a solution of sodium iodide.

$Cl_2 + I^- \rightarrow I_2 + Cl^-$

Potassium dichromate solution is added to an acidified solution of sodium sulfite.

$Cr_2O_7^{2-} + H^+ + SO_3^{2-} \rightarrow Cr^{3+} + SO_4^{2-} + H_2O$

Sodium iodate, potassium iodide, and dilute sulfuric acid are mixed.

$I^- + H^+ + IO_3^- \rightarrow I_2 + H_2O$

Quick Quiz #19

Directions: Please write the chemical equations for each statement below.

1. Manganese(IV) oxide is added to warm, concentrated hydrochloric acid.

2. Chlorine gas is bubbled into cold, dilute potassium hydroxide.

XX. Precipitation Reactions

These problems involve mixing two solutions. Each solution is a water solution of an ionic compound. From the mixture of the two solutions, at least one insoluble precipitate will form. The other ions present are probably soluble and are called spectator ions; they are NOT included in the net ionic equations. You must know the solubility rules to do these problems.

Examples

A solution of silver nitrate is added to a solution of hydrochloric acid.

$Ag^+ + Cl^- \rightarrow AgCl$ (All nitrates are soluble.)

A solution of silver nitrate is added to a solution of potassium chromate.

$Ag^+ + CrO_4^{2-} \rightarrow Ag_2CrO_4$

A solution of lead nitrate is added to a solution of sodium chloride.

$Pb^{2+} + Cl^- \rightarrow PbCl_2$

A solution of iron(III) nitrate is added to a strong sodium hydroxide solution.

$Fe^{3+} + OH^- \rightarrow Fe(OH)_3$

A solution of strontium chloride is added to a solution of sodium sulfate.

$Sr^{2+} + SO_4^{2-} \rightarrow SrSO_4$

Quick Quiz #20

Directions: Please write the chemical equations for each statement below.

1. Equimolar solutions of nickel(II) nitrate and cesium hydroxide are mixed.

2. Aqueous ammonium carbonate is added to a solution of nickel(II) chloride.

3. Equimolar solutions of zinc acetate and cesium hydroxide are mixed.

XXI. Complex Ions

A complex ion is an ion containing one or more molecules or ions bonded to a central metal ion. Examples of complex ions include: $Cu(NH_3)_4^{2+}$, $Ni(NH_3)_4^{2+}$, $Zn(NH_3)_4^{2+}$, $Ag(NH_3)^{2+}$, $FeSCN^{2+}$, $Pb(OH)_3^-$, $Al(OH)_4^-$, $Zn(OH)_2^{2-}$, and $Cr(OH)_4^-$. Examples of transition metals that form complexes (including their coordination number in parentheses) include: Cu^{2+} (4), Al^{3+} (6), Fe^{3+} (6), and Ag^+ (2). When in doubt as to the coordination number, double the charge on the ion.

Common ligands include: NH_3, OH^-, I^-, and CO.

Examples

A concentrated solution of ammonia is added to a solution of zinc nitrate.

$Zn^{2+} + NH_3 \rightarrow Zn(NH_3)_4^{2+}$ or $Zn^{2+} + NH_3 + H_2O \rightarrow Zn(OH)_2 + NH_4^+$

(The concentration of NH_3 determines which product.)

A solution of iron(III) iodide is added to a solution of ammonium thiocyanate.

$Fe^{3+} + SCN^- \rightarrow Fe(SCN)_6^{3-}$

A solution of copper(II) nitrate is added to a strong solution of ammonia.

$Cu^{2+} + NH_3 \rightarrow Cu(NH_3)_4^{2+}$

A concentrated potassium hydroxide solution is added to solid aluminum hydroxide.

$OH^- + Al(OH)_3 \rightarrow Al(OH)_4^-$

Sodium cyanide solution is added to a solution of silver nitrate.

$CN^- + Ag^+ \rightarrow [Ag(CN)_2]^-$

Quick Quiz #21

Directions: Please write the chemical equations for each statement below.

1. A solution of ammonium thiocyanate is added to a solution of iron(III) chloride.

2. A solution of diamminesilver(I) bromide is treated with dilute nitric acid.

3. Excess hydrochloric acid is added to a solution containing the tetraamminecadmium(II) ion.

XXII. Strong Acid + Strong Base → Salt + H_2O (neutralization)

Acid–base reactions require both an acid and a base as reactants. Acid–base reactions are sometimes called proton-transfer reactions because an H^+ moves from the acid to the base. If you can spot this happening, even with nontraditional acids and bases, it will be an acid–base reaction. Traditional acids are easily identified from the formula. When hydrogen is the first element, it is an acid. If the formula is written this way, all hydrogens at the beginning of the formula will react with the base. There are two important exceptions: H_2 and H_2O. H_2 is never an acid. Although water is not normally considered an acid, in some cases it can act as one. If it does, it will lose only one proton. In fact, you may often find it advantageous to think of the formula of water as HOH, since it normally reacts as H^+ and OH^-. Another traditional way to write organic (carbon-based) acids is to have the formula end in "COOH." If the formula is written this way, there will probably be lots of other hydrogens, but only the one after the COO is acidic or donated. Two types of common bases are hydroxides (OH^-) and carbonates (CO_3^{2-}). These are both anions. In reactions each will be associated with a cation. The cation will not affect its basic properties. When hydroxides react with an acid, one product will be water. When carbonates react with an acid, the products will include carbon dioxide and water.

Examples

A strong solution of sodium hydroxide is added to a strong solution of hydrochloric acid.

$H^+ + OH^- \rightarrow H_2O$

Equal volumes of 0.1-molar sulfuric acid and 0.1-molar potassium hydroxide are mixed.

$H^+ + OH^- \rightarrow H_2O$ -

• •

Quick Quiz #22

Directions: Please write the chemical equations for each statement below.

1. A nitric acid solution of unknown concentration in which a few drops of phenolphthalein had been added was titrated with a known concentration of sodium hydroxide.

2. Perchloric acid is mixed with a solution of rubidium hydroxide.

XXIII. Organic Reactions

Addition of Br₂ or Cl₂ to alkene → halogenated alkane	
Ethene gas is bubbled through bromine water. $Br_2 + H_2C{=}CH_2 \rightarrow BrH_2C\text{-}CH_2Br$ *(1,2-dibromoethane)*	$-\overset{\mid}{C}{=}\overset{\mid}{C}- + X_2 \rightarrow -\overset{\mid}{\underset{X}{C}}-\overset{\mid}{\underset{X}{C}}-$ X = Br or Cl
Addition of Br₂ or Cl₂ to alkyne → halogenated alkane	
An excess of chlorine gas is added to pure acetylene. $Cl_2 + HC{\equiv}CH \rightarrow CHCl_2\text{-}CHCl_2$

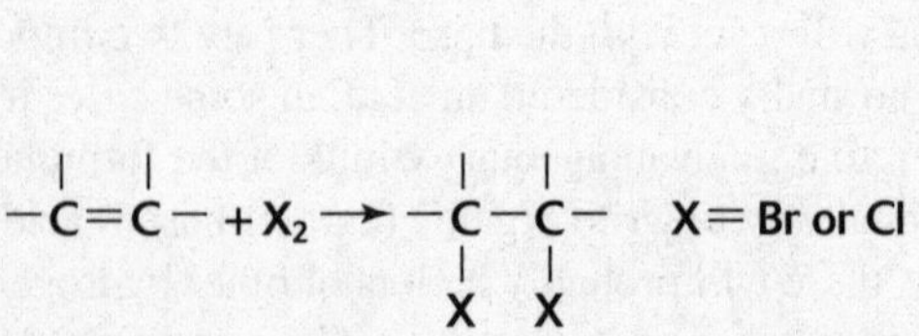

Addition of H₂ to alkene → alkane

2-butene is combined with hydrogen gas in the presence of a nickel catalyst.

$$C_4H_8 + H_2 \rightarrow C_4H_{10}$$

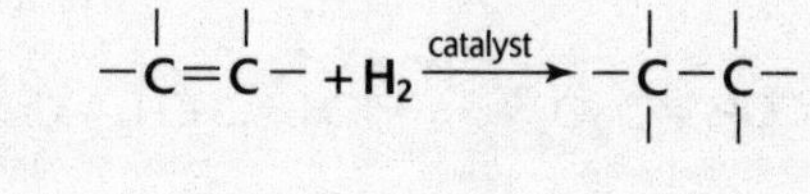

$$-\overset{|}{C}=\overset{|}{C}- + H_2 \xrightarrow{\text{catalyst}} -\overset{|}{\underset{|}{C}}-\overset{|}{\underset{|}{C}}-$$

Addition of H₂O to alkene → alcohol

Gaseous ethanol and steam are mixed.

$$CH_2{=}CH_2 + H_2O \rightarrow CH_3CH_2OH$$

$$-\overset{|}{C}=\overset{|}{C}- + H_2O \xrightarrow{H^+} -\overset{|}{\underset{|}{C}}-\overset{|}{\underset{OH}{C}}-$$

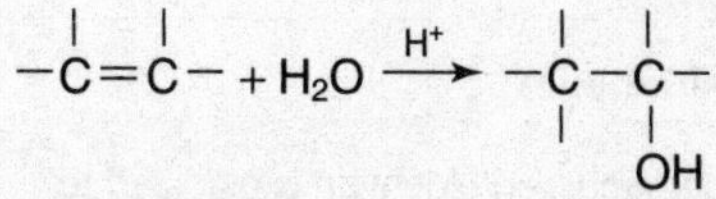

Addition of HX to alkenes or alkynes → halogenated alkane

A sample of pure 2-butene is treated with hydrogen chloride gas.

$$\overset{\overset{\displaystyle Cl}{\displaystyle |}}{}$$

$$CH_3CH{=}CHCH_3 + HCl \rightarrow CH_3CH_2{-}CHCH_3$$

$$-\overset{|}{C}=\overset{|}{C}- + HX \longrightarrow -\overset{|}{\underset{X}{C}}-\overset{|}{\underset{X}{C}}- \quad X = F, Cl, Br, \text{ or } I$$

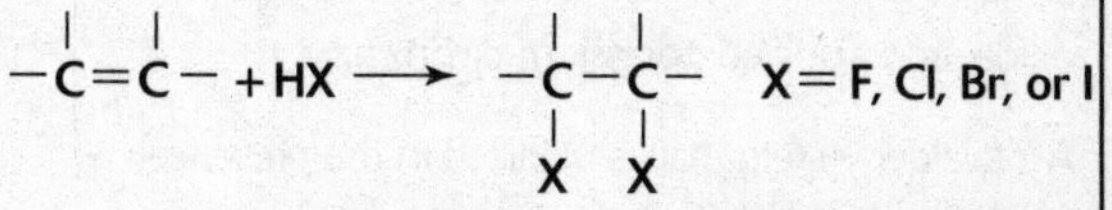

Dehydration of alcohol → alkene

Ethanol vapor is passed over hot aluminum oxide powder acting as a catalyst.

$$CH_3CH_2OH \xrightarrow{Al_2O_3} CH_2 = CH_2 + H_2O$$

$$-\overset{|}{C}-\overset{|}{\underset{OH}{C}}- \xrightarrow{H_2SO_4} -\overset{|}{C}=\overset{|}{C}- + H_2O$$

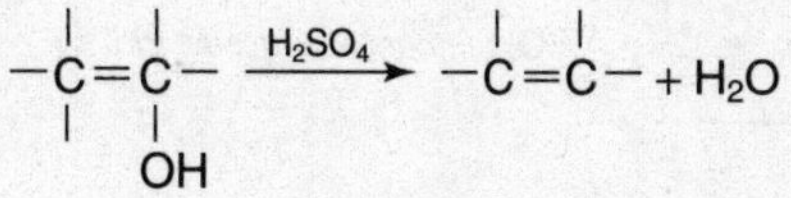

Halogenation of aromatic rings

Pure chlorine gas is bubbled through liquid benzene and the mixture heated in the presence of iron(III) chloride acting as a catalyst.

$$Cl_2 + C_6H_6 \xrightarrow{FeCl_3} C_6H_5Cl + HCl$$

benzene $+ X_2 \xrightarrow{Fe}$ benzene$-X$ $\quad X = Br$ or Cl

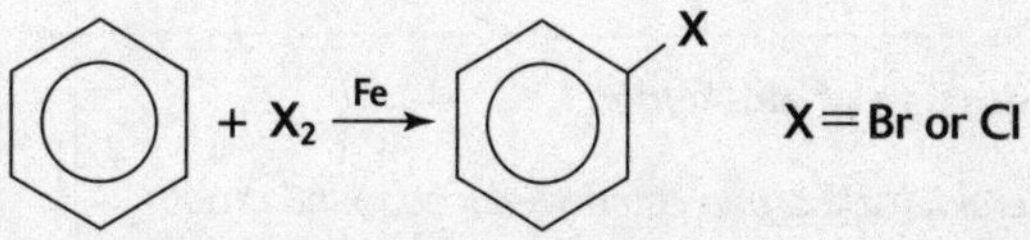

Nitration of aromatic rings

Nitric acid is added to benzene and the mixture is heated in the presence of sulfuric acid acting as a catalyst.

$$C_6H_6 + HNO_3 \xrightarrow{H_2SO_4} C_6H_5NO_2 + H_2O$$

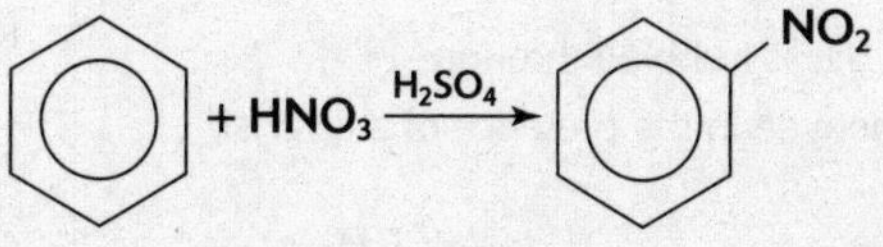

benzene $+ HNO_3 \xrightarrow{H_2SO_4}$ benzene$-NO_2$

Oxidation of primary alcohol → aldehyde

Ethanol is mixed with chromic acid and the mixture is heated.

$$CH_3CH_2OH + Cr_2O_7^{2-} + H^+ \rightarrow CH_3CHO + Cr^{3+} + H_2O$$

Primary

$$RCH_2OH \xrightarrow{[O]} R-\overset{\|}{\underset{O}{C}}-H \xrightarrow{[O]} R-\overset{\|}{\underset{O}{C}}-OH$$

Oxidation of primary alcohol → carboxylic acid

Ethanol is mixed with excess chromic acid and the mixture is heated.

$$CH_3CH_2OH + Cr_2O_7^{2-} + H^+ \rightarrow CH_3COOH + Cr^{3+} + H_2O$$

Secondary

$$R-\overset{|}{\underset{OH}{C}}H-R' \xrightarrow{[O]} R-\overset{\|}{\underset{O}{C}}-R'$$

Oxidation of secondary alcohol → ketone

Propan-2-ol is mixed with potassium dichromate and the mixture is heated in the presence of sulfuric acid acting as a catalyst.

Tertiary

$$R-\overset{\overset{\displaystyle R'}{\displaystyle |}}{\underset{\underset{\displaystyle R''}{\displaystyle |}}{C}}-OH \xrightarrow{[O]} \text{no reaction}$$

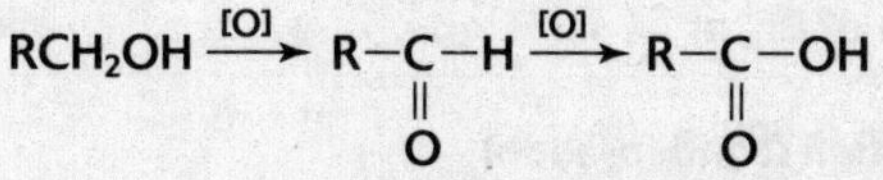

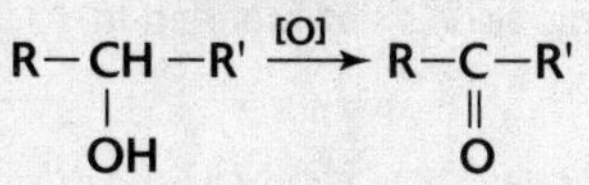

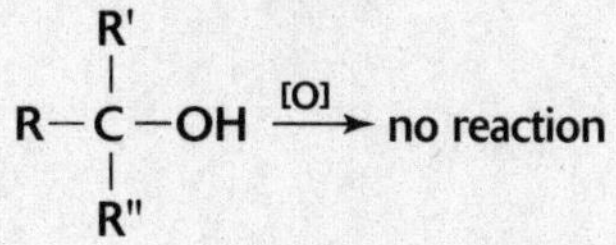

(continued)

$$CH_3-\underset{\underset{CH_3}{|}}{\overset{\overset{H}{|}}{C}}OH + COH + Cr_2O_7{}^{2-} \xrightarrow{H^+} CH_3-\overset{\overset{O}{\parallel}}{C}-CH_3 + Cr^{3+} + H_2O$$

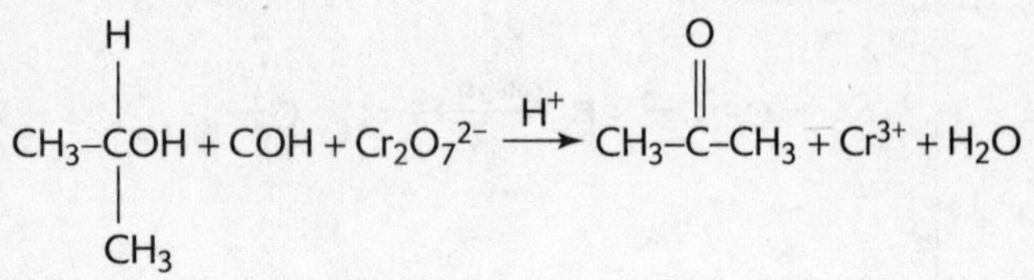

oxidation of aldehydes Under acidic conditions, an aldehyde is oxidized to a carboxylic acid. Under alkaline conditions, a salt is formed instead. Suitable oxidizing agents include potassium permanganate, nitric acid, chromium(VI) oxide, and acidified potassium dichromate. Acetalaldehye (ethanal) is oxidized in the presence of an acidified solution of potassium dichromate. $$CH_3\overset{\overset{H}{	}}{C}=O \xrightarrow{H^+,\ K_2Cr_2O_7} CH_3\overset{\overset{O}{\parallel}}{C}-OH \text{ (ethanoic or acetic acid)}$$	

$$R-\overset{\overset{[O]}{}}{\underset{\underset{O}{\parallel}}{C}}H \xrightarrow{[O]} R-\underset{\underset{O}{\parallel}}{C}-OH$$

Aldehyde Carboxylic acid

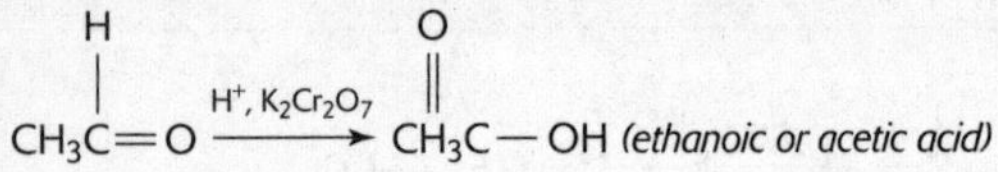

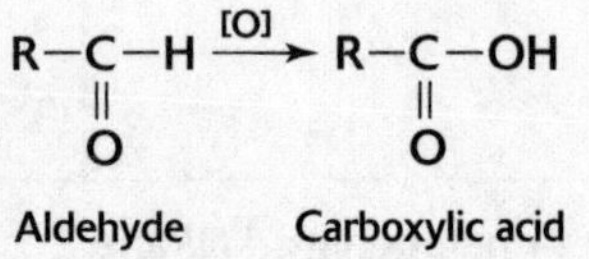

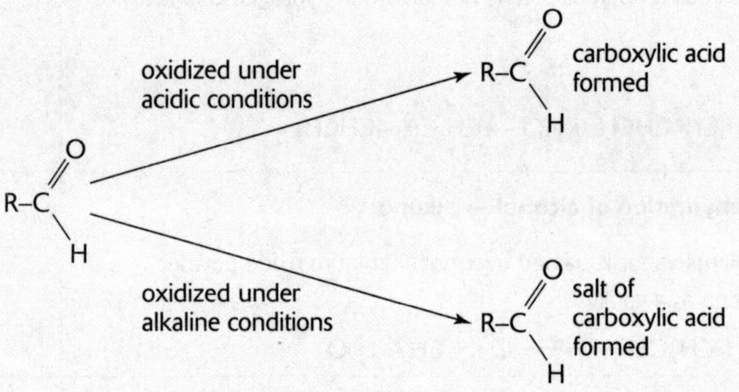

reduction of aldehydes *The aldehyde group can be reduced to the group -CH₂OH, changing the aldehyde into a primary alcohol.* Hydrogen gas is bubbled through propionaldehyde in the presence of a catalyst.	$$R-\underset{\underset{O}{\parallel}}{C}-H \xrightarrow{H^+} R-CH_2-OH$$ Aldehyde Primary alcohol

$$H_3C-\overset{\overset{H_2}{\overset{|}{C}}}{\underset{\underset{H}{\overset{|}{C}}}{}} + H\!-\!H \longrightarrow H_3C-\overset{\overset{H_2}{\overset{|}{C}}}{\underset{\underset{H}{\overset{|}{C}}}{}}\overset{H\ O}{\underset{}{}}H$$

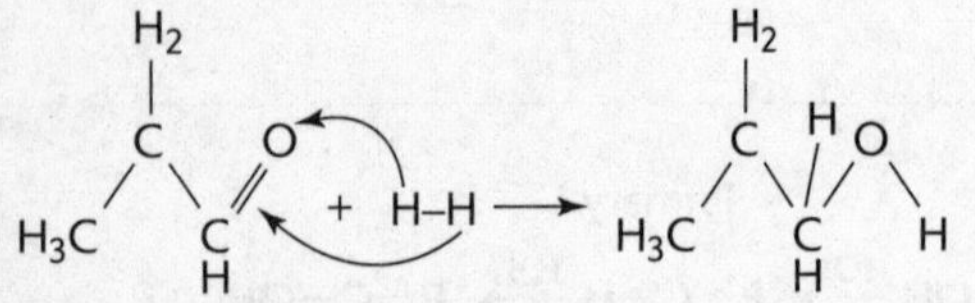

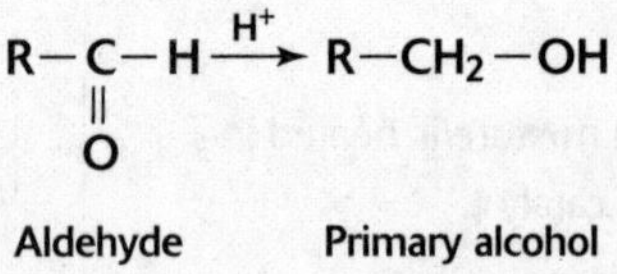

esterification (condensation) **(carboxylic acid + alcohol → ester + water)** Acetic acid (ethanoic acid) is slowly added to methanol. $CH_3COOH + CH_3OH \rightarrow CH_3COOCH_3 + H_2O$	$$R-\underset{\underset{O}{\parallel}}{C}-OH + R'OH \underset{}{\overset{H^+}{\rightleftharpoons}} R-\underset{\underset{O}{\parallel}}{C}-OR' + H_2O$$

formation of an ether (condensation) **(alcohol + acid → ether + water)**	
Methyl alcohol is mixed with a small amount of sulfuric acid and then the mixture is warmed gently. $$CH_3OH + HOCH_3 \xrightarrow{H_2SO_4} CH_3OCH_3 + H_2O$$	$$-\overset{\mid}{C}=\overset{\mid}{\underset{\overset{\mid}{OH}}{\underset{H}{C}}}- \xrightarrow{H_2SO_4} -\overset{\mid}{C}=\overset{\mid}{C}- + H_2O$$
reduction of ketone → secondary alcohol	
Hydrogen gas is bubbled through propanone. $$\underset{CH_3}{\overset{CH_3}{C}}=O + H_2 \longrightarrow CH_3-\underset{\underset{CH_3}{\mid}}{\overset{\overset{OH}{\mid}}{C}}-H \quad (CH_3CHCH_3) \quad \underset{OH}{}$$ Propan-2-ol is the product.	$$R-\underset{O}{\overset{\mid\mid}{C}}-R' \xrightarrow{[H]} R-\underset{OH}{\overset{\overset{H}{\mid}}{C}}-R'$$ Ketone Secondary alcohol

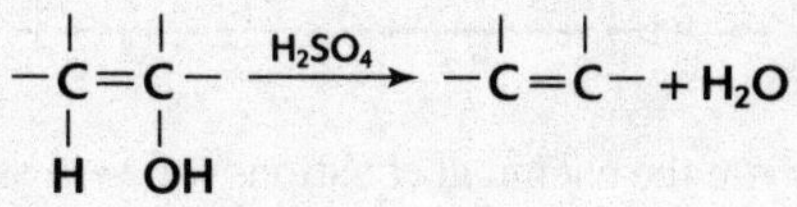

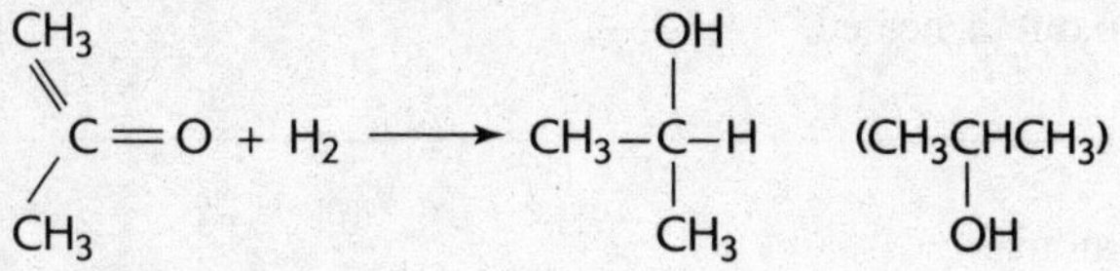

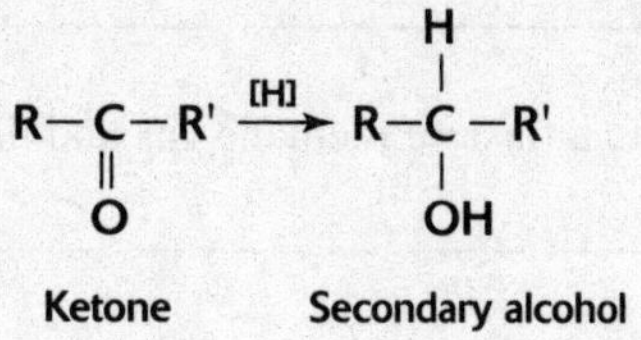

Examples

Ethanol and formic acid (methanoic acid) are mixed and warmed.

$$C_2H_5OH + HCOOH \rightarrow HCOOC_2H_5 + H_2O$$

Ethene (ethylene) gas is bubbled through a solution of bromine.

$$C_2H_4 + Br_2 \rightarrow C_2H_4Br_2$$

Propanol is burned completely in air.

$$C_3H_7OH + O_2 \rightarrow CO_2 + H_2O$$

Quick Quiz #23

Directions: Please write the chemical equations for each statement below.

1. Ethanol is heated in the presence of sulfuric acid.

____

2. Chlorine gas is added to a flask of methane gas and the mixture is heated.

____

3. Chloromethane is bubbled through a solution of warm ammonia.

____

Quick Quiz Answers

Quick Quiz #1

1. $C_3H_6 + H_2O \rightarrow C_3H_7OH$
2. $C_4H_8 + HCl \rightarrow CH_3CH_2CHClCH_3$
3. $Br_2 + C_2H_2 \rightarrow C_2H_2Br_4$
4. $C_2H_4 + Cl_2 \rightarrow C_2H_4Cl_2$
5. $Al + Br_2 \rightarrow AlBr_3$

Quick Quiz #2

1. $Fe(OH)_3 \rightarrow Fe_2O_3 + H_2O$
2. $HNO_2 \rightarrow N_2O_3 + H_2O$
3. $I^- + H_2O \rightarrow I_2 + H_2 + OH^-$

Quick Quiz #3

1. $Pb + Cu^{2+} + SO_4^{2-} \rightarrow PbSO_4 + Cu$
2. $Sr + H^+ + SO_4^{2-} \rightarrow SrSO_4 + H_2$

Quick Quiz #4

1. $CH_3COOH + MgCO_3 \rightarrow CH_3COO^- + Mg^{2+} + CO_2 + H_2O$
2. $NH_4^+ + OH^- \rightarrow NH_3 + H_2O$
3. $Ba^{2+} + CrO_4^{2-} \rightarrow BaCrO_4$
4. $H^+ + MnS \rightarrow Mn^{2+} + H_2S$
5. $Mg_3N_2 + H_2O \rightarrow Mg(OH)_2 + NH_3$

Quick Quiz #5

1. $Mg_3N_2 + O_2 \rightarrow MgO + N_2$
2. $O_2 + NH_3 \xrightarrow{Pt} NO_2 + H_2O$
3. $Na + O_2 \rightarrow Na_2O$
4. $B_2H_6 + O_2 \rightarrow B_2O_3 + H_2O$

Quick Quiz #6

1. $K_2O + H_2O \rightarrow K^+ + OH^-$
2. $Na_2O + H_2O \rightarrow Na^+ + OH^-$

Quick Quiz #7

1. P_4O_{10} (or P_2O_5) $+ H_2O \rightarrow H_3PO_4$
2. $SO_2 + H_2O \rightarrow H_2SO_3$ *(Sulfurous acid is a weak acid. Do NOT write it as $H^+ + HSO_3^-$)*

Quick Quiz #8

1. $CuO + H^+ \rightarrow Cu^{2+} + H_2O$
2. $MgO + H^+ \rightarrow Mg^{2+} + H_2O$

Quick Quiz #9

1. $CO_2 + OH^- \rightarrow CO_3^{2-} + H_2O$
2. $N_2O_5 + NH_3 \rightarrow NH_4^+ + NO_3^- + H_2O$

Quick Quiz #10

1. $CO_2 + Na_2O \rightarrow Na_2CO_3$
2. $K_2O + SO_3 \rightarrow K_2SO_4$

Quick Quiz #11

1. $Ca + H^+ \rightarrow Ca^{2+} + H_2$
2. $Pb + HSO_4^- \rightarrow PbSO_4 + SO_2 + H_2O$ *(exception)*

Quick Quiz #12

1. $Si + OH^- \rightarrow SiO_4^{4-} + H_2$
2. $Sn + OH^- \rightarrow SnO_2^{2-} + H_2$

Quick Quiz #13

1. $H^+ + NO_2^- \rightarrow HNO_2$
2. $H^+ + C_2O_4^{2-} \rightarrow H_2C_2O_4$

Quick Quiz #14

1. $H_2SO_3 + N_2H_4 \rightarrow HSO_3^- + N_2H_5^+$

Quick Quiz #15

1. $OH^- + H_2PO_4^- \rightarrow H_2O + PO_4^{3-}$
2. $H_2C_2O_4 + OH^- \rightarrow C_2O_4^{2-} + H_2O$
3. $H_3PO_4 + OH^- \rightarrow H_2PO_4^- + H_2O$

Quick Quiz #16

1. $HPO_4^{2-} + H^+ \rightarrow H_2PO_4^-$
2. $H^+ + NH_3 \rightarrow NH_4^+$

Quick Quiz #17

1. $H^+ + CO_3^{2-} \rightarrow CO_2 + H_2O$
2. $CH_3COOH + MgCO_3 \rightarrow Mg^{2+} + CH_3COO^- + H_2O + CO_2$

Quick Quiz #18

1. $CaO + SO_3 \rightarrow CaSO_4$
2. $BaO + CO_2 \rightarrow BaCO_3$

Quick Quiz #19

1. $MnO_2 + H^+ + Cl^- \rightarrow Mn^{2+} + Cl_2 + H_2O$
2. $Cl_2 + OH^- \rightarrow Cl^- + ClO^- + H_2O$

Quick Quiz #20

1. $Ni^{2+} + OH^- \rightarrow Ni(OH)_2$
2. $Ni^{2+} + CO_3^{2-} \rightarrow NiCO_3$
3. $Zn^{2+} + OH^- \rightarrow Zn(OH)_2$

Quick Quiz #21

1. $SCN^- + Fe^{3+} \rightarrow [Fe(SCN)]^{2+}$ or $[Fe(SCN)_6]^{3-}$
2. $[Ag(NH_3)_2]^+ + Br^- + H^+ \rightarrow AgBr + NH_4^+$
3. $H^+ + [Cd(NH_3)_4]^{2+} \rightarrow Cd^{2+} + NH_4^+$

Quick Quiz #22

1. $H^+ + OH^- \rightarrow H_2O$
2. $H^+ + OH^- \rightarrow H_2O$

Quick Quiz #23

1. $C_2H_5OH \xrightarrow{H^+} C_2H_5\text{-}O\text{-}C_2H_5$
2. $CH_4 + Cl_2 \rightarrow CH_3Cl + HCl$
3. $CH_3Cl + NH_3 \rightarrow H^+ + Cl^-$ (or $[CH_3NH_3]^+ + Cl^-$)

Practice Sets

Practice Set #1

1. Chlorine gas is bubbled into a cold solution of dilute potassium hydroxide.
2. Hydrogen peroxide is added to an acidified solution of lithium bromide.
3. Dilute sulfuric acid is added to a solution of calcium chloride.
4. Ethanol is completely burned in air.
5. Small pieces of zinc metal are immersed in a solution of copper(II) sulfate.
6. Sulfur dioxide gas is bubbled into a beaker of distilled water.
7. Excess concentrated sulfuric acid is added to solid magnesium phosphate.
8. Phosphine (phosphorus trihydride) gas is bubbled into liquid boron trichloride.

9. Solid zinc hydroxide is added to aqueous ammonia.

10. Solid copper(II) sulfide is burned in oxygen.

Practice Set #2

1. A solution of iron(II) nitrate is left out in an open beaker for a considerable amount of time.
2. Hot iron(II) oxide powder is exposed to an atmosphere of hydrogen gas.
3. A solution of sodium hydrogen carbonate is added to a weak solution of acetic acid.
4. Solid ammonium carbonate is heated.
5. Small pellets of lithium metal are placed into a container of nitrogen gas.
6. Glacial acetic acid is added to pure liquid methanol.
7. Hydrogen sulfide gas is bubbled through a sodium hydroxide solution.
8. Hydrogen peroxide is added to an acidified solution of potassium dichromate.
9. Excess dilute nitric acid is added to a solution containing the tetramminecadmium(II) ion.
10. Water is added to a sample of pure phosphorus trichloride.

Practice Set #3

1. Solutions of sodium dihydrogen phosphate and sodium hydroxide are mixed.
2. Crystals of copper(II) chloride are added to a concentrated solution of ammonia.
3. 3*M* solutions of sodium iodide and lead nitrate are mixed.
4. A solution of sodium iodide is electrolyzed.
5. Small pellets of pure copper are immersed in dilute nitric acid.
6. Steam is added to propene gas in the presence of a catalyst.
7. Dinitrogen trioxide gas is bubbled through distilled water.
8. Oxygen gas and ammonia gas are mixed together in the presence of a platinum catalyst.
9. Ethyl acetate is treated with a solution of sodium hydroxide.
10. Pieces of calcium oxide are exposed to carbon dioxide gas.

Practice Set #4

1. A concentrated solution of hydrochloric acid is added to solid sodium permanganate.
2. Distilled water is added to a beaker that contains solid barium oxide.
3. Solid ammonium carbonate is added to a saturated solution of barium hydroxide.
4. Small strips of aluminum are added to a solution of silver nitrate.
5. A small piece of magnesium is heated strongly in pure nitrogen gas.
6. Ethyl acetate is treated with a solution of potassium hydroxide.
7. A solution of nickel(II) sulfate is added to a concentrated ammonia solution.
8. Pieces of calcium metal are added to a dilute solution of hydrochloric acid.
9. Water is added to a flask containing pure sodium hydride.
10. Tin(II) nitrate is added to an acidified solution of potassium dichromate.

Practice Set Answers

Practice Set #1

1. $Cl_2 + OH^- \rightarrow Cl^- + ClO^- (ClO_3^-) + H_2O$
2. $H_2O_2 + Br^- + H^+ \rightarrow Br_2 + H_2O$
3. $Ca^{2+} + SO_4^{2-} \rightarrow CaSO_4$
4. $C_2H_5OH + O_2 \rightarrow CO_2 + H_2O$
5. $Zn + Cu^{2+} \rightarrow Zn^{2+} + Cu$
6. $SO_2 + H_2O \rightarrow H_2SO_3$
7. $H_2SO_4 + Mg_3(PO_4)_2 \rightarrow H_3PO_4 + MgSO_4$ *(or $Mg^{2+} + SO_4^{2-}$, $Mg^{2+} + HSO_4^-$, $Mg(HSO_4)_2$)*
8. $PH_3 + BCl_3 \rightarrow H_3PBCl_3$ (or PH_3BCl_3)
9. $NH_3 + Zn(OH)_2 \rightarrow [Zn(NH_3)_4]^{2+}$
10. $CuS + O_2 \rightarrow SO_2 + Cu$ *(or CuO or Cu_2O)*

Practice Set #2

1. $Fe^{2+} + O_2 + H_2O \rightarrow Fe_2O_3$ (or $Fe(OH)_3$)
2. $H_2 + FeO \rightarrow H_2O + Fe$
3. $HCO_3^- + CH_3COOH \rightarrow CH_3COO^- + H_2O + CO_2$
4. $(NH_4)_2CO_3 \rightarrow NH_3 + H_2O + CO_2$
5. $Li + N_2 \rightarrow Li_3N$
6. $CH_3COOH + CH_3OH \rightarrow CH_3COOCH_3 + H_2O$
7. $H_2S + OH^- \rightarrow S^{2-} + H_2O$
8. $H_2O_2 + H^+ + Cr_2O_7^{2-} \rightarrow Cr^{3+} + O_2 + H_2O$
9. $Cd(NH_3)_4^{2+} + H^+ \rightarrow Cd^{2+} + NH_4^+$
10. $H_2O + PCl_3 \rightarrow H^+ + Cl^- + H_3PO_3$

Practice Set #3

1. $OH^- + H_2PO_4^- \rightarrow PO_4^{3-} + H_2O$
2. $CuCl_2 + NH_3 \rightarrow Cu(NH_3)_4^{2+} + Cl^-$
3. $Pb^{2+} + I^- \rightarrow PbI_2$
4. $I^- + H_2O \rightarrow I_2 + H_2 + OH^-$
5. $Cu + H^+ + NO_3^- \rightarrow Cu^{2+} + NO + H_2O$
6. $C_3H_6 + H_2O \rightarrow CH_3CHOHCH_3$
7. $N_2O_3 + H_2O \rightarrow HNO_2$
8. $O_2 + NH_3 \rightarrow NO + H_2O$
9. $CH_3CO_2CH_2CH_3 + OH^- \rightarrow CH_3CO_2^- + CH_3CH_2OH$
10. $CaO + CO_2 \rightarrow CaCO_3$

Practice Set #4

1. $H^+ + Cl^- + NaMnO_4 \rightarrow Mn^{2+} + Cl_2 + H_2O + Na^+$
2. $BaO + H_2O \rightarrow Ba^{2+} + OH^-$
3. $(NH_4)_2CO_3 + Ba^{2+} + OH^- \rightarrow NH_3 + BaCO_3 + H_2O$
4. $Al + Ag^+ \rightarrow Al^{3+} + Ag$
5. $Mg + N_2 \rightarrow Mg_3N_2$
6. $CH_3COOC_2H_5 + OH^- \rightarrow C_2H_5OH + CH_3COO^-$
7. $NH_3 + Ni^{2+} \rightarrow [Ni(NH_3)_6]^{2+}$
8. $H^+ + Ca \rightarrow Ca^{2+} + H_2$
9. $NaH + H_2O \rightarrow Na^+ + OH^- + H_2$
10. $Sn^{2+} + Cr_2O_7^{2-} + H^+ \rightarrow Sn^{4+} + Cr^{3+} + H_2O$

Laboratory Experiments

Approximately 5–10% of the AP Chemistry Exam is devoted to questions involving laboratory experiments. Understanding basic laboratory concepts and being able to analyze sample data will likely make the difference between a 4 or a 5 on the exam. The questions involving laboratory experiments can be categorized into four main groups:

1. making observations of chemical reactions and substances
2. recording data
3. calculating and interpreting results based on the quantitative data obtained
4. communicating effectively the results of experimental work

Some colleges report that some students, while doing well on the written exam, have been at serious disadvantage when they arrive at college because of inadequate or nonexistent laboratory experience in AP Chemistry at the high school. Completion of all recommended 22 laboratory experiments is *essential* to doing the best possible on the AP Chemistry Exam. Meaningful laboratory work is important in fulfilling the requirements of a college-level course of a laboratory science and in preparing you for sophomore-level chemistry courses in college. Issues of college accreditation are also factors that must be considered, since colleges are giving you college laboratory credit for work that was *supposed* to be completed in the high school setting. "Dry labs," that is substituting real laboratory situations with worksheets or slide shows, are unacceptable in preparing you for college-level work. Because chemistry professors at some institutions will ask to see a record of the laboratory work that you did in AP Chemistry before making a decision about granting credit, placement, or both, you must keep a neat, well-organized laboratory notebook in such a fashion that the reports can be readily reviewed.

Students involved in laboratory experiments in AP Chemistry should be familiar with basic laboratory equipment, which will include but not be limited to:

- beakers, flasks, test tubes, crucibles, evaporating dishes, watch glasses, burners, plastic and glass tubing, stoppers, valves, spot plates, funnels, reagent bottles, wash bottles and droppers.

Students should also be familiar with measuring equipment, which will include, but not be limited to:

- balances (to the nearest 0.001 g), thermometers, barometers, graduated cylinders, burets, volumetric pipets, graduated pipets, volumetric flasks, ammeters and voltmeters, pH meters, and spectrophotometers.

Students should also have familiarity, involving more than a single day's experience, in such general types of chemical laboratory work as:

- synthesis of compounds (solid and gas)
- separations (precipitations and filtration, dehydration, centrifugation, distillation, chromatography)
- observing and recording phase changes (solid-liquid-gas)
- titration using indicators and meters
- spectophotometry/colorimetry
- devising and utilizing a scheme for qualitative analysis of ions in solution
- gravimetric analysis

The review of laboratory experiments in this book are not meant to replace detailed laboratory procedures, disposal and safety concerns. Under NO circumstances are the scenarios for the labs to be used as directions for actually performing the laboratory work.

Experiment 1: Determination of the Empirical Formula of a Compound

Background: Many elements combine with oxygen or other nonmetals in various ratios; i.e., FeO, Fe_2O_3, Fe_3O_4. This phenomenon demonstrates the Law of Multiple Proportions. In this experiment, you will analyze the ratios in which lead and chlorine can combine and from the data provided, be able to determine the empirical formulas of the compounds produced.

Scenario: A student was given 2.982 grams of a sample of pure anhydrous lead chloride, Compound A. The student added the sample and a small amount of water to the test tube and heated it in a fume hood, liberating chlorine gas and creating Compound B. A flask filled with 0.500 *M* NaOH and gently swirled helped to trap the chlorine gas (see Figure 1).

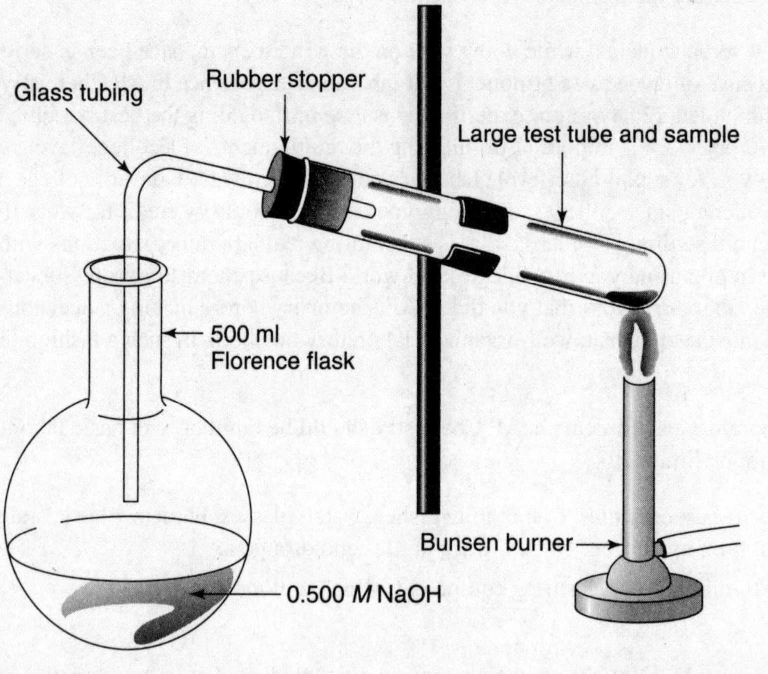

Figure 1

The student then heated Compound B, driving off the remaining water, and determined the mass of Compound B as 2.364 g. The student then reduced Compound B with hydrogen gas to form elemental lead (see Figure 2). The chlorine in Compound B was driven off as $HCl_{(g)}$. This lead was massed and found to weigh 1.770 g.

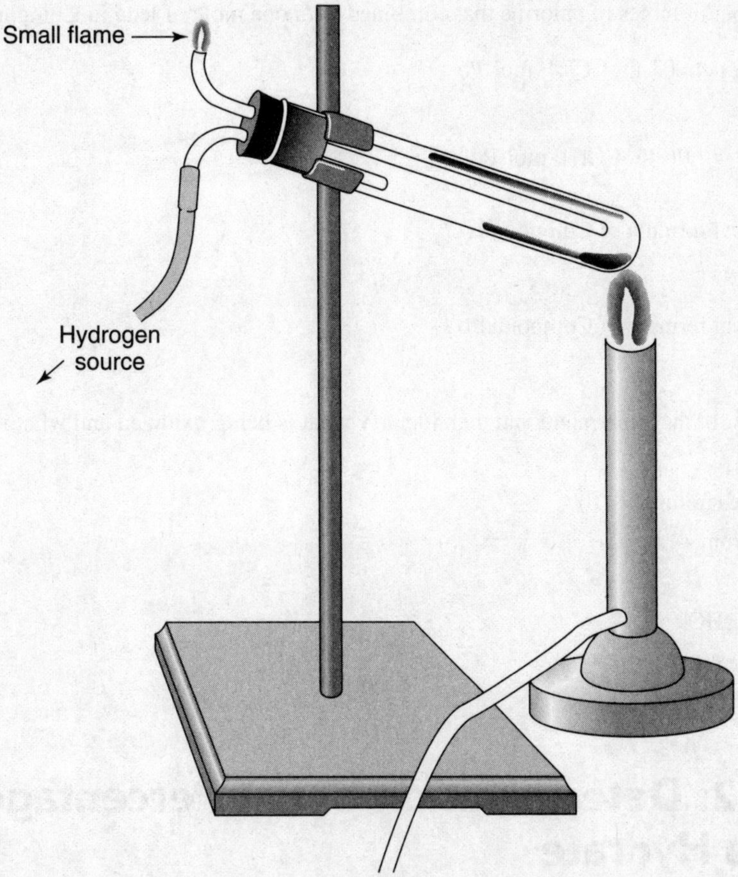

Figure 2

Analysis:

1. Determine the mass of chlorine in Compounds A and B.

   2.982 g A − 1.770 g Pb = 1.212 g Cl in A

   2.364 g B − 1.770 g Pb = 0.594 g Cl in B

2. Using the masses of lead and chlorine from the experiment, what relationship exists for Compounds A and B?

   A: 1.770 g Pb : 1.212 g Cl

   B: 1.770 g Pb : 0.594 g Cl

3. Using information from Question 2, calculate the number of grams of chlorine that would combine with 1 mole of lead in Compounds A and B.

   $$\text{A: } \frac{1.212 \text{ g Cl}}{1.770 \cancel{\text{ g Pb}}} \times \frac{207.2 \cancel{\text{ g Pb}}}{1 \text{ mol Pb}} = 141.9 \text{ g Cl} \cdot \text{mol Pb}^{-1}$$

   $$\text{B: } \frac{0.594 \text{ g Cl}}{1.770 \cancel{\text{ g Pb}}} \times \frac{207.2 \cancel{\text{ g Pb}}}{1 \text{ mol Pb}} = 69.5 \text{ g Cl} \cdot \text{mol Pb}^{-1}$$

4. Calculate the number of moles of chlorine that combined with one mole of lead in Compounds A and B.

A: $\frac{141.9 \text{ g Cl}}{35.45 \text{ g Cl/mol}} = 4.003 \text{ mol Cl} : 1 \text{ mol Pb}$

B: $\frac{69.5 \text{ g Cl}}{35.45 \text{ g Cl/mol}} = 1.96 \text{ mol Cl} : 1 \text{ mol Pb}$

5. What is the empirical formula of Compound A?

$PbCl_4$

6. What is the empirical formula of Compound B?

$PbCl_2$

7. Write the equations for the experiment and then identify what is being oxidized and what is being reduced.

$PbCl_4 \rightarrow PbCl_2 + Cl_2$

Oxidation: Chlorine (from –1 to 0)

Reduction: Lead (from +4 to +2)

$PbCl_2 + H_2 \rightarrow Pb + 2HCl$

Oxidation: Hydrogen (from 0 to +1)

Reduction: Lead (from +2 to 0)

Experiment 2: Determination of the Percentage of Water in a Hydrate

Background: Many solid chemical compounds will absorb some water from the air over time. In many cases, this amount is small and is only found on the surface of the crystals. Other chemical compounds, however, absorb large amounts of water from the air and chemically bind the water into the crystal structure. The majority of these compounds are ionic salts (metallic cation other than H^+ and nonmetallic anion other than OH^- or O^{2-}). To remove the water from many of these hydrates, one only needs to gently heat the compound to slightly above the temperature of boiling water. When one heats the hydrate, the crystalline structure will change and often a color change occurs. For example, $CuCl_2 \cdot 2\,H_2O$, copper (II) chloride dihydrate is green as the hydrate; as the anhydride, $CuCl_2$, it is brownish-yellow. When hydrates lose water spontaneously, they are said to effloresce. The degree of efflorescence is a function of the relative humidity. Some compounds will spontaneously absorb water from the air. These compounds are known as desiccants and are said to be hygroscopic (hydrophilic). When desiccants absorb so much water that they dissolve, they are said to be deliquescent. Do not confuse production of water vapor as an absolute indicator of dehydration since many organic compounds such as carbohydrates will produce water vapor upon decomposition. This decomposition is not reversible but is usually reversible in the case of an anhydride (that is, adding water to the anhydride will convert it back to the hydrate). In general, the proportion of water in the hydrate is a mole ratio (whole integer or a multiple of ½) to that of the salt.

Scenario: A student placed some blue $CoCl_2$ on a watch glass and observed that over time it changed to violet and then to red. Upon heating the red compound gently, she observed that it changed back to violet and then to blue. She then took a sample of sodium sulfate decahydrate whose large crystals appeared colorless and transparent and observed over time that they changed to a fine white powder. She then added water to the fine white powder, dissolving it. Upon gently heating this mixture, the large, colorless transparent crystals reappeared. Then, she took 1.700 g of a green nickel sulfate hydrate and heated the hydrate completely in a crucible (see Figure 1).

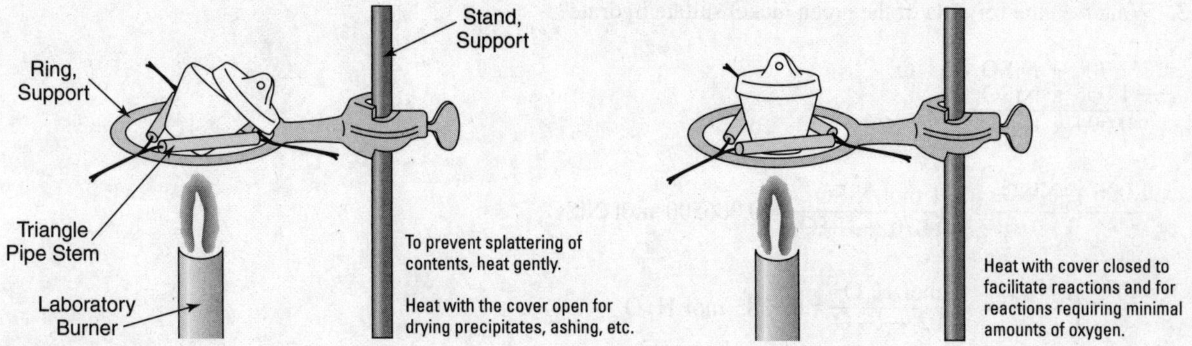

Figure 1

She allowed it to cool in a desiccator (see Figure 2),

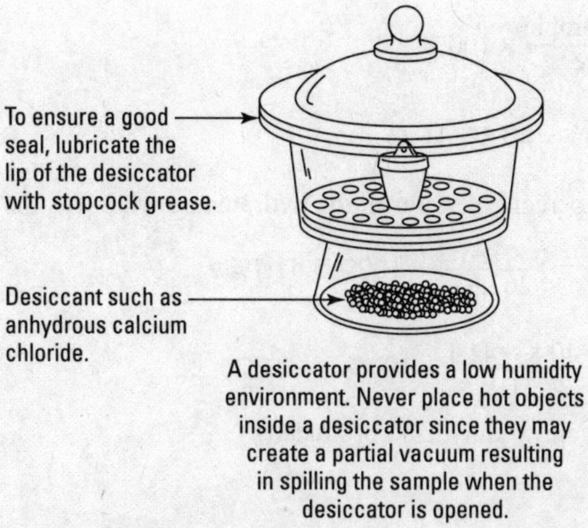

To ensure a good seal, lubricate the lip of the desiccator with stopcock grease.
Desiccant such as anhydrous calcium chloride.
A desiccator provides a low humidity environment. Never place hot objects inside a desiccator since they may create a partial vacuum resulting in spilling the sample when the desiccator is opened.

Figure 2

and then reweighed it and discovered it weighed 1.006 grams. The anhydride produced was yellow.

Analysis:

1. Describe the processes occurring with the cobalt chloride.

   Three color changes were observed: blue, violet and red. From the information provided, the blue form appeared to be the anhydride, $CoCl_2$. When exposed briefly to air containing water vapor, the anhydrous cobalt chloride turned violet, $CoCl_2 \cdot 2H_2O$. Upon further standing in air, the dihydrate was converted to the fully hydrated form, $CoCl_2 \cdot 6\,H_2O$. The color of the anhydride-hydrate depended upon the relative humidity of the air to which it was exposed.

2. Describe the processes occurring with the sodium sulfate decahydrate.

   It appeared that the large, well-defined crystals of sodium sulfate decahydrate, $Na_2SO_4 \cdot 10\,H_2O$, lost water when exposed to air and converted to the anhydrous form, Na_2SO_4. This process is known as efflorescence. It would appear that the relative humidity of the air was rather low for this to occur. When rehydrated and gently dried, the hydrate reappeared indicating a reversible reaction:

   $Na_2SO_4 \cdot 10\,H_2O + \text{heat} \rightleftharpoons Na_2SO_4 + 10\,H_2O$

3. What was the formula of the green nickel sulfate hydrate?

$$\begin{array}{r} 1.700\ \text{g NiSO}_4\cdot ?\text{H}_2\text{O} \\ -1.006\ \text{g NiSO}_4 \\ \hline 0.694\ \text{g H}_2\text{O} \end{array}$$

$$\frac{1.006\ \cancel{\text{g NiSO}_4}}{1} \times \frac{1\ \text{mol NiSO}_4}{154.76\ \cancel{\text{g NiSO}_4}} = 0.006500\ \text{mol NiSO}_4$$

$$\frac{0.694\ \cancel{\text{g H}_2\text{O}}}{1} \times \frac{1\ \text{mol H}_2\text{O}}{18.02\ \cancel{\text{g H}_2\text{O}}} = 0.0385\ \text{mol H}_2\text{O}$$

$$\frac{0.0385\ \text{mol H}_2\text{O}}{0.006500\ \text{mol NiSO}_4} = \frac{5.93}{1.00} = \text{NiSO}_4\cdot 6\text{H}_2\text{O}^*$$

4. What was the percentage, by mass, of the water in the hydrate based upon this experiment?

$$\%\ \text{water} = \frac{\text{mass of H}_2\text{O in sample}}{\text{mass of hydrate}} \times 100\%$$

$$\frac{0.694\ \text{g H}_2\text{O}}{1.700\ \text{g NiSO}_4\cdot 6\ \text{H}_2\text{O}} \times 100\% = 40.8\%\ \text{H}_2\text{O}$$

5. What would be the theoretical percent of water in the hydrate and what was the percent error?

$$\%\ \text{H}_2\text{O} = \frac{\text{part water}}{\text{whole mass}} \times 100\% = \frac{6 \times 18.02}{262.87} \times 100\% = 41.1\%$$

$$\%\ \text{error} = \frac{\text{obs} - \text{exp}}{\text{exp}} \times 100\% = \frac{40.8 - 41.1}{41.1} \times 100\% = -0.7\%$$

6. What was the formula for the yellow anhydride produced?

$NiSO_4$

**$NiSO_4$ exists in two forms. The β-form is stable at 40°C and changes to the blue α-form at room temperature. The α-form is an aquamarine to bluish-green color.*

Experiment 3: Determination of Molar Mass by Vapor Density

Background: The Ideal Gas Law can be used to determine the approximate* molecular mass of a gas through the equation $MM = \frac{g \cdot R \cdot T}{P \cdot V}$. In this experiment, a small amount of a volatile liquid is placed into a flask (of which you know the volume) and allowed to vaporize. A small pinhole in the system allows the pressure of the gas to equalize with the air pressure. The temperature of the vapor will be assumed to be the temperature of the boiling water in which the flask is immersed. At this point, you know *g, R, T, V*, and *P*. You will then be able to calculate the apparent *MM*.

Scenario: A student obtained a sample of an unknown volatile liquid and placed it into a 0.264 L flask. The student covered the flask with a piece of aluminum foil which contained a very small pin hole. The student then immersed the flask into a boiling water bath, which she measured as 100.5°C and allowed the liquid to vaporize, forcing out the air in the flask. (See Figure 1 for set-up.)

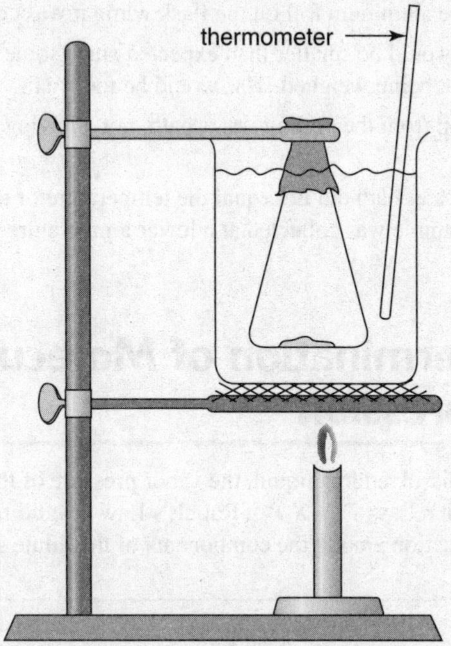

Figure 1

**The gas or vapor may deviate significantly from ideality since it is not that far above the temperature of its boiling point.*

When there was no more liquid visible in the flask, the student then placed the flask into cold water so that the vapor could condense. She dried the flask thoroughly and then reweighed the flask and determined the mass of the condensed vapor to be 0.430 g. The student then checked the barometric pressure of the room and found it to be 750. torr.

Analysis:

1. Calculate the molecular mass of the unknown. What possible sources of error were not accounted for in the calculations?

$$MM = \frac{g \cdot R \cdot T}{P \cdot V} = \frac{0.430 \text{ g} \cdot 0.0821 \not{L} \cdot \not{atm} \cdot 373.5 \not{K}}{\text{mol} \cdot \not{K} \cdot (750./760 \not{atm}) \cdot 0.264 \not{L}} = 50.6 \text{ g} \cdot \text{mol}^{-1}$$

Possible sources of error might include:

(a) mass of air

(b) thermometer immersion point

(c) diffusion effects (air/vapor)

(d) the B.P. of the water at 100.5°C at 750. torr could indicate either a faulty thermometer or that she was not using distilled water. Calibrations factored in the analysis for the thermometer or correctional factors for the type of water could have been made.

2. Explain how the following errors would affect the calculated molecular mass:

(a) She removed the flask prematurely from the hot water bath leaving some of the unknown in the liquid phase.

The mass of the condensate would be larger than expected since it would include the mass of the vapor and the mass of the liquid. *MM* would be higher than expected.

(b) She did not dry off the flask properly and left a few drops of water on the outside of the flask.

The mass of the condensate would be larger than expected since it would include the mass of the vapor and the mass of the drops of water. *MM* would be higher than expected.

(c) She was not careful to keep the aluminum foil on the flask while it was cooling.

The calculated mass of vapor would be smaller than expected since some of the vapor would have escaped from the flask prior to the flask being weighed. *MM* would be too small.

(d) She removed the flask too soon from the boiling water bath, not allowing it a chance to reach the temperature of the hot water.

Since the temperature of the water bath did not equal the temperature of the vapor, the temperature value used would be too large since the sample was collected at a lower temperature than the boiling water. *MM* would be too large.

Experiment 4: Determination of Molecular Mass by Freezing Point Depression

Background: If a nonvolatile solid is dissolved in a liquid, the vapor pressure of the liquid solvent is lowered and can be determined through the use of Raoult's Law, $P_1 = X_1P_1°$. Raoult's Law is valid for ideal solutions wherein $\Delta H = 0$ and in which there is no chemical interaction among the components of the dilute solution (see Figure 1).

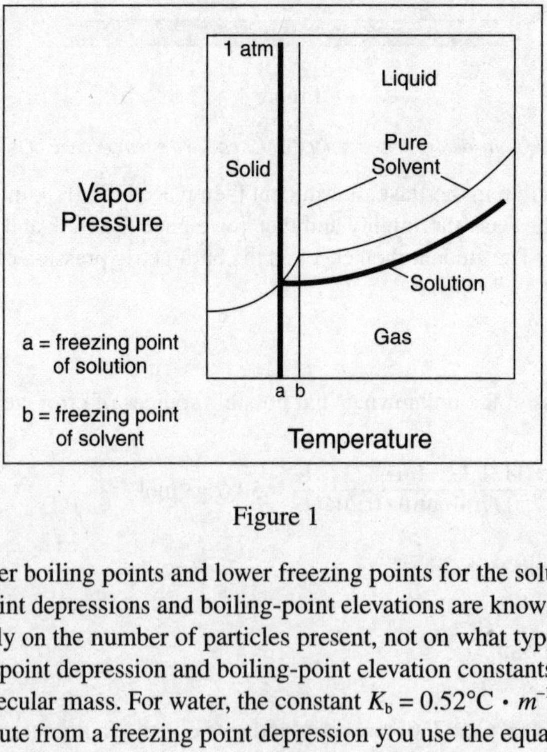

Figure 1

This phenomenon results in higher boiling points and lower freezing points for the solution as compared to the pure solvent. Vapor pressure, freezing point depressions and boiling-point elevations are known as colligative properties. Colligative properties depend only on the number of particles present, not on what type of particles they are. Each solvent has its own unique freezing point depression and boiling-point elevation constants — values that must be factored into an equation to solve for molecular mass. For water, the constant $K_b = 0.52°C \cdot m^{-1}$ and $K_f = 1.86°C \cdot m^{-1}$. To determine the molecular mass of a solute from a freezing point depression you use the equation

$$\Delta T_f = i \cdot K_f \cdot m = i \cdot K_f \cdot \frac{\text{moles of solute}}{\text{kg of solvent}} = i \cdot K_f \cdot \frac{\frac{g\ \text{solute}}{MM_{\text{solute}}}}{\text{kg solvent}}$$

which can be rearranged to produce

$$MM_{\text{solute}} = \frac{i \cdot K_f \cdot \text{g solute}}{\text{kg of solvent} \cdot \Delta T_f}$$

where *i*, known as the van't Hoff or dissociation factor, represents the degree to which the solute ionizes. For non-ionic compounds, $i = 1$; for NaCl, $i = 2$ since for every one mole of NaCl there results two moles of ions, Na^+ and Cl^-; $i = 3$ for $NiBr_2$, and so on. The van't Hoff factor is only approximate except in infinitely dilute solutions. Otherwise, one must use activity coefficients for the ions at their concentrations.

Figure 2 shows the cooling curve for a pure solvent and for a solution. Supercooling may result. Should this occur as the crystals begin to form, the temperature will increase slightly and then remain relatively constant as the pure solvent freezes.

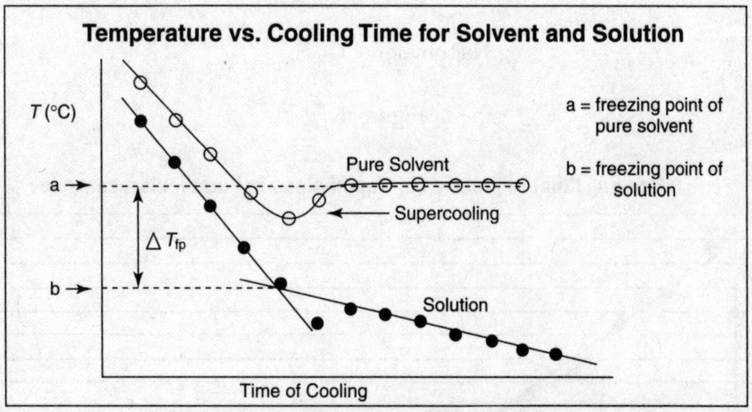

Figure 2: Freezing Point Graph for Pure Solvent and for Solution

Scenario: A student set up an apparatus to determine the molecular mass through freezing point depression (see Figure 3) of naphthalene (see Figure 4). The student measured out 52.0 grams of paradichlorobenzene and 4.0 grams of naphthalene, placed them in a test tube in a hot-water bath and allowed the mixture to completely melt. The mixture was stirred well. The tube was then removed from the hot-water bath, dried and allowed to cool while it was gently stirred to minimize supercooling. Temperature readings were taken every 60 seconds until the mixture solidified and the temperature stabilized. A graph was drawn of the results (see Figure 5).

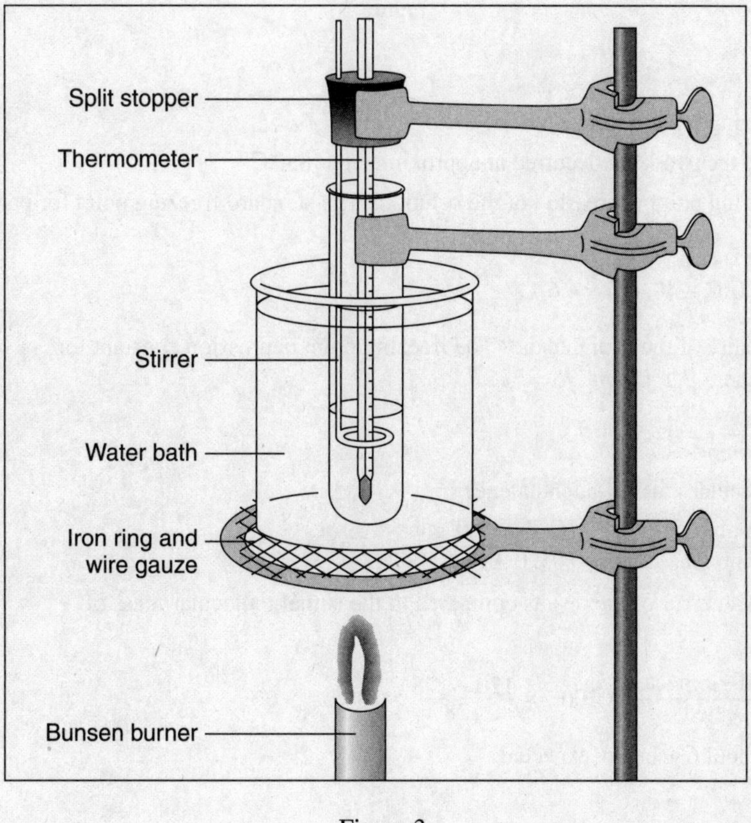

Figure 3

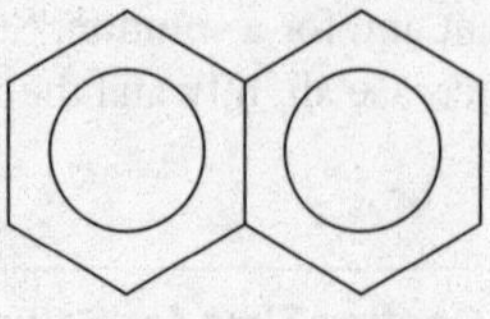

Figure 4

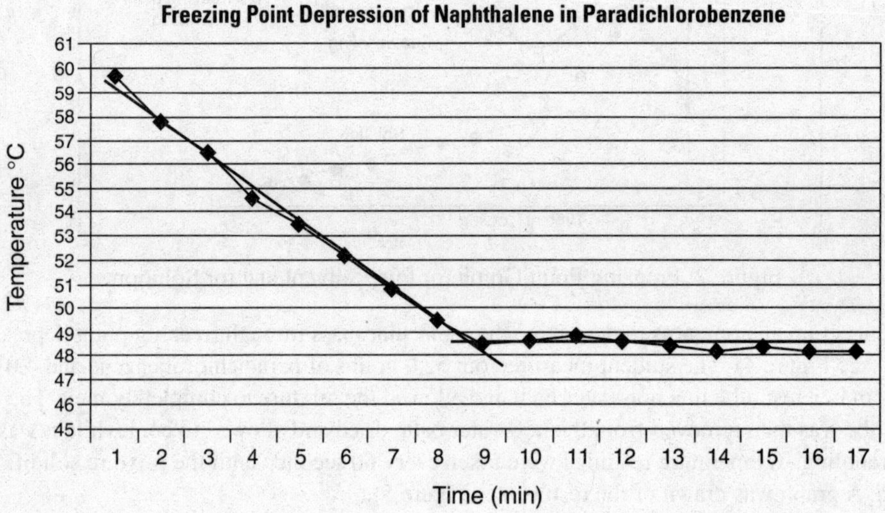

Figure 5

Analysis:

1. What was the freezing point of the solution?

   The intersection of the two lines occurred at approximately 48.4°C

2. What was the freezing point depression of the solution? The standard freezing point for paradichlorobenzene is 53.0°C.

   $\Delta T_f = T_f^\circ - T_f = 53.0°\text{C} - 48.4°\text{C} = 4.6°\text{C}$

3. What was the molality of the naphthalene? The freezing point depression constant for paradichlorobenzene is 7.1°C · m^{-1}.

   $$m = \frac{\Delta T_f}{K_f} = \frac{4.6°\text{C}}{7.1°\text{C} \cdot m^{-1}} = 0.65m$$

4. What was the molecular mass of naphthalene?

   $$MM_{\text{solute}} = \frac{K_f \cdot \text{g solute}}{\text{kg solvent} \cdot \Delta T_f} = \frac{7.1 \cancel{°\text{C}} \cdot \cancel{\text{kg}} \cdot 4.0\ \text{g}}{\text{mol} \cdot 0.0520\ \cancel{\text{kg}} \cdot 4.6 \cancel{°\text{C}}} = 120\ \text{g} \cdot \text{mol}^{-1}$$

5. What was the percent error of the results compared to the actual molecular mass of 128 g · mol^{-1}?

   $$\%\ \text{error} = \frac{\text{observed} - \text{expected}}{\text{expected}} \times 100\% = \frac{120 - 128}{128} \times 100\% = -6\%$$

   The results were about 6% below expected.

Experiment 5: Determination of the Molar Volume of a Gas

Background: Avogadro's law ($V_1n_2 = V_2n_1$), where moles, $n = \dfrac{\text{grams}}{MW(\text{grams/mole})}$ expresses the relationship between molar mass, the actual mass and the number of moles of a gas. The molar volume of a gas at STP, $\overline{V}_{STP}$, is equal to the volume of the gas measured at STP divided by the number of moles; $\overline{V}_{STP} = \dfrac{V_{STP}}{n}$. Dalton's Law of Partial Pressure ($P_{total} = P_1 + P_2 + P_3 + \ldots$) and the derivation, $P_i = \dfrac{n_i}{n_{total}} \cdot P_{total}$ will also be used in this experiment to predict the volume occupied by one mole of hydrogen gas at STP.

Scenario: A student cut a 4.60 cm piece of pure magnesium ribbon. The student then prepared a gas collecting tube with HCl at the bottom and water at the top and placed the magnesium in a copper cage into the water end. The tube was then inverted (see Figure 1). The HCl being more dense flowed down the tube and then reacted with the magnesium, producing bubbles of gas. After all of the magnesium had reacted, the student then transferred the gas collecting tube carefully to a large cylinder filled with water and adjusted the gas collecting tube so that the water level in the tube was even with the water level in the cylinder. The student then read the volume of the gas in the collecting tube as 40.44 cm^3. The temperature of the water was 26.3°C and the air pressure of the room was 743 mm of Hg.

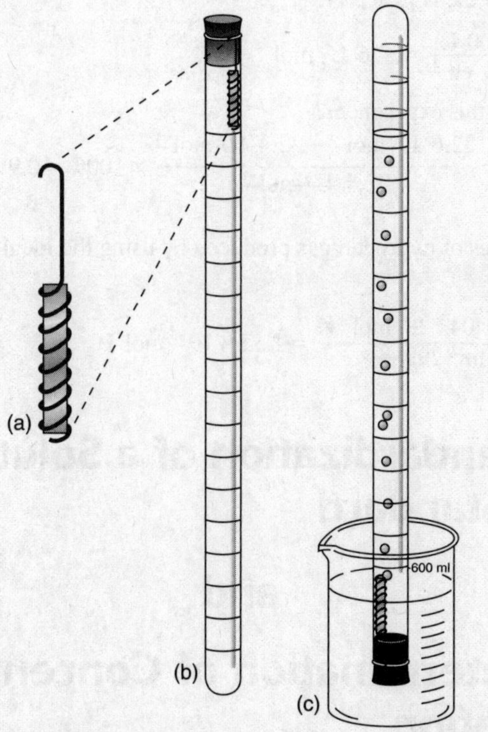

Figure 1

Analysis:

1. Given that 1.00 m of the pure Mg ribbon weighs 0.816 g, determine the mass of Mg used in the experiment.

$$\frac{4.60\ \cancel{\text{cm Mg}}}{1} \times \frac{1.00\ \cancel{\text{m Mg}}}{100.\ \cancel{\text{cm Mg}}} \times \frac{0.816\ \text{g Mg}}{1.00\ \cancel{\text{m Mg}}} = 0.0375\ \text{g Mg}$$

2. Calculate the number of moles of Mg used in the experiment.

$$\frac{0.0375\ \cancel{\text{g Mg}}}{1} \times \frac{1\ \text{mol Mg}}{24.3\ \cancel{\text{g Mg}}} = 0.00154\ \text{mol Mg}$$

3. Calculate the partial pressure of the hydrogen gas in the mixture. The vapor pressure of the water at 26.3 °C is 25.7 mm Hg.

$$P_{H_2} = P_{tot} - P_{H_2O}$$

$$= 743 \text{ mm Hg} - 26 \text{ mm Hg} = 717 \text{ mm Hg}$$

4. Calculate the volume of the hydrogen gas at STP, assuming that the gas temperature equals the temperature of the aqueous HCl.

$$T_1 = 26°\text{C} + 273 = 299\text{K}$$

$$V_2 = V_1 \frac{P_1}{P_2} \times \frac{T_2}{T_1} = 40.44 \text{ cm}^3 \times \frac{717 \cancel{\text{mm Hg}}}{760 \cancel{\text{mm Hg}}} \times \frac{273 \cancel{\text{K}}}{299 \cancel{\text{K}}} = 34.8 \text{ cm}^3$$

5. Write the balanced net ionic equation for the reaction.

$$Mg_{(s)} + 2H^+_{(aq)} \rightarrow H_{2(g)} + Mg^{2+}_{(aq)}$$

6. Determine the number of moles of $H_{2(g)}$ produced, based on the moles of Mg used.

$$\frac{0.00154 \cancel{\text{mol Mg}}}{1} \times \frac{1.00 \text{ mol } H_2}{1.00 \cancel{\text{mol Mg}}} = 0.00154 \text{ mol } H_{2(g)}$$

7. Calculate the molar volume of the $H_{2(g)}$ at STP.

$$\bar{V}_{STP} = \frac{34.8 \cancel{\text{cm}^3 H_2}}{0.00154 \text{ mol } H_2} \times \frac{1.000 \text{ L}}{1000 \cancel{\text{cm}^3}} = 22.6 \text{ L} \cdot \text{mol}^{-1}$$

8. What was the percent error in this experiment?

$$\% \text{ error} = \frac{\text{obs} - \text{exp}}{\text{exp}} \times 100\% = \frac{22.6 \cancel{\text{L} \cdot \text{mol}^{-1}} - 22.4 \cancel{\text{L} \cdot \text{mol}^{-1}}}{22.4 \cancel{\text{L} \cdot \text{mol}^{-1}}} \times 100\% = 0.9\%$$

9. Determine the number of moles of hydrogen gas produced by using the Ideal Gas Law.

$$PV = nRT$$

$$n = \frac{P \cdot V}{R \cdot T} = \frac{717/760 \cancel{\text{atm}} \cdot 0.04044 \cancel{\text{L}} \cdot \text{mol} \cdot \cancel{\text{K}}}{0.0821 \cancel{\text{L}} \cdot \cancel{\text{atm}} \cdot 299 \cancel{\text{K}}} = 1.55 \times 10^{-3} \text{ mol } H_2$$

Experiment 6: Standardization of a Solution Using a Primary Standard

and

Experiment 7: Determination of Concentration by Acid-Base Titration

Background: A neutralization reaction results when a strong acid reacts with a strong base and is represented by the following net-ionic equation:

$$H^+_{(aq)} + OH^-_{(aq)} \rightarrow H_2O_{(l)}$$

The equilibrium constant for this reaction at room temperature is approximately 10^{14}. The magnitude of the equilibrium constant shows that the reaction proceeds essentially to the product side, using up nearly all of the ions present as limiting reactants. If both H^+ and OH^- are present in equal quantities as reactants, the resulting solution will be neutral, because water is the only product of the reaction. When weak acids are titrated with strong bases, the resulting solution will be basic because the conjugate base of the weak acid will form. When weak bases are titrated with strong acids, the resulting solution will be acidic because the conjugate acid of the weak base will form.

In Part I of this experiment a titration will be performed by titrating a standardized solution of HCl with a NaOH solution whose concentration is not known. One cannot make a standardized solution of NaOH directly by weighing out an exact amount of NaOH and diluting it with distilled water since solid NaOH absorbs both H_2O and CO_2. The titration will allow the concentration of the OH^- to be calculated accurately. The equivalence point is the point in the titration when enough titrant has been added to react exactly with the substance in solution being titrated and will be determined by using an indicator. The end point, the point in the titration at which the indicator changes color, will be very close to 7. At this point, a drop of acid or base added to the solution will change the pH by several pH units.

In Part II, a weak acid is titrated with the strong base from Part I and the equivalence point will be somewhat higher than 7 (8 – 9). By titrating a known amount of solid acid with the standardized NaOH, it will be possible to determine the number of moles of H^+ the acid furnished. From this information, one can obtain the equivalent mass (EM_a) of the acid:

$$EM_a = \frac{\text{grams acid}}{\text{moles of } H^+}$$

However, the equivalent mass of the acid may or may not be the same as the molecular mass of the acid since some acids produce more than one mole of H^+ per mole of acid. In order to find the molecular mass from the EM_a, the number of ionizable hydrogen ions per acid molecule is required.

If a graph is drawn of pH versus mL of NaOH added, there will be a significant change in pH in the vicinity of the equivalence point. It is important to understand that the equivalence point will not be at pH 7, but will be slightly higher. The value of the equilibrium constant for the dissociation of the acid can be obtained from this graph. Since a weak acid is being studied in Part II, the dissociation can be represented as

$$HA + H_2O \rightleftharpoons H_3O^+ + A^-$$

which results in the equilibrium expression:

$$K_a = \frac{[H_3O^+][A^-]}{[HA]}$$

This can be rearranged to read $[H_3O^+] = K_a \times \frac{[HA]}{[A^-]}$

When the acid is half neutralized, half of the number of moles of HA originally present will be converted to the conjugate base A^-. So $[HA] = [A^-]$ and K_a will be equal to $[H_3O^+]$ since $[HA] / [A^-] = 1$. Therefore, when the acid is half-neutralized, pH = pK_a. The point at which the pH is equal to pK_a can be seen in Figure 1.

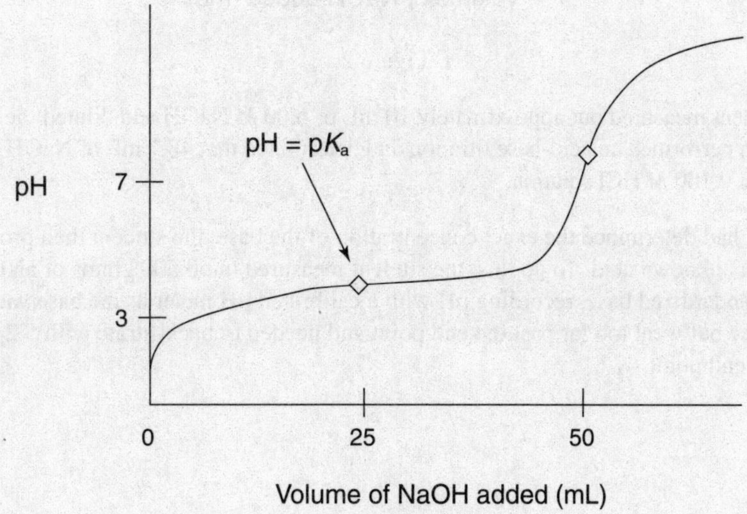

Figure 1

If one were to titrate a weak diprotic acid such as maleic acid with the known NaOH solution, the graph would show two separate inflections — representing the neutralization of each hydrogen — assuming the pK_a values differ by 4 or more pK units (see Figure 2). The dissociation of a diprotic acid occurs in two separate steps:

$$H_2A + H_2O \rightleftharpoons H_3O^+ + HA^-$$
$$HA^- + H_2O \rightleftharpoons H_3O^+ + A^{2-}$$

and results in two separate equilibrium expressions:

$$K_{a_1} = \frac{[H_3O^+][HA^-]}{[H_2A]}$$

$$K_{a_2} = \frac{[H_3O^+][A^{2-}]}{[HA^-]}$$

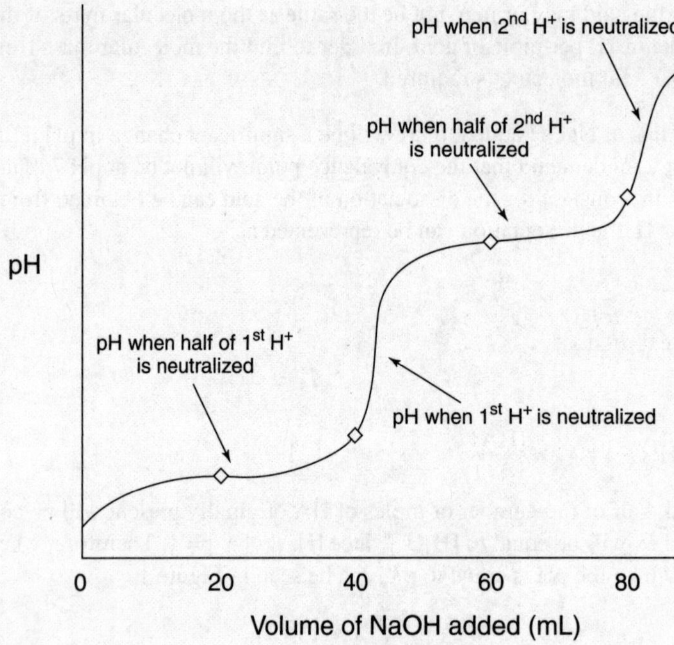

Figure 2

Scenario: Part 1: A student measured out approximately 10 mL of 6.00 *M* NaOH and diluted the base to approximately 600 mL. The student then performed an acid-base titration and determined that 48.7 mL of NaOH solution were needed to neutralize 50.0 mL of a 0.100 *M* HCl solution.

Part 2: Once the student had determined the exact concentration of the base, the student then proceeded to determine the equivalent mass of an unknown acid. To do this, the student measured out 0.500 grams of an unknown solid acid and titrated it with the standardized base, recording pH with a calibrated pH meter as the base was added. The student added 43.2 mL of the base but went too far past the end point and needed to back-titrate with 5.2 mL of the 0.100 *M* HCl to exactly reach the end point.

Analysis:

1. Calculate the molarity of the NaOH solution from Part I.

$$50.0\ \cancel{\text{mL}} \times \frac{0.100\ \cancel{\text{mol HCl}}}{1000\ \cancel{\text{mL}}} \times \frac{1\ \text{mol NaOH}}{1\ \cancel{\text{mol HCl}}} \times \frac{1}{0.0487\ \text{L}} = 0.103\ M\ \text{NaOH}$$

2. The graph of the titration from this experiment is presented in Figure 3. Determine the K_a or K_a's.

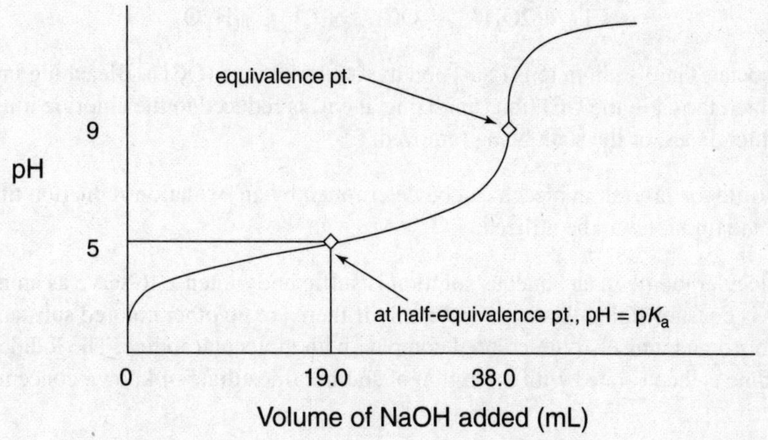

Figure 3

$K_a = 10^{-pK_a} = 10^{-5} = 1 \times 10^{-5}$

3. What is the pH at the equivalence point?

The pH at the equivalence point appears to be around 9. Therefore, $[OH^-] \approx 10^{-5} M$

4. Why is the equivalence point not a pH of 7?

The neutralization reaction is $HA + OH^- \rightarrow A^- + H_2O$, where HA is the weak acid and A^- is its conjugate base. This assumes that HA is a monoprotic acid. Because the principal product of this reaction is the weak base, A^-, the resulting solution will be basic with a pH greater than 7.

5. Determine the EM_a of the solid acid.

$$43.2\ \cancel{\text{mL}} \times \frac{0.103\ \text{mol OH}^-}{1000\ \cancel{\text{mL}}} = 0.00445\ \text{mol OH}^-\ \text{dispensed from buret}$$

$$5.2\ \cancel{\text{mL}} \times \frac{0.100\ \text{mol H}^+}{1000\ \cancel{\text{mL}}} = 0.00052\ \text{mol H}^+\ \text{used in back-titration}$$

$(0.00445 - 0.00052)$ mol = 0.00393 mol OH^- actually used to neutralize

Since H^+ from the acid reacts in a 1:1 mole ratio with OH^-, the number of moles of H^+ furnished by the acid must also be 0.00393.

$$\text{equivalent mass} = \frac{\text{grams of acid}}{\text{moles of H}^+} = \frac{0.500\ \text{g}}{0.00393\ \text{mol}} = 127\ \text{g/mol}$$

6. Referring to the Appendix, which indicator(s) would have been the most appropriate to use?

Phenolphthalein would have been a good choice because the pH at the equivalence point falls within the range over which this indicator changes its color.

7. Does the solid acid appear to be monoprotic or diprotic and why?

This acid appears to be monoprotic because the titration curve (see Figure 3 above) only shows one inflection point so far as plotted. Another end-point (equivalence point) is generally hard to find using only indicators above pH=10.5 since the indicator equilibrium reaction $HIn \rightleftharpoons H^+ + In^- (K_{HIn} = 10^{-12})$ interacts and interferes.

Experiment 8: Determination of Concentration by Oxidation-Reduction Titration

Background: Commercially available bleaching solutions contain NaOCl, sodium hypochlorite. Sodium hydroxide is reacted with chlorine gas to produce the hypochlorite ion, OCl^-.

$$Cl_{2\,(g)} + 2OH^-_{(aq)} \rightarrow OCl^-_{(aq)} + Cl^-_{(aq)} + H_2O_{(l)}$$

In solution, NaOCl dissociates into sodium ions (Na^+) and hypochlorite ions (OCl^-). Bleaching involves an oxidation-reduction reaction in which the Cl in the OCl^- ion (oxidizing agent) is reduced to the chloride ion (Cl^-). The reducing agent is either a dye, which fades, or the stain being removed.

The amount of hypochlorite ion present in bleach can be determined by an oxidation-reduction titration. In this experiment, an iodine-thiosulfate titration will be utilized.

The brown color of molecular iodine in an aqueous solution is sufficiently intense to serve as an indicator, the brown color disappearing as I_2 is consumed, but this is possible only if there are no other colored substances present to interfere. "Soluble" starch forms an intensely blue-colored complex with molecular iodine. The iodide ion is oxidized to form iodine, I_2. This iodine is then titrated with a solution of sodium thiosulfate of known concentration. Three steps are involved:

1. An acidified solution of iodide ion and hypochlorite ion is oxidized to iodine:

   $$2H^+_{(aq)} + OCl^-_{(aq)} + 2I^-_{(aq)} \rightarrow Cl^-_{(aq)} + I_{2\,(aq)} + H_2O_{(l)}$$

2. However, iodine is not very soluble in water. Therefore, an aqueous solution of iodide ion is added to the iodine to form the complex ion, triiodide ion, $I_3^-{}_{(aq)}$. In dilute concentrations, the triiodide ion is yellow and in concentrated solutions it is a dark reddish-brown.

   $$I_{2\,(aq)} + I^-_{(aq)} \rightarrow I^-_{3\,(aq)}$$

3. Finally, the triiodide ion is titrated with a known solution of thiosulfate ions, which forms iodide ions:

   $$I^-_{3\,(aq)} + 2S_2O_3^{2-}{}_{(aq)} \rightarrow 3I^-_{(aq)} + S_4O_6^{2-}{}_{(aq)}$$

In this step the reddish brown color of the triiodide begins to fade to yellow and finally to clear, indicating only iodide ions present. However, this is not the best procedure for determining when all of the I_3^- has disappeared since it is not a sensitive reaction and the change from pale yellow to colorless is not distinct. A better procedure is to add a soluble starch solution shortly prior to reaching the end point, since if it is added to soon, too much iodine or triiodide ion may be present forming a complex that may not be reversible in the titration. The amount of thiosulfate used is proportional to the amount of hypochlorite ion present.

The experimental error involved in measuring small volumes of liquids is usually greater than the error when measuring larger volumes. Diluted samples will be prepared, called aliquots, to improve the accuracy.

Scenario: A student diluted 50.00 mL of a commercial bleach to 250.00 mL in a volumetric flask and then titrated a 20. mL aliquot. The titration required 35.50 mL of 0.10000 *M* $Na_2S_2O_3$ solution. The price of the gallon jug of bleach was \$1.00. The density of the bleach was 1.15 g • mL^{-1}.

Analysis:

1. Calculate the number of moles of $S_2O_3^{2-}$ ion required for titration.

$$= \frac{35.50 \text{ mL } Na_2S_2O_3 \text{ sol'n}}{1} \times \frac{1 \text{ L sol'n}}{1000 \text{ mL } Na_2S_2O_3 \text{ sol'n}} \times$$

$$\frac{0.10000 \text{ mol } Na_2S_2O_3}{1 \text{ L sol'n}} \times \frac{1 \text{ mol } S_2O_3^{2-}}{1 \text{ mol } Na_2S_2O_3} = 3.550 \times 10^{-3} \text{ mol } S_2O_3^{2-}$$

2. Calculate the number of moles of I_2 produced in the titration mixture.

$$2S_2O_3^{2-}{}_{(aq)} + I_{2\,(aq)} \rightarrow S_4O_6^{2-}{}_{(aq)} + 2I^-{}_{(aq)}$$

$$\frac{3.550 \times 10^{-3}\ \cancel{\text{mol } S_2O_3^{2-}}}{1} \times \frac{1 \text{ mol } I_2}{2\ \cancel{\text{mol } S_2O_3^{2-}}} = 1.775 \times 10^{-3} \text{mol } I_2$$

3. Calculate the number of moles of OCl^- ion present in the diluted bleaching solution that was titrated.

$$\frac{1.775 \times 10^{-3}\ \cancel{\text{mol } I_2}}{1} \times \frac{1 \text{ mol } OCl^-}{1\ \cancel{\text{mol } I_2}} = 1.775 \times 10^{-3} \text{ mol } OCl^-$$

4. Calculate the mass of NaOCl present in the diluted bleaching solution titrated.

$$\frac{1.775 \times 10^{-3}\ \cancel{\text{mol } OCl^-}}{1} \times \frac{1\ \cancel{\text{mol NaOCl}}}{1\ \cancel{\text{mol } OCl^-}} \times \frac{74.44 \text{ g NaOCl}}{1\ \cancel{\text{mol NaOCl}}} = 0.1321 \text{ g NaOCl}$$

5. Determine the volume of commercial bleach present in the diluted bleach solution titrated (aliquot).

$$\frac{20.00\ \cancel{\text{mL diluted bleach sol'n}}}{1} \times \frac{50.0 \text{ mL commercial bleach}}{250.0\ \cancel{\text{mL diluted bleach sol'n}}}$$

$$= 4.00 \text{ mL commercial bleach}$$

6. Calculate the mass of commercial bleach titrated.

$$\frac{4.00\ \cancel{\text{mL commercial bleach}}}{1} \times \frac{1.15 \text{ g commerical bleach}}{1.00\ \cancel{\text{mL commercial bleach}}} = 4.60 \text{ g commercial bleach}$$

7. Determine the percent NaOCl in the commercial bleach.

$$\frac{\text{part}}{\text{whole}} \times 100\% = \frac{0.1321 \text{ g NaOCl}}{4.60 \text{ g commercial bleach}} \times 100\% = 2.87\%$$

8. Calculate the mass of 1.00 gallon of the commercial bleach. 1 U.S. gallon = 3785 mL.

$$= \frac{1.00\ \cancel{\text{gal comm. bleach}}}{1} \times \frac{3785\ \cancel{\text{mL}}}{1\ \cancel{\text{gal}}} \times \frac{1.15 \text{ g comm. bleach}}{1\ \cancel{\text{mL comm. bleach}}} = 4.35 \times 10^3 \text{ g}$$

9. Calculate the cost of 100. g of the commercial bleach.

$$\frac{100.\ \cancel{\text{g comm. bleach}}}{1} \times \frac{1.00\ \cancel{\text{gal comm. bleach}}}{4.35 \times 10^3\ \cancel{\text{g comm. bleach}}}$$

$$\times \frac{\$1.00}{1.00\ \cancel{\text{gal comm. bleach}}} = \$0.0230$$

10. Determine the cost of the amount of commercial bleach required to supply 100. g of NaOCl.

$$\frac{100.\ \cancel{\text{g NaOCl}}}{1} \times \frac{100.\ \cancel{\text{g comm.bleach}}}{2.87\ \cancel{\text{g NaOCl}}} \times \frac{\$0.0230}{100.\ \cancel{\text{g comm.bleach}}} = \$0.801$$

Experiment 9: Determination of Mass and Mole Relationship in a Chemical Reaction

Background: This experiment uses the concept of continuous variation to determine mass and mole relationships. Continuous variation keeps the total volume of two reactants constant, but varies the ratios in which they combine. The optimum ratio would be the one in which the maximum amount of both reactants of known concentration are consumed and the maximum amount of product(s) is produced. Since the reaction is exothermic, and heat is therefore a product, the ratio of the two reactants that produces the greatest amount of heat is a function of the actual stoichiometric relationship. Other products that could be used to determine actual molar relationships might include color intensity, mass of precipitate formed, amount of gas evolved, and so on.

Scenario: The active ingredient in commercial bleach is NaClO (see Experiment 8). A student was given a sample of commercial bleach which was labeled 5.20% NaClO by mass. The student was then directed to prepare 300. mL of a 0.500 *M* NaClO solution. The student was also directed to prepare 300. mL of a 0.500 *M* solution of sodium thiosulfate, $Na_2S_2O_3$ in 0.200 *M* sodium hydroxide. Both solutions were then allowed to reach a room temperature of 25.0°C. Keeping a constant final volume of 50.0 mL of solution, the student mixed various amounts of sodium hypochlorite and sodium thiosulfate together, stirring well, and recorded the maximum temperature (±0.2°C) of the solution with a calibrated temperature probe. The change in temperature (ΔT) is equal to $T_{final} - 25.0$°C. A chart and graph of the data is given in Figure 1.

Trial #	ΔT(°C)	mL NaClO	mL $Na_2S_2O_3$	vol ratio
1	0	0	50	x
2	3.9	5	45	1:9
3	8.1	10	40	1:4
4	11.3	15	35	1:2.3
5	14.7	20	30	1:1.5
6	18.8	25	25	1:1
7	22.6	30	20	1.5:1
8	27.6	35	15	2.3:1
9	31.9	40	10	4:1
10	12	45	5	9:1
11	0.1	50	0	x

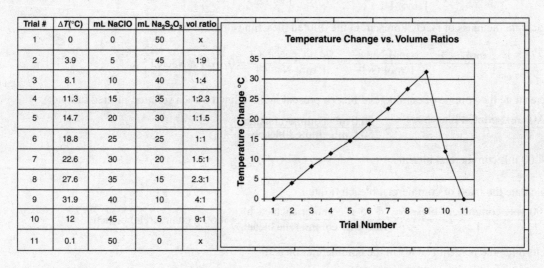

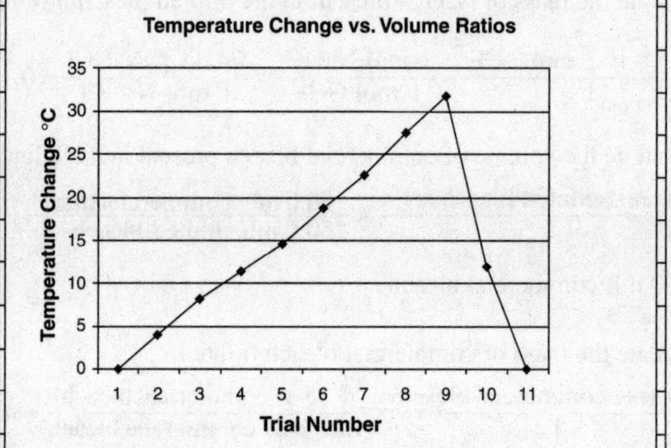

Figure 1

Analysis:

1. Write the net ionic equations involved in this experiment.

$$4OCl^-_{(aq)} + S_2O_3^{2-}{}_{(aq)} + 2\,OH^-_{(aq)} \rightarrow 2\,SO_4^{2-}{}_{(aq)} + 4Cl^-_{(aq)} + H_2O_{(l)}$$

2. Show the steps necessary to produce the 0.500 *M* sodium hypochlorite solution.

The commercial bleach was 5.20% NaClO. The directions required making a 0.500 *M* solution. *MM* of NaClO = 74.44 g • mol^{-1}. 300. mL of solution should contain 11.2 g NaClO:

$$\frac{300.\,\cancel{\text{mL sol'n}}}{1} \times \frac{1\,\cancel{\text{L sol'n}}}{1000\,\cancel{\text{mL sol'n}}} \times \frac{0.500\,\cancel{\text{mole NaClO}}}{1\,\cancel{\text{L sol'n}}} \times \frac{74.44\text{ g NaClO}}{1\,\cancel{\text{mole NaClO}}} = 11.2\text{ g NaClO}$$

To obtain 11.2 g of NaClO, using a 5.20% solution, would require 215 g of bleach solution, diluted to 300. mL with distilled water:

$$\frac{11.2\,\cancel{\text{g NaClO}}}{1} \times \frac{100.\text{ g sol'n}}{5.20\,\cancel{\text{g NaClO}}} = 215\text{ g bleach sol'n diluted to 300. mL}$$

3. Show the steps necessary to produce the 300. mL of 0.500 *M* sodium thiosulfite in 0.200 *M* NaOH.

(a) 0.200 *M* NaOH

$$\frac{300.\,\cancel{\text{mL sol'n}}}{1} \times \frac{1\,\cancel{\text{L sol'n}}}{1000\,\cancel{\text{mL sol'n}}} \times \frac{0.200\,\cancel{\text{mol NaOH}}}{1\,\cancel{\text{L sol'n}}} \times \frac{40.00\text{ g NaOH}}{1\,\cancel{\text{mol NaOH}}}$$

= 2.40 g NaOH

(b) 0.500 *M* $Na_2S_2O_3$

$$\frac{300.\ \cancel{\text{mL sol'n}}}{1} \times \frac{1\ \cancel{\text{L sol'n}}}{1000\ \cancel{\text{mL sol'n}}} \times \frac{0.500\ \cancel{\text{mol } Na_2S_2O_3}}{1\ \cancel{\text{L sol'n}}} \times \frac{158.12\ \text{g } Na_2S_2O_3}{1\ \cancel{\text{mol } Na_2SO_3}}$$

$= 23.7$ g $Na_2S_2O_3$

To make the solution, add 2.40 g of NaOH and 23.7 g $Na_2S_2O_3$ to a graduated cylinder. Dilute to 300. mL with distilled water.

4. Why must the volume of solution produced remain constant?

The amount of heat evolved should be proportional to the mole ratios of the reactants involved. If varying volumes of reactants were allowed, calculations would need to be performed for each mixture so that a valid comparison could be made.

5. Referring to the graph produced, what is the limiting reactant on the line with the positive slope? With the negative slope?

Positive Slope: The mL and mole ratio for equivalency is 4 NaClO to 1 $Na_2S_2O_3$ (see #1 above). In examining the data table, it can be seen that the $Na_2S_2O_3$ is in excess, with the NaClO being the limiting reactant; for example, in Trial 7, for 30 mL of 0.500 *M* NaClO,

$$\frac{30.\ \cancel{\text{mL NaClO}}}{1} \times \frac{1\ \text{mL } Na_2S_2O_3}{4\ \cancel{\text{mL NaClO}}} = 7.5\ \text{mL } Na_2S_2O_3$$

would be needed for equivalency, but 20. mL of $Na_2S_2O_3$ was used.

Negative Slope: In examining the data table, it can be seen that the NaClO is in excess and that the $Na_2S_2O_3$ is the limiting reactant.

6. Why should the point of intersection of the two best-fit lines be used to find the molar ratio rather than ratio associated with the greatest temperature change?

The exact ratios that would have produced the greatest temperature change may not have been used.

7. If 20. mL of the sodium hypochlorite solution was at 25.0°C and 30. mL of the sodium thiosulfate solution was initially at 35.0°C before they were mixed, and after they were mixed together the final temperature was 34.0 °C, what would be the actual temperature change of the mixture?

A temperature correction factor would be needed:

$$\frac{(20.\ \text{mL} \cdot 25.0^\circ\text{C}) + (30.\ \text{mL} \cdot 35.0^\circ\text{C})}{50.\ \text{mL}} = 31.0^\circ\text{C}$$

If the measured temperature is 34.0°C, ΔT should be reported as 34.0°C − 31.0°C = 3.0°C

8. What is the purpose of having sodium hydroxide in both reactants?

The bleach solution is a base. Diluting the bleach in a base of approximately the same molarity does not appreciably change the temperature when the bleach is diluted as there is no chemical reaction occurring.

9. What conclusions can be drawn from Trial 9?

According to the balanced net ionic equation

$$4OCl^-_{(aq)} + S_2O_3^{2-}{}_{(aq)} + 2OH^-_{(aq)} \rightarrow 2SO_4^{2-}{}_{(aq)} + 4Cl^-_{(aq)} + H_2O_{(l)}$$

4 moles of OCl^- are required for every 1 mole of $S_2O_3^{2-}$. In trial 9, the trial which showed the greatest temperature change, 40. mL of NaClO was used for 10 mL of $Na_2S_2O_3$.

$$\frac{40.\ \cancel{\text{mL NaClO}}}{1} \times \frac{1\ \cancel{\text{L}}}{1000\ \cancel{\text{mL}}} \times \frac{0.500\ \text{mol NaClO}}{1\ \cancel{\text{L sol'n}}} = 0.020\ \text{mol } ClO^-$$

$$\frac{10.\ \cancel{\text{mL } Na_2S_2O_3}}{1} \times \frac{1\ \cancel{\text{L}}}{1000\ \cancel{\text{mL}}} \times \frac{0.500\ \text{mol } Na_2S_2O_3}{1\ \cancel{\text{L sol'n}}} = 0.0050\ \text{mol } S_2O_3^{2-}$$

$$\frac{0.020\ \text{mol } ClO^-}{0.0050\ \text{mol } S_2O_3^{2-}} = 4{:}1\ \text{molar ratio}$$

Experiment 10 A: Determination of the Equilibrium Constant, K_a, for a Chemical Reaction

Background: Weak acids, upon dissolving in water, dissociate slightly according to the following equation:

$$HA + H_2O \rightleftharpoons H_3O^+ + A^-$$

The equilibrium expression for this dissociation is: $K_a = \dfrac{[H_3O^+][A^-]}{[HA]}$

Most weak acids dissociate 5% or less, that is, 95% or more of the acid remains as HA. The smaller the value of K_a, the weaker the acid.

If the acid contains more than one ionizable hydrogen, the acid is known as a polyprotic acid. Specifically, diprotic acids, such as sulfuric acid, H_2SO_4, contain two ionizable hydrogens and triprotics, such as phosphoric acid, H_3PO_4, contain three ionizable hydrogens.

In the case of a diprotic acid, the dissociation occurs in two steps and a separate equilibrium constant exists for each step:

$$H_2A + H_2O \rightleftharpoons H_3O^+ + HA^- \qquad K_{a_1} = \frac{[H_3O^+][HA^-]}{[H_2A]}$$

$$HA^- + H_2O \rightleftharpoons H_3O^+ + A^{2-} \qquad K_{a_2} = \frac{[H_3O^+][A^{2-}]}{[HA^-]}$$

The second dissociation generally occurs to a smaller extent than the first dissociation so that K_{a_2} is smaller than K_{a_1}. Exceptions are generally bio-molecules in specific solvent media.

This experiment will determine K_a for a monoprotic weak acid.

A common weak acid, acetic acid, dissociates according to the following equation:

$$\underset{\text{acid}}{HC_2H_3O_2} + \underset{\text{base}}{H_2O} \rightleftharpoons \underset{\substack{\text{conjugate}\\\text{acid}}}{H_3O^+} + \underset{\substack{\text{conjugate}\\\text{base}}}{C_2H_3O_2^-}$$

The equilibrium expression for this dissociation is:

$$K_a = \frac{[H_3O^+][C_2H_3O_2^-]}{[HC_2H_3O_2]} = 1.8 \times 10^{-5}\,M$$

If $[HC_2H_3O_2] = [C_2H_3O_2^-]$, the two terms cancel, resulting in $[H_3O^+] = 1.8 \times 10^{-5}\,M$.

$$K_a = \frac{[H_3O^+]\cancel{[C_2H_3O_2^-]}}{\cancel{[HC_2H_3O_2]}} = 1.8 \times 10^{-5}\,M$$

Scenario: A student prepared three solutions by adding 12.00, 18.50, and 35.00 mL of a $7.50 \times 10^{-2}\,M$ NaOH solution to 50.00 mL of a 0.100 *M* solution of a weak monoprotic acid, HA. The solutions were labeled X, Y and Z respectively. Each of the solutions were diluted to a total volume of 100.00 mL with distilled water. The pH readings of these solutions, obtained through the use of a calibrated pH meter, were (X) 6.50, (Y) 6.70 and (Z) 7.10.

Analysis:

1. Convert the pH of each solution to an equivalent H_3O^+ concentration.
   $-pH = \log_{10}[H_3O^+]$

   Step 1: Enter pH

   Step 2: Change sign by pressing +/– key

Step 3: Press "2nd" then "log" or "inv" then "log"

X: $3.16 \times 10^{-7}\ M\ H_3O^+$

Y: $2.00 \times 10^{-7}\ M\ H_3O^+$

Z: $7.94 \times 10^{-8}\ M\ H_3O^+$

2. For each solution, calculate the number of moles of acid added.

The moles of acid was constant for each solution,

$$\frac{50.00\ \cancel{mL}}{1} \times \frac{1\ \cancel{L}}{1000\ \cancel{mL}} \times \frac{0.100\ \text{moles HA}}{1\ \cancel{L}} = 5.00 \times 10^{-3}\ \text{mol HA}$$

3. For each solution, calculate the number of moles of OH^- added.

$$\text{X: } \frac{12.00\ \cancel{mL}}{1} \times \frac{1\ \cancel{L}}{1000\ \cancel{mL}} \times \frac{7.50 \times 10^{-2}\ \text{mol OH}^-}{\cancel{L}} = 9.00 \times 10^{-4}\ \text{mol OH}^-$$

$$\text{Y: } \frac{18.50\ \cancel{mL}}{1} \times \frac{1\ \cancel{L}}{1000\ \cancel{mL}} \times \frac{7.50 \times 10^{-2}\ \text{mol OH}^-}{\cancel{L}} = 1.39 \times 10^{-3}\ \text{mol OH}^-$$

$$\text{Z: } \frac{35.00\ \cancel{mL}}{1} \times \frac{1\ \cancel{L}}{1000\ \cancel{mL}} \times \frac{7.50 \times 10^{-2}\ \text{mol OH}^-}{\cancel{L}} = 2.69 \times 10^{-3}\ \text{mol OH}^-$$

4. For each solution, determine the concentration of HA and of A^- ion present at equilibrium.

$$\text{X: } [\text{HA}] = \frac{\text{initial moles HA} - \text{moles OH}^-\ \text{added}}{\text{volume sol'n}}$$

$$[\text{HA}] = \frac{5.00 \times 10^{-3} - 9.00 \times 10^{-4}}{0.10000\ \text{L}} = 4.10 \times 10^{-2}\ M$$

moles A^- formed = moles OH^- added

$$[\text{A}^-] = \frac{9.00 \times 10^{-4}\ \text{mol A}^-}{0.10000\ \text{L}} = 9.00 \times 10^{-3}\ M$$

$$\text{Y: } [\text{HA}] = \frac{\text{initial moles HA} - \text{moles OH}^-\ \text{added}}{\text{volume sol'n}}$$

$$[\text{HA}] = \frac{5.00 \times 10^{-3} - 1.39 \times 10^{-3}}{0.10000\ \text{L}} = 3.61 \times 10^{-2}\ M$$

moles A^- formed = moles OH^- added

$$[\text{A}^-] = \frac{1.39 \times 10^{-3}\ \text{mol A}^-}{0.10000\ \text{L}} = 1.39 \times 10^{-2}\ M$$

$$\text{Z: } [\text{HA}] = \frac{\text{initial moles HA} - \text{moles OH}^-\ \text{added}}{\text{volume sol'n}}$$

$$[\text{HA}] = \frac{5.00 \times 10^{-3} - 2.69 \times 10^{-3}}{0.10000\ \text{L}} = 2.31 \times 10^{-2}\ M$$

moles A^- formed = moles OH^- added

$$[\text{A}^-] = \frac{2.69 \times 10^{-3}\ \text{mol A}^-}{0.10000\ \text{L}} = 2.69 \times 10^{-2}\ M$$

5. Determine the reciprocal of the A^- ion concentration for each solution.

$$\text{X: } \frac{1}{9.00 \times 10^{-3}} = 1.11 \times 10^{+2}\ M^{-1}$$

$$\text{Y: } \frac{1}{1.39 \times 10^{-2}} = 7.19 \times 10^{1}\ M^{-1}$$

$$\text{Z: } \frac{1}{2.63 \times 10^{-2}} = 3.80 \times 10^{1}\ M^{-1}$$

6. Plot the reciprocal of the A^- ion concentration on the ordinate against the H_3O^+ ion concentration on the abscissa. Draw a straight "best-fit" line (see Figure 1).

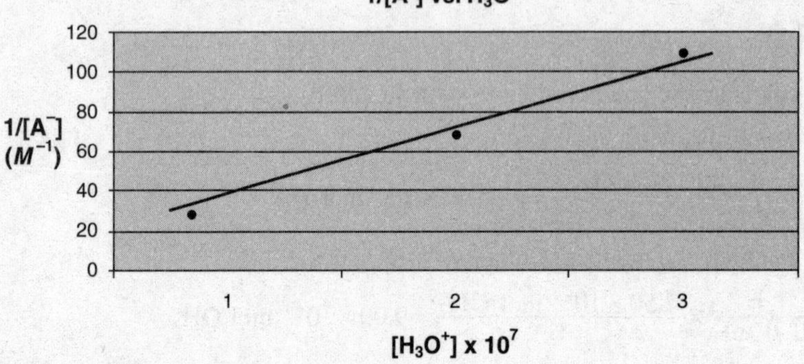

Figure 1

7. Determine the slope of the line.

$$\text{Slope} = \frac{\Delta y}{\Delta x} = \frac{\Delta[1/A^-]}{\Delta[H_3O^+]} = \frac{1.11 \times 10^2 - 3.80 \times 10^1}{(3.16 \times 10^{-7}) - (7.94 \times 10^{-8})} = 3.08 \times 10^8$$

8. Determine the initial concentration of the acid, HA.

$$= \frac{5.00 \times 10^{-3} \text{ mol HA}}{0.10000 \text{ L}} = 5.00 \times 10^{-2}\ M$$

9. Determine the K_a for the weak acid.

$$\frac{1}{\text{slope}} = \frac{\Delta[H_3O^+]}{\Delta[1/A^-]} = [H_3O^+] \cdot [A^-]$$

$$K_a = \frac{1}{HA^* \cdot \text{slope}} = \frac{1}{5.00 \times 10^{-2} \cdot (3.08 \times 10^8)} = 6.49 \times 10^{-8}\ M$$

*= *concentration of HA prior to dissociation or neutralization*

Experiment 10 B: Determination of the Equilibrium Constant, K_{sp}, for a Chemical Reaction

Background: Lead iodide is relatively insoluble, with a solubility of less than 0.002 *M* at 20°C. Lead iodide dissolved in water is represented as:

$$PbI_{2\,(s)} \rightleftharpoons Pb^{2+}{}_{(aq)} + 2I^-{}_{(aq)}$$

The solubility product expression (K_{sp}) for this reaction is:

$$K_{sp} = [Pb^{2+}][I^-]^2$$

If lead iodide is in a state of equilibrium in solution, the product of the molar concentration of lead ions times the square of the molar concentration of the iodide ions will be equal to a constant. This constant does not depend upon how the state of equilibrium was achieved.

When standard solutions of lead nitrate, $Pb(NO_3)_2$ and potassium iodide, KI, are mixed in the presence of KNO_3, a yellow precipitate of lead(II) iodide, PbI_2, forms. The potassium nitrate helps to keep the solution at a nearly constant ionic molarity and promotes the formation of well-defined crystals of lead iodide. The lead iodide will be allowed to come to equilibrium in the solution by mixing the solution very well and then allowing the precipitate to settle completely by centrifuging. The iodide ion, I^-, is colorless and not able to be directly measured in a spectrophotometer (see Figure 1). Therefore, the I^- will be oxidized to I_2, which is brown in water, by an acidified potassium nitrite, KNO_2, solution. The concentration of I_2 is rather small; however, the absorption of light at 525 nm is sufficient to allow detection of the I_2 molecule. $[Pb^{2+}]$ in solution will be determined from the initial state of the system, the measured $[I^-]$ and the relationship between $[Pb^{+2}]$ and $[I^-]$ in the equilibrium expression.

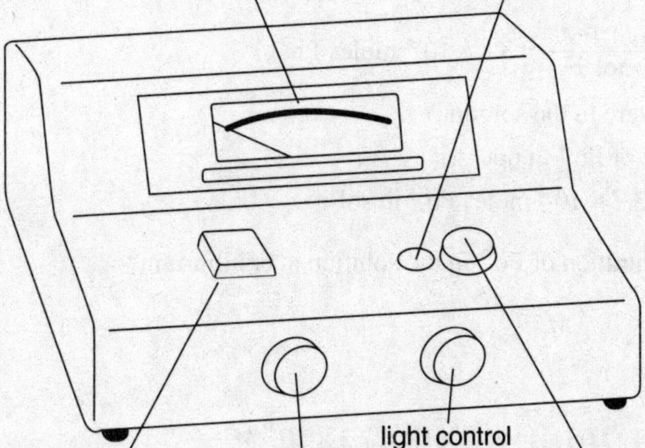

Figure 1

Scenario: A student mixed 5.0 mL of 0.015 *M* $Pb(NO_3)_2$ with 3.0 mL of 0.030 *M* KI in 2.0 mL of 0.200 *M* KNO_3. The test tube was shaken for 15 minutes and the solid precipitate of lead(II) iodide was allowed to settle. The tube was centrifuged to remove any excess lead(II) iodide from the supernatant. To the supernatant, she added KNO_2 to oxidize the I^- to I_2. The supernatant was then analyzed for I_2 by using a spectrophotometer. She then made known dilutions of a 0.10 *M* potassium iodide solution in acidified KNO_2 to create a calibration curve to be able to determine the I^- in the supernatant.

Analysis:

1. How many moles of Pb^{2+} were initially present?

$$\frac{5.0\ \cancel{\text{mL sol'n}}}{1} \times \frac{1\ \cancel{\text{L sol'n}}}{1000\ \cancel{\text{mL sol'n}}} \times \frac{0.015\ \text{mol Pb}(\text{NO}_3)_2}{1\ \cancel{\text{L sol'n}}}$$

$= 7.5 \times 10^{-5}$ mol $Pb(NO_3)_2$ yielding 7.5×10^{-5} mol Pb^{2+}

2. How many moles of I^- were initially present?

$$\frac{3.0\ \cancel{\text{mL sol'n}}}{1} \times \frac{1\ \cancel{\text{L sol'n}}}{1000\ \cancel{\text{mL sol'n}}} \times \frac{0.030\ \text{mol KI}}{1\ \cancel{\text{L sol'n}}}$$

$= 9.0 \times 10^{-5}$ mol KI yielding 9.0×10^{-5} mol I^-

3. From known dilutions of KI in acidified KNO_2, a calibration curve was created. From the calibration curve, it was determined that the concentration of I^- at equilibrium in the supernatant was 1.4×10^{-3} mole/liter. How many moles of I^- were present in 10. mL of the final solution?

$$\frac{1.4\times10^{-3}\text{ moles}}{\cancel{L}}\times\frac{0.010\ \cancel{L}}{1}=1.4\times10^{-5}\text{ mol I}^-\text{ in sol'n at equil.}$$

4. How many moles of I^- precipitated?

moles I^- originally present – moles of I^- in solution

$= 9.0 \times 10^{-5} - 1.4 \times 10^{-5} = 7.6 \times 10^{-5}$ moles I^- ppt.

5. How many moles of Pb^{2+} precipitated?

There are twice as many moles of I^- as there are Pb^{2+}, therefore,

$$\frac{7.6\times10^{-5}\ \cancel{\text{mol I}^-}}{1}\times\frac{1.00\text{ mol Pb}^{2+}}{2.00\ \cancel{\text{mol I}^-}}=3.8\times10^{-5}\text{ moles Pb}^{2+}$$

6. How many moles of Pb^{2+} were in the solution?

total moles of Pb^{2+} – moles of Pb^{2+} in ppt

$= 7.5 \times 10^{-5} - 3.8 \times 10^{-5} = 3.7 \times 10^{-5}$ moles Pb^{2+} in sol'n

7. What was the molar concentration of Pb^{2+} in the solution at equilibrium?

$$\frac{3.7\times10^{-5}\text{ mol Pb}^{2+}}{0.010\text{ L}}=3.7\times10^{-3}\ M$$

8. Determine K_{sp}

$K_{sp} = [Pb^{2+}]\,[I^-]^2 = (3.7 \times 10^{-3}\ M)\,(1.4 \times 10^{-3}\ M)^2 = 7.3 \times 10^{-9}\ M^3$

9. The published value of K_{sp} at 25°C for PbI_2 is 7.1×10^{-9}. Determine the percent error.

$$\%\text{ error}=\frac{\text{obs}-\text{exp}}{\text{exp}}\times100\%=\frac{(7.3\times10^{-9}-7.1\times10^{-9})}{7.1\times10^{-9}}\times100\%=2.8\ \%$$

Experiment 10 C: Determination of the Equilibrium Constant, K_c, for a Chemical Reaction

Background: Many reactions do not go to completion. Rather, they reach an intermediate state in which both reactants and products are present simultaneously. When the concentrations of all species remain constant at a particular temperature over time, a state of equilibrium has been achieved. The equilibrium constant, K_c, relates the concentrations of products to reactants at equilibrium. K_c values significantly greater than 1 indicate that the products are favored, while K_c values significantly less that 1 indicate that the reactants are more predominant.

In this experiment the equilibrium between iron(III) ions, Fe^{3+}, and thiocyanate ions, SCN^-, will be investigated. The equilibrium equation is:

$$Fe^{3+}_{(aq)} + SCN^-_{(aq)} \rightleftharpoons FeSCN^{2+}_{(aq)}$$

From the equation, an equilibrium expression can be created:

$$K_c=\frac{[FeSCN^{2+}]}{[Fe^{3+}][SCN^-]}$$

The $FeSCN^{2+}$ ion is red. The degree of color is proportional to the concentration. The concentration of $FeSCN^{2+}$ will be found through the use of a calibrated spectrophotometer whose most optimal wavelength was determined in which a known concentration of $FeSCN^{2+}$ is made up and the wavelength varied for maximum absorbance. Since the $FeSCN^{2+}$ is red, the wavelength of the light in the spectrophotometer should be the complement color and appear blue-violet. Then, with the spectrophotometer set at this optimal wavelength, the absorbances of various known concentration of $FeSCN^{2+}$ will be recorded and graphed. From this graph the concentration of the $FeSCN^{2+}$ at equilibrium will be extrapolated through Beer's law.

Scenario: A student determined that the optimal wavelength for the absorbance of $FeSCN^{2+}$ experiment was 445 nm. Then the student prepared samples of known concentrations of $FeSCN^{2+}$ ranging from 4.0×10^{-5} *M* to 1.4×10^{-4} *M*. The samples were then examined by means of a spectrophotometer and their transmittances recorded. From the transmittance, the absorbance was calculated and graphed. Next, he mixed 5.0 mL of 2.0×10^{-3} *M* $Fe(NO_3)_3$ with 5.0 mL of 2.0×10^{-3} *M* KSCN. This solution was then analyzed in the spectrophotometer and through extrapolation, he was able to determine that the concentration of $FeSCN^{2+}$ at equilibrium was 1.3×10^{-4} *M*.

Analysis:

1. How many moles of Fe^{3+} and SCN^- were initially present?

$$\frac{0.0050\ \cancel{\text{L sol'n}}}{1} \times \frac{2.0 \times 10^{-3}\ \text{moles } Fe^{3+}}{\cancel{\text{L sol'n}}} = 1.0 \times 10^{-5}\ \text{moles } Fe^{3+}$$

$$\frac{0.0050\ \cancel{\text{L sol'n}}}{1} \times \frac{2.0 \times 10^{-3}\ \text{moles } SCN^-}{\cancel{\text{L sol'n}}} = 1.0 \times 10^{-5}\ \text{moles } SCN^-$$

2. How many moles of $FeSCN^{2+}$ were in the mixture at equilibrium?

Total volume of sol'n = 5.0 mL + 5.0 mL = 10.0 mL

$$\frac{1.3 \times 10^{-4}\ \text{moles } FeSCN^{2+}}{\cancel{\text{L sol'n}}} \times \frac{0.0100\ \cancel{\text{L sol'n}}}{1} = 1.3 \times 10^{-6}\ \text{moles } FeSCN^{2+}$$

3. How many moles of Fe^{3+} and SCN^- were used up in making the $FeSCN^{2+}$?

The balanced equation at equilibrium is:

$$Fe^{3+}{}_{(aq)} + SCN^-{}_{(aq)} \rightleftharpoons FeSCN^{2+}{}_{(aq)}$$

The ratio of Fe^{3+} to SCN^- is 1:1 and the ratio of Fe^{3+} and SCN^- to $FeSCN^{2+}$ is 1:1

Therefore, 1.3×10^{-6} moles of Fe^{3+} and 1.3×10^{-6} moles of SCN^- were used in making the $FeSCN^{2+}$.

4. How many moles of Fe^{3+} and SCN^- remain in the solution at equilibrium?

initial # of moles – # of moles used up in making $FeSCN^{2+}$

$= 1.0 \times 10^{-5}$ moles Fe^{3+} – 1.3×10^{-6} moles Fe^{3+} = 8.7×10^{-6} moles Fe^{3+}

$= 1.0 \times 10^{-5}$ moles SCN^- – 1.3×10^{-6} moles SCN^- = 8.7×10^{-6} moles SCN^-

5. What are the concentrations of Fe^{3+}, SCN^-, and $FeSCN^{2+}$ at equilibrium?

$$[Fe^{3+}] = \frac{8.7 \times 10^{-6}\ \text{moles } Fe^{3+}}{0.01\ \text{L sol'n}} = 8.7 \times 10^{-4}\ M\ Fe^{3+}$$

$$[SCN^-] = \frac{8.7 \times 10^{-6}\ \text{moles } SCN^-}{0.01\ \text{L sol'n}} = 8.7 \times 10^{-4}\ M\ SCN^-$$

$[FeSCN^{2+}] = 1.3 \times 10^{-4}$ *M* $FeSCN^{2+}$

6. Determine K_c for the reaction.

$$Fe^{3+}{}_{(aq)} + SCN^-{}_{(aq)} \rightleftharpoons FeSCN^{2+}{}_{(aq)}$$

$$K_c = \frac{[FeSCN^{2+}]}{[Fe^{3+}][SCN^-]} = \frac{1.3 \times 10^{-4}\ M}{(8.7 \times 10^{-4})^2\ M^2} = 1.7 \times 10^2\ M^{-1}$$

Experiment 11: Determination of Appropriate Indicators for Various Acid-Base Titrations

and

Experiment 19: Preparation and Properties of Buffer Solutions

Background: Strong acids generally dissociate into ions nearly completely. The hydronium ion concentration of a strong monoprotic acid solution is therefore essentially equal to the concentration of the acid in solution*. In mono-hydroxy strong bases, the hydroxide ion generally dissociates nearly completely and the hydroxide ion concentration is equivalent to the concentration of the base in solution**. In 1909, Sören Sörenson proposed the system that we use today in measuring the concentration of acids and bases. This system is based on exponents to overcome the difficulties of dealing with small numbers.

$$pH = \log\frac{1}{[H^+]} = -\log[H^+] \qquad [H_3O^+] = 10^{-pH}$$

$$pOH = \log\frac{1}{[OH^-]} = -\log[OH^-] \qquad [OH^-] = 10^{-pOH}$$

Since $K_w = 1.0 \times 10^{-14} = [H^+] \cdot [OH^-]$; $\log K_w = -14.00 = \log[H^+] + \log[OH^-]$; $[-\log[H^+]] + [-\log[OH^-]] = -[-14.00]$, then pH + pOH = 14.00***

For weak acids, those that do not dissociate completely (usually 5% dissociation or less), hydronium ion concentration is not equal to the concentration of the acid in solution (it is less). In weak bases, as well, the concentration of the hydroxide ion is not equal to the concentration of the base (it is less).

In the case of a weak acid, acetic acid, which is represented by HAc, the dissociation reaction can be written as:

$$HAc_{(aq)} + H_2O_{(l)} \rightleftharpoons Ac^-_{(aq)} + H_3O^+_{(aq)}$$

The equilibrium expression is therefore:

$$K_a = \frac{[H_3O^+][Ac^-]}{[HAc]} = 1.8 \times 10^{-5}\ M$$

The concentration of the acetic acid that has not dissociated is considered to be approximately equal to the initial concentration of the acid because the extent of the dissociation of weak acids is small. However, often it is not negligible and then to solve for the equilibrium concentrations, use of the quadratic equation or other special mathematics is needed.

** more accurately as the anion of the acid*

*** more accurately as the cation of the base*

**** temperature dependent*

In hydrolysis, a salt reacts with water. The species that hydrolyze do so because a weak acid or a weak base is formed. The reaction may produce a solution that is acidic, basic or neutral according to the following chart:

Strong base + strong acid	*No hydrolysis — neutral*
NaOH + HCl	Salt formed — NaCl $H^+ + OH^- \rightleftharpoons H_2O$ $K = \frac{1}{[H^+][OH^-]} = \frac{1}{K_w}$ Methyl Red (end point = pH 5) Bromthymol Blue (end point = pH 7) Phenolphthalein (end point = pH 9)
Strong base + weak acid	***Basic — only anion hydrolyzes***
NaOH + HAc	Salt formed — NaAc $Ac^- + H_2O \rightleftharpoons HAc + OH^-$ $K_b = \frac{[HAc][OH^-]}{[Ac^-]} \times \frac{[H^+]}{[H^+]} = \frac{K_w}{K_{HAc}}$ Phenolphthalein (end point = pH 9)
Weak base + strong acid	***Acidic — only cation hydrolyzes***
NH_3 + HCl	Salt formed — NH_4Cl $NH_4^+ + H_2O \rightleftharpoons NH_3 + H_3O^+$ $K_a = \frac{[NH_3][H_3O^+]}{[NH_4^+]} \times \frac{[OH^-]}{[OH^-]} = \frac{K_w}{K_{NH_3}}$ Methyl Red (end point = pH 5) or Methyl Orange (end point = pH 4)
Weak base + weak acid	***Variable pH— both ions hydrolyze. pH depends upon extent of hydrolysis of each ion involved.***
NH_3 + HCN	Salt formed — NH_4CN $NH_4^+ + H_2O \rightleftharpoons NH_3 + H_3O^+$ $CN^- + H_2O \rightleftharpoons HCN + OH^-$ $K_a = \frac{[NH_3][HCN]}{[NH_4^+][CN^-]} \times \frac{[H^+][OH^-]}{[H^+][OH^-]} = \frac{K_w}{K_b NH_3 \times K_a HCN}$ pH of $NH_4CN_{(aq)}$ is greater than 7 because CN^- ($K_b = 2.0 \times 10^{-5}$) is more basic than NH_4^+ ($K_a = 5.6 \times 10^{-10}$) is acidic.

If solutions undergo only very small changes in pH after small amounts of strong acids or bases are added, the solution is called a buffer. Buffers may be prepared by either combining a weak acid and a salt of the acid or by adding a weak base to a salt of the base. Where both ions of a salt can hydrolyze, that salt may also act as a buffer (for example, NH_4Ac, pH=7.0). The solutions that result may have a common ion and resist changes in pH.

The simplest quantitative method for determining pH is with the use of indicators. An indicator is a colored substance usually derived from plant material that can exist in either an acid or base form. The two forms have different colors. If one knows the pH at which the indicator turns from one form to the other, one can then determine from the observed color whether the solution has a pH higher or lower than this value. Methyl orange changes color over the pH interval from 3.1 to 4.4. Below pH 3.1 it is in the acid form, which is red. In the interval from 3.1 to 4.4 it is gradually converted to the basic form, which is yellow. By pH 4.4 the conversion is complete.

See the Appendix for a chart of acid-base indicators.

Scenario: Part I: pH of a Strong Acid

A student obtains 100.0 mL of 0.100 *M* HCl. The student prepares serial dilutions of the acid to obtain solutions of the following concentrations: 0.0500 *M,* 0.0100 *M,* 0.00500 *M* and 0.00100 *M.* The student determines the pH of each of the solutions with a pH meter and then from an assortment of indicators available and using Appendix E, adds the appropriate indicator to samples of the solutions produced.

Part II: pH of a Weak Acid

This time the student obtains 100.0 mL of 0.100 *M* acetic acid solution and repeats the steps from Part I.

Part III: pH of Various Salt Solutions

0.100 *M* solutions of NH_4Ac, NaCl, NaAc, NH_4Cl, $NaHCO_3$ and Na_2CO_3 are available. The student measures each solution with the calibrated pH meter and also adds appropriate indicators to samples of each solution and observes color changes.

Part IV: pH of Buffer Solutions

The student prepares a buffer solution by adding 4.00 g of sodium acetate to 200 mL of 0.250 *M* acetic acid. The student then obtains 4 beakers labeled 1, 2, 3 and 4. To beakers 1 and 2 she adds 50.0 mL of the buffer solution. To beakers 3 and 4 she adds 50.0 mL of distilled water. She then uses a calibrated pH meter and obtains the pH of the solutions in the beakers. To beakers 1 and 3, she pipets 25.0 mL of 0.250 *M* HCl, mixes well and determines the pH using the calibrated pH meter. She also selects an appropriate indicator and records the color produced. To beakers 2 and 4 she adds 25.0 mL of 0.250 *M* NaOH and repeats the process as she did with the HCl. The pH of each beaker was as follows: (1) 4.32, (2) 5.25, (3) 1.01, (4) 12.88.

Analysis: Because the data obtained from this lab is quite extensive, sample questions will be asked to determine knowledge of the processes involved.

1. A solution from Part I was determined to have a pH of 1.00. Determine the pOH, the $[H_3O^+]$ and the $[OH^-]$.

   $pOH = 14.00 - pH = 14.00 - 1.00 = 13.00$

   $[H^+] = 10^{-pH} = 10^{-1.00} = 0.100\ M$

   $[OH^-] = 10^{-pOH} = 10^{-13.00} = 1.00 \times 10^{-13}\ M$

2. A solution from Part I had an $[OH^-]$ of 2.00×10^{-12} *M.* Determine the pH.

   $pOH = -\log[OH^-] = -\log(2.00 \times 10^{-12}) = 11.70$

   $pH = 14.00 - pOH = 14.00 - 11.70 = 2.30$

3. The pH of a 0.100 *M* acetic acid solution in Part II was found to be 2.87. Calculate the K_a of acetic acid.

   $[H_3O^+] = 10^{-2.87} = 1.35 \times 10^{-3}\ M$ at equilibrium

   $$HAc_{(aq)} + H_2O_{(l)} \rightleftharpoons Ac^-_{(aq)} + H_3O^+_{(aq)}$$

	[HAc]	[Ac⁻]	$[H_3O^+]$
I	0.100 *M*	0	~0
C	−0.00135	+0.00135	+0.00135
E	~0.099	0.00135	0.00135

$$K_a = \frac{[Ac^-][H_3O^+]}{[HAc]} = \frac{(0.00135)(0.00135)}{0.099} = 1.8 \times 10^{-5}$$

4. Calculate the hydrolysis constant K_h for the ammonium chloride solution from Part III. Assume that $[NH_4^+]$ is the same as the initial concentration of ammonium chloride.

From collected data, pH = 5.13, so $[H_3O^+] = 10^{-5.13} = 7.4 \times 10^{-6}\ M$

$$NH_4^+ + H_2O \rightleftharpoons NH_3 + H_3O^+$$

	$[NH_4^+]$	$[NH_3]$	$[H_3O^+]$
I	0.100 *M*	0	~0
C	-7.4×10^{-6}	$+7.4 \times 10^{-6}$	$+7.4 \times 10^{-6}$
E	~0.100	7.4×10^{-6}	7.4×10^{-6}

$$K_h = \frac{[NH_3][H_3O^+]}{[NH_4^+]} = \frac{(7.4 \times 10^{-6})(7.4 \times 10^{-6})}{0.100} = 5.5 \times 10^{-10}$$

5. **Part IV:** Calculate the theoretical pH of the original buffer solution, assuming the volume change due to the addition of the solid is negligible.

$$0.200\ \cancel{L} \times \frac{0.250 \text{ mol HAc}}{\cancel{L}} = 0.0500 \text{ mol HAc}$$

$$\frac{4.00\ \cancel{\text{g NaAc}}}{1} \times \frac{1\ \cancel{\text{mol NaAc}}}{82.034\ \cancel{\text{g NaAc}}} \times \frac{1 \text{ mol Ac}^-}{1\ \cancel{\text{mol NaAc}}} = 0.0488 \text{ mol Ac}^-$$

Since, $\dfrac{[HAc]}{[Ac^-]} = \dfrac{n_{HAc}/V_{sol'n}}{n_{Ac^-}/V_{sol'n}}$

Then, $[H^+] = K_a \cdot \dfrac{n_{HAc}}{n_{Ac^-}} = 1.8 \times 10^{-5} \cdot \dfrac{0.0500 - x \text{ mol HAc}}{0.0488 - x \text{ mol Ac}^-} = 1.84 \times 10^{-5}\ M^*$

where x is negligible

*extra significant figure

$pH = -\log [H^+] = -\log (1.84 \times 10^{-5}) = 4.73$

6. Calculate the theoretical pH of the buffer solution with the added HCl (beaker 1).

$$0.0500\ \cancel{L} \times \frac{0.250 \text{ mol HAc}}{\cancel{L}} = 0.0125 \text{ mol HAc}$$

$$0.0500\ \cancel{L} \times \frac{0.0488 \text{ mol Ac}^-}{0.200\ \cancel{L}} = 0.0122 \text{ mol Ac}^-$$

$$0.0250\ \cancel{L} \times \frac{0.250 \text{ mol H}^+}{\cancel{L}} = 0.00625 \text{ mol H}^+$$

$$Ac^- + H^+ \rightleftharpoons HAc$$

	$[Ac^-]$	$[H^+]$	$[HAc]$
I	0.0122 *M*	0.00625	0.0125
C	−0.00625	−0.00625	+0.00625
E	0.00595	~0	0.01875

$$[H^+] = K_a \times \frac{n_{HAc}}{n_{Ac^-}} = 1.8 \times 10^{-5} \times \frac{0.01875 \text{ mol HAc}}{0.00595 \text{ mol Ac}^-} = 5.67 \times 10^{-5}\ M$$

$pH = -\log [H^+] = -\log (5.67 \times 10^{-5}) = 4.25$

7. **Part IV:** Calculate the theoretical pH of the buffer solution with the added NaOH (beaker 2).

$$0.0500\ \cancel{L} \times \frac{0.250\ \text{mol HAc}}{\cancel{L}} = 0.0125\ \text{mol HAc}$$

$$0.0500\ \cancel{L} \times \frac{0.488\ \text{mol Ac}^-}{0.200\ \cancel{L}} = 0.0122\ \text{mol Ac}^-$$

$$0.0250\ \cancel{L} \times \frac{0.250\ \text{mol OH}^-}{\cancel{L}} = 0.00625\ \text{mol OH}^-$$

$$\text{HAc} + \text{OH}^- \rightleftharpoons \text{Ac}^- + \text{H}_2\text{O}$$

	[HAc]	[OH⁻]	[Ac⁻]
I	0.0125 *M*	0.00625	0.0122
C	–0.00625	–0.00625	+0.00625
E	0.00625	~0	0.01845

$$[\text{H}^+] = K_a \times \frac{n_{\text{HAc}}}{n_{\text{Ac}^-}} = 1.8 \times 10^{-5} \times \frac{0.00625\ \text{mol HAc}}{0.01845\ \text{mol Ac}^-} = 6.10 \times 10^{-6}\ M$$

$$\text{pH} = -\log\,[\text{H}^+] = -\log\,(6.10 \times 10^{-6}) = 5.21$$

8. Calculate the theoretical pH of the distilled water and added HCl (beaker 3).

$$[\text{H}^+] = 0.0250\ \cancel{L} \times \frac{0.250\ \text{mol H}^+}{\cancel{L}} \times \frac{1}{(0.0250 + 0.0500)\text{L}} = 8.33 \times 10^{-2}\ M$$

$$\text{pH} = -\log\,[\text{H}^+] = -\log\,(8.33 \times 10^{-2}) = 1.08$$

9. Calculate the theoretical pH of the distilled water and added NaOH (beaker 4).

$$[\text{OH}^-] = 0.0250\ \cancel{L} \times \frac{0.250\ \text{mol OH}^-}{\cancel{L}} \times \frac{1}{(0.0250 + 0.0500)\text{L}} = 8.33 \times 10^{-2}\ M$$

$$\text{pOH} = -\log\,[\text{OH}^-] = -\log\,(8.33 \times 10^{-2}) = 1.08$$

$$\text{pH} = 14.00 - \text{pH} = 14.00 - 1.08 = 12.92$$

10. A 0.1 *M* solution of an acid was tested with the following indicators and the following colors observed:

Phenolphthalein: clear
Thymol blue: yellow
Methyl orange: yellow
Bromthymol blue: blue
Alizarin yellow: yellow
Methyl red: yellow

Using the Appendix, what is the approximate pH of the solution? What two indicators would you use to find the pH more precisely and why?

From the indicators that were used, the following is a summary of their properties:

Phenolphthalein: range 8.3 to 10.0	Lower color-colorless; Upper color-dark pink
Bromthymol blue: range 6.0 to 7.6	Lower color-yellow; Upper color-blue
Thymol blue: range 8.1 to 9.5	Lower color-yellow; Upper color-blue
Alizarin yellow: range 9.9 to 11.8	Lower color-yellow; Upper color-dark orange
Methyl orange: range 2.5 to 4.4	Lower color-red; Upper color-yellow
Methyl red: range 4.4 to 6.2	Lower color-red; Upper color-yellow
m-Cresol purple: range 7.5 to 9.0	Lower color-yellow; Upper color-violet

Using the Appendix, you would choose bromthymol blue (range 6.0 to 7.6, Lower color-yellow; Upper color-blue) and *m*-Cresol purple (range 7.5 to 9.0, Lower color-yellow; Upper color-violet) because bromthymol blue's high-end color (blue) ends where *m*-cresol purple's low-end color (yellow) begins. The pH would be between 7.5–8.5.

Experiment 12: Determination of the Rate of a Reaction and Its Order

Background: Reaction rates depend on several criteria: the concentration of the reactants, the nature of the reaction, temperature, and presence of catalysts. The rate of most reactions increases when the concentration of any reactant increases. For the reaction

$$aA + bB \rightarrow cC$$

the rate can be expressed by the rate equation, rate = $k[A]^x[B]^y$. The values of x and y are usually whole number integers ranging from 0 to 3 and can only be determined by examining lab data. These numbers represent the order of the reactant. If the order of the reactant is 0, then increasing the concentration of that reactant has no effect on the rate. If the reactant order is 1, then doubling the concentration of that reactant will double the rate of the reaction. If the reactant order is 2, then doubling the concentration of that reactant will increase the rate 4 times. And if the reactant order is 3, then doubling the concentration of that reactant will increase the reaction rate eight times. It is possible to have reactant orders that are fractions or that are negative. To obtain the overall order of the reaction, simply add the reactant orders.

k is known as the rate-specific constant. It is a value, unique for each reaction, that allows the rate law to exist. It is constant for the reaction as long as the temperature does not change. It depends principally upon the nature of the reactants and the temperature at which the reaction occurs. For reactions between ions in aqueous solution, it is affected by the total concentration of ions in the solution.

Svante Arrhenius proposed that a minimum amount of energy was necessary for a reaction to proceed. This minimum amount of energy is called the activation energy, E_a. The Arrhenius equation

$$k = Ae^{-E_a/RT}$$

relates the temperature to the rate specific constant, *k*. A more useful derivation of this equation is

$$\ln k = \frac{-E_a}{RT} + \ln A$$

where *A* is called the collision frequency factor constant and considers the collision frequency and the geometry of colliding species, which in this experiment will be ignored. *R* is the universal gas constant. This equation follows the straight line relationship: $y = mx + b$. A plot of the natural logarithm of *k* versus $1/T$ gives a straight line. The slope of the graph will be used to determine the activation energy.

This experiment studies the kinetics or reaction mechanisms, and their rates, when iodine is added to acetone:

$$CH_3{-}\overset{\overset{\displaystyle O}{\|}}{C}{-}CH_3 + I_2 \longrightarrow CH_3{-}\overset{\overset{\displaystyle O}{\|}}{C}{-}CH_2I + H^+ + I^-$$

Therefore a rate law can be created:

$$\text{rate} = k\,(\text{acetone})^x \cdot [I_2]^y \cdot [H^+]^z$$

It is known that the amount of iodine does not affect the rate of the reaction. Therefore, the rate order of I_2 is 0. Investigating the reaction in terms of the change in the concentration of iodine over time gives the relationship

$$\text{rate} = \frac{-\Delta[I_2]}{\Delta t}$$

The negative sign cancels the negative value of the change in I_2 which is due to the disappearance of I_2, making the rate a positive value. Since the rate of the overall reaction does not depend on the iodine, the reaction rate can be studied by making the iodine the limiting reactant present in excess acetone and H^+, concentrations high enough so that their concentrations do not change significantly through the course of the reaction. One simply then measures the time required for the I_2 to be consumed by varying the concentrations of H^+ and acetone — easily determined since I_2 is yellow in solution.

Scenario: A student prepared a data table for the results that he got in doing this experiment:

Mixture	*[Acetone]*	*[H⁺]*	*$[(I_2)_0]$*	*Time (sec)*	*Temp. (°C)*	*rate*
I	0.80 *M*	0.20	0.0010	240	25°C	4.2×10^{-6}
II	1.60	0.20	0.0010	120	25°C	8.3×10^{-6}
III	0.80	0.40	0.0010	120	25°C	8.3×10^{-6}
IV	0.80	0.20	0.00050	120	25°C	4.2×10^{-6}

Analysis:

1. Determine the rate order for each reactant.

$\text{rate} = k \cdot [\text{acetone}]^x \cdot ([I_2]_0)^y \cdot [H^+]^z$

$\text{rate I} = 4.2 \times 10^{-6} = k \cdot (0.80)^x \cdot (0.0010)^y \cdot (0.20)^z$

$\text{rate II} = 8.3 \times 10^{-6} = k \cdot (1.60)^x \cdot (0.0010)^y \cdot (0.20)^z$

Ratio of Rate II to Rate I:

$$\frac{\text{rate II}}{\text{rate I}} = \frac{8.3 \times 10^{-6}}{4.2 \times 10^{-6}} = 2.0 = \frac{\cancel{k} \cdot (1.60)^x \cdot \cancel{(0.0010)^y} \cdot \cancel{(0.20)^z}}{\cancel{k} \cdot (0.80)^x \cdot \cancel{(0.0010)^y} \cdot \cancel{(0.20)^z}}$$

$\log 2 = x \cdot \log 2$; $\mathbf{x = 1}$

$\text{rate III} = 8.3 \times 10^{-6} = k \cdot (0.80)^x \cdot (0.0010)^y \cdot (0.40)^z$

$\text{rate IV} = 4.2 \times 10^{-6} = k \cdot (0.80)^x \cdot (0.00050)^y \cdot (0.20)^z$

Ratio of rate III to rate IV:

$$\frac{\text{rate III}}{\text{rate IV}} = \frac{8.3 \times 10^{-6}}{4.2 \times 10^{-6}} = 2.0 = \frac{\cancel{k \cdot (0.80)^x \cdot (0.00050)^y} \cdot (0.40)^z}{\cancel{k \cdot (0.80)^x \cdot (0.00050)^y} \cdot (0.20)^z}$$

$\log 2 = z \cdot \log 2$; $\mathbf{z = 1}$

Ratio of rate IV to rate I:

$$\frac{\text{rate IV}}{\text{rate I}} = \frac{4.2 \times 10^{-6}}{4.2 \times 10^{-6}} = 1.0 = \frac{\cancel{k \cdot (0.80)^x} \cdot (0.00050)^y \cdot \cancel{(0.20)^z}}{\cancel{k \cdot (0.80)^x} \cdot (0.0010)^y \cdot \cancel{(0.20)^z}}$$

$\log 1 = y \log 0.5$; $\mathbf{y = 0}$

As the concentration of the acetone doubles, the rate doubles; $x = 1$.

As the concentration of the H^+ doubles, the rate doubles; $z = 1$.

The concentration of the I_2 has no effect on the rate; $y = 0$.

2. Determine the rate specific constant, *k*, for the reaction.

$$k = \frac{\text{rate}}{[\text{acetone}][H^+]}$$

$$\text{Mixture1:} \quad k = \frac{4.2 \times 10^{-6}}{(0.80)(0.20)} = 2.6 \times 10^{-5}$$

$$\text{Mixture2:} \quad k = \frac{8.3 \times 10^{-6}}{(1.60)(0.20)} = 2.6 \times 10^{-5}$$

Mixture3: $k = \dfrac{8.3 \times 10^{-6}}{(0.80)(0.20)} = 2.6 \times 10^{-5}$

Mixture4: $k = \dfrac{4.2 \times 10^{-6}}{(0.80)(0.20)} = 2.6 \times 10^{-5}$

Average: $k = 2.6 \times 10^{-5}$

3. Given the following information, predict the time required for the reaction to reach completion:

Acetone	HCl	I_2	H_2O
25 mL	25 mL	25 mL	25 mL
3.2 *M*	4.0 *M*	0.020 *M*	—

Total volume of mixture = 25 mL + 25 mL + 25 mL + 25 mL = 1.0×10^2 mL

Concentration of each after mixing:

$$\text{Acetone: } \frac{0.025\ \cancel{L}}{1} \times \frac{3.2\ \text{moles}}{\cancel{L}} \times \frac{1}{0.10\ \text{L sol'n}} = 0.80\ M$$

$$\text{HCl: } \frac{0.025\ \cancel{L}}{1} \times \frac{4.0\ \text{moles}}{\cancel{L}} \times \frac{1}{0.10\ \text{L sol'n}} = 1.0\ M$$

$$I_2\text{: } \frac{0.025\ \cancel{L}}{1} \times \frac{0.020\ \text{moles}}{\cancel{L}} \times \frac{1}{0.10\ \text{L sol'n}} = 0.0050\ M$$

rate = $k \cdot [\text{acetone}]^x \cdot ([I_2]_o)^y \cdot [H^+]^z$

$= 2.6 \times 10^{-5} \cdot (0.80)^1 \cdot (0.0050)^0 \cdot (1.0)^1 = 2.1 \times 10^{-5}$ moles $\cdot$ L^{-1} $\cdot$ sec^{-1}

4. The student used the ratios in Mixture I and ran the experiment at two different temperatures. Calculate the rate, the rate constant, log k and $1/T$ for each temperature studied. From the data, plot k versus $1/T$ and determine the activation energy. Given that the activation energy for the reaction is 8.6×10^4 Joules, calculate the % error.

25 °C 240 seconds

40 °C 45 seconds

Begin by creating a table summarizing the known information and leaving room for calculated results:

[Acetone]	$[H^+]$	$[I_2]_o$	Temp (°C)	Time (sec)	rate	*k*	log *k*	$1/T$ (K^{-1})
0.80 *M*	0.20	0.0010	25	240	4.2×10^{-6}	2.6×10^{-5}	−4.58	3.36×10^{-3}
0.80	0.20	0.0010	40	45	2.2×10^{-5}	1.4×10^{-4}	−3.86	3.19×10^{-3}

rate = $k \cdot [\text{acetone}]^1 \cdot ([I_2]_o)^0 \cdot [H^+]^1$

rate = $[I_2]_0 \cdot \text{time}^{-1}$

At 25°C = 298 K:

$$\text{rate} = \frac{0.0010\ M}{240\ \text{sec}} = 4.2 \times 10^{-6}$$

$$k = \frac{4.2 \times 10^{-6}}{(0.80)(0.20)} = 2.6 \times 10^{-5}$$

At 40°C = 313 K:

$$\text{rate} = \frac{0.0010\ M}{45\ \text{sec}} = 2.2 \times 10^{-5}$$

$$k = \frac{2.2 \times 10^{-5}}{(0.80)(0.20)} = 1.4 \times 10^{-4}$$

$$\text{slope} = \frac{y_2 - y_1}{x_2 - x_1} = \frac{-3.86 + 4.58}{3.19 \times 10^{-3} - 3.36 \times 10^{-3}} = -4.24 \times 10^{3}$$

$$E_a = -2.30 \times R \times \text{slope}$$
$$= -2.30 \times \frac{8.31}{\text{mol}} \times (-4.24 \times 10^{3})$$
$$= 8.10 \times 10^{4}\ \text{J} \cdot \text{mol}^{-1}$$

$$\%\ \text{error} = \frac{\text{obs} - \text{exp}}{\text{exp}} \times 100\% = \frac{8.1 \times 10^{4} - 8.6 \times 10^{4}}{8.6 \times 10^{4}} \times 100\%$$

$$= -5.8\%$$

Experiment 13: Determination of Enthalpy Changes Associated with a Reaction and Hess's Law

Background: Thermochemistry is the study of heat changes and transfers associated with chemical reactions. In this thermochemical laboratory study, you will determine the enthalpy change that occurs when a strong base, sodium hydroxide, reacts with a strong acid, hydrochloric acid. Other mixtures studied will include ammonium chloride mixed with sodium hydroxide and ammonia mixed with hydrochloric acid. These three reactions are represented as:

$$NaOH_{(aq)} + HCl_{(aq)} \rightarrow NaCl_{(aq)} + H_2O_{(l)}$$
$$NH_4Cl_{(aq)} + NaOH_{(aq)} \rightarrow NH_{3\,(aq)} + NaCl_{(aq)} + H_2O_{(l)}$$
$$NH_{3\,(aq)} + HCl_{(aq)} \rightarrow NH_4Cl_{(aq)}$$

So that there is no gain nor loss of heat, thermochemical reactions that are called "adiabatic" are carried out in well-insulated containers called calorimeters. The reactants and products in the calorimeter are called the chemical system. Everything else is called the surroundings, and includes the air above the calorimeter, the water in the calorimeter, the thermometer and stirrer, etc.

Hess's Law, or the law of constant heat summation, states that at constant pressure, the enthalpy change for a process is not dependent on the reaction pathway, but is dependent only upon the initial and final states of the system. The enthalpy changes of individual steps in a reaction can be added or subtracted to obtain the net enthalpy change for the overall reaction.

An exothermic reaction occurs when the enthalpy of the reactants is greater than the enthalpy of the products, $-\Delta H$ ($\Delta H = \Sigma\Delta H_{f\ \text{products}} - \Sigma\Delta H_{f\ \text{reactants}}$). In endothermic reactions, the enthalpy of the reactants is lower than that of the products, $+\Delta H$.

Some of the heat transferred to the surroundings during an exothermic reaction are absorbed by the calorimeter and its parts. In order to account for this heat, a calorimeter constant or heat capacity of the calorimeter is required and usually expressed in $J \cdot °C^{-1}$.

Scenario: A student constructed a 'coffee cup calorimeter' (see Figure 1). To determine the heat capacity of the calorimeter, the student placed 50.0 mL of room temperature distilled water in the calorimeter. A calibrated temperature probe recorded the temperature as 23.0°C. The student then added 50.0 mL of warm distilled water (61.0°C) to the calorimeter and recorded the temperature every 30 seconds for the next three minutes. The calorimeter was then emptied and dried. Next, the student measured the temperature change when 50.0 mL of 2.00*M* HCl was added to 50.0 mL of 2.00*M* NaOH. Again, temperature change was recorded every 30 seconds for three minutes. The same procedure was followed for 2.00*M* NH_4Cl with 2.00*M* NaOH and finally, 2.00*M* NH_3 with 2.00*M* HCl.

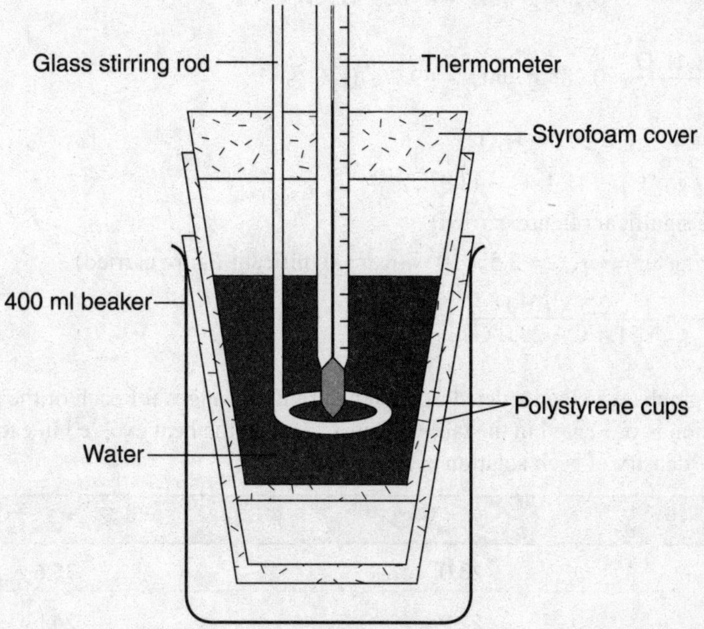

Figure 1

Analysis:

1. A graph was constructed to determine the heat capacity of the calorimeter (see Figure 2). From the graph, determine the heat capacity of the calorimeter. The specific gravity of water at 23.0°C is 0.998 and at 61.0°C it is 0.983.

	A	B
1	30	41.15
2	60	40.9
3	90	40.42
4	120	40.1
5	150	39.91
6	180	39.47
7	Time(sec)	Temperature (°C)

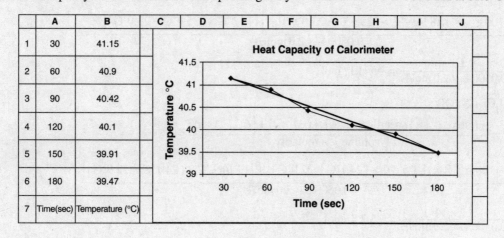

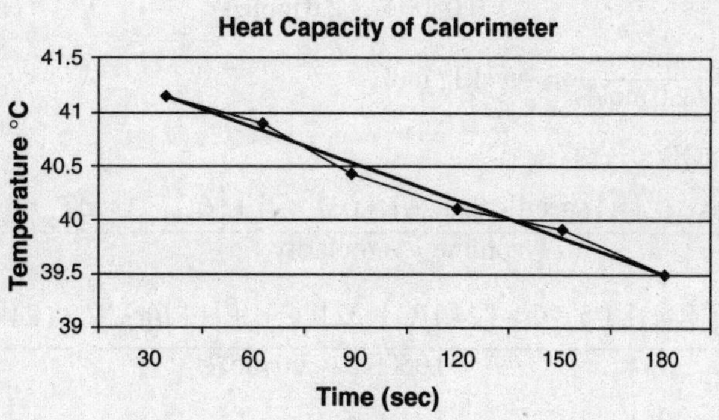

Figure 2

Extrapolating the regression line to the Y axis (0 seconds) gives a temperature of 41.4°C at the moment the room temperature and warm water were mixed.

Average temperature of room temperature and warm water:

$$\frac{23.0°\text{C} + 61.0°\text{C}}{2} = 42.0°\text{C}$$

$$C_{\text{calorimeter}} = \frac{q_{\text{calorimeter}}}{(T_{\text{mix}} - T_{\text{initial}})}$$

$q_{\text{calorimeter}} = -q_{\text{water}}$

q_{water} = (mass water) · (specific heat) · ($T_{\text{mix}} - T_{\text{avg}}$)

At 23.0°C: $\frac{50.0 \text{ mL } H_2O}{1} \times 0.983 \text{ g} \cdot \text{mL}^{-1} = 49.9 \text{ g } H_2O$

At 61.0°C: $\frac{50.0 \text{ mL } H_2O}{1} \times 0.983 \text{ g} \cdot \text{mL}^{-1} = 49.1 \text{ g } H_2O$

Total mass = 49.9 g + 49.1 g = 99.0 *g* H_2O

= (99. 0 g) · (4.18 J / g · °C) · (41.4 °C – 42.0°C)

= -2.5×10^2 J (extra significant figure carried)

Heat gained by calorimeter = $-q_{\text{water}}$ = 2.5×10^2 J (extra significant figure carried)

$$C_{\text{calorimeter}} = \frac{q_{\text{calorimeter}}}{(T_{\text{mix}} - T_{\text{initial}})} = \frac{2.5 \times 10^2 \text{ J}}{(41.4°\text{C} - 23.0°\text{C})} = 14 \text{ J} \cdot °\text{C}^{-1}$$

2. In the same fashion, graphs were constructed of the temperature changes for each of the three reactions. A summary of the information is presented in the table below. Calculate the heat evolved in each reaction (kJ/mol of product). Assume the density of each solution = 1.00 g · mL^{-1}.

	T_{initial} (°C)	$T_{\text{at mixing}}$ (°C)
HCl + NaOH	23.0	35.6
NH_4Cl + NaOH	22.9	24.1
NH_3 + HCl	23.0	33.1

(a) HCl + NaOH

$$q_{\text{rxn}} = \frac{-[(\text{mass}_{\text{sol'n}}) \times (\text{specific heat}_{\text{sol'n}}) \times (\Delta T_{\text{sol'n}})] + [C_{\text{calorimeter}} \times \Delta T_{\text{sol'n}}]}{\text{volume}_{\text{sol'n}} \times \text{molarity}}$$

$$= \frac{[100 \text{ g}_{\text{sol'n}} \times 4.18 \text{ J/g} \cdot \cancel{°\text{C}} \times (35.6\cancel{°\text{C}} - 23.0\cancel{°\text{C}})] + [14 \text{ J/}\cancel{°\text{C}} \times (35.6\cancel{°\text{C}} - 23.0\cancel{°\text{C}})]}{0.0500 \cancel{\text{L}} \times 2.0 \text{ mole/}\cancel{\text{L}}}$$

$$= \frac{-5.4 \times 10^3 \text{ J}}{0.0500 \cancel{\text{L}} \times 2.0 \text{ mol/}\cancel{\text{L}}} = -54 \text{ kJ / mol}$$

(b) NH_4Cl + NaOH

$$q_{\text{rxn}} = \frac{-[(\text{mass}_{\text{sol'n}}) \times (\text{specific heat}_{\text{sol'n}}) \times (\Delta T_{\text{sol'n}})] + [C_{\text{calorimeter}} \times \Delta T_{\text{sol'n}}]}{\text{volume}_{\text{sol'n}} \times \text{molarity}}$$

$$= \frac{-[100. \text{g}_{\text{sol'n}} \times 4.18 \text{ J/g} \cdot \cancel{°\text{C}} \times (24.1\cancel{°\text{C}} - 22.9\cancel{°\text{C}})] + [14 \text{ J/g} \cdot \cancel{°\text{C}} \times (24.1\cancel{°\text{C}} - 22.9\cancel{°\text{C}})]}{0.0500 \text{ L} \times 2.0 \text{ mol/}\cancel{\text{L}}}$$

$$= \frac{-5.2 \times 10^2 \text{ J}}{0.0500 \cancel{\text{L}} \times 2.0 \text{ mol/}\cancel{\text{L}}} = -5.2 \text{ kJ/mol}$$

(c) $NH_3 + HCl$

$$q_{rxn} = \frac{-[(\text{mass}_{\text{sol'n}}) \times (\text{specific heat}_{\text{sol'n}}) \times (\Delta T_{\text{sol'n}})] + [C_{\text{calorimeter}} \times \Delta T_{\text{sol'n}}]}{\text{volume}_{\text{sol'n}} \times \text{molarity}}$$

$$= \frac{[100\ \text{g}_{\text{soln}} \times 4.18\ \text{J/g}^\circ\cancel{\text{C}} \times (33.1^\circ\cancel{\text{C}} - 23.0^\circ\cancel{\text{C}})] + [14\ \text{J}/^\circ\cancel{\text{C}} \times (33.1^\circ\text{C} - 23.0^\circ\text{C})]}{0.0500\ \cancel{\text{L}} \times 2.0\ \text{mole}/\cancel{\text{L}}}$$

$$= \frac{-4.4 \times 10^3\ \text{J}}{0.0500\ \cancel{\text{L}} \times 2.0\ \text{mol}/\cancel{\text{L}}} = -44\ \text{kJ/mol}$$

3. Write the net ionic equation, including the ΔH's, for the first two reactions studied and rearrange the equation(s) where necessary to produce the third reaction and its ΔH.

$$H^+_{(aq)} + \cancel{OH^-_{(aq)}} \rightarrow \cancel{H_2O_{(l)}} \qquad \Delta H = -54\ \text{kJ} \cdot \text{mol}^{-1}$$

$$NH_{3\,(aq)} + \cancel{H_2O_{(l)}} \rightarrow NH_4^+{}_{(aq)} + \cancel{OH^-_{(aq)}} \qquad \Delta H = +5.2\ \text{kJ} \cdot \text{mol}^{-1}$$

$$NH_{3\,(aq)} + H^+_{(aq)} \rightarrow NH_4^+{}_{(aq)} \qquad \Delta H = -49\ \text{kJ} \cdot \text{mol}^{-1}$$

4. Calculate the percent error between the measured ΔH and the calculated ΔH.

$$\%\ \text{error} = \frac{\text{obs} - \text{exp}}{\text{exp}} \times 100\% = \frac{-44 - (-49)}{-49} \times 100\% = -10\%$$

Experiment 14: Separation and Qualitative Analysis of Cations and Anions

Background: Qualitative analysis answers the question "What is and what is not present?". Although technology has replaced many of the "wet chemistry" techniques that are employed in these lab procedures, nevertheless, the technology does not replace the understanding that comes from knowing the reactions. The techniques employed in "wet chemistry" such as decanting, filtering, centrifuging, proper methods of determining pH, washing, and so on are beyond the scope of this review. Furthermore, the detailed qualitative schemes for each reaction, other than being presented in a condensed flowchart style (see the Appendix), are also beyond the scope of a review. Instead, a "Test Tube Mystery" problem will be proposed. The solution of this "mystery" will require you to have mastered the techniques and understanding of some of the reactions in qualitative analysis.

Scenario: Following is a list of solutions used in this "mystery".

- 0.1M $Ni(NO_3)_2$
- 0.1M $SnCl_4$ in 3M HCl
- 0.1M $Cu(NO_3)_2$
- 0.1M $Ca(NO_3)_2$
- 0.1M $Al(NO_3)_3$
- 0.1M $AgNO_3$
- 3M H_2SO_4
- 6M NH_3
- 6M NaOH
- 6M HCl

A student was given 10 test tubes labeled 1–10. Each tube contained a different solution from the list above. Samples of the solutions in each tube were mixed in all possible combinations and the results presented in the following table. From the information presented and the use of the Appendix, logically determine the contents of each test tube, write formulas of precipitates where necessary and support your reasoning.

	1	2	3	4	5	6	7	8	9	10
1	X	H	H, S AMMONIA SMELL*	NR	NR	NR	NR	GREEN SOL'N.	NR	P WHITE
2	X	X	NR	H	P, D WHITE	P GREEN	P, D, H WHITE	P BLUE	P WHITE	P BROWN
3	X	X	X	H	P WHITE	P, D BLUE	P, D, H WHITE	P, D BLUE	NR	P, D BROWN
4	X	X	X	X	NR	NR	NR	NR	NR	P WHITE (small P)
5	X	X	X	X	X	NR	NR	NR	NR	NR
6	X	X	X	X	X	X	NR	NR	NR	NR
7	X	X	X	X	X	X	X	NR	NR	P WHITE
8	X	X	X	X	X	X	X	X	NR	NR
9	X	X	X	X	X	X	X	X	X	NR
10	X	X	X	X	X	X	X	X	X	X

X = either this is a duplicate (1 + 2 is the same as 2 + 1) or it is a mixture of identical solutions (1 + 1).

P = precipitate

G = gas

D = precipitate dissolves in excess reagent

NR = no reaction

S = smoke

H = heat evolved

observed odor in tube 3 before mixing

Analysis:

Test Tube 1: 6*M* HCl: Had to be a strong acid since when mixed with tube 3 it got hot and I had already identified tube 3 as NH_3 by odor. When mixed with samples from test tube 2, the reaction produced a great deal of heat, therefore tube 1 had to contain a strong acid. Could be either 6*M* HCl or 3*M* H_2SO_4. When mixed with test tube 3, a white smoke was produced. I concluded that the smoke was NH_4Cl, therefore, by default, test tube 1 had to contain 6*M* HCl. To confirm that this test tube contained HCl, I mixed samples from test tube 1 with test tube 10, which I believed to contain Ag^+ from prior data in the table, and a white precipitate of AgCl was formed.

Test Tube 2: 6*M* NaOH: When samples of this test tube were mixed with samples from test tube 1, a great deal of heat was produced. The same occurred when I mixed samples of this tube with test tube 4. Therefore, test tube 2 had to contain a strong base since I had already identified test tube 1 as a strong acid. The only strong base among the choices was 6*M* NaOH. When I mixed samples from test tube 2 with samples from test tube 10 which I thought contained Ag^+, a brownish-gray precipitate was formed, indicative of AgOH. When I mixed samples of test tube 2 with samples from test tube 7, which I believed contained Sn^{4+}, a precipitate formed, which I believed to be $Sn(OH)_4$. Upon adding more solution from test tube 2, the precipitate dissolved, consistent with a shift in equilibrium. When I mixed samples from test tube 2 with samples from test tube 6, which I believed contained Ni^{2+}, a green precipitate was produced, $Ni(OH)_2$.

Test Tube 3: 6*M* NH_3: I *carefully* smelled all tubes to begin with and this tube was definitely ammonia. Since I was able to identify this tube initially, I then mixed a small amount of known ammonia with all other tubes. As I mixed the ammonia with the other tubes, I noticed considerable heat being produced in tubes 1, 4 and 7, which I suspected was due to an acid present. With tube 1, smoke appeared, which led me to believe that tube 1 was the HCl which produced a white cloud (smoke) of NH_4Cl. Tubes 1 and 3 were now ruled out. I then noticed precipitates formed in tubes 8 (blue), tube 6 (blue), tube 5 (white), tube 10 (brownish-grey) and tube 7 (white). When excess ammonia was added to tube 10, the precipitate dissolved. When excess ammonia was added to test tube 8, the precipitate dissolved and the solution turned dark blue indicative of Cu^{2+}. When I added excess ammonia to test tube 6, the precipitate dissolved and the solution turned a medium blue color, indicative of the presence of $Ni(NH_3)_6^{2+}$.

Test Tube 4: 3*M* H_2SO_4: Test tube 4 had to contain an acid since when I mixed it with test tube 3 which I had concluded contained a base, it got hot. Since I had already identified test tube 1 as 6*M* HCl I was left with the choice of this tube containing either the 3*M* H_2SO_4 or $SnCl_4$ in 3*M* HCl. When I mixed test tube 4 with tube 2 the reaction produced a great amount of heat. Therefore, I concluded that this tube had to contain a strong acid. I was able to rule out the $SnCl_4$ earlier (see test tube 7), therefore this tube must have contained the H_2SO_4.

Test Tube 5: 0.1*M* $Al(NO_3)_3$: When I mixed samples of test tube 5 with a sample from test tube 3, a white precipitate formed. No heat was evident. The white precipitate could have been either $Al(OH)_3$ or $Sn(OH)_4$, however, since no heat was produced and the $Al(NO_3)_3$ did not contain an acid, it can be concluded that test tube 5 contained $Al(NO_3)_3$. When I mixed samples of test tube 5 which I believed contained Al^{3+} with samples of test tube 2 which I believed contained OH^-, a white precipitate formed which I believed to be $Al(OH)_3$. When I added more solution from test tube 2, increasing the OH^- concentration, the precipitate dissolved, consistent with a shift in equilibrium.

Test Tube 6: 0.1*M* $Ni(NO_3)_2$: I was able to identify this tube through observation since the Ni^{2+} ion is green. No other solution in the list should have had a green color. I was able to confirm this when I mixed samples of test tube 6 with test tube 3 (ammonia) producing $Ni(NH_3)_6^{2+}$, a known light blue solution. When I mixed samples from test tube 6 with test tube 4 which I believed to contain OH^-, a green precipitate formed consistent with the color of $Ni(OH)_2$.

Test Tube 7: 0.1*M* $SnCl_4$ in 3*M* HCl: When I mixed samples from tube 3 (6*M* NH_3) with samples from test tube 7, a white precipitate formed and heat was produced. Tube 7 could contain Al^{3+} or Sn^{4+}. Since heat was produced, an acid must have been present. Between the two choices, only $SnCl_4$ was originally mixed with acid, therefore I concluded that test tube 7 contained $SnCl_4$. When I mixed samples of test tube 7 with samples from test tube 2 that I believed contained OH^-, a white precipitate formed, consistent with $Sn(OH)_4$. Upon adding more NaOH, the precipitate dissolved resulting from a shift in equilibrium.

Test Tube 8: 0.1*M* $Cu(NO_3)_2$: I was able to identify this tube by observation, knowing that the Cu^{2+} ion is blue. No other solution in the list should have a blue color. I confirmed this by forming $Cu(NH_3)_4^{2+}$ (dark blue solution) with samples from test tube 3 that I had initially identified as NH_3.

Test Tube 9: 0.1*M* $Ca(NO_3)_2$: When I mixed samples from test tube 9 with samples from test tube 2 that I had already identified as OH^-, a white precipitate was produced consistent with $Ca(OH)_2$.

Test Tube 10: 0.1*M* $AgNO_3$: When I mixed samples from test tube 10 with samples from test tube 2 that I had already identified as OH^-, a brownish-gray precipitate consistent with the color of AgOH formed. Since I had already ruled out test tube 9 and this was the last tube that needed identification, I can conclude that test tube 10 contained Ag^+. Finally, when I mixed the samples of test tube 10, which I believed to contain Ag^+, with samples from test tube 1 which contained what I believed to be HCl, a white precipitate formed consistent with the color of AgCl.

Experiment 15: Synthesis of a Coordination Compound and Its Chemical Analysis

and

Experiment 17: Colorimetric or Spectrophotometric Analysis

Background: Coordination compounds or complexes are an exciting branch of chemistry and area where much research is focused today. There are several types of coordination compounds. One type of coordination compound consists of a cation bonded to a complex ion, often highly colored, e.g., $K_2[Ni(CN)_4]$, potassium tetracyanonickelate(II). The complex ion, the section in square brackets, consists of a centrally located metallic ion, surrounded by ligands. Ligands may be either polar molecules or simple anions. The bonding within this complex ion is through coordinate covalent bonds. Another type of coordination compound forms when neither the ligands nor the central atom has a charge, e.g., $[Cr(CO)_6]$, hexacarbonylchromium(0), or when the central atom does have a charge, e.g., $[Ni(H_2O)_2(NH_3)_4](NO_3)_2$, tetraamminediaquanickel(II) nitrate.

The rate of reaction involving the formation of complex ions is often very rapid. Given this fact, the ion that is formed is usually the most stable, consistent with the principles of equilibrium and subject to shift. Labile reactions are reactions that involve very fast reversible complex ion formation. However, complex ions may not be labile, that is they do not exchange ligands rapidly and are referred to as nonlabile. These complex ions exchange ligands slowly in substitution reactions and may be favored more kinetically than thermodynamically. Adding a catalyst and thereby changing the rate of formation of the product(s) may change the nature of the complex ion produced. An easy method to determine whether a complex ion is labile or not is to note whether a color change occurs in a solution containing the ion when a good complexing ligand is added.

Chemists are involved in both synthesis, that is creating compounds, and analysis, determing the nature of compounds. In this lab, a coordination compound containing Ni^{2+}, NH_3 and Cl^- will be synthesized. Once it has been synthesized, the next step will be to analyze the coordination compound to determine its exact formula.

When the compound that is synthesized is irradiated with white light, some of the light at particular wavelengths will be selectively absorbed. To determine the wavelength(s) of light absorbed, we can expose a solution of the compound to varying wavelengths of monochromatic light and record the responses. If a particular wavelength of light is not absorbed, the intensity of the light directed at the solution (I_o) will match the intensity of the light transmitted by the solution (I_t). For wavelengths of light absorbed, the intensity will be measurably less intense, therefore, $I_t < I_o$.

$$\%T = \frac{I_t}{I_o} \times 100\%$$

The ratio of I_t to I_o can be helpful in identification when unknown concentrations and characteristics are compared to known values. The lowest percent transmittance ($\%T$) is found at the wavelength to which the sample is most sensitive. This wavelength is known as the analytical wavelength, λ_{max}. Once the analytical wavelength has been determined, then it is possible to investigate or determine: 1) concentration of the solution (c); 2) pathway of light through the solution (b); and 3) the molar absorptivity (ε) of the solution. When multiplied together, these three variables provide the absorbance (A) of the solution, as expressed by Beer's law:

$$A = \varepsilon bc$$

The spectrophotometer used has two scales–absorbance (log scale, 0–2) and percent transmittance (linear scale, 0–100). Most readings are taken from the transmittance scale and then converted to absorbance through the relationship

$$A = 2.000 - \log(\%T)$$

Beer's law allows us to determine concentration since absorbance is directly proportional to it. To negate influences due to cuvette differences, or differences between sample tubes, a reference solution is made containing all of the components except the species being analyzed. From this reference point, accurate absorbances can then be determined. This data is then plotted (absorbance vs. known concentrations) and the unknown concentration then extrapolated from the Beer's law plot. Factors that limit this technique include: 1) sensitivity of the instrument being used — usually best between 10 and 90%*T*, 2) the magnitude of the molar absorptivity (ε), 3) fluctuations due to pH changes, and 4) temperature changes.

Scenario: A student reacted green nickel chloride hexahydrate ($NiCl_2 \cdot 6\,H_2O$) with NH_3. A solid bluish purple solid was produced:

$$Ni^{2+}{}_{(aq,\ green)} + 2Cl^-{}_{(aq)} + nNH_{3\,(aq)} \rightarrow Ni\left(NH_3\right)_n Cl_{2(s,\text{bluish purple})}$$

However, NH_3 in water produces a small amount of hydroxide ion:

$$NH_{3\,(aq)} + H_2O_{(l)} \rightleftharpoons NH_4^+{}_{(aq)} + OH^-{}_{(aq)} \quad K_b = 1.75 \times 10^{-5}$$

So the student simultaneously produced green $Ni(OH)_2$

$$Ni^{2+}{}_{(aq)} + 2OH^-{}_{(aq)} \rightleftharpoons Ni(OH)_{2\,(s)}$$

resulting in an impure synthesis. To maximize the yield of the coordination compound, the products were separated based on their solubilities by heating the products in a small amount of water at 60°C. Further treatment to ensure that no $Ni(OH)_2$ remained involved cooling the solution mixture to 0°C and washing the product with cold ethanol, filtering out the crystals and finally washing them with cold, concentrated NH_3. The crystals were then dried and weighed to determine yield of product.

After the coordination compound was made, it was then analyzed to determine: (1) the mass percent of NH_3 in the compound and (2) the mass percent of Ni^{2+} in the compound.

The analysis of NH_3 began by adding excess HCl to the synthesized compound according to the following reaction:

$$Ni\left(NH_3\right)_n Cl_{2(s)} + nH_3O^+{}_{(aq)} \rightleftharpoons nNH_4^+{}_{(aq)} + Ni^{2+}{}_{(aq)} + nH_2O + 2Cl^-{}_{(aq)}$$

The student was not told the coordination number of the compound, so "*n*" was used to represent the number of ammonia ligands surrounding the nickel(II) ion. After the reaction has reached completion, additional HCl was then titrated back with a standardized NaOH solution:

$$H_3O^+{}_{(aq)} + OH^-{}_{(aq)} \rightarrow 2H_2O_{(l)}$$

At the equivalence point, the point at which the moles of OH^- equals the moles of H_3O^+, an indicator mixture of bromcresol green and methyl red with a suitable end point, was used to determine the equivalence point (pH of 5.1). The reason that the equivalence point is at 5.1 is that the ammonium ion present as a product hydrolyzes resulting in an acidic solution:

$$NH_4^+{}_{(aq)} + H_2O_{(l)} \rightleftharpoons NH_{3\,(aq)} + H_3O^+{}_{(aq)}$$

To determine the mass percent of Ni^{2+} in the compound one takes advantage of the fact that the $[Ni(NH_3)_n]^{2+}$ ion absorbs light. To determine the wavelength of light which this ion absorbs, the analytical wavelength, λ_{max}, was determined. Fifty mL aliquots of standardized solutions of $[Ni(NH_3)_n]^{2+}$ were made up by mixing nickel(II) sulfate hexahydrate in water with excess NH_3 and the absorbances plotted. The reason that $NiSO_4 \cdot 6H_2O$ was used to provide the $[Ni(NH_3)_n]^{2+}$ was that its molecular weight is known. Furthermore, SO_4^{2-} is less likely to disturb the $[Ni(NH_3)_n]^{2+}$ coordination than would Cl^- and the $NiCl_2 \cdot 6H_2O$ deliquesces. The absorbing species, $[Ni(NH_3)_n]^{2+}$, is identical in both the known and unknown solutions, therefore, the molar absorptivity, ε, would be the same. The molar ratio of Ni^{2+} between $Ni(NH_3)_nCl_2$ and $NiSO_4 \cdot 6H_2O$ is 1:1, making direct comparisons possible.

Data:

I. Synthesis

a. Mass of $NiCl_2 \cdot 6H_2O$ used = 7.00 g

b. Mass of (impure) synthesized $Ni(NH_3)_nCl_2$ produced = 5.50 g

II. Mass Percent of NH_3 in $Ni(NH_3)_nCl_2$

a. molarity of NaOH solution = 0.100*M*

b. molarity of HCl solution = 0.250*M*

c. volume of HCl solution added = 25.0 mL

d. volume of NaOH solution required = 29.6 mL

e. mass of $Ni(NH_3)_nCl_2$ used in titration = 0.130 g

III. Mass Percent of Ni^{2+} in $Ni(NH_3)_nCl_2$

a. molar mass of $NiSO_4 \cdot 6\,H_2O$ = 262.88 g · mol^{-1}

b. mass of $NiSO_4 \cdot 6\,H_2O$ = 0.3000 g

c. mass of $Ni(NH_3)_nCl_2$ = 0.3500 g

d. initial color of $NiSO_4$ solution = blue-green

e. initial color of $Ni(NH_3)_nCl_2$ solution = bluish-purple

f. final color of $NiSO_4$ after NH_3 added = bluish-purple

g. final color of $Ni(NH_3)_nCl_2$ after NH_3 added = bluish-purple

IV. *%T* for the standard $[Ni(NH_3)_n]^{2+}$

Wavelength (nm)	*%T of the standard $[Ni(NH_3)_n]^{2+}$ sol'n*
540	42.6
560	38.3
580	35.9
600	32.6
620	42.7
640	48.3

Approximate λ_{max} of $[Ni(NH_3)_n]^{2+}$ ion (nm) = 600 nm

%T of the standard $[Ni(NH_3)_n]^{2+}$ solution at 600 nm = 32.6

%T of the unknown $[Ni(NH_3)_n]^{2+}$ = 22.4

V. Analysis

Mass Percent of NH_3 in $Ni(NH_3)_nCl_2$

Recap: Excess HCl was added to the synthesized $Ni(NH_3)_nCl_2$ to form NH_4^+. The solution was then titrated with NaOH to reach an endpoint of 5.1.

1. Determine the number of moles of HCl originally.

$$\frac{25.0\ \cancel{\text{mL HCl}}}{1} \times \frac{1\ \cancel{\text{L}}}{1000\ \cancel{\text{mL}}} \times \frac{0.250\ \text{mol HCl}}{1\ \cancel{\text{L sol'n}}} = 0.00625\ \text{moles HCl}$$

2. Determine the number of moles of NaOH added.

$$\frac{29.6\ \cancel{\text{mL NaOH}}}{1} \times \frac{1\ \cancel{\text{L}}}{1000\ \cancel{\text{mL}}} \times \frac{0.100\ \text{mol NaOH}}{1\ \cancel{\text{L sol'n}}} = 0.00296\ \text{moles NaOH}$$

3. Determine the number of moles of HCl that remained after the NH_3 was neutralized.

$$\frac{29.6 \text{ \sout{mL NaOH}}}{1} \times \frac{1 \text{ \sout{L}}}{1000 \text{ \sout{mL}}} \times \frac{0.100 \text{ \sout{mol NaOH}}}{1 \text{ \sout{L sol'n}}} \times \frac{1 \text{ mol HCl}}{1 \text{ \sout{mol NaOH}}} = 0.00296 \text{ mol HCl}$$

4. Determine the number of moles of NH_3 in the $Ni(NH_3)_nCl_2$ sample.

= 0.00625 mol HCl – 0.00296 mol NaOH = 0.00329 mol HCl used to react with the NH_3

$$\frac{0.00329 \text{ \sout{mol HCl}}}{1} \times \frac{1 \text{ mol } NH_3}{1 \text{ \sout{mol HCl}}} = 0.00329 \text{ mol } NH_3$$

5. Calculate the mass of NH_3 in the $Ni(NH_3)_nCl_2$ sample.

$$\frac{0.00329 \text{ \sout{mol NH}}_3}{1} \times \frac{17.04 \text{ g } NH_3}{1 \text{ \sout{mol NH}}_3} = 0.0561 \text{ g } NH_3$$

6. Calculate the mass percent of NH_3 in $Ni(NH_3)_nCl_2$.

$$= \frac{0.0561 \text{ g } NH_3}{0.130 \text{ g } Ni(NH_3)_n Cl_2} \times 100\% = 43.2\%$$

Mass Percent of Ni^{2+} in $Ni(NH_3)_nCl_2$

Recap: 50. mL samples of known concentration of $[Ni(NH_3)_n]^{2+}$ were made up by using $NiSO_4 \cdot 6\,H_2O$. The concentrations were then plotted versus their absorbance. The unknown solution's absorbance was then extrapolated from this graph and used in the calculation for the mass percent of Ni^{2+}.

7. Calculate the number of moles of $NiSO_4 \cdot 6\,H_2O$ added to form the standard solution.

$$\frac{0.3000 \text{ \sout{g NiSO}}_4\cdot 6H_2O}{1} \times \frac{1 \text{ mol } NiSO_4 \cdot 6H_2O}{262.88 \text{ \sout{g NiSO}}_4 \cdot 6H_2O} = 0.0041 \text{ mol of } NiSO_4 \cdot 6H_2O$$

8. Calculate the number of moles of $Ni(NH_3)_nCl_2$ in the standard solution.

$$\frac{0.001141 \text{ \sout{mol of NiSO}}_4\cdot 6H_2O}{1} \times \frac{1 \text{ mol } Ni(NH_3)_n Cl_2}{1 \text{ \sout{mol of NiSO}}_4 \cdot 6H_2O}$$

= 0.001141 mol $Ni(NH_3)_nCl_2$

9. Calculate the concentration of $Ni(NH_3)_nCl_2$ in the standard solution.

$$\frac{0.001141 \text{ mol } Ni(NH_3)_n Cl_2}{50.0 \text{ \sout{mL}}} \times \frac{1000. \text{ \sout{mL}}}{1 \text{ L}} = 0.0228\,M$$

10. Calculate the absorbance of the standard (known) and unknown solutions of $[Ni(NH_3)_n]^{2+}$ from their measured transmittance.

absorbance of standard solution = 2.000 – log (32.6) = 0.487

absorbance of unknown solution of $Ni(NH_3)_nCl_2$ = 2.000 – log (22.4) = 0.650

11. Calculate the concentration of the unknown solution of $Ni(NH_3)_nCl_2$, given that

$$\frac{A_s}{c_s} = \varepsilon b = \frac{A_{syn}}{c_{syn}}$$

where A_s = absorbance of $[Ni(NH_3)_n]^{2+}$ from standard solution, A_{syn} = absorbance of $[Ni(NH_3)_n]^{2+}$ from synthesized $Ni(NH_3)_nCl_2$, c_s = concentrations of standard solution and c_{syn} = concentrations of synthesized solution.

$$\frac{0.650}{1} \times \frac{0.0228 \text{ mol}}{\text{L}} \times \frac{1}{0.487} = 0.0304\,M$$

12. Calculate the concentration of the $Ni^{2+}{}_{(aq)}$ ion in the unknown solution.

$$\frac{0.0304 \text{ \sout{mol Ni(NH}}_3)_n \text{\sout{Cl}}_2}{\text{L}} \times \frac{1 \text{ mol } Ni^{2+}}{1 \text{ \sout{mol Ni(NH}}_3)_n \text{\sout{Cl}}_2} = 0.0304\,M$$

13. Calculate the mass of $Ni^{2+}_{(aq)}$ ion in 50.0 mL of the unknown solution.

$$\frac{0.0304\ \cancel{\text{mol Ni}^{2+}}}{\cancel{\text{L}}} \times \frac{58.69\ \text{g Ni}^{2+}}{1\ \cancel{\text{mol Ni}^{2+}}} \times \frac{50.0\ \cancel{\text{mL sol'n}}}{1} \times \frac{1\ \cancel{\text{L}}}{1000\ \cancel{\text{mL}}} = 0.0892\ \text{g Ni}^{2+}$$

14. Calculate the mass percent of $Ni^{2+}_{(aq)}$ in the unknown solution.

$$\frac{0.0892\ \text{g Ni}^{2+}_{(aq)}}{0.350\ \text{g Ni}(\text{NH}_3)\text{Cl}_2} \times 100\% = 25.5\%$$

Empirical Formula and Percent Yield of $Ni(NH_3)_nCl_2$

15. Determine the mass percent of Cl^- in $Ni(NH_3)_nCl_2$

$= 100\% - (\text{mass }\%\ Ni^{2+}_{(aq)}) + (\text{mass }\%\ NH_3)$

$= 100\% - (25.5\% + 43.1\%) = 31.4\%$

16. Determine the empirical formula of $Ni(NH_3)_nCl_2$.

mass % Ni^{2+} = 25.5%

mass % NH_3 = 43.1%

mass % Cl^- = 31.4%

Assuming 100. g $Ni(NH_3)_nCl_2$

$$\frac{25.5\ \cancel{\text{g Ni}^{2+}}}{1} \times \frac{1\ \text{mol Ni}^{2+}}{58.69\ \cancel{\text{g Ni}^{2+}}} = 0.434\ \text{mol Ni}^{2+}$$

$$\frac{43.1\ \cancel{\text{g NH}_3}}{1} \times \frac{1\ \text{mol NH}_3}{17.04\ \cancel{\text{g NH}_3}} = 2.53\ \text{mol NH}_3$$

$$\frac{31.4\ \cancel{\text{g Cl}^-}}{1} \times \frac{1\ \text{mol Cl}^-}{35.45\ \cancel{\text{g Cl}^-}} = 0.886\ \text{mol Cl}^-$$

The Lowest Common Multiplier (LCM) is 0.434, which gives an actual ratio of

$$\text{Ni}^{2+}\frac{0.434}{0.434} : \text{NH}_3\frac{2.53}{0.434} : \text{Cl}^-\frac{0.886}{0.434} = 1.00 : 5.83 : 2.04$$

Lowest whole number ratio = $1Ni^{2+}$: $6NH_3$: $2Cl^-$

Therefore, the empirical formula is $Ni(NH_3)_6Cl_2$

MM of $Ni(NH_3)_6Cl_2 = 231.83\ g \cdot mol^{-1}$

17. Determine the theoretical yield of product in grams.

$$\frac{7.00\ \cancel{\text{g NiCl}_2\cdot 6\text{H}_2\text{O}}}{1} \times \frac{1\ \text{mol NiCl}_2\cdot 6\text{H}_2\text{O}}{237.71\ \cancel{\text{g NiCl}_2\cdot 6\text{H}_2\text{O}}} = 0.0294\ \text{mol}$$

moles of $NiCl_2 \cdot 6H_2O$ = moles $Ni(NH_3)_6Cl_2$ = 0.0294 mol

$$\frac{0.0294\ \cancel{\text{mol Ni}(\text{NH}_3)_6\text{Cl}_2}}{1} \times \frac{231.83\ \text{g Ni}(\text{NH}_3)_6\text{Cl}_2}{1\ \cancel{\text{mol Ni}(\text{NH}_3)_6\text{Cl}_2}} = 6.82\ \text{g Ni}(\text{NH}_3)_6\text{Cl}_2$$

18. Determine the actual % yield of the impure product.

$$= \frac{\text{actual yield of product}}{\text{theoretical yield of product}} \times 100\%$$

$$= \frac{5.50\ \text{g Ni}(\text{NH}_3)_6\text{Cl}_{2\ \text{impure}}}{6.83\ \text{g Ni}(\text{NH}_3)_6\text{Cl}_{2\ \text{pure}}} \times 100\% = 80.5\%$$

Experiment 16: Analytical Gravimetric Determination

Background: Analytical gravimetric analysis is a method for determining the amount of a given substance in a solution by precipitation, filtration, drying, and weighing. The steps generally follow the pattern of weighing the sample, dissolving the sample in an appropriate solvent, forming a precipitate, filtering the precipitate, drying the precipitate and then finally weighing the precipitate. From the data obtained and through mass-mass stoichiometry, the nature of the sample can be determined. In this experiment, a sample of alum, $KAl(SO_4)_2 \cdot 12H_2O$, will be analyzed for the sulfate content and compared to the theoretical percent found from the formula.

The precipitate that will be formed in this experiment is barium sulfate. The precipitate is neither typically "curdy" nor gelatinous, but rather forms very fine crystals.

Scenario: A student obtained a Büchner funnel, a piece of Whatman No. 42 filter paper, and a filter flask. She then weighed out 1.059 grams of alum and dissolved it in 50.0 mL of distilled water. She then calculated how much 0.200 *M* $Ba(NO_3)_2$ she would need to totally precipitate all of the sulfate ion present in solution. She carefully added twice this amount to the alum solution, stirring constantly. She then heated the solution to just under the boiling point for 15 minutes and then allowed the solution to stand overnight. The next day she discovered that fine crystals had appeared in the solution. She weighed the filter paper and determined its mass on an analytical balance as 1.675 g. She then filtered the solution through the Büchner funnel containing the filter paper and collected the crystals. The filter paper was removed and allowed to dry in a drying oven set at 50°C to avoid charring of the paper. She returned later and weighed the paper and crystals and determined their total mass to be 2.715 grams.

Analysis:

1. Write the balanced equation for the reaction.

   $KAl(SO_4)_2 \cdot 12\,H_2O + 2Ba(NO_3)_2 \rightarrow KNO_3 + Al(NO_3)_3 + 2BaSO_4 + 12H_2O$

2. Calculate how much 0.200 *M* $Ba(NO_3)_2$ would be needed to totally precipitate all of the sulfate ion present in the alum solution.

$$\frac{1.059\ \cancel{g\ KAl(SO_4)_2 \cdot 12H_2O}}{1} \times \frac{1\ \cancel{mol\ KAl(SO_4)_2 \cdot 12H_2O}}{474.46\ \cancel{g\ KAl(SO_4)_2 \cdot 12H_2O}}$$

$$\times \frac{2\ \cancel{mol\ Ba(NO_3)_2}}{1\ \cancel{mol\ KAl(SO_4)_2 \cdot 12H_2O}} \times \frac{1\ \cancel{L\ Ba(NO_3)_2}}{0.200\ \cancel{mol\ Ba(NO_3)_2}} \times \frac{1000\ mL}{1\ \cancel{L}}$$

$$= 22.3\ mL$$

3. What was the percent sulfate ion in the alum based upon the experiment?

   2.715 g paper + barium sulfate – 1.675 g paper = 1.040 g $BaSO_4$

$$\frac{1.040\ \cancel{g\ BaSO_4}}{1} \times \frac{1\ \cancel{mol\ BaSO_4}}{233.37\ \cancel{g\ BaSO_4}} \times \frac{1\ \cancel{mol\ SO_4^{2-}}}{1\ \cancel{mol\ BaSO_4}} \times \frac{96.04\ g\ SO_4^{2-}}{1\ \cancel{mol\ SO_4^{2-}}} = 0.4281\ g\ SO_4^{2-}$$

$$\%\ sulfate = \frac{part}{whole} \times 100\% = \frac{0.4281\ g\ SO_4^{2-}}{1.059\ g\ KAl(SO_4)_2 \cdot 12H_2O} \times 100\% = 40.43\%$$

4. What would the theoretical % sulfate be in the alum?

$$= \frac{192.08\ g\ SO_4^{2-}}{474.46\ g\ KAl(SO_4)_2 \cdot 12H_2O} \times 100\% = 40.48\%$$

5. What was the % error in this investigation?

$$\%\ error = \frac{obs - exp}{exp} \times 100\% = \frac{40.43 - 40.48}{40.48} \times 100\% = -0.15\%$$

Experiment 18: Separation by Chromatography

Background: Methods to separate mixtures can be based on many principles such as differences in solubility, boiling and freezing points, polarity, density, and so on. In chromatography, differences in polarity can be used to separate mixtures and identify their components. Molecular sizes and shapes are also used in sieving (gel) and recognition (host-guest) chromatography. Common methods include: 1) paper; 2) thin layer; 3) column; 4) high performance liquid (HPLC); and 5) gas (GC) or vapor phase chromatography (VPC). No matter what method of chromatography is employed, it is a powerful analytical tool that involves a stationary phase (either a liquid or solid) and a mobile phase (either a liquid or gas). The stationary phase attracts the components of the mixture. The medium of the stationary phase may be polar, attracting polar components of the mixture, or it may be non-polar, attracting non-polar and excluding polar components. In paper chromatography, the mobile phase or solvent travels through the stationary phase (the paper) depositing components of the mixture along the way on the stationary phase based upon differences in intermolecular interactions. The leading edge of the solvent is known as the solvent front. The movement of the mobile phase, due to capillary action, through the stationary phase and selectively depositing components is characterized by determining a retention or retardation factor (R_f):

$$R_f = \frac{\text{distance traveled by component (cm)}}{\text{distance traveled by solvent front (cm)}}$$

R_f values can range from 0.0 which indicates that the component did not travel at all, to a maximum of 1.0, which indicates that the component traveled to the solvent front, resulting in no or little retention. It is best to determine the solvent characteristics for a good separation prior to determining the R_f.

Scenario: A student was given a sample containing a mixture of food dyes. The sample appeared green. The student was also given four commercial grade samples of FDC food dyes including Blue 1, Blue 2, Red 3 and Yellow 5. The student spotted the chromatography paper with the known dyes and the unknown mixture, making sure the paper dried before each application, and then placed the paper into a developing chamber that contained a small amount of eluting solvent (see Figure 1). After the solvent front had reached a point near the top of the paper, the paper was removed, a line was marked to show the solvent front and the paper dried. The chromatogram is shown in Figure 2.

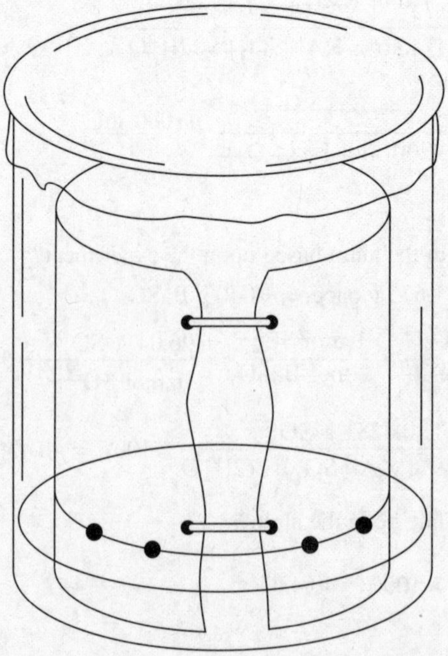

Figure 1

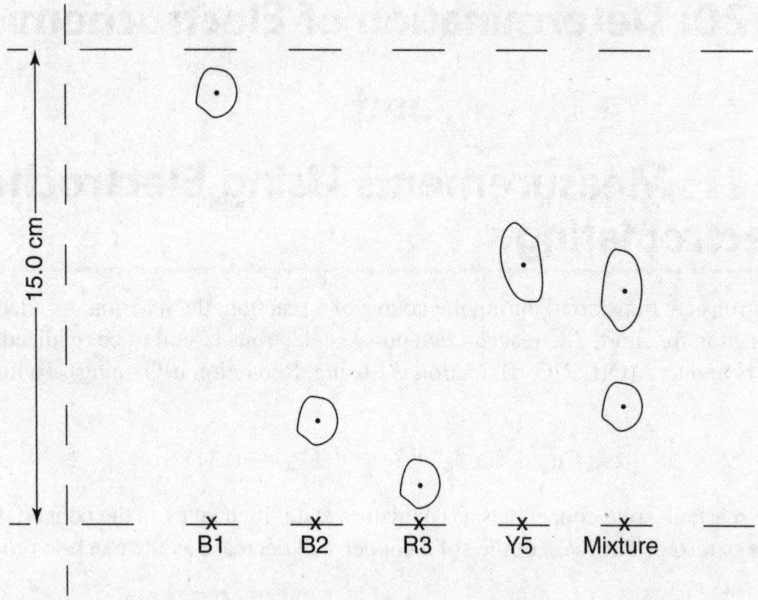

Figure 2 (not to scale)

Analysis:

1. Using a cm ruler, determine the length of the solvent front.

   The chromatogram indicates the solvent traveled 15.0 cm.

2. Measure the distance that each component traveled, measuring from the middle of the spot to the point of application and determine R_f.

Dye	R_f
FDC* Blue 1	$R_f = \frac{13.9}{15.0}$ $= 0.927$
FDC Blue 2	$R_f = \frac{3.3}{15.0}$ $= 0.22$
FDC Red 3	$R_f = \frac{1.0}{15.0}$ $= 0.067$
FDC Yellow 5 **	$R_f = \frac{7.9}{15.0}$ $= 0.52$
Unknown Mixture	1 at 3.4 cm $R_f = 0.23$ 1 at 7.8 cm $R_f = 0.53$

**FDC — Food, Drug and Cosmetic Act*

***Causes hyperactivity in some children*

3. What conclusions can you make regarding the unknown mixture?

   The unknown mixture clearly shows that it was composed of FDC Blue 2 and FDC Yellow 5. Since blue dye mixed with yellow dye gives green dye, the color of the unknown sample, this further supports the conclusion.

Experiment 20: Determination of Electrochemical Series

and

Experiment 21: Measurements Using Electrochemical Cells and Electroplating

Background: When electrons are transferred during the course of a reaction, the reaction is called an oxidation-reduction reaction, or redox reaction for short. The reactant that donates electrons is said to be oxidized and the species that gains electrons is said to be reduced (OIL RIG- Oxidation is Losing, Reduction is Gaining). To illustrate oxidation, examine the half-reaction

$$\text{ox: } Cu_{(s)} \rightarrow Cu^{2+}_{(aq)} + 2e^- \qquad E^\circ_{ox} = -0.34V$$

Here you can see that the reactant, solid copper, has a 0 oxidation state. It changes to the copper(II) ion by losing 2 electrons and is said to be oxidized. The mass of the solid copper will decrease as the reaction proceeds.

In the reduction reaction

$$\text{red: } Ag^+_{(aq)} + e^- \rightarrow Ag_{(s)} \qquad E^\circ_{red} = 0.799V$$

the Ag^+ ion is reduced to the silver atom. If the summation of the voltages is positive, the reaction is said to be spontaneous and work can be done. If the summation of the voltages is negative, then work must be done on the system, through the use of a battery, to cause the reaction to occur. In the example above, if a copper wire was placed in a solution of silver nitrate, the copper wire would oxidize to Cu^{2+} ions and silver ions in solution would be reduced and begin to collect on the copper wire as silver atoms.

In Part I of this experiment, different metals will be added to solutions of different aqueous ions to determine whether a spontaneous redox reaction occurs. Also tested will be the colors of three halogens and their corresponding halide ion in mineral oil. Halogens such as $Br_{2(aq)}$, $Cl_{2(aq)}$ and $I_{2(aq)}$ dissolve in non-polar solvents such as mineral oil to give a characteristic color. And finally in Part I, various combinations of these halogens and halides will be mixed and observations recorded.

In Part II, cells will be constructed to determine the relative magnitudes of E and E^0, the determination of a solubility product and a formation constant. In both parts, the relative activity of elements will be determined.

Scenario: Part I

A student obtained a 24-well plate and placed samples of solid metals into solutions of various metallic ions. The results are presented in Table 1 below:

Table 1

	$Cu_{(s)}$	$Mg_{(s)}$	$Pb_{(s)}$
$Cu^{2+}_{(aq)}$	X	rxn	rxn
$Mg^{2+}_{(aq)}$	no rxn	X	no rxn
$Pb^{2+}_{(aq)}$	no rxn	rxn	X

rxn=reaction occurs

Next, drops of bromine water, chlorine water and iodine water were mixed in samples of mineral oil and the color of the oil and evidence of a reaction were recorded in the Table 2 below. Also tested was the halide ion mixed with mineral oil.

Table 2	
Bromine water $(Br_2)_{(aq)}$ + mineral oil	Orange-brown
Chlorine water $(Cl_2)_{(aq)}$ + mineral oil	Faint greenish-yellow
Iodine water $(I_2)_{(aq)}$ + mineral oil	Pink
$Br^-_{(aq)}$ + mineral oil	Colorless
$Cl^-_{(aq)}$ + mineral oil	Colorless
$I^-_{(aq)}$ + mineral oil	Colorless

Another plate was set up with bromine water, chlorine water and iodine water mixed with samples of $Br^-_{(aq)}$, $Cl^-_{(aq)}$ and $I^-_{(aq)}$ to see if the halogens could be reduced by any of the halide ions. The results of such mixtures are presented in the Table 3 below:

Table 3

	$Br^-_{(aq)}$	$Cl^-_{(aq)}$	$I^-_{(aq)}$
$Br_{2(aq)}$	no rxn	mineral oil was orangish-brown	mineral oil was pink
$Cl_{2(aq)}$	mineral oil was orangish-brown	no rxn	mineral oil was pink
$I_{2(aq)}$	mineral oil was pink	mineral oil was pink	no rxn

Scenerio: Part II

A student constructed an electrochemical cell as shown in Figure 1:

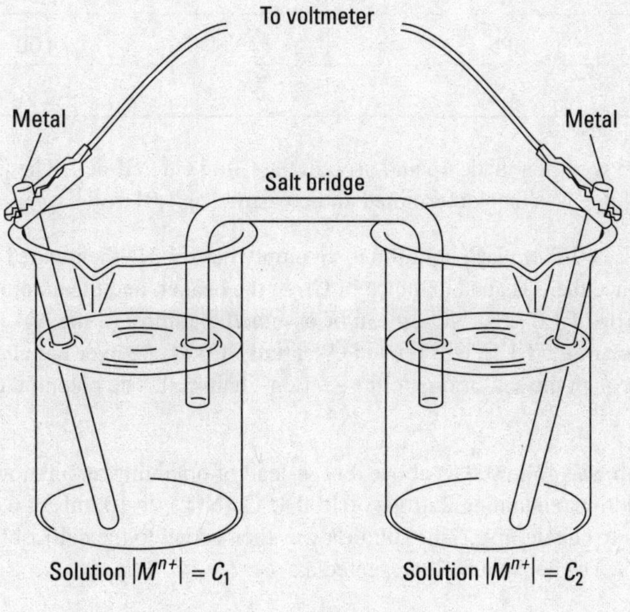

Figure 1

The student began by constructing a half-cell using Zn as a reference electrode in 1.0 *M* $Zn^{2+}_{(aq)}$. The voltages between the Zn electrode and other electrodes in 1.0 *M* solutions of their metallic ion at 25°C are presented in Table 4 below. A salt bridge of 1.0 *M* KNO_3 connected the two half-cells. With the voltmeter set to read a positive voltage, the wire connected to the + terminal on the meter, usually a red wire, was connected to the cathode, the location where reduction was supposedly occurring (RED CAT). The other wire coming from the meter labeled negative and usually black in color, was connected to the anode, the location where oxidation was supposedly occurring (AN OX). However, anode and cathode definitions are for the electrodes in solutions. The anodes produce e^- and the cathodes receive them, so that the signs outside the solutions reverse.

Table 4

	Voltage (V)	*Anode*	*Cathode*
Zn–Ag	1.40	Zn	Ag
Zn–Cu	0.99	Zn	Cu
Zn–Fe	0.55	Zn	Fe
Zn–Mg	0.60	Mg	Zn
Zn–Pb	0.48	Zn	Pb

Next, the student used three different combinations of metals for both anodes and cathodes and measured the potential difference. The results are presented in Table 5.

Table 5

Anode	*Cathode*	*Measured Potential Difference*
Fe	Cu	0.50
Mg	Pb	1.00
Pb	Cu	0.51

A 0.0100 *M* $Cu(NO_3)_2$ solution was then made up and used in the Cu^{2+} | Cu half-cell. The $[Zn^{2+}_{(aq)}]$ was kept at 1.0 *M* in the Zn | Zn^{2+} half-cell. The voltage was then determined and measured as 1.01 volts.

The student then added 10. mL of 1.0 *M* NaCl solution to an empty beaker. He then added one drop of 1.0 *M* $AgNO_3$ to the beaker and stirred well. Since there is an abundance of Cl^- in the beaker, and the amount of NaCl (10. mL) is magnitudes greater than the one drop of 1.0 *M* $AgNO_3$, it can be assumed that most of the $Ag^+_{(aq)}$ will combine with the $Cl^-_{(aq)}$ and that the concentration of the $Cl^-_{(aq)}$ will remain essentially 1.0 *M*. A silver metal electrode was immersed in this solution and connected through the salt bridge to the Zn | Zn^{2+} half-cell. The potential difference was measured as 0.91 volts.

And finally, the same procedure was followed as above, but instead of obtaining an unknown concentration of silver ion, the student prepared a solution containing 2 drops of 1.00 *M* $Cu(NO_3)_2$ in 10. mL of 6.00 *M* NH_3. The student determined that it took 20. drops to equal 1 mL. This solution was then added to the cell containing the copper electrode. The voltage was read as 0.56 V. The cell can be represented as:

$$Zn_{(s)} \mid Zn^{2+}_{(aq)}\ (1.00\ M) \parallel Cu^{2+}_{(aq)}(?\ M) \mid Cu_{(s)}$$

Analysis:

1. Examine Table 1. Write balanced net ionic equations where reactions occurred and identify the oxidizing agent (OA) and the reducing agent (RA) for each equation.

$Cu^{2+}_{(aq)} + Mg_{(s)} \rightarrow Cu_{(s)} + Mg^{2+}_{(aq)}$ OA = $Cu^{2+}_{(aq)}$; RA = $Mg_{(s)}$

$Cu^{2+}_{(aq)} + Pb_{(s)} \rightarrow Cu_{(s)} + Pb^{2+}_{(aq)}$ OA = $Cu^{2+}_{(aq)}$; RA = $Pb_{(s)}$

$Pb^{2+}_{(aq)} + Mg_{(s)} \rightarrow Pb_{(s)} + Mg^{2+}_{(aq)}$ OA = $Pb^{2+}_{(aq)}$; RA = $Mg_{(s)}$

2. Referring to a table of standard reduction potentials, list the metals studied in order of increasing ease of oxidation.
Copper < Lead < Magnesium

3. Referring to Table 1, list the metallic ions studied in order of increasing ease of reduction.
$Mg^{2+}_{(aq)} < Pb^{2+}_{(aq)} < Cu^{2+}_{(aq)}$

4. Explain briefly what was occurring in Tables 2 and 3 and write the balanced net ionic equations for reactions which occurred.
"*Like dissolves like*" is a fundamental rule of solubility. Mineral oil is non-polar. Therefore, one would expect non-polar solutes to dissolve in it. Halide ions are charged particles, therefore one would not expect them to dissolve in a non-polar solvent like mineral oil, but should dissolve in water, a polar solvent. From the data, it appears that the non-polar halogens dissolved in the non-polar mineral oil. When aqueous solutions of halide ions and halogens are mixed together, the color of the mineral oil layer should indicate whether a reaction had occurred or not. If the color of the halogen appeared in the mineral oil from what initially began as the halide ion, then one can conclude that the halide ion was oxidized to the halogen; e.g., $2Br^-_{(aq)}$ (colorless)→ $Br_{2\,(l)} + 2e^-$ (orangish-brown). The mixtures in which reactions occurred were:

$Br_{2\,(aq)} + 2I^-_{(aq)} \rightarrow 2Br^-_{(aq)} + I_{2\,(aq)}$

$Cl_{2\,(aq)} + 2Br^-_{(aq)} \rightarrow 2Cl^-_{(aq)} + Br_{2\,(aq)}$

$Cl_{2\,(aq)} + 2I^-_{(aq)} \rightarrow 2Cl^-_{(aq)} + I_{2\,(aq)}$

The most reactive halogen was chlorine, followed by bromine and then iodine which appeared to not react. This order agrees with their order of reactivity in the periodic table.

5. In reference to Table 4 above and using a chart of E^0_{red} potentials, determine the potentials had hydrogen been used as a reference electrode instead of the Zn electrode and calculate the differences.

Reduction Rxn	***Voltages (V) Using Zn***	***E^0_{red} Voltages (V) Using H_2 (Chart)***	***Difference (V)***
$Ag^+ + e^- \rightarrow Ag$	1.40	0.80	0.60
$Cu^{2+} + 2e^- \rightarrow Cu$	0.99	0.34	0.65
$Fe^{3+} + 3e^- \rightarrow Fe$	0.55	−0.04	0.59
$Mg^{2+} + 2e^- \rightarrow Mg$	0.60	−2.37	2.97
$Pb^{2+} + 2e^- \rightarrow Pb$	0.48	−0.13	0.61
$Zn^{2+} + 2e^- \rightarrow Zn$	0.00	−0.76	0.76

6. For each reaction studied in Part II, Table 5, write a balanced redox equation.

$Cu^{2+}{}_{(aq)} + Fe_{(s)} \rightarrow Cu_{(s)} + Fe^{2+}{}_{(aq)}$

$Pb^{2+}{}_{(aq)} + Mg_{(s)} \rightarrow Pb_{(s)} + Mg^{2+}{}_{(aq)}$

$Cu^{2+}{}_{(aq)} + Pb_{(s)} \rightarrow Cu_{(s)} + Pb^{2+}{}_{(aq)}$

7. For each reaction in #3 above, predict the potentials from the data obtained and found in Table 4 and compare it to the measured values found in Table 5.

Redox Rxn	*Predicted Voltages*	*Measured Voltage*
$Cu^{2+}{}_{(aq)} + Fe_{(s)} \rightarrow Cu_{(s)} + Fe^{2+}{}_{(aq)}$	0.99 + (–0.55) = 0.44	0.50
$Pb^{2+}{}_{(aq)} + Mg_{(s)} \rightarrow Pb_{(s)} + Mg^{2+}{}_{(aq)}$	0.48 + 0.60 = 1.08	1.00
$Cu^{2+}{}_{(aq)} + Pb_{(s)} \rightarrow Cu_{(s)} + Pb^{2+}{}_{(aq)}$	0.99 + (–0.48) = 0.51	0.51

8. Using the Nernst equation, predict the expected voltage of the cell which contained the 0.0100 M $Cu^{2+}{}_{(aq)}$ solution and compare it to the actual voltage obtained.

$Zn_{(s)} + Cu^{2+}{}_{(aq)} \rightarrow Zn^{2+}{}_{(aq)} + Cu_{(s)}$ $\qquad E° = 1.00\text{ V}$

$$E = E^0 - \frac{0.0592}{n}\log Q = 1.00V - \frac{0.0592}{2}\log\frac{[Zn^{2+}]}{[Cu^{2+}]}$$

$$= 1.00V - \frac{0.0592}{2}\log\frac{1}{0.0100} = 0.94V$$

This compares favorably to the 1.01 V that was actually measured.

9. Using the data from the cell containing the unknown $Ag^{+}{}_{(aq)}$ solution, calculate the K_{sp} of AgCl.

$Zn_{(s)} + 2Ag^{2+}{}_{(aq)} \rightarrow Zn^{2+}{}_{(aq)} + 2Ag_{(s)}$ $\quad E° = 1.56V$

ox: $Zn_{(s)} \rightarrow Zn^{2+}{}_{(aq)} + 2e^-$ $\qquad E°_{ox} = 0.76\text{ V}$

red: $Ag^{+}{}_{(aq)} + e^- \rightarrow Ag_{(s)}$ $\qquad E°_{red} = 0.80\text{ V}$

$E° = E°_{ox} + E°_{red} = 0.76\text{ V} + 0.80\text{ V} = 1.56\text{ V}$

$$E = E^0 - \frac{0.0592}{n}\log Q = E^0 - \frac{0.0592}{2}\log\frac{[Zn^{2+}]}{[Ag^+]^2}$$

$$0.91 = 1.56 - \frac{0.0592}{2}\log\frac{1}{[Ag^+]^2}$$

$$\log\frac{1}{[Ag^+]^2} = 21.959 \rightarrow \frac{1}{[Ag^+]^2} = 9.1\times10^{21} \qquad [Ag^+] = 1.0\times10^{-11}$$

$$K_{sp} = [Ag^+][Cl^-] = (1.0\times10^{-11})\times(1) = 1.0\times10^{-11}$$

The actual K_{sp} for AgCl is 1.56×10^{-10} at 25ºC.

10. From the data on the cell containing the $Cu^{2+}{}_{(aq)}$ and $NH_{3(aq)}$ mixture, write the reaction and determine the formation constant, K_f and compare it to the accepted value for K_f of 2×10^{13} M^{-4}.

$Zn_{(s)} + Cu^{2+}{}_{(aq)} \rightarrow Zn^{2+}{}_{(aq)} + Cu_{(s)}$ $\qquad E = 0.56\text{ V};$ $\qquad E° = 1.10\text{ V}$

In a 6.0 M NH_3 solution, most of the $Cu^{2+}{}_{(aq)}$ will combine with NH_3 to form $Cu(NH_3)_4{}^{2+}{}_{(aq)}$ as evidenced by the magnitude of K_f.

$$Cu^{2+}{}_{(aq)} + 4NH_{3(aq)} \rightleftharpoons Cu(NH_3)_4^{2+}{}_{(aq)}$$

It is the uncomplexed $Cu^{2+}{}_{(aq)}$ ion concentration that needs to be determined through the Nernst equation

$$E = E^0 - \frac{0.0592}{n}\log Q = E^0 - \frac{0.0592}{2}\log\frac{[Zn^{2+}]}{[Cu^{2+}]}$$

$$0.56\text{V} = 1.10\text{V} - \frac{0.0592}{2}\log\frac{1}{[Cu^{2+}]}$$

$$\log\frac{1}{[Cu^{2+}]} = 18.2$$

$$\frac{1}{[Cu^{2+}]} = 1.75 \times 10^{18}\ M^{-1}$$

$$[Cu^{2+}] = 5.71 \times 10^{-19}\ M$$

Since 20. drops = 1 mL, 1 drop = 0.050 mL; and 2 drops were added, $V_1 = 0.10$ mL

$$[Cu(NH_3)_4{}^{2+}] = \frac{V_1 \times M_1}{V_2} = \frac{0.10\ \cancel{\text{mL}} \times 1.0\ M}{10.1\ \cancel{\text{mL}}} = 0.010\ M$$

The formation constant, K_f, is derived from the following equation:

$$Cu^{2+} + 4NH_3 \rightleftharpoons Cu(NH_3)_4{}^{2+}$$

$$K_f = \frac{[Cu(NH_3)_4{}^{2+}]}{[Cu^{2+}][NH_3]^4} = \frac{0.0099}{(5.71\times10^{-19})\times(6.0)^4} = 1.3\times10^{13}$$

$$\%\ \text{error} = \frac{\text{obs} - \text{exp}}{\text{exp}} \times 100\% = \frac{1.3\times10^{13} - 2\times10^{13}}{2\times10^{13}} \times 100\% = -3\%$$

Experiment 22: Synthesis, Purification, and Analysis of an Organic Compound

Background: When acids react with alcohols, an ester and water is formed:

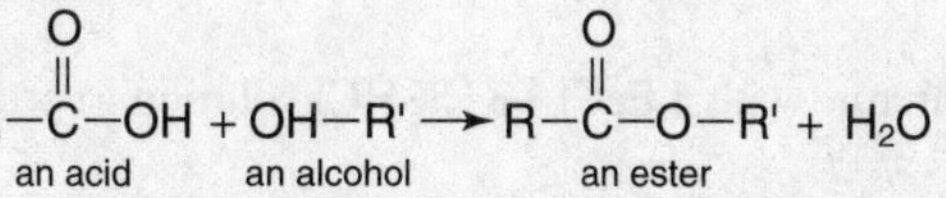

Aspirin, also known as acetylsalicylic acid (ASA), can be synthesized when the carboxyl group in acetic acid (–COOH) reacts with the (–OH) group in the salicylic acid molecule:

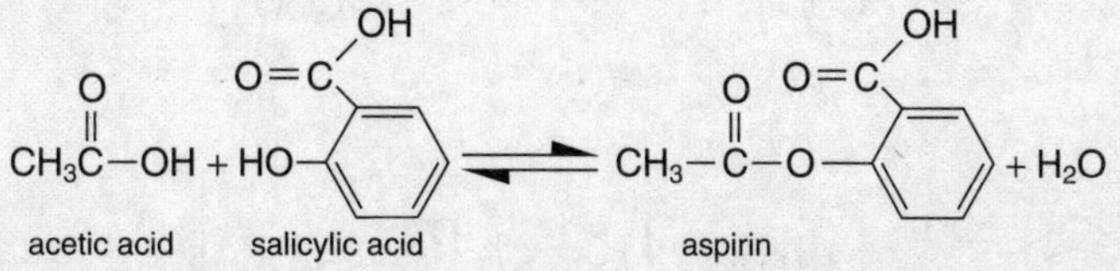

However, the driving force in this reaction is not large, so one usually ends up with an equilibrium mixture of water, salicylic acid, ASA and acetic acid. A better approach to produce ASA (aspirin) is to react acetic anhydride with salicylic acid in the presence of phosphoric or sulfuric acid acting as a catalyst:

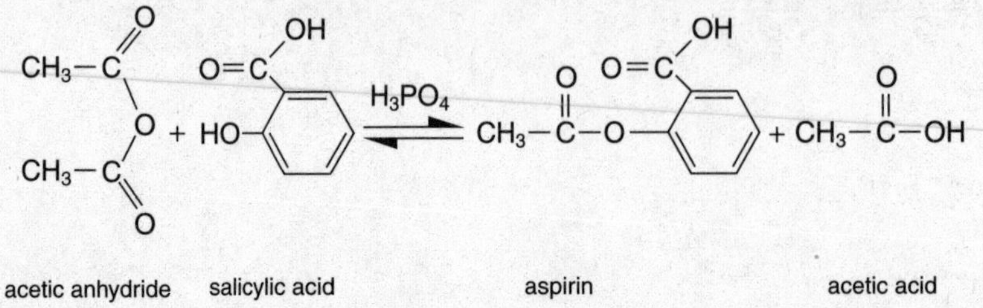

The driving forces in this reaction produce a much higher yield of ASA. One method to determine purity involves determining the melting point of the aspirin produced and comparing it with the known value. If the product is pure, it will have a very distinct melting point. If the sample is impure, there will be a resulting melting range. The final melting point will be lower than the known value by an amount roughly proportional to the amount of impurity present.

A much more definitive method of determining the purity of the aspirin is to analyze the sample through colorimetry. Salicylic acid, not being very soluble in water, is probably the major impurity in the ASA produced. In the presence of Fe^{3+} ion, salicylic acid forms a highly colored magenta or purple complex. By measuring the absorbance of this light and comparing it to known absorbances, it is possible to determine the percent salicylic acid present in the ASA. For a discussion of colorimetry and Beer's law, see Experiments 15 and 17.

Scenario: A student prepared ASA starting with 2.00 g of salicylic acid and 5.00 mL of acetic anhydride (density = 1.08 g · mL^{-1}). After the product was dried, it weighed 1.90 grams. The student then hydrolyzed the ASA with sodium hydroxide and heated the mixture to produce the salicylate dianion:

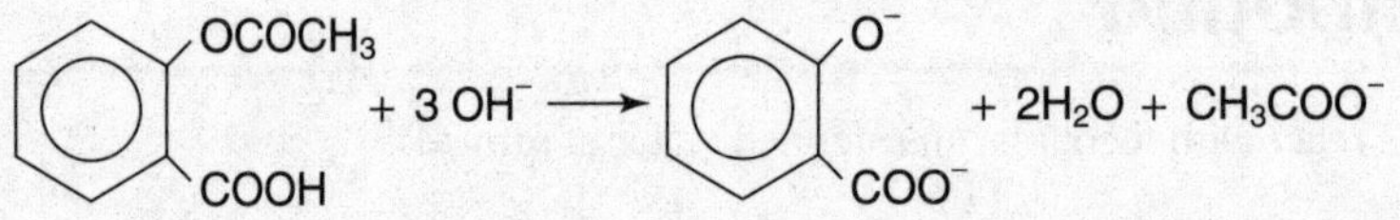

Next, the student then acidified the mixture with a $FeCl_3$–KCl–HCl solution to produce the magenta complex of tetraaquosalicylatoiron(III) ion:

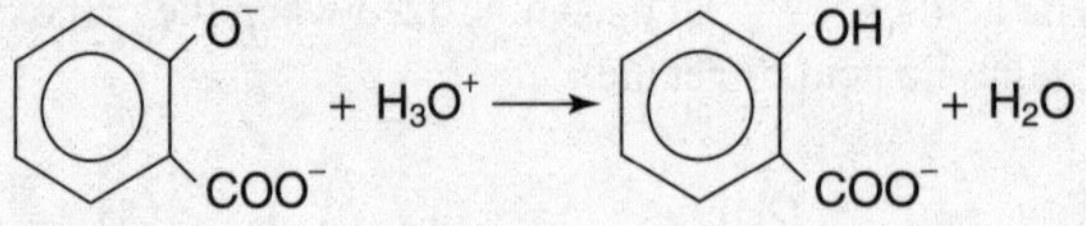

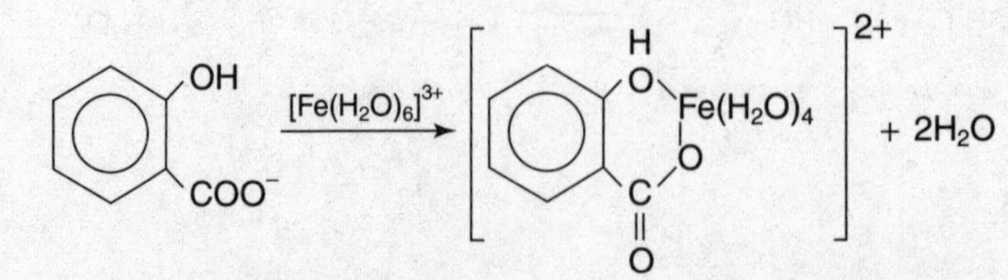

Since the ratio of ASA to the complex ion produced is 1:1, the concentration of the complex ion as determined through colorimetry is the same concentration as that of the ASA. The complex ion is sensitive to pH, therefore care was taken to keep the pH in the range of 0.5–2.0 to avoid formation of di- and trisalicylate complexes of iron(III).

Before the concentration could be determined through colorimetry, the student needed to know the wavelength of light that was most absorbed by the complex ion in order to set the spectrophotometer properly. The student calibrated the spectrophotometer by setting the transmittance to 100% with the $FeCl_3$–KCl–HCl solution as a reference. The optimal wavelength was found to be 525 nm (see Figure 1).

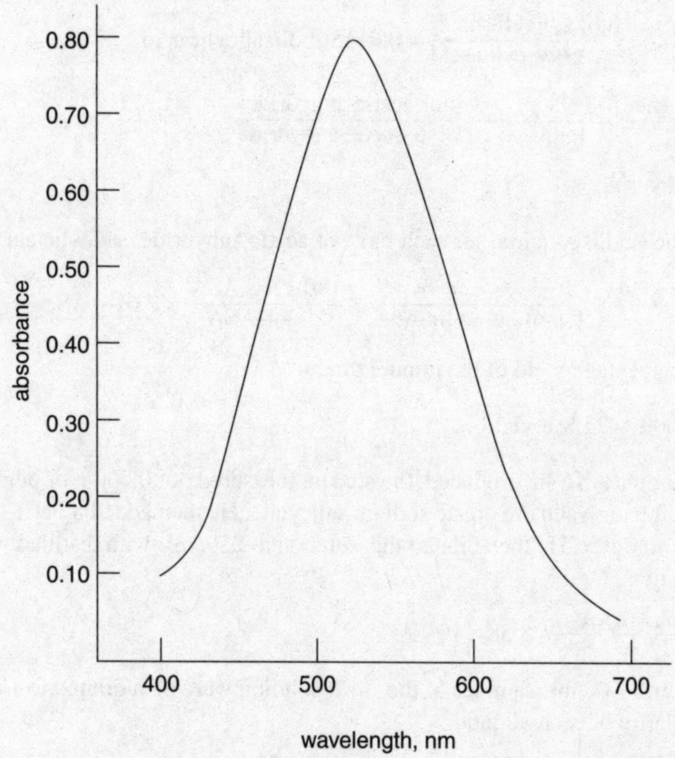

Figure 1

Various known concentrations of the stock solution of the complex ion were colormetrically analyzed and a Beer's law plot drawn (see Figure 2). The ASA that was produced was then treated as described earlier and then colorimetrically analyzed with the concentration determined through extrapolation of the Beer's law plot.

Finally, a small sample of the ASA was determined to have a final melting point of 134°C.

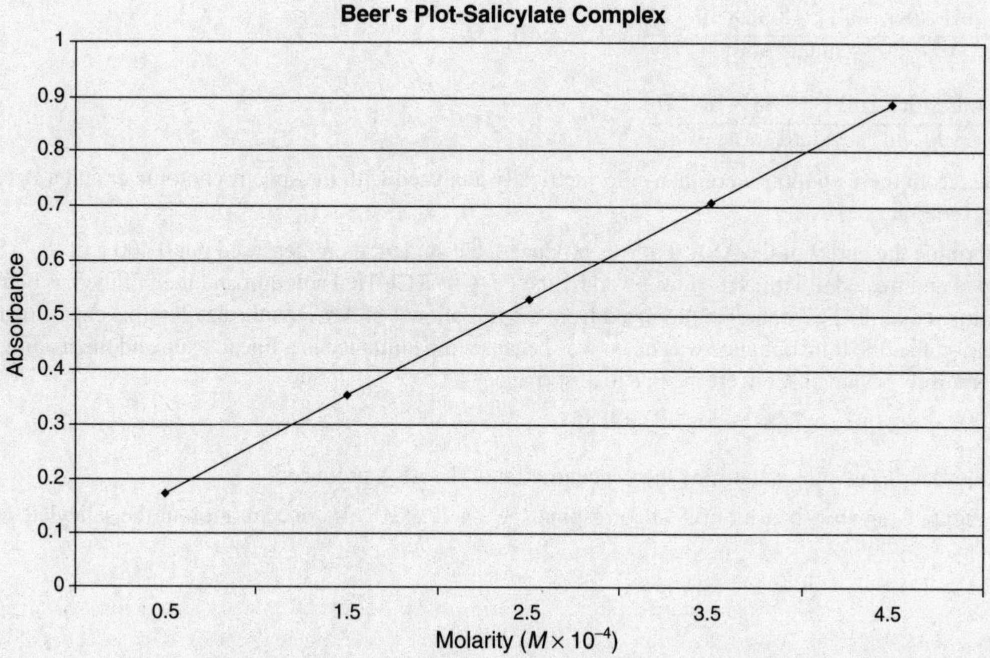

Figure 2

Analysis:

1. Calculate the theoretical yield of ASA to be obtained in this synthesis.

$$\frac{2.00 \text{ \sout{g salicylic acid}}}{1} \times \frac{1 \text{ mol salicylic acid}}{138.1 \text{ \sout{g salicylic acid}}} = 0.0145 \text{ mol salicylic acid}$$

$$\frac{5.00 \text{ \sout{mL acetic anhydride}}}{1} \times \frac{1.08 \text{ \sout{g}}}{1 \text{ \sout{mL}}} \times \frac{1 \text{ mol acetic anhydride}}{102.1 \text{ \sout{g acetic anhydride}}}$$

$= 0.053$ mol acetic anhydride

Since 1 mol of salicylic acid is required for each mole of acetic anhydride, salicylic acid is the limiting reagent.

$$\frac{0.0145 \text{ \sout{mol salicylic acid}}}{1} \times \frac{1 \text{ \sout{mol ASA}}}{1 \text{ \sout{mol salicylic acid}}} \times \frac{180.17 \text{ g ASA}}{1 \text{ \sout{mol ASA}}} = 2.61 \text{ g ASA}$$

2. What was the actual percentage yield of the impure product?

$$\% \text{ yield} = \frac{1.90 \text{ g}}{2.61 \text{ g}} \times 100\% = 72.8\% \text{ yield}$$

3. To analyze the purity of the ASA he produced, the student measured out 0.400 g of pure, analytical reagent grade ASA and then treated it with NaOH to create sodium salicylate. He then added a $FeCl_3$–KCl–HCl solution to create a purple salicylate complex. He then diluted this solution to 250. mL with distilled water. Determine the molarity of the stock solution.

$$\frac{0.400 \text{ \sout{g ASA}}}{0.250 \text{ L}} \times \frac{1 \text{ mol ASA}}{180.17 \text{ \sout{g ASA}}} = 8.88 \times 10^{-3}\, M$$

4. 5.00, 4.00, 3.00, 2.00 and 1.00 mL samples of the stock solution were then diluted to 100. mL with distilled water. Determine the molarity of each aliquot.

$$\frac{(5.00 \text{ mL stock sol'n}) \cdot (8.88 \times 10^{-3}\, M)}{100. \text{ mL standard sol'n}} = 4.44 \times 10^{-4}\, M$$

$$\frac{(4.00 \text{ mL stock sol'n}) \cdot (8.88 \times 10^{-3}\, M)}{100. \text{ mL standard sol'n}} = 3.55 \times 10^{-4}\, M$$

$$\frac{(3.00 \text{ mL stock sol'n}) \cdot (8.88 \times 10^{-3}\, M)}{100. \text{ mL standard sol'n}} = 2.66 \times 10^{-4}\, M$$

$$\frac{(2.00 \text{ mL stock sol'n}) \cdot (8.88 \times 10^{-3}\, M)}{100. \text{ mL standard sol'n}} = 1.78 \times 10^{-4}\, M$$

$$\frac{(1.00 \text{ mL stock sol'n}) \cdot (8.88 \times 10^{-3}\, M)}{100. \text{ mL standard sol'n}} = 8.88 \times 10^{-5}\, M$$

5. Samples from these aliquots were then colormetrically analyzed with the spectrophotometer and a Beer's plot drawn (see Figure 2).

   To determine the purity of the ASA that was produced, the student then measured out 0.400 g of the ASA that he produced and treated it with NaOH followed by the Fe–Cl_3–KCl–HCl solution and then diluted as before. The transmittance of the Fe^{3+} complex produced from a 5 mL aliquot of ASA synthesized in this experiment was 14%. The reason that the transmittance was taken was because transmittance is a linear scale and the readings were more precisely obtained. Convert the *%T* to absorbance.

   $A = 2.000 - \log(\%T) = 2.000 - \log(14) = 0.854$

6. From the Beer's law plot, determine the concentration of the ASA produced.

   From Figure 2, an absorbance of 0.854 corresponds to a $4.27 \times 10^{-4}\, M$ concentration of the salicylate complex.

7. Calculate the mass of ASA in the sample produced.

$$= \frac{4.27 \times 10^{-4} \cancel{\text{mol ASA}}}{\cancel{\text{L}}} \times \frac{180.17 \text{ g ASA}}{1 \cancel{\text{mol ASA}}} \times \frac{100. \cancel{\text{mL standard sol'n}}}{1}$$

$$\times \frac{1 \cancel{\text{L}}}{1000 \cancel{\text{mL}}} \times \frac{250. \cancel{\text{mL}}}{5.00 \cancel{\text{mL}}} = 0.385 \text{ g}$$

8. Calculate the percent ASA in the sample produced.

$$\frac{0.385 \text{ g ASA}}{0.400 \text{ g sample}} \times 100\% = 96.3\%$$

9. The melting point of the ASA produced was determined as 134°C as compared to the known value of 135°C. Comment on the disparity.

The melting point of the ASA is very close to known literature values. The melting occurred over a very narrow range and was distinct. This confirms a fairly pure synthesis of 96.3%.

Laboratory Manual Resources

1. Vonderbrink, SallyAnn, *Laboratory Experiments for Advanced Placement Chemistry,* Flinn Scientific, Inc., Publishers, Batavia, IL, 1995.
2. Chemical Education Resources, Inc., *Modular Laboratory Program in Chemistry,* Palmyra, PA.

PART II

PRACTICE EXAMS

PERIODIC TABLE OF THE ELEMENTS

1 **H** 1.0079																	2 **He** 4.0026
3 **Li** 6.941	4 **Be** 9.012											5 **B** 10.811	6 **C** 12.011	7 **N** 14.007	8 **O** 16.00	9 **F** 19.00	10 **Ne** 20.179
11 **Na** 22.99	12 **Mg** 24.30											13 **Al** 26.98	14 **Si** 28.09	15 **P** 30.974	16 **S** 32.06	17 **Cl** 35.453	18 **Ar** 39.948
19 **K** 39.10	20 **Ca** 40.08	21 **Sc** 44.96	22 **Ti** 47.90	23 **V** 50.94	24 **Cr** 51.00	25 **Mn** 54.93	26 **Fe** 55.85	27 **Co** 58.93	28 **Ni** 58.69	29 **Cu** 63.55	30 **Zn** 65.39	31 **Ga** 69.72	32 **Ge** 72.59	33 **As** 74.92	34 **Se** 78.96	35 **Br** 79.90	36 **Kr** 83.80
37 **Rb** 85.47	38 **Sr** 87.62	39 **Y** 88.91	40 **Zr** 91.22	41 **Nb** 92.91	42 **Mo** 95.94	43 **Tc** (98)	44 **Ru** 101.1	45 **Rh** 102.91	46 **Pd** 105.42	47 **Ag** 107.87	48 **Cd** 112.41	49 **In** 114.82	50 **Sn** 118.71	51 **Sb** 121.75	52 **Te** 127.60	53 **I** 126.91	54 **Xe** 131.29
55 **Cs** 132.91	56 **Ba** 137.33	57 ***La** 138.91	72 **Hf** 178.49	73 **Ta** 180.95	74 **W** 183.85	75 **Re** 186.21	76 **Os** 190.2	77 **Ir** 192.22	78 **Pt** 195.08	79 **Au** 196.97	80 **Hg** 200.59	81 **Ti** 204.38	82 **Pb** 207.2	83 **Bi** 208.98	84 **Po** (209)	85 **At** (210)	86 **Rn** (222)
87 **Fr** (223)	88 **Ra** 226.02	89 **†Ac** 227.03	104 **Rf** (261)	105 **Db** (262)	106 **Sg** (266)	107 **Bh** (264)	108 **Hs** (277)	109 **Mt** (268)	110 **Ds** (271)	111 **Rg** (272)							

* Lanthanide Series	58 **Ce** 140.12	59 **Pr** 140.91	60 **Nd** 144.24	61 **Pm** (145)	62 **Sm** 150.4	63 **Eu** 151.97	64 **Gd** 157.25	65 **Tb** 158.93	66 **Dy** 162.50	67 **Ho** 164.93	68 **Er** 167.26	69 **Tm** 168.93	70 **Yb** 173.04	71 **Lu** 174.97
† Actinide Series	90 **Th** 232.04	91 **Pa** 231.04	92 **U** 238.03	93 **Np** 237.05	94 **Pu** (244)	95 **Am** (243)	96 **Cm** (247)	97 **Bk** (247)	98 **Cf** (251)	99 **Es** (252)	100 **Fm** (257)	101 **Md** (258)	102 **No** (259)	103 **Lr** (260)

STANDARD REDUCTION POTENTIALS IN AQUEOUS SOLUTION AT 25°C

Half-reaction			E°(V)
$F_{2(g)} + 2e^-$	→	$2F^-$	2.87
$Co^{3+} + e^-$	→	Co^{2+}	1.82
$Au^{3+} + 3e^-$	→	$Au_{(s)}$	1.50
$Cl_{2(g)} + 2e^-$	→	$2Cl^-$	1.36
$O_{2(g)} + 4H^+ + 4e^-$	→	$2H_2O_{(l)}$	1.23
$Br_{2(l)} + 2e^-$	→	$2Br^-$	1.07
$2Hg^{2+} + 2e^-$	→	$Hg_2{}^{2+}$	0.92
$Hg^{2+} + 2e^-$	→	$Hg_{(l)}$	0.85
$Ag^+ + e^-$	→	$Ag_{(s)}$	0.80
$Hg_2{}^{2+} + 2e^-$	→	$2Hg_{(l)}$	0.79
$Fe^{3+} + e^-$	→	Fe^{2+}	0.77
$I_{2(s)} + 2e^-$	→	$2I^-$	0.53
$Cu^+ + e^-$	→	$Cu_{(s)}$	0.52
$Cu^{2+} + 2e^-$	→	$Cu_{(s)}$	0.34
$Cu^{2+} + e^-$	→	Cu^+	0.15
$Sn^{4+} + 2e^-$	→	Sn^{2+}	0.15
$S_{(s)} + 2H^+ + 2e^-$	→	$H_2S_{(g)}$	0.14
$2H^+ + 2e^-$	→	$H_{2(g)}$	0.00
$Pb^{2+} + 2e^-$	→	$Pb_{(s)}$	−0.13
$Sn^{2+} + 2e^-$	→	$Sn_{(s)}$	−0.14
$Ni^{2+} + 2e^-$	→	$Ni_{(s)}$	−0.25
$Co^{2+} + 2e^-$	→	$Co_{(s)}$	−0.28
$Cd^{2+} + 2e^-$	→	$Cd_{(s)}$	−0.40
$Cr^{3+} + e^-$	→	Cr^{2+}	−0.41
$Fe^{2+} + 2e^-$	→	$Fe_{(s)}$	−0.44
$Cr^{3+} + 3e^-$	→	$Cr_{(s)}$	−0.74
$Zn^{2+} + 2e^-$	→	$Zn_{(s)}$	−0.76
$H_2O_{(l)} + 2e^-$	→	$H_{2(g)} + 2OH^-$	−0.83
$Mn^{2+} + 2e^-$	→	$Mn_{(s)}$	−1.18
$Al^{3+} + 3e^-$	→	$Al_{(s)}$	−1.66
$Be^{2+} + 2e^-$	→	$Be_{(s)}$	−1.70
$Mg^{2+} + 2e^-$	→	$Mg_{(s)}$	−2.37
$Na^+ + e^-$	→	$Na_{(s)}$	−2.71
$Ca^{2+} + 2e^-$	→	$Ca_{(s)}$	−2.87
$Sr^{2+} + 2e^-$	→	$Sr_{(s)}$	−2.89
$Ba^{2+} + 2e^-$	→	$Ba_{(s)}$	−2.90
$Rb^+ + e^-$	→	$Rb_{(s)}$	−2.92
$K^+ + e^-$	→	$K_{(s)}$	−2.92
$Cs^+ + e^-$	→	$Cs_{(s)}$	−2.92
$Li^+ + e^-$	→	$Li_{(s)}$	−3.05

Note: Unless otherwise stated, assume that for all questions involving solutions and/or chemical equations, the system is in water at room temperature.

ADVANCED PLACEMENT CHEMISTRY EQUATIONS AND CONSTANTS

ATOMIC STRUCTURE

$E = h\nu \qquad c = \lambda\nu$

$\lambda = \dfrac{h}{m\upsilon} \qquad p = m\upsilon$

$E_n = \dfrac{-2.178 \times 10^{-18}}{n^2}$ joule

EQUILIBRIUM

$K_a = \dfrac{[H^+][A^-]}{[HA]}$

$K_b = \dfrac{[OH^-][HB^+]}{[B]}$

$K_w = [OH^-][H^+] = 1.0 \times 10^{-14}$ @ 25°C

$= K_a \times K_b$

pH = – log [H^+], pOH = – log [OH^-]

14 = pH + pOH

$\text{pH} = \text{p}K_a + \log\dfrac{[A^-]}{[HA]}$

$\text{pOH} = \text{p}K_b + \log\dfrac{[HB^+]}{[B]}$

$\text{p}K_a = -\log K_a, \ \text{p}K_b = -\log K_b$

$K_p = K_c(RT)^{\Delta n}$

where Δn = moles product gas – moles reactant gas

THERMOCHEMISTRY/KINETICS

$\Delta S° = \Sigma S°$ products $- \Sigma S°$ reactants

$\Delta H° = \Sigma \Delta H_f°$ products $- \Sigma \Delta H_f°$ reactants

$\Delta G° = \Sigma \Delta G_f°$ products $- \Sigma \Delta G_f°$ reactants

$\Delta G° = \Delta H° - T\Delta S°$

$= -RT \ln K = -2.303\ RT \log K$

$= -n \mathcal{F} E°$

$\Delta G = \Delta G° + RT \ln Q = \Delta G° + 2.303\ RT \log Q$

$q = mc\Delta T$

$C_p = \dfrac{\Delta H}{\Delta T}$

$\ln[A]_t - \ln[A]_0 = -kt$

$\dfrac{1}{[A]_t} - \dfrac{1}{[A]_0} = kt$

$\ln k = \dfrac{-E_a}{R}\left(\dfrac{1}{T}\right) + \ln A$

E = energy
ν = frequency
λ = wavelength
p = momentum
υ = velocity
n = principal quantum number
m = mass

Speed of light, $c = 3.0 \times 10^8$ m • s^{-1}

Planck's constant, $h = 6.63 \times 10^{-34}$ J • s

Boltzmann's constant, $k = 1.38 \times 10^{-23}$ J • K^{-1}

Avogadro's number $= 6.022 \times 10^{23}$ mol^{-1}

Electron charge, $e = -1.602 \times 10^{-19}$ coulomb

1 electron volt per atom = 96.5 kJ • mol^{-1}

Equilibrium Constants

K_a (weak acid)
K_b (weak base)
K_w (water)
K_p (gas pressure)
K_c (molar concentrations)

$S°$ = standard entropy
$H°$ = standard enthalpy
$G°$ = standard free energy
$E°$ = standard reduction potential
T = temperature
n = moles
m = mass
q = heat
c = specific heat capacity
C_p = molar heat capacity at constant pressure
E_a = activation energy
k = rate constant
A = frequency factor

Faraday's constant, $\mathcal{F}$ = 96,500 coulombs per mole of electrons

Gas constant, $R = 8.31$ J • mol^{-1} • K^{-1}
= 0.0821 L • atm • mol^{-1} • K^{-1}
= 8.31 volt • coulomb • mol^{-1} • K^{-1}

GASES, LIQUIDS, AND SOLUTIONS

$$PV = nRT$$

$$\left(P + \frac{n^2a}{V^2}\right)(V - nb) = nRT$$

$$P_A = P_{total} \times X_A, \text{ where } X_A = \frac{\text{moles A}}{\text{total moles}}$$

$$P_{total} = P_A + P_B + P_C + \ldots$$

$$n = \frac{m}{M}$$

$$K = °C + 273$$

$$\frac{P_1V_1}{T_1} = \frac{P_2V_2}{T_2}$$

$$d = \frac{m}{V}$$

$$u_{rms} = \sqrt{\frac{3kT}{m}} = \sqrt{\frac{3RT}{m}}$$

$$KE \text{ per molecule} = \tfrac{1}{2}mv^2$$

$$KE \text{ per mole} = \tfrac{3}{2}RT$$

$$\frac{r_1}{r_2} = \sqrt{\frac{M_2}{M_1}}$$

molarity, M = moles solute per liter solution

molality, m = moles solute per kilogram solvent

$$\Delta T_f = i \cdot K_f \times \text{molality}$$

$$\Delta T_b = i \cdot K_b \times \text{molality}$$

$$\pi = i \cdot M \cdot R \cdot T$$

$$A = a \cdot b \cdot c$$

P = pressure
V = volume
T = temperature
n = number of moles
d = density
m = mass
v = velocity

u_{rms} = root-mean-square speed
KE = kinetic energy
r = rate of effusion
M = molar mass
π = osmotic pressure
i = van't Hoff factor
K_f = molal freezing point depression constant
K_b = molal boiling point elevation constant
A = absorbance
a = molar absorptivity
b = path length
c = concentration
Q = reaction quotient
I = current (amperes)
q = charge (coulombs)
t = time (seconds)
$E°$ = standard reduction potential
K = equilibrium constant

OXIDATION-REDUCTION; ELECTROCHEMISTRY

$$Q = \frac{[C]^c [D]^d}{[A]^a [B]^b}, \text{ where } aA + bB \rightarrow cC + dD$$

$$I = \frac{q}{t}$$

$$E_{cell} = E°_{cell} - \frac{RT}{n\mathcal{F}} \ln Q = E°_{cell} - \frac{0.0592}{n} \log Q \text{ @ } 25°C$$

$$\log K = \frac{n \cdot E°}{0.0592}$$

Gas constant, $R = 8.31 \text{ J} \cdot \text{mol}^{-1} \cdot \text{K}^{-1}$
$= 0.0821 \text{ L} \cdot \text{atm} \cdot \text{mol}^{-1} \cdot \text{K}^{-1}$
$= 8.31 \text{ volt} \cdot \text{coulomb} \cdot \text{mol}^{-1} \cdot \text{K}^{-1}$

Boltzmann's constant, $k = 1.38 \times 10^{-23} \text{ J} \cdot \text{K}^{-1}$

K_f for H_2O = $1.86 \text{ K} \cdot \text{kg} \cdot \text{mol}^{-1}$

K_b for H_2O = $0.512 \text{ K} \cdot \text{kg} \cdot \text{mol}^{-1}$

1 atm = 760 mm Hg
= 760 torr

STP = 0.000°C and 1.000 atm

Faraday's constant, $\mathcal{F}$ = 96,500 coulombs per mole of electrons

CUT HERE

Multiple-Choice Answer Sheet for Practice Exam 1

Remove this sheet and use it to mark your answers.

Section I
Multiple-Choice Questions

1 Ⓐ Ⓑ Ⓒ Ⓓ Ⓔ	26 Ⓐ Ⓑ Ⓒ Ⓓ Ⓔ	51 Ⓐ Ⓑ Ⓒ Ⓓ Ⓔ
2 Ⓐ Ⓑ Ⓒ Ⓓ Ⓔ	27 Ⓐ Ⓑ Ⓒ Ⓓ Ⓔ	52 Ⓐ Ⓑ Ⓒ Ⓓ Ⓔ
3 Ⓐ Ⓑ Ⓒ Ⓓ Ⓔ	28 Ⓐ Ⓑ Ⓒ Ⓓ Ⓔ	53 Ⓐ Ⓑ Ⓒ Ⓓ Ⓔ
4 Ⓐ Ⓑ Ⓒ Ⓓ Ⓔ	29 Ⓐ Ⓑ Ⓒ Ⓓ Ⓔ	54 Ⓐ Ⓑ Ⓒ Ⓓ Ⓔ
5 Ⓐ Ⓑ Ⓒ Ⓓ Ⓔ	30 Ⓐ Ⓑ Ⓒ Ⓓ Ⓔ	55 Ⓐ Ⓑ Ⓒ Ⓓ Ⓔ
6 Ⓐ Ⓑ Ⓒ Ⓓ Ⓔ	31 Ⓐ Ⓑ Ⓒ Ⓓ Ⓔ	56 Ⓐ Ⓑ Ⓒ Ⓓ Ⓔ
7 Ⓐ Ⓑ Ⓒ Ⓓ Ⓔ	32 Ⓐ Ⓑ Ⓒ Ⓓ Ⓔ	57 Ⓐ Ⓑ Ⓒ Ⓓ Ⓔ
8 Ⓐ Ⓑ Ⓒ Ⓓ Ⓔ	33 Ⓐ Ⓑ Ⓒ Ⓓ Ⓔ	58 Ⓐ Ⓑ Ⓒ Ⓓ Ⓔ
9 Ⓐ Ⓑ Ⓒ Ⓓ Ⓔ	34 Ⓐ Ⓑ Ⓒ Ⓓ Ⓔ	59 Ⓐ Ⓑ Ⓒ Ⓓ Ⓔ
10 Ⓐ Ⓑ Ⓒ Ⓓ Ⓔ	35 Ⓐ Ⓑ Ⓒ Ⓓ Ⓔ	60 Ⓐ Ⓑ Ⓒ Ⓓ Ⓔ
11 Ⓐ Ⓑ Ⓒ Ⓓ Ⓔ	36 Ⓐ Ⓑ Ⓒ Ⓓ Ⓔ	61 Ⓐ Ⓑ Ⓒ Ⓓ Ⓔ
12 Ⓐ Ⓑ Ⓒ Ⓓ Ⓔ	37 Ⓐ Ⓑ Ⓒ Ⓓ Ⓔ	62 Ⓐ Ⓑ Ⓒ Ⓓ Ⓔ
13 Ⓐ Ⓑ Ⓒ Ⓓ Ⓔ	38 Ⓐ Ⓑ Ⓒ Ⓓ Ⓔ	63 Ⓐ Ⓑ Ⓒ Ⓓ Ⓔ
14 Ⓐ Ⓑ Ⓒ Ⓓ Ⓔ	39 Ⓐ Ⓑ Ⓒ Ⓓ Ⓔ	64 Ⓐ Ⓑ Ⓒ Ⓓ Ⓔ
15 Ⓐ Ⓑ Ⓒ Ⓓ Ⓔ	40 Ⓐ Ⓑ Ⓒ Ⓓ Ⓔ	65 Ⓐ Ⓑ Ⓒ Ⓓ Ⓔ
16 Ⓐ Ⓑ Ⓒ Ⓓ Ⓔ	41 Ⓐ Ⓑ Ⓒ Ⓓ Ⓔ	66 Ⓐ Ⓑ Ⓒ Ⓓ Ⓔ
17 Ⓐ Ⓑ Ⓒ Ⓓ Ⓔ	42 Ⓐ Ⓑ Ⓒ Ⓓ Ⓔ	67 Ⓐ Ⓑ Ⓒ Ⓓ Ⓔ
18 Ⓐ Ⓑ Ⓒ Ⓓ Ⓔ	43 Ⓐ Ⓑ Ⓒ Ⓓ Ⓔ	68 Ⓐ Ⓑ Ⓒ Ⓓ Ⓔ
19 Ⓐ Ⓑ Ⓒ Ⓓ Ⓔ	44 Ⓐ Ⓑ Ⓒ Ⓓ Ⓔ	69 Ⓐ Ⓑ Ⓒ Ⓓ Ⓔ
20 Ⓐ Ⓑ Ⓒ Ⓓ Ⓔ	45 Ⓐ Ⓑ Ⓒ Ⓓ Ⓔ	70 Ⓐ Ⓑ Ⓒ Ⓓ Ⓔ
21 Ⓐ Ⓑ Ⓒ Ⓓ Ⓔ	46 Ⓐ Ⓑ Ⓒ Ⓓ Ⓔ	71 Ⓐ Ⓑ Ⓒ Ⓓ Ⓔ
22 Ⓐ Ⓑ Ⓒ Ⓓ Ⓔ	47 Ⓐ Ⓑ Ⓒ Ⓓ Ⓔ	72 Ⓐ Ⓑ Ⓒ Ⓓ Ⓔ
23 Ⓐ Ⓑ Ⓒ Ⓓ Ⓔ	48 Ⓐ Ⓑ Ⓒ Ⓓ Ⓔ	73 Ⓐ Ⓑ Ⓒ Ⓓ Ⓔ
24 Ⓐ Ⓑ Ⓒ Ⓓ Ⓔ	49 Ⓐ Ⓑ Ⓒ Ⓓ Ⓔ	74 Ⓐ Ⓑ Ⓒ Ⓓ Ⓔ
25 Ⓐ Ⓑ Ⓒ Ⓓ Ⓔ	50 Ⓐ Ⓑ Ⓒ Ⓓ Ⓔ	75 Ⓐ Ⓑ Ⓒ Ⓓ Ⓔ

CUT HERE

Practice Exam 1

Section I: Multiple-Choice Questions

Time: 90 minutes

75 questions

No calculators allowed

This section consists of 75 multiple-choice questions. Mark your answers carefully on the answer sheet.

1. The ground-state electron configuration for an arsenic atom, showing the number of electrons in each subshell is

A. $1s^2 2s^2 2p^6 3s^2 3p^6 4s^1 3d^{10} 4p^4$
B. $1s^2 2s^2 2p^6 3s^2 3p^6 4s^2 3d^{10} 4p^3$
C. $1s^2 2s^2 2p^6 3s^2 3p^6 4s^1 3d^{10} 4p^3$
D. $1s^2 2s^2 2p^6 3s^2 3p^6 4s^2 3d^9 4p^4$
E. none of the above are correct

For Questions 2–5, choose from the following:

A. Calculation of the change in energy between electrons in two different energy levels of a hydrogen atom.
B. Used to calculate momentum.
C. Used to calculate the energy of an electron within a specific energy level of a hydrogen atom.
D. Used to calculate the energy of a proton.
E. Used to calculate the wavelength of a moving particle.

2. $p = m \cdot \upsilon$

3. $\lambda = \dfrac{h}{m \cdot v}$

4. $\Delta E = h \cdot v = R_H \left(\dfrac{1}{n_i^2} - \dfrac{1}{n_f^2} \right)$

5. $E_n = \dfrac{-2.178 \times 10^{-18}}{n^2}$ joules

6. Gaseous atoms of which of the following elements are paramagnetic: Mg, V, Co, Cd, As?

A. Mg and As only
B. Cd and As only
C. Mg, V, and Co only
D. V, Co, and As only
E. V, Co, and Cd only

7. ΔE, in kilojoules per mole, when a hydrogen electron in the first excited state ($n = 2$) is completely removed from the atom is approximately

A. -640 kJ · mol^{-1}
B. -320 kJ · mol^{-1}
C. 0 kJ · mol^{-1}
D. 160 kJ · mol^{-1}
E. 320 kJ · mol^{-1}

8. Which general statement regarding the properties of elements arranged in the periodic table is correct?

A. Atomic sizes decrease going down a group or family.
B. Atomic sizes increase going from Fr in Group I to F in Group VII.
C. Atomic sizes decrease going from left to right in a period.
D. All atoms in the same group have the same size.
E. Shielding decreases as one moves down a group or family.

GO ON TO THE NEXT PAGE

For Questions 9–12, choose from the following:

A. Döbereiner
B. Mendeleev
C. Mosley
D. Newlands
E. Thompson

9. Developed early periodic table based on increasing atomic mass.

10. Similar groups of three elements.

11. Law of octaves.

12. Correlation between atomic number and chemical properties of elements.

13. Which of the following molecules has the shortest bond length?

A. Br_2
B. I_2
C. Cl_2
D. N_2
E. O_2

For Questions 14–18, choose from the following:

A. Dispersion forces
B. Permanent dipole-dipole interactions
C. Non-polar molecule containing polar bonds
D. Hydrogen bonding
E. Polar covalent compound

14. A white, odorless, crystalline solid melts after about ten seconds in a burner flame. It is soluble in water and insoluble in carbon tetrachloride. Neither the melted material nor its aqueous solution conducts electricity. The compound would be best described as a __________.

15. The very high heat of vaporization of H_2O is mainly a result of _____.

16. The type of bonds found in SO_2

17. The sublimation of dry ice is an endothermic process. The energy absorbed is required to overcome _____.

18. ___________ would be the strongest force between molecules of HCl.

19. Which of the following does NOT have a zero dipole moment?

A. SF_6
B. C_6H_6
C. SO_2
D. CO_2
E. PF_5

20. Predict the hybridization and molecular geometry of BrF_5.

A. sp^3d^2, square pyramidal
B. sp^3, square planar
C. sp^3d, T-shaped
D. sp^2, seesaw
E. sp, trigonal pyramidal

21. 3.978 grams of copper oxide was heated in a stream of hydrogen gas and produced 0.901 grams of water. What is the formula for copper oxide?

A. CuO
B. CuO_2
C. Cu_2O
D. $CuO \cdot 2H_2O$
E. Cu_2O_3

22. A common ingredient found in over-the-counter (OTC) medicines for an upset stomach is bismuth subsalicylate, $C_7H_5BiO_4$. A student analyzed 3.62 grams of the medication and discovered that it contained 627 mg of bismuth. Assuming that there is no other bismuth-containing compound in the medication and using the information provided in the table below for $C_7H_5BiO_4$, what percent (by mass) of the medication is bismuth subsalicylate?

Element	*Moles*	*Grams*
C	7	84.07
H	5	5.05
Bi	1	209.00
O	4	64.00
Total	—	362.12

A. 3.65%
B. 19.5%
C. 27.4%
D. 30.0%
E. 73.0%

23. 5.50 grams of gas A and 5.50 grams of gas B are sealed in a rigid container at a constant temperature. The total pressure of the system is 9.00 atm. Which of the following about the partial pressure of gas B is correct?

A. The partial pressure of gas B is equal to ½ the total pressure.
B. In addition to the information provided, one needs to know the relative molecular mass of B in order to determine the partial pressure of gas B.
C. In addition to the information provided, one needs to know the total volume of the container in order to calculate the partial pressure of gas B.
D. In addition to the information provided, one needs to know the temperature of the gas mixture in order to calculate the partial pressure of gas B.
E. In addition to the information provided, one needs to know the average distance traveled between molecular collisions.

24. A sample of neon has a volume of 250. cm^3 at 2.00 atm of pressure. At constant temperature, what would the pressure have to be in order for the gas to have a volume of 5.00×10^2 cm^3?

A. 1.00 atm
B. 3.33 atm
C. 15.7 atm
D. 21.5 atm
E. 43.0 atm

25. 1.85 L of a gas is collected over water at 98.64 kPa and 22.0°C. The vapor pressure of water at 22.0°C is 2.64 kPa. Which of the following would be the proper setup for solving for the final volume of the dry gas at STP?

A. $1.85\,\text{L} \times \frac{(98.64\,\cancel{\text{kPa}})(273\,\cancel{\text{K}})}{(101.325\,\cancel{\text{kPa}})(295\,\cancel{\text{K}})}$

B. $1.85\,\text{L} \times \frac{(96.00\,\cancel{\text{kPa}})(273\,\cancel{\text{K}})}{(101.325\,\cancel{\text{kPa}})(295\,\cancel{\text{K}})}$

C. $1.85\,\text{L} \times \frac{(96.00\,\cancel{\text{kPa}})(295\,\cancel{\text{K}})}{(101.325\,\cancel{\text{kPa}})(273\,\cancel{\text{K}})}$

D. $1.85\,\text{L} \times \frac{(98.64\,\cancel{\text{kPa}})(295\,\cancel{\text{K}})}{(101.325\,\cancel{\text{kPa}})(273\,\cancel{\text{K}})}$

E. $1.85\,\text{L} \times \frac{(96.00\,\cancel{\text{kPa}})(22\,\cancel{^\circ\text{C}})}{(101.325\,\cancel{\text{kPa}})(0\,\cancel{^\circ\text{C}})}$

26. The density of an unknown gas is 4.00 grams per liter at 4.00 atmospheres pressure and 127°C. What is the molecular weight of this gas? $R = 0.0821$ liter · atm / (mole · K).

A. 11.8 g · mol^{-1}
B. 32.8 g · mol^{-1}
C. 88.0 g · mol^{-1}
D. 94.1 g · mol^{-1}
E. 138 g · mol^{-1}

27. Which gas will diffuse twice as fast as SO_2 ($MW = 64$)?

A. He ($MW = 4$)
B. CH_4 ($MW = 16$)
C. O_2 ($MW = 32$)
D. HI ($MW = 128$)
E. None of the above. All gases at the same temperature diffuse at the same rate.

28. Real gases will often exhibit a measured volume greater than that which is calculated from the ideal gas law because

A. molecules will vary in size.
B. collisions between molecules are not elastic.
C. significant intermolecular attractions exist between molecules.
D. high temperatures result in a significant increases in pressures.
E. larger molecules will take up more room in a container, thereby decreasing the volume of the container.

29. The critical temperature of a substance is the

A. temperature above which a gas cannot be made to liquefy, no matter how much pressure is applied.
B. temperature at which the pressure above the liquid is equal to the vapor pressure of the liquid.
C. temperature below which a gas cannot be made to liquefy, no matter how much pressure is applied.
D. temperature at which the solid, liquid, and vapor phases are all in equilibrium.
E. temperature at which liquid and solid phases are in equilibrium at one atmosphere of pressure.

GO ON TO THE NEXT PAGE

30. Given the heating curve above, the temperature(s) at which the gas condenses is

A. 10°C
B. 55°C
C. 95°C
D. between 25°C and 55°C
E. between 55°C and 95°C

31. The standard enthalpies of formation of SO_2 and SO_3 are –297 and –396 kJ/mol, respectively. Calculate the standard enthalpy of reaction for the reaction:

$$SO_2 + \frac{1}{2}O_2 \rightarrow SO_3$$

A. –298 kJ/mol
B. –149 kJ/mol
C. –99 kJ/mol
D. +99 kJ/mol
E. +693 kJ/mol

32. The initial temperature of 150. g of ethanol was 22.0°C. What would be the correct setup to determine the final temperature of the ethanol if 3240 J of energy was used to raise its temperature? The specific heat capacity of ethanol is 2.44 $J \cdot {}^{\circ}C^{-1} \cdot g^{-1}$.

A. $3240\ J = 150.\ g \times 2.44\ J \cdot {}^{\circ}C^{-1} \cdot g^{-1} \times (22.0^{\circ}C - T_f)$
B. $3240\ J = 150.\ g \times 2.44\ J \cdot {}^{\circ}C^{-1} \cdot g^{-1} \times (T_f - 22.0^{\circ}C)$
C. $3240\ J = 150.\ g \times 2.44\ J \cdot {}^{\circ}C^{-1} \cdot g^{-1} \times$ x $(T_f + 22.0^{\circ}C)$
D. $3240\ J = (150.\ g \div 2.44\ J \cdot {}^{\circ}C^{-1} \cdot g^{-1}) \times (T_f - 22.0^{\circ}C)$
E. $3240\ J = (150.\ g \div 2.44\ J \cdot {}^{\circ}C^{-1} \cdot g^{-1}) \times (-22.0^{\circ}C + T_f)$

For Questions 33–34:

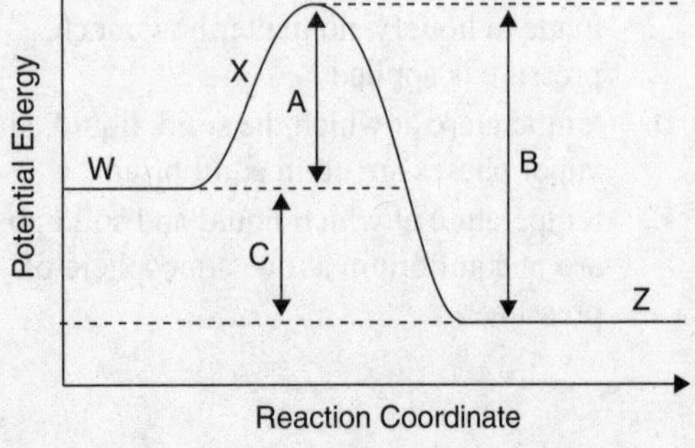

33. Which letter (or expression) represents the activation energy (E_a) in the diagram above?

A. A
B. B
C. C
D. B – A
E. B – C

34. Which letter (or expression) represents the enthalpy of reaction (ΔH) in the diagram above?

A. A
B. B
C. C
D. B – A
E. B – C

35. A 25.0 mL sample is drawn from a bottle labeled "98.09% by weight H_2SO_4, density 1.642 g/mL". What is the molarity of the sample?

A. 8.78 *M*
B. 10.5 *M*
C. 16.4 *M*
D. 18.2 *M*
E. 98.09 *M*

36. What is the molarity of a solution containing 6.00% acetic acid (CH_3COOH) by weight and which has a density of 1.05 g/mL? (*MW* CH_3COOH = 60.05 $g \cdot mol^{-1}$)

A. 0.300 *M*
B. 0.600 *M*
C. 1.05 *M*
D. 1.36 *M*
E. 3.22 *M*

37. 40.0 grams of substance X dissolves in 100.0 grams of CS_2 (B.P. = 46.23°C; K_b = 3.25°C/*m*) to produce a solution that has a boiling point of 49.48°C. Which of the following could be X?

A. S_8
B. C_2H_6
C. CH_3OH
D. NaCl
E. none of the above

38. What is the vapor pressure of a mixture of 9.01 grams of water and 0.500 mol sugar at 29°C? The vapor pressure of water at 29°C is 30.0 torr.

A. 3.75 torr
B. 7.50 torr
C. 15.0 torr
D. 30.0 torr
E. 60.0 torr

39. $FeO_{(s)} + CO_{(g)} \rightleftharpoons Fe_{(s)} + CO_{2(g)}$ $\Delta H = -10.5$ kJ

When the substances in the equation above are at equilibrium at pressure *P* and temperature *T*, the equilibrium can be shifted to favor the products by

A. adding a catalyst
B. increasing the pressure by adding an inert gas such as helium
C. decreasing the temperature
D. increasing the temperature
E. keeping the temperature constant while increasing the pressure of the system

40. At 25°C, the K_{sp} for AgCl is 1.8×10^{-10}. To determine the standard free-energy change at 25°C for the reaction $AgCl_{(s)} \rightleftharpoons Ag^+_{(aq)} + Cl^-_{(aq)}$, you would set up the problem as

A. $x = \sqrt{1.8 \times 10^{-10}}$
B. $x = (1.8 \times 10^{-10})^2$
C. $-(8.314)(25)(\ln 1.8 \times 10^{-10})$
D. $-(8.314)(298)(\ln 1.8 \times 10^{-10})$
E. $-(1.8 \times 10^{-10})^2 + \log(1.8 \times 10^{-10})$

41. What are the products of the following Brønsted acid-base reaction?

$$HSO_4^-{}_{(aq)} + S^{2-}{}_{(aq)} \rightleftharpoons ?$$

A. $SO_{3(g)} + H_2O_{(l)}$
B. $H_2SO_{4(aq)} + S^{3-}{}_{(aq)}$
C. $SO_4^{2-}{}_{(aq)} + HS^-{}_{(aq)}$
D. $H_3O^+{}_{(aq)} + H_2S_{(aq)}$
E. $H_2S_{(aq)} + H_2O_{(l)}$

42. All Brønsted acids are Lewis acids, but not all Lewis acids are Brønsted acids. Which of the following are Lewis acids but not Brønsted acids?

I. HCl
II. CO_2
III. HCN
IV. SO_2
V. BCl_3

A. I
B. II and IV
C. I and III
D. II, IV, and V
E. I, II, III, IV, and V

43. What is the pOH of a solution prepared by adding distilled water to 0.3099 grams of sodium oxide (Na_2O) to reach a final volume of 100. mL?

A. 1.00
B. 2.00
C. 6.50
D. 10.00
E. 13.00

44. When the acids HClO, H_2SO_3, H_3BO_3, $HClO_3$, and $HClO_2$ are arranged in order of increasing strength (weakest acid first), the correct order is

A. $HClO_3 < HClO_2 < HClO < H_2SO_3 < H_3BO_3$
B. $H_2SO_3 < H_3BO_3 < HClO < HClO_2 < HClO_3$
C. $HClO < HClO_2 < HClO_3 < H_3BO_3 < H_2SO_3$
D. $H_3BO_3 < H_2SO_3 < HClO < HClO_2 < HClO_3$
E. $H_2SO_3 < H_3BO_3 < HClO_3 < HClO_2 < HClO$

45. 7.50 grams of a diprotic acid is dissolved in distilled water to make exactly 200. mL of solution. What is the molar mass of the acid if 20.0 mL of this solution required 20.0 mL of 1.50 *M* NaOH for neutralization? Assume that both protons of the acid are titrated.

A. $8.50\ g \cdot mol^{-1}$
B. $16.0\ g \cdot mol^{-1}$
C. $25.0\ g \cdot mol^{-1}$
D. $50.0\ g \cdot mol^{-1}$
E. $100.\ g \cdot mol^{-1}$

GO ON TO THE NEXT PAGE

46. A 0.050 *M* solution of a monoprotic weak acid is 20.0% ionized. What is the ionization constant of the acid?

A. 2.50×10^{-3}
B. 3.00×10^{-2}
C. 4.00×10^{-1}
D. 1.00
E. 2.50×10^{0}

47. The K_a of a particular indicator is 3.0×10^{-5}. The color of HIn is red and that of In^- is yellow. A student added a few drops of this indicator to a HCl solution and then titrated it against a NaOH solution. What is the $[H^+]$ at the point the indicator changes color and what is the color?

A. 3.0×10^{-5}, red
B. 3.0×10^{-5}, orange
C. 3.0×10^{-5}, yellow
D. 1.0×10^{-7}, orange
E. 7.00, no color

48. Which of the following salts are basic?

Na_2CO_3, $FeCl_3$, KNO_3, $NH_4C_2H_3O_2$, $ZnSO_4$, $Ba(NO_3)_2$, RbF

A. Na_2CO_3 and RbF
B. $FeCl_3$ and $ZnSO_4$
C. $Ba(NO_3)_2$
D. $NH_4C_2H_3O_2$ and $Ba(NO_3)_2$
E. KNO_3 and RbF

49. An ammonia solution was determined to have a pH of 11.00. What was the original concentration (*M*) of $NH_{3(aq)}$? Assume for this problem that K_b $NH_3 = 2 \times 10^{-5}$.

A. 0.01 *M*
B. 0.02 *M*
C. 0.03 *M*
D. 0.04 *M*
E. 0.05 *M*

50. How long does it take 2.50 *M* of reactant to decrease in concentration to 0.75 *M* if the rate constant is 0.25 *M*/min?

A. 60. sec
B. 2.5 min
C. 3.5 min
D. 5.0 min
E. 7.0 min

51. The energy diagram for the reaction $A + B \rightarrow C + D$ is shown below. The addition of a catalyst to this reaction would NOT cause a change in which of the indicated energy differences?

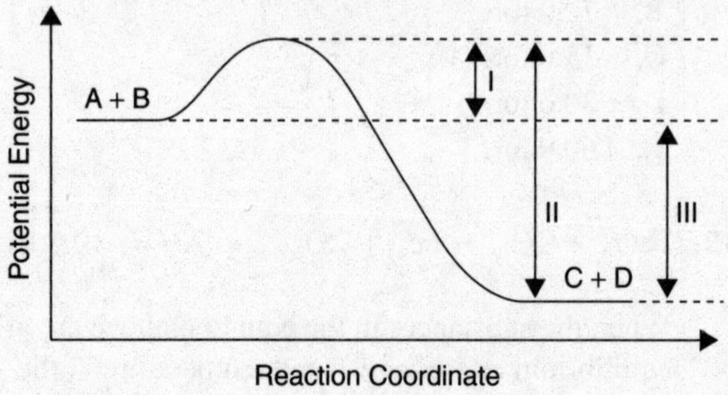

A I only
B II only
C III only
D I and III only
E I, II, and III

For Questions 52–54:

$$H_{2(g)} + I_{2(g)} \rightarrow 2HI_{(g)}$$
$$K_c = 57.0 \text{ at } 700.\text{ K}$$

52. The rate constant k_r for the decomposition of HI is ________ the rate constant k_f for the synthesis of HI.

A. smaller than
B. larger than
C. equal to
D. not related to
E. the reciprocal of

53. If the value of k_f for the synthesis of HI is 5.70×10^{-2}, the value of k_r for the decomposition of HI is

A. 4.00×10^{-7}
B. 2.00×10^{-5}
C. 1.00×10^{-4}
D. 1.00×10^{-3}
E. 1.00×10^{3}

54. If a catalyst is added to the system, which of the following choices is true?

A. K_c will not be affected.
B. K_c will increase in value.
C. K_c will decrease in value.
D. k_f and k_r will increase by the same proportion.
E. Both choices A and D are correct.

55. $ICl_{(s)} + H_2O_{(l)} \rightarrow HCl_{(aq)} + HOI_{(aq)}$

Which of the following is true regarding the equation written above?

A. I is oxidized and Cl is reduced.
B. Cl is oxidized and I is reduced.
C. O is oxidized and I is reduced.
D. O is reduced and Cl is oxidized.
E. This is not a redox reaction.

56. Pure calcium metal can be obtained by the electrolysis of calcium chloride. How many grams of calcium metal can be produced by passing 0.965 amperes of electricity through molten calcium chloride for 1.00 hour?

A. 0.144g
B. 0.289g
C. 0.721g
D. 1.12g
E. 2.24kg

57. What is the correct setup to determine the potential of a cell made up of $Zn|Zn^{2+}$ and $Sn|Sn^{2+}$ half-cells at 25°C if $[Zn^{2+}] = 0.50\ M$ and $[Sn^{2+}] = 0.15\ M$?

A. $0.62\text{ V} - \dfrac{0.0591\text{ V}}{2}\log\dfrac{0.15}{0.50}$

B. $0.62\text{ V} - \dfrac{0.0591\text{ V}}{2}\log\dfrac{0.50}{0.15}$

C. $0.62\text{ V} + \dfrac{0.0591\text{ V}}{2}\log\dfrac{0.50}{0.15}$

D. $0.0591\text{ V} - \dfrac{0.62\text{ V}}{2}\log\dfrac{0.50}{0.15}$

E. $0.62\text{ V} - \dfrac{0.0591\text{ V}}{2^2}\ln\dfrac{0.50}{0.15}$

58. When written and balanced correctly, the alpha decay of Ra-226 is:

A. ${}^{226}_{88}Ra \rightarrow {}^{4}_{2}He + {}^{222}_{86}Rn$
B. ${}^{224}_{88}Ra \rightarrow {}^{2}_{4}He + {}^{222}_{84}Rn$
C. ${}^{228}_{90}Ra \rightarrow {}^{4}_{2}He + {}^{222}_{86}Rn$
D. ${}^{224}_{86}Ra \rightarrow {}^{4}_{2}He + {}^{222}_{86}Rn$
E. ${}^{226}_{90}Ra \rightarrow {}^{4}_{2}He + {}^{222}_{88}Rn$

59. When written and balanced correctly, positron emission of K-40 is represented as

A. ${}^{40}_{18}K \rightarrow {}^{40}_{18}Ar + {}^{0}_{0}e$
B. ${}^{40}_{19}K \rightarrow {}^{40}_{20}Ar + {}^{0}_{-1}e$
C. ${}^{40}_{19}K \rightarrow {}^{40}_{17}Ar + {}^{0}_{2}e$
D. ${}^{40}_{20}K \rightarrow {}^{40}_{19}Ar + {}^{0}_{1}e$
E. ${}^{40}_{19}K \rightarrow {}^{40}_{18}Ar + {}^{0}_{1}e$

For Questions 60–64, choose answers from the following:

A. ${}^{0}_{-1}e$
B. ${}^{4}_{2}He$
C. ${}^{0}_{+1}e$
D. ${}^{49}_{24}Cr$
E. ${}^{90}_{39}Y$

60. ${}^{234}_{90}Th \rightarrow {}^{234}_{91}Pa + ?$

61. ${}^{90}_{38}Sr \rightarrow {}^{0}_{-1}e + ?$

62. ${}^{135}_{60}Nd \rightarrow {}^{135}_{59}Pr + ?$

63. ${}^{135}_{60}Mn \rightarrow {}^{0}_{+1}e + ?$

64. ${}^{170}_{78}Pt \rightarrow {}^{166}_{76}Os + ?$

65. How many hydrogen and carbon atoms are in the following structure?

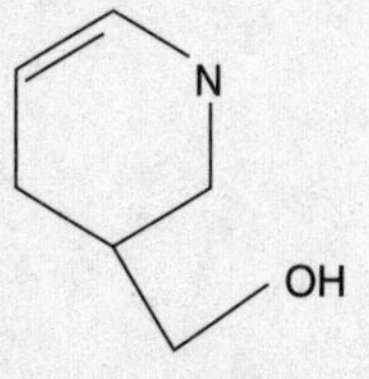

A. 5 carbons, 10 hydrogens
B. 6 carbons, 11 hydrogens
C. 6 carbons, 12 hydrogens
D. 6 carbons, 14 hydrogens
E. 7 carbons, 12 hydrogens

GO ON TO THE NEXT PAGE

66. The proper name for the following compound is

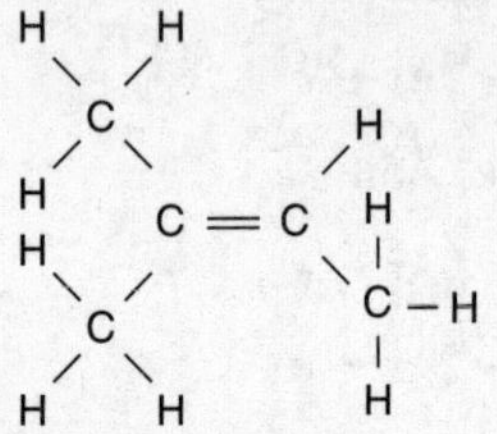

A. *cis*-2-pentene
B. *trans*-2-pentene
C. 2-methyl-2-butene
D. 3-methyl-1-butene
E. 2-methyl-2-butene

67. The correct name for the following compound is

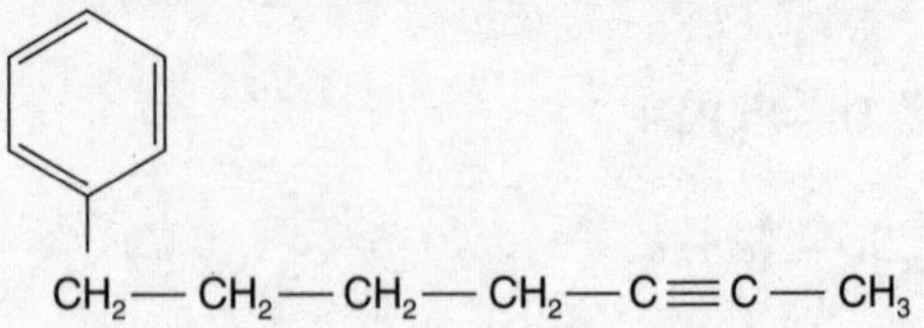

A. 4-phenyloctane
B. 5-phenyl-3-heptene
C. 7-phenyl-2-heptyne
D. 2-phenyl-7-heptyne
E. none of the above are correct

68. The name of the following compound

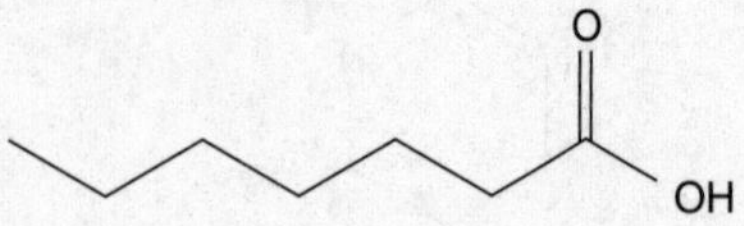

is

A. heptanone
B. heptyl ether
C. heptanol
D. heptanoic acid
E. heptanal

69. The name of the following compound

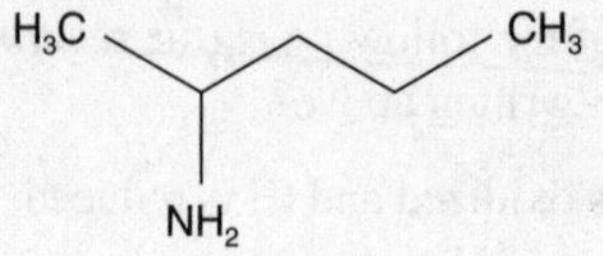

is

A. 2-pentamide
B. 2-aminopentane
C. 4-aminopentane
D. 4-amidopentane
E. 4-aminopentane

70. The name of the following compound

$$CH_3COCH(CH_3)_2$$

is

A. methyl propyl ether
B. propanone
C. methyl propyl ester
D. methyl isopropyl ketone
E. butanoic acid

71. The name of the following compound

is

A. 1-methoxypropane
B. methyl propyl ether
C. methyl butyl ether
D. methyl propyl ketone
E. both (A) and (B)

72. A student wished to produce only carbon dioxide and water vapor from the combustion of methane, CH_4. To accomplish this, the student should burn CH_4

A. in limited oxygen.
B. in a vacuum.
C. in excess oxygen.
D. at a very low temperature.
E. at a very high pressure.

73. A certain organic compound has a vapor pressure of 132 mm Hg at 54°C. To determine the vapor pressure of 2.00 moles of the compound at 37°C, taking the heat of vaporization for the compound to be 4.33×10^4 J/mole, you would use

 A. the Arrhenius equation
 B. the Clausius-Clapeyron equation
 C. the combined gas laws
 D. the ideal gas law
 E. Raoult's law

74. What would be the O—C—O bond angle in oxalic acid?

$$\begin{array}{ccccccc} & & O & & O & & \\ & & \| & & \| & & \\ H-O-&C&-&C&-O-H \end{array}$$

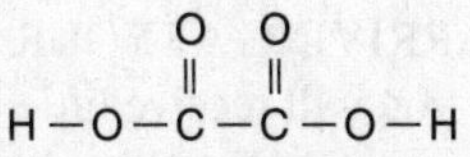

 A. 60°
 B. 90°
 C. 109°
 D. 120°
 E. 180°

75. Which of the following does NOT show hydrogen bonding?

 A. ammonia, NH_3
 B. hydrazine, N_2H_4
 C. hydrogen peroxide, H_2O_2
 D. dimethyl ether, CH_3OCH_3
 E. methyl alcohol, CH_3OH

STOP

Section II: Free-Response Questions*

CHEMISTRY

Section II

(Total time—95 minutes)

Part A

Time—55 minutes

YOU MAY USE YOUR CALCULATOR FOR PART A

CLEARLY SHOW THE METHOD USED AND THE STEPS INVOLVED IN ARRIVING AT YOUR ANSWERS. It is to your advantage to do this, because you may obtain partial credit if you do and you will receive little or no credit if you do not. Attention should be paid to significant figures.

Answer Questions 1, 2, and 3. The Section II score weighting for each question is 20%.

1. Nitric oxide (NO) is a very reactive, poisonous gas with adverse effects on the environment. Produced in internal combustion engines and electrical generating stations, NO has been implicated in depletion of the ozone layer, formation of photochemical smog, and acid rain. In an experiment to investigate ozone-depleting compounds, nitric oxide and ozone were mixed at 200.°C and the following gaseous equilibrium concentrations were measured:

$$[NO] = 0.25\ M$$
$$[O_3] = 0.30\ M$$
$$[NO_2] = [O_2] = 0.60\ M$$

(a) Write the balanced reaction at equilibrium.

(b) What is the mole fraction of $O_{2(g)}$ in the equilibrium mixture?

(c) Write the equilibrium expression for K_c.

(d) Calculate the value of K_c and interpret the magnitude.

(e) Calculate K_p in terms of K_c.

(f) When the mixture was cooled to a lower temperature, 25% of the $O_{2(g)}$ was converted back into $O_{3(g)}$. Calculate K_c at this lower temperature.

(g) A different experiment was conducted in which 0.75 moles of $NO_{(g)}$ was mixed with 0.75 moles of $O_{3(g)}$ in a 5.0-liter reaction vessel at 200.°C. Calculate $[O_2]$ at equilibrium at this temperature.

*You may use the charts on pages 387–390 with this section.

2. Given a 0.050 M H_3PO_4 solution ($K_{a_1} = 7.5 \times 10^{-3}$; $K_{a_2} = 6.2 \times 10^{-8}$), calculate the:

(a) pH of the solution

(b) the equilibrium concentration of H_3PO_4

(c) the equilibrium concentration of $H_2PO_4^-$

(d) the equilibrium concentration of HPO_4^{2-}

3. A student obtained the following rate constants at various temperatures for a particular reaction.

Temperature (K)	***Rate constant (s^{-1})***
200.	0.236
300.	0.301
400.	0.340
500.	0.366
600.	0.385
700.	0.399
800.	0.409

(a) Sketch a graph that plots ln k (y-axis) vs. T^{-1} (x-axis)

(b) Determine the slope of the line.

(c) Determine the equation of the line.

(d) Determine the activation energy for this reaction in J/mol.

If you finish before time is called, you may check your work on this part only. Do not turn to the other part of the test until you are told to do so.

STOP

CHEMISTRY

Part B

Time—40 minutes

NO CALCULATORS MAY BE USED FOR PART B

Answer Question 4 below. The Section II score weighting for this question is 10%.

4. For each of the following three reactions, in Part (i) write a balanced reaction and in Part (ii) answer the question about the reaction. In Part (i), coefficients should be in terms of lowest whole numbers. Assume that solutions are aqueous unless otherwise indicated. Represent substances in solutions as ions if the substances are extensively ionized. Omit formulas for any ions or molecules that are unchanged by the reaction. You may use the empty space at the bottom of the next page for scratch work, but only equations that are written in the answer boxes will be graded.

Example:

(i) A strip of magnesium metal is added to a solution of silver(I) nitrate.

$$Mg + 2Ag^{+} \rightarrow Mg^{2+} + 2Ag$$

(ii) Which substance is oxidized in the reaction?

Mg is oxidized.

(a) Excess concentrated potassium hydroxide solution is added to solid aluminum hydroxide.

(i) Write the balanced equation for the reaction described.

(ii) Name any complex ion formed in the reaction.

(b) Zinc metal is placed in a solution of copper(II) sulfate.

(i) Write the balanced equation for the reaction described above.

(ii) Describe the change in color of the solution that occurs as the reaction proceeds.

(c) Pentane is combusted in air.

(i) Write the balanced equation for the reaction described above.

(ii) How many molecules of products are formed?

Answer Questions 5 and 6. The Section II score weighting for these questions is 15% each.

Your responses to these questions will be graded on the basis of the accuracy and relevance of the information cited. Explanations should be clear and well organized. Examples and equations may be included in your responses where appropriate. Specific answers are preferable to broad, diffuse responses.

5. (a) Draw Lewis structures for

(i) BF_3

(ii) N_2O

(b) Determine the molecular geometries including all idealized bond angles for ClNO where the N atom is in the center of the molecule.

(c) Classify XeF_4 as polar or non-polar and explain why.

(d) Describe the orbital hybridization scheme used by the central atom in its sigma bonding for the following molecules. How many pi bonds are contained in each molecule?

(i) XeF_4

(ii) XeF_2

6. 3 moles of $PCl_{3(g)}$ and 2 moles of $Cl_{2(g)}$ were introduced into an empty sealed flask and allowed to reach equilibrium with the product, $PCl_{5(g)}$. It was experimentally determined that the overall forward reaction was second order and the reverse reaction was first order in PCl_5.

(a) Write the equilibrium expression for the reaction.

(b) Draw a graph showing how the concentrations of all species change over time until equilibrium is achieved.

(c) Write a possible rate law for the forward reaction.

(d) List four factors that influence the rate of a reaction and explain each factor using chemical principles.

(e) What is an activated complex?

(f) Explain the concepts behind the Maxwell-Boltzmann distribution and sketch a diagram to explain the concepts.

STOP

Answer Key for Practice Exam 1

Section I: Multiple-Choice Questions

1. B
2. B
3. E
4. A
5. C
6. D
7. E
8. C
9. B
10. A
11. D
12. C
13. D
14. E
15. D
16. C
17. A
18. B
19. C
20. A
21. A
22. D
23. B
24. A
25. B
26. B
27. B
28. C
29. A
30. C
31. C
32. B
33. A
34. C
35. C
36. C
37. E
38. C
39. C
40. D
41. C
42. D
43. A
44. D
45. D
46. A
47. B
48. A
49. E
50. E
51. C
52. A
53. D
54. E
55. E
56. C
57. B
58. A
59. E
60. A
61. E
62. C
63. D
64. B
65. B
66. E
67. C
68. D
69. B
70. D
71. E
72. C
73. B
74. D
75. D

Answers and Explanations for Practice Exam 1

Multiple Choice

1. B.

2. B.

3. E.

4. A.

5. C.

6. D.

7. E. $\Delta E = 0 - E_2$

$$E_2 = \frac{-2.178 \times 10^{-18}\,\not{\text{J}}}{2^2} \times \frac{6.022 \times 10^{23}}{1\,\text{mol}} \times \frac{1\,\text{kJ}}{10^3\,\not{\text{J}}}$$

when rounded

$$E_2 = \frac{-2 \times 10^{-18}\,\not{\text{J}}}{2^2} \times \frac{6 \times 10^{23}}{1\,\text{mol}} \times \frac{1\,\text{kJ}}{10^3\,\not{\text{J}}}$$

$\approx -300\ \text{kJ} \cdot \text{mol}^{-1}$

$\Delta E = 0 - (-300\ \text{kJ} \cdot \text{mol}^{-1}) \approx 320\ \text{kJ} \cdot \text{mol}^{-1}$

8. C.

9. B.

10. A.

11. D.

12. C.

13. D. All bonds are covalent because the electronegativity difference is 0 for all examples. However, N_2 is the only molecule given that forms a triple bond. Triple bonds are stronger (and shorter) than comparable double or single bonds.

14. E.

15. D.

16. C.

17. A.

18. B.

19. C. SO_2 is bent. The polarity vectors point from the sulfur to the two oxygens (the head of the arrow pointing in the direction of greatest electronegativity). Because the molecule is bent, the vectors will not cancel out. Instead they should add to give a resultant vector that bisects the O-S-O angle and points from the S to a point in between the two oxygen atoms.

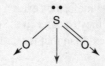

20. **A.** The central bromine atom makes five bonds to fluorine and has one lone pair of electrons for a total of six electron domains.

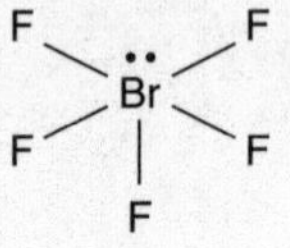

21. **A.** $\frac{\overset{0.9}{\cancel{0.901 g H_2O}}}{1} \times \frac{\overset{8}{\cancel{16.00}} g O}{\underset{9}{\cancel{18.02 g H_2O}}} \approx 0.8 g O$

$(0.8 \cancel{g O})(1 \text{ mol O} / 16.00 \cancel{g O}) \approx 0.05 \text{ mol O}$

$3.978 \text{ g total} - 0.8 \text{ g O} \approx 3.2 \text{ g Cu}$

$(3.2 \cancel{g Cu})(1 \text{ mol Cu} / 63.55 \cancel{g Cu}) \approx 0.05 \text{ mol Cu}$

$\frac{0.05 \text{ mol Cu}}{0.05 \text{ mol O}} = 1:1 \rightarrow CuO$

22. **D.** $\frac{627 \cancel{mg Bi}}{3.62 \text{ g medication}} \times \frac{1 \cancel{g Bi}}{10^3 \cancel{mg Bi}} \times \frac{362.12 \text{ g } C_7H_5BiO_4}{209.00 \cancel{g Bi}} \times 100\% = 30.0\%$

Hint: Do NOT spend time doing the math above. Examine the numbers and cancel where possible. The problem above can be done without a calculator and simplifies to

$\frac{\overset{3}{\cancel{627 mg Bi}}}{\underset{1}{\cancel{3.62}} \text{ g medication}} \times \frac{1 \cancel{g Bi}}{10^3 \cancel{mg Bi}} \times \frac{\overset{\sim 100}{\cancel{362.12}} \text{ g } C_7H_5BiO_4}{\underset{1}{\cancel{209.00 g Bi}}} \times 100\% \approx 30\%$

23. **B.** In examining the equation, $P_B = X_B \cdot P_T$, the partial pressure of gas B (P_B) is determined by knowing the total pressure of all gases (given as 9.00 atm) and the mol fraction of gas B (X_B). Since you were given the number of grams of gas B in order to determine moles, you would need to know the relative molecular mass of gas B.

24. **A.** $P_2 = \frac{P_1V_1}{V_2} = \frac{2.00 \text{ atm} \times \overset{1}{\cancel{250. cm^3}}}{\underset{2}{\cancel{5.00 \times 10^2 cm^3}}} = 1.00 \text{ atm}$

25. **B.** $P_{\text{dry gas}} = P_{\text{total}} - P_{H_2O} = 98.64 \text{ kPa} - 2.64 \text{ kPa} = 96.00 \text{ kPa}$

$T_1 = (22.0°C + 273) = 295 \text{ K}$

$V_2 = V_1\frac{P_1}{P_2} \times \frac{T_2}{T_1} = 1.85 \text{ L} \times \frac{(96.00 \cancel{kPa})(273 \cancel{K})}{(101.325 \cancel{kPa})(295 \cancel{K})}$

26. **B.** Because $d = \frac{m}{V} = \frac{P \cdot M}{R \cdot T}$; therefore, $M = \frac{d \cdot R \cdot T}{P}$

$T = 127°C + 273 = 400. \text{ K}$

$M = \frac{\cancel{4.00 g} \cdot 0.0821 \cancel{L} \cdot \cancel{atm} \cdot 400. \cancel{K}}{\cancel{L} \cdot \text{mol} \cdot \cancel{K} \cdot \cancel{4.00 atm}} \approx 32 \text{ g} \cdot \text{mol}^{-1}$

27. **B.** $\frac{r_{CH_4}}{r_{SO_2}} = \frac{\sqrt{MM_{SO_2}}}{\sqrt{MM_{CH_4}}} = \frac{\sqrt{64 \text{ g} \cdot \text{mol}^{-1}}}{\sqrt{16 \text{ g} \cdot \text{mol}^{-1}}} = \sqrt{4} = 2$

28. **C.** The deviation from ideal behavior is large at high pressure and low temperature. At high pressures, and thus high densities, the intermolecular distances can become quite short, and attractive forces between molecules become significant. Neighboring molecules exert a relatively long-range attractive force on one another, which will reduce the momentum that they transfer to the container walls. The observed pressure exerted by the gas under these conditions will be less than that for an Ideal Gas. Since *P* and *V* of gases are inversely proportion, less pressure means greater volume.

29. **A.** This is the definition of critical temperature.

30. **C.** Condensation occurs when a gas turns into a liquid.

31. **C.**

$$\begin{array}{ll} SO_{2(g)} \rightarrow \cancel{S_{(s)}} + O_{2(g)} & \Delta H = 297\,\text{kJ} \\ \cancel{S_{(s)}} + \tfrac{3}{2}O_{2(g)} \rightarrow SO_{3(g)} & \Delta H = -396\,\text{kJ} \\ \hline SO_{2(g)} + \tfrac{1}{2}O_{2(g)} \rightarrow SO_{3(g)} & \Delta H = -99\,\text{kJ} \end{array}$$

32. **B.** $q = m \times c \times (T_f - T_i) = 3240$ J

$= (150.\text{ g}) \times (2.44\text{ J} \cdot {}^\circ\text{C}^{-1} \cdot \text{g}^{-1}) \times (T_f - 22.0^\circ\text{C}) = 3240$ J

For information only:

$3240\ J = 366\ J\ (T_f - 22.0^\circ C)$

$8.85 = T_f - 22.0^\circ C$

$T_f = 30.9^\circ C$

33. **A.** Activation energy is the energy that must be overcome in order for a chemical reaction to occur and is denoted by E_a. Graphically, it represents the height of the potential barrier. For chemical reactions to have a noticeable rate, there should be a significant number of molecules with energies equal to or greater than the activation energy.

34. **C.**

35. **C.** $$\frac{98.09\,\cancel{\text{g H}_2\text{SO}_4}}{100.\,\cancel{\text{g sol'n.}}} \times \frac{1.642\,\cancel{\text{g sol'n.}}}{1\,\cancel{\text{mL sol'n.}}} \times \frac{10^3\,\cancel{\text{mL sol'n.}}}{1\,\text{L sol'n.}} \times \frac{1\,\text{mol H}_2\text{SO}_4}{\cancel{98.09\,\text{g H}_2\text{SO}_4}} = 16.4\,M$$

36. **C.** $$\frac{{}^{1}\cancel{6.00\,\text{g a.a.}}}{100.\,\cancel{\text{g sol'n}}} \times \frac{1.05\,\cancel{\text{g sol'n}}}{1\,\cancel{\text{mL sol'n}}} \times \frac{10^3\,\cancel{\text{mL sol'n}}}{1\,\text{L sol'n}} \times \frac{1\,\text{mol a.a.}}{{}_{\sim 10}\cancel{60.05\,\text{g a.a.}}} \approx 1.05\,M$$

37. **E.** $\Delta T_{BP} = 49.48^\circ\text{C} - 46.23^\circ\text{C} = 3.25^\circ\text{C}$; $\Delta T_{BP} = K_b m$

$$m = \frac{\Delta T_{BP}}{K_b} = \frac{3.25^\circ\cancel{\text{C}}}{3.25^\circ\cancel{\text{C}}/m} = 1.00\,m$$

$$\frac{{}^{1}\cancel{100.0\,\text{g CS}_2}}{1} \times \frac{1.00\,\text{mol } X}{{}_{10}\cancel{1000\,\text{g CS}_2}} = 0.100\,\text{mol } X$$

$$\frac{40.0\,\text{g } X}{0.100\,\text{mol } X} = 400.\,\text{g } X \cdot \text{mol}^{-1}$$

None of the choices are close to 400. g · mol^{-1}

38. **C.**

$$\frac{{}^{1}\cancel{9.01\,\text{g H}_2\text{O}}}{1} \times \frac{1\,\text{mol H}_2\text{O}}{{}_{2}\cancel{18.02\,\text{g H}_2\text{O}}} = 0.500\,\text{mol H}_2\text{O}$$

$$\text{mol fraction H}_2\text{O} = \frac{0.500\,\text{mol H}_2\text{O}}{0.500\,\text{mol H}_2\text{O} + 0.500\,\text{mol sugar}} = 0.500$$

$VP_{solution} = VP_{solvent} \cdot X_A = (30.0\text{ torr})\ (0.500) = 15.0$ torr

39. **C.** Because heat is produced by the reaction, removing heat (cooling) would have the same effect as removing a product.

40. **D.** Because the reaction is at equilibrium, $Q = K_{sp}$

$\Delta G^\circ = -RT \ln K_{sp} = -(8.314\text{ J} \cdot \cancel{\text{K}^{-1}})\ (298\ \cancel{\text{K}})\ (\ln 1.8 \times 10^{-10})$

For information only:

$\Delta G^\circ = 5.56 \times 10^4\ J = 55.6\ kJ.$

Note that ΔG° is >> 1 which is in agreement with K_{sp} << 1.

41. C. Brønsted acid (proton donor): $HSO_4^-{}_{(aq)} \rightarrow SO_4^{2-}{}_{(aq)} + H^+{}_{(aq)}$

Brønsted base (proton acceptor): $S^{2-}{}_{(aq)} + H^+{}_{(aq)} \rightarrow HS^-{}_{(aq)}$

42. D. Brønsted acids, by definition, are proton donors; therefore, each Brønsted acid must contain at least one hydrogen atom. Choices II, IV, and V do not contain hydrogen. A Lewis acid must be able to accept an electron pair.

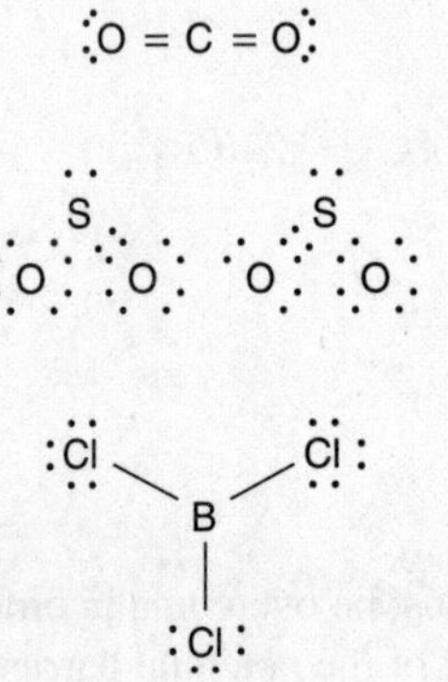

43. A. $Na_2O_{(s)} + H_2O_{(l)} \rightarrow 2Na^+{}_{(aq)} + 2OH^-{}_{(aq)}$

$Na_2O \approx 62\ g \cdot mol^{-1}$

$$\frac{{}^{1}\cancel{0.3099\,g\,Na_2O}}{100.\,\cancel{mL}} \times \frac{1\,\cancel{mol\,Na_2O}}{{}_{\sim 200}\cancel{62\,g\,Na_2O}} \times \frac{2\,mol\,OH^-}{1\,\cancel{mol\,Na_2O}} \times \frac{10^3\,\cancel{mL}}{1\,L} \approx 0.1\,M\,OH^-$$

44. D. Acids with the most electronegative central atom (Cl in this case) will be the strongest; i.e., the greater the electronegativity of the central atom, the stronger will be the acid. The larger difference in electronegativity between the hydrogen and the other atom shifts the bonding pair of electrons toward the other atom thus weakening the bond between the hydrogen and the other atom, resulting in the bond between the atom and hydrogen becoming more easily broken. For example: $HF > H_2O > NH_3 > CH_4$ or $HCl > H_2S > PH_3 > SiH_4$. Keeping the central atom the same, acid strength increases with more oxygen.

45. D. $2NaOH_{(aq)} + H_2A_{(aq)} \rightarrow Na_2A_{(aq)} + 2H_2O_{(l)}$

$$\frac{{}^{10}\cancel{20.0\,mL\,NaOH}}{1} \times \frac{1\,\cancel{L}}{10^3\,\cancel{mL}} \times \frac{1.50\,\cancel{mol\,NaOH}}{1\,\cancel{L}} \times \frac{1\,mol\,H_2A}{{}_{1}\cancel{2\,mol\,NaOH}} = 1.50 \times 10^{-2}\,mol\,H_2A$$

$$\frac{{}^{5}\cancel{7.50}\,g\,H_2A}{{}_{1}\cancel{1.50} \times 10^{-2}\,mol\,H_2A} \times \frac{{}^{1}\cancel{20.0\,mL}}{{}_{10}\cancel{200.\,mL}} = 50.0\,g \cdot mol^{-1}$$

46. A. $[H^+] = [A^-] = 0.200 \times 0.050\,M = 0.0100\,M$

$[HA] = (0.050 - 0.0100)\,M = 0.040\,M$

$$K_a = \frac{[H^+][A^-]}{[HA]} = \frac{(0.0100)^2}{0.040} = 2.50 \times 10^{-3}$$

47. B. When $[HIn] \approx [In^-]$, the color of the indicator changes and is a mixture of the two colors; in this case it should be orange.

$$\frac{[HIn]}{[In^-]} = \frac{[H^+]}{K_a} = 1 \qquad [H^+] = K_a = 3.0 \times 10^{-5}$$

If $[HIn] / [In^-] \geq 10$, the color will be that of HIn (in this case red).

If $[HIn] / [In^-] \leq 0.1$, the color will be that of In^- (in this case yellow).

For information only: pH = 4.52

48. **A.** Na_2CO_3 is a basic salt because NaOH is a strong base and H_2CO_3 is a weak acid. RbF is an alkaline salt because RbOH is strong and HF is weak. $FeCl_3$ is an acid salt because $Fe(OH)_3$ is weak base and HCl is a strong acid. KNO_3 is a neutral salt. Both HNO_3 and KOH are strong. $NH_4C_2H_3O_2$ is indeterminate unless the relative K_a and K_b values are supplied. Both NH_4OH and $HC_2H_3O_2$ are weak. $ZnSO_4$ is an acid salt. The first ionization of H_2SO_4 is strong and $Zn(OH)_2$ is weak. $Ba(NO_3)_2$ is neutral because both $Ba(OH)_2$ and HNO_3 are strong.

49. **E.** $NH_{3(aq)} + H_2O_{(l)} \rightleftharpoons NH_4^+{}_{(aq)} + OH^-{}_{(aq)}$

$pH = -\log[H^+] \quad 11.00 = -\log[H^+] \quad [H^+] = 1.0 \times 10^{-11}\,M$

$$[OH^-] = \frac{K_w}{[H_3O^+]} = \frac{1.00 \times 10^{-14}}{1.0 \times 10^{-11}} = 1.0 \times 10^{-3}\,M$$

$[OH^-] = [NH_4^+]$ Let x = original concentration of ammonia.

$$K_b = 2 \times 10^{-5} = \frac{(1.00 \times 10^{-3})(1.00 \times 10^{-3})}{x - 1.00 \times 10^{-3}} \qquad \text{Assuming } 1.00 \times 10^{-3} \text{ is } x = 0.05\,M$$

50. **E.** The units of the rate constant (M / min) imply that this is a zero-order reaction in which the rate = k. Therefore, the rate law is

$[A] = -kt + [A_0]$

$(0.75\,M) = -(0.25\,M/\text{min})t + (2.50\,M)$

$-1.75\,M = (-0.25\,M/\text{min})t$

$t = 7.0$ min

51. **C.** Catalysts lower activation energy (arrow I). By lowering the activation energy, the energy change represented by arrow II is also lowered. The overall ΔH (arrow III) is not affected.

52. **A.** $K_c = k_f / k_r = 57.0$. The rate constant for the decomposition of HI (k_r) would be 57.0 times smaller than the rate constant (k_f) for the synthesis of HI.

53. **D.** $K_c = k_f / k_r$

$k_r = k_f / K_c = (5.70 \times 10^{-2}) / 57.0 = 1.00 \times 10^{-3}$

54. **E.** Catalysts lower the activation barrier for both the forward and reverse reactions by the same amount; i.e., rates become larger by the same proportion. Therefore, the ratio of k_f / k_r remains constant and $k_f / k_r = K_c$.

55. **E.** Begin by assigning oxidation numbers.

ICl: I = +1, Cl = −1 In binary compounds, the more electronegative element is assigned to have a negative oxidation number. Cl is more electronegative than I.

H_2O: H = +1, O = −2

HCl: H = +1, Cl = −1

HOI: H = +1, O = −2, I = +1

56. **C.** ANODE: $2Cl^-{}_{(aq)} \rightarrow Cl_{2(g)} + 2e^-$ (AN OX—oxidation occurs at the anode)

CATHODE: $Ca^{2+}{}_{(aq)} + 2e^- \rightarrow Ca_{(s)}$ (RED CAT—reduction occurs at the cathode)

Amount of charge passing through cell:

$$\frac{\overset{\sim 1}{\cancel{0.965\,A}}}{1} \times \frac{1\,\cancel{C/s}}{1\,\cancel{A}} \times \frac{60\,\cancel{s}}{1\,\cancel{min}} \times \frac{60\,\cancel{min}}{1\,\cancel{hr}} \times \frac{1.00\,\cancel{hr}}{1} \times \frac{1\,F}{\underset{\sim 10^5}{\cancel{96{,}500\,C}}} \approx 3.6 \times 10^{-2}\,F$$

Amount of calcium formed:

$$\frac{3.6 \times 10^{-2}\,\cancel{F}}{1} \times \frac{1\,\cancel{mol\,Ca}}{1\,\cancel{F}} \times \frac{\overset{\sim 40}{\cancel{40.08}}\,g\,Ca}{1\,\cancel{mol\,Ca}} \approx 0.72\,g\,Ca$$

57. **B.** Begin by writing the two half reactions (remember to use the diagonal rule to decide which species is being oxidized and which species is being reduced).

$$\text{OX: } Zn_{(s)} \rightarrow Zn^{2+}_{(aq)} + 2e^- \qquad E^\circ_{ox} = 0.76\ V$$
$$\text{RED: } Sn^{2+}_{(aq)} + 2e^- \rightarrow Sn_{(s)} \qquad E^\circ_{red} = -0.14\ V$$
$$Zn_{(s)} + Sn^{2+}_{(aq)} \rightarrow Zn^{2+}_{(aq)} + Sn_{(s)} \qquad E^\circ = 0.62\ V$$

$$E = E^\circ - \frac{0.0591\ V}{n}\log Q = 0.62\ V - \frac{0.0591\ V}{2}\log\frac{[Zn^{2+}]}{[Sn^{2+}]}$$

$$= 0.62\ V - \frac{0.0591\ V}{2}\log\frac{0.50}{0.15} = 0.60\ V$$

58. **A.** Subtract 4 from the mass number; subtract 2 from the atomic number; add a helium nucleus ^4_2He.

59. **E.** Mass number stays the same. Subtract 1 from the atomic number.

Add a positron $^{0}_{+1}e$.

60. **A.** For Questions 60–64, remember that the sum of the reactant superscripts must be equal to the sum of the product superscripts and the sum of the reactant subscripts must be equal to the sum of the product subscripts.

61. **E.**

62. **C.**

63. **D.**

64. **B.**

65. **B.**

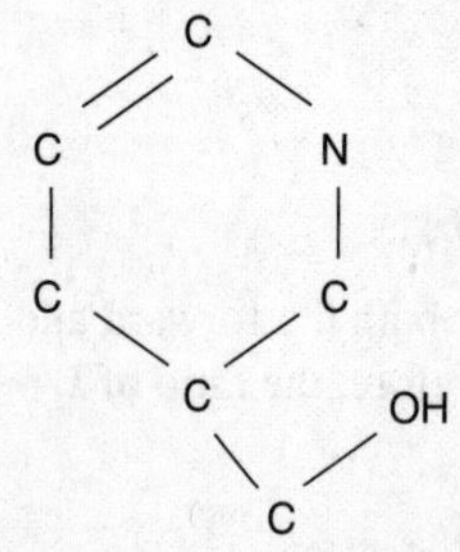

66. **E.** If you missed this problem, review nomenclature of alkenes.

67. **C.** If you missed this problem, review nomenclature of alkynes.

68. **D.**

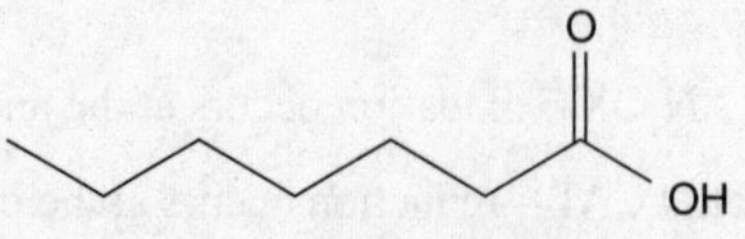

If you missed this problem, review nomenclature of carboxylic acids.

69. **B.** If you missed this problem, review nomenclaure of amides.

70. **D.** If you missed this problem, review nomenclature of ketones.

71. **E.** If you missed this problem, review nomenclature of ethers.

72. **C.** Hydrocarbon fuels, when combusted under actual (non-ideal) combustion conditions, produce several intermediate products in addition to carbon dioxide and water and include the unburned hydrocarbon, carbon monoxide, oxides of nitrogen, hydroxyl radicals, and the hydrogen ions.

73. B. To do this problem, you would use the Clausius-Clapeyron equation:

$$\log \frac{P_2}{P_1} = \frac{\Delta H_{vap}}{2.303R}\left(\frac{T_2 - T_1}{T_2 T_1}\right)$$

where

$T_1 = 54°C + 273 = 327$ K

$T_2 = 37°C + 273 = 310$ K

P_1 (132 mm Hg) is the vapor pressure of the liquid at T_1 (327K)

P_2 (x) is the vapor pressure of the liquid at T_2 (310K)

R is a universal gas constant: 8.314 joules/(mole · K)

74. D. Count the double bond around the central carbons atom as a single electron pair when determining geometry or bond angle. There are a total of 3 electron pairs around each C atom—counting the double bond as just one electron pair. The result is trigonal planar geometry with a bond angle of 120°.

75. D. Hydrogen bonding is a very strong intermolecular force that occurs between molecules containing an H atom that is bonded to fluorine, oxygen, or a nitrogen atom. In choice (D), the hydrogens are bonded to carbon, not to F, O, or N.

Free Response

Question 1

Maximum Points for Question 1
Part (a): 1 point
Part (b): 2 points
Part (c): 1 point
Part (d): 2 points
Part (e): 1 point
Part (f): 2 points
Part (g): 2 points
Total points: 11

1. Nitric oxide (NO) is a very reactive, poisonous gas with adverse effects on the environment. Produced in internal combustion engines and electrical generating stations, NO has been implicated in depletion of the ozone layer, formation of photochemical smog, and acid rain. In an experiment to investigate ozone-depleting compounds, nitric oxide and ozone were mixed at 200.°C and the following gaseous equilibrium concentrations were measured: *[NO] = 0.25 M* *$[O_3]$ = 0.30 M* *$[NO_2] = [O_2]$ = 0.60 M*	***1 point possible***

(continued)

(a) Write the balanced reaction at equilibrium. $NO_{(g)} + O_{3(g)} \rightleftharpoons NO_{2(g)} + O_{2(g)}$	*1 point for correctly balanced equation.*
(b) What is the mole fraction of $O_{2(g)}$ in the equilibrium mixture? mol fraction for O_2: $\frac{\text{moles}O_2}{\text{mol}NO + \text{mol}O_3 + \text{mol}NO_2 + \text{mol}O_2}$ $= \frac{0.60}{0.25 + 0.30 + 0.60 + 0.60} = 0.34$ ***Note:*** The volume was not necessary since mole fraction is independent of a constant volume.	***2 points possible*** *1 point for correct setup.* *1 point for correct answer.*
(c) Write the equilibrium expression for K_c. $K_c = \frac{[NO_2][O_2]}{[NO][O_3]}$	***1 point possible*** *1 point for correct expression.*
(d) Calculate the value of K_c and interpret the magnitude. $K_c = \frac{(0.60)(0.60)}{(0.25)(0.30)} = 4.8$ Because $K_c > 1$, the product of the equilibrium concentrations of $NO_{2(g)}$ and $O_{2(g)}$ is greater than the product of the equilibrium concentrations of $NO_{(g)}$ and $O_{3(g)}$.	***2 points possible*** *1 point for correct setup and value for K_c.* *1 point for correct interpretation of K_c.*
(e) Calculate K_p in terms of K_c. $K_p = K_c (RT)^{\Delta n}$ Because $\Delta n_{gas} = 0$; $K_p = K_c = 4.8$	***1 point possible*** *1 point for correct setup and answer.*
(f) When the mixture was cooled to a lower temperature, 25% of the $O_{2(g)}$ was converted back into $O_{3(g)}$. Calculate K_c at this lower temperature. moles NO_2 reacting = moles O_2 reacting = moles O_3 formed = (0.25) (0.60*M*) = 0.15 *M* [NO] = 0.25 + 0.15 = 0.40 *M* $[O_3]$ = 0.30 + 0.15 = 0.45 *M* $[NO_2] = [O_2]$ = 0.60 - 0.15 = 0.45 *M* $K_c = (0.45)^2 / (0.40)(0.45) = 1.1$	***2 points possible*** *1 point for correct setup.* *1 point for correct K_c.*
(g) A different experiment was conducted in which 0.75 moles of $NO_{(g)}$ was mixed with 0.75 moles of $O_{3(g)}$ in a 5.0-liter reaction vessel at 200.°C. Calculate $[O_2]$ at equilibrium at this temperature. let *x* = number of moles that react	***2 points possible***

	[NO]	*[O₃]*	*[NO₂]*	*[O₂]*
Initial (I)	(0.75 / 5.0)	(0.75 / 5.0)	0	0
Change (C)	$-x / 5.0$	$-x / 5.0$	$+x / 5.0$	$+x / 5.0$
Equlibrium (E)	$\frac{(0.75 - x)}{5.0}$	$\frac{(0.75 - x)}{5.0}$	$x / 5.0$	$x / 5.0$

$K_c = \frac{[NO_2][O_2]}{[NO][O_3]} = \frac{(x/5.0)^2}{[(0.75 - x)/5.0]^2} = 4.8$	*1 point for correct setup.*
(determined in part d)	
$x / (0.75 - x) = (4.8)^{0.5}$	
$x = 0.51$ mol	
$[O_2] = 0.51$ mol / 5.0 L = 0.10 *M*	*1 point for correct value for* $[O_2]$.

Question 2

Maximum Points for Question 2
Part (a): 2 points
Part (b): 2 points
Part (c): 2 points
Part (d): 2 points
Total points: 8

2. Given a 0.050 M H_3PO_4 *solution*

($K_{a_1} = 7.5 \times 10^{-3}$; $K_{a_2} = 6.2 \times 10^{-8}$), calculate the:

(a) pH of the solution

2 points possible

$H_3PO_{4(aq)} + H_2O_{(l)} \rightleftharpoons H_2PO_4^-{}_{(aq)} + H_3O^+{}_{(aq)}$

	H_3PO_4	H_3O^+	$H_2PO_4^-$
Initial Conc. (*M*)	0.050	~ 0	0
Change (*M*)	$-x$	$+x$	$+x$
Final Conc. (*M*)	$(0.050 - x)$	x	x

$$K_{a_1} = \frac{[H^+][H_2PO_4^-]}{[H_3PO_4]} = 7.5 \times 10^{-3} = \frac{(x)(x)}{0.050 - x} = \frac{x^2}{0.050 - x}$$

1 point for correct setup.

The magnitude of K_{a_1} is relatively large (almost 10^{-2}), which makes it likely that the acid will undergo greater than 5% dissociation.

$(7.5 \times 10^{-3})(0.050 - x) = (x^2)$

$x^2 = 3.75 \times 10^{-4} - 7.5 \times 10^{-3}x$

$ax^2 + bx + c = 0$

$x^2 + 7.5 \times 10^{-3}x - 3.75 \times 10^{-4} = 0$

$$x = \frac{-b \pm \sqrt{b^2 - 4ac}}{2a}$$

$x = 1.6 \times 10^{-2}$

(continued)

$[H_3O^+] = 1.6 \times 10^{-2}\ M$ $pH = -\log[1.6 \times 10^{-2}] = 1.80$	*1 point for correct calculation of pH.*
(b) the equilibrium concentration of H_3PO_4 $[H_3PO_4] = (0.050 - x)$ $[H_3PO_4] = 0.050 - 0.016 = 3.4 \times 10^{-2}\ M$	***2 points possible*** *1 point for correct setup.* *1 point for correct answer.*
(c) the equilibrium concentration of $H_2PO_4^-$ Let y = concentration of HPO_4^- produced during the second dissociation.	***2 points possible***

	$H_2PO_4^-$	H_3O^+	HPO_4^{2-}
Initial Conc. (*M*)	1.6×10^{-2}	1.6×10^{-2}	0
Change (*M*)	$-y$	$+y$	$+y$
Final Conc. (*M*)	$1.6 \times 10^{-2} - y$	$1.6 \times 10^{-2} + y$	$+y$

$K_{a_2} = \frac{[H^+][HPO_4^{2-}]}{[H_2PO_4^-]} = 6.2 \times 10^{-8} = \frac{(1.6 \times 10^{-2} + y)(y)}{1.6 \times 10^{-2} - y}$	*1 point for correct setup.*
Because the value of K_{a_2} is much smaller than the value of K_{a_1}, the amount of $H_3O^+_{(aq)}$ added during the second dissociation is negligible. Second dissociation: $H_2PO_4^-{}_{(aq)} + H_2O_{(l)} \rightleftharpoons HPO_4^{2-}{}_{(aq)} + H_3O^+{}_{(aq)}$ $[H_2PO_4^-] = 1.6 \times 10^{-2}\ M$	*1 point for correct answer.*
(d) the equilibrium concentration of HPO_4^{2-} $K_{a_2} = \frac{[H^+][HPO_4^{2-}]}{[H_2PO_4^-]} = 6.2 \times 10^{-8} \approx \frac{(\cancel{1.6 \times 10^{-2}})(y)}{\cancel{1.6 \times 10^{-2}}}$ Because $K_{a_2} \ll 1$, $y \ll 1.6 \times 10^{-2}$; so, $1.6 \times 10^{-2} \pm y \approx 1.6 \times 10^{-2}$. Because 1.6×10^{-2} now appears in both the numerator and denominator, they cancel each other out, leaving $y = 6.2 \times 10^{-8} = [HPO_4^{2-}]$.	***2 points possible*** *1 point for correct setup.* *1 point for correct answer.*

Question 3

Maximum Points for Question 3
Part (a): 2 points
Part (b): 2 points
Part (c): 2 points
Part (d): 2 points
Total points: 8

3. A student obtained the following rate constants at various temperatures for a particular reaction.

2 points possible

Temperature (K)	***Rate constant (s^{-1})***
200.	0.236
300.	0.301
400.	0.340
500.	0.366
600.	0.385
700.	0.399
800.	0.409

(a) Sketch a graph that plots ln k (y-axis) vs. T^{-1} (x-axis).

1 point for correct values for T^{-1} and ln k.

Temperature (K)	***T^{-1}***	***Rate constant k (s^{-1})***	***ln k***
200	0.00500	0.236	–1.444
300	0.00333	0.301	–1.201
400	0.00250	0.340	–1.079
500	0.00200	0.366	–1.005
600	0.00167	0.385	–0.955
700	0.00143	0.399	–0.919
800	0.00125	0.409	–0.894

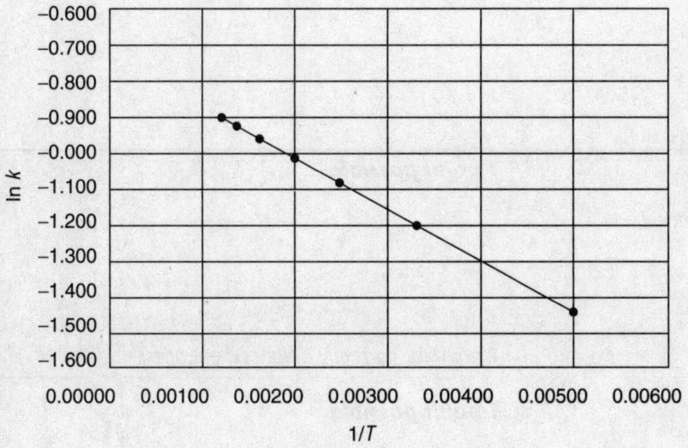

1 point for correctly drawn graph.

(b) Determine the slope of the line.	***2 points possible***
slope = $(y_2 - y_1) / (x_2 - x_1)$	*1 point for correct setup.*
= (–1.444 + 0.894) / (0.00500 – 0.00125) = –147	*1 point for correct answer.*
(c) Determine the equation of the line.	***2 points possible***
$y = mx + b$	
m = slope = –147	*1 point for correct setup.*
$b = y - mx$ = –1.444 – (–147) (0.00500) = –0.71	
$y = -147x - 0.71$	*1 point for correct answer.*
(d) Determine the activation energy for this reaction in J/mol.?	***2 points possible***
slope = $-E_a / R$	*1 point for correct setup.*
E_a = –slope (R) = – (–147 K) (8.314 J / K · mol)	
E_a = 1,222 J/mol	*1 point for correct answer.*

Question 4

Maximum Points for Question 4
Part (a) (i): 1 point
Part (a) (ii): 1 point
Part (b) (i): 1 point
Part (b) (ii): 1 point
Part (c) (i): 1 point
Part (c) (ii): 1 point
Total points: 6

4.	***1 point possible***
(a) Excess concentrated potassium hydroxide solution is added to solid aluminum hydroxide.	
(i) Write the balanced equation for the reaction described.	
$OH^- + Al(OH)_3 \rightarrow [Al(OH)_4]^-$	*1 point for correctly balanced equation.*
(ii) Name any complex ion formed in the reaction.	***1 point possible***
Tetrahydroxoaluminate.	*1 point for correct name of the complex ion.*
(b) Zinc metal is placed in a solution of copper(II) sulfate.	***1 point possible***
(i) Write the balanced equation for the reaction described above.	
$Zn + Cu^{2+} \rightarrow Zn^{2+} + Cu$	*1 point for correctly balanced equation.*

(ii) Describe the change in color of the solution that occurs as the reaction proceeds. The blue color of the solution due to the presence of the hydrated copper(II) ion fades as the copper(II) ion reacts and the colorless hydrated zinc(II) ion forms.	***1 point possible*** *1 point for correct color change and explanation.*
(c) Pentane is combusted in air. *(i) Write the balanced equation for the reaction described above.* $C_5H_{12} + 8O_2 \rightarrow 5CO_2 + 6H_2O$	***1 point possible*** *1 point for correctly balanced equation.*
(ii) How many molecules of products are formed? 1 molecule of pentane produces 11 molecules of products.	***1 point possible*** *1 point for correct number of molecules formed.*

Question 5

Maximum Points for Question 5
Part (a) (i): 1 point
Part (a) (ii): 1 point
Part (b): 2 points
Part (c): 2 points
Part (d)(i): 2 points
Part (d) (ii): 2 points
Total points: 10

5. *(a) Draw Lewis structures for* (i) BF_3 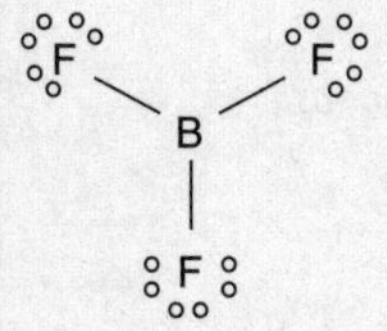	***1 point possible*** *1 point for correct diagram.*
(ii) N_2O 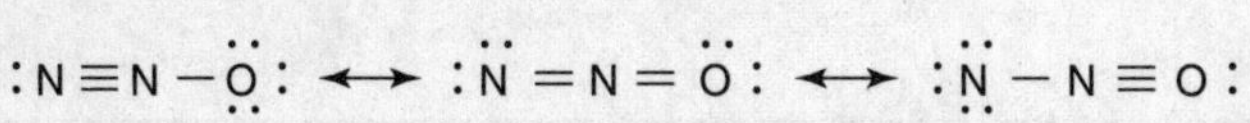	***1 point possible*** *1 point for correct diagram.*

(b) Determine the molecular geometries including all idealized bond angles for ClNO where the N atom is in the center of the molecule 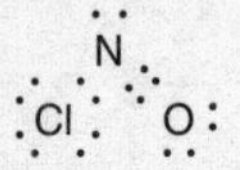 Because the central N atom is surrounded by four electron pairs, three bond pairs (O is double-bonded) and one lone pair, the geometry is bent or V shaped with the Cl-N-O angle approximately 120°.	***2 points possible*** *1 point for correct geometry.* *1 point for correct bond angle.*
(c) Classify XeF_4 as polar or non-polar and explain why. Non-polar because XeF_4 has a square planar geometry according to VSEPR, and thus the four Xe → F bond dipoles will cancel giving a non-polar molecule. 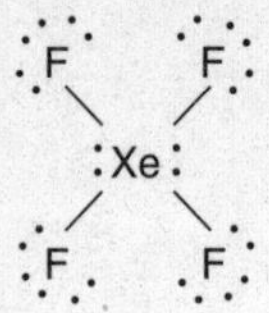	***2 points possible*** *1 point for correct conclusion.* *1 point for correct explanation.*
(d) Describe the orbital hybridization scheme used by the central atom in its sigma bonding for the following molecules. How many pi bonds are contained in each molecule? (i) XeF_4 sp^3d^2 hybrid orbitals, 0 pi bonds 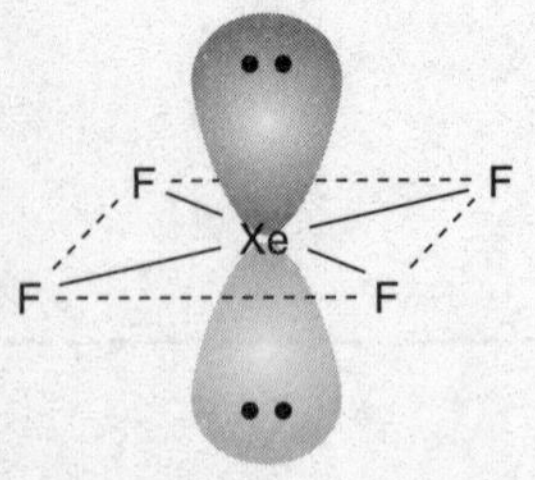	***2 points possible*** *1 point for correct hybridization.* *1 point for correct number of pi bonds.*
(ii) XeF_2 sp^3d hybrid orbitals, 0 pi bonds 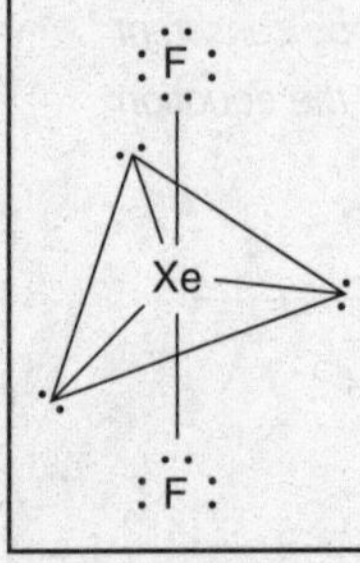	***2 points possible*** *1 point for correct hybridization.* *1 point for correct number of pi bonds.*

Question 6

Maximum Points for Question 6
Part (a): 1 point
Part (b): 1 point
Part (c): 1 point
Part (d): 4 points
Part (e): 1 point
Part (f): 2 points
Total points: 10

6. 3 moles of $PCl_{3(g)}$ and 2 moles of $Cl_{2(g)}$ were introduced into an empty sealed flask and allowed to reach equilibrium with the product, $PCl_{5(g)}$. It was experimentally determined that the overall forward reaction was second order and the reverse reaction was first order in PCl_5.

(a) Write the equilibrium expression for the reaction.

$PCl_{3(g)} + Cl_{2(g)} \rightleftharpoons PCl_{5(g)}$

$$K_c = \frac{[PCl_5]}{[Cl_3][Cl_2]}$$

1 point possible

1 point for correct equation.

(b) Draw a graph showing how the concentrations of all species change over time until equilibrium is achieved.

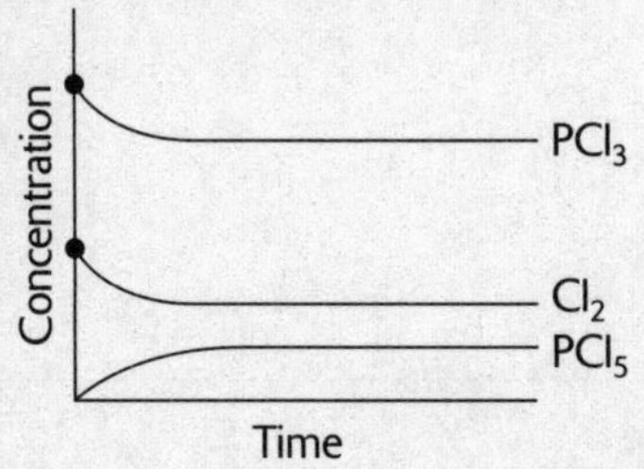

1 point possible

1 point for correct graph. Graph must include:

- *points on ordinate take into account the initial amounts of the three substances.*
- *the PCl_5 line rises while the other lines fall.*
- *lines are curved at start and flatten after equilibrium has been achieved.*
- *the concentration changes should be consistent with the fact that all coefficients in the equation are 1.*

(c) Write a possible rate law for the forward reaction.

rate = $k[PCl_3]\,[Cl_2]$

1 point possible

1 point for being first order for each reactant and incorporating k into the equation.

Note: *Other rate laws given full credit if consistent with overall second order; i.e., rate law = $k[Cl_2]^2$.*

(d) List four factors that influence the rate of a reaction, and explain each factor using chemical principles. ■ Nature of the reactants. In the case of solid reactants, if we reduce the physical size of the reactants through grinding, we are in essence increasing the total surface area that collisions can take place. This will have an enhanced effect on rate of product formation. Gaseous reactants have a higher kinetic energy, and therefore the impact energy will be greater resulting in a higher rate of product formation. ■ A higher concentration of reactants leads to more effective collisions per unit time, which leads to an increasing reaction rate (except for zero order reactions). Similarly, a higher concentration of products tends to be associated with a lower reaction rate. ■ Medium. The rate of a chemical reaction depends on the medium in which the reaction occurs. It may make a difference whether a medium is aqueous or organic; polar or non-polar; or liquid, solid, or gaseous. ■ Temperature. Increasing the temperature increases the average kinetic energy of the molecules. This will increase the impact energy enough to overcome the activation energy. ■ Catalyst. Catalysts (e.g., enzymes) lower the activation energy of a chemical reaction and increase the rate of a chemical reaction without being consumed in the process. Catalysts work by increasing the frequency of collisions between reactants, altering the orientation of reactants so that more collisions are effective, reducing intra-molecular bonding within reactant molecules, or donating electron density to the reactants. The presence of a catalyst helps a reaction to proceed more quickly to equilibrium. Aside from catalysts, other chemical species can affect a reaction. The quantity of hydrogen ions (the pH of aqueous solutions) can alter a reaction rate. Other chemical species may compete for a reactant or alter orientation, bonding, electron density, etc., thereby decreasing the rate of a reaction.	***4 points possible*** *1 point for each factor (including explanation from points listed).*
(e) What is an activated complex? An activated complex is a short-lived, high-energy, unstable intermediate that is formed during a reaction. When chemical substances collide in a reaction, a high-energy, unstable, transitory species known as activated complex is formed. The activated complex is an unstable arrangement of the atoms which must form either the original reactants or some new products. If the collision is effective it comes apart to form new products, and if the collision is ineffective it comes apart to reform the reactants.	***1 point possible*** *1 point for correct explanation using any of the concepts listed.*

(f) Explain the concepts behind the Maxwell-Boltzmann distribution, and sketch a diagram to explain the concepts.

2 points possible

In order for a molecular collision to be effective it must meet two conditions: (1) the collision must have enough impact energy to overcome the activation energy. The activation energy is the minimum energy determined by the temperature necessary for the product to form. This impact energy must be sufficient so that bonds can be broken within the reactant molecules and new bonds formed to produce the products, and (2) the molecules must also have proper positioning for effective collisions to occur. In any particular mixture of moving molecules, the velocity of the molecules will vary a great deal, from very slow particles (low energy) to very fast particles (high energy). Most of the particles however will be moving at a speed very close to the average. The Maxwell-Boltzmann distribution shows how the speeds (and hence the energies) of a mixture of moving particles varies at a particular temperature.

1 point for correct explanation using any of the concepts listed (sufficient energy of collision or proper positioning of molecules).

The Maxwell-Boltzmann Distribution

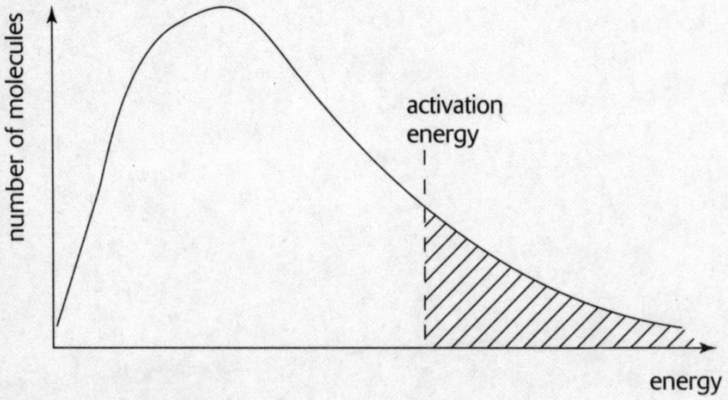

1 point for correct sketch.

From the sketch, notice that

- no molecules are at zero energy
- few molecules are at high energy
- there is no maximum energy value

For a reaction to occur, the particles involved need a minimum amount of energy—the activation energy (E_a). If a particle is not in the shaded area, then it will not have the required energy so it will not be able to participate in the reaction.

CUT HERE

Multiple-Choice Answer Sheet for Practice Exam 2

Remove this sheet and use it to mark your answers.

Section I
Multiple-Choice Questions

1 Ⓐ Ⓑ Ⓒ Ⓓ Ⓔ	26 Ⓐ Ⓑ Ⓒ Ⓓ Ⓔ	51 Ⓐ Ⓑ Ⓒ Ⓓ Ⓔ
2 Ⓐ Ⓑ Ⓒ Ⓓ Ⓔ	27 Ⓐ Ⓑ Ⓒ Ⓓ Ⓔ	52 Ⓐ Ⓑ Ⓒ Ⓓ Ⓔ
3 Ⓐ Ⓑ Ⓒ Ⓓ Ⓔ	28 Ⓐ Ⓑ Ⓒ Ⓓ Ⓔ	53 Ⓐ Ⓑ Ⓒ Ⓓ Ⓔ
4 Ⓐ Ⓑ Ⓒ Ⓓ Ⓔ	29 Ⓐ Ⓑ Ⓒ Ⓓ Ⓔ	54 Ⓐ Ⓑ Ⓒ Ⓓ Ⓔ
5 Ⓐ Ⓑ Ⓒ Ⓓ Ⓔ	30 Ⓐ Ⓑ Ⓒ Ⓓ Ⓔ	55 Ⓐ Ⓑ Ⓒ Ⓓ Ⓔ
6 Ⓐ Ⓑ Ⓒ Ⓓ Ⓔ	31 Ⓐ Ⓑ Ⓒ Ⓓ Ⓔ	56 Ⓐ Ⓑ Ⓒ Ⓓ Ⓔ
7 Ⓐ Ⓑ Ⓒ Ⓓ Ⓔ	32 Ⓐ Ⓑ Ⓒ Ⓓ Ⓔ	57 Ⓐ Ⓑ Ⓒ Ⓓ Ⓔ
8 Ⓐ Ⓑ Ⓒ Ⓓ Ⓔ	33 Ⓐ Ⓑ Ⓒ Ⓓ Ⓔ	58 Ⓐ Ⓑ Ⓒ Ⓓ Ⓔ
9 Ⓐ Ⓑ Ⓒ Ⓓ Ⓔ	34 Ⓐ Ⓑ Ⓒ Ⓓ Ⓔ	59 Ⓐ Ⓑ Ⓒ Ⓓ Ⓔ
10 Ⓐ Ⓑ Ⓒ Ⓓ Ⓔ	35 Ⓐ Ⓑ Ⓒ Ⓓ Ⓔ	60 Ⓐ Ⓑ Ⓒ Ⓓ Ⓔ
11 Ⓐ Ⓑ Ⓒ Ⓓ Ⓔ	36 Ⓐ Ⓑ Ⓒ Ⓓ Ⓔ	61 Ⓐ Ⓑ Ⓒ Ⓓ Ⓔ
12 Ⓐ Ⓑ Ⓒ Ⓓ Ⓔ	37 Ⓐ Ⓑ Ⓒ Ⓓ Ⓔ	62 Ⓐ Ⓑ Ⓒ Ⓓ Ⓔ
13 Ⓐ Ⓑ Ⓒ Ⓓ Ⓔ	38 Ⓐ Ⓑ Ⓒ Ⓓ Ⓔ	63 Ⓐ Ⓑ Ⓒ Ⓓ Ⓔ
14 Ⓐ Ⓑ Ⓒ Ⓓ Ⓔ	39 Ⓐ Ⓑ Ⓒ Ⓓ Ⓔ	64 Ⓐ Ⓑ Ⓒ Ⓓ Ⓔ
15 Ⓐ Ⓑ Ⓒ Ⓓ Ⓔ	40 Ⓐ Ⓑ Ⓒ Ⓓ Ⓔ	65 Ⓐ Ⓑ Ⓒ Ⓓ Ⓔ
16 Ⓐ Ⓑ Ⓒ Ⓓ Ⓔ	41 Ⓐ Ⓑ Ⓒ Ⓓ Ⓔ	66 Ⓐ Ⓑ Ⓒ Ⓓ Ⓔ
17 Ⓐ Ⓑ Ⓒ Ⓓ Ⓔ	42 Ⓐ Ⓑ Ⓒ Ⓓ Ⓔ	67 Ⓐ Ⓑ Ⓒ Ⓓ Ⓔ
18 Ⓐ Ⓑ Ⓒ Ⓓ Ⓔ	43 Ⓐ Ⓑ Ⓒ Ⓓ Ⓔ	68 Ⓐ Ⓑ Ⓒ Ⓓ Ⓔ
19 Ⓐ Ⓑ Ⓒ Ⓓ Ⓔ	44 Ⓐ Ⓑ Ⓒ Ⓓ Ⓔ	69 Ⓐ Ⓑ Ⓒ Ⓓ Ⓔ
20 Ⓐ Ⓑ Ⓒ Ⓓ Ⓔ	45 Ⓐ Ⓑ Ⓒ Ⓓ Ⓔ	70 Ⓐ Ⓑ Ⓒ Ⓓ Ⓔ
21 Ⓐ Ⓑ Ⓒ Ⓓ Ⓔ	46 Ⓐ Ⓑ Ⓒ Ⓓ Ⓔ	71 Ⓐ Ⓑ Ⓒ Ⓓ Ⓔ
22 Ⓐ Ⓑ Ⓒ Ⓓ Ⓔ	47 Ⓐ Ⓑ Ⓒ Ⓓ Ⓔ	72 Ⓐ Ⓑ Ⓒ Ⓓ Ⓔ
23 Ⓐ Ⓑ Ⓒ Ⓓ Ⓔ	48 Ⓐ Ⓑ Ⓒ Ⓓ Ⓔ	73 Ⓐ Ⓑ Ⓒ Ⓓ Ⓔ
24 Ⓐ Ⓑ Ⓒ Ⓓ Ⓔ	49 Ⓐ Ⓑ Ⓒ Ⓓ Ⓔ	74 Ⓐ Ⓑ Ⓒ Ⓓ Ⓔ
25 Ⓐ Ⓑ Ⓒ Ⓓ Ⓔ	50 Ⓐ Ⓑ Ⓒ Ⓓ Ⓔ	75 Ⓐ Ⓑ Ⓒ Ⓓ Ⓔ

CUT HERE

Practice Exam 2

Time: 90 minutes

75 questions

No calculators allowed

This section consists of 75 multiple-choice questions. Mark your answers carefully on the answer sheet.

For Questions 1–5, choose from the following:

- **A.** Bohr
- **B.** Einstein
- **C.** Heisenberg
- **D.** Rutherford
- **E.** Thompson

1. The electron can exist in any one of a set of discrete energy levels.

2. The atom contains an extremely small, positively charged nucleus.

3. As the wavelength of light used to locate an electron decreases, the error in determining its position decreases and the error in determining its momentum increases.

4. The charge-to-mass ratio of an electron.

5. When light with certain frequencies strikes a piece of metal, it emits electrons from the metal.

6. A permissible set of four quantum numbers for an outermost *p* electron in a single As atom when it is in its ground state is

- **A.** 4, 0, 0, +½
- **B.** 4, 2, +1, −½
- **C.** 4, 1, −1, +½
- **D.** 4, −1, 0, +½
- **E.** 5, 1, −1, −½

7. Which statement is false?

- **A.** Alkali metals generally have low ionization energies.
- **B.** Metallic character decreases as one moves right in the periodic table.
- **C.** NaO_2 is the formula for sodium peroxide.
- **D.** Te and Po are metalloids.
- **E.** Aluminum oxide displays amphoteric properties.

For Questions 8–10, choose from the following:

I = metals

II = nonmetals

III = metalloids

8. Form acidic hydroxyl compounds (oxyacids).

- **A.** I
- **B.** II
- **C.** III
- **D.** I and II
- **E.** Neither I, II, or III

9. Have one to five electrons in the outermost shell, usually not more than three.

- **A.** I
- **B.** II
- **C.** III
- **D.** I and II
- **E.** Neither I, II, or III

10. Readily form cations by loss of electrons.

- **A.** I
- **B.** II
- **C.** III
- **D.** I and II
- **E.** Neither I, II, or III

GO ON TO THE NEXT PAGE

11. A correct Lewis structure for aluminum trichloride, $AlCl_3$ is

A.
 : Cl : Al : Cl :

 : Cl :
 ..

B. ..
 Cl : Al : Cl
 ..
 Cl

C. Cl – Al – Cl
 |
 Cl

D. $[: \ddot{C}l :]^-$ Al^{3+} $[: \ddot{C}l :]^-$
 $[: \ddot{C}l :]^-$

E. $\begin{bmatrix} Cl \diagdown \quad \diagup Cl \\ Al \\ | \\ Cl \end{bmatrix}^{+3}$

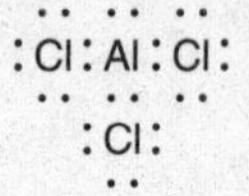

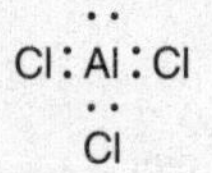

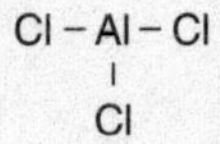

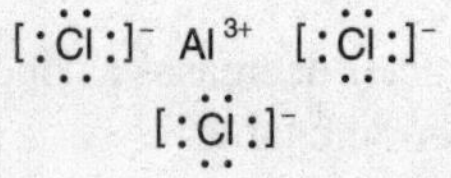

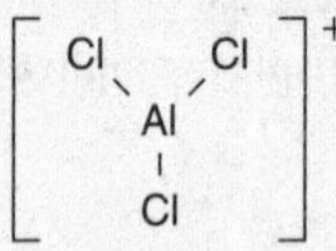

12. Which compound is most likely to be ionic?

A. CH_3OH
B. $ScBr_3$
C. NO_2
D. ClO_2
E. S_8

13. Which bond would be the least polar?

A. H—F
B. B—F
C. Cl—F
D. Ca—F
E. Na—Cl

14. Which species would be a free radical (has an unpaired, single electron)?

A. N_2O
B. NO_2^-
C. NO_2^+
D. OH
E. CO

15.

Bond Energies	
N—N	$193 \ kJ \cdot mol^{-1}$
N=N	$418 \ kJ \cdot mol^{-1}$
N≡N	$941 \ kJ \cdot mol^{-1}$
H—H	$436 \ kJ \cdot mol^{-1}$
H—N	$389 \ kJ \cdot mol^{-1}$

Use the bond energies in the table above to determine ΔH for the formation of hydrazine, N_2H_4, from nitrogen and hydrogen according to this equation:

$$N_{2(g)} + 2H_{2(g)} \rightarrow N_2H_{4(g)}$$

A. $\Delta H = -711 \ kJ$
B. $\Delta H = -64 \ kJ$
C. $\Delta H = +64 \ kJ$
D. $\Delta H = +711 \ kJ$
E. $\Delta H = +980 \ kJ$

16. For which of the following molecules are resonance structures necessary to describe the bonding satisfactorily?

A. H_2O
B. SO_2
C. CO_2
D. NH_3
E. PF_3

17. The geometry of the SO_3^{2-} ion is best described as

A. trigonal planar
B. trigonal pyramidal
C. square planar
D. bent
E. T-shape

18. Pi bonding occurs in each of the following species EXCEPT

A. CO_2
B. C_2H_2
C. CN^-
D. C_6H_6
E. C_2H_6

19. 20.9 grams of bismuth reacts with an excess of fluorine. How much product is formed?

A. 20.9 g
B. 26.6 g
C. 36.8 g
D. 41.8 g
E. 62.7 g

20. $C_2H_3F_{(l)} + O_{2(g)} \rightarrow CO_{2(g)} + H_2O_{(g)} + HF_{(g)}$

When the equation above is balanced, the sum of all coefficients is

A. 9
B. 11
C. 12
D. 15
E. 19

21. Acetylene (C_2H_2) burns in oxygen to produce carbon dioxide and water. Starting with 260. grams of acetylene and 320. grams of oxygen, how many grams of carbon dioxide can be produced?

A. 110. g
B. 352 g
C. 461 g
D. 523 g
E. 880. g

For Questions 22–23: Methanol can be produced by the combustion of carbon monoxide gas with hydrogen gas.

22. If 84 kg of carbon monoxide gas reacts with 16 kg of hydrogen gas, how much methanol could theoretically be produced?

A. 1.0×10^3 mol
B. 2.0×10^3 mol
C. 3.0×10^3 mol
D. 4.0×10^3 mol
E. 5.0×10^3 mol

23. If only 4.8×10^4 g of methanol was produced, what was the actual yield?

A. 5.0%
B. 10.%
C. 25.0%
D. 50.%
E. 75.%

24. 5.00 L of a gas is known to contain 0.300 mol. If the amount of gas is increased to 1.80 mol, what new volume will result (temperature and pressure are held constant)?

A. 0.108 L
B. 0.833 L
C. 8.98 L
D. 22.4 L
E. 30.0 L

25. 5.00 L of a gas is collected at 100. K and then allowed to expand to 20.0 L. What must the new temperature be in order to maintain the same pressure?

A. 50.0 K
B. 100. K
C. 200. K
D. 300. K
E. 400. K

GO ON TO THE NEXT PAGE

26. A mixture of 3.01×10^{23} molecules of N_2 and 6.02×10^{23} molecules of N_2O has a total pressure of 2.00 atm. What is the partial pressure of N_2?

A. 0.333 atm
B. 0.500 atm
C. 0.667 atm
D. 1.00 atm
E. 1.50 atm

27. A sample of nitrogen gas is sealed in a closed container with constant volume. The container is heated until the absolute temperature is tripled. Which of the following is also tripled?

A. Volume of the gas molecules
B. Density of the gas
C. The molecular mass of the gas
D. The velocity of the gas molecules
E. none of the above

28. How many nitrogen molecules are contained in a 8.21-L flask at 227°C and a pressure of 380. torr (mm of Hg)? Assume ideal behavior.

A. 3.04×10^{21}
B. 6.02×10^{22}
C. 6.02×10^{23}
D. 6.02×10^{24}
E. 1.20×10^{25}

29. A student places 20.18 grams of neon gas into a flexible gas container. Into another flexible gas container he places 64.07 grams of sulfur dioxide gas. Both containers are maintained at the same temperature and pressure. Which of the following statements regarding these two gas samples is FALSE?

A. The volume of the container containing the neon gas is the same as the volume of the container containing the sulfur dioxide gas.
B. The number of atoms of neon gas is the same as the number of molecules of sulfur dioxide gas.
C. The density of the neon gas is less than that of the sulfur dioxide sample.
D. The average kinetic energy of the neon atoms is the same as the average kinetic energy of the sulfur dioxide molecules.
E. The average speed of the neon atoms is the same as the average speed of the sulfur dioxide molecules.

30.

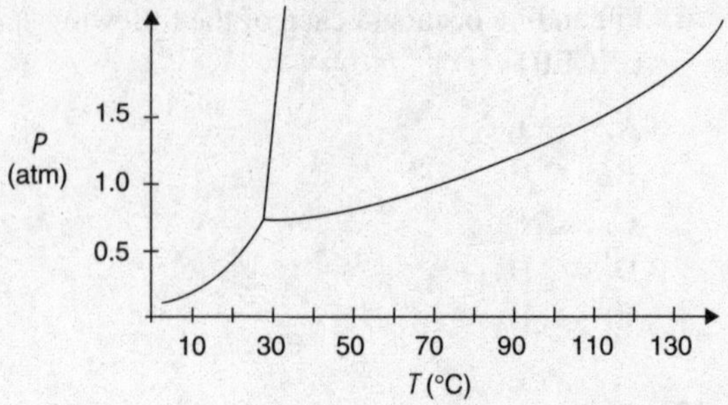

For the substance represented in the phase diagram above, which of the phases is most dense and which is the least dense at 20°C?

	Most Dense	Least Dense
(A)	Solid	Liquid
(B)	Solid	Gas
(C)	Liquid	Gas
(D)	Gas	Liquid
(E)	The diagram gives no information about densities.	

31. Given:

$$CH_{4(g)} + 2O_{2(g)} \rightarrow CO_{2(g)} + 2H_2O_{(l)}$$
$$\Delta H° = -889.1 \text{ kJ}$$
$$\Delta H_f° \; H_2O_{(l)} = -285.8 \text{ kJ/mole}$$
$$\Delta H_f° \; CH_{4(g)} = -75.8 \text{ kJ/mole}$$

What is the approximate standard heat of formation of carbon dioxide, $\Delta H_f° \; CO_{2(g)}$, as calculated from the data above?

A. −390 kJ/mole
B. 0 kJ/mole
C. 200 kJ/mole
D. 390 kJ/mole
E. 700 kJ/mole

32. When a 3.2 g sample of the rocket fuel hydrazine, N_2H_4, is burned in a bomb calorimeter which contains 1000. g of water, the temperature rises from 26.2°C to 28.2°C. If the $C_{calorimeter}$ for the bomb is 865 J/°C, what is $q_{reaction}$ for the combustion of one mole of hydrazine? The specific heat of water is 4.18 J / (g · °C).

A. −3.2 kJ/mol
B. −7.23 kJ/mol
C. -1.01×10^2 kJ/mol
D. -6.23×10^2 kJ/mol
E. -3.33×10^3 kJ/mol

33. Given the pairs of substances below, choose the substance within each pair having the larger standard entropy at 25°C.

(i) Ethyl alcohol or dimethyl ether.
(ii) Neon or xenon.

A. ethyl alcohol and neon
B. ethyl alcohol and xenon
C. dimethyl ether and neon
D. dimethyl ether and xenon
E. all choices have the same standard entropy at 25°C

34. Given the following information in the table below for the synthesis of ammonia from nitrogen and hydrogen gases, which of the following choices is true for the reaction below?

$$N_{2(g)} + 3H_{2(g)} \rightleftharpoons 2NH_{3(g)}$$

	$\Delta H_f°$ (kJ · mol^{-1})	$S°$ (J · mol^{-1} · K^{-1})
$N_{2(g)}$	0	191.5
$H_{2(g)}$	0	131.0
$NH_{3(g)}$	−46	193.0

A. $\Delta H° = -200.$ J/K; $\Delta S° = -92$ kJ
B. $\Delta H° = 92$ kJ; $\Delta S° = -200.$ J/K
C. $\Delta H° = -92$ kJ; $\Delta S° = 200.$ J/K
D. $\Delta H° = -92$ kJ; $\Delta S° = -200.$ J/K
E. $\Delta H° = 92$ kJ; $\Delta S° = 200.$ J/K

35. Referring to the table in problem #34 and assuming that the values of $\Delta H°$ and $\Delta S°$ for the ammonia synthesis reaction are still valid at 527°C, which of the following choices is correct?

A. $\Delta G = 68$ kJ; reaction is unfavorable at high temperatures.
B. $\Delta G = 68$ kJ; reaction is favorable at high temperatures.
C. $\Delta G = -68$ kJ; reaction is unfavorable at high temperatures.
D. $\Delta G = -68$ kJ; reaction is favorable at high temperatures.
E. None of the above.

36. A student is required to prepare a 25.0 *m* solution of methanol (CH_3OH; $MW = 32.05$ g · mol^{-1}). She started with 160.25 grams of methanol ($d = 0.7918$ g · mL^{-1}). How much distilled water should she use?

A. 100. mL
B. 200. mL
C. 300. mL
D. 400. mL
E. More information is required in order to do this problem.

37. How many milliliters of 6.00-*M* HCl must be diluted to obtain 4.00 liters of 3.00-*M* HCl?

A. 1.00×10^3 mL
B. 1.50×10^3 mL
C. 1.75×10^3 mL
D. 2.00×10^3 mL
E. 2.75×10^3 mL

38. What is the mole fraction of ethanol, C_2H_5OH, in an aqueous solution that has a density of 0.789 g · mL^{-1} and in which the ethanol concentration is 4.50 *m*?

A. 0.0046
B. 0.090
C. 0.15
D. 0.35
E. 0.72

GO ON TO THE NEXT PAGE

39. What is the molecular weight of substance Y if a solution that contains 30.0 grams of Y per kilogram of water freezes at – 0.93°C? Y is a non-ionizing solute.

k_f H_2O = 1.86°C/*m*

A. 30. g/mol
B. 60. g/mol
C. 90. g/mol
D. 120 g/mol
E. 150 g/mol

40. A physician studying hemoglobin dissolves 33.3 mg of the protein in water at 27°C to make 1.00 mL of solution in order to measure its osmotic pressure.

At equilibrium, the solution has an osmotic pressure of 0.00821 atm. What is the molar mass (*MM*) of the hemoglobin?

A. 1.00×10^1 g/mol
B. 1.00×10^2 g/mol
C. 1.00×10^3 g/mol
D. 1.00×10^4 g/mol
E. 1.00×10^5 g/mol

41. A solution is made by adding 0.100 mol of KI and 0.0100 mol of KCl to a final volume of 0.100 L. A silver nitrate solution of unknown concentration is slowly added. Which precipitate will form first? K_{sp} AgI = 8.5×10^{-17}; K_{sp} AgCl = 1.8×10^{-10}.

A. AgCl
B. AgI
C. ICl
D. Both will precipitate at the same time
E. Neither, both are soluble.

42. At 500.°C, the equilibrium constant K_c for the reaction $N_{2(g)} + 3H_{2(g)} \rightleftharpoons 2NH_{3(g)}$ is 6.00×10^{-2}. 5.00 moles of $N_{2(g)}$, 4.00 moles of $H_{2(g)}$, and 8.00 moles of $NH_{3(g)}$ were introduced into a 5.00-L flask. Which of the following is true?

A. The reaction will proceed from left to right, increasing the concentration of NH_3 and decreasing the concentrations of N_2 and H_2 until $Q_c = K_c$.
B. The reaction will proceed from right to left, increasing the concentration of NH_3 and decreasing the concentrations of N_2 and H_2 until $Q_c = K_c$.
C. The reaction will proceed from left to right, decreasing the concentration of NH_3 and increasing the concentrations of N_2 and H_2 until $Q_c = K_c$.
D. The reaction will proceed from right to left, decreasing the concentration of NH_3 and increasing the concentrations of N_2 and H_2 until $Q_c = K_c$.
E. The reaction is at equilibrium. No changes will occur.

43. Given the following bases, which one is NOT an example of an Arrhenius base?

I. NH_3
II. CN^-
III. NO_2^-
IV. KOH

A. I, II, and III
B. IV
C. II and III
D. All are examples of Arrhenius bases.
E. None of them are examples of Arrhenius bases.

44. The conjugate acid and conjugate base of HSO_4^- are, respectively,

A. H_3O^+ and OH^-
B. H_3O^+ and SO_4^{2-}
C. H_2SO_4 and OH^-
D. H_2SO_4 and SO_4^{2-}
E. SO_4^{2-} and H_2SO_4

45. Choose the stronger acid from each of the following pairs:

(I)	$BF_{3(aq)}$	$BBr_{3(aq)}$
(II)	$Fe^{2+}{}_{(aq)}$	$Fe^{3+}{}_{(aq)}$
(III)	$H_3PO_{4(aq)}$	$H_3AsO_{4(aq)}$
(IV)	$HNO_{2(aq)}$	$HNO_{3(aq)}$
(V)	$CH_3COOH_{(aq)}$	$CHCl_2COOH_{(aq)}$
(VI)	$HS^-{}_{(aq)}$	$Br^-{}_{(aq)}$
(VII)	$CH_{4(aq)}$	$NH_4^+{}_{(aq)}$
(VIII)	$ClO_2^-{}_{(aq)}$	$ClO_3^-{}_{(aq)}$

A. $BF_{3(aq)}$, $Fe^{2+}{}_{(aq)}$, $H_3PO_{4(aq)}$, $HNO_{2(aq)}$, $CH_3COOH_{(aq)}$, $HS^-{}_{(aq)}$, $CH_{4(aq)}$, and $ClO_2^-{}_{(aq)}$

B. $BBr_{3(aq)}$, $Fe^{3+}{}_{(aq)}$, $H_3AsO_{4(aq)}$, $HNO_{3(aq)}$, $CHCl_2COOH_{(aq)}$, $Br^-{}_{(aq)}$, $NH_4^+{}_{(aq)}$, and $ClO_3^-{}_{(aq)}$

C. $BF_{3(aq)}$, $Fe^{3+}{}_{(aq)}$, $H_3PO_{4(aq)}$, $HNO_{3(aq)}$, $CHCl_2COOH_{(aq)}$, $Br^-{}_{(aq)}$, $NH_4^+{}_{(aq)}$, and $ClO_3^-{}_{(aq)}$

D. $BF_{3(aq)}$, $Fe^{3+}{}_{(aq)}$, $H_3PO_{4(aq)}$, $HNO_{3(aq)}$, $CH_3COOH_{(aq)}$, $Br^-{}_{(aq)}$, $CH_{4(aq)}$, and $ClO_3^-{}_{(aq)}$

E. $BBr_{3(aq)}$, $Fe^{2+}{}_{(aq)}$, $H_3AsO_{4(aq)}$, $HNO_{3(aq)}$, $CHCl_2COOH_{(aq)}$, $Br^-{}_{(aq)}$, $CH_{4(aq)}$, and $ClO_3^-{}_{(aq)}$

46. What is the pH of a solution made by titrating 35.0 mL of 0.150 *M* HCl with 15.0 mL of 0.200 *M* NH_3? You may use the following true log relationships.

number	*– log₁₀*
0.030	1.52
0.035	1.46
0.040	1.40
0.045	1.35
0.050	1.30

A. 0.30
B. 1.35
C. 7.00
D. 9.35
E. 12.65

47. A buffer is formed by adding 500. mL of 0.20 *M* $HC_2H_3O_2$ to 500. mL of 0.10 *M* $NaC_2H_3O_2$. What would be the maximum amount of HCl that could be added to this solution without exceeding the capacity of the buffer?

A. 0.010 mol
B. 0.050 mol
C. 0.10 mol
D. 0.15 mol
E. 0.20 mol

48. N_2O_3 gas is bubbled through water and produces

A. NO
B. NO_2
C. HNO_2
D. HNO_3
E. HNO_4

49. Acetaldehyde, CH_3CHO, decomposes by second-order kinetics with a rate constant of 0.334 $M^{-1} \cdot s^{-1}$ at 500.°C. How much time would it take for 70.% of the acetaldehyde to decompose in a sample that has an initial concentration of 0.0100 *M*?

A. 423 seconds
B. 500 seconds
C. 699 seconds
D. 750 seconds
E. 873 seconds

50. Sometimes a small increase in temperature often produces a large increase in the rate of a chemical reaction. The best explanation for this is

A. higher temperatures decrease the activation energy of the reaction.
B. higher temperatures increase the effectiveness of the collisions between the reactant molecules.
C. higher temperatures decrease the number of collisions per second between the reactant molecules.
D. higher temperatures increase the concentration of the reactants, altering the volume of the reactants.
E. higher temperatures have no effect on the rate of a chemical reaction.

GO ON TO THE NEXT PAGE

51. Which of the following choices below shows nitrogen increasing in oxidation number?

A. $NO < N_2O < NO_2 < NO_3^- = N_2O_5 < NH_4^+$
B. $NH_4^+ < N_2O < NO < NO_2 < NO_3^- = N_2O_5$
C. $N_2O_5 = NH_4^+ < N_2O = NO < NO_2 < NO_3^-$
D. $N_2O_5 = NO_3^- < NO_2 < NO < N_2O < NH_4^+$
E. $N_2O < N_2O_5 < NO_2 < NH_4^+ < N_2O_5 < NO$

52. Arrange the following oxidizing agents in order of increasing strength under standard-state conditions: $Br_{2(l)}$, $Cr_2O_7^{2-}{}_{(aq)}$, and $Fe^{3+}{}_{(aq)}$.

A. $Cr_2O_7^{2-}{}_{(aq)} < Br_{2(l)} < Fe^{3+}{}_{(aq)}$
B. $Fe^{3+}{}_{(aq)} < Br_{2(l)} < Cr_2O_7^{2-}{}_{(aq)}$
C. $Br_{2(l)} < Cr_2O_7^{2-}{}_{(aq)} < Fe^{3+}{}_{(aq)}$
D. $Fe^{3+}{}_{(aq)} < Cr_2O_7^{2-}{}_{(aq)} < Br_{2(l)}$
E. $Cr_2O_7^{2-}{}_{(aq)} < Fe^{3+}{}_{(aq)} < Br_{2(l)}$

53. $Sn^{2+}{}_{(aq)} + IO_4^-{}_{(aq)} \rightarrow Sn^{4+}{}_{(aq)} + I^-{}_{(aq)}$

The balanced net ionic equation for the equation above in acidic solution is:

A. $2Sn^{2+}{}_{(aq)} + 16H^+{}_{(aq)} + 2IO_4^-{}_{(aq)} \rightarrow 2Sn^{4+}{}_{(aq)} + 2I^-{}_{(aq)} + 8H_2O_{(l)}$
B. $Sn^{2+}{}_{(aq)} + 8H^+{}_{(aq)} + IO_4^-{}_{(aq)} \rightarrow Sn^{4+}{}_{(aq)} + I^-{}_{(aq)} + 4H_2O_{(l)}$
C. $3Sn^{2+}{}_{(aq)} + 8H^+{}_{(aq)} + IO_4^-{}_{(aq)} \rightarrow 3Sn^{4+}{}_{(aq)} + I^-{}_{(aq)} + 4H_2O_{(l)}$
D. $4Sn^{2+}{}_{(aq)} + 8H^+{}_{(aq)} + IO_4^-{}_{(aq)} \rightarrow 4Sn^{4+}{}_{(aq)} + I^-{}_{(aq)} + 4H_2O_{(l)}$
E. $8Sn^{2+}{}_{(aq)} + 8H^+{}_{(aq)} + IO_4^-{}_{(aq)} \rightarrow 8Sn^{4+}{}_{(aq)} + I^-{}_{(aq)} + 4H_2O_{(l)}$

For Questions 54–56 use the information in the table below:

$I_{2(s)} + 2e^- \rightarrow 2I^-{}_{(aq)}$	$E°_{red} = 0.53$ V
$Br_{2(l)} + 2e^- \rightarrow 2Br^-{}_{(aq)}$	$E°_{red} = 1.07$ V
$Cl_{2(g)} + 2e^- \rightarrow 2Cl^-{}_{(aq)}$	$E°_{red} = 1.36$ V

54. Molecular bromine (Br_2) is added to a solution containing NaCl and NaI at 25°C? Assuming all species are in their standard state, what is $E°$?

A. –1.604 V
B. –0.54 V
C. 0.00 V
D. 0.54 V
E. 1.60 V

55. What is the value for $\Delta G°$?

A. -1.0×10^{-5}
B. -1.0×10^{-1}
C. -1.0×10^{2}
D. 1.0×10^{2}
E. 1.0×10^{5}

56. What would be the correct set-up to determine the value for K_c?

A. $10^{(2)\ (0.54)\ /\ (0.0591)}$
B. $10^{(2)\ (0.54)\ (0.0591)}$
C. $10^{(2)\ /\ (0.54)\ (0.0591)}$
D. $10^{(2)\ (0.54)\ +\ (0.0591)}$
E. $10^{(0.54)\ *\ (0.0591)\ /\ 2}$

57. When written and balanced correctly, the beta decay of I-131 is represented as

A. ${}^{131}_{53}I \rightarrow {}^{131}_{54}Xe + {}^{0}_{-1}e$
B. ${}^{131}_{53}I \rightarrow {}^{131}_{52}Te + {}^{0}_{1}e$
C. ${}^{131}_{53}I \rightarrow {}^{131}_{55}Cs + {}^{0}_{-2}e$
D. ${}^{131}_{54}I \rightarrow {}^{131}_{53}I + {}^{0}_{1}e$
E. ${}^{131}_{52}I + {}^{0}_{-1}e \rightarrow {}^{131}_{51}Xe$

58. When written and balanced correctly, electron capture from Hg-197 is represented as

A. ${}^{197}_{80}Hg + {}^{0}_{1}e \rightarrow {}^{197}_{81}Au$
B. ${}^{197}_{80}Hg + {}^{1}_{-1}e \rightarrow {}^{198}_{79}Au$
C. ${}^{197}_{80}Hg + {}^{1}_{0}e \rightarrow {}^{198}_{80}Au$
D. ${}^{197}_{80}Hg + {}^{0}_{-1}e \rightarrow {}^{197}_{79}Au$
E. ${}^{197}_{80}Hg + {}^{0}_{0}e \rightarrow {}^{197}_{80}Au$

For Questions 59–63, use the following answer choices:

A. beta decay
B. positron emission
C. electron capture
D. alpha emission
E. gamma-ray emission

59. ${}^{8}_{5}B \rightarrow {}^{8}_{4}B + {}^{0}_{+1}e$

60. ${}^{125}_{53}I + {}^{0}_{-1}e \rightarrow {}^{125}_{52}Te + hv$

61. ${}^{210}_{86}Rn \rightarrow {}^{206}_{84}Po + {}^{4}_{2}He$

62. ${}^{14}_{6}C \rightarrow {}^{14}_{7}N + {}^{0}_{-1}e$

63. ${}^{56}_{28}Ni \rightarrow {}^{56}_{28}Ni + \gamma$

64. Thallium-206 decays to lead-206 with a half-life of 4.20 minutes. If you started with 5.12 moles of thallium, approximately how many atoms of Tl-206 would be left after 37.8 minutes?

A. 6.02×10^{19}
B. $6.02. \times 10^{20}$
C. $6.02. \times 10^{21}$
D. $6.02. \times 10^{22}$
E. $6.02. \times 10^{23}$

65. The correct name for the following molecule

$$H_3C - CH_2 - C \equiv C - HC - CH_2 - CH_3$$
$$|$$
$$CH_2 - CH_3$$

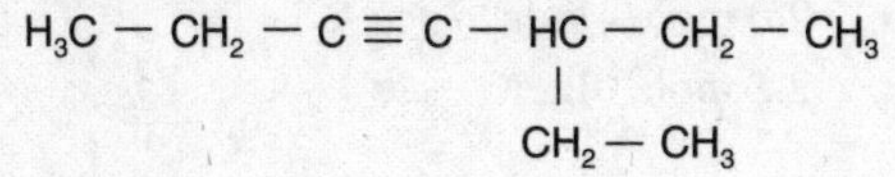

is

A. 3-ethyl-4-heptyne
B. 5-ethyl-3-heptyne
C. 5-ethyl-4-heptyne
D. 2-heptyl-ethane
E. 3-ethyl-3-heptyne

66. The correct name for the following alcohol

$$\begin{array}{c} HO \\ | \\ H_3C - CH_2 - C - CH_2 - CH_3 \\ | \\ CH_3 \end{array}$$

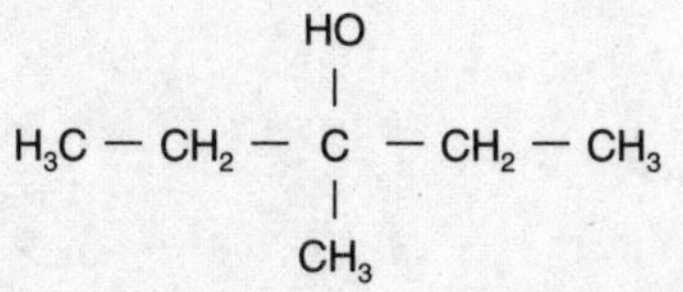

is

A. 3-methyl-3-pentanol
B. 3-pentyl-3-ol
C. 3-methyl-hexanol
D. 2-ethyl-2-butanol
E. iso-hexanol

67. The name of the following compound

$$\begin{array}{c} H \quad H \quad O \\ | \quad | \quad \| \\ H - C - C - C - N\begin{array}{c}H\\H\end{array} \\ | \quad | \\ H \quad H \end{array}$$

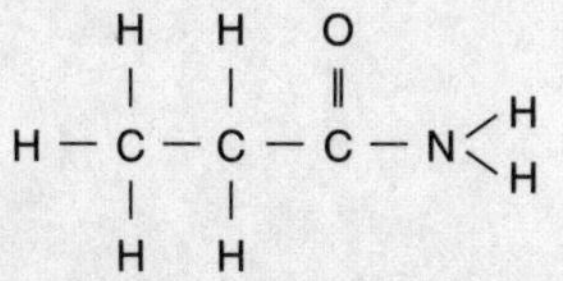

is

A. ethyl-methylamide
B. propyl amide
C. propamine
D. propanimide
E. propanamide

68. The name of the following compound

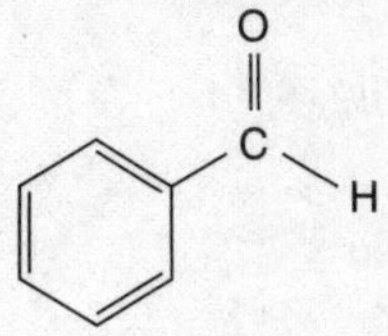

is

A. phenylaldehye
B. benzaldehyde
C. hexanal
D. toluene
E. benzone

69. The name of the following compound

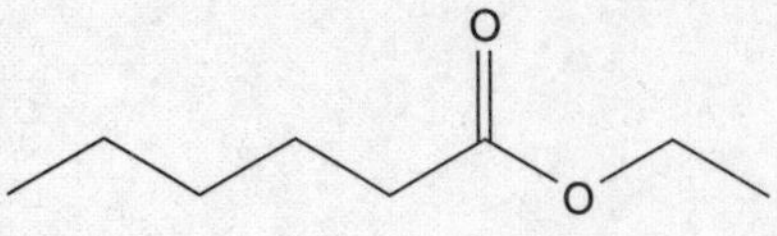

is

A. 3-hexanone
B. propyl-ethyl ester
C. ethyl butanoate
D. propyl ethanoate
E. diethyl ester

70. Which of the following compounds would form enantiomers because the molecule is chiral?

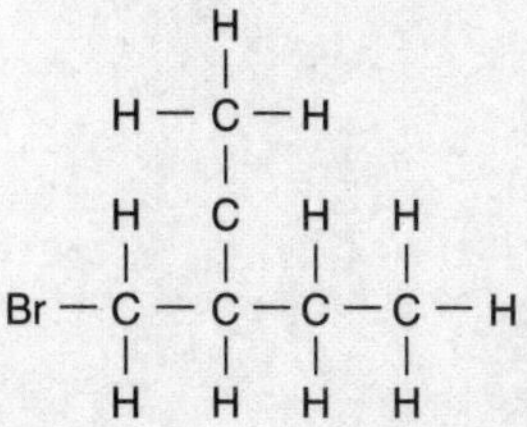

1-bromo-2-methylbutane

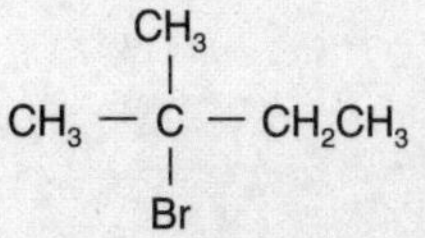

2-bromo-2-methylbutane

A. 1-bromo-2-methylbutane
B. 2-bromo-2-methylbutane
C. both
D. neither
E. cannot be answered since not enough information is provided

GO ON TO THE NEXT PAGE

For Questions 71–74:

A. alcohol
B. carboxylic acid
C. ester
D. ether
E. ketone

71. The product of the reaction of an alcohol and a carboxylic acid.

72. The product of the reaction of an alkene and water.

73. The product formed by the oxidation of a secondary alcohol.

74. The product formed by the condensation reaction of alcohols.

75. Acetaldehyde, CH_3CHO, decomposes into methane gas and carbon monoxide gas. This is a second-order reaction (rate is proportional to the concentration of the reactant). The rate of decomposition at 140°C is 0.10 mole · liter^{-1} · sec^{-1} when the concentration of acetaldehyde is 0.010 mole · liter^{-1}. What is the rate of the reaction when the concentration of acetaldehyde is 0.050 mole/liter?

A. 0.50 mole · liter^{-1} · sec^{-1}
B. 1.0 mole · liter^{-1} · sec^{-1}
C. 1.5 mole · liter^{-1} · sec^{-1}
D. 2.0 mole · liter^{-1} · sec^{-1}
E. 2.5 mole · liter^{-1} · sec^{-1}

STOP

Section II: Free-Response Questions*

CHEMISTRY

Section II

(Total time—95 minutes)

Part A

Time—55 minutes

YOU MAY USE YOUR CALCULATOR FOR PART A.

CLEARLY SHOW THE METHOD USED AND THE STEPS INVOLVED IN ARRIVING AT YOUR ANSWERS. It is to your advantage to do this, since you may obtain partial credit if you do and you will receive little or no credit if you do not. Attention should be paid to significant figures.

Answer Questions 1, 2, and 3. The Section II score weighting for each question is 20%.

1. HCN is a weak acid ($K_a = 4.9 \times 10^{-10}$) used in the steel industry, manufacturing of acrylic resin plastics, gold extraction, dyeing, explosives, and engraving. Given a 0.10 *M* solution of HCN, calculate

(a) $[H_3O^+]$

(b) $[CN^-]$

(c) [HCN]

(d) $[OH^-]$

(e) pH

(f) pOH

(g) K_b

(h) percent dissociation

2. 5.0 mg / mL of a certain drug solution decays by first-order kinetics with a rate constant of 0.0005 / day.

(a) What is the concentration of drug remaining after 120 days?

(b) What is $t_{1/2}$ for the drug solution?

(c) How long will it take to reach 90.% of the original concentration?

** You may use the charts on pages 387–390 with this section.*

3. Answer the following questions regarding the electrochemical cell at standard conditions diagrammed below.

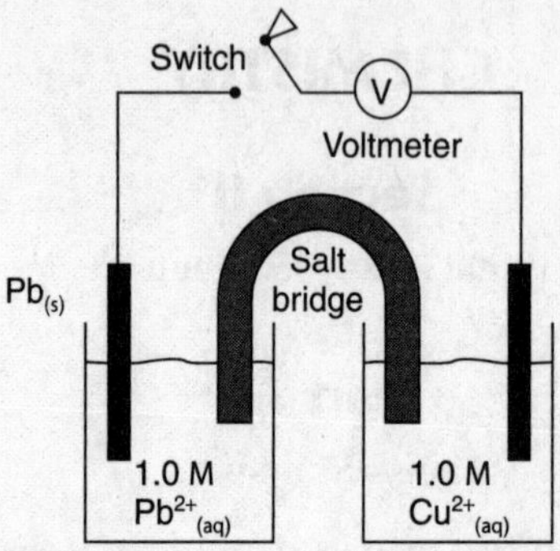

(a) Write the oxidation half-reaction.

(b) Write the reduction half-reaction.

(c) Write the balanced net-ionic equation and determine the cell voltage.

(d) Identify the anode and the cathode.

(e) If 25.0 mL of 3 *M* $Cu(NO_3)_2$ is added to the half-cell on the right, explain what will happens to the cell voltage.

(f) If 3.00 grams of solid KCl is added to each half-cell, explain what will happen to the cell voltage.

(g) If 25.0 mL of distilled water is added to both half-cells, explain what will happen.

If you finish before time is called, you may check your work on this part only. Do not turn to the other part of the test until you are told to do so.

STOP

CHEMISTRY

Part B

Time—40 minutes

NO CALCULATORS MAY BE USED FOR PART B.

Answer Question 4 below. The Section II score weighting for this question is 10%.

4. For each of the following three reactions, in part (i) write a balanced reaction and in part (ii) answer the question about the reaction. In part (i), coefficients should be in terms of lowest whole numbers. Assume that solutions are aqueous unless otherwise indicated. Represent substances in solutions as ions if the substances are extensively ionized. Omit formulas for any ions or molecules that are unchanged by the reaction. You may use the empty space at the bottom of the next page for scratch work, but only equations that are written in the answer boxes will be graded.

Example:

(i) A strip of magnesium metal is added to a solution of silver(I) nitrate.

$$Mg + 2Ag^+ \rightarrow Mg^{2+} + 2Ag$$

(ii) Which substance is oxidized in the reaction?

Mg is oxidized.

(a) Solid calcium oxide is added to distilled water.

(i) Write the balanced equation for the reaction described.

(ii) Is the resulting solution acidic, basic, or neutral? Explain.

(b) Solid sodium chlorate is strongly heated and decomposes, resulting in a change in the oxidation numbers of both chlorine and oxygen.

(i) Write the balanced equation for the reaction described.

(ii) What is the oxidation number of chlorine before and after the reaction?

(c) A solution of ethanoic (acetic) acid is added to a solution of sodium hydroxide.

(i) Write the balanced equation for the reaction described.

(ii) Explain why a mixture of equal volumes of equimolar solutions of ethanoic acid and sodium hydroxide is basic.

Practice Exam 2

Answer Questions 5 and 6. The Section II score weighting for these questions is 15% each.

Your responses to these questions will be graded on the basis of the accuracy and relevance of the information cited. Explanations should be clear and well organized. Examples and equations may be included in your responses where appropriate. Specific answers are preferable to broad, diffuse responses.

5. Explain each of the following in terms of (1) inter- and intra- atomic or molecular forces and (2) structure.

(a) ICl has a boiling point of 97°C, whereas NaCl has a boiling point of 1400°C.

(b) $KI_{(s)}$ is very soluble in water, whereas $I_{2(s)}$ has a solubility of only 0.03 grams per 100 grams of water.

(c) Solid Ag conducts an electric current, whereas solid $AgNO_3$ does not.

(d) PCl_3 has a measurable dipole moment, whereas PCl_5 does not.

(e) The carbon-to-carbon bond energy in C_2H_5Cl is less than it is in C_2H_3Cl.

6. If one completely vaporizes a measured amount of a volatile liquid, the molecular weight of the liquid can be determined by measuring the volume, temperature, and pressure of the resulting gas. When using this procedure, one must use the ideal gas equation and assume that the gas behaves ideally. However, if the temperature of the gas is only slightly above the boiling point of the liquid, the gas deviates from ideal behavior.

(a) Explain the postulates of the ideal gas equation.

(b) Explain why, if measured just above the boiling point, the molecular weight deviates from the true value.

(c) Would the molecular weight of a real gas be higher or lower than that predicted by the van der Waals equation and explain why?

STOP

Answer Key for Practice Exam 2

Section I: Multiple-Choice Questions

1. A
2. D
3. C
4. E
5. B
6. C
7. C
8. B
9. A
10. A
11. D
12. B
13. C
14. D
15. C
16. B
17. B
18. E
19. B
20. D
21. B
22. C
23. D
24. E
25. E
26. C
27. E
28. B
29. E
30. B
31. A
32. C
33. D
34. D
35. A
36. B
37. D
38. B
39. B
40. E
41. B
42. D
43. A
44. D
45. C
46. D
47. B
48. C
49. C
50. B
51. B
52. B
53. D
54. D
55. C
56. A
57. A
58. D
59. B
60. C
61. D
62. A
63. E
64. C
65. B
66. A
67. E
68. B
69. C
70. A
71. C
72. A
73. E
74. D
75. E

Answers and Explanations for Practice Exam 2

Multiple Choice

1. **A.** If you missed this question, refer to the chart “Important People, Experiments, and Theories” in Chapter 1.
2. **D.** If you missed this question, refer to the chart “Important People, Experiments, and Theories” in Chapter 1.
3. **C.** If you missed this question, refer to the chart “Important People, Experiments, and Theories” in Chapter 1.
4. **E.** If you missed this question, refer to the chart “Important People, Experiments, and Theories” in Chapter 1.
5. **B.** If you missed this question, refer to the chart “Important People, Experiments, and Theories” in Chapter 1.
6. **C.** If you missed this question, refer to “The Aufbau Process” in Chapter 1.
7. **C.** NaO_2 is sodium superoxide. Sodium peroxide is Na_2O_2.
8. **B.** If you missed this question, refer to the chart “Chemical Properties and Periodicity” in Chapter 2.
9. **A.** If you missed this question, refer to the chart “Chemical Properties and Periodicity” in Chapter 2.
10. **A.** If you missed this question, refer to the chart “Chemical Properties and Periodicity” in Chapter 2.
11. **D.** $AlCl_3$ is ionic (metal-nonmetal). By convention and to be technically correct, the metal ion is placed in the center with its charge (in this case +3). Since the aluminum atom loses three electrons to become the Al^{3+} ion, and each chlorine atom gains one electron to become a chloride ion (Cl^-), we draw the three chlorine ions around the aluminum ion. This is an example of an incomplete octet.
12. **B.** Ionic compounds are composed of a metallic cation and a non-metallic anion.
13. **C.** The further apart atoms are located in the periodic table, the more polar their bonds will be.
14. **D.** The hydroxyl radical is the neutral form of the hydroxide ion (OH^-).

    $\dot{\text{O}}\text{H}$

15. **C.**

    $N_{2(g)} + 2H_{2(g)} \rightarrow N_2H_{4(g)}$

    $N{\equiv}N + 2(H{-}H) \rightarrow N{-}N + 4(N{-}H)$

    1 $N{\equiv}N$ needs to be broken: 1(941 kJ) = 941 kJ

    2 H—H bonds need to be broken: 2(436 kJ) = 872 kJ

    1 N—N bond need to be formed: 1(193 kJ) = 193 kJ

    4 N—H bonds need to be formed: 4(389 kJ) = 1556 kJ

    $\Delta H = \Sigma$B.E. bonds broken $-$ ΣB.E. bonds formed = (941 kJ + 872 kJ) $-$ (193 kJ + 1556 kJ) = 64 kJ

16. **B.**

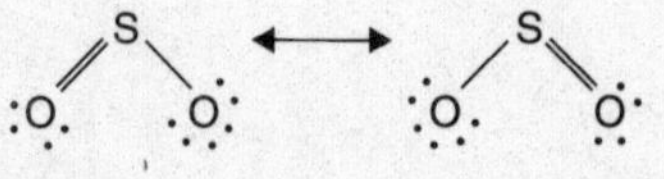

17. B. SO_3^{2-} conforms to AB_3E with 4 electron pairs around S.

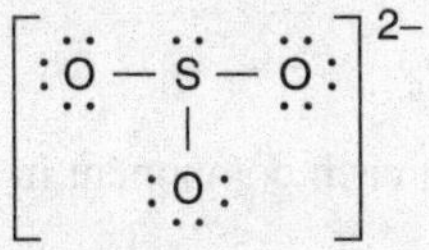

18. E. Double or triple bonds are required for pi bonding. Ethane, C_2H_6 is the only molecule listed that does not contain double or triple bonds.

19. B. The product is BiF_3: $2Bi_{(s)} + 3F_{2(g)} \rightarrow 2BiF_{3(s)}$

$$\frac{\overset{1}{\cancel{20.9\text{ g Bi}}}}{1} \times \frac{1\ \cancel{\text{mole Bi}}}{{}_{10}\cancel{209\text{ g Bi}}} \times \frac{\cancel{2\text{ mol BiF}_3}}{\cancel{2\text{ mol Bi}}} \times \frac{266\text{ g BiF}_3}{1\ \cancel{\text{mol BiF}_3}} = 26.6\text{ g BiF}_3$$

20. D. $2C_2H_3F_{(l)} + 5O_{2(g)} \rightarrow 4CO_{2(g)} + 2H_2O_{(g)} + 2HF_{(g)}$

21. B. Begin by writing a balanced equation: $2C_2H_{2(g)} + 5O_{2(g)} \rightarrow 4CO_{2(g)} + 2H_2O_{(g)}$

$$\frac{\overset{10}{\cancel{260.\text{ g C}_2\text{H}_2}}}{1} \times \frac{1\text{ mol }\cancel{\text{C}_2\text{H}_2}}{\cancel{26\text{ g C}_2\text{H}_2}} \times \frac{\overset{2}{\cancel{4\text{ mol CO}_2}}}{{}_{1}\cancel{2\text{ mol C}_2\text{H}_2}} \times \frac{44\text{ g CO}_2}{1\ \cancel{\text{mol CO}_2}} = 880\text{ g CO}_2$$

$$\frac{\overset{2\ \cancel{10}}{\cancel{320.\text{ g O}_2}}}{1} \times \frac{1\ \cancel{\text{mol O}_2}}{{}_{1}\cancel{32\text{ g O}_2}} \times \frac{\cancel{4\text{ mol CO}_2}}{{}_{1}\cancel{5\text{ mol O}_2}} \times \frac{44\text{ g CO}_2}{1\ \cancel{\text{mol CO}_2}} = 352\text{ g CO}_2$$

Oxygen is the limiting factor, therefore 352 g of CO_2 is the maximum amount that can be produced.

22. C. Begin by writing a balanced equation: $2H_{2(g)} + CO_{(g)} \rightarrow CH_3OH_{(l)}$

Next, determine the limiting factor:

$$\frac{\overset{3}{\cancel{84\text{ kg CO}}}}{1} \times \frac{10^3\ \cancel{\text{g CO}}}{1\ \cancel{\text{kg CO}}} \times \frac{1\ \cancel{\text{mole CO}}}{{}_{1}\cancel{28\text{ g CO}}} \times \frac{1\text{ mol CH}_3\text{OH}}{1\ \cancel{\text{mol CO}}} = 3.0 \times 10^3\text{ mol CH}_3\text{OH}^*$$

$$\frac{\overset{4}{\cancel{16\text{ kg H}_2}}}{1} \times \frac{10^3\ \cancel{\text{g H}_2}}{1\ \cancel{\text{kg H}_2}} \times \frac{1\ \cancel{\text{mol H}_2}}{{}_{1}\cancel{2\text{ g H}_2}} \times \frac{1\text{ mol CH}_3\text{OH}}{{}_{1}\cancel{2\text{ mol H}_2}} = 4.0 \times 10^3\text{ mol CH}_3\text{OH}$$

* *CO is the limiting factor*

23. D. $CH_3OH = 32\text{ g} \cdot \text{mol}^{-1}$

$$\frac{3.00 \times 10^3\ \cancel{\text{mol CH}_3\text{OH}}}{1} \times \frac{32\text{ g CH}_3\text{OH}}{1\ \cancel{\text{mol CH}_3\text{OH}}} = 9.6 \times 10^4\text{ g CH}_3\text{OH (theoretical yield)}$$

$$\frac{\overset{1}{\cancel{4.8 \times 10^4\text{ g CH}_3\text{OH}}}}{{}_{2}\cancel{9.6 \times 10^4\text{ g CH}_3\text{OH}}} \times 100\% = 50\%\text{ yield}$$

24. E. $V_1n_2 = V_2n_1 \rightarrow (5.00\text{ L})(1.80\text{ mol}) = (V_2)(0.300\text{ mol})$

$V_2 = 30.0\text{ L}$

Practice Exam 2

25. **E.** $T_2 = \frac{V_2 T_1}{V_1} = \frac{{}^{4}\cancel{20.0\,L} \times 100.\,K}{{}_{1}\cancel{5.00\,L}} = 400.\,K$

26. **C.** $P_{total} = P_{N_2} + P_{N_2O}$; therefore, $P_{N_2} = P_{total} - P_{N_2O}$

Begin by calculating the number of moles of each component in the mixture.

$$n_{N_2} = \frac{3.01 \times 10^{23}\ \cancel{\text{molecules}N_2}}{6.02 \times 10^{23}\ \cancel{\text{molecules}}/\text{mole}} = 0.500\ \text{moles}$$

$$n_{N_2O} = \frac{6.02 \times 10^{23}\ \cancel{\text{molecules}N_2O}}{6.02 \times 10^{23}\ \cancel{\text{molecules}}/\text{mole}} = 1.00\ \text{moles}$$

$n_{total} = 0.500\ \text{mol} + 1.00\ \text{mol} = 1.50\ \text{moles}$

Next, calculate the mole fraction N_2:

$$X_{N_2} = \frac{0.500\ \cancel{\text{moles}}}{1.500\ \cancel{\text{moles}}} = 0.333$$

$P_{N_2} = X_{N_2} \times P_{total} = 0.333 \times 2.00\ \text{atm} = 0.667\ \text{atm}$

27. **E.** The question involves Gay-Lussac's Law that states that at constant volume, the pressure exerted by a given mass of gas varies directly with the absolute temperature. The correct answer would have been pressure.

28. **B.** $T = 227°C + 273 = 500.\ K$

$$PV = nRT;\ \text{therefore}, n = \frac{P \cdot V}{R \cdot T} = \frac{(380.\ \cancel{\text{torr}}/760\ \cancel{\text{torr}} \cdot \cancel{\text{atm}^{-1}}) \cdot {}^{100}\cancel{8.21\,L}}{{}_{1}\cancel{0.0821\,L} \cdot \cancel{\text{atm}} \cdot \text{mol}^{-1} \cdot \cancel{K^{-1}} \cdot 500.\ \cancel{K}} = 0.100\ \text{mol}$$

$0.100\ \cancel{\text{mol}} \cdot (6.02 \times 10^{23}\ \text{molecules} \cdot \cancel{\text{mol}^{-1}}) = 6.02 \times 10^{22}\ \text{molecules}$

29. **E.** The molar mass of neon is 20.18 g · mol^{-1} and the molar mass of sulfur dioxide is 64.07 g · mol^{-1}. So both containers contain exactly one mole of gas. Using the equation $PV = nRT$, and since $n = 1$ for both gases, and the pressure and temperature are the same, the volume of both containers will be the same. Since there are the same numbers of moles of gas, i.e., 1, each container will contain 6.02×10^{23} particles of gas. Since one mole of neon gas weighs less than one mole of sulfur dioxide gas, density (mass/volume) will be lower for the neon gas. Average kinetic energy is determined by the temperature of the system. Since both containers are at the same temperature, the kinetic energy of the particles is the same. Since lighter particles travel faster at the same temperature, the neon atoms will be traveling faster than the sulfur dioxide molecules; therefore, (E) is false.

30. **B.** Answer obtained through inspection.

$$\begin{array}{ll}
\cancel{CH_{4(g)}} + 2O_{2(g)} \rightarrow CO_{2(g)} + \cancel{2H_2O_{(l)}} & \Delta H° \approx -890\ \text{kJ/mol} \\
\cancel{2H_2O_{(l)}} \rightarrow \cancel{2H_{2(g)}} + O_{2(g)} & \Delta H° \approx +580\ \text{kJ/mol} = 2 \times 290 \\
C_{(s)} + \cancel{2H_{2(g)}} \rightarrow \cancel{CH_{4(g)}} & \Delta H° \approx -80\ \text{kJ/mol} \\
\hline
C_{(s)} + O_{2(g)} \rightarrow CO_{2(g)} & \Delta H_f° \approx -390\ \text{kJ/mol}
\end{array}$$

31. **A.**

32. **C.** $q_{reaction} = -(q_{water} + q_{bomb})$

$q_{reaction} = -(4.18\ \text{J} / (\text{g} \cdot °\text{C}) \times m_{water} \times \Delta t + C \text{ x } \Delta t)$

$q_{reaction} = -(4.18\ \text{J} / (\text{g} \cdot °\text{C}) \times m_{water} + C)\Delta t$

$q_{reaction} = -(4.18\ \text{J} / (\cancel{\text{g}} \cdot °\cancel{\text{C}}) \times 1000.\ \cancel{\text{g}} + 865\ \text{J}/°\cancel{\text{C}})(28.2°\cancel{\text{C}} - 26.2°\cancel{\text{C}})$

$\approx -(4000\ \text{J} + 900\ \text{J})(2.0) = -9{,}800\ \text{J} \approx -1 \times 10^4\ \text{J}$

$$q_{reaction} = \frac{-1 \times 10^4\ \text{J}}{{}_{1}\cancel{3.2\,g\,N_2H_4}} \times \frac{{}^{10}\cancel{32\,g\,N_2H_4}}{1\ \text{mol}\ N_2H_4} = -1 \times 10^5\ \text{J/mol or } -1 \times 10^2\ \text{kJ/mol}$$

33. D. Dimethyl ether. Ethyl alcohol can form hydrogen bonds and therefore can form a more orderly arrangement than dimethyl ether which cannot form hydrogen bonds.

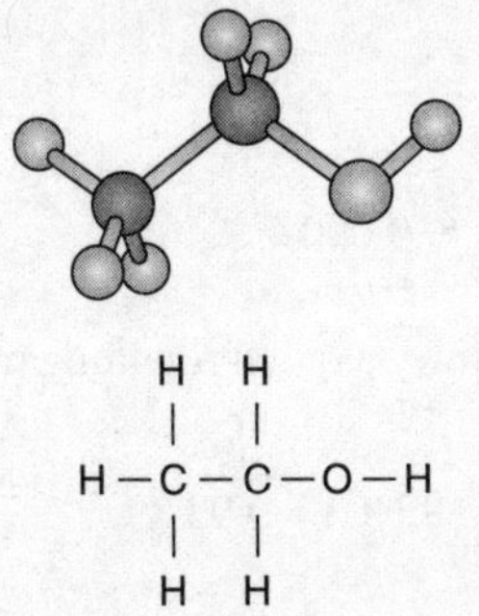

Ethyl alcohol, C_2H_6O

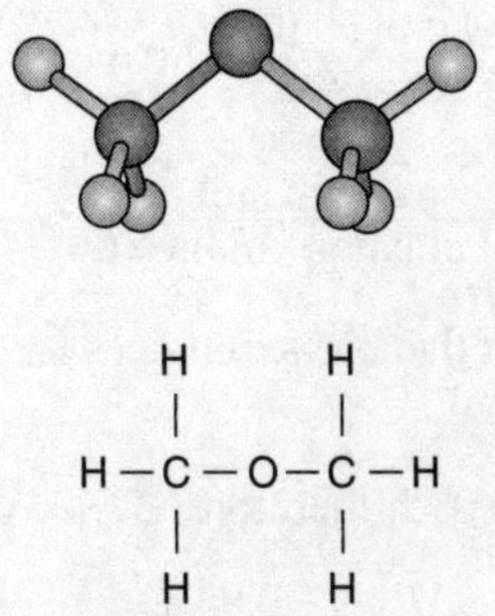

Dimethyl ether, C_2H_6O

Xenon. The xenon atom has more particles (protons, neutrons, and electrons) than neon. Since there are more particles in the xenon atom, the probability is higher for disorder.

34. D.

$N_{2(g)} + 3H_{2(g)} \rightleftharpoons 2NH_{3(g)}$

$\Delta H° = \Sigma \Delta H_f°_{\text{(products)}} - \Sigma \Delta H_f°_{\text{(reactants)}}$

$= [2\ \cancel{mol}\ NH_3 \times (-46\ kJ/\cancel{mol})] - [(1\ \cancel{mol}\ N_2 \times 0\ kJ/\cancel{mol}) + (3\ \cancel{mol}\ H_2 \times 0\ kJ/\cancel{mol})]$

$= -92\ kJ$

$\Delta H° < 0$ means that the enthalpy of reaction favors the products of the reaction.

$\Delta S° = \Sigma S°_{\text{(products)}} - \Sigma S°_{\text{(reactants)}}$

$= [2\ \cancel{mol\ NH_3}\ °\ 190^*\ J \cdot \cancel{mol^{-1}} \cdot K^{-1}] - [(1\ \cancel{mol\ N_2} \times 190^*\ J \cdot \cancel{mol^{-1}} \cdot K^{-1}) + (3\ \cancel{mol\ H_2} \times 130^*\ J \cdot \cancel{mol^{-1}} \cdot K^{-1})$

$\approx (380 - 190 - 390)\ J/K$

$\approx -200\ J/K$

$\Delta S° < 0$ means that the entropy of reaction is unfavorable (nonspontaneity is favored) because there is a significant increase in the order of the system when N_2 and H_2 combine to form NH_3.

* *numbers were rounded to facilitate solving the problem without a calculator*

35. A. $527°C + 273 = 800.\ K$

$\Delta G = \Delta H - T\Delta S$

$= -92{,}000\ J - [800.\ \cancel{K}\ (-200.\ J/\cancel{K})]$

$= -92{,}000\ J - (-160{,}000\ J)$

$= 68{,}000\ J = 68\ kJ$

Because the entropy term ($-T\Delta S$) becomes larger as the temperature increases, the reaction changes from one which is favorable at low temperatures to one that is unfavorable at high temperatures.

36. B.

density $H_2O = 1.00\ g \cdot mL^{-1}$

$$\frac{{}^{5}\cancel{160.25\,g\,CH_3OH}}{1} \times \frac{1\ \cancel{mol\,CH_3OH}}{{}_{1}\cancel{32.05\,g\,CH_3OH}} \times \frac{1\ \cancel{kg\,H_2O}}{25.0\ \cancel{moles\,CH_3OH}} \times \frac{10^3\ \cancel{g\,H_2O}}{1\ \cancel{kg\,H_2O}} \times \frac{1\,mL\,H_2O}{1.00\ \cancel{g\,H_2O}} = 200.\,mL\,H_2O$$

Note: The density of methanol was not needed to solve this problem.

37. D. $M_iV_i = M_fV_f$ $(6.00\ \cancel{M})(V_i) = (3.00\ \cancel{M})(4.00\ \cancel{L})$ $V_i = 2.00\text{ L} = 2.00 \times 10^3\text{ mL}$

38. B.

$$\frac{1.00\ \cancel{\text{kg H}_2\text{O}}}{1} \times \frac{10^3\ \cancel{\text{g}}}{1.00\ \cancel{\text{kg}}} \times \frac{1\text{ mol H}_2\text{O}}{18\ \cancel{\text{g H}_2\text{O}}} \approx 50\text{ mol H}_2\text{O}$$

$$\text{mol fraction ethanol} = \frac{\text{mol ethanol}}{\text{mol ethanol} + \text{mol H}_2\text{O}} = \frac{\sim 5}{\sim 5 + 50} \approx 0.090$$

Hint: Notice how far apart the answer choices are. This allows a quick rounding of numbers in order to save time doing the math.

39. B. Pure water freezes at 0.0°C; therefore, $\Delta T_{FP} = 0°C - (-0.93°C) = 0.93°C$

$$\Delta T_{FP} = k_f \cdot m;\ \text{therefore } m = \frac{\Delta T_{FP}}{k_f} = \frac{0.93°\cancel{C}}{1.86°\cancel{C}/m} = 0.50\ m$$

So, 1 kg of solvent contains 0.50 mol of substance Y.

$$\frac{30.0\text{ g Y}}{0.50\text{ mol}} = 60.\text{ g/mol}$$

40. E. 27°C + 273 = 300. K

$$M = \frac{\pi}{RT} = \frac{{}^{1}\cancel{0.00821\text{ atm}}}{\left({}_{10}\cancel{0.0821}\text{ L}\cdot\cancel{\text{atm}}\cdot\text{mol}^{-1}\cdot\cancel{\text{K}^{-1}}\right)300.\ \cancel{\text{K}}} = 3.33 \times 10^{-4}\ M$$

$$n = M \cdot V = \frac{3.33 \times 10^{-4}\text{ mol}}{\cancel{\text{L}}} \times \frac{1.00\ \cancel{\text{mL sol'n}}}{1} \times \frac{1\ \cancel{\text{L}}}{10^3\ \cancel{\text{mL}}} = 3.33 \times 10^{-7}\text{ mol}$$

$$MM = \frac{{}^{10}\cancel{33.3\text{ mg}}}{1} \times \frac{1\text{ g}}{10^3\ \cancel{\text{mg}}} \times \frac{1}{{}_{1}\cancel{3.33} \times 10^{-7}\text{ mol}} = 1.00 \times 10^5\text{ g/mol}$$

41. B. For AgI: Let $x = [Ag^+]$ at which precipitation begins.

$[Ag^+][I^-] = (x)(0.100\text{ mol} \div 0.100\text{ L}) = 8.5 \times 10^{-17}$

$$x = \frac{8.5 \times 10^{-17}}{(0.100 \div 0.100)} = \frac{8.5 \times 10^{-17}}{1.00} = 8.5 \times 10^{-17}$$

AgI will begin to precipitate when $[Ag^+] = 8.5 \times 10^{-17}\ M$

For AgCl: Let $y = [Ag^+]$ at which precipitation begins.

$[Ag^+][Cl^-] = (y)(0.0100\text{ mol} \div 0.100\text{ L}) = 1.8 \times 10^{-10}$

$$y = \frac{1.8 \times 10^{-10}}{(0.0100 \div 0.100)} = 1.8 \times 10^{-9}\ M$$

AgCl will begin to precipitate when $[Ag^+] = 1.8 \times 10^{-9}\ M$

Therefore, AgI begins to precipitate at a lower silver ion concentration than AgCl.

42. D. $N_{2(g)} + 3H_{2(g)} \rightleftharpoons 2NH_{3(g)}$

$$Q_c = \frac{[NH_3]^2}{[N_2][H_2]^3} = \frac{(8.00\text{ mol}/5.00\text{L})^2}{(5.00\text{ mol}/5.00\text{L})(4.00\text{ mol}/5.00\text{L})^3} = \frac{\cancel{64} \times 25}{5 \times \cancel{64}} = 5$$

Because Q_c is greater than K_c, the reaction will proceed from right to left, decreasing the concentration of NH_3 and increasing the concentrations of N_2 and H_2 until $Q_c = K_c = 6.00 \times 10^{-2}$.

43. **A.** A Brønsted base is capable of accepting a proton. $NH_{3(aq)} + H^+_{(aq)} \rightarrow NH_4^+{}_{(aq)}$; $CN^-{}_{(aq)} + H^+_{(aq)} \rightarrow HCN_{(aq)}$; $NO_2^-{}_{(aq)} + H^+_{(aq)} \rightarrow HNO_{2(aq)}$. An Arrhenius base provides hydroxide ions to a solution $KOH_{(aq)} \rightarrow K^+_{(aq)} + OH^-{}_{(aq)}$.

44. **D.** Conjugate acid (*addition of a proton to a base forms its conjugate acid*):

$H^+ + HSO_4^- \rightarrow H_2SO_4$. *Conjugate base (removal of a proton from an acid forms its conjugate base)*: $HSO_4^- \rightarrow H^+ + SO_4^{2-}$.

45. **C.**

(I) BF_3 because the B-F bond is more polar than the B-Br bond.

(II) Fe^{3+} because it is more electropositive than Fe^{2+}.

(III) H_3PO_4 because P has a higher electronegativity than As.

(IV) HNO_3 because acid strength increases with the number of oxygen atoms.

(V) $CHCl_2COOH$ because the chlorine is more electronegative than hydrogen and attracts electrons toward itself, making the O-H bond more polar; therefore, the hydrogen atom in the carboxyl group (-COOH) is more easily ionized.

(VI) $Br^-{}_{(aq)}$ does not undergo hydrolysis and therefore does not affect pH. $HS^-{}_{(aq)}$ is the conjugate base of the weak acid H_2S and therefore has an affinity for $H^+_{(aq)}$ ions ($HS^-{}_{(aq)} + H_2O_{(l)} \rightleftharpoons H_2S_{(aq)} + OH^-{}_{(aq)}$) making the solution mildly basic. Therefore, the solution containing $Br^-{}_{(aq)}$ would have a lower pH than a solution containing $HS^-{}_{(aq)}$.

(VII) NH_4^+ has a higher positive charge and nitrogen is more electronegative than carbon.

(VIII) ClO_3^- (the conjugate base of $HClO_3$) is a stronger acid than ClO_2^- (the conjugate base of $HClO_2$) because $HClO_3$ is a stronger acid (more oxygen) than $HClO_2$.

46. **D.** $HCl_{(aq)} + NH_{3(aq)} \rightarrow NH_4Cl_{(aq)}$

$$\frac{15.0\,\cancel{\text{mL NH}_3}}{1} \times \frac{1\,\cancel{\text{L}}}{10^3\,\cancel{\text{mL}}} \times \frac{0.200\text{ mol NH}_3}{\cancel{\text{L sol'n}}} = 3.00 \times 10^{-3}\text{ mol NH}_3$$

$$\frac{35.0\,\cancel{\text{mL HCl}}}{1} \times \frac{1\,\cancel{\text{L}}}{10^3\,\cancel{\text{mL}}} \times \frac{0.150\text{ mol HCl}}{\cancel{\text{L sol'n}}} = 5.25 \times 10^{-3}\text{ mol HCl}$$

$(5.25 \times 10^{-3}) - (3.00 \times 10^{-3}) = 2.25 \times 10^{-3}$ mol HCl left over

Note: Even though NH_4^+ hydrolyzes to produce H^+, the amount is negligible compared to the H^+ contributed by HCl; therefore, the $[H^+]$ contributed by NH_4^+ will be ignored.

$$[H^+] = \frac{2.25 \times 10^{-3}\text{ mol}}{35.0\,\cancel{\text{mL}} + 15.0\,\cancel{\text{mL}}} \times \frac{10^3\,\cancel{\text{mL}}}{1\text{ L}} = 0.045\,M$$

pH = –log $[H^+]$ = –log 0.045 according to the table = 1.35

Notice that the answer choices are fairly spread apart. This allows you to round numbers with a considerable amount of leeway.

47. **B.** 0.05 moles would be the maximum amount that would react completely with the given amount of the weak base: moles $C_2H_3O_2^-$ = (0.50 L) (0.10 *M*) = 0.050 moles. Because the acid and base react in a 1:1 mole ratio, 0.050 moles of HCl would use up all of the acetate ion.

48. **C.** Dinitrogen trioxide is the anhydride of nitrous acid, HNO_2 ($N_2O_3 + H_2O \rightarrow 2HNO_2$). Dinitrogen pentoxide is the anhydride of nitric acid, HNO_3 ($N_2O_5 + H_2O \rightarrow 2HNO_3$).

Practice Exam 2

49. **C.** rate = $k(CH_3CHO)^2$

$$\frac{1}{[CH_3CHO]} - \frac{1}{[CH_3CHO]_0} = kt$$

The initial concentration of acetaldehyde is 0.0100 *M*. The final concentration is only 30.% as large, or 0.00300 *M*:

$$\frac{1}{(0.00300)} - \frac{1}{(0.0100)} = 0.334t$$

t = 699 seconds ~ 11.7 minutes

It therefore takes about 12 minutes for 70.% of the acetaldehyde to decompose at this temperature.

50. **B.** In order for a reaction to occur, a collision must occur; the collision must be of sufficient energy to break the necessary bonds and be of proper orientation. Factors affecting reaction rates are concentration of the reacting species found in the rate law, temperature and the presence or absence of a catalyst.

51. **B.**

NO: N = +2

N_2O: N = +1

NO_2: N = +4

NO_3^-: N = +5

N_2O_5: N = +5

NH_4^+: N = −3 (H will have a +1 ox. number because it is bonded to N, a nonmetal)

52. **B.** Refer to the $E°_{red}$ table. The strength of the oxidizing agents increases on moving up in the table. $Cr_2O_7^{2-}{}_{(aq)}$ ($E°_{red}$ = 1.33 V) has the greatest tendency to be reduced (largest $E°_{red}$), and $Fe^{3+}{}_{(aq)}$ ($E°_{red}$ = 0.77 V) has the least tendency to be reduced (smallest $E°_{red}$). Therefore the answer is $Fe^{3+}{}_{(aq)} < Br_{2(l)} < Cr_2O_7^{2-}{}_{(aq)}$.

53. **D.**

OX: $Sn^{2+}{}_{(aq)} \rightarrow Sn^{4+}{}_{(aq)}$

$Sn^{2+}{}_{(aq)} \rightarrow Sn^{4+}{}_{(aq)} + 2e^-$

RED: $IO_4^-{}_{(aq)} \rightarrow I^-{}_{(aq)}$

$IO_4^-{}_{(aq)} \rightarrow I^-{}_{(aq)} + 4H_2O_{(l)}$

$8H^+{}_{(aq)} + IO_4^-{}_{(aq)} \rightarrow I^-{}_{(aq)} + 4H_2O_{(l)}$

$8H^+{}_{(aq)} + IO_4^-{}_{(aq)} + 8e^- \rightarrow I^-{}_{(aq)} + 4H_2O_{(l)}$

Balance electrons

OX: $4(Sn^{2+}{}_{(aq)} \rightarrow Sn^{4+}{}_{(aq)} + 2e^-)$

$4Sn^{2+}{}_{(aq)} \rightarrow 4Sn^{4+}{}_{(aq)} + 8e^-$

Add half reactions:

$4Sn^{2+}{}_{(aq)} \rightarrow 4Sn^{4+}{}_{(aq)} + \cancel{8e^-}$

$8H^+{}_{(aq)} + IO_4^-{}_{(aq)} + \cancel{8e^-} \rightarrow I^-{}_{(aq)} + 4H_2O_{(l)}$

$4Sn^{2+}{}_{(aq)} + 8H^+{}_{(aq)} + IO_4^-{}_{(aq)} \rightarrow 4Sn^{4+}{}_{(aq)} + I^-{}_{(aq)} + 4H_2O_{(l)}$

54. D. Begin by predicting what the overall reaction will be. Using a standardized reduction potential table, any species on the left of a given half-cell reaction will react spontaneously with a species that appears on the right of any half-cell reaction located *above* it (also known as the diagonal rule). Referring to the information provided in the problem, we see that Br_2 will oxidize I^- but will not oxidize Cl^-. Therefore, the only redox reaction that will occur spontaneously under standard-state conditions is:

OX:	$2I^-_{(aq)} \rightarrow I_{2\,(s)} + \cancel{2e^-}$	$E^\circ_{ox} = -0.53\text{ V}$
RED:	$Br_{2\,(l)} + \cancel{2e^-} \rightarrow 2Br^-_{(aq)}$	$E^\circ_{red} = 1.07\text{ V}$
	$2I^-_{(aq)} + Br_{(l)} \rightarrow I_{2\,(s)} + 2Br^-_{(aq)}$	$E^\circ = 0.54\text{ V}$

55. C. $\Delta G^\circ = -nFE^\circ_{cell}$ $\quad -(2\text{ mol})(96{,}500\text{ J}\cdot\text{V}^{-1}\cdot\text{mol}^{-1})(0.54\text{ V}) = -1.0 \times 10^2\text{ kJ}$

Hint: Notice that the answer choices are magnitudes apart. It would not be necessary to do the math in order to determine the correct answer.

56. A. $K_c = 10^{nE^\circ/0.0591} = 10^{(2)(0.54)/(0.0591)} = 10^{18}$

57. A. Mass number stays the same. Add 1 to the atomic number. Add an electron ${}^{0}_{-1}e$.

58. D. Mass number stays the same. Subtract 1 from the atomic number. Add an electron ${}^{0}_{-1}e$.

59. B. If you missed this question, go back and review decay modes.

60. C. If you missed this question, go back and review decay modes.

61. D. If you missed this question, go back and review decay modes.

62. A. If you missed this question, go back and review decay modes.

63. E. If you missed this question, go back and review decay modes.

64. C. 37.8 minutes is equal to 9 half-lives (37.8 min / 4.20 min = 9.00 half-lives).

$$\left(\frac{1}{2}\right)^9 = \frac{1}{512}$$

$$\frac{\overset{1}{\cancel{5.12\text{ mol Tl}-206}}}{1} \times \frac{6.02 \times 10^{23}\text{ atoms Tl}-206}{1\ \cancel{\text{mol Tl}-206}} \times \frac{1}{\underset{100}{\cancel{512}}} = 6.02 \times 10^{21}\text{ atoms Tl}-206$$

65. B. If you missed this question, refer to nomenclature of alkynes.

66. A. If you missed this question, refer to nomenclature of alcohols.

67. E. The common name is propionamide. It is the amide of propionic acid. If you missed this question, refer to the nomenclature of amides.

68. B. If you missed this question, refer to nomenclature of aromatic compounds.

69. C. It is also known as ethyl butyrate and is used as a common pineapple flavoring.

70. A. The second carbon atom in 2-bromo-2-methylbutane contains two identical CH_3 substituents. As a result, this compound is achiral and does not form enantiomers.

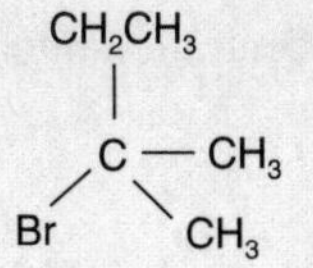

2-bromo-2-methylbutane

The second carbon atom in 1-bromo-2-methylbutane carries four different substituents: H, $BrCH_2$, CH_3, and CH_2CH_3. As a result, this molecule is chiral and it forms enantiomers.

$$
\begin{array}{ccc}
CH_2CH_3 & & CH_2CH_3 \\
| & & | \\
C-CH_3 & \text{and} & C-H \\
BrCH_2 \quad H & & BrCH_2 \quad CH_3
\end{array}
$$

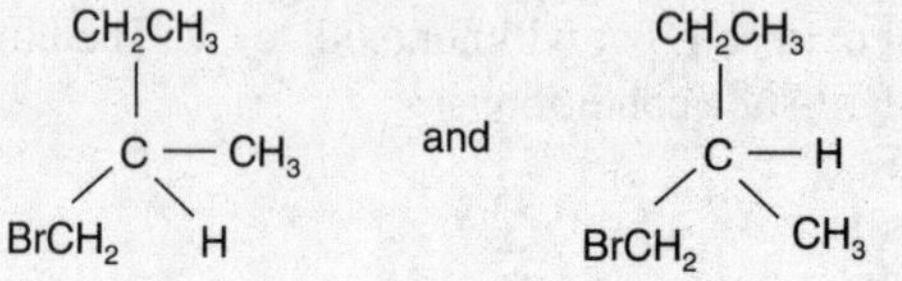

71. C. An example of esterification is the production of ethyl acetate by the reaction of ethanol with acetic acid.

$$CH_3CH_2OH + CH_3COOH \longrightarrow CH_3COOCH_2CH_3 + H_2O$$

72. A. An example is the production of ethanol by the addition of water to ethylene.

$$C_2H_4 + H_2O \longrightarrow CH_3CH_2OH$$

73. E. A secondary alcohol has the general structure

$$
\begin{array}{c}
R' \\
| \\
R''-C-OH \\
| \\
H
\end{array}
$$

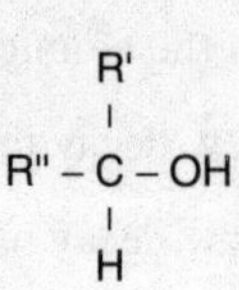

where the R' and R'' (which may be the same or different) represent hydrocarbon fragments. An example is the oxidation of isopropyl alcohol to acetone.

$$(CH_3)_2CH-OH \xrightarrow{hotCu} (CH_3)_2C=O + H_2$$

74. D. A condensation reaction is characterized by the joining of two molecules and the elimination of a water molecule. In the example below, two methyl alcohol molecules react to form dimethyl ether.

$$2CH_3OH \xrightleftharpoons{Al_2O_3} CH_3OCH_3 + H_2O$$

75. E. Begin this problem by writing a balanced equation.

$$CH_3CHO_{(g)} \to CH_{4(g)} + CO_{(g)}$$

Next, write a rate expression.

$$\text{rate} = k(\text{conc. } CH_3CHO)^2$$

Because you know the rate and the concentration of CH_3CHO, solve for k, the rate-specific constant.

$$k = \frac{\text{rate}}{\left(\text{conc.} CH_3CHO\right)^2} \to \frac{0.10 \text{ mole/liter} \cdot \text{sec}}{(0.01 \text{ mole/liter})^2} = 1.0 \times 10^3 \text{ liters} \cdot \text{mole}^{-1} \cdot \text{sec}^{-1}$$

Finally, substitute the rate-specific constant and the new concentration into the rate expression.

$$\text{rate} = \frac{1.0 \times 10^{-3} \text{ liter}}{1 \text{ mole} \cdot \text{sec}} \times \left(\frac{0.050 \text{ mole}}{1 \text{ liter}}\right)^2 = 2.5 \text{ moles} \cdot \text{liter}^{-1} \cdot \text{sec}^{-1}$$

Free Response

Question 1

Maximum Points for Question 1
Part (a): 2 points
Part (b): 2 points
Part (c): 2 points
Part (d): 2 points
Part (e): 2 points
Part (f): 2 points
Part (g): 2 points
Total points: 14

1. HCN is a weak acid ($K_a = 4.9 \times 10^{-10}$) used in the steel industry, manufacturing acrylic resin plastics, gold extraction, dyeing, explosives, and engraving. Given a 0.10 M solution of HCN, calculate	**2 points possible**
(a) $[H_3O^+]$	
$HCN_{(aq)} + H_2O_{(l)} \rightleftharpoons H_3O^+_{(aq)} + CN^-_{(aq)}$	

	HCN	*H_3O^+*	*CN^-*
initial (*M*)	0.10	~ 0	0
change (*M*)	$-x$	$+x$	$+x$
equilibrium (*M*)	$0.10 - x$	x	x

$$K_a = \frac{[H_3O^+][CN^-]}{[HCN]} = 4.9 \times 10^{-10} = \frac{x^2}{0.1 - x} \approx \frac{x^2}{0.1} \quad x = 7.0 \times 10^{-6}$$

1 point for correct setup.

$[H_3O^+] = 7.0 \times 10^{-6}$ *M*

1 point for correct answer.

(b) $[CN^-]$	**2 points possible**
According to the table above, $x = [CN^-] = 7.0 \times 10^{-6}$ *M*	*1 point for correct setup.*
	1 point for correct answer.
(c) [HCN]	**2 points possible**
According to the table above, $[HCN] = 0.10 - x$	*1 point for correct setup.*
$= 0.10 - 7.0 \times 10^{-6} \approx 0.10$ *M*	*1 point for correct answer.*

(d) [OH⁻] $[OH^-] = K_w / [H_3O^+] = 1.0 \times 10^{-14} / 7.0 \times 10^{-6}$ $= 1.4 \times 10^{-9}$	***2 points possible*** *1 point for correct setup.* *1 point for correct answer.*
(e) pH $pH = -\log [H_3O^+] = -\log (7.0 \times 10^{-6}) = 5.15$	***2 points possible*** *1 point for correct setup.* *1 point for correct answer.*
(f) pOH pOH = 14.00 – pH = 14.00 – 5.15 = 8.85	***2 points possible*** *1 point for correct setup.* *1 point for correct answer.*
(g) K_b $K_b = \frac{K_w}{K_a} = \frac{1.0 \times 10^{-14}}{4.9 \times 10^{-10}} = 2.0 \times 10^{-5}$	***2 points possible*** *1 point for correct setup.* *1 point for correct answer.*
(h) percent dissociation $\% \text{ dissociation} = \frac{[HCN]_{dissociated}}{[HCN]_{initial}} \times 100\%$ $= \frac{7.0 \times 10^{-6} M}{0.10 M} \times 100\% = 0.0070\%$	***2 points possible*** *1 point for correct setup.* *1 point for correct answer.*

Question 2

Maximum Points for Question 2
Part (a): 3 points
Part (b): 3 points
Part (c): 3 points
Total points: 9

2. 5.0 mg / mL of a certain drug solution decays by first-order kinetics with a rate constant of 0.0005 / day. *(a) What is the concentration of drug remaining after 120 days?* $\ln [A] = -kt + \ln [A_0]$ $= -(.0005 / \text{day})(120 \text{ day}) + \ln (5 \text{ mg / mL})$ $\ln [A] = -0.06 + 1.609 = 1.549$ [A] = 4.71 mg / mL	***3 points possible*** *2 points for correct setup of problem and showing work.* *1 point for correct answer.*

(b) What is $t_{1/2}$ for the drug solution? $t_{1/2} = 0.693 / k = 0.693 / 0.0005/\text{day} = 1{,}386$ days	***3 points possible*** *2 points for correctly setting up problem and showing work.* *1 point for correct answer.*
(c) How long will it take to reach 90.% of the original concentration? 0.90(5 mg / mL) = 4.5 mg / mL $\ln [A] = -kt + \ln [A_0]$, $t = (\ln [A] - \ln [A_0]) / -k$ $= (\ln 4.5 - \ln 5.0) / -0.0005 = 210$ days	***3 points possible*** *2 points for correctly setting up problem and showing work.* *1 point for correct answer.*

Question 3

Maximum Points for Question 3
Part (a): 1 point
Part (b): 1 point
Part (c): 2 points
Part (d): 2 points
Part (e): 2 points
Part (f): 1 point
Part (g): 1 point
Total points: 10

3. Answer the following questions regarding the electrochemical cell at standard conditions diagrammed below. 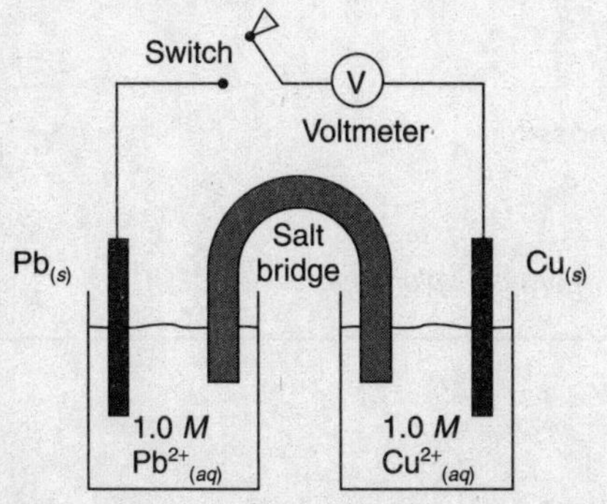 *(a) Write the oxidation half-reaction.* Because you know that the overall cell voltage ($E°$) must be positive, first determine whether Pb or Cu will be oxidized (or reduced) based on looking at the $E°_{red}$ table. $Pb_{(s)} \rightarrow Pb^{2+}_{(aq)} + 2e^-$	***1 point possible*** *1 point for correctly writing the oxidation half-reaction.*

(b) Write the reduction half-reaction. $Cu^{2+}_{(aq)} + 2e^- \rightarrow Cu_{(s)}$	***1 point possible*** *1 point for correctly writing the reduction half-reaction.*
(c) Write the balanced net-ionic equation and determine the cell voltage. OX: $Pb_{(s)} \rightarrow Pb^{2+}_{(aq)} + \cancel{2e^-}$ $\quad E^\circ_{ox}: 0.13\,V$ RED: $Cu^{2+}_{(aq)} + \cancel{2e^-} \rightarrow Cu_{(s)}$ $\quad E^\circ_{red}: 0.34\,V$ $Pb_{(s)} + Cu^{2+}_{(aq)} \rightarrow Pb^{2+}_{(aq)} + Cu_{(s)}$ $\quad E^\circ = 0.47\,V$	***2 points possible*** *1 point for correctly writing the balanced net-ionic equation.* *1 point for correctly determining the cell voltage.*
(d) Identify the anode and the cathode. AN OX. Because oxidation occurs at the anode, lead is the anode. RED CAT: Because reduction occurs at the cathode, copper is the cathode.	***2 points possible*** *1 point for correctly identifying the anode.* *1 point for correctly identifying the cathode.*
(e) If 25.0 mL of 3M $Cu(NO_3)_2$ is added to the half-cell on the right, explain what will happens to the cell voltage. Because Cu^{2+} is a reactant in the overall cell reaction, increasing the concentration of Cu^{2+} will shift the reaction to the right, thereby increasing the cell voltage. Furthermore, because $Q = [Pb^{2+}] / [Cu^{2+}]$, increasing $[Cu^{2+}]$ will decrease Q. In the Nernst equation, $E = E^\circ - \frac{0.0591V}{n} \log Q$, if Q decreases, then the voltage (E) increases. The Nernst equation is discussed in more detail below.	***2 points possible*** *1 point for use of the Nernst equation.* *1 point for correct conclusion.*
(f) If 3.00 grams of solid KCl is added to each half-cell, explain what will happen to the cell voltage. $KCl_{(s)} \rightarrow K^+_{(aq)} + Cl^-_{(aq)}$. Adding Cl^- to the solution containing Pb^{2+} ions will cause $PbCl_2$ to precipitate out, decreasing the concentration of Pb^{2+}. This will result in a smaller Q, and hence a higher voltage. Adding Cl^- to the solution containing Cu^{2+} will have no effect because $CuCl_2$ is soluble.	***1 point possible*** *1 point for correct explanation.*
(g) If 25.0 mL of distilled water is added to both half-cells, explain what will happen. Because $Q = [Pb^{2+}] / [Cu^{2+}]$, diluting both solutions by the same amount will have no effect on Q or the voltage.	***1 point possible*** *1 point for correct explanation.*

Question 4

Maximum Points for Question 4
Part (a) (i): 1 point
Part (a) (ii): 1 point
Part (b) (i): 1 point
Part (b) (ii): 1 point
Part (c) (i): 1 point
Part (c) (ii): 1 point
Total points: 6

4. (a) Solid calcium oxide is added to distilled water. *(i) Write the balanced equation for the reaction described.* $CaO + H_2O \rightarrow Ca^{2+} + OH^-$	***1 point possible*** *1 point for correctly balanced equation.*
(ii) Is the resulting solution acidic, basic, or neutral? Explain. Basic. Metal oxides form basic compounds in water.	***1 point possible*** *1 point for correct explanation of why it is basic.*
(b) Solid sodium chlorate is strongly heated and decomposes, resulting in a change in the oxidation numbers of both chlorine and oxygen. *(i) Write the balanced equation for the reaction described.* $2NaClO_3 \rightarrow 2NaCl + 3O_2$	***1 point possible*** *1 point for correctly balanced equation.*
(ii) What is the oxidation number of chlorine before and after the reaction? Chlorine has an oxidation number of +5 in $NaClO_3$ and –1 in NaCl.	***1 point possible*** *1 point for correct oxidation number before and after reaction.*
(c) A solution of ethanoic (acetic) acid is added to a solution of sodium hydroxide. *(i) Write the balanced equation for the reaction described.* $HC_2H_3O_2 + OH^- \rightarrow H_2O + C_2H_3O_2^-$	***1 point possible*** *1 point for correctly balanced equation.*
(ii) Explain why a mixture of equal volumes of equimolar solutions of ethanoic acid and sodium hydroxide is basic. Because equal numbers of moles of both reactants are initially present, they are both consumed without any excess of either one. The reason the solution is basic is because the principal product of the reaction, the acetate ion, is a weak base in water.	***1 point possible*** *1 point for correct explanation of why solution is basic.*

Question 5

Maximum Points for Question 5
Part (a): 2 points
Part (b): 2 points
Part (c): 2 points
Part (d): 2 points
Part (e): 2 points
Total points: 10

5. Explain each of the following in terms of (1) inter- and intra- atomic or molecular forces and (2) structure. *(a) ICl has a boiling point of 97°C, whereas NaCl has a boiling point of 1400°C.* ICl is a covalently bonded, molecular solid; NaCl is an ionic solid. There are dipole forces between ICl molecules but electrostatic forces between Na^+ and Cl^- ions. Dipole forces in ICl are much weaker that the ionic bonds in NaCl. I and Cl are similar in electronegativity—generates only partial δ^+ and δ^- around molecule. Na and Cl differ greatly in electronegativity—greater electrostatic force. When heated slightly, ICl boils because energy supplied (heat) overcomes weak dipole forces.	***2 points possible*** *1 point each for any two of the reasons listed on the left.*
(b) $KI_{(s)}$ is very soluble in water, whereas $I_{2(s)}$ has a solubility of only 0.03 grams per 100 grams of water. KI is an ionic solid, held together by ionic bonds. I_2 is a molecular solid, held together by covalent bonds. KI dissociates into K^+ and I^- ions. I_2 slightly dissolves in water, maintaining its covalent bond. Solubility rule: Like dissolves like. H_2O is polar; KI is polar; I_2 is not polar.	***2 points possible*** *1 point each for any two of the reasons listed on the left.*
(c) Solid Ag conducts an electric current, whereas solid $AgNO_3$ does not. Ag is a metal. $AgNO_3$ is an ionic solid. Ag structure consists of Ag^+ cations surrounded by mobile or "free" electrons. $AgNO_3$ structure consists of Ag^+ cations electrostatically attracted to NO_3^- polyatomic anions—no free or mobile electrons.	***2 points possible*** *1 point each for any two of the reasons listed on the left.*

<table>
<tr><td>

(d) PCl_3 has a measurable dipole moment, whereas PCl_5 does not.

PCl_3 Lewis structure

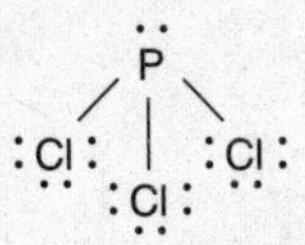

PCl_3—note the lone pair of unshared electrons.

PCl_3 is triangular pyramidal, and all pyramidal structures are polar.

PCl_5 Lewis structure

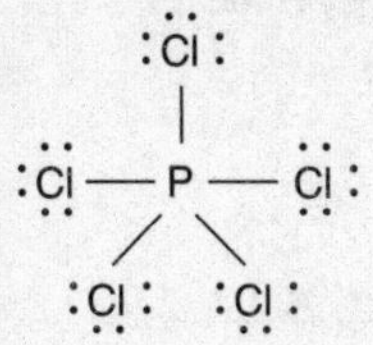

PCl_5 has no unshared electrons on P.

PCl_5 is trigonal bipyramidal and thus perfectly symmetrical, so there is no polarity; all dipoles cancel.

</td><td>

2 points possible

1 point each for any two of the reasons listed on the left.

</td></tr>
<tr><td>

(e) The carbon-to-carbon bond energy in C_2H_5Cl is less than it is in C_2H_3Cl.

C_2H_3Cl has a double bond between the carbon atoms

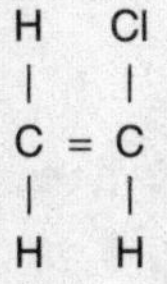

whereas C_2H_5Cl contains a single bond between the carbon atoms

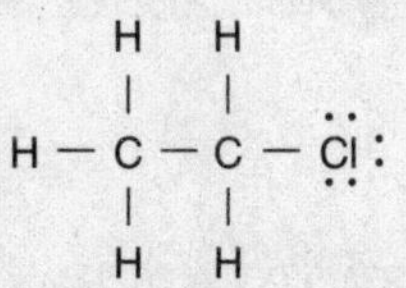

Less energy is required to break a single bond than a double bond.

</td><td>

2 points possible

1 point for indicating that C_2H_5Cl has a single bond between the carbon atoms and that C_2H_3Cl has a single bond between the carbon atoms.

1 point for indicating that a double bond requires more energy to break than a single bond.

</td></tr>
</table>

Question 6

Maximum Points for Question 6
Part (a): 4 points
Part (b): 4 points
Part (c): 2 points
Total points: 10

6. If one completely vaporizes a measured amount of a volatile liquid, the molecular weight of the liquid can be determined by measuring the volume, temperature, and pressure of the resulting gas. When using this procedure, one must use the ideal gas equation and assume that the gas behaves ideally. However, if the temperature of the gas is only slightly above the boiling point of the liquid, the gas deviates from ideal behavior.	***4 points possible***
(a) Explain the postulates of the ideal gas equation. The ideal gas equation, $PV = nRT$, stems from three relationships known to be true for gases:	*1 point for correctly stating the formula for the ideal gas equation.*
■ the volume is directly proportional to the number of moles: $V \sim n$ ■ the volume is directly proportional to the absolute temperature: $V \sim T$ ■ the volume is inversely proportional to the pressure: $V \sim 1/P$	*1 point for stating each of the three postulates.*
(b) Explain why, if measured just above the boiling point, the molecular weight deviates from the true value.	***4 points possible***
n, the symbol used for the moles of gas, can be obtained by dividing the mass of the gas by the molecular weight. In effect, n = mass · molecular weight^{-1} ($n = m \cdot MW^{-1}$). Substituting this relationship into the ideal gas law gives $P \cdot V = \frac{m \cdot R \cdot T}{MW}$	*1 point for stating the equation to determine molecular weight of a gas.*
Solving this equation for the molecular weight yields $MW = \frac{m \cdot R \cdot T}{P \cdot V}$	*1 point for concept that ideal gas molecules do not occupy space.*
Real gas behavior deviates from the values obtained using the ideal gas equation because the ideal equation assumes that: (1) the molecules do not occupy space, and (2) there is no attractive force between the individual molecules. However, at low temperatures (just above the boiling point of the liquid), these two postulates are not true and one must use an alternative equation known as the van der Waals equation, which accounts for these factors.	*1 point for concept that there are no attractive forces between individual gas molecules in an ideal gas.* *1 point for stating that the van der Waals equation accounts for these factors.*
At normal conditions of temperature and pressure, van der Waals forces are negligible. As the pressure increases, molecules are forced closer together, and/or the temperature decreases (molecules slow down ~ less kinetic energy), and van der Waals forces become more significant. Only at conditions of high pressure and/or low temperature are the molecules able to participate in van der Waals forces noticeably—only at these conditions will these gases liquefy.	*1 point for relationship that attraction between molecules increases as temperature is lowered (less kinetic energy).*

(c) Would the molecular weight of a real gas be higher or lower than that predicted by the van der Waals equation and explain why?	***2 points possible***
Because the attraction between the molecules becomes more significant at the lower temperatures due to a decrease in kinetic energy of the molecules, the compressibility of the gas is increased. This causes the product $P \cdot V$ to be smaller than predicted. $P \cdot V$ is found in the denominator in the equation listed above, so the molecular weight tends to be higher than its ideal value.	*1 point for stating that gases with lower temperatures have less kinetic energy.* *1 point for correct explanation that the molecular weight of a real gas tends to be higher than that of an ideal gas.*

Appendix

Mathematical Operations

Significant Figures

In order to receive full credit in Section II, the essay section, you must be able to express your answer with the correct number of significant figures (s.f.). There are slight penalties on the AP Chemistry Exam for not doing so. The "Golden Rule" for significant figures is that *your answer cannot contain more significant figures than the least accurately measured quantity. Do not use conversion factors for determining significant figures.* Review the following rules for determining significant figures. Underlined numbers are significant.

- Any digit that is not zero is significant. $\underline{123}$ = 3 s.f.
- Zeros between significant figures (captive zeros) are significant. $\underline{80601}$ = 5 s.f.; $\underline{10.001}$ = 5 s.f.
- Zeros to the left of the first nonzero digit (leading zeros) are not significant. $0.00\underline{2}$ = 1 s.f.
- If a number is equal to or greater than 1, than all of the zeros written to the right of the decimal point (trailing zeros) count as significant figure. $\underline{9.00}$ = 3 s.f. The number 100 has only one significant figure ($\underline{1}00$), but written as 100. (note the decimal point), it has three significant figures. $\underline{400}$. = 3 s.f.
- For numbers less than 1, only zeros that are at the end of the number and zeros that are between nonzero digits are significant. $0.0\underline{70}$ = 2 s.f.
- For addition or subtraction, the limiting term is the one with the smallest number of decimal places, so count the decimal places. For multiplication and division, the limiting term is the number that has the least number of significant figures, so count the significant figures.

  11.01 + 6.**2** + 8.995 = 26.**2** (one decimal place)

  $32.010 \times \underline{501} = 1.60 \times 10^4$ (three significant figures)

Logs and Antilogs

You will use your calculator in Section II to determine logs and antilogs. There are two types of log numbers that you will use on the AP Exam: $\log_{10}$, or log, and natural log, or ln. Log base 10 of a number is that exponent to which 10 must be raised to give the original number. Therefore, the log of 10 is 1 because 10^1 is 10. The log of 100 is 2 because 10^2 is 100. The log of 0.001 is –3, and so on.

Scientific Notation

Try to use scientific notation when writing your answers. For example, instead of writing 1,345,255 write 1.345255×10^6. Remember always write one digit, a decimal point, the rest of the digits (making sure to use only the correct number of significant figures), and then times 10 to the proper power. An answer such as 0.000045 should be written 4.5×10^{-5} (2 s.f.). Also, don't forget that when you multiple exponents you add them, and when you divide exponents you subtract them. Your chemistry text book or math book probably has a section that covers significant figures, logs, antilogs, scientific notation, and the like. If your math background or algebra skills are weak, you must thoroughly review and polish these skills before attempting to do the problems in this book.

Absolute error = Experimental value – Accepted value

$$\% \text{ error} = \frac{\text{actual} - \text{measured}}{\text{actual}} \times 100\%$$

Consider the following expression:

$$\frac{(32.56 \times 0.4303 \times 0.08700)}{4.3422} \times 100\%$$

The % error for each term is

Term	***Calculation***	***% Error***
32.5**6** ± 0.01	[(32.56 + 0.01) – 32.56/32.56] · 100%	0.0307
0.430**3** ± 0.0001	[(0.4303 + 0.0001) – 0.4303/0.4303] · 100%	0.0232
0.0870**0** ± 0.00001	[(0.08700+ 0.001) – 0.08700/0.08700 · 100%	0.0115
4.342**2** ± 0.0001	[(4.3422 + 0.0001) – 4.3422/4.3422] · 100%	0.0023

Adding up the % errors: 0.0307 + 0.0232 + 0.0115 + 0.0023 = 0.0677% and

$$\frac{(32.56 \times 0.4303 \times 0.08700)}{4.3422} \times 100\% = 28.07147 \text{ with } 0.0677\% \text{ error}$$

reported as 28.07 ± 0.01

Use the term with the largest possible error (32.56 ± 0.01) for significant numbers.

Two types of errors may affect the accuracy of a measured value:

(a) determinate errors—errors that are instrumental, operative, and involved in the methodology. These types of errors can be avoided or corrected.

(b) indeterminate errors—accidental and/or random. These types of errors cannot be estimated or predicted except through the use of probability theory and follow a Gaussian distribution.

Precision

Often an actual or accepted value is not known. If this is the case, the accuracy of the measurement cannot be reported because one does not know how close or far one is from the actual value. Instead, experiments are repeated several times, and a measurement of how close together the values lie (precision) is done. It is the goal that experiments that give reproducible results will also give accurate results.

$$\text{Absolute deviation} = |\text{measured} - \text{mean}|$$

Average deviation or average difference = average of all the absolute deviations.

$$\text{Percent deviation} = \frac{\text{average deviation}}{\text{mean}} \times 100\%$$

Example: Given three masses of the same object: 1.51 g, 1.63 g, 1.48 g

$$\text{Mean or average} = \frac{1.51 + 1.63 + 1.48}{3} = 1.54$$

Absolute deviation of each value for mean:

$$|1.51 - 1.54| = 0.03$$
$$|1.63 - 1.54| = 0.09$$
$$|1.48 - 1.54| = 0.06$$

$$\text{Average deviation} = \frac{0.03 + 0.09 + 0.06}{3} = 0.06$$

$$\text{Relative deviation for relative difference} = \frac{\text{average deviation}}{\text{mean}} \times 100\%$$

$$= \frac{0.06}{1.54} \times 100\% = 3.9\%$$

This says that the three measurements are within 3.9% of the average (and hopefully) true value of the object.

Rounding Off Numbers

318.04 = 318.0 (the 4 is smaller than 5)

318.06 = 318.1 (the 6 is greater than 5)

318.05 = 318.0 (the 0 before the 5 is an even number)

318.15 = 318.2 (the 1 before the 5 is an odd number)

Mathematics Self-Test

Try taking this short mathematics self-test. If you understand these math problems and get the answers correct, you're ready to go on. If you miss problems in this area, you need to back up and review those operations with which you are uncomfortable.

Determine the number of significant figures in the following numbers.

1. 100
2. 100.01
3. 0.010
4. 1234.100

Round the following numbers to the number of significant figures indicated and express in scientific notation.

5. 100.075 rounded to 3 significant figures
6. 140 rounded to 2 significant figures
7. 0.000787 rounded to 2 significant figures

Perform the following math operations, expressing your answers to the proper number of significant figures.

8. $(4.5 \times 10^{-3}) + (5.89 \times 10^{-4})$
9. $(5.768 \times 10^{9}) \times (6.78 \times 10^{-2})$
10. (5.661×10^{-9}) divided by (7.66×10^{-8})
11. $8.998 + 9.22 + 1.3 \times 10^{2} + 0.006$

Determine:

12. log of 98.71

13. log 0.0043

14. ln of 3.99

15. ln of 0.0564

16. log (0.831/0.111)

17. ln $(1.5^2/3.0 \times 10^{-4})$

Evalute:

18. $e^{7.82}$

Solve for x:

19. log $(12.0/x) = 3.0$

20. $40.1 = 5.13^x$

Answers to Mathematics Self-Test

1. 1 significant figure
2. 5 significant figures
3. 2 significant figures
4. 7 significant figures
5. 1.00×10^2
6. 1.4×10^2
7. 7.9×10^{-4}
8. 5.1×10^{-3}
9. 3.91×10^8
10. 7.39×10^{-2}
11. 1.5×10^2
12. 1.994
13. –2.4
14. 1.38
15. –2.88
16. 0.874
17. 8.9
18. 2.49×10^3
19. $x = 0.012$
20. $x = 2.26$

Common Polyatomic Ions

Anions −1	Anions −2	Anions −3
acetate, CH_3COO^-	carbonate, CO_3^{2-}	Arsenate, AsO_4^{3-}
amide, NH_2^-	chromate, CrO_4^{2-}	Borate, BO_3^{3-}
azide, N_3^-	dichromate, $Cr_2O_7^{2-}$	Citrate, $C_6H_5O_7^{3-}$
benzoate, $C_6H_5COO^-$	manganate, MnO_4^{2-}	Phosphate, PO_4^{3-}
bromate, BrO_3^-	metasilicate, SiO_3^{2-}	
chlorate, ClO_3^-	monohydrogen phosphate, HPO_4^{2-}	**Anions −4**
chlorite, ClO_2^-	oxalate, $C_2O_4^{2-}$	silicate, SiO_4^{4-}
cyanate, OCN^-	peroxide, O_2^{2-}	
cyanide, CN^-	peroxydisulfate, $S_2O_8^{2-}$	**Cations +1**
dihydrogen phosphate, $H_2PO_4^-$	phthalate, $C_8H_4O_4^{2-}$	Ammonium, NH_4^+
formate, $HCOO^-$	selenate, SeO_4^{2-}	Hydronium, H_3O^+
hydrogen carbonate, HCO_3^-	sulfite, SO_3^{2-}	
(bicarbonate)	tartrate, $C_4H_4O_6^{2-}$	
hydrogen sulfate, HSO_4^-	tellurate, TeO_4^{2-}	
hydrogen sulfide, HS^-	tetraborate, $B_4O_7^{2-}$	
(bisulfide or hydrosulfide)	thiosulfate, $S_2O_3^{2-}$	
hydroxide, OH^-	tungstate, WO_4^{2-}	
hypochorite, ClO^-	zincate, ZnO_2^{2-}	
iodate, IO_3^-		
nitrate, NO_3^-		
nitrite, NO_2^-		
perchlorate, ClO_4^-		
permanganate, MnO_4^-		
thiocyanate, SCN^-		
triiodide, I_3^-		
vandate, VO_3^-		

Common Strong Acids and Bases

Common Strong Acids	Common Strong Bases
HNO_3 nitric acid	LiOH lithium hydroxide
HCl hydrochloric acid	NaOH sodium hydroxide
H_2SO_4 sulfuric acid	KOH potassium hydroxide
$HClO_4$ perchloric acid	RbOH rubidium hydroxide
HBr hydrobromic acid	CsOH cesium hydroxide
HI hydroiodic acid	$Mg(OH)_2$ magnesium hydroxide
	$Ca(OH)_2$ calcium hydroxide
	$Sr(OH)_2$ strontium hydroxide
	$Ba(OH)_2$ barium hydroxide
	Additional strong bases include: oxides of group I and II cations (Na_2O, BaO, CaO, etc.) which react with water to give the cation and the hydroxide ion (i.e. $Na_2O + H_2O \rightarrow Na^+ + OH^-$). The hydride ion ($H^-$) gives OH^- and H_2 in water. The nitride ion (N^{3-}) gives OH^- and NH_3 in water. The carbide ion (C^{4-}) gives OH^-, acetylene (C_2H_2) and H_2 in water.

Common Weak Acids	Common Weak Bases
$HC_2H_3O_2$ acetic acid (HAc)	$C_3H_5O_2NH_2$ alanine
$H_2C_6H_6O_6$ ascorbic acid	NH_3 ammonia (NH_4OH in water)
H_3BO_3 boric acid	$(CH_3)_2NH$ dimethylamine
$HC_4H_7O_2$ butanoic acid	$C_2H_5NH_2$ ethylamine
H_2CO_3 carbonic acid	$C_2H_3O_2NH_2$ glycine
H_2CrO_4 chromic acid	N_2H_4 hydrazine
$H_3C_6H_5O_7$ citric acid	CH_3NH_2 methylamine
$HCHO_2$ formic acid	$(CH_3)_3N$ trimethylamine
$HC_7H_{13}O_2$ heptanoic acid	Additional weak bases include most anions (PO_4^{3-}, F^-, HCO_3^-, CO_3^{2-}, SO_3^{2-}, etc.). Example: $PO_4^{3-} + H_2O \rightarrow HPO_4^{2-} + OH^-$
$HC_6H_{11}O_2$ hexanoic acid	
HCN hydrocyanic acid	
HF hydrofluoric acid	
$HC_3H_5O_3$ lactic acid	
HNO_2 nitrous acid	
$HC_8H_{15}O_2$ octanoic acid	
$H_2C_2O_4$ oxalic acid	

Common Strong Acids and Bases
Common Weak Acids
$HC_5H_9O_2$ pentanoic acid
H_3PO_4 phosphoric acid
$HC_3H_5O_2$ propanoic acid
H_2SO_3 sulfurous acid
$HC_5H_3N_4O_3$ uric acid
Additional weak acids—protonated nitrogen cations such as NH_4^+, $CH_3NH_3^+$, etc.; highly charged metal cations such as Fe^{3+}, Al^{3+}, Cr^{3+}, etc.; and oxides of nonmetals (acid anhydrides) such as CO_2, SO_2, SO_3, NO_2, ClO_3, etc. Note the nonmetal retains its oxidation number.

Range	*Indicator*	*Lower Color*	*Upper Color*
0.0–2.5	Methyl violet	Yellow-green	Violet
0.5–2.0	Malachite green HCl	Yellow	Blue
1.0–2.8	Thymol blue	Red	Yellow
1.2–4.0	Benzopurpurin	Violet	Red
1.3–3.0	Orange IV	Red	Yellow
1.5–2.6	Naphthol yellow S	Colorless	Yellow
2.1–2.8	*p*-phenylazoaniline	Orange	Yellow
2.5–4.4	Methyl orange	Red	Yellow
3.0–4.7	Bromophenol blue	Orange-yellow	Violet
3.0–5.0	Congo red	Blue	Red
3.5–6.3	Gallein	Orange	Red
3.8–5.4	Bromcresol green	Yellow	Blue
4.0–5.8	2,5 dinitrophenol	Colorless	Yellow
4.2–4.6	Ethyl orange	Colorless	Yellow
4.4–6.2	Methyl red	Salmon	Orange
4.5–8.3	Litmus	Red	Blue
4.8–6.2	Chlorphenol red	Yellow	Red
5.1–6.5	Propyl red	Pink	Yellow
5.4–6.8	Bromocresol purple	Green-yellow	Violet
5.6–7.2	Alizarin	Yellow	Red
6.0–7.6	Bromthymol blue	Yellow	Blue
6.0–7.6	Bromoxylenol blue	Orange-yellow	Blue
6.4–8.2	Phenol red	Yellow	Red-violet
7.1–8.8	Cresol red	Yellow	Violet
7.5–9.0	*m*-cresol purple	Yellow	Violet
8.1–9.5	Thymol blue	Yellow	Blue
8.3–10.0	Phenolphthalein	Colorless	Dark pink
8.6–9.8	*o*-Cresolphthalein	Colorless	Pink
9.5–10.4	Thymolphthalein	Colorless	Blue
9.9–11.8	Alizarin yellow R	Yellow	Dark orange
10.6–13.4	Methyl blue	Blue	Pale violet
11.1–12.8	Acid fuchsin	Red	Colorless
11.4–13.0	Indigo carmine	Blue	Yellow
11.7–12.8	2,4,6-trinitrotoluene	Colorless	Orange
12.0–14.0	Trinitrobenzene	Colorless	Orange

Flame Test	
BLUE	
Azure	Lead, selenium, $CuCl_2$ (and other copper compounds when moistened with HCl); $CuBr_2$ appears azure blue, then is followed by green.
Light Blue	Arsenic and some of its compounds; selenium.
Blue-green	Phosphates moistened with sulfuric acid; B_2O_3.
GREEN	
Emerald Green	Copper compounds other than halides (when not moistened with HCl), thallium compounds.
Greenish-blue	$CuBr_2$; arsenic; lead; antimony.
Pure green	Thallium and tellurium compounds.
Yellow-green	Barium; possibly molybdenum; borates with (H_2SO_4).
Faint green	Antimony and ammonium compounds.
Whitish green	Zinc.
RED	
Carmine	Lithium compounds (masked by barium or sodium) are invisible when viewed through green glass, appear violet through cobalt glass.
Scarlet	Calcium compounds (masked by barium) appear greenish when viewed through cobalt glass and green through green glass.
Crimson	Strontium compounds (masked by barium) appear violet through cobalt glass, yellowish through green glass.
VIOLET	Potassium compounds other than silicates, phosphates, and borates; rubidium and cesium are similar. Color is masked by lithium and/or sodium, appears purple-red through cobalt glass and bluish through green glass.
YELLOW	Sodium, even the smallest amount, invisible when viewed through cobalt glass.